COST ACCOUNTING
Theory and Applications

Paul M. Fischer , PhD, CPA

Professor of Accounting
University of Wisconsin-Milwaukee

Werner G. Frank , PhD, CPA

Professor of Accounting
University of Wisconsin-Madison

Published by

A72 **SOUTH-WESTERN PUBLISHING CO.**

CINCINNATI   WEST CHICAGO, IL   DALLAS   PELHAM MANOR, NY   PALO ALTO, CA

ISBN: 0-538-01720-1

Library of Congress Catalog Card Number: 84-51588

1 2 3 4 5 6 7 D 10 9 8 7 6 5 4

Printed in the United States of America

PREFACE

In writing this text, we were challenged by the objective of treating the relevant issues of cost accounting in an efficient and up-to-date manner. The text, which is designed to be covered in one semester, develops a theory of analyzing profits within a firm and then integrates this concept into each chapter. Each chapter provides the student with sound theory and a logical, problem-solving approach. Common operations research and statistical tools are used whenever appropriate.

In each chapter, many illustrations and examples are used because we believe that they expedite the learning process. Also, these illustrations provide the necessary guidance for solving end-of-chapter exercises and problems. The exercises are intended to cover single concepts, while the problems are more comprehensive, often integrating several concepts.

The topical flow of the text reflects what we believe is a logical learning sequence. Chapters 1 through 3 develop the concept of how to measure profits within a firm. These chapters include discussions of cost concepts, job order and process costing techniques, and the tools of statistical analysis that are needed in subsequent chapters. Chapters 4 through 6 analyze the response of profits to changes in costs and revenues, and include the use of tools from the areas of statistics and operations research. Chapters 7 and 8 extend these tools to capital budgeting decisions, which impact on future time periods. In these chapters, the analytic tools needed for considering the acquisition of new assets and the replacement of assets are discussed. All relevant tax considerations and the effects of recent tax acts are also discussed.

Chapters 9 through 11 present the procedures for costing individual production units. Both the standard cost and the actual cost methods are fully developed, including complications caused by inventories of partially complete units and the occurrence of spoiled units. Unique scheduling approaches provide a means of solving a wide variety of problems. Chapter 12 considers the special issues for decision making and accounting that result from costs which are shared in common by several products.

Chapters 13 through 15 integrate many of the concepts of earlier chapters. Chapter 13 discusses budgeting and financial simulation models for a firm. Chapter 14 discusses transfer pricing and applies the model of analyzing profitability to measuring the performance of segments of a firm. Chapter 15 extends the tools of cost accounting to areas of quantitative analysis, including inventory control, learning curves, and critical path analysis.

A study guide, which is available as a supplemental learning tool for students, provides an outline of each chapter, followed by true-false items, multiple choice questions, and problems that are carefully structured to allow a step-by-step solution. Many of these items are taken from CPA and CMA exams.

Permission has been received from the Institute of Management Accounting of the National Association of Accountants to use questions and/or unofficial answers from past CMA examinations. Permission has also been received from the American Institute of Certified Public Accountants to use questions and/or unofficial answers from past CPA examinations.

We are grateful to the Literary Executor of the late Sir Ronald A. Fisher, F.R.S., to Dr. Frank Yates, F.R.S., and to Longman Group Ltd., London, for permission to reprint Table III, Distribution of *t*, from their book, *Statistical Tables for Biological, Agricultural and Medical Research* (6th edition, 1974).

We are most appreciative of the many students at the University of Wisconsin-Madison and the University of Wisconsin-Milwaukee for helping us test and refine our manuscript and problem materials. We especially acknowledge the work of Tom Klammer in providing significant help in developing the end-of-chapter materials. We also thank Cheryl Witt, John Arevalo, and Tom Taugher for verifying solutions. We thank posthumously the editing and typing contribution of Pearl Fischer, and we sincerely thank Nancy Taylor for completing this work.

Paul M. Fischer
Werner G. Frank

CONTENTS

One

Role of Cost Accounting in Decision Making

This chapter will introduce the role of accounting information in the management of a firm. It will demonstrate the types of analyses the controller provides to a firm's managers, so that they may plan and control their segments of the firm in a way that will optimize the performance of the firm. To understand the basic methods of accounting for the operations of a firm, the commonly held views of costs and revenues will be discussed in terms of their responses to the firm's volume. A theory of how to analyze profits within a firm will then be developed. This theory will become the foundation for specialized accounting procedures in subsequent chapters. Various decisions for which accounting data are crucial will be briefly studied in order to indicate the use of accounting information in the day-to-day decision making of a firm.

THE ACCOUNTANT'S VIEW OF COSTS AND REVENUES

Effective planning requires that management consider the response of a firm's costs and revenues to changes in volume. For example, a question that might be asked is, "How much will costs increase next year, if volume increases 20%?" Alternatively, management might be content with next year's projected profit, but wonders what would happen to profit if revenues fell 5% short of the projection.

Again, the behavior of costs and revenues with respect to volume must be considered.

Costs and Volume

To illustrate the relationship of costs and volume, assume that you are the cost accountant for a company that manufactures a saver switch, a device that cuts off the air conditioner in a car under heavy acceleration. You have not yet committed yourself to any production method. Economic analysis would suggest that, for any given production level, there is an optimum scale of plant that would most economically produce the switch. Optimum scale is defined as that plant size which results in the lowest average cost per unit. In Illustration 1-1, Part A, a long-run cost curve shows the monthly cost of producing various outputs, each using the appropriate scale of plant. Although the curve is not continuous, it has been drawn by connecting the alternative plant sizes. The curve is based on the common assumption that total cost increases quickly at first, then increases slowly as the optimum scale of plant is reached. Beyond the optimum scale of plant, diseconomies of scale set in and costs begin to rise more quickly. Diseconomies of scale suggest that a larger plant is inefficient and results in a higher average cost per unit. Notice that just below the graph of Part A of Illustration 1-1, the per unit costs at 3 scales of plant are calculated. The lowest average cost per unit, $5.50, occurs at plant scale B.

Assume that your firm builds a plant such as that suggested at scale B. Once the plant exists, you may be committed to one method of production. No longer do you have the complete freedom of action suggested by the economist's long-run cost curve. Ideally, your plant was built to produce 60,000 units per month, although it is possible to vary production about this target volume. To estimate the costs of production at other output levels, you might study the composition of costs at the 60,000-unit output. In Illustration 1-1, Part A, the predicted $330,000 cost included the following components:

Materials, .125 pounds of plastic at $16 per pound	$2
Labor, .2 hour at $10 per hour	2
Total materials and labor costs per unit	$4
Total materials and labor costs for 60,000 switches	$240,000
Add monthly cost of leasing and operating plant	90,000
Total estimated cost	$330,000

Based on this analysis, you might conclude that $90,000 of the cost will not change, even if output falls short of or exceeds 60,000 units. Such a cost is said to be fixed in nature. It would also appear that the remaining cost will change at the rate of $4 per unit as volume changes. Costs which respond proportionately with output are termed variable costs. As the accountant, your view of costs can be constructed as shown in Illustration 1-1, Part B. This graph includes a relevant cost range between 35,000 and 65,000 units per year. In this range, the cost function is shown as a solid line to indicate that the function is assumed to be accurate. Beyond this range, the function is shown as a broken line to indicate that the use of the function at these volumes is less accurate. The relevant cost range

Illustration 1-1
Response of Cost to
Changes in Volume

Part A
Economist's View of
Costs—Long-Run

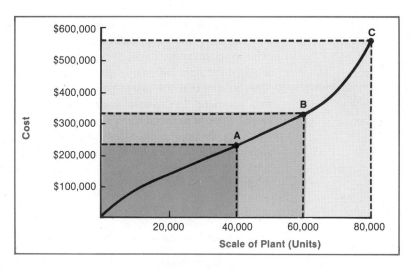

Calculation of average cost per unit:

Plant Scale	Average Cost per Unit
A	$240,000 ÷ 40,000 = $6.00
B	330,000 ÷ 60,000 = 5.50
C	560,000 ÷ 80,000 = 7.00

Illustration 1-1
Response of Cost to
Changes in Volume

Part B
Accountant's View of
Costs—Plant Scale B

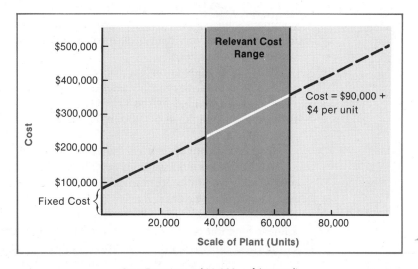

Cost Function = $90,000 + $4 per unit

is the area in which the linear cost function, $90,000 per period plus $4 per switch, is applicable. Specifically, you would defend the cost function in this range by making the following assumptions:

1. The fixed cost of production, $90,000, will remain constant over a given range of output. However, it is likely that this cost would change at outputs beyond this range.

2. The production function is given. Only one combination of labor, materials, and capital (equipment) will be used to build the switch at volumes within the relevant cost range. If you were to depart substantially from the 60,000-unit level, alternative ratios of inputs might be used.

3. You believe that the prices paid for the inputs will not be impacted by your firm's demand. In this case, your demand for labor and materials will not affect the $10-per-hour labor cost or $16-per-pound materials cost. You assume that input markets are sufficiently competitive to be insensitive to your demands within a reasonable range around 60,000 units of output. If demand changed significantly, however, input prices might vary. For instance, input prices might react if your demand doubles or is reduced by 50%.

Revenues and Volume

To project profit at alternative volumes, management must estimate the price at which units will sell. In many cases, this process will be very subjective, since there may be little data from which to make an estimate, especially for a new product such as your saver switch. Economic theory states that, in most cases, the revenue curve for a product is a nonlinear function of units sold. This function is only viewed as linear in a market characterized by pure competition. Except in the case of the perfectly competitive market, economic theory holds that higher unit volume is achieved only at lower prices for all units sold. The response of revenue to volume is thus less than proportional. The revenue line has a declining slope, which approaches zero.

Part A of Illustration 1-2 shows an economist's possible estimate of total revenue at alternative monthly sales of your saver switch. The total revenue at any volume, when divided by the volume, results in the price at which the units will be sold. For example, at 60,000 units, the price per unit would be $6 ($360,000 ÷ 60,000 units).

The accountant's view of the revenue function is derived from economic analysis but differs in its applications. The accountant agrees that the optimum price might be derived from economic theory, but once the price is chosen, the firm may be committed to the chosen price in the short run. Price lists and promotions are based on the chosen price. Thus, once the price is established, revenue becomes a linear function, equal to the price multiplied by the units sold. In the example of the saver switch, assume that you establish the price at $6 per unit. Economic analysis already suggests that sales will be 60,000 units per month. However, you may reason that sales could vary between 40,000 and 70,000 units per month, depending on competition and economic conditions. This range could be termed the relevant revenue range, since it defines the range of revenue which may result from a given price.

Part B of Illustration 1-2 shows the linear revenue function. The graph indicates the most likely sales volume as provided by economic analysis. It also defines the relevant revenue range of volume that may result at a chosen price. Revenue outside the relevant revenue range is indicated by a broken line.

Illustration 1-2
Comparison of Revenue
Functions

Part A
Economist's View

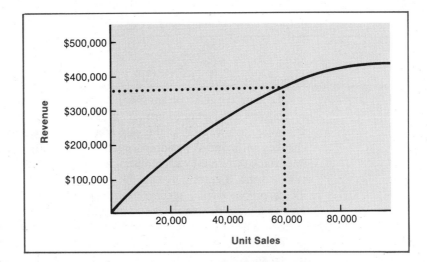

Illustration 1-2
Comparison of Revenue
Functions

Part B
Accountant's View

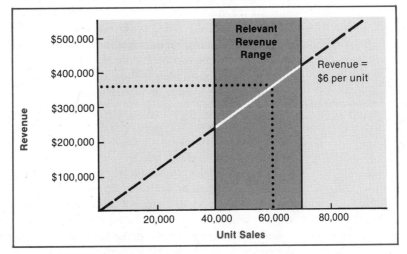

The Ultimate Relevant Range

The following comparison of the relevant cost range with the relevant revenue range shows that they are not the same, but that there is a range of volumes satisfying the limitations of both the cost and revenue relevant ranges.

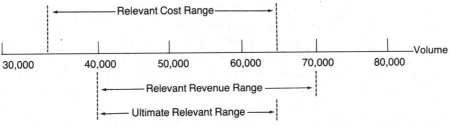

In this example, the "ultimate relevant range" is 40,000 to 65,000 units.

When the term **relevant range** is used in this text, it will be defined as this ultimate relevant range.

ANALYZING PROFITABILITY WITHIN THE FIRM

To date, your accounting education has probably focused on the reporting procedures for the entire firm. You have mastered the presentation of income for an entire firm as well as the preparation of a balance sheet and a statement of changes in financial position for the firm. While such statements are of prime importance to investors, creditors, and government agencies, they are of limited value to the operating management of the firm. The problem is that these statements, prepared for external reporting, report only the aggregate success of all the firm's activities during the accounting period. These statements do not analyze the performance of the firm's various segments, which are responsible for the overall performance of the firm. All firms, except very small ones, are subdivided into manageable segments such as product lines or sales territories. Each segment is in turn managed so as to maximize its performance and, in the process, maximize the profits of the firm. Thus, profit maximization may be delegated to managers of workable operating segments who are most familiar with and able to respond to the opportunities and problems of a given market.

It is the responsibility of the firm's chief accountant, often called the **controller** or **comptroller,** to provide the cost data needed by segment managers. The controller's original function was to provide financial data for external statements. This function was then expanded to the providing of data to production management. The controller's responsibility now includes the providing of cost and revenue data to sales segments.

The financial information provided by the controller must not only meet the needs of a particular segment, but it must also be capable of aggregation. For example, the financial results of the actions of product managers within a division should, when combined, indicate the financial performance of the division. The combined results of all the divisions should, in turn, measure the performance of the entire firm. The actual segments used to analyze performance should parallel the organization chart of the firm. The model used to analyze performance must be usable for planning future actions and later comparing actual performance to the plan.

Contribution Theory

The theory of profits within a firm is based on contribution theory. This theory compares the revenue of a segment with the specific costs of a segment. Specific costs are incurred only for the segment and could be avoided if the segment were discontinued. Examples would include the labor and materials used to build a product, along with depreciation, rent, and administrative costs incurred solely for the benefit of the product. No attempt is made to charge a segment with an allocated share of costs used in common with other segments. Thus, if two product lines share a building, neither would be charged for its use. Since all segments share the use of the firm's president and staff, no segment would be charged for these salaries.

Net income implies that all of the firm's costs have been deducted from revenue. It is thus useful for measuring the performance of an entire firm. Since there will always be some common costs that will not be charged to segments, the net income concept is not readily applicable to segments. The performance of a segment can only be measured by its contribution, defined as revenue less specific segment costs.

To understand contribution analysis, assume that a firm has three divisions: boats, golf equipment, and bowling equipment. The boat division is divided into 3 main product lines: sailboats, fishing boats, and sport boats. Each product line within the boat division contributes to the boat division's contribution. Illustration 1-3 demonstrates the concept of contribution analysis for this firm.

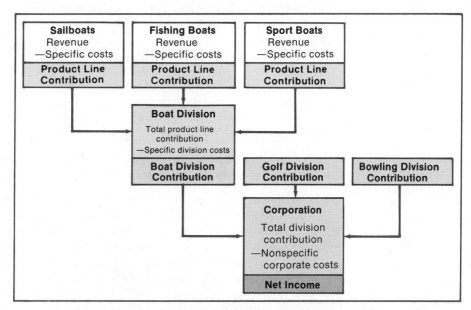

The contribution of each product line is the revenue of the line less all specific costs of the line. Included would be the labor and materials used to manufacture each boat, plus costs common to all boats produced within a line. The sum of the product lines' contributions is available to cover the costs which are first specific at the division level. Such costs would include division management and the cost of the common production facilities used by all product lines. The sum of the product lines' contributions is available to cover the specific costs of the division, so that the division may make a contribution to the firm. The sum of the divisions' contributions is available to cover the costs which are first specific at the firm-wide level. Such costs would include the corporate headquarters staff as well as any other services or facilities shared by divisions. If the total contributions of the divisions is sufficient to cover these costs, there will be net income. Net income is finally calculable, since all costs are specific at the corporate level.

Illustration 1-3 does not exhaust the opportunities for contribution analysis within this firm. Very likely the contribution of each model boat to the product line's contribution would be analyzed. It is also likely that the contribution of each product line by sales territories would be studied.

The controller's measurement of the performance of segment managers should result in a keen awareness of the concept of responsibility accounting. No revenue or cost should be attached to a segment unless it is controllable by the segment's management. It is not reasonable to hold a segment responsible for revenues or costs over which it has no authority. Therefore, the management level to which contribution analysis may be applied is limited. Where there is no direct responsibility for revenue at a management level, contribution cannot be measured. Responsibility accounting requires that only costs be measured in such cases. Thus, when the performance of a supervisor in the hull molding department for sailboats is being measured, only specific costs will be considered. The direct role of the supervisor in maximizing contribution is to minimize costs. It is not prudent, however, to minimize costs without maintaining quality. Thus, it would be more accurate to state that the supervisor should minimize cost subject to maintaining a given quality level.

To differentiate between segments that do have revenue responsibility and those that do not, the term **contribution center** will be used to refer to segments where there is both revenue and cost responsibility, and the term **cost center** will refer to segments which have only direct responsibility for costs.

The Planning and Control Cycle

The role of contribution analysis is best understood by reviewing the planning and control cycle of a firm. This cycle includes the following basic steps:

1. Preliminary planning: The controller collects the needed cost information and identifies costs by segments. Each segment uses the information to build a tentative plan for future periods in order to maximize its contribution.
2. Evaluation of preliminary plans: The controller assembles the plans of the segments into a comprehensive plan for the firm. The segment plans are checked at the corporate level for compatibility. The comprehensive plan must provide adequate forecast net income for the firm and be supportable with the firm's financial resources. If a segment's plans are unacceptable, they will be returned to the segment for modification.
3. Master plan: The controller will combine final segment plans into a master budget or profit plan for the entire firm. Each segment will receive a budget which identifies that segment's responsibility for the future period.
4. Performance control: The controller will compare actual performance by each segment with that segment's budget. Variances will be studied for possible corrective action. Typically the budget will be flexible, adjusting for output levels different from the planned levels. This flexibility will allow cost analysis to be correlated to actual output.

Throughout the planning and control cycle, the focus is on maximizing the firm's profit by maximizing the contribution of each segment. Management must, however, be careful to identify possible opportunities for suboptimization. Suboptimization occurs when a segment maximizes its contribution in such a manner that the overall profit of the firm is reduced. In other words, the increase in one segment's contribution is more than offset by another segment's loss of contribution. In the previous illustration, for example, each dealer might be required to place a large minimum order of fishing boats, which could increase the sales of fishing boats at the expense of sail and sport boat sales. Another example might be that of a production supervisor eliminating the final cleanup of boats to minimize costs, which could result in dealers reducing their purchases to the point that the reduction in cost is more than offset by a loss in revenue. One of the functions performed in the evaluation of preliminary plans is the identification and elimination of obvious cases of suboptimization.

GUIDELINES FOR DECISION MAKING

The discussion so far has centered on the overall performance of a segment. It should be obvious that the performance of the segment reflects the quality of the individual decisions concerning the operations of the segment. It is therefore important that the controller provide segment decision makers with the data needed to aid their analysis and to make wise decisions. Analytic models should be available for use when the decision being studied will have a material impact on the segment's contribution. Major examples of decisions that require financial evaluation would include the acquisition of new equipment, entering new sales territories, marketing new products, dropping existing products, and buying parts from outside suppliers rather than continuing to manufacture the parts. Many of these decisions will impact on several future periods. For example, a machine purchased today may provide labor savings for 10 years. If the machine costs $6,145, and the labor savings are $1,000 per year, is the investment wise? It is not appropriate to compare the total savings of $10,000 (10 × $1,000) to the $6,145 cost, because the interest that could be earned on the $6,145 investment is being ignored. The $1,000 per year must be viewed as a return of the $6,145 investment plus interest on the investment. By using capital budgeting techniques, discussed in Chapter 7, the interest on the investment can be computed. If the interest rate provides a sufficient return, the investment should be made; if not, the acquisition should be vetoed.

There are several general guidelines for analyzing major decisions. These guidelines, which will be explained in detail and demonstrated in later chapters, are as follows:

1. Decisions should recognize the uncertainty inherent in estimates of future results, such as how many units will be sold or what future labor rates will be. It is tempting to just incorporate one best estimate into the analysis, but this procedure is dangerous. Instead, possible alternative estimates should be considered. For example, the one best estimate might be replaced with a weighted average estimate, which would be based on several estimates weighted by their likelihood of occurring. Another alternative would be to determine how sensitive the decision is to the correctness of the estimates. If projected sales are off by 10%, would the same decision still be made? Such evaluations are called sensitivity analysis.

2. Decisions should incorporate the effect of variations in volume and future costs. If, for example, a new product is being considered, its production cost

must be estimated. Since sales may vary from period to period, the cost of production should be stated in a way that allows adjustment for alternative volumes. Therefore, a knowledge of cost behavior—the response of costs to changes in volume—is necessary. Typically there are some costs, called fixed costs, that do not respond to changes in volume and are estimated at a given amount per period. Other costs, called **variable costs,** change with volume and are estimated as a cost per unit of output.

3. For decision-making purposes, the cost of a unit of output should be only the variable costs that would have been saved if that single unit had not been built. Even though a fixed cost is specific to a product, there is no reason to state cost on a per-unit-of-output basis, except to comply with external accounting requirements. To understand this concept, assume that a donut shop rents an automated donut maker for $600 per month and that the materials cost $.05 per donut. The per unit cost of a donut, for decision purposes, is $.05. If the cost of a unit were to include the $600 per month, dividing by expected output would be necessary. If sales are estimated at 5,000 donuts per month, the rent per donut would be $.12. This $.12 would be the allocated fixed cost per unit, but it should not be considered for future decision processes, because the $600 per month is a common cost of all units. For example, assume that a one-time contract to sell 1,000 extra donuts at $.08 is available. The decision to produce the 1,000 additional donuts should be based on the contribution of these donuts, that is, the difference between the additional revenue of $.08 per donut and the additional cost of $.05 per donut. The order would thus contribute $30 ($.03 × 1,000) toward covering the $600 per month fixed cost.

4. If decisions involve assets currently owned, the opportunity cost of these assets must be considered. The historical cost is not usually relevant. **Opportunity cost** is the value of the asset in its most profitable alternative use. In other words, if the asset is not used for the decision, what is the most profitable use for the asset and what is it worth in that use? Consider the following examples.
   a. The replacement of an existing machine is being considered. If it is replaced, the most advantageous action is to sell the old machine. The opportunity cost is the old machine's market value.
   b. The discontinuance of a manufacturing operation is being considered. A building would no longer be needed. It would be more profitable to rent out the building than to sell it. The opportunity cost is the rental value.
   c. It is nearing the end of the year, and a book publisher has in stock 1,000 current-year tax guides that cost $10 a book to produce. The publisher has an opportunity to sell the books for $2 each to a foreign university desiring a "feel" for U.S. taxation. The only other option is to sell the books to a paper recycler for $.10 each. The opportunity cost used to consider the foreign university's offer is $.10 per book, which is the only alternative opportunity.

5. For any decision, only those costs and revenues that will change from their current levels should be considered. Including costs and revenues that will not change complicates and confuses the analysis. For example, assume that a major automobile manufacturer is considering the building of a limited production convertible. It could compare the entire future corporate income

statements with and without the convertibles. But it would make more sense to just compare the added costs with added revenues caused by the convertible. These cost and revenue changes caused by the decision are termed the **incremental** costs and revenues. The process of considering only incremental changes is termed **relevant cost/revenue analysis.**

6. Income taxes are a penalty for earning profits. Decisions that increase profit cause incremental tax payments. Thus, every decision should be analyzed for its tax impact. When the added tax burden is deducted from the contribution of a decision, the contribution is reported "net of tax." No decision can ignore tax.

7. Decision analysis should attempt to quantify all cost and revenue ramifications. However, it will often be impossible to make a reasonable estimate. In such cases, the unquantifiable potential ramifications should be stated, so that it is possible for the decision maker to at least consider them subjectively. For example, the introduction of a new product might indirectly lower sales of other products in a firm's line, and the added *quantified* contribution may not be great enough to offset any *unquantified* loss of current sales. Or leasing an asset may be more expensive than buying it, but the added cost of leasing may be worth the unquantified convenience.

EXAMPLES OF COST ANALYSIS

To become better acquainted with the role of cost analysis in decision making, consider some of the typical analyses made by a corporate controller. The following examples will be kept simple, because they are designed to set the stage for the cost analysis methods used in subsequent chapters. This knowledge of basic analysis methods will provide a context for the tools to be mastered in these chapters.

Case 1: Budgeting for Control

Description. The controller has observed a problem concerning cost control in the shipping department. In past years, the sales of the corporation have been fairly constant, and thus the activity levels in the shipping department have not varied much from period to period. Each month, a budget was developed for the shipping department. The budget was usually based on the average expenditures of the past several periods adjusted for known cost increases, such as an increase in labor rates. The budget was quoted as a single planned amount, such as $40,000 for the month. This type of budget is called a **static budget,** since it is a single figure which is not adjustable for alternate levels of activity.

In recent periods, the shipping supervisor has experienced a dramatic increase in activity due to increasing sales. Since more labor and materials have been used to meet the demands, the shipping department has been exceeding budget. Though the controller says that some cost overrun is reasonable due to increased sales, the supervisor feels pressured if cost overruns are generated. The supervisor is already getting complaints from sales managers that shipments are behind schedule, but is unwilling to improve services at the expense of greater cost overruns. The supervisor has told the controller that the department's budget should automatically be increased proportionate to the units shipped. Thus, if the budget was $40,000 for 10,000 units, it would be increased to $60,000 if 15,000 units are shipped.

Analysis. The controller felt that the budget procedure should be changed from a static approach to a flexible budget approach, which states cost as a function of activity. The controller believes that some of the shipping department's costs are fixed regardless of units shipped. A cost study revealed that such costs, including rent, depreciation, and supervision, amount to $15,000 per month. The remaining costs, primarily labor and packaging materials, are approximately $2.50 per unit. Based on this study, the controller has developed the following formula for the shipping department:

Flexible budget for a month = $15,000 per month + $2.50 per unit

At the end of each month, the supervisor's performance will be evaluated by comparing the actual cost incurred with a flexible budget applied to the units shipped. For example, if the shipping department spends $49,204 to ship 13,000 units, performance would be analyzed as follows:

Actual cost for 13,000 units	$49,204
Flexible budget for 13,000 units [$15,000 + ($2.50 × 13,000 units)]	47,500
Unfavorable variance	$ 1,704

Assuming that the flexible budget is accurate, the supervisor is now being credited for the level of activity.

Case 2: Profit Projection

Description. The controller has been asked to help the board of directors analyze the profit potential of a company that they are considering purchasing. The company is a small local firm, the Appleton Cheese Factory. While the current earnings of the firm are not impressive, it is felt that the firm has potential. If Appleton's product line were promoted by $90,000 in advertising and sold by the purchasing firm's sales force, it is believed that sales could increase by 40%. Salespeople would receive a 5% commission on all sales.

The following summarized income statement for the past year was prepared:

Sales	$800,000
Cost of goods sold	600,000
Gross profit	$200,000
Less selling and administrative expenses	150,000
Income before tax	$ 50,000
Less provision for tax (40%)	20,000
Net income	$ 30,000

Analysis. The controller must divide costs into two groups if future profits are to be estimated. The costs that vary with sales must be separated from those that are fixed and remain constant at alternative sales levels. The controller determined that the cost of goods sold includes $120,000 of rent, depreciation, and supervision that will remain constant even if sales increase 40%. The remaining $480,000 of cost of goods sold is believed to vary in direct proportion to sales, which means that the variable cost of production is estimated to be 60% ($480,000 ÷ $800,000) of sales. The selling and administrative expenses include a fee of 10% of sales, currently paid to manufacturers representatives that sell all of the product line. The remaining expenses of $70,000 [$150,000 − (.10 × $800,000)] do not respond to changes in volume. Based on this analysis, the controller predicted the following results for the next year:

Sales (current sales of $800,000 increased 40%)		$1,120,000
Less variable costs:		
Production costs (.6 × $1,120,000)	$672,000	
Selling commissions (.05 × $1,120,000)	56,000	728,000
Contribution to fixed costs that do not change with volume		$ 392,000
Less fixed costs:		
Production costs	$120,000	
Current selling and administrative expenses	70,000	
Additional advertising	90,000	280,000
Estimated income before tax		$ 112,000
Less provision for tax (40%)		44,800
Estimated net income		$ 67,200

Case 3: Product Line Drop Decision

Description. Hardwood Inc. is a manufacturer of furniture. It has recently hired a new controller to replace the former controller, who retired. The first day on the job, the controller is asked to confirm an analysis which indicates that the children's furniture line is losing money and should be discontinued. The president intends to eliminate the line but wants the new controller's comments. The following summarized income statement for the children's furniture line for the preceding period was prepared by the former controller:

Sales		$900,000
Less cost of goods sold		700,000
Gross profit		$200,000
Less other expenses:		
Sales commissions (10% of sales)	$90,000	
Advertising and promotion	60,000	
Administrative costs	80,000	230,000
Net loss, excluding tax effects		$ 30,000

The controller suspects that the reported loss includes some allocated costs that would continue, even if the line is dropped. The former controller had said that every cost must be covered if the corporation is to have net income, so every product must cover its fair share of costs.

Analysis. The new controller's research produced the following results:

1. The cost of goods sold included $540,000 of costs that varied directly with sales. These costs included primarily labor and materials. Of the remaining costs, $70,000 were for out-of-pocket costs that did not vary with output but

would be eliminated if the children's furniture line were discontinued. The remaining $90,000 is the depreciation of the building and equipment. If the children's furniture line is discontinued, the best alternative for the building and equipment is to lease it to a cabinet maker for $5,000 per month.

2. The 10% sales commissions would be saved, but that could mean less income to existing salespeople. Dissatisfied salespeople might leave the firm.

3. Only $30,000 of the $60,000 advertising and promotion expense was incurred specifically for the children's furniture line. The remainder is a portion of corporate costs, which were allocated by sales dollars.

4. Administrative costs include $35,000 incurred by the children's furniture line that would be eliminated. The remainder is an allocation of corporate costs based on various measures such as floor space and sales dollars. The investigation shows that there would be no immediate reduction in corporate administrative costs if the children's furniture line were dropped; but in time, $20,000 could be saved through a restructuring of procedures.

Based on this analysis, the new controller restructured the income statement as follows, using contribution analysis:

Sales		$900,000
Less variable costs that vary directly with sales:		
Manufacturing costs (60%)	$540,000	
Sales commissions (10%)	90,000	630,000
Contribution to fixed costs		$270,000
Less product line fixed costs that would be avoided by discontinuance:		
Out-of-pocket manufacturing costs	$ 70,000	
Opportunity cost of using plant and equipment (rental value, 12 x $5,000)	60,000	
Advertising and promotion	30,000	
Administrative costs	35,000	195,000
Product line contribution to common corporate costs in the short run		$ 75,000
Less corporate cost reductions possible in the long run (administrative savings)		20,000
Product line contribution to corporate costs in the long run		$ 55,000

The controller pointed out that the following costs, formerly allocated to the product line, would not cease upon discontinuance of the line:

Depreciation in excess of rental value	$ 30,000
Allocated corporate advertising and promotion	30,000
Allocated corporate administrative costs that will not be eliminated in the long run	25,000
Total	$ 85,000

These costs are what caused a $55,000 contribution to become a $30,000 loss. The controller also added the following subjective considerations:

1. Would the loss of salespeople, due to a reduction in commissions, hurt the sales of other lines?

2. Would other lines suffer a loss of future sales because some customers are won over to the firm by its unique children's line?

1. Why might a manager want to consider the response of a firm's cost to changes in volume?

2. What is the difference between variable costs and fixed costs?

3. What is the relevant cost range, and what assumptions must be made about the cost function within this range?

4. How can accountants defend revenue as a linear function equal to price times units?

5. What is the contribution theory?

6. What is responsibility accounting?

7. Define a cost center. How does this differ from a contribution center?

8. What is suboptimization, and how might obvious cases of suboptimization be eliminated?

9. For what purpose might an accountant unitize fixed costs?

10. You have rented a carpet cleaner at $30 per day to clean all of the carpets in your home. The cleaning will take 8 hours and will use 4 bottles of carpet shampoo at $5 per bottle. Your neighbor offers to pay you $8 to clean a living room carpet, which will take 2 hours and will require one bottle of shampoo. In deciding whether to clean your neighbor's carpet, what costs do you consider relevant?

11. Would your answer to Question 10 be the same if the carpet cleaner could only be rented on a per-hour basis?

12. Define opportunity cost.

13. What is relevant cost/revenue analysis, and what is the reason for its use?

14. What is the difference between a static budget and a flexible budget? Which is more advantageous?

15. In decision making, what is wrong with the statement that every cost must be covered if the corporation is to have net income, so every product must cover its fair share of costs?

Exercise 1. Ken Kiefer is investigating the construction of a plant which would manufacture small digital clocks for installation in automobile dashboards. After consulting with industrial engineers and accountants, he has estimated the following operating costs of various sizes of plants:

Yearly Output	Annual Operating Cost
10,000 units	$190,000
20,000	240,000
30,000	280,000
40,000	300,000
50,000	360,000
60,000	510,000

After analyzing the above data and making sales forecasts, Kiefer decides to proceed with a plant of 40,000 units-per-year output. Further investigation yields the following cost breakdown:

Annual Output	Fixed Costs	Variable Costs
30,000 units	$60,000	$180,000
40,000	60,000	240,000
50,000	60,000	300,000

(1) Graph the long-run total cost curve faced by the firm, based on the operating costs of various sizes of plants. Indicate the range of output over which increasing economies of scale occur.

(2) Plot the cost curve for the plant with a 40,000 units-per-year output. Indicate the relevant cost range, and state the cost function.

Exercise 2. During July, Kennar Company incurred total manufacturing costs of $666,000 for an output of 53,000 units. Of these costs, $242,000 were incurred for supervisory salaries, depreciation, factory lease costs, and other costs considered to be fixed. The cost relationships are expected to remain unchanged over outputs between 45,000 and 70,000 units per month.

What manufacturing costs can Kennar Company expect to incur in August if (a) output rises to 65,000 units; (b) falls to 48,000 units?

Exercise 3. Kneller Brewing Company, a small Pennsylvania brewer, has hired an economist to determine the demand for the firm's super-premium *Oktoberfest* brand. After extensive market research, the following data are presented:

Price per Barrel	Quantity Sold per Month
$ 4	10,000 barrels
7	8,000
10	6,000
13	4,000
16	2,000

Based on the above data, the brewery expands *Oktoberfest* plant capacity from 4,000 to 6,000 barrels per month. Kneller's sales representatives feel that the price of $10 per barrel can actually be maintained over outputs between 4,200 and 7,500 barrels per month.

(1) Using the information supplied, plot the economist's total revenue curve for *Oktoberfest.*

(2) Assume that Kneller decides on a price of $10 per barrel. Plot the accountant's revenue curve and indicate the relevant revenue range. What is the expected revenue if sales are 6,000 barrels?

Exercise 4. The Garment Division of Sta-Rite Company manufactures two kinds of clothes hangers: Model A, an inexpensive wire hanger, and Model D, a deluxe plastic hanger. The Model D hanger sells for $0.30 per unit; variable costs are $0.18 per unit. In the upcoming year, the division expects to incur fixed costs of $180,000, 35% of which are incurred only because of Model D production. Expected sales of Model D are 750,000 units.

Calculate Model D's contribution to next year's Garment Division fixed costs at the expected sales level.

Exercise 5. Leffler Recycling Inc. has estimated the following costs and revenues for their scrap paper reprocessing operation:

Quantity Processed per Month	Cost	Revenue
0	$10,000	0
20,000 lbs.	16,000	$10,000
40,000	22,000	20,000
60,000	28,000	30,000
80,000	34,000	40,000
100,000	40,000	50,000

(1) Graph the cost and revenue data for the firm's paper reprocessing operation and estimate the profit at an output of 75,000 pounds per month.
(2) Confirm the profit estimate in (1) by mathematically calculating the reprocessing operation's cost and revenue functions and solving each for an output of 75,000 pounds.

Exercise 6. Miller-Castle Company produces glass products for sale to the retail and food service markets. The selling price of its most popular drinking glass, the 9-oz. Deluxe, is $14 per case. Variable costs, including shipping costs, are $8 per case; the remaining $6 per case contributes to the firm's fixed costs and to profit.

Miller-Castle is operating well below capacity and has received a special order from a European hotel chain for 10,000 cases of 9-oz. Deluxe glasses. The chain is willing to pay $12 per case, but insists that the glasses be labeled with the hotel insignia; the cost of labeling is estimated at $3.75 per case. Shipping costs of $1.30 per case would be avoided, however, since the buyer will be responsible for shipping the glasses. All other costs are unchanged.

Calculate the contribution of the special order. Should Miller-Castle accept the order?

Exercise 7.

(1) As a graduate student at State University, your tuition is $1,250 per year, or 1/3 the cost of tuition at a comparable private college. Your economics professor suggests that the most significant cost of obtaining a degree is the earnings forgone by not working full time while at school, or about $19,000 per year. Is the professor correct in this assertion?
(2) Highlands Products has bagpipe-making equipment, which originally cost $60,000. The equipment is being depreciated at $12,000 per year (no salvage) and has 2 years' remaining depreciable life. The bottom has fallen out of the bagpipe market, however, and the equipment has no market value. Highlands would like to use the equipment to make rubber storage bladders. In evaluating this new product decision, what is the relevant cost of the old equipment?
(3) Over the past three years, Sundowner Company has spent $270,000 in research and development costs to perfect its new suntan oil. Of this amount, $120,000 was spent in the current year. In evaluating whether

to go ahead with production of the new product, what amount of research costs should be considered?

(4) A large supermarket purchases 150 cases of grapefruit for $18 per case. Fruit sales are poor, however, and the manager must quickly sell the 100 remaining cases before they spoil. Although a case normally retails for $23, the manager thinks all the grapefruit could be sold by cutting the price to $15 per case. The fruit can also be sold to a juice company for $17 or to a cannery for $16. In deciding whether to sell to the juice company, what is the opportunity cost of a case of grapefruit?

(5) Bangor Fireworks Co. devotes exactly one half of their Albany plant to production of *Super Sparklers*. The 100,000-square-foot building rents for $8 per square foot per month. Bangor also leases a warehouse for $425,000 per month. If production of *Super Sparklers* was discontinued, all warehouse activities could be moved into the vacated space. What is the cost of *Super Sparklers* production space?

Exercise 8. Wolff Construction is evaluating a one-year contract to supply cement to a dam project in Arkansas. The contract requires Wolff to supply between 11,000 and 15,000 tons of cement at $400 per ton. Wolff estimates its variable costs to be $280 per ton. Fixed costs total $200,000. Income taxes are 40%.

(1) What is the aftertax income of the project if 15,000 tons are produced and sold?

(2) Would the project be profitable if only 11,000 tons were produced and sold?

Exercise 9. As controller for the Glenview Village board, you are concerned about the sudden rise in payroll costs at the Glenview Welfare Services Agency. Last year, the wages and salaries expense for the agency was $111,000. Payroll costs have shot up to $160,000 in the year just ended. The agency supervisor argues that the agency's case load has increased from 12,000 cases last year to 18,000 cases this year, and that the payroll should increase accordingly—by 50%. An investigation shows that the agency employs one supervisor, who handles no cases and is paid $27,000. Each case requires, on the average, one hour of caseworker time. Caseworkers are paid $7 per hour.

(1) Using the supervisor's 50% rule, what amount should have been spent on payroll this year?

(2) Develop a flexible budget for payroll costs, based on the number of cases handled. Using this budget, how much should have been spent on payroll this year?

(3) Compare the budget figures in (1) and (2) with the $160,000 actually spent. Are they higher or lower?

Exercise 10. Aero Products Company, a designer and builder of ultra-light aircraft, also designs and constructs hot-air balloons. The balloons sell for $22,000 each. Almost all the costs of building a balloon are variable costs, which total $17,500 per balloon. The only fixed cost is depreciation on the building in which the balloon panels are cut and sewn. The building is being depreciated at $15,000 per year over 15 years. The building could be leased as a warehouse for $14,000 per year. Aero Products expects to sell only 3 balloons per year for the foreseeable future.

Determine the impact on the firm of dropping the balloon line.

PROBLEMS

Problem 1-1. Applied Research Inc. has developed a solar-powered radio which it hopes to export to developing countries. After extensive market study and engineering research, the following prices and unit costs have been determined for planning the scale of plant:

Output	Price per Unit	Average Cost per Unit
20,000 units	$20.00	$20.00
40,000	16.00	12.50
60,000	12.50	9.00
80,000	10.00	8.00
100,000	7.50	9.00

Required

(1) On the same graph, plot the total revenue and total cost curves faced by the firm. At which scale of plant is the firm's profit maximized?
(2) Confirm your estimate in (1) by mathematically calculating the profit earned at various outputs. What is the firm's profit at the profit-maximizing output?
(3) At what level of output is unit cost minimized? How does this output compare with the profit-maximizing output in (1)?

Problem 1-2. On the basis of the long-run revenue and cost projections in Problem 1-1, Applied Research Inc. constructs a plant with a scale of 60,000 radios per year. The company's marketing department feels that the $12.50 unit price can be maintained over all outputs between 45,000 and 72,000 units. Cost data for the plant are as follows:

Variable costs:
Materials ....$2.10 per unit
Labor .... 2.60 per unit
Overhead .... 0.30 per unit
Fixed costs:
Factory lease expense $120,000
Selling expenses 85,000
Administrative expenses 55,000

The projected costs are expected to remain unchanged over outputs between 55,000 and 72,000 units.

Required

(1) On the same graph, plot the revenue and cost curves for the 60,000-unit plant scale. Indicate the relevant range for each curve and the ultimate relevant range for the firm.
(2) Prepare the flexible budget cost function for radio production.
(3) What amount of profit would the firm earn if production and sales are (a) 63,000 units; (b) 58,000 units?
(4) Sales next year are expected to rise to 85,000 units. Should the firm rely on its present cost and revenue estimates to project profits?

Problem 1-3. Tri-Star Company has two divisions: the Office Machines Division and the Meter Division. The Office Machines Division manufactures mechanical cash registers and adding machines, while the Meter Division produces gas and water meters for residential homes. Both divisions share the same production building, together with corporate administrative offices, although each has its own assembly line. Revenue and cost data for the firm are as follows:

Product	Price	Materials, Labor, Variable Overhead	Produced and Sold
Cash registers	$240	$150 per unit	950 units
Adding machines	100	55	1,400 units
Gas meters	180	100	2,700 units
Water meters	110	98	1,200 units

Sales commissions of 5% and 2-1/2% of the selling price are paid on cash registers and adding machines, respectively. No commission is paid on either gas meters or water meters.

Shipping expenses of $8 per unit are incurred on all cash registers and adding machines. Shipping charges for the heavier gas and water meters are $14 per unit.

Each division has its own marketing department. Marketing expenses, which are fixed in nature, were $40,000 for the Office Machines Division. Of this amount, 30% were incurred solely for cash register sales and 20% for adding machine sales. The remaining 50% cannot be charged to either product. Marketing expenses for the Meter Division were $25,000. Since these were incurred entirely for displays in trade shows in which both products appeared, they are not charged to the products.

The company provides maintenance, management and computer services to both divisions. Cost breakdowns are as follows:

Item	Total Amount	Company Headquarters	Office Machines Div.	Meter Div.
Maintenance Expense	$ 45,000	20%	40%	40%
Computer Services	30,000	40	35	25
Management	100,000	35	45	20

The company's land and building are leased on a long-term lease for $35,000 per year. This cost would have to be paid even if one or the other division were closed.

Required
(1) Calculate the products' contribution to the division, the divisions' contribution to common corporate costs, and net income.
(2) Should either division be shut down; b) should any products be discontinued?

Problem 1-4. The New Trier School District is in a dilemma. Although enrollment has fallen 10% over the last year, from 6,500 students to 5,850 students, costs fell by only $400,000, to $5,100,000. In an effort to control costs, the school board has developed the following figures:

Building maintenance:
Capital expenditures .... $14,000 per school
Maintenance workers' salaries .... $66,000 per school
Maintenance supplies .... $ 2.50 per student

Teaching materials: $22,000 + $3.75 per student

Transportation: Each bus costs $1,225 per year to lease.

School board expenses:
    Salaries . . . . $32,000 per year
    Other expenses . . . . $ 3,000 per year

Administrative salaries:
    Principal . . . . $35,000 per school
    Vice-principal . . . . $24,000 per school
    Secretaries . . . . $16,000 per school
    Teachers . . . . $18,000 per teacher

Other activities: $1,000 per school + $.25 per student

State law requires one teacher for every 27 students. About one half of all students ride buses; the buses hold 35 students each. The New Trier School District operates 8 schools. Despite declining enrollments, public pressure prevents them from closing schools.

Required
(1) Prepare a budget for the school system for the upcoming year, using an enrollment of 5,850 students. Organize your information according to the following columnar format (round all figures to the nearest whole unit):

Cost Item	Costs Based Solely on Number of Schools	Costs Based Solely on Number of Students	Costs Based on Other Factors
Building maintenance: Capital expenditures	$112,000	–	–

(2) Compare your budgeted cost estimate with actual costs. By how much do these amounts differ?

Problem 1-5. Enterprise Billings Co. is a professional billings service that contracts with doctors, lawyers, accountants, and other professionals to manage all their customer billings. The client is paid 92% of the face amount of the billings. The difference between what is collected and what is paid out is the revenue of the service. Uncollectible accounts are an expense borne by the billing service. Enterprise would like to open an office in an area of the country completely new to it. The following data have been gathered:

- One office worker is required for each $400,000 in billings or portion thereof. Office workers are paid $12,000 per year.
- Uncollectible accounts average 1-1/2% of gross billings.
- The monthly lease on a computer required to maintain records is $1,200.
- Past experience has shown that supplies expense averages 0.2% of billings.
- Office rent is $350 per month.
- A full-time office manager is paid $24,000 per year.
- Advertising expense is budgeted at $2,800 during the first year's operations.

Enterprise is unsure of the amount of billings it can capture in the new area. The president of the company, on the basis of past experience and a limited market study, feels that $1,600,000 in billings is realistic. The president is also concerned as to how sensitive the firm will be to billing levels slightly above or below the estimate. A private consultant, engaged by the firm's shareholders, has estimated $1,305,000 to be the most likely level of billings.

Required

(1) What profit will the office earn if billings reach the $1,600,000 estimate?
(2) What profit will the firm earn if billings are (a) 10% below the estimate; (b) 10% above?
(3) What profit will be earned at the consultant's estimate of billings?

Problem 1-6. Miami-Atlas Corp. manufactures solar heating panels in its plant in southern Florida. Currently, the Florida plant is operating at capacity. The cost of manufacturing a solar panel in its Florida plant is as follows:

Materials	$200
Labor (22 hours @ $5 per hr.)	110
Overhead (all variable)	115
	$425

The company would like to expand its operations to the midwest by opening a 100,000-square-foot plant in Michigan. Miami-Atlas feels that wage rates are about 15% higher in Michigan than in Florida, but this increase would be offset by lower utility rates. Overhead per unit is expected to decrease by 12%.

The firm expects to expand sales by 750 panels. The panels built in the new plant will be sold at a price of $700 per panel. The factory will employ its own staff of 5 salespeople, each paid a $17,000 per year salary plus a commission of 2% on sales. The firm will continue its practice of displaying its product at four major trade shows. On the average, a display costs $6,000 per show.

One half of the plant's equipment will be purchased new for $175,000 and depreciated straight-line over ten years with no salvage value. The company leases similar equipment at its Florida plant for $15,000 per year. The remaining equipment is unused equipment from the Florida plant. The equipment is fully depreciated and has no market value.

Most management functions are located at the firm's Miami plant. These costs are expected to rise from $150,000 to $190,000 after the new plant begins operation. Management of the plant itself is expected to cost $47,000 per year.

Miami-Atlas has spent $27,000 in research and development costs in each of the past three years, adapting its solar panels to the cold midwestern climate. Total research and development costs for this application are expected to fall to $23,000 per year after the plant is in operation, since the major design work will have been completed.

Property tax rates in Michigan are $10 per thousand square feet of building area.

It is anticipated that the value of the plant will not change over the next several years.

Calculate the new plant's contribution to the firm's fixed costs, after all specific fixed costs of the expansion have been covered. Should Miami-Atlas build the new plant?

Problem 1-7. Rayco Corp. manufactures turbine blades for aircraft jet engines and automobile turbochargers. The automobile turbine blades are selling poorly, and Rayco is considering dropping the line. The blades are sold in sets of twelve at $450 per set. Materials cost $125 per set; labor and variable overhead are an additional $245 per set. Equipment used in production originally cost $280,000 and is being depreciated over ten years (straight-line, no salvage value). This equipment could be leased to another firm for $2,000 per month. Rayco leases manufacturing space for the line for $3,200 per month. The lease is immediately cancelable, or the space could be subleased for $2,800 per month. Administrative expenses for the firm are $275,000. Administrative expenses could be reduced 15% in the first year by dropping the line, and by a further 10% of the original amount in the second year. Marketing expenses are $123,000, which includes a 5% commission paid on sales of the blade sets, and the salaries of 3 sales representatives who are paid $17,000 per year. Other expenses could be reduced by $25,000 by dropping the line. Shipping costs for the sets are $12 per set. Rayco expects to sell 3,200 sets per year for the foreseeable future.

Determine the impact on the firm of dropping the automobile blade line.

Problem 1-8. Woodlawn Farms operates a gardening supply store and a lawn care service whose accounting records are mixed. Susan Mills, the owner of the operation, feels that the lawn care service does not contribute as much to the firm's total profit as the store. She has asked her accountant to show the performance of each operation in the income statement. The accountant has provided the proprietor with the following income statement and additional data:

Woodlawn Farms
Income Statement
For Year Ended December 31, 19X7

	Store	Lawn Care	Combined
Sales	$330,000	$220,000	$550,000
Sales returns and allowances	16,000	0	16,000
Net sales	$314,000	$220,000	$534,000
Cost of goods sold	205,000	0	205,000
Gross margin	$109,000	$220,000	$329,000
Wages and salaries expense	$ 78,000	$112,000	$190,000
Depreciation expense	4,000	15,000	19,000
Insurance	6,000	4,000	10,000
Maintenance	4,000	7,000	11,000
Fuel	0	13,000	13,000
Advertising	2,400	1,600	4,000
Total expenses	$ 94,400	$152,600	$247,000
Net income	$ 14,600	$ 67,400	$ 82,000

- Cost of goods sold: The cost of goods sold for the store is completely variable.

- Wages and salaries: Wages and salaries expense pertains to the employees of each operation, except for the salary of the proprietor, $38,000, which was allocated equally to each operation. Of the remainder, 1/4 is estimated to be fixed and 3/4 is variable for each operation.
- Depreciation: The depreciation expense pertains to the specific equipment of each operation, except for $2,000 depreciation on the store building, which was allocated to each operation on the basis of gross sales. The store building houses the administrative offices of the lawn care service and provides storage space for materials and equipment.
- Insurance: Insurance expense was allocated to each division on the basis of gross sales. A more detailed investigation yielded the following breakdown:

Policy	Premium
Policies covering store equipment	$ 3,500
Policies covering lawn service equipment	5,800
Life and health insurance for proprietor	700
	$10,000

- Maintenance: Maintenance expenses were incurred on the specific equipment of each operation and are considered to be fixed in nature.
- Fuel: All fuel costs relate to gasoline for the trucks used in the lawn care operation. Fuel costs vary proportionately with sales.
- Advertising: Advertising expense was allocated to each division on the basis of gross sales. All advertisements include references to both the store and the lawn care service. Total advertising expenditures would not be reduced, even if one of the operations were discontinued.

Required

Prepare a contribution format income statement for the Woodlawn Farm's 19X7 operations. Treat each operation as a separate division, and show each division's contribution to its specific fixed costs, the divisions' contribution to common costs, and net income.

Two

Cost Concepts and Behavior; Job Order and Process Costing

The costs of a firm are described in many ways, depending on the particular use of the cost data. The previous chapter, for example, focused on identifying costs with segments. It is also common to describe costs according to their functional type, such as manufacturing and nonmanufacturing. The important distinction between these functional types is that, for external reporting purposes, manufacturing costs are allocated in some manner to each unit produced. Thus, manufacturing costs are also termed product costs to connote their status as costs which are inventoriable. Thus, there is likely to be a delay between the time a manufacturing cost is incurred and the time it is expensed. In contrast, nonmanufacturing costs, such as warehouse rent and advertising, are not unitized or inventoried. Rather, they are expensed with the passage of time and are called period costs.

This chapter also describes costs according to their behavior. Cost behavior is the way in which costs respond to changes in output. For example, manufacturing costs tend to vary with respect to units produced, and clerical costs may vary with respect to invoices prepared. A major concern in analyzing cost behavior is distinguishing between variable costs that respond in a linear manner to changes in output and fixed costs that are unaffected by reasonable changes in output. As you study this chapter, you should focus on cost concepts as they apply to both decision making and the preparation of the firm's financial statements.

MANUFACTURING COSTS

Manufacturing costs are typically divided into three major groups: materials, direct labor, and overhead. Each has its unique attributes in terms of planning and control. Therefore, the behavior of each cost must be analyzed. It is also necessary to understand how these cost components are combined into the cost of a unit produced. Unfortunately, there are usually two product costs: the cost used for decision purposes and the cost used for external reporting purposes.

Materials and Direct Labor

Materials are the purchased components that are used in the manufacturing of a product. Direct labor is the workers' time that can be directly traced to the production of a unit. Materials and direct labor are sometimes collectively termed **prime costs,** since in many cases they constitute the major portion of manufacturing costs. Both materials and direct labor costs should be based on physical quantities, such as 2 pounds of chemical X and 3 hours of labor. The physical quantities are then multiplied by current unit costs to arrive at a dollar budget.

Materials purchased include both raw materials which are to be processed as well as parts which are to be assembled into a complete unit. For example, a transmission purchased by a truck manufacturer is categorized as materials. Materials are directly traceable to each unit, and thus the materials cost varies directly with the number of units. Typically, the allowable use of materials per unit is determined by developing a materials list from the blueprints or other design plans for the product.

Including an item in the materials category presumes that its cost and use will be closely controlled. Some materials costs, however, are too insignificant in terms of their cost per unit to warrant this attention. Such materials costs are included in overhead as indirect materials. An example would be the grease used to lubricate a new car.

Direct labor should vary in direct proportion to the number of units produced. To be included in the category of direct labor, it should be possible to physically observe the time it takes to perform a given operation on an individual product unit. For example, the time that it takes to install the engine and transmission in a new car can be observed. Typically, industrial engineers use time and motion studies to determine the allowable labor per unit.

Some labor costs are not included in the direct labor cost category because they cannot reasonably be identified with each unit produced. Examples would be the cleaning and maintenance in a car assembly operation. Such labor costs are included in overhead as indirect labor. Also included in overhead are labor fringe benefits, such as pensions and insurance, which do not vary directly with hours worked. It is also common to record overtime and shift premiums as a part of overhead rather than as direct labor.

Arriving at the labor cost is complicated by the fact that a unit may be produced by workers who receive differing pay to reflect differing skills and/or seniority, as in the following example:

Worker	Hours	Pay per Hour	Total
Jones	2.0	$ 8	$16
Smith	1.0	10	10
Avery	.5	12	6
		Total labor cost per unit	$32

To simplify accounting for labor, a firm may derive an average direct labor cost per hour, based on the average mix of labor used. In this example, the average cost per hour would be $9.14 ($32 ÷ 3.5 hours). Thus, the budgeted labor cost per unit would be stated as 3.5 hours at $9.14 per hour. Chapter 9 will discuss the recording of labor costs in detail, including the problem that occurs when the actual mix of labor pay categories differs from the budgeted mix.

Overhead

Overhead, broadly defined, includes all manufacturing costs other than the costs which are separately identified as materials and direct labor. As noted earlier, minor amounts of materials are included in overhead as indirect materials, and some labor costs are included in overhead as indirect labor. In addition to indirect materials, indirect labor, and labor-related costs such as fringe benefits and over-time premiums, overhead may include major cost items such as supervision, rent, depreciation, utilities, and maintenance.

Although the component costs of overhead may be studied in detail, overhead is typically studied only in the aggregate for planning, control, and reporting purposes. The accountant's job is to study the response of the total set of overhead costs with respect to output.

Overhead is the most difficult cost to analyze from a cost behavior standpoint. It includes indirect materials and indirect labor, which vary directly with output and are termed **variable costs.** It also includes items such as rent and depreciation, which are not responsive to changes in output. Costs which have no observable relation to output are termed **fixed costs.**

Some overhead costs have both fixed and variable components. These costs are termed **mixed costs, semivariable costs,** or **semifixed costs.** An example of a mixed cost is electricity, which has a fixed cost per month plus a variable cost per unit of consumption.

Other overhead costs are fixed over given ranges of output, but shift upward at certain output levels. Supervision might cost $500 per supervisor per week. Each supervisor may be able to oversee the production of 1,000 units per week. At each 1,000-unit increase, supervision would shift up $500. Thus, the supervision would be a $500 fixed cost between 0 and 999 units and a $1,000 fixed cost between 1,000 and 1,999 units. Shifting fixed costs such as this are termed **step costs.** Although the steps are budgeted at discrete quantities, the points at which the steps occur are likely to be somewhat movable in reality. For example, one supervisor might be temporarily able to oversee 1,250 units. It is also likely that if production temporarily dipped from 1,800 to 950 units, the two supervisors would be retained.

Illustration 2-1 is a summary of how the variable, fixed, mixed, and step overhead cost functions combine to form the total overhead cost function. It is important to note that while overhead may be theoretically viewed as a sum of these cost types, the distinctions are lost in practice, since overhead is usually budgeted and controlled only as an aggregate figure. The underlying cost behaviors are described to help you understand the nature of overhead and its measurement, which is discussed in Chapter 3. In practice, you can expect to calculate only the budgeted total overhead cost.

Variable Overhead. Recall that variable overhead includes, among other items, materials and labor which were not studied in detail because of their low individual values. Since such items are included in variable overhead, it is most common to study only the response of the total aggregated set of variable overhead costs with respect to output. Therefore, the industrial engineering methods often used to estimate direct materials and direct labor are not used to analyze overhead costs. Instead, other approaches are used, including the statistical methods discussed in Chapter 3. These methods study previous levels of overhead and attempt to relate them to output.

While prime costs have precise variability, overhead may have a more general type of variability. For example, one might confidently say that direct labor costs $14 per unit, but be reluctant to state that variable overhead actually costs $3 per unit, even though a statistical study produces this figure. One might rather say that variable overhead tends to be about $3 per unit. Although one more unit might not cost exactly $3, variable overhead would increase by approximately $3,000 if output were increased from 4,000 to 5,000 units.

Another difference between variable overhead costs and direct labor and materials costs is that variable overhead may not be determined on a per-unit-of-output basis. For instance, it would be difficult to study the total variable overhead cost of a department on a per-unit-of-output basis when several different types of units are produced. In such cases, variable overhead is studied with respect to a more general measure of activity which is applicable to varying products.

The most common factor used to measure variability is direct labor hours, since many types of overhead exist in support of the direct labor force. Thus, it is reasonable to expect overhead to vary with direct labor hours. The use of direct labor hours is also convenient, and it aids in the costing of products. Since labor hours are a statistic that will already be measured in order to control labor cost, variable overhead stated on the basis of cost per direct labor hour may easily be added to the product cost.

In some heavily mechanized departments, variable overhead may vary more predictably with machine hours than with direct labor hours. In these departments, the variable overhead may be stated as a function of machine hours. For product costing purposes, it would be necessary to know the machine hours per unit of product in order to build the total product cost. However, firms would be reluctant to use this approach if it is too costly to maintain a record of machine hours.

Fixed Overhead. Nonaccountants often tend to view fixed costs as meaning costs fixed "in concrete," which is not usually the case. Fixed costs are merely those costs which have no direct observable relationship to output. Since overhead is usually studied as a function of direct labor hours, fixed costs may refer to costs that have no good correlation to direct labor hours. Some components of fixed costs may

Illustration 2-1
**Analysis of Weekly
Overhead Cost**

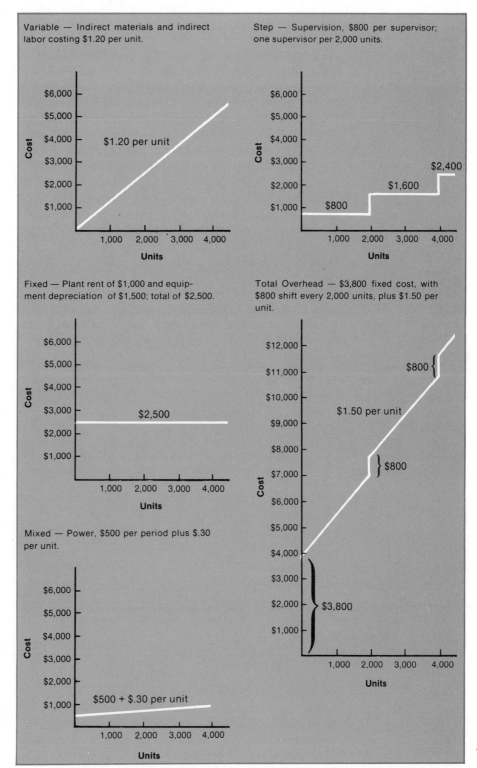

Variable — Indirect materials and indirect labor costing $1.20 per unit.

$1.20 per unit

Step — Supervision, $800 per supervisor; one supervisor per 2,000 units.

$2,400

$1,600

$800

Fixed — Plant rent of $1,000 and equipment depreciation of $1,500; total of $2,500.

$2,500

Total Overhead — $3,800 fixed cost, with $800 shift every 2,000 units, plus $1.50 per unit.

$800

$1.50 per unit

$800

$3,800

Mixed — Power, $500 per period plus $.30 per unit.

$500 + $.30 per unit

change from period to period, but the relationship is not to output. For example, heating cost does not vary with output but does vary with the outside temperature.

Some fixed costs are currently controllable, while others are not. Those that are currently controllable are termed discretionary fixed costs. Such costs may be adjusted and/or eliminated in the next period. For example, the supervisor's salary may be altered or eliminated and maintenance costs may be adjusted. Other fixed costs may not be readily changed in the short run and are termed nondiscretionary. Those costs for which a commitment has been made are termed sunk costs. An example would be the rent on a factory under a long-term lease.

It should be noted that, at some point in time, all fixed costs are controllable by someone, and thus all are initially discretionary. For example, factory rent was discretionary when the ten-year lease was signed, but becomes essentially nondiscretionary during the lease term. The supervisor's salary is not discretionary at the supervisor's level of management, but it is a decision controllable by the supervisor's superior. In summary, whether or not a fixed cost is discretionary is determined by the time frame and the level of management involved.

Mixed Overhead. When total overhead for a department is studied in the aggregate, it will tend to appear as a mixed cost, because it includes variable and fixed costs as well as mixed individual cost components. Illustration 2-2 is a graph of monthly total overhead costs for a given department.

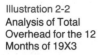

Illustration 2-2
Analysis of Total
Overhead for the 12
Months of 19X3

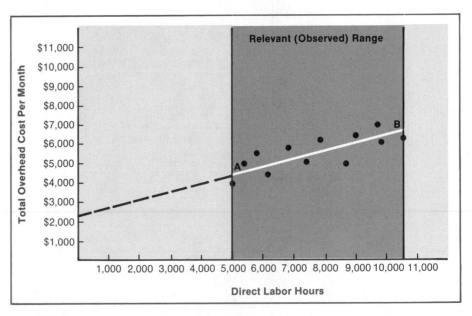

Each point on the graph represents the total overhead cost and the number of direct labor hours worked for each month. Line AB is the straight line that comes closest to the set of observations, for which the range of output is from 5,000 to 10,500 direct labor hours. The broken line is an extrapolation of the solid line to the y axis. Based on the entire line, total overhead could be expressed as $2,300 fixed cost plus $.43 per direct labor hour, derived as follows:

$$\frac{\text{Change in cost}}{\text{Change in direct labor hours}} = \frac{\$6,800 - \$2,300}{10,500 - 0 \text{ hours}} = \frac{\$4,500}{10,500} = \$.429$$

Step Overhead. Although step costs tend to exist in most firms, they are often treated as either fixed or variable overhead costs. The reason for such treatment is that accounting is a tool which serves management's needs, and analyses which do not produce benefits exceeding their costs cannot be justified. If the range of activity being studied is small enough, so that all outputs are contained in a single step, the relevant range should be specified and the cost treated as fixed for analytical purposes. In the range of 2,000 to 4,000 units in Illustration 2-1, for example, the supervisor's cost is fixed at $1,600.

If the range of activity covers many steps, on the other hand, little error is introduced by treating the step cost as a variable cost. In such cases, the steps are like the teeth of a fine tooth saw, which appear to be a straight line. For example, if one supervisor can oversee 2,000 direct labor hours per month and the range of activity being considered is 100,000 to 200,000 direct labor hours, the cost of supervisors' salaries should be treated as a variable cost.

Calculating Unit Costs

After the manufacturing costs have been analyzed, the cost components are combined to form the cost of an individual production unit. To illustrate the calculations, assume that a firm makes only one product, the Super Frisbee, in a single process. The estimated prime costs (materials and direct labor), which were established using industrial engineering methods, are as follows:

Super plastic (5 oz. @ $.30 per oz.)	$1.50
Paint (1 oz. @ $.40 per oz.)	.40
Purchased package	.30
Labor (1/4 hr. per unit @ $8 per hr.)	2.00
Prime cost per unit	$4.20

Major fixed overhead cost components include factory and machinery rent and supervision. Variable and mixed overhead cost components include electricity, maintenance, and fringe benefits. Based on a study of these costs in the aggregate, the budget for overhead may be expressed as follows:

Overhead = $18,000 per month + $3.60 per direct labor hour (DLH)

Although this cost function is applicable to a range of 1,000 to 4,000 direct labor hours per month, recall that the variable overhead cost per unit may not be as precise an estimate as the prime cost per unit.

Variable Cost per Unit. The increment in total manufacturing cost that occurs as each additional unit is produced is termed the **variable** or **direct cost** per unit. It is the prime cost, composed of direct materials and direct labor, plus the variable overhead applicable to a unit. For a Super Frisbee, the estimated variable cost per unit would be as follows:

```
Materials:
    Super plastic (5 oz. @ $.30 per oz.)  . . . . . . . . $1.50
    Paint (1 oz. @ $.40 per oz.) . . . . . . . . . . . . . .    .40
    Purchased package  . . . . . . . . . . . . . . . . . . .    .30    $2.20
Direct labor (1/4 hr. @ $8 per DLH)  . . . . . . . . . .            2.00
Variable overhead (1/4 hr. @ $3.60 per DLH) . . . .              .90
    Total variable cost per unit  . . . . . . . . . . . . . .        $5.10
```

Though fixed costs might appear to be ignored, the total manufacturing cost would be stated as $18,000 per month plus $5.10 per unit. Even on a per unit basis, fixed costs may be considered. For example, if a Super Frisbee sells for $9, each unit contributes $3.90 ($9 sales price - $5.10 variable cost) to covering fixed costs. Once fixed costs are covered, each unit would contribute $3.90 to the firm's profit.

Some accountants see no reason to unitize costs other than those that are variable. They endorse "variable" or "direct costing," a method in which only variable costs are inventoried. This position and its merits will be discussed in Chapter 6.

Full Cost per Unit. The full cost of a unit is the variable cost per unit plus an allocated share of the fixed overhead cost. The calculation of the full cost of a unit, including applied fixed overhead, is also termed **absorption costing,** since each unit absorbs a pro rata share of the fixed overhead cost. Full-unit costing is currently required for external reporting and tax purposes. For product costing purposes, the budgeted fixed overhead is usually applied to units, using the same application base as is used for variable overhead. Thus, fixed overhead is typically applied on the basis of direct labor hours. For example, if the $18,000 of fixed overhead for Super Frisbee is applied on the basis of next month's anticipated 3,000 direct labor hours, the full cost of each unit would be calculated as follows:

```
Materials:
    Super plastic (5 oz. @ $.30 per oz.)  . . . . $1.50
    Paint (1 oz. @ $.40 per oz.) . . . . . . . . . . .    .40
    Purchased package  . . . . . . . . . . . . . . .    .30    $2.20
Direct labor (1/4 hr. @ $8 per DLH)  . . . . . .            2.00
Overhead:
    Variable (1/4 hr. @ $3.60 per DLH) . . . . . $ .90
    Fixed (1/4 hr. @ $6 per DLH)  . . . . . . . .  1.50    2.40
Total full cost per unit  . . . . . . . . . . . . . . .        $6.60
```

There is a problem, however, with using each month's anticipated labor hours to apply fixed overhead. Erratic changes in unit cost will occur, even though the budgeted fixed production cost remains constant. Such changes in the cost per unit due to fluctuating output are illustrated in the following example:

Month	Fixed Cost	Direct Labor Hours (DLH)	Fixed Cost per DLH	Fixed Cost per Unit (1/4 DLH)	Budgeted Variable Cost	Full Cost per Unit
January	$18,000	3,000	$6.00	$1.50	$5.10	$6.60
February	18,000	2,500	7.20	1.80	5.10	6.90
March	18,000	4,500	4.00	1.00	5.10	6.10

To the extent that price is based on cost, full costing could also produce some irrational results. For example, when demand is down and a lower price should be considered in order to stimulate demand, the unit cost would increase. When demand is up and a higher price may be warranted, the unit cost would decrease.

To eliminate these erratic swings in unit cost from month to month, it is common to use average monthly labor hours, which would be the expected annual labor hours divided by 12. This approach evens out the cost per unit, but it presents a new problem. The cost applied to units produced during the month may exceed or fall short of the actual fixed cost for the month. If average monthly production of 3,750 labor hours were used in the preceding example and fixed overhead is applied at a rate of $4.80 per DLH ($18,000 ÷ 3,750 DLH), the disparity that would occur is illustrated as follows:

Month	Actual Fixed Cost	Fixed Cost Applied to Units	Variance
January	$18,000	3,000 × $4.80 = $14,400	$3,600 underapplied
February	18,000	2,500 × $4.80 = $12,000	6,000 underapplied
March	18,000	4,500 × $4.80 = $21,600	3,600 overapplied

On a monthly basis, underapplied overhead is typically carried on the balance sheet as a deferred charge, while overapplied overhead is carried as a deferred credit. At year end, the net over- or underapplied overhead for the year is an adjustment to the manufacturing cost of the units produced during the year.

The full cost approach can clearly cause confusion. Applying the fixed cost on a per unit basis may make fixed overhead appear to be a variable cost which increases in total as each unit is manufactured. Based on the full cost computation for Super Frisbees and using 12,000 expected units, it might appear that each unit costs $6.60 to produce. More useful for management's purposes is the statement made previously that it costs $18,000 per month to allow production to proceed, and that the incremental cost per unit is $5.10. Budgets can then be constructed to reflect true cost behavior, and better information for selling decisions is provided. For example, if the Super Frisbee company has an opportunity to produce a special order of 500 units, which can be sold for $6.40 each without affecting future orders, should the order be accepted? Clearly the price covers the incremental cost of $5.10 per unit, even though it does not cover the $6.60 full cost.

NONMANUFACTURING COSTS

Nonmanufacturing costs include the costs of making sales and processing the resulting orders. To analyze these costs properly, three major types of nonmanufacturing costs may be identified.

Physical Distribution Costs

Physical distribution costs are also commonly called order-filling costs. They represent the costs necessary to move units from the production facility to the customer and to complete the sales transaction. The activities involved include warehousing, order processing, shipping, recording of the sale, and collection. Costs subsequent to the sale, such as warranty repairs, may also be included in this category.

Physical distribution costs bear a resemblance to production costs. They exhibit similar cost behavior, having fixed, variable, and mixed cost components. The activities are often repetitive and standardized and will often lend themselves to cost accounting methods already in use for production costs. The primary problem is identifying the factors which explain the behavior of these costs.

Promotional Costs

Promotional costs, which are the costs of efforts made to generate sales, are also termed order-getting costs. The most common examples are sales force compensation, advertising, and sales promotion. Though it is appropriate to have the objective of minimizing production and physical distribution costs, the objective in managing promotional costs should be to maximize sales results per dollar of expenditure. Promotional efforts should be directed to markets or segments with the greatest potential contribution.

A study of promotional costs for most firms will reveal that they contain some variable costs, such as sales commissions and premiums, but the majority of costs are discretionary fixed costs. Common examples of discretionary fixed costs are advertising, sales salaries, and dealer promotions.

Administrative and Financial Costs

Administrative and financial costs can be viewed as the core of necessary costs to manage and finance the entire firm. Included are central management and related costs, income taxes, and interest costs. Most administrative and financial costs are of the fixed discretionary type. An exception is income taxes, which vary with the reported income of the firm.

Analysis of Nonmanufacturing Costs

The application of modern accounting methods to nonmanufacturing costs has lagged far behind the application of these methods to manufacturing costs. While almost all production firms closely scrutinize manufacturing costs, many of the same firms do little to study nonmanufacturing costs. Several reasons for this disparity in the use of analytic tools may be identified.

1. Only manufacturing costs are unitized into a cost per unit to be included in the inventory. The cost assigned to inventory is an asset and must be verifiable. When sold, the cost of the unit is released from the inventory and is reported on the income statement. Thus, a firm's income statement and balance sheet rely heavily on the value assigned to each unit. In contrast, all nonmanufacturing costs are period costs which expire with the passage of time. No matter what sophistication is used to analyze them, the expense is not changed, and thus the income for the period is not affected. Unlike the situation for manufacturing costs, external reporting and tax requirements provide no motivation for studying the behavior of nonmanufacturing costs.

2. In the past, some firms analyzed nonmanufacturing costs in order to study the profitability of various market segments. These firms usually deducted production costs to determine a segment's gross profit, and then proceeded to deduct an allocated share of all nonmanufacturing costs to arrive at the net

income for each segment. When nonmanufacturing costs were fully allocated, segments received costs over which they had no control, and many of the cost-dollars allocated to segments could not be logically justified. With such an approach, it was common to identify segments producing a loss. While it would appear that such a segment should be eliminated, further analysis might show that many of the allocated costs would not cease if the segment were eliminated. This type of analysis questioned the credibility of methods used for allocating nonmanufacturing costs and slowed the development of better analytic tools.

3. If nonmanufacturing costs are to be planned and controlled, their cost behavior with respect to activity levels must be determined. The problem is that there are many different types of nonmanufacturing costs, each with a possibly unique factor of variability which explains the behavior of costs. For example, clerical costs may correlate to invoices prepared, warehouse costs may correlate to cubic space occupied, and shipping may correlate to weight and distance. The ability to relate the bulk of nonmanufacturing costs to a single factor such as units produced or direct labor hours does not exist as it does for manufacturing costs. Therefore, the analysis of nonmanufacturing costs may be more difficult, more expensive, and more time-consuming than is required for production costs.

Today it is generally realized that the analysis of nonmanufacturing costs must have two goals. First, nonmanufacturing cost behavior must be studied carefully, so that the various cost functions may be planned and controlled. Second, cost functions should be identified for analyzing the profitability of market segments and for making pricing, promotion, and other marketing decisions. For performance evaluation purposes, segments should be charged only for variable costs and fixed costs that may be specifically identified with the segment, thus allowing contribution analysis as described in Chapter 1 to be applied.

COST FLOWS IN A MANUFACTURING FIRM

Income statement preparation for a manufacturing firm is complicated by the detailed procedures needed to determine a cost of goods sold for the period. Illustration 2-3 traces the flow of costs within a manufacturing company. Note the following features of the illustration:

1. The total set of inputs into the production plant are termed the total manufacturing cost. Included are:
   a. Materials issued (*not* materials purchased). Since there may be an inventory of materials at the start and at the end of the period, issuances do not usually equal purchases.
   b. Direct labor.
   c. Overhead. Under full costing, both variable and fixed overhead are included in the total manufacturing cost entering the production plant. Since all costs entering the production plant are unitized, fixed costs will be unitized. If direct costing is used, fixed overhead would not enter the production plant as part of the total manufacturing cost. Instead, it would be expensed as a period cost. Thus, only variable costs would be unitized.

Illustration 2-3
Cost Flows for a
Manufacturing Firm

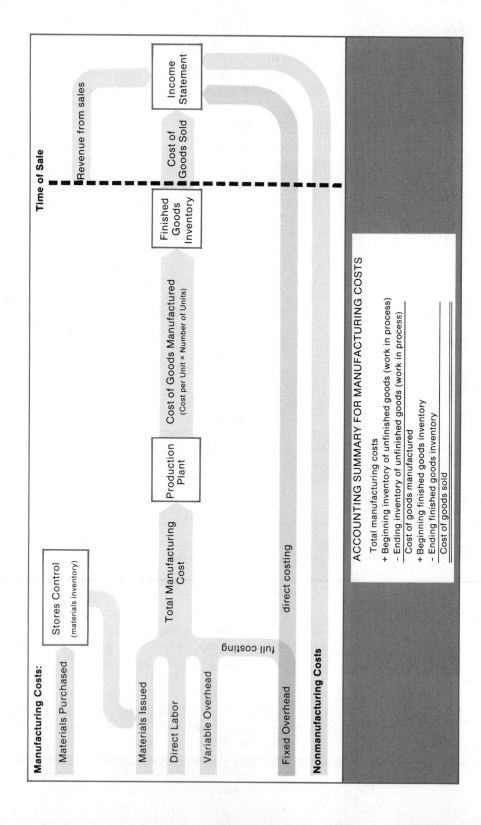

ACCOUNTING SUMMARY FOR MANUFACTURING COSTS

  Total manufacturing costs
+ Beginning inventory of unfinished goods (work in process)
− Ending inventory of unfinished goods (work in process)
  Cost of goods manufactured
+ Beginning finished goods inventory
− Ending finished goods inventory
  Cost of goods sold

2. From an accounting standpoint, the production plant is where input costs are unitized. The total manufacturing cost enters as dollars of material, direct labor, and overhead. It leaves as a cost per unit of output. If there were no beginning or ending inventory of work in process (unfinished units), the total manufacturing cost and the cost of goods manufactured would be equal. Only their composition would differ. This is demonstrated by the following example, which assumes no inventories of work in process:

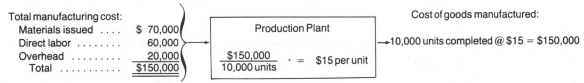

Total manufacturing cost:
Materials issued	$ 70,000
Direct labor	60,000
Overhead	20,000
Total	$150,000

Production Plant

$$\frac{\$150,000}{10,000 \text{ units}} = \$15 \text{ per unit}$$

Cost of goods manufactured:

10,000 units completed @ $15 = $150,000

When partially complete units exist in the beginning and/or ending work in process inventory, a special procedure is used to calculate unit cost. As explained in Chapter 11, the procedure involves dividing the period's costs by equivalent production units (EPUs).

3. The cost of goods manufactured is a cost per unit multiplied by the number of units transferred to finished goods. The cost of goods sold is the same unit cost multiplied by the number of units sold. If there were no beginning or ending inventories of finished goods, the cost of goods manufactured would equal the cost of goods sold.

4. To the left of the vertical dashed line, all accounting procedures for manufacturing costs are cost rearrangements. No expenses are recognized until a unit is sold and becomes a part of the cost of goods sold.

5. The Accounting Summary for Manufacturing Costs at the bottom of Illustration 2-3 shows that it is easy to compute the cost of goods sold if the total manufacturing cost is calculated properly. After the total manufacturing cost has been determined, an adjustment is made for beginning and ending work in process inventories to arrive at the cost of goods manufactured. The cost of goods manufactured is adjusted for finished goods inventories to produce the cost of goods sold.

Illustration 2-4 is a numerical example of the cost flow diagram just studied. Inventory values for work in process are given, since the EPU procedure has not been presented. It is assumed that Crews Company produces a single product, wood carvings, from a single material, a block of wood. The fifo inventory method is used. The carvings are sold for $6 each. Illustration 2-4 is the basis for the income statement on page 39.

Rather than encumber the income statement with all of the manufacturing cost data, it is common to place some or all of the supporting figures in a separate schedule. One approach is to include the cost of goods sold in the income statement and to prepare a separate cost of goods sold schedule. Another approach is to begin the cost of goods sold section of the income statement with the cost of goods manufactured and to include the finished goods inventories to arrive at the cost of goods sold. A supporting manufacturing cost schedule or a cost of goods manufactured schedule details the cost of goods manufactured.

Illustration 2-4
Numerical Example of
Cost Flows

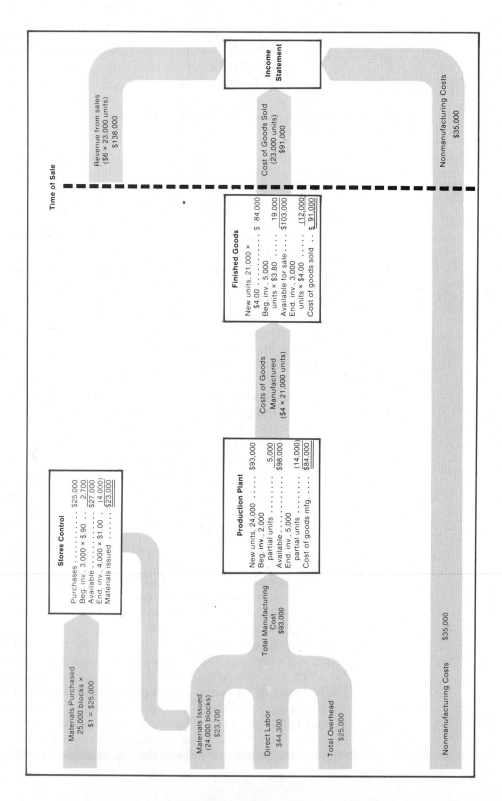

Income Statement

Revenue from sales
($6 × 23,000 units)
$138,000

Cost of Goods Sold
(23,000 units)
$91,000

Nonmanufacturing Costs
$35,000

Time of Sale

Finished Goods

New units, 21,000 × $4.00	$ 84,000
Beg. inv., 5,000 units × $3.80	19,000
Available for sale	$103,000
End inv., 3,000 units × $4.00	(12,000)
Cost of goods sold	$ 91,000

Costs of Goods
Manufactured
($4 × 21,000 units)

Stores Control

Purchases	$25,000
Beg. inv., 3,000 × $.90	2,700
Available	$27,000
End inv., 4,000 × $1.00	(4,000)
Materials issued	$23,000

Production Plant

New units, 24,000	$93,000
Beg. inv., 2,000 partial units	5,000
Available	$98,000
End inv., 5,000 partial units	(14,000)
Cost of goods mfg.	$84,000

Total Manufacturing
Cost
$93,000

Materials Purchased
25,000 blocks ×
$1 = $25,000

Materials Issued
(24,000 blocks)
$23,700

Direct Labor
$44,300

Total Overhead
$25,000

Nonmanufacturing Costs
$35,000

Crews Company
Income Statement
For Year Ended December 31, 19X1

Sales (23,000 units @ $6)			$138,000
Cost of goods sold:			
Materials purchased	$25,000		
Beginning inventory, materials	2,700		
Materials available	$27,700		
Ending inventory, materials	4,000		
Materials issued		$23,700	
Direct labor		44,300	
Overhead		25,000	
Total manufacturing cost		$93,000	
Beginning inventory, work in process		5,000	
Total cost to account for		$98,000	
Ending inventory, work in process		14,000	
Cost of goods manufactured		$ 84,000	
Beginning inventory, finished goods		19,000	
Goods available for sale		$103,000	
Ending inventory, finished goods		12,000	
Cost of goods sold			91,000
Gross margin			$ 47,000
Nonmanufacturing costs			35,000
Net income			$ 12,000

BASIC METHODS OF UNITIZING COSTS

It is the accountant's responsibility to combine the individual elements of materials, labor, and overhead entering a plant during a period into a cost per unit of output to be transferred to the finished goods inventory. The two basic methods of unitizing costs are the job order and process cost methods. Job order costing is typically used for high value, individually unique units, such as large boats, buildings, and custom processed orders. Job order methods calculate the actual cost of a unit or set of units in an order, often termed a batch. Materials used and direct labor hours worked are directly charged to each job order. It is not possible, however, to charge overhead directly to each job, since overhead is an aggregated set of costs, most of which cannot be reasonably traced to individual jobs. Overhead is charged to jobs by determining an average rate for overhead, typically as a function of direct labor hours.

In contrast to job order costing, process costing does not attempt to calculate the cost of each unit or batch produced. It is commonly used for mass-produced, identical units for which there is no need to know the cost of every unit. Process costing techniques charge materials, direct labor, and overhead to identifiable processes (production steps) through which units pass. Once costs are gathered by processes, an average cost per process is determined by dividing the cost of the process by the number of units produced. The cost of a unit is the sum of the average costs of the processes through which the unit passes. Thus, under process costing, only an average, and never a specific, cost per unit is available.

Job Order Costing Techniques

The essential document that allows a job order cost system to function is a job cost sheet which accompanies each unit or batch. The materials issued to and direct labor hours worked for each job are entered on the job sheets. Overhead is applied to each job, usually on the basis of direct labor hours. Before a firm attempts to calculate an overhead application rate, however, it must estimate the overhead for the forthcoming period. The overhead estimate is usually based on the flexible budget which is already in use for planning and controlling overhead expenditures. This budget is flexible with respect to output, since it is stated as a fixed sum per period plus a cost per unit of activity. To illustrate, assume that Skyler Company has developed the following flexible budget:

Total monthly overhead = $4,000 per month + $1.60 per DLH

The variable portion may be clearly identified with each job, using the $1.60 per direct labor hour rate. Since full costing will be required for external reporting, the fixed cost must also be allocated to each job by dividing the $4,000 fixed cost by direct labor hours. If the monthly average direct labor hours are estimated to be 3,200, the fixed overhead application rate would be $1.25 per direct labor hour ($4,000 ÷ 3,200 hours). The total overhead application rate per direct labor hour would thus be $2.85 ($1.60 variable overhead plus $1.25 fixed overhead).

To trace the flow of costs for Skyler Company for January, 19X2, the following facts will be used:

1. Skyler produces custom bookcases primarily for libraries. The jobs in production during January were as follows:

Job Order	January 1 Inventory Cost	January Costs	Transferred Out	January 31 Inventory Costs
210	$7,240.00	$ 5,126.50	$12,366.50	
211		11,320.50	11,320.50	
212		13,420.00	13,420.00	
213		17,620.50	17,620.50	
214		18,927.00	18,927.00	
215		14,550.00	14,550.00	
216		4,213.00		$4,213.00
Total	$7,240.00	$85,177.50	$88,204.50	$4,213.00

2. Jobs 210 through 214 have been sold and shipped. Job 215 remains in the finished goods inventory, and Job 216 remains in work in process.
3. Materials information:

	Jan. 1 Inventory	Purchases	Issuances	Jan. 31 Inventory
Wood	$3,000	$38,000	$36,000	$5,000
Hardware	1,800	15,600	15,000	2,400
Total	$4,800	$53,600	$51,000	$7,400

4. Direct labor, 3,150 hours at $8 per hour totals $25,200.

5. Actual overhead expenses:

Payroll taxes	$2,030
Employee pension contribution	2,410
Supervision	1,500
Insurance	300
Depreciation expense	800
Supplies	1,700
Power	760
Total	$9,500

6. Overhead applied to manufacturing is 3,150 direct labor hours × $2.85 per direct labor hour, or $8,977.50.

On the basis of these facts, the summary journal entries and the ledger control accounts (with entry numbers in parentheses) would be prepared as shown in Illustration 2-5. Illustration 2-6, which is a job cost sheet for Job 211, shows the recording of materials, direct labor, and overhead for a specific job. The estimates for cost and direct labor hours on the job card are for cost control purposes only and are not the basis of any accounting entries.

Illustration 2-5
Job Order Costing

Entry No.	Entry		
1.	Materials - Wood	38,000.00	
	Materials - Hardware	15,600.00	
	Accounts Payable		53,600.00
	To record purchases of raw materials.		
2.	Work in Process	51,000.00	
	Materials - Wood		36,000.00
	Materials - Hardware		15,000.00
	To record issuances of raw materials to production. Materials issued are recorded for each job. See Illustration 2-6 for an example of materials issued to Job 211.		
3.	Work in Process (3,150 hours × $8 per DLH)	25,200.00	
	Wages Payable		25,200.00
	To record direct labor cost applicable to work in process. Direct labor is also posted to each job in process. See Illustration 2-6 for an example of materials issued to Job 211.		
4.	Overhead Control	9,500.00	
	Payroll Taxes Payable		2,030.00
	Wages Payable (for supervision)		1,500.00
	Employee Pension Contributions Payable		2,410.00
	Prepaid Insurance (expired insurance)		300.00
	Accumulated Depreciation		800.00
	Supplies Inventory (for supplies used)		1,700.00
	Utilities Payable		760.00
	To record incurrence of overhead expenses for the period.		
5.	Work in Process (3,150 hours × $2.85 per DLH)	8,977.50	
	Overhead Control		8,977.50
	To record overhead applied to work in process. See Illustration 2-6 for overhead applied to Job 211.		

Entry No.	Entry		
6.	Finished Goods	88,204.50	
	Work in Process		88,204.50
	To record completion of Jobs 210 through 215 and the transfer of their costs from work in process to finished goods. As each job is completed, the total materials, labor, and overhead on each job card is the basis for the entry for the transfer of costs to finished goods.		
7.	Cost of Goods Sold	73,654.50	
	Finished Goods		73,654.50
	To record sale of Jobs 210 through 214. The total cost recorded for each job is transferred to Cost of Goods Sold at the time of sale.		

Ledger

Materials—Wood

Jan. 1 Balance	3,000.00	(2) Issued . . .	36,000.00
(1) Purchases .	38,000.00		
Jan. 31 Balance	5,000.00		

Materials—Hardware

Jan. 1 Balance	1,800.00	(2) Issued . . .	15,000.00
(1) Purchases .	15,600.00		
Jan. 31 Balance	2,400.00		

Work in Process

Jan. 1 Balance (Job 210)	7,240.00	(6) Transferred to finished goods:	
(2) Wood used .	36,000.00	Job 210 . .	12,366.50
(2) Hardware used	15,000.00	211 . .	11,320.50
(3) Labor used .	25,200.00	212 . .	13,420.00
(5) Overhead applied . . .	8,977.50	213 . .	17,620.50
		214 . .	18,927.00
		215 . .	14,550.00
Jan. 31 Balance (Job 216)	4,213.00		

Overhead Control

(4) Expenses .	9,500.00	(5) Applied . . .	8,977.50
Jan. 31 Balance	522.50		

Finished Goods

(6) Received from work in process:		(7) Sold and shipped:	
Job 210 . .	12,366.50	Job 210 . .	12,366.50
211 . . .	11,320.50	211 . .	11,320.50
212 . . .	13,420.00	212 . .	13,420.00
213 . . .	17,620.50	213 . .	17,620.50
214 . . .	18,927.00	214 . .	18,927.00
215 . . .	14,550.00		
Jan. 31 Balance (Job 215)	14,550.00		

Cost of Goods Sold

(7) Sold and shipped:			
Job 210 . .	12,366.50		
211 . . .	11,320.50		
212 . . .	13,420.00		
213 . . .	17,620.50		
214 . . .	18,927.00		
Total	73,654.50		

Illustration 2-6
Job Cost Card

Skyler Company

Job Order No. 211

Purchaser: STORE BANK PUBLIC SCHOOLS
34124 HIGHWAY 175
OCONOMOWOC WI 53066-3472

Description: BOOKSHELVES PER QUOTATION NO. 352
Date ordered: DEC. 15, 19X1
Date promised: JAN. 10, 19X2
Date shipped: JAN. 9, 19X2
Cost estimate: $11,600 including 360 direct labor hours

| | MATERIALS | | | LABOR | | | OVERHEAD APPLIED | |
Date	Reqn. No.	Amount	Date	Hrs.	Rate	Amount	Rate	Amount
JAN. 5	127	$4,236.00	JAN. 5	70	$8.00	$ 560.00	$2.85	$199.50
JAN. 6	132	1,124.00	JAN. 6	80	8.00	640.00	2.85	228.00
JAN. 8	133	2,163.00	JAN. 7	90	8.00	720.00	2.85	256.50
			JAN. 8	110	8.00	880.00	2.85	313.50
TOTALS		$7,523.00		350		$2,800.00		$997.50

TOTAL JOB COST $11,320.50

In reviewing the entries and ledger accounts of Illustration 2-5, the following observations should be made:

1. A perpetual inventory is used for raw materials, so that materials may be recorded as they are issued to jobs. The subsidiary ledger cards for each item of the wood and hardware inventories are not included in the example. Only the two major control accounts are shown.

2. Work in process is also a perpetual inventory. Each cost card for jobs in process is actually a subsidiary ledger. The sum of costs on each job card at any point in time is the total work in process inventory. As shown on page 42, the total cost for Job 210 is the beginning work in process inventory. The cost assigned to Job 216 is the ending work in process inventory. As jobs are completed, the work in process inventory is credited for the sum of the costs on each completed job card.

3. The finished goods inventory is also a perpetual inventory. As a job is completed, the job's cost is added to the finished goods inventory. When the job is sold, the inventory is credited for the cost of the job. At any point in time, the total finished goods inventory is the sum of the costs found on the job cards for the unsold units.

4. There will generally be a disparity between total overhead expenses incurred in a period and the overhead applied to jobs. In this example, $9,500 of expenses were incurred, while only $8,977.50 was applied to work in process. This disparity results because actual expenses may not agree with the amount originally budgeted, and, in the case of fixed overhead, because the actual labor hours worked do not agree with the number of hours built into the predetermined application rate. For example, overhead was applied on the basis of 3,150 direct labor hours, while the predetermined rate was based on 3,200 hours. Therefore, $62.50 of fixed overhead is unapplied (50 hours below the basis for application × $1.25 per direct labor hour).

The disparity between overhead expense and overhead applied is carried on the monthly balance sheet as a deferred debit or credit. If there is a net under- or overapplied balance at year end, it may not be deferred to the next year. Technically, the cost of all units produced during the year should be adjusted for this disparity. Since the majority of units produced will have been sold, however, the concept of materiality permits adjusting the cost of goods sold for the entire disparity.

Process Costing Techniques

Process costing is appropriate when identical products are built using standard, repetitive operations. In process costing, materials, direct labor, and overhead are charged only to departments and not specifically to units or job orders. The cost of processing a single unit is an average cost derived by dividing the process cost during a given period by output. The cost of a unit passing through multiple processes is the sum of the average costs of the processes utilized.

To illustrate process costing techniques, assume that Conney River Paddle Company produces a single-size canoe paddle. Paddles are first cut and shaped in the Shaping Department and then are sanded and varnished in the Finishing Department. Illustration 2-7 reveals that materials, direct labor, and overhead are debited directly to the using department.

Illustration 2-7
Process Costing

Work in Process - Shaping Department

Incurred and recorded during Jan.	Materials	$ 27,000	Transferred out	$ 55,000*
	Direct labor	16,000		
	Overhead	12,000	(Per unit cost = $\dfrac{\$\,55{,}000}{20{,}000\ units}$ = $2.75)	
	Total cost	$ 55,000		

Work in Process - Finishing Department

	Materials	$ 13,000	Transferred out (cost of	
Incurred and recorded during Jan.	Direct labor	26,000	goods manufactured)	$103,000*
	Overhead	9,000		
	Prior department cost (recorded on Jan. 31)	55,000	(Per unit cost = $\dfrac{\$103{,}000}{20{,}000\ units}$ = $5.15)	
	Total cost	$103,000		

Finished Goods (FIFO Cost Method)

	Inventory, Jan. 1 (4,000 units @ $4.90)	$ 19,600	Cost of goods sold:	
Posted Jan. 31	Cost of goods manufactured (20,000 units @ $5.15)	103,000	(4,000 units @ $4.90)	$ 19,600
			(17,000 units @ $5.15)	87,550
				$107,150*
	Inventory, Jan. 31 (3,000 units @ $5.15)	$ 15,450		

Cost of Goods Sold

Jan. 31	$107,150		

*Calculated Jan. 31

Budgets may be used to plan and control department costs, but budgeted figures are not recorded. When overhead occurs solely within a department, no overhead application rate is needed, since total actual costs for the period are calculated at the end of the period only. If there were overhead costs common to the two departments, some method would be needed to allocate the common cost, as discussed in Chapter 14.

By nature, a process cost system based on actual costs uses periodic inventory procedures. No unit cost is available until the end of the period, when the total cost is divided by units produced. In Illustration 2-7, the total and per unit cost of the shaping process is not known until January 31, 19X1. At that time, the following entry records the transfer of the cost of units sent to the Finishing Department:

Work in Process—Finishing Department	55,000	
Work in Process—Shaping Department		55,000

The cost of units entering a process from a previous process are termed prior department costs. Prior department costs are, in a sense, internally procured materials. The prior department cost procedure allows costs to be "rolled" down the assembly line. Each department inherits all costs incurred to date, which allows the final total cost to emerge from the last process. This principle could be described as a "snowball" principle, since each unit picks up added costs as it rolls down the line, and finally arrives at a cumulative total. Once the prior department cost is known and charged to the Finishing Department, a final total and per unit cost can be computed and charged to Finished Goods. The final step is to calculate the cost of goods sold.

In the illustration, it is assumed that there is no inventory of work in process at the beginning or end of the process. This assumption was made in order to avoid the complication resulting from the EPU concept, which is discussed in Chapter 11.

Although the illustration used periodic inventory procedures, most major industrial firms that use process costing will use perpetual inventory procedures in order to have a unit cost available at any time during a period. As discussed in Chapter 11, these procedures will usually be based on standard costs. A standard cost is a predetermined estimate on a per-unit-of-output basis. As units are completed, they are moved from one process to another and to finished goods at the predetermined standard cost. However, each process will likely show a difference, termed a variance, between the actual cost for a period and the standard cost of the unit produced. This variance may be subdivided in order to explain its causes.

1. Define product costs and period costs.

2. What are prime costs?

3. What are the three major categories of manufacturing costs, and what is included in each?

4. Briefly describe how you would expect each of the following overhead costs to change as output increases:

   (1) Supervision
   (2) Fringe benefits for direct labor
   (3) Plant insurance
   (4) Maintenance
   (5) Depreciation
   (6) Power
   (7) Heat

5. What types of costs might one find included in overhead? How do these costs separately behave?

6. What are discretionary fixed costs? Is it correct to say that at some point in time all fixed costs are discretionary? Why or why not?

7. When is it appropriate to treat step costs as fixed? variable?

8. It is common to allocate fixed overhead to each unit produced. What problems occur when using the various application bases?

9. Identify the three major types of nonmanufacturing costs. Why might a firm want to analyze these costs?

10. What are some reasons that nonmanufacturing costs are not studied and controlled as closely as costs directly associated with the manufacturing process?

11. If direct or variable costing is used, where do fixed overhead costs enter the cost flows of a manufacturing firm?

12. What is the total manufacturing cost? What is the cost of goods manufactured? When would these amounts be equal?

13. Describe briefly the two basic methods of unitizing costs.

14. When using a job order cost system, at the end of the period there will usually be a balance in the overhead control account. Why? How is this balance normally handled?

15. Does using a process cost system automatically preclude using a periodic inventory?

16. What is a variance? For what type of costing system is a variance likely to occur?

Exercise 1. Alumco Company manufactures aluminum storm windows. In making each 10-unit lot, four operations must be performed. Cutting of the aluminum takes 1.5 hours by an employee paid $8.50 per hour. Glass cutting is done in .7 hours at $9 per hour. The assembling takes 2.5 hours at a pay rate of $12 per hour. The finishing and inspecting is completed in 6 minutes per window at $7 per hour.

What is the labor cost to build a 10-window-unit lot? What is the average cost per hour of labor?

Exercise 2. Blough Inc., which manufactures a successful new product, is installing a new cost accounting system.

Last year's data showed a cost of $18.50 per unit for material. Three hours of direct labor at $5 per hour were required each unit. Sales and production were 5,000 units.

Overhead included indirect labor, 40% of which varied with direct labor hours. Supplies consisted of items that were used in the manufacturing process but that were too small to account for separately. The use of power and computer time was dependent upon the level of output. The actual costs were:

Indirect labor	$30,000
Plant depreciation	15,000
Supplies	4,500
Power	3,000
Production computer time	6,000

The company expects a 20% increase in sales next year. The additional demand can be produced in the current plant.

Classify the overhead items. Formulate a production budget for next year for materials, labor, fixed overhead, and variable overhead per direct labor hour.

Exercise 3. Walsh Co. is analyzing the various components of its overhead account. For each overhead item listed below, draw a rough sketch of how the cost would behave as output increases. Graph output per year on the horizontal axis and total cost on the vertical axis.

- Power: Power cost consists of a monthly meter charge, plus a charge per thousand kilowatt-hours used. The rate per thousand kilowatt-hours decreases at distinct points as usage increases.
- Depreciation on factory equipment: All depreciation is calculated using the sum-of-the-years-digits method.
- Property taxes: The property tax is assessed as a fixed percentage of assessed value.
- Fire insurance: Fire insurance is paid quarterly.
- Indirect labor: Indirect labor includes the wages of six employees classified as indirect labor and includes maintenance functions.
- Rent for materials warehouse: For production rates below 70% of normal capacity, one warehouse is adequate to store raw materials. For outputs beyond this level, an additional warehouse must be leased.

Exercise 4. A manufacturer of mini tractors expects to incur the following costs to produce its normal output, 1,000 units. Variable overhead varies as a function of direct labor hours.

	Overhead Estimates
Direct labor (7,500 hrs.)	$75,000
Indirect labor	8,000 V
Indirect labor	22,000 F
Direct materials	90,000
Power	2,500 V
Supplies	3,000 F
Equipment depreciation	5,000

(1) Calculate the variable and fixed overhead rates per direct labor hour.
(2) Calculate the variable cost per unit.
(3) Calculate the full cost per unit.

Exercise 5. Easy Rider Inc. produces lawn mowers. The company uses the full cost method to value its mowers for inventory purposes. Fixed overhead for the period is expected to be $14,000. Variable costs are estimated as:

Materials	$25.00 per unit
Direct labor	18.00
Variable overhead	5.50
Total	$48.50 per unit

Calculate the full cost per unit if the output is: (1) 700 units; (2) 1,000 units; (3) 1,400 units.

Exercise 6. Best Sock Co. uses the full cost of its product to make decisions about accepting special orders. The costs of manufacturing and selling the socks are:

Materials	$15.00 per case
Direct labor ($7.80 per hr. × 1.5 hrs.)	$11.70 per case
Variable overhead	$3,000 per 1,000 cases
Fixed overhead	$250,000
Variable selling expenses	$.75 per case
Fixed selling expenses	$60,000

Fixed overhead and fixed selling expenses are applied on the basis of normal production of 200,000 cases.

CheapMart Discount Stores have offered to purchase 150 cases of socks for $31.50 per case. The normal variable selling expenses would be reduced by $.05 per case. The special order would not impact on other sales.

The policy of the company is to accept only orders that cover their share of fixed costs. Are fixed costs covered in this case? Should Best Sock Co. accept this offer? Explain.

Exercise 7. The following information relates to Whitewall Tire Company for the current manufacturing period:

Direct labor	$25,000
Materials purchased	15,000
Materials beginning inventory	2,500
Materials ending inventory	5,500
Overhead (all variable)	6,000

Of the 5,000 units manufactured, 80% were sold. There was no beginning inventory of work in process or finished goods.

Calculate the cost of goods sold under direct costing, using the following flow diagram:

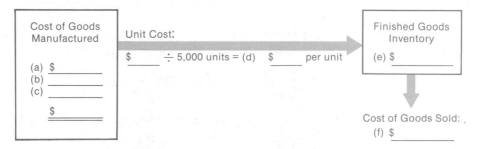

Exercise 8. **Maxi Computer Company** runs a job order shop for its large computer line. Cost data relating to Job 444 are:

July 17: Materials issued, $ 429.50; hours worked, 55
July 18: Materials issued, 1,250.00; hours worked, 70
July 19: Materials issued, 130.00; hours worked, 60
July 21: Materials issued, 0 ; hours worked, 25

For this type of job, the average labor rate is $13.50. The variable overhead application rate is $5.35 per hour. The budget for fixed overhead is $24,000 and is applied using a normal 16,000 hours for the period.

Develop a job order card in good form, showing the costs for materials, labor, and overhead, and the total cost.

Exercise 9. **Hard Hammer Company** makes hammers in 2 processes, molding and finishing. During the period, 12,000 units with an inventoriable cost of $48,000 were transferred from the Molding Department to Finishing. Materials used in the Finishing Department for the period were $7,600. Labor hours amounted to 800 hours at $10.50 per hour. Overhead is applied at a rate of $2.50 per direct labor hour for the department.

Calculate the cost per hammer as it moves from (1) Molding to Finishing (2) to Finished Goods. There are no beginning or ending work in process inventories in either department.

Prepare the entires to record the flow of costs from the Molding Department to Finished Goods.

PROBLEMS

Problem 2-1. Given on page 50 are a number of graphs of cost behavior and a list of expenses. For each of the graphs, the vertical axis describes the total cost of the activity, while the horizontal axis describes output for a calendar year.

(1) Straight-line depreciation on production equipment.
(2) Packaging department total labor cost.
(3) Total maintenance expense on factory equipment.
(4) Unemployment taxes on factory labor payroll.
(5) Bonus expense for the plant manager. The bonus is 1/2% of the plant's contribution to the division's fixed cost. The bonus cannot exceed $15,000 per year.

(6) Cost of direct materials purchased subject to quantity discounts which increase from 2% to 10% as larger and larger quantities are used.

(7) Depreciation on production equipment, using sum-of-the-years-digits method.

(8) Total payroll cost for product inspectors; each inspector can inspect 1,250 units per day; planned output is between 250,000 and 750,000 units per year.

(9) Cost of electricity. The price schedule per thousand kilowatt-hours is as follows:

Usage per Year (in 000s of kwh)	Price per 1,000 kwh
0-10,000	$ 6
10,001-20,000	7
20,001-30,000	9
Over 30,000	12

(10) Operating costs of corporate aircraft used by factory managers.

(11) Lease cost of company computer system which serves the factory. All factory departments use equal portions of computer time.

(12) Property taxes paid on factory building. The property tax rate falls from $.16 per $1,000 of assessed value (16 mils) to 8 mils if capacity utilization is below 75%.

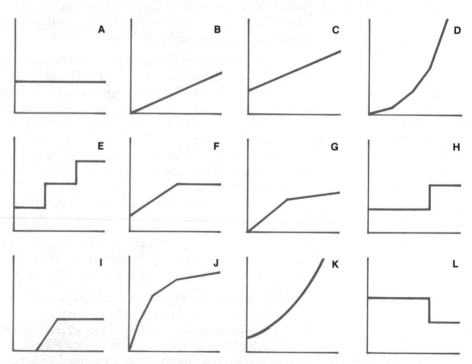

Match each expense with the cost graph which best describes how the cost changes as output changes. Each graph may be used more than once or not at all.

Problem 2-2. Harris Corporation is bidding on a contract to produce 2,500 widgets. It is estimated that the materials and labor costs for the project will be as follows:

Plastic $11,000
Paint   1,500
Labor:

Dept.	Rate	Hours
Molding	$9	200
Painting	7	140
Finishing	8	60

In a recent month, when 8,000 direct labor hours were worked, the following overhead costs were incurred:

Power (40% is fixed) $3,000
Indirect labor (variable)   6,000
Rent   4,500
General overhead (fixed)   4,300
General overhead (variable)   5,000

Required

(1) Calculate the average wage rate for the contract. Use a schedule to show how the rate is determined.
(2) How many average labor hours are needed to produce one unit?
(3) Develop a budget formula for the total overhead cost.
(4) Calculate the variable product cost per unit. In a schedule, show variable cost per unit for each item: plastic, paint, direct labor, and variable overhead.
(5) Continue the schedule developed in (4) to show the full cost per unit. (Hint: What is the fixed application rate per direct labor hour, using 8,000 direct labor hours?)

Problem 2-3. Palmetto Industries produces a variety of transmissions for garden tractors, trenching machines, and other types of light- and medium-duty equipment. In July, Palmetto produced 4,000 gearboxes. Each gearbox requires 3 direct labor hours to produce. Overhead information for the plant is as follows:

(1) The only indirect material is 3 quarts of transmission fluid per unit. The average cost of fluid is $.80 per quart.
(2) Light and power costs, which are considered to be variable, totaled $1,800 in July.
(3) Separate maintenance records are kept for building and machinery maintenance expenses. Building maintenance averages $675 per month, regardless of output. Machinery maintenance expenses are $300 per month, plus $.15 per gearbox.
(4) Air conditioning of the plant costs $1,600 per month from May to September; from October to April, heating costs are $1,200 per month.
(5) The plant needs one supervisor for each 2,500 gearboxes produced per month. Supervisors are paid $2,000 per month.
(6) The plant leases a computer at a cost of $1,000 per month. The computer, which maintains inventory and payroll records and schedules production, is large enough to handle all outputs within plant capacity.

(7) Overtime must be paid at the additional rate of $4 per direct labor hour for all outputs above 20,000 DLH per month.

(8) Property taxes paid on factory building are $700 per month, regardless of output level.

(1) Develop a monthly overhead budget for Palmetto Industries, using direct labor hours as a base, Step costs should be treated as fixed, but the location of the steps should be specified. Palmetto's relevant production range is 3,000 to 8,000 units per month. Organize your data using the following columns:

Variable Costs			Fixed Costs	
cost item	cost per unit	cost per DLH	costs	comments

(2) In July, Palmetto incurred overhead costs of $27,000. Palmetto expects production in August to reach 5,500 units. Using the budget developed in (1), what is the expected overhead cost in August?

Probelm 2-4. Kowalski Inc. expects the following costs for overhead, based on a normal level of 4,000 direct labor hours for the period:

Variable Overhead		Fixed Overhead	
Materials handling	$1,500	Depreciation	$3,000
Supplies	1,400	Property taxes	500
Indirect labor	2,600	Supervision	2,500

Two hours of labor are necessary to produce each unit. The product cost for materials and labor combined is $4.50 per unit.

Required

(1) Determine the overhead budget for Kowalski Inc. Use direct labor hours as a base.

(2) Determine the full cost of a unit, based on production of 1,500, 2,000, and 2,500 units. Apply the total fixed overhead to each of the alternative quantities, using direct labor hours as a base.

(3) Determine the full cost per unit, applying the fixed overhead in terms of the normal level of 4,000 direct labor hours.

(4) For the production of 1,500, 2,000, and 2,500 units, apply fixed overhead, using the normal production rate. Determine the over- or underapplied overhead at each level.

Problem 2-5. Nelson Manufacturing Company produces a single product, with the following per unit costs based on 2,750 direct labor hours per period:

Materials	$18.50
Direct labor	12.00
Variable overhead	3.20
Fixed overhead	3.00

To produce 1 unit, 1.5 hours of direct labor are required. During the period, 2,000 units were started, completed, and sold. The sales price is $50 per unit. The nonmanufacturing costs were: variable selling, $1.75 per unit; and fixed selling, $7,500.

Ch. 2

52

Prepare an income statement for 19X0, including an adjustment to Cost of Goods Manufactured for under- or overapplied overhead. There were no beginning or ending finished goods inventories.

Problem 2-6. Peanut Products Co. roasts and packages peanuts for consumption as snacks. The snacks sell for $1.25 per bag. Cost and production data for the processing operation are as follows:

Materials (oil, salt, peanuts, and packaging): $.35 per bag
Direct labor (.05 DLH per bag): average wage rate is $6 per DLH
Selling expenses: $3,100 per month
Administrative costs: $4,200 per month

Peanut Product's accounting staff has just completed a study of overhead costs in order to improve cost control. The results of the study are summarized as follows:

Item	Cost per Month	Variable	Fixed
Heat, light, and power	$2,400	25%	75%
Indirect materials	1,250	100	-
Plant supervision	3,000	20	80
Depreciation	980	-	100
Maintenance	2,250	60	40

In a normal month, 1,520 direct labor hours are worked. Fixed overhead is allocated on the basis of normal DLHs. Any under- or overapplied fixed overhead is closed with an adjustment to Cost of Goods Sold.

In September, 19X7, Peanut Products produced and sold 42,000 bags of peanuts. There were no beginning or ending inventories.

(1) Calculate an overhead budget and the overhead application rates for fixed and variable overhead.
(2) Prepare a full cost income statement, including an adjustment for under- or overapplied overhead for September.

Problem 2-7. Armand-Flint Corporation manufactures structural steel components for engineering projects. The cost of goods sold is based on actual costs incurred during the period. Data for September, 19X8, are as follows:

Materials inventory, September 1	$12,000
Work in process, September 1	26,350
Finished goods inventory, September 1	12,250
Materials purchases	61,100
Direct labor hours worked (6,300 hours @ $8.15 per hour)	51,345
Selling expenses:	
Salaries	7,500
Commissions	2,320
Other	1,300
General and administrative expenses	17,800
Variable overhead:	
Indirect labor	9,720
Indirect materials—10% of direct materials cost entering production	?
Fixed overhead	38,500

Materials inventory, September 30	15,500
Work in process, September 30	24,000
Finished goods inventory, September 30	18,400
Revenues	182,400

Required (1) Prepare a flowchart showing the flow of costs through Armand-Flint's accounting records.

(2) Prepare an income statement showing the results of September's operations.

Problem 2-8 (AICPA adapted, 5/76). Management of Bicent Company estimates the following unit costs for the one product it manufactures:

Direct materials (all variable)	$30.00
Direct labor (all variable)	19.00
Manufacturing overhead:	
Variable cost	6.00
Fixed cost (based on 10,000 units per year)	5.00
Selling, general, and administrative expenses:	
Variable cost per unit manufactured	4.00
Fixed cost (based on 10,000 units per year)	2.80

The projected selling price is $80 per unit. The fixed costs remain fixed within the relevant range of 4,000 to 16,000 units of production.

Management has also projected the following data for the year:

Beginning inventory	2,000 units
Production	9,000
Available for sale	11,000 units
Sales	7,500
Ending inventory	3,500 units

Required (1) What is the inventoriable cost per unit, using full costing:

(2) Prepare a projected full cost income statement for 19X6. Charge the under- or overapplied fixed manufacturing overhead to Cost of Goods Sold.

Problem 2-9. Ross Company manufactures aluminum awnings at its plant in Arizona. Its results for the current year are summarized as follows:

Ross Company
Income Statement
For Year Ended December 31, 19X7

Sales		$720,000
Cost of goods sold:		
Direct materials (all variable)	$186,000	
Direct labor (all variable)	138,000	
Overhead (fixed and variable)	228,000	
Cost of goods sold	$552,000	
Adjustment for underapplied overhead	30,000	
Adjusted cost of goods sold		582,000
Gross profit		$138,000
Selling expenses	$ 62,000	
Office and other administrative expenses	47,000	109,000
Net income		$ 29,000

Ross Company started, completed, and sold 6,000 awnings in 19X7. There were no beginning or ending inventories. Of the total overhead, $108,000 is considered variable. Fixed overhead was applied to production, using an expected production level of 7,500 units.

During 19X8, Ross expects unit sales to increase by 20%. Fixed overhead cost is expected to increase by 10%. Selling expenses will increase by $12,000 due to an increase in the commission rate. Unit labor costs will rise by 15%. To cover these rising costs, Ross will raise the price of its awnings by 25%. All other costs will remain unchanged.

Required   Prepare a projected income statement for 19X8.

Problem 2-10. TRZ Corporation manufactures diesel/electric freight locomotives at its Albany plant. The production rate averages one locomotive per month. On August 31, work in process consisted of one job, Job 36, whose job card is as follows:

TRZ Corporation

Job No.: 36

FOR: GULF NORTHERN RAILROAD
BANGOR, MAINE

PRODUCT: MODEL 150
DATE ORDERED: FEBRUARY 15, 19X6
DATE INITIATED: AUGUST 5, 19X6
DATE COMPLETED:

MATERIALS		DIRECT LABOR			APPLIED OVERHEAD	
Week	Cost	Week	Hours	Cost	Date	Amount
AUG. 2	$97,000	AUG. 2	880	$10,560		
9	51,000	9	1,920	23,040		
16	20,000	16	1,875	22,500		
23	44,000	23	1,950	23,400		
30	19,000	30	895	10,740	AUG. 31	$101,520
END OF MONTH		END OF MONTH				
SEPT. 1		SEPT. 1				
8		8				
15		15				
Total $		Total $			Total $	

JOB SUMMARY
Materials . . . . $_____
Direct labor . . . . _____
Applied overhead . . . . _____
Total manufacturing cost . . $_____

Job 36 was completed on September 9. Jobs 37 and 38, for Texas Coast Lines, were initiated on September 6th and 28th, respectively. These jobs, ordered in March, were for locomotives identical to Job 36. Job 37 was completed on September 29th.

The average labor rate in the plant is $12 per hour. Materials and labor costs incurred during September were:

Week	Job 36		Job 37		Job 38	
	Materials	Labor Hours	Materials	Labor Hours	Materials	Labor Hours
Sept. 1	$32,000	300				
6	9,000	180	$90,000	1,650		
13			73,000	2,300		
20			84,000	2,400		
27			36,000	1,600	$61,000	320
End of month						
Total	$41,000	480	$283,000	7,950	$61,000	320

Overhead is applied to production at the rate of $13.50 per DLH. Actual overhead expenses for September were $123,500. Any under- or overapplied overhead is carried into the next month and closed to Cost of Goods Sold at year end.

Required

(1) Prepare job cost cards for Jobs 37 and 38, using the illustration as an example.
(2) Calculate the value of the beginning and ending work in process inventories for September.
(3) Prepare journal entries for September, summarizing TRZ's production activities. All accounts are updated at the end of each week and at the month's end.

Problem 2-11. Wand-Art Company manufactures customized shelving units for convenience stores, liquor stores, and other small retailers. Accounting information for January is as follows:

- Work in process:

	Job	Materials	Labor	Overhead
January 1:	150	$875	12 hours	12 hours
	151	330	7	7
January 31:	172	415	3	3

- Finished goods inventory, January 1: $12,500
- Finished goods inventory, January 31: $16,700
- Materials records:

	Inventory, January 1	Purchases	Issuances	Inventory, January 31
Aluminum	$3,150	$16,750	$ 7,350	?
Steel	4,200	5,150	8,150	?
Hardware	1,075	3,235	3,060	?
	$8,425	$25,135	$18,560	

- Direct labor hours worked: 420 hours
- Overhead:

Heat, light, and power	$2,125
Depreciation	4,750
Plant management	3,750
Indirect labor	2,235
Insurance	640
Total	$13,500

Labor is charged at the rate of $12.50 per direct labor hour. Overhead is charged to production at a rate of $31.50 per direct labor hour. Over- or underapplied overhead is treated as an adjustment to Cost of Goods Sold at year end on December 31. All jobs are numbered consecutively, and all work not in ending inventory has been completed and transferred out.

Required (1) Calculate the value of the beginning work in process inventory.

(2) Prepare journal entries and T accounts recording Wand-Art's operations for January.

(3) What is the value, at the end of January, of (a) the 3 materials inventories, (b) Work in Process, and (c) Cost of Goods Sold?

Problem 2-12. DFV Winters manufactures open-wheel racing cars in the Formula Atlantic and Formula Super-Vee classification. All production is accounted for using job order costing. Information for the January, 19X6 operations is as follows:

- Materials inventories:

	Inventory, January 1	Purchases	Issuances	Inventory, January 31
Structural aluminum	$ 1,800	$ 19,600	$ 20,400	$ 1,000
Wheel assemblies	5,500	52,000	48,000	9,500
Engines	14,500	79,000	84,300	9,200
Miscellaneous parts	8,700	136,300	141,250	3,750
	$30,500	$286,900	$293,950	$23,450

- Work in process:

	Job	Materials	Labor	Overhead
January 1:	12	$17,200	276 hours	276 hours
	13	4,500	20	20
January 31:	24	21,500	292	292

- Hours worked during month: 3,600 hours @ $12 per hour (same rate applied last month)

- Overhead:

Factory	$24,000
Depreciation	12,300
Plant management	29,000
Overtime	4,750
Other	3,950
Total	$74,000

- Finished goods inventories:

January 1: 0
January 31, (Job 23):

Materials	$21,652
Direct labor	3,700
Applied overhead	6,398
Total	$31,750

- Sales: 11 cars at $42,750 each

- Other expenses:

Shipping	$18,700
Research and testing	34,000
Administration	17,000

Overhead is applied to production at the rate of $20.75 per hour (same as rate applied last month). Under- or overapplied overhead is closed into Cost of Goods Sold at month's end.

Required   Prepare an income statement for January. It may be useful to prepare T accounts to organize the manufacturing cost data.

Problem 2-13. Felixstone Company manufactures precision valves for large industrial engines. The valves pass through two departments during manufacture: the Casting Department, where the valves are cast, and the Finishing Department, where the valves are ground and polished. During a recent month, both departments transferred out 125,000 valves. There were no beginning or ending work in process or finished goods inventories. Manufacturing cost data for the company are as follows:

	Casting Department	Finishing Department
Materials	$57,500	$9,750
Labor	2,000 hours	2,500 hours
Overhead:		
Plant management	$ 2,700	$1,600
Heat, light, and power	12,200	9,700
Depreciation	13,500	7,150
Other	3,600	2,050

The labor rate in the Casting Department is $11.50 per hour; in the Finishing Department, $10.40 per hour.

Required   (1) Prepare journal entries and T accounts to record the manufacturing operations for the month.
(2) What is the unit cost of the valves transferred (a) to the Finishing Department, (b) to Finished Goods?

Problem 2-14. Essex Company is a manufacturer of plastic products, including an inexpensive line of plastic flower pots and planters. These products go through two processes: Molding, in which raw plastic is molded into the desired shape, and Finishing, where the pieces are trimmed and decorations, if any, are applied. In a recent month, the following production costs were incurred:

	Molding Department	Finishing Department
Materials	$47,145	$ 7,440
Labor	23,400	11,400
Overhead	23,150	7,350

To control overhead costs, Essex applies overhead to production at the rate of $11.90 per direct labor hour for Molding and $3.90 per direct labor hour for Finishing. The average wage rates are $12 per hour and $6 per hour in Molding and Finishing, respectively. Any difference between overhead applied and over-head incurred is closed into Cost of Goods Sold at the end of the month.

The beginning finished goods inventory consisted of 12,500 units valued at $19,375. Sales during the month were 78,500 units. Essex uses the fifo inventory method for its finished goods inventory. There were no beginning or ending work in process inventories. Production for both departments was 75,000 units.

Prepare journal entries and T accounts to record the month's operations. Be sure to calculate the cost of goods sold for the period.

Three

Determining the Relationship of Costs to Volume

In Chapter 2, the discussion of cost concepts indicated that not all costs respond proportionately to changes in volume. In the analysis of total costs, therefore, it was necessary to incorporate the various cost behavior patterns exhibited by different types of costs. In this chapter, several different methods of determining these behavior patterns are examined.

The discussion in Chapter 2 also indicated that the allowable materials costs can be determined by examining the design plans for a product, and that the allowable direct labor requirements can be determined by time and motion studies. Engineering studies, however, are not usually used to determine the allowable overhead costs, because there are many individual overhead cost categories and because overhead costs are indirectly related to production activities.

Approaches to determining overhead costs are described in this chapter. These approaches, which are applied to overhead account categories or to the aggregate overhead cost, can also be applied to nonmanufacturing costs. Some of the methods rely on the judgment of experienced cost analysts or operating managers; others take advantage of the more objective results provided by statistical analysis of past cost data.

NONSTATISTICAL APPROACHES TO ESTIMATING COST RELATIONSHIPS

Three methods which primarily utilize the judgment of the individual determining the cost behavior are: (1) the classification of accounts, (2) the subjective judgment of cost variability, and (3) graphic approximations based on past cost data. These methods may be used for almost any application in many different types of organizations, and they may be applied when only limited data are available. Since the data requirements are modest, cost estimates can usually be put together quickly and at relatively low cost. In addition, if the operating manager has a "good feel" for the operations, the manager can incorporate into the estimates the effects of many factors that might not be apparent from an extensive analysis of the data by a less experienced individual.

On the other hand, the quality of the analysis based on nonstatistical methods is very dependent on the analytical capabilities of the manager. An individual may be a good manager and yet may have a distorted idea of how costs will change in response to changes in activity. In addition, the subjective element means that two different managers faced with similar operating situations may arrive at two very different cost estimates. This element of subjectivity makes it difficult to rely on a given individual's cost estimates.

Classification of Accounts

The simplest approach to developing cost variability information is to list accounts and account balances for a recent period and then categorize each account in terms of whether, in general, it is expected to be a variable cost or a fixed cost. For a more elaborate breakdown, additional categories can be added for mixed costs (with some portion variable and the remainder fixed) and step costs. In practice, no cost category corresponds exactly to only one of these classifications. Nevertheless, such a breakdown is a substantial improvement to simply treating the total cost as though it would change proportionately with changes in volume (i.e., as though it were entirely variable), or ignoring cost variability altogether (i.e., treating it as fixed).

To illustrate the account classification procedure, assume that you are the manager of a department that assembles butcher block tables. You are estimating the level of costs for the next month (July). For July, production volume in the department is expected to be 30% higher than in June, when 1,800 direct labor hours were worked. While July costs will increase, they should not increase by 30%, since some of the costs are fixed. Using this information and the additional information contained in the June cost report, shown in Part A of Illustration 3-1, you have developed the cost estimates shown in Part B.

For this operation, you consider materials, direct labor, and supplies to be variable. Since orders for table tops and pedestals are expected to increase from 1,000 to 1,300, the number of workers will increase from 10 to 13, and July costs for supplies will be 30% greater than the June supply costs.

The indirect labor cost is an example of a step cost. In June, the indirect labor consists of the wages of one forklift operator, who can keep up to ten workers supplied with materials and transport their finished tables to the loading dock. Since the number of workers increases to 13 in July, two operators will be needed. Although two operators could accommodate a doubling of production, you will probably use some of their time in July to accomplish other tasks, such as rearranging inventory. Their total time will still be charged as indirect labor.

Illustration 3-1
Cost Analysis Based on
the Classification of
Accounts Approach

Part A
June Cost Report

Number of tables assembled		1,000
Costs incurred:		
Materials issued:		
Butcher block tops	$50,000	
Pedestals	10,000	$60,000
Direct labor:		
1,800 hours @ $5 per hour (10 workers)		9,000
Manufacturing overhead:		
Supplies (glue, sandpaper, etc.)	$ 2,000	
Indirect labor (wages for one forklift		
operator)	1,000	
Electricity and other utilities	1,000	
Supervisory salary	1,500	
Depreciation of equipment	2,000	
Rental of factory space	1,000	8,500
Total factory cost		$77,500
Full cost per table ($77,500 ÷ 1,000)		$77.50 per table

Illustration 3-1
Cost Analysis Based on
the Classification of
Accounts Approach

Part B
Estimate of July Costs
Based on Analysis of
Accounts

	Type of Cost	June	July
Materials	Variable cost	$60,000	$78,000 (1.3 × $60,000)
Direct Labor	Variable cost	$ 9,000	$11,700 (1.3 × $9,000)
Manufacturing overhead:			
Supplies	Variable cost	$ 2,000	$ 2,600 (1.3 × $2,000)
Indirect Labor	Step cost	1,000	2,000 (1 forklift operator for each 10 workers)
Utilities	Mixed cost	1,000	1,180 ($400 + 1.3 × $600)
Supervisor Salary	Fixed cost	1,500	1,500 (Same as in June)
Depreciation	Fixed cost	2,000	2,000 (Same as in June)
Rent	Fixed cost	1,000	1,000 (Same as in June)
Total manufacturing overhead		$ 8,500	$10,280
Total factory cost		$77,500	$99,980
Number of tables assembled		1,000	1,300
Full cost per table		$77.50	$76.91

The utilities cost is an example of a mixed cost. There is a base, or "connect" charge, with the remainder of the utility bill based on usage. Some of this usage, such as the electricity used for lights, will not change much from June to July, while another portion, such as the electricity used to power machinery, will vary proportionately with production volume. You estimate that the fixed component of utilities is $400, and you increase the variable component by 30%.

The remaining costs (your salary, the depreciation, and the rent) are fixed. When these costs are added to the other costs, the July estimated costs total $99,980, or $76.91 per table.

While a cost analysis based on account classification may be done quickly, the characterization of a given account will vary from situation to situation, especially if the account categories are broad. Indirect labor, for example, may be primarily variable in one business setting but essentially fixed in another. An understanding of how the organization operates and a knowledge of what kind of costs are included in each account are essential to achieving reasonably accurate cost estimates with the account classification approach.

Subjective Estimates by Managers

Since most managers are accustomed to working with accounting cost reports for their own operations, it is reasonable to expect that managers would have an idea of how the costs of their operations are affected by variations in volume. One method that accountants sometimes use to develop cost variability information is to ask the managers directly about their perceptions of how individual costs may change in response to changes in activity. Starting with an estimate of costs at a typical activity level or with last period's actual costs, the manager could be asked how much costs would change if the activity in the department were to increase 20% or decrease by 20%, for example. Two sets of costs at two different activity levels would be sufficient to identify the amount of fixed and variable costs, but to uncover any step costs, a third set of cost data for some intermediate activity level would be necessary.

To illustrate this approach, assume that the information shown in Illustration 3-2 was compiled from your responses to questions about the effect of a 20% increase or a 20% decrease in volume in the Table Assembly Department. In this schedule, the variable and fixed costs are easily identified. The variable costs decrease or increase by 20% in response to a 20% change in activity, while the fixed costs remain unchanged. Indirect labor is easily identified as a step cost, but without further investigation, it is not known exactly where the costs "step up" from $1,000 to $2,000.

Illustration 3-2
Manager's Estimates of
Cost Variability

	Estimated Costs for a 20% Decrease in Volume (800 Tables)	Costs at the Current (June) Volume (1,000 Tables)	Estimated Costs for a 20% Increase in Volume (1,200 Tables)
Materials	$48,000	$60,000	$72,000
Direct labor	7,200	9,000	10,800
Supplies	1,600	2,000	2,400
Indirect labor	1,000	1,000	2,000
Supervisory salary	1,500	1,500	1,500
Utilities (see Illus. 3-3)	880	1,000	1,120
Depreciation	2,000	2,000	2,000
Rent	1,000	1,000	1,000
Total cost	$63,180	$77,500	$92,820

The utilities costs are identified as a mixed cost because the 20% change in activity leads to a smaller change (12%) in the total utilities cost. In Illustration 3-3, the utilities costs are plotted after the variable and fixed components have been determined by using the following procedure:

1. Find the unit variable cost by dividing the cost change by the change in activity.
   ($1,000 − $880) ÷ (1,000 − 800 tables) = $120 ÷ 200 tables = $.60 per table
2. Find the total variable cost for one of the observations by multiplying the unit variable cost by the total number of units.
   $.60 × 1,000 tables = $600
3. Find the total fixed cost by subtracting the total variable cost from the total cost.
   $1,000 − $600 = $400

Illustration 3-3
Plot of Utilities Costs for
the Table Assembly
Department

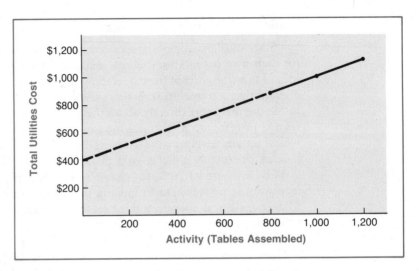

If the Table Assembly Department's total overhead cost, Y, were character-ized as a function of the number of tables produced, X, the following formulas would be applicable:

For the production of 1,000 tables or less:

$$Y = \$5,900 + \$2.60X \qquad (3.1)$$

For the production of more than 1,000 tables:

$$Y = \$6,900 + \$2.60X \qquad (3.2)$$

The $5,900 of fixed cost in Formula 3.1 is the total indirect labor cost ($1,000), the fixed portion of utilities costs ($400), supervisory salary ($1,500), depreciation ($2,000), and rent ($1,000). The extra $1,000 of fixed cost in Formula 3.2 represents the wages of the additional forklift operator required for larger production volumes. The variable overhead cost of $2.60 per table is the total of the cost of supplies ($2 per table) and the variable portion of utilities ($.60 per table). When the July production level of 1,300 tables is substituted for X in Formula 3.2, a total overhead cost of $10,280 [$6,900 + ($2.60 × 1,300)] for July is estimated.

Graphic Approximations

A severe limitation of the two approaches considered in the previous para-graphs is that they are based on only a few cost observations. Cost estimates based on many cost observations are more reliable. In this section, methods which consider numerous data points in arriving at estimates of fixed and variable costs are discussed and illustrated.

Scattergraph Method. Cost analysts often plot a series of past data points and then visually fit a straight line to these data. To illustrate this approach, called the scattergraph method, the monthly data for factory overhead costs and volume for the Table Assembly Department are shown in Part A of Illustration 3-4. The overhead cost data are plotted as a function of volume. This data plot, often called a scattergram or scattergraph, is shown in Part B.

After the data points are plotted, a straight line is drawn by inspection to show the cost-volume relationship. The line shown in Part C of Illustration 3-4 is a reasonable fit to the cost and volume data. The *y* intercept is $2,725, the fixed cost component. The line passes through the point where *y* is $8,825 and *x* is 1,000 units. Thus, the slope of the line is $6.10 per unit, the variable cost component [($8,825 − $2,725) ÷ 1,000 units].

Illustration 3-4
Graphic Analysis of
Overhead Costs

Part A
Monthly Overhead
Cost Data

19X0	Overhead Cost	Production Volume	19X1	Overhead Cost	Production Volume
July	$ 8,462.20	950	January	$11,045.90	1,420
August	10,437.60	1,210	February	8,233.00	910
September	7,865.30	850	March	9,999.00	1,120
October	10,667.30	1,400	April	11,991.70	1,600
November	7,616.10	800	May	7,784.60	900
December	10,735.00	1,250	June	8,500.00	1,000

Illustration 3-4
Graphic Analysis of
Overhead Costs

Part B
Scattergraph of
Monthly Data

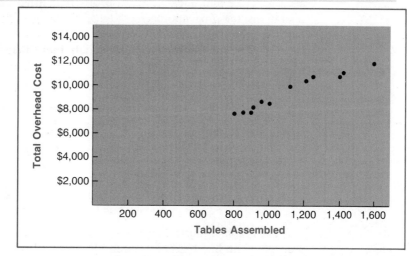

Illustration 3-4
Graphic Analysis of
Overhead Costs

Part C
Straight Line Fitted
to Cost Data

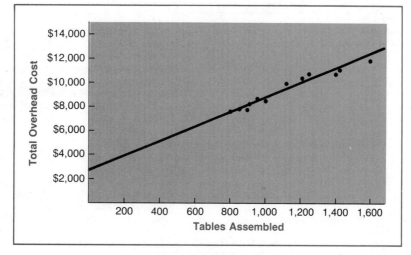

Cost analysts use their own judgment in fitting the line, so that the distance from the points to the line is minimized, or as many points lie above the line as below it. Since there are no hard-and-fast rules for such freehand fits, cost analysts are free to incorporate steps in the cost function, to fit a smooth curve instead of a straight line, or to use their knowledge (or imagination) about the operations of the business. The scattergraph method thus provides a maximum amount of flexibility, but a minimum of objectivity.

High-Low Method. Another simple approach for fitting a line to a set of data is to connect the highest and lowest points. This method, called the high-low method, has the major disadvantage that the highest and lowest points may be unrepresentative of the majority of the cost observations. The high and/or low observations may be influenced by factors that come into play only for very large or very small activity levels. It is also possible that these extreme observations are the result of an unusual set of circumstances, such as a strike, a shortage of materials, or a large and unexpected rush order. If the event is not typical of normal operations, the usual approach is to discard that observation and select one that is more representative (the next highest or lowest).

To illustrate the high-low method, assume that the November and April observations from Illustration 3-4 are not unusual. The unit variable and total fixed costs are calculated as follows:

	Cost	Volume
High month (April, 19X1)	$11,991.70	1,600 units
Low month (November, 19X0)	7,616.10	800
Difference	$ 4,375.60	800 units

Variable overhead cost: $4,375.60 ÷ 800 units = $5.4695 per unit
Fixed overhead cost: April: $11,991.70 − (1,600 units) ($5.4695) = $3,240.50
November: $7,616.10 − (800 units) ($5.4695) = $3,240.50

The graph in Illustration 3-5 is identical to the graph in Illustration 3-4, except that the white line has been added to connect the high and low points.

Illustration 3-5
High-Low Analysis of
Overhead Costs

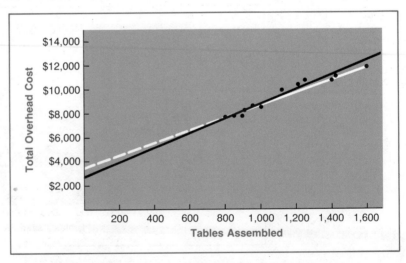

A straight-line cost function captures the behavior of variable costs, fixed costs, and mixed costs. It does not, however, reflect the cost behavior of step costs or costs which behave in a curvilinear fashion over the relevant range of activity. Nevertheless, a linear cost function is often a satisfactory description of cost behavior, especially if the range of activity under study is not too wide, and if the steps in a cost function are not too large relative to the total cost. If a linear approximation is not satisfactory, then narrowing the range of activity or dividing the overall range into several smaller pieces and fitting separate linear cost functions to each (developing a *piece-wise linear cost function*) will often provide acceptable results.

STATISTICAL ANALYSIS OF TOTAL OVERHEAD COSTS

Statistical cost analysis is becoming more common as firms of all types and sizes find it increasingly practical to use computers in their accounting activities. Computerized information systems enable the accountant to retrieve the data necessary for such an analysis, while statistical programs eliminate the computational drudgery associated with this approach.

Simple Linear Regression

Many of the limitations of the judgmental approaches to estimating cost-volume relationships can be overcome by using statistical regression techniques. Regression analysis can provide parameter estimates for the line which best fits the cost and volume data. **Best fit** is used here in the sense that if the distance from each of the data points to the line is squared and the squares summed, this sum would be less than the sum for any other line. Squaring the distances treats both positive and negative deviations from the line in the same way—the squared deviations are positive. Minimizing the squared distances enables differential calculus procedures to be used to derive the formulas for the slope and intercept parameter values.

Regression analysis can also provide measures of the uncertainty or variability associated with an estimated cost-volume relationship. These measures are useful in establishing a range for the cost estimates which might be expected for a given prediction of cost.

The simplest cost function fitted to a set of cost and volume observations is a straight line using only one explanatory factor. The expression for such a straight line is:

$$Y' = a + bX \tag{3.3}$$

The following symbols will be used to describe the calculations involved in simple linear regression.

Symbol	Statistical Meaning	Accounting Interpretation
Y'	The fitted or estimated values of Y, the dependent variable	The estimated total cost for the period
Y	The actual or observed values of Y	The actual total cost for the period

X	The actual or observed values of X, the independent, or explanatory, variable	The actual volume or activity level for the period
a	The Y intercept	The estimate of the fixed cost component over the relevant range
b	The slope of the line	The estimate of the variable cost component over the relevant range
n	The number of paired observations of X and Y used to fit the line to the n data points	The number of cost and volume observations

The sums of the Y values (ΣY), the X values (ΣX), the product of X and Y (ΣXY), and the squared X values (ΣX^2) are substituted into the following standard least squares regression formulas to calculate the values for a and b:[1]

$$a = \frac{(\Sigma Y)(\Sigma X^2) - (\Sigma X)(\Sigma XY)}{n(\Sigma X^2) - (\Sigma X)^2} \tag{3.4}$$

$$b = \frac{n(\Sigma XY) - (\Sigma X)(\Sigma Y)}{n(\Sigma X^2) - (\Sigma X)^2} \tag{3.5}$$

To illustrate the use of these formulas, the overhead cost data and production volume data from Illustration 3-4 are simplified by dividing by 1,000. The values for a and b are calculated in Illustration 3-6.

These statistical estimates indicate that the Table Assembly Department's fixed overhead is somewhat less ($3,036 vs. $3.240) and the variable overhead slightly more ($5.73 vs. $5.47) than the amounts calculated using the high-low method.

Once the regression slope coefficient, b, and the intercept coefficient, a, have been calculated, Formula 3.3 may be used to predict the total overhead cost for other activity levels. If last year's overhead cost relationships in the Table Assembly Department can be expected next month, a production volume of 1,300 tables would be expected to result in an overhead cost of approximately $10,491 [$3,036 + ($5.7347)(1,300)]. This estimate is about 2% ($211) larger than the $10,280 estimated by the department manager, as shown in Part B of Illustration 3-1.

Statistical analysis also provides goodness-of-fit measures. The coefficient of correlation, R, is a measure that indicates how well a given regression model fits the observed data. The correlation coefficient takes on values between 0 and $\pm$ 1. Zero indicates no association between the two variables, which suggests a

---

[1] These formulas are derived by solving simultaneously the following two equations, referred to in statistics as the normal equations for fitting a straight line using the least squares method:

$$\Sigma Y = na + b\Sigma X$$
$$\Sigma XY = a\Sigma X + b\Sigma X$$

Illustration 3-6
Calculation of Least
Squares Regression
Estimates

	Total Overhead Cost, Y (Thousands)	Volume, X (Thousands)	X²	XY	Y²
19X0 July	$ 8.4622	0.95	0.9025	$ 8.0391	$ 71.6088
Aug.	10.4376	1.21	1.4641	12.6295	108.9435
Sept.	7.8653	0.85	0.7225	6.6855	61.8629
Oct.	10.6673	1.40	1.9600	14.9342	113.7913
Nov.	7.6161	0.80	0.6400	6.0929	58.0050
Dec.	10.7350	1.25	1.5625	13.4188	115.2402
19X1 Jan.	11.0459	1.42	2.0164	15.6852	122.0119
Feb.	8.2330	0.91	0.8281	7.4920	67.7823
Mar.	9.9990	1.12	1.2544	11.1989	99.9800
Apr.	11.9917	1.60	2.5600	19.1867	143.8009
May	7.7846	0.90	0.8100	7.0061	60.6000
June	8.5000	1.00	1.0000	8.5000	72.2500
Totals	$113.3377	13.41	15.7205	$130.8689	$1,095.8768
	ΣY	ΣX	ΣX^2	ΣXY	ΣY^2

$$a = \frac{(\$113.3377)(15.7205) - (13.41)(\$130.8689)}{(12)(15.7205) - (13.41)(13.41)} = \frac{\$26.7734}{8.8179} = \$3.0363 \text{ (or \$3,036 per month)}$$

$$b = \frac{(12)(\$130.8689) - (13.41)(\$113.3377)}{8.8179} = \frac{\$50.5682}{8.8179} = \$5.7347 \text{ (or \$5.73 per table)}$$

$$\text{Averages: } \bar{Y} = \frac{\$113.3377}{12} = \$9.4448 \qquad \bar{X} = \frac{13.41}{12} = 1.1175$$

fixed cost. A value of $+1$ indicates perfect positive correlation; i.e., as X increases, Y increases, with the computed Y values exactly equal to the actual Y values. A value of -1 indicates perfect negative correlation; i.e., as X increases, Y decreases.

In Illustration 3-7, a computer printout of a regression analysis for the Table Assembly Department shows a value of 0.975 for R.[2] In practice, the cost analyst may have to accept correlations much lower than the 0.975 coefficient obtained from these data.

If the correlation coefficient is squared, the resulting statistic, R^2 (the coefficient of determination), will take on the value of zero if no correlation exists between X and Y. Similarly, a value of 1.0 indicates that X and Y are perfectly correlated. R^2 is interpreted as the percentage of variability in the dependent variable, Y, which is explained by the variability in the independent variable, X. For the Table Assembly Department, R^2 is computed as shown in Illustration 3-8.

The actual monthly overhead costs, the predicted costs, and the differences between the actual and predicted costs are listed in Columns 1, 2, and 3, respectively.[3] Column 4 of Illustration 3-8 contains the squared differences between the actual and predicted costs. Column 5 contains the differences between the actual monthly overhead (Column 1) and the average monthly overhead, $9.4448. Column 6 contains the squares of these differences.

---

[2]Computer printouts are shown in the text to emphasize that computers are routinely used in statistical cost estimation. The statistical formulas used to compute the values shown in this printout, along with the application of some of the less commonly used statistical concepts, are in the appendix to this chapter.

[3]The deviations of the actual overhead costs from the overhead predicted by the regression cost model, $Y' = \$3.0363 + \$5.7347X$, are also shown in the column labeled "RESIDUAL" in the computer printout, Illustration 3-7.

```
THE REGRESSION EQUATION IS:
Y = 3.0363 + 5.7347 X1

                                    STAN. DEV.    T RATIO =
 CONSTANT     COLUMN    COEFFICIENT  OF COEF.     COEF./STAN. DEV.
              --        3.0363       0.4735       6.41
 X1           C2        5.7347       0.4137       13.86

THE STANDARD ERROR OF ESTIMATE, S, IS:
S = 0.3547
WITH (12 - 2) = 10 DEGREES OF FREEDOM (D.F.)

THE COEFFICIENT OF CORRELATION, R, IS:
R = 0.975


R SQUARED = 95.1 PERCENT
R SQUARED = 94.6 PERCENT, ADJUSTED FOR D.F.


          X1        Y         PRED. Y
 ROW      C2        C1        VALUE      RESIDUAL
 1        0.95      8.462     8.484      -0.022
 2        1.21      10.438    9.975       0.463
 3        0.85      7.865     7.911      -0.046
 4        1.40      10.667    11.065     -0.398
 5        0.80      7.616     7.624      -0.008
 6        1.25      10.735    10.205      0.530
 7        1.42      11.046    11.180     -0.134
 8        0.91      8.233     8.255      -0.022
 9        1.12      9.999     9.459       0.540
 10       1.60      11.992    12.212     -0.220
 11       0.90      7.785     8.198      -0.413
 12       1.00      8.500     8.771      -0.271
```

Illustration 3-8   Computation of R^2 Statistic

	(1) Actual Overhead Costs (Y)	(2) Predicted Overhead Costs (Y')	(3) Difference (Residual) ($Y - Y'$)	(4) Squared Residual ($Y - Y'$)^2	(5) Variation Around Avg. Overhead ($Y - \overline{Y}$)	(6) Squared Variation ($Y - \overline{Y}$)^2
19X0, July	$ 8.4622	$ 8.4843	$-0.0221	0.0005	$-0.9826	0.9655
Aug.	10.4376	9.9753	0.4623	0.2137	0.9928	0.9857
Sept.	7.8653	7.9108	-0.0455	0.0021	-1.5795	2.4948
Oct.	10.6673	11.0649	-0.3976	0.1581	1.2225	1.4945
Nov.	7.6161	7.6241	-0.0080	0.0001	-1.8287	3.3441
Dec.	10.7350	10.2047	0.5303	0.2812	1.2902	1.6646
19X1, Jan.	11.0459	11.1796	-0.1337	0.0179	1.6011	2.5635
Feb.	8.2330	8.2549	-0.0219	0.0005	-1.2118	1.4685
Mar.	9.9990	9.4592	0.5398	0.2914	0.5542	0.3071
Apr.	11.9917	12.2118	-0.2201	0.0484	2.5469	6.4867
May	7.7846	8.1975	-0.4129	0.1705	-1.6602	2.7563
June	8.5000	8.7710	-0.2710	0.0734	-0.9448	0.8926
Totals	$113.3377	$113.3381	$- .0004*	1.2578	$ 0.0001*	25.4239

*Total is different from zero because of rounding.

The sum of the squared residuals (the unexplained part of the monthly costs) in Column 4 is 1.2578, and the sum of the variations in monthly costs in Column 6 is 25.4239. The ratio of the unexplained variation is $1.2578 \div 25.4239$, or 0.05. Since 5% has not been explained, the explained portion must be $100\% - 5\%$, or 95%. Accordingly, 0.95 is the value of R^2 for this simple linear regression overhead cost model.

The R^2 value is equal to the proportion of the total monthly variability (variance) of the Y values (the overhead costs) explained by the corresponding variability of X (production volume). The concept of R^2 can be further explained by considering that the total variation between the monthly costs and the average monthly cost $(Y - \bar{Y})$ is made up of two parts: (1) the deviation of the actual cost value from the value predicted by the fitted regression line $(Y - Y')$, and (2) the deviation of the predicted values from the average value $(Y' - \bar{Y})$. These deviations are shown graphically in Illustration 3-9.

Illustration 3-9
Graphic Analysis of R^2

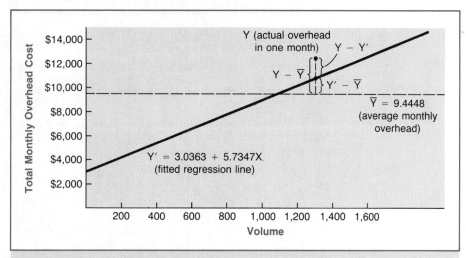

$$R^2 = \text{Portion of the variability in total overhead cost explained by volume}$$

$$= 1 - \text{Unexplained portion of variability}$$

$$= 1 - \frac{\Sigma(Y-Y')^2}{\Sigma(Y-\bar{Y})^2}$$

$$= 1 - \frac{\$1.2578}{\$25.4239} = 1.0 - 0.05 = 0.95$$

The closer the fit of a regression line to a set of data, the smaller the deviations between the actual and predicted values. If all the monthly costs were to lie exactly on the regression line, there would be no deviation of the actual Y values from the line. In that case, 100% of the variation in monthly costs would be explained, and there would be perfect correlation between costs and volume. Both R and R^2 would be equal to 1.

Illustration 3-10 shows different sets of cost-volume data with differing correlations. Each of the graphs shows a set of data with roughly similar slopes and intercepts, but the correlations, R, vary from .98 to .45, and the R^2 values vary from .95 to .20. Figure 1 is the plot of the actual overhead cost data for the Table Assembly Department.

The variability of a set of data can be described by the variance, σ^2, and the standard deviation, σ. Because variances due to several independent sources can

Illustration 3-10
Cost-Volume Data
Displaying Varying
Degrees of Association

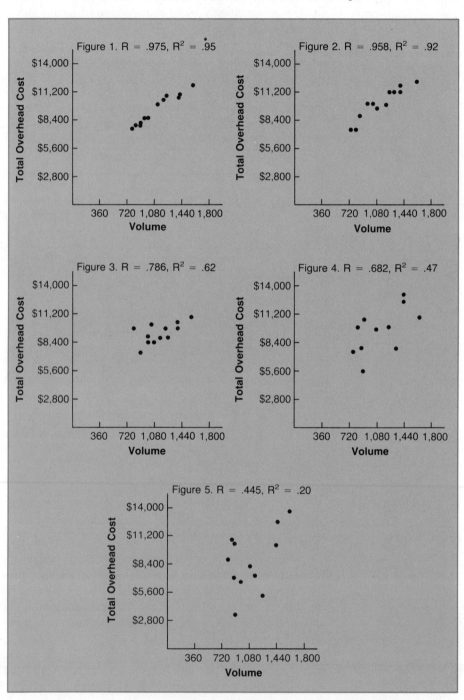

be added together to arrive at the total variance, while the individual standard deviations cannot be added, variances are often incorporated in statistical calculations. On the other hand, since fluctuations around a mean value can be more easily visualized in terms of standard deviations, the value of the standard deviation, rather than the variance, is often provided when data sets are being described.

The standard deviation for a set of data is calculated by using either of the following formulas:

$$\sigma = \sqrt{\frac{\Sigma(Y - \bar{Y})^2}{n}} \tag{3.6}$$

$$\sigma = \sqrt{\frac{\Sigma Y^2}{n} - \bar{Y}^2} \tag{3.7}$$

For the Table Assembly Department, the standard deviation of the twelve overhead cost observations measures the fluctuations of the individual monthly cost observations around the average monthly overhead cost for the twelve-month period. Using Formula 3.7, calculations of the standard deviation and the variance for the department's overhead yield the following results:

$$\sigma = \sqrt{\frac{1{,}095.8768}{12} - (9.4448)^2} = \sqrt{2.1188} = 1.4556$$

$$\sigma^2 = 2.1188$$

The twelve overhead cost observations are just one sample from among many which might have been chosen. To estimate the standard deviation of the population of overhead costs, S, and the corresponding variance, S^2, an adjustment for the appropriate degrees of freedom ($d.f.$) is made by substituting $n - 1$ for n in Formulas 3.6 and 3.7.[4] The values for S and S^2 are:

$$S = \sqrt{\frac{1{,}095.8768}{11} - (9.4448)^2} = \sqrt{10.4209} = 3.2281$$

$$S^2 = 10.4209$$

If the relationship between overhead cost and volume is ignored, a reasonable prediction of the overhead for any month would be the average overhead of the past twelve months, $9.4448. If that 12-month average, $\bar{Y}$, were used to predict overhead for each of the twelve months, there would be prediction errors of varying size (equal to $Y - \bar{Y}$) in each month, although the sum of the prediction errors, $\Sigma(Y - \bar{Y})$, would be equal to zero. In this prediction context, the unadjusted standard deviation, σ (1.4556), and variance, σ^2 (2.1188), and the corresponding values as adjusted for degrees of freedom, S (3.2281), and S^2 (10.4209), could be viewed as measures of the prediction accuracy of the mean overhead cost.

---

[4]One degree of freedom is lost because the mean overhead cost is not known and must be estimated from the data. Without this adjustment, the variability of overhead from month to month would be understated.

If the relationship between overhead cost and volume is taken into account, better predictions of monthly overhead can be made. If the regression cost model, $Y' = \$3.0363 + \$5.7347\ X$, is used to predict overhead in the past twelve months, smaller prediction errors (equal to $Y - Y'$, the residuals) would result. The unadjusted standard deviation of these prediction errors is 0.3239. Using volume to explain overhead costs thus reduces the unadjusted variance to 0.1049, which is only 5% of the unadjusted variance of the original data, 2.1188. This 5% verifies the meaning of the R^2 value of 0.95; i.e., 95% of the variance is explained, and 5% is unexplained.

To adjust the standard deviation and the variance of the residuals from the regression for the appropriate degrees of freedom, $n - 2$ must be used in the denominator. Two degrees of freedom are lost because two parameters, the slope and the intercept, are estimated from the data. The adjusted standard deviation is 0.3547 and the adjusted variance is 0.1259. The adjusted standard deviation appears in Illustration 3-7 as the standard error of the estimate.

Uncertainty in Statistical Estimates

As mentioned in the previous section, the variable and fixed cost (slope and intercept) estimates provided by the least squares regression formulas give the "best" single values, or point estimates, that can be computed from the cost and production data of the Table Assembly Department. However, these values are based on twelve specific observations, and if some other set of monthly data had been selected, somewhat different values would have been obtained. In statistical terms, the sample of cost observations was only one of many which might have been collected from the entire population of monthly costs.

Instead of relying on a single point estimate, it may be more helpful to provide the range of values, called a **confidence interval,** which would include the unknown population parameter. If the R^2 value is close to 1.0, these intervals will be very small. On the other hand, if the association between monthly overhead costs and production levels is not strong, as shown by a low R^2 value, then these intervals will be quite large. If the intervals are large, the portion of the total costs that are fixed and the portion that are variable will not be readily identifiable. Therefore, an analysis based on the estimate of fixed and variable costs could be subject to large errors.

To construct a confidence interval for one of the estimated values, a measure of its variability is needed. As noted previously, the standard deviation provides a measure of this variability. Standard deviations are usually part of the printout of most computer regression programs. Since ready access to computers is common, the details of the calculations are not shown. The appropriate formulas for manual calculations are provided in the appendix to this chapter.

It should be kept in mind that in order to make valid statistical inferences about confidence intervals, it is crucial that certain conditions relating to the statistical distribution of the cost data be met. These conditions are discussed in the appendix section on least squares statistical assumptions.

Uncertainty Associated with the Estimate of a Regression Coefficient. The computer printout (Illustration 3-7) shows that the standard deviation of the intercept coefficient, s_a, is \$0.4735 and that of the slope coefficient, s_b, is \$0.4137. To establish a range corresponding to some given confidence level for variable overhead, for example, the end points for the interval can be obtained by adding and subtracting the appropriate multiple of the standard deviation of the slope coefficient, \$0.4137. This multiplier will vary according to the confidence level chosen—the greater the confidence desired, the larger the multiple will have to be. If the sample size is large (more than 30 observations), a table based on the normal curve can be used. For smaller sample sizes, such as in this illustration, a t distribution should be used. The t table reproduced in the appendix to this textbook shows the required number of standard deviations for any one of six confidence levels.

The amount of uncertainty connected with the calculation of a given regression estimate depends both on the number of observations used (12 in this case) and the number of parameters that are calculated from the data (2 here: the intercept and the slope coefficients). Accordingly, the degrees of freedom are calculated by subtracting the number of parameters from the number of observations ($d.f. = 12 - 2 = 10$), and the value from the t table is obtained in the row for 10 degrees of freedom. For a 95% confidence interval, the interval includes 95% of the area under the curve, leaving 2 1/2% in each tail. Since the table of t values is a "one-tailed" table, the required value of t is in the column labeled 0.025, or 2.228. The required confidence interval is then calculated as:

$$P\% \text{ confidence interval} = \frac{\text{Point}}{\text{estimate}} \pm \left(\begin{array}{c}\text{Appropriate } t \\ \text{from } t \text{ table}\end{array}\right)\left(\begin{array}{c}\text{Standard deviation} \\ \text{of point estimate}\end{array}\right) \quad \textbf{(3.8)}$$

$$95\% \text{ confidence interval} = \$5.7347 \pm (2.228 \times \$0.4137)$$
$$= \$4.81 \text{ to } \$6.66$$

In other words, with 95% confidence, the range of \$4.81 to \$6.66 per unit will contain the variable costs.

The standard deviation of the coefficient for an explanatory variable is also sometimes used to evaluate the quality of a given regression model. For example, the underlying logic behind the overhead cost model for the Table Assembly Department is that the number of tables assembled in a given month will influence that month's overhead cost. If the production levels do not have an effect on overhead costs, then information about the number of tables produced in a month would be irrelevant in predicting the month's overhead, and total overhead would appear to be a fixed cost. A regression analysis using production as an explanatory variable would result in a coefficient of zero for that variable.

To test whether the data from the Table Assembly Department are consistent with the (null) hypothesis that the production level is not related to overhead costs, the difference between the point estimate of \$5.7347 and zero can be measured in terms of standard deviations. For the Table Assembly Department data, the point estimate is 13.86 standard deviations away from zero (\$5.7347 estimated variable cost per unit ÷ \$0.4137 standard deviation). This distance is referred to as the **t ratio,** whose significance can be checked by referring to a t table. In this case, a value of 13.86 for t, with 10 degrees of freedom, is highly significant, since it corresponds to a confidence level so large that it is not found in the t table. Thus, the coefficient for production is not likely to be zero, and production levels undoubtedly do influence overhead costs, which are, in part, variable.

If the t ratio for a coefficient is small, the actual value of that coefficient could easily be zero, and using the computed value may produce misleading results. A rule of thumb often used is that the t ratio should be at least 2. For regressions based on a large number of observations, this corresponds roughly to a 95% confidence level.

Although the t ratio for both the slope and intercept coefficients is shown in Illustration 3-7, it is the estimate of variable costs, using the slope coefficient, that is most often needed by accountants. Estimates of the total cost at zero volume (shutdown of operations), using the intercept coefficient, are usually ignored, since zero volume is normally well outside the relevant range.

Uncertainty Associated with Predicted Costs. The overhead cost model expressed earlier as $Y' = a + bX$ (Formula 3.3) does not recognize any variability in the dependent variable, cost, except the effect of the production level, X. A more realistic cost model would recognize that actual monthly overhead costs are influenced by a variety of factors, which in the aggregate cause the costs to fluctuate in a random fashion around the value predicted on the basis of production alone. This cost model can be stated as:

$$Y = a + bX + u \tag{3.9}$$

where u represents the combined influence of all other unspecified factors. On average, u should be zero; but in any given month, u may be some positive or negative amount. It may be referred to as the residual, the disturbance term, or the noise in the model. The least squares regression model assumes that the residual has a normal distribution with a mean (average) value of zero and an unspecified but constant standard deviation, regardless of the X value. Substituting Y' for $a + bX$ in Formula 3.9 gives:

$$Y = Y' + u, \text{ or } u = Y - Y' \tag{3.10}$$

Since u is the difference between the actual and predicted values of Y, u may also be viewed as the prediction error. As noted earlier, the least squares regression technique computes values for the parameters a and b, which will minimize the sum of the squared u values for the particular X and Y values in the data set. These computed values for a and b will also force the mean residual value, $\bar{u}$, to be zero.

The estimated standard deviation of the residuals (adjusted for degrees of freedom) is referred to as the standard error of estimate, s_e. It may also be described as the standard deviation of Y about the regression line. The computer printout in Illustration 3-7 indicates that the value of s_e for the overhead regression is $0.3547, or $355 in terms of the original data.

The standard error of estimate is often used to identify data extremes for possible investigation. Since estimates should not be based on data which reflect some atypical factor, such as a strike, a quick way to isolate such an extreme would be to determine whether any observation is more than two standard errors away from the regression line. Assuming that the true cost function is identical with the estimate, no more than about 5%, or 1 in 20, of the observations would lie beyond the two-standard-error range as a result of random, or chance, factors.

A plot of the Table Assembly Department's monthly overhead with the original regression line is shown in Illustration 3-11. The area between the dashed lines represents the limits established by the standard error of estimate, $\pm$ \$710 (2 $\times$ \$355). As can be seen, all of the monthly observations lie within these limits. If an extreme point had been noted and determined to be the result of some unusual, nonrecurring event, that observation would have been deleted from the data set and new regression estimates would have been calculated.

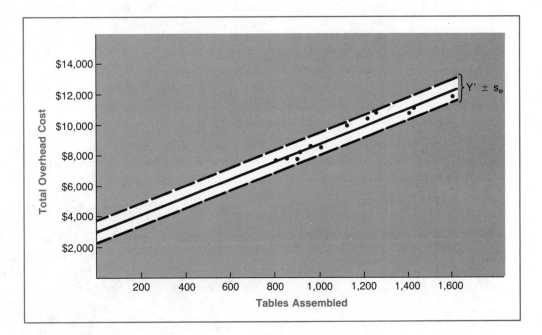

Prediction Intervals. The cost function based on regression estimates for the Table Assembly Department should facilitate a good prediction of overhead cost for July. However, the actual overhead cost for July may differ from this prediction because of the random influence of factors other than volume, and because the regression estimates used to predict overhead may not be precise. To show the effect of the uncertainty due to these causes, it is useful to construct a prediction interval which, with a specified confidence level, would be expected to contain the actual overhead cost of a given future month. Such a prediction interval (*PI*) can be constructed using the following formula:

$$PI = Y' \pm (t)(s_p) \tag{3.11}$$

where s_p is the standard deviation for a prediction.

The prediction interval formula computes an amount on either side of a point estimate (*Y'*). For the Table Assembly Department, the point estimate of July overhead is \$10.4914 [\$3.0363 + (\$5.7347)(1.3)], or \$10,491 in terms of the original data. If it is desired that the prediction interval will contain the overhead cost with 95% confidence, reference to the *t* table gives a value for *t* of 2.228 for 10 degrees of freedom and 2 1/2% in each tail.

The value of s_p for the Table Assembly Department's overhead costs is $0.3768, determined according to a formula given in the appendix to this chapter. The value of s_p is slightly larger than the standard error of estimate (s_e), $0.3547, because the regression estimates of the variable (slope) and fixed (intercept) cost components may not be precise. If the regression fit is good, however, and if the month's predicted production level is not expected to be too far from the average, then the standard error of estimate may be used as a reasonable measure of the overhead's month-to-month variability due to factors other than production volume. Therefore, assuming that the standard error of estimate ($0.3547) is a reasonable approximation of s_p in Formula 3.11, a 95% prediction interval would cover $0.7903(2.228 standard deviations × $0.3547) on either side of the point estimate. The prediction interval would be:

$$PI = \$10.4914 \pm \$0.7903$$
$$= \$ 9.7011 \text{ to } \$11.2817$$

Illustration 3-12
Prediction Interval for
Overhead Cost Data

In Illustration 3-12, the prediction interval is shown as the shaded area between the solid lines. The limits established by the standard error of estimate, as shown in Illustration 3-11, are included for comparative purposes.

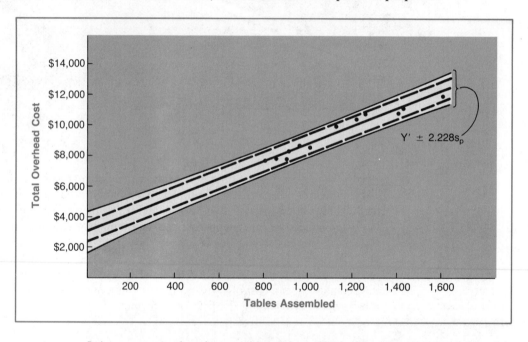

It is not certain that the variable cost on which the point estimate is based is exactly $5.7347 per unit. The greater the production level for the month, the greater the impact of this uncertainty about the *true* variable cost. Earlier in the chapter, a 95% confidence interval for the variable cost estimate was constructed. This confidence interval was $4.81 to $6.66 per unit. If the $4.81 estimate for variable cost were used, the point estimate of July overhead would be $9.2893 [$3.0363 + ($4.81)(1.3)], or $9.289. The prediction interval based on this point estimate would then be $9.2893 ± $0.7903, or $8.4990 to $10.0796 ($8,499 to

$10,080). On the other hand, if the variable cost were as high as $6.66 per unit, then the July overhead estimate would be $11.6943, and the prediction interval would be $10.9040 to $12.4846 ($10,904 to $12,485).

Although it is likely that the variable cost is closer to $5.7347 than either $4.81 or $6.66, the actual value of s_p (0.3768) for the overhead cost regression allows for this uncertainty regarding the regression parameter estimates by expanding the prediction interval to be $9.6519 to $11.3309, calculated as follows:

$$
\begin{aligned}
PI &= \$10.4914 \pm (\$2.228)(0.3768) \\
&= \$10.4914 \pm \$0.8395 \\
&= \$\ 9.6519 \text{ to } \$11.3309
\end{aligned}
$$

This more accurate interval of $1,679 ($9,652 to $11,331) may be more helpful to management in evaluating alternatives and subsequent performance.

Multiple Linear Regression

In the discussion of simple regression, the cost model used to explain monthly overhead costs had only one explanatory variable, the level of production for the month. Often the cost predictions can be improved by using multiple linear regression, which incorporates several explanatory variables. For example, if a single department produces both toasters and mixers, the overhead for a month in which three fourths of the production was toasters may be quite different from the overhead for a month in which most of the output was mixers, even though the total number of appliances produced was the same in both months. Therefore, a separate explanatory variable for each product should be used in order to take into account the cost impact of different products.

With multiple regression, the following estimate of monthly overhead might be derived:

$$Y = \$60,000 + 10X_1 + 20X_2$$

where X_1 is the number of toasters produced in the month, and X_2 is the number of mixers produced. This cost function provides a more accurate estimate of monthly overhead by taking into account the fact that the variable overhead cost of mixers is twice the variable overhead cost of toasters.

Dummy (Shift) Variables

In addition to explanatory variables which reflect quantitative factors, it is also possible to use qualitative or categorical variables. These qualitative variables are often referred to as **dummy variables.** Dummy variables take on a value of 1 if some characteristic is present, or a value of 0 if it is not present.

One use of dummy variables in cost analysis is to reflect seasonal factors. For example, if utility costs are expected to be higher in winter months, then winter could be incorporated as a dummy variable in the following simple cost model:

$$Y = a + b_1 X_1 + b_2 X_2 \tag{3.12}$$

where Y is the total monthly overhead cost, X_1 is the production level, and X_2 is a dummy variable for winter. For winter months, X_2 would be given a value of

1, and for other months, X_2 would be 0. The coefficient of the dummy variable, b_2, would be the amount by which the average monthly costs in winter differ from costs in other months.

A different use of dummy variables is to identify the amount of the shift in step costs over different ranges of production. As applied to the overhead costs of the Table Assembly Department, a dummy variable, X_2, could take on a value of 1 if production exceeded 1,000 tables and a value of 0 for lower production levels. Based on the same data used for the simple regression (except that costs and volumes were not divided by 1,000), the results of such a multiple regression are shown in Illustration 3-13 and summarized as follows:

$$Y = \$4,635.4712 + \$3.8167X_1 + \$1088.3263X_2$$
$$(t = 9.95) \qquad (t = 7.52) \qquad (t = 4.33)$$
$$R^2 = 0.98$$

Illustration 3-13
Table Assembly
Department Multiple
Regression Analysis
(Unscaled Data)

where Y is total monthly overhead cost in dollars, X_1 is the number of tables assembled in units, and X_2 is the dummy variable which indicates whether production exceeded 1,000 tables.

The large t values for the coefficients (in parentheses) indicate that all the coefficients are significant at more than a 95% level. Notice that the multiple

```
THE REGRESSION EQUATION IS:
Y =   4635.4712   + 3.8167 X1 + 1088.3263 X2

                                          STAN. DEV.        T RATIO =
                                           OF COEF.      COEF./STAN. DEV.
 CONSTANT       COLUMN      COEFFICIENT
                  --          4635.4712     465.8062           9.95
 X1               C2             3.8167       0.5075           7.52
 X2               C3          1088.3263     251.1896           4.33

THE STAN. DEV. OF Y ABOUT REGRESSION LINE IS:
S = 212.8
WITH ( 12 - 3) =   9 DEGREES OF FREEDOM (D.F.)

R SQUARED = 98.4 PERCENT
R SQUARED = 98.0 PERCENT, ADJUSTED FOR D.F.

               X1          Y       PRED. Y
 ROW           C2         C5        VALUE      RESIDUAL
 1            950       8462.2      8261.3       200.9
 2           1210      10437.6     10342.0        95.6
 3            850       7865.3      7879.7       -14.4
 4           1400      10667.3     11067.2      -399.9
 5            800       7616.1      7688.8       -72.7
 6           1250      10735.0     10494.7       240.3
 7           1420      11045.9     11143.5       -97.6
 8            910       8233.0      8108.7       124.3
 9           1120       9999.0      9998.5         0.5
 10          1600      11991.7     11830.5       161.2
 11           900       7784.6      8070.5      -285.9
 12          1000       8500.0      8452.2        47.8
```

regression has simultaneously computed the estimates of monthly fixed costs ($4,635), unit variable costs ($3.82 per table), and the cost of an additional forklift operator ($1,088) when production exceeds 1,000 tables per month.

Choosing Among Alternative Regression Models

To determine which regression model to use in a given application, the following practical and statistical factors should be considered:

1. The model should make good economic sense. Unless there is some rational basis for expecting that costs behave in the way that corresponds to the model, the observations may be the result of chance or spurious correlation. For example, over the past five years, sales salaries in a firm may show a significant positive correlation with units sold, which would indicate that sales salaries are a variable cost. However, the sales staff may not have grown at all, and the relationship may only reflect the fact that over this period both sales units and annual salaries (reflecting inflation) have increased. The observed correlation in this case is not due to an economic cost-volume relationship.

2. There should be a good overall fit of the data to the regression model. Other factors being equal, a model with a higher R^2 and a lower standard error of estimate is preferable to a model with a poorer fit to the given data.

3. Highly significant values for the regression coefficients of the explanatory variables are desirable. A rule of thumb often used is that the t values should be at least 2. Values less than 2 for large data sets mean that a 95% confidence interval for the regression coefficient would include 0, which would imply that the variable in question has no identifiable impact on the dependent variable which is being predicted.

   A low t value can occur when the regression model includes a variable which has no real explanatory power. Low t values can also occur when two variables which are closely correlated are both included in a multiple regression model. Such variables are referred to as **collinear,** and this problem is called **multicollinearity.** In such a situation, it is difficult to determine how much of the overall variability can be attributed separately to each variable.

   When multicollinearity is present, the R^2 value for the multiple regression model with both of the highly correlated independent variables will typically not be much greater than the R^2 value for the simpler model with only one of the explanatory variables. Since about the same results are obtained with the simpler model, only the single variable with the highest correlation to the dependent variable is usually included.

4. The model chosen should be easy to implement. If predictions for the future require new data, the ease of obtaining accurate values for the independent variables should be considered. If one model uses data that will be costly or difficult to obtain, it may be better to use another model whose data requirements are less severe.

Case Study: Choosing a Regression Model for Selling Expenses

In previous sections of this chapter, manufacturing costs were emphasized. The same approaches developed for estimating these costs can be applied to marketing and administrative expenses. To illustrate the process of selecting a regression model for such expenses, assume that you are the accountant in charge of estimating the total monthly selling expenses for Rogers Co., a regional wholesaler of building hardware. You have listed the following variables and your reason for believing that each variable influences the monthly selling expenses (Y):

1. X_1—the dollar sales for the current month. (Reason: The higher the sales in any month, the more Rogers probably spent to make the sales and process the sales orders.)
2. X_2—the number of calls made by Rogers' sales force during the month. (Reason: On the average, since there is a certain variable cost per call, the more calls in a given month, the higher the total selling costs for the month.)
3. X_3—the value of building permits issued in the previous month in the region served by Rogers. (Reason: The greater the amount of construction, the more building hardware Rogers will sell and the higher Rogers' selling expenses will probably be. The one-month lag reflects the average lag between the time builders receive a building permit and the time orders are placed for building hardware.)

You have collected monthly data for 24 months and have fitted the data to seven different models. The results are summarized in Part A of Illustration 3-14. Models No. 1, No. 2, and No. 3 are single-variable models, while Models No. 4, No. 5, No. 6, and No. 7 use two or more of the listed variables.

Of the single-variable models, Model No. 2, which contains X_2, gives the best fit to the data. It explains more of the variance (about 43%) in the 24 monthly cost observations than either Models No. 1 or No. 3, since its R^2 value is .43. It also has the smallest standard error of estimate of any of the single-variable models.

You could have known in advance which single-variable model would provide the best fit to the data if you knew which of the three independent variables, X_1, X_2, or X_3, was most highly correlated with the selling expenses, Y. Part B of Illustration 3-14 shows a correlation matrix, which contains the coefficients of correlation, R, among all the variables being considered in this analysis. Only half of the matrix is shown, since the lower left half of the matrix is the same as the upper right half. The top row of the matrix indicates that X_2, sales calls, has the highest correlation with Y, selling expenses. If only one explanatory variable is used, then the model with X_2 will give the best fit.

Your selection of a regression model may, however, depend on how you intend to use it. If the major use of the model is to estimate total selling expenses for the next month, the number of sales calls which will be made in that month must be estimated before selling expenses can be predicted. If estimates of future calls are subject to sizable errors, then those errors will affect the selling expense estimate. In this case, you might choose to use Model No. 3, in spite of its lower R^2. Since the input for Model No. 3 (building permits issued in the previous month) is known at the time you forecast selling expenses, the value of the explanatory variable is not subject to errors of estimating.

An even better fit to the data may be obtained by using a cost model with more than one explanatory variable. If good estimates are available for all the explanatory variables, you will probably use Model No. 4, which is based on both dollar

Illustration 3-14
Analysis of Rogers Co.
Monthly Selling Expenses

Part A
Summary of Regression
Results

	Model	Adjusted Stan. Error of Estimate*	Adjusted R^{2*}
1.	$Y = \$15,654 + \$0.569X_1$ $(t=2.8)$	$2,697	0.23
2.	$Y = \$12,300 + 24.5X_2$ $(t=4.3)$	2,326	0.43
3.	$Y = \$15,723 + .0063X_3$ $(t=2.8)$	2,687	0.23
4.	$Y = \$9,732 + \$0.534X_1 + 23.7X_2$ $(t=3.9)$ $(t=5.3)$	1,813	0.65
5.	$Y = \$15,563 + \$0.263X_1 + .0036X_3$ $(t=0.52)$ $(t=0.66)$	2,732	0.21
6.	$Y = \$10,611 + 22.0X_2 + .0050X_3$ $(t=4.4)$ $(t=3.1)$	1,979	0.59
7.	$Y = \$9,575 + \$0.73X_1 + 24.6X_2 - .0023X_3$ $(t=2.1)$ $(t=5.1)$ $(t=-0.6)$	1,842	0.64

*Values have been adjusted for the appropriate degrees of freedom.

Illustration 3-14
Analysis of Rogers Co.
Monthly Selling Expenses

Part B
Correlation Matrix for
Variables

	Y	X_1	X_2	X_3
Y	1.00	0.51	0.67	0.52
X_1		1.00	0.05	0.91
X_2			1.00	0.17
X_3				1.00

sales and the number of sales calls. This model explains about 65% of the monthly variability in selling expenses, it has a much lower standard error of estimate than Model No. 2, and it has highly significant t values for the coefficients of both explanatory variables.

It might be assumed that the best model would be Model No. 7, which incorporates all three explanatory variables. However, after an adjustment for the degrees of freedom is made, the goodness-of-fit statistics (standard error of estimate and R^2) are actually poorer for this more complex model. In addition, the low t value for X_3, − 0.6,[5] indicates that little reliance can be placed on the computed value for that coefficient. The actual marginal impact of X_3 could as easily be positive as negative. Although Model No. 7 will probably give selling expense predictions which are just about the same as Model No. 4, it should not be used for other applications which make use of the values for the individual regression coefficients. For example, because of the high degree of association of the X_1 and X_3 values (the correlation between the two is 0.91), it would be dangerous to rely on the 0.73 coefficient for X_1 and the −0.0023 coefficient for X_3 as providing the separate marginal effects of a change in dollar sales (X_1) or in permits issued (X_3) on monthly selling expenses.

[5]Conventionally, the t value is given the same sign as the related coefficient. In using the t value to evaluate the significance of a regression coefficient, however, a minus sign may be ignored.

Pitfalls in Applying Statistical Regression[6]

In practice, cost analysis involves more than just plugging numbers into a formula. Statistical analysis can be misused, unless accountants are aware of the limitations as well as the advantages of this powerful technique. Some of these limitations are discussed in the following paragraphs.

Problems with the Data. Statistical analysis is usually based on a particular set of historical data. Managers, however, are attempting to predict the future rather than observe the past. Accountants must be careful to adjust their observed historical relationships to reflect any changes expected in the future.

The data set used in least squares calculations is the raw material for statistical analysis. If this raw material is faulty, then the results will be faulty also. It is essential that the basic data be recorded correctly. It is also essential that a consistent accounting method be used to record accruals, deferrals, allocations, and expenses. Otherwise, the costs recorded for certain periods may be distorted. Certain supply items, for example, may be expensed as purchased, rather than inventoried and charged to expense as used. The total cost of supplies for the year may be approximately correct, but the individual monthly figures in such a situation will present a misleading picture of cost behavior. Significant clerical errors or inconsistencies in recording data can often be identified by comparing the predicted value of each observation with the value actually recorded.

The choice of the number of observations to use is also important. The greater the number of observations, the smaller the sampling errors will be. Small sample sizes, for example, will lead to larger values for s_e and s_p. Moreover, if too few observations are used, the results may be dependent on peculiarities in the individual observations that happened to be chosen for analysis. The high-low method, which uses only two data points, is subject to this problem.

On the other hand, it usually requires time, effort, and cost to secure additional observations. Also, older observations tend to include data that are not representative of the situation being analyzed. For the Table Assembly Department, for example, additional observations beyond July of the previous year could be used. The more distant the observations are from the present, however, the more likely it is that a different cost pattern existed at that time because of differences in prices, production methods, and design of the tables being produced. As a result of these considerations, the additional benefits should be balanced against the additional costs and disadvantages in determining the number of observations to use.

Just as it is important to consider the number of observations to use, the time period covered by a single observation should be considered. Daily data, in most cases, are not adequate for statistical regression analysis. Many accounting systems are not designed to process all information daily, but record most costs weekly, biweekly, or monthly. If the time period is too short, the recorded cost and activity data may be mismatched, since the recorded costs cover one calendar period and the recorded activity covers a different period. Moreover, the shorter the time period, the more any irregularities or "noise" will influence the results.

---

[6]For a detailed discussion of this subject, see "Multiple Regression Analysis of Cost Behavior" by George Benston, *The Accounting Review,* October, 1966, pp. 657-672.

On the other hand, time periods should not be too long. Just as short time periods emphasize momentary irregularities, time periods that are too long can actually smooth out the variations that should be measured in the cost analysis. In addition, as many shorter time periods are combined into longer ones, the number of observations to work with is reduced.

The choice of the number and nature of the observations may also have an effect on the amount of variability present in a data set. Since regression analysis can only detect how variations in one variable are associated with variations in another, statistical analysis of data covering only a limited range of activity will not provide useful results.

Each cost study must be viewed individually. The objective of the cost analyst should be to select a time period long enough to capture the basic features of the cost variability patterns, and short enough to provide a reasonable number of observations.

Problems with the Model. Another set of limitations is the particular model used to describe the costs relating to a set of activities. The account classification, the high-low, as well as the simple regression approaches all assume that the total cost can be divided into costs that are either fixed or variable in a linear manner with respect to volume. More complicated cost relationships involving step costs or the effect of several variables are ignored. If the actual relationships are complex, however, models which are simplified may give poor predictions and lead to erroneous conclusions.

Other problems may result from violating certain statistical assumptions on which the least squares regression results are based. These assumptions are that the residuals should: (a) be independent, (b) have a constant variance, (c) be normally distributed, and (d) have an expected value of zero for any given observation. These assumptions, which are discussed in more detail in the appendix to this chapter, must be satisfied before reliance is placed on any statistical results.

APPENDIX 3: ADDITIONAL INFORMATION ON USING STATISTICAL PROCEDURES IN COST ESTIMATION

Statistical Formulas
For Simple
Regression

Occasionally it is necessary to compute the values of certain regression statistics rather than obtaining them from a computer printout. The formulas for the coefficient of correlation, R (page 68), the standard error of estimate, s_e (page 76), the standard error of a prediction, s_p (page 77), and the standard errors (standard deviations) of the slope coefficient, s_b, and the intercept coefficient, s_a (page 75), are given below. Along with each formula, the value of the statistic for the Table Assembly Department cost data (Illustration 3-6) is also calculated and shown. These values may be compared to the numbers shown on the computer printout in Illustration 3-7. (The slight differences in the last decimal place are due to differences in rounding.)

Coefficient of correlation, R:

$$R = \frac{n(\Sigma XY) - (\Sigma X)(\Sigma Y)}{\sqrt{n(\Sigma X^2) - (\Sigma X)^2 \times n(\Sigma Y^2) - (\Sigma Y)^2}} \qquad \text{(A3.1)}$$

$$R = \frac{(12)(\$130.8689) - (13.41)(\$113.3377)}{\sqrt{(12)(15.7205) - (13.41)^2} \times \sqrt{(12)(\$1,095.8768) - (\$113.3377)^2}}$$

$$R = \frac{\$50.5682}{\$51.8671} = .9750$$

Standard error of estimate (standard deviation of the predicted Y^1), s or s_e:

$$s_e = \sqrt{\frac{\Sigma(Y-Y')^2}{n-2}} = \sqrt{\frac{\Sigma u^2}{n-2}} \qquad \text{(A3.2)}$$

or

$$s_e = \sqrt{\frac{\Sigma Y^2 - a(\Sigma Y) - b(\Sigma XY)}{n-2}} \qquad \text{(A3.3)}$$

Using A3.2,

$$s_e = \sqrt{\frac{\$1.2578}{10}} = \$.3547$$

Standard error of a prediction, s_p:*

$$s_p = s_e \sqrt{1 + \frac{1}{n} + \frac{\left(X_0 - \frac{\Sigma X}{n}\right)^2}{\Sigma X^2 + \frac{(\Sigma X)^2}{n}}} \qquad \text{(A3.4)}$$

$$= \$.3547 \sqrt{1 + \frac{1}{12} + \frac{\left(1.3 - \frac{13.41}{12}\right)^2}{15.7205 - \frac{(13.41)^2}{12}}} = (\$.3547)(1.0624) = \$0.3768$$

Standard error of the slope, s_b:

$$\qquad \text{(A3.5)}$$

$$s_b = \frac{s_e}{\sqrt{\Sigma(X-X)^2}}$$

or

$$s_b = \frac{s_e}{\sqrt{\Sigma X^2 - \bar{X}\Sigma X}} \qquad \text{(A3.6)}$$

Using A3.6,

$$s_b = \frac{\$.3547}{\sqrt{15.7205 - (1.1175)(13.41)}} = \frac{\$.3547}{.8572} = \$.4138$$

* Since the standard error of a prediction depends on the X value to be used in making the prediction, the X value should be specified. The specified X value is referred to as X_0 in the formula.

Standard error of the intercept, s_a:

$$s_a = s_e \sqrt{\frac{1}{n} + \frac{\overline{X}^2}{\Sigma X^2 - \overline{X}\Sigma X}} \qquad\qquad \textbf{(A3.7)}$$

$$= \$.3547 \sqrt{\frac{1}{12} + \frac{(1.1175)^2}{15.7205 - (1.1175)(13.41)}} = (\$.3547)(1.3352) = \$.4736$$

**Statistical
Assumptions**

It is possible to use the least squares regression estimates for the slope and intercept of a straight line to obtain the parameter values for the line which best fits a particular set of data. However, if statistical inferences about appropriate confidence intervals are to be made, it is necessary to go behind the raw data to see whether the major least squares assumptions have been met for the particular situation being analyzed. These assumptions are described as follows:

1. The residuals should be independent. Knowing the value of one residual or prediction error should not help in predicting what the next residual should be. Sometimes, however, the influence of a factor will cause several adjacent observations to be either consistently above or below the predicted values. This situation is likely to occur when the data are a time series (data from adjacent calendar periods), as opposed to cross-sectional data (data from different organizations or activities for the same time period).

   Dependence among residuals can occur, for example, if management adds employees to increase production but is reluctant to cut its labor force proportionately when demand falls off and production decreases. Economists have noted that this tendency exists for the economy as a whole, and refer to it as a ratchet effect. Part A of Illustration A3-1 shows such a situation.

   A lack of independence among adjacent observations may be detected by plotting the observations in sequence. The systematic correlation between consecutive observations of the same variable is called autocorrelation or serial correlation. Often, computer regression programs will calculate the Durbin-Watson statistic, d, which reflects the degree of autocorrelation present in the residuals. A value for d around 2.0 indicates no serious autocorrelation of the residuals. As a rule of thumb, a value for d outside the range of 1.0 to 3.0 would be an indication of autocorrelation. Serious autocorrelation can often be eliminated by working with first differences of the data (the change in costs and activity from one period to the next) rather than the actual values.

2. The residuals should have a constant variance at all levels of activity. It is assumed that the variability of the unexplained costs (the residuals) should be the same, regardless of the size of the expected costs for the period. Statisticians refer to this constant variance as homoscedasticity, and to the nonconstant variance of the residuals as heteroscedasticity. An example of heteroscedasticity is shown in Part B of Illustration A3-1, where the absolute values of the residuals increase as the costs increase. If this condition is serious, it can often be corrected by an appropriate transformation of the data.

3. The residuals should be normally distributed. To see if the residuals have a normal distribution, a histogram of the residuals can be compared to the bell-shaped pattern expected for a normal distribution. More formal approaches include conducting statistical tests for departures from a normal

distribution, such as plotting the residuals on normal probability paper. Such a plot, which may be generated by a computer regression program, will appear as a straight line if the residuals are normally distributed.

4. The residuals should have an expected value of zero for any given observation. This assumption is often difficult to test, since the least squares calculations will force the average (mean) of the residuals to be zero. Clues about the possible violation of this assumption are sometimes provided by plotting the residuals against the values of the explanatory variables used in the regression analysis.

Illustration A3-1
Some Violations of Least Squares Regression Assumptions

Part A
Dependence Among Residuals

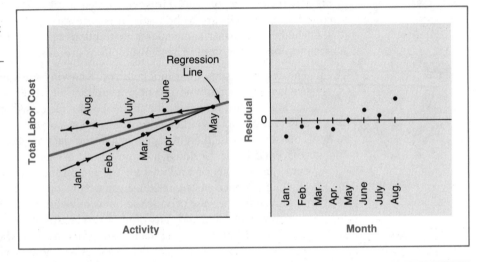

Illustration A3-1
Some Violations of Least Squares Regression Assumptions

Part B
Residuals with Nonconstant Variance

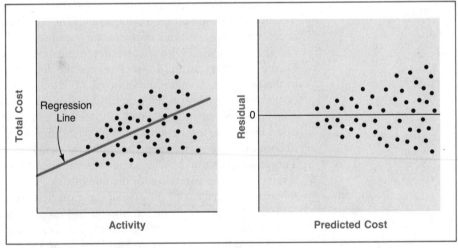

Handling Nonlinear
Relationships

The basic regression model is a linear model. It is based on the assumption that the value of the dependent variable can be explained by a fixed component and one or more variable components which are constant per unit over some relevant range. If prices or efficiency change significantly over a given range of activity, however, a linear model may not give good results. In such cases, a curvilinear relationship may be modeled by transforming the variables. For example, by using the logarithm, the square or square root, or the inverse of the X value rather than the X value itself, the relationship between the transformed variables may be approximately linear. A simple polynomial expression, such as $Y = a + b_1 X + b_2 X^2$, also may be helpful in modeling cost relationships that are not linear.

The need to fit cost data to a nonlinear model may be evidenced by a scattergram plot of the data or by observing a residuals pattern in which there is a systematic underestimate of costs over certain ranges and consistent overestimates for other ranges. Sometimes it is possible to know in advance that a linear model will not be appropriate. An example of this situation is the effect of continuing improvement in production efficiency as volume increases. In Chapter 15, least squares regression will be used to model a nonlinear cost function resulting from the learning that goes on in certain production situations.

1. Discuss the advantages and disadvantages of statistical versus nonstatistical methods of estimating cost behavior.

2. The senior accountant of the Kemwel Corp. explained to a recently hired accounting clerk how costs were classified as either variable, fixed, mixed, or step for budgeting purposes. As an example of a fixed cost, the senior accountant mentioned plant heating and cooling costs for the firm's 150,000-square-foot plant. The clerk, who handles cash disbursements, knows that heating and cooling costs for the New England firm normally double in winter as opposed to summer, and wonders how such costs could be classified as fixed. Is the accountant's classification correct? Explain.

3. (a) What is squared when the method of least squares is used?
   (b) What values are minimized in the least squares technique?

4. A simple, single-variable, least squares regression equation has the form: $Y = a + bX$. Explain, in accounting terms, the meaning of each of the elements in the equation, as applied to a cost estimation situation.

5. Explain the meaning of the coefficient of correlation and the coefficient of determination. What range of values can these statistics take?

6. What does the standard error of estimate measure, and how is it calculated?

7. Boswick, the cost accountant of Tampco Inc., would like to calculate a prediction interval for the estimated total cost based on next month's activity level, as well as confidence intervals for the variable cost per unit and the fixed cost per month. What are the appropriate standard deviation statistics which should be used to calculate each interval?

8. How are degrees of freedom calculated for regression estimates?

9. Explain the purpose of the t ratio and how it is calculated.

10. Describe the meaning and identification of an extreme data point.

11. Define dummy or shift variable. Give an example of such a variable in an overhead cost application.

12. What factors are important in evaluating the usefulness of a linear regression model for budgeting purposes?

13. In selecting data to be used in statistical analyses of costs, what factors should an accountant consider?

Exercise 3-1. As an aid toward better control of overhead costs, Watertown Company has asked its accountant to perform an analysis of its overhead accounts to determine an overall overhead budget. Information regarding Watertown's principal overhead accounts and direct labor hours (DLH) is shown at the top of page 91.

Using the classification of accounts method, prepare a monthly overhead budget for Watertown.

	June (1,500 DLH)	July (2,000 DLH)	August (2,500 DLH)
Indirect Materials	$ 225	$ 300	$ 375
Factory Supervision	2,300	2,400	2,500
Property Taxes—Factory	400	400	400
Heat, Light, and Power	775	800	825
Depreciation—Factory Equip.	400	400	400

Exercise 3-2. Rawlins Company is a small manufacturer of canvas tents and awnings. During the past three quarters, its production rate and overhead costs have fluctuated widely. To forecast overhead costs for the fourth quarter, you have been asked to analyze past overhead costs. A summary of the past nine months' performance is as follows:

	Production Level	Total Overhead Cost
January	1,000 DLH	$4,000
February	1,500	5,000
March	2,000	6,250
April	1,800	5,500
May	2,700	7,000
June	3,500	8,200
July	4,000	9,000
August	3,700	8,300
September	2,900	7,200

Rawlins expects to work 1,800 hours in October, 1,800 hours in November, and 1,400 hours in December.

(1) Using the scattergraph method, plot the above points and determine, by inspection, an overhead budget.
(2) Using the budget formula developed in (1), calculate the amount of total overhead cost to be budgeted for the fourth quarter (October-December).

Exercise 3-3. Perfex Industries produces a wide variety of agricultural fertilizers and pesticides at its plant in Arizona. The company's management is reviewing its budgeting procedures in order to prepare for the coming fiscal year. Overhead costs for the past six quarters are as follows:

Year	Quarter	Activity	Total Overhead Cost
19X7	III	15,000 DLH	$ 80,000
	IV	12,000	92,200
19X8	I	19,000	97,500
	II	20,000	104,000
	III	26,000	124,000
	IV	22,000	108,000

In the last quarter of 19X7, the company was struck by repair and maintenance employees. A combination of regular and outside employees were utilized to provide essential services, at considerable cost to the company. The area was also affected by an unexpected, severe water shortage, causing industrial water rates to almost triple. Perfex uses a considerable amount of water in its production processes as well as for cleaning.

Using the high-low method, calculate an overhead budget formula for the coming year for Perfex Industries.

Exercise 3-4. Determine whether each of the statements regarding least squares regression lines is true or false. Explain why each false statement is incorrect.

(1) Given a properly fit linear regression equation, there will always be as many data points above the line as below the line.

(2) Given a properly fit linear regression equation, the sum of the data point deviations above and below the line is zero.

(3) A linear regression line always passes through at least one data point.

(4) A coefficient of determination of 90% implies that 90% of all predictions made using the regression equation will be correct.

(5) In a linear regression of overhead costs against an activity variable, a negative constant (fixed cost term) implies that the regression analysis is in error.

(6) The standard error of a prediction is the sum of the standard error of the slope and the standard error of the intercept.

(7) In a regression analysis based on a given set of overhead cost and volume data, a 95% confidence interval for the estimate of unit variable overhead cost will be *smaller* than a 90% confidence interval for that parameter.

(8) The linear regression equations yield that straight line which passes through the maximum number of data points.

(9) A single-variable linear regression analysis may yield a higher adjusted coefficient of determination than a multiple linear regression analysis using the same independent variable.

(10) In choosing among different regression models, the accountant should always choose the regression which has the highest R^2 value, regardless of whether there is any common-sense relationship between the independent and the dependent variable.

Exercise 3-5. Cascade Corporation has used linear regression analysis as an aid in developing overhead budgets. The following equation for total monthly overhead has been derived:

$$Y = \$7,342 + \$1.69X_1$$

where X_1, the explanatory variable, is the total machine hours per month. Cascade would like to forecast its overhead for next month, when 4,200 direct machine hours are expected to be used. The standard error of a prediction at the projected activity level is $695. Cascade's managers wish to use a prediction interval with 90% confidence and 30 degrees of freedom.

Calculate a 90% prediction interval for next month's overhead.

Exercise 3-6. Standard Products Company produces a line of precision-machined metal components for industrial gas turbines. As the first step in a comprehensive study of overhead, the accountant has gathered cost and operating data and has fit a regression line. The results are shown at the top of page 93.

Using this information, calculate the coefficient of determination (R^2) for the regression equation, and explain its meaning.

Activity per Month (X)	Actual Cost (Y)
5,100 DLH	$ 4,300
12,000	6,430
14,990	7,620
19,700	9,400
24,050	11,300
22,500	9,800
18,650	9,100

Equation: $Y = \$2,367 + 0.354X$

Exercise 3-7. The sales manager of Eagleton Company has performed some simple statistical analyses in order to understand the cost behavior of the sales department. A simple linear regression model, using the number of sales calls per month as an explanatory variable, yielded the following linear regression equation:

$$Y = \$6,720 + \$42.78X$$

where X is the number of sales calls made per month, and Y is the total selling cost per month.

The standard errors for the intercept coefficient and the slope coefficient and the number of observations are as follows:

$$S_a = \$1,372$$

$$S_b = \$19.01$$

$$n = 30 \text{ (28 degrees of freedom)}$$

Construct 90%, 95%, and 99% confidence intervals around the estimates for the fixed and variable components of the total selling cost. Calculate the t ratio for both parameters and comment on their statistical significance.

Exercise 3-8. Buckton Engineering uses linear regression estimates in its cost budgeting process. The results of a recent regression analysis of overhead costs has yielded the following data:

$$Y = \$7,260 + \$4.13X$$

$$S_p = \$1,227$$

$$S_a = \$1,597$$

$$S_b = \$0.97$$

$$\text{degrees of freedom} = 18$$

$$Y = \text{total monthly overhead}$$

$$X = \text{direct machine hours per month}$$

Buckton would like to forecast its overhead for the coming month, when 1,700 machine hours are expected to be used.

(1) Estimate the total overhead cost for the coming month.

(2) Calculate a confidence interval for the fixed overhead component and the unit variable cost at both the 90% and 95% confidence levels.

(3) Calculate a 90% and a 95% prediction interval for next month's expected overhead.

Exercise 3-9. (*Note: Some formulas required to work this exercise are given in Appendix 3.*) As the accountant for A & A Manufacturing Company, you would like to apply statistical regression techniques to cost data in order to prepare better cost forecasts. You have calculated the least squares linear regression equation, $Y = \$4,499 + \$2.939X$, after gathering the following data:

Activity per Month (X)	Actual Overhead Cost per Month (Y)
1,220 DLH	$8,100
1,300	8,510
1,450	8,600
1,525	8,870
1,560	9,345
1,405	8,520
1,375	8,445

(1) Calculate the coefficient of determination, the standard error of estimate, and the standard error of a prediction for a month in which X_o is 1,400 DLH.

(2) Prepare a 90% prediction interval for estimated total overhead cost for next month, when 1,400 direct labor hours are expected to be used.

Exercise 3-10. Rockford Speedy Cab Company has asked you to aid it in developing a more sophisticated budgeting system than the one currently in use. Among the data necessary are revenue forecasts for the upcoming months. After consulting with Rockford's managers, drivers, and dispatchers, you conclude that revenue might be directly related to the number of passengers carried per month, the total number of miles driven, or the number of convention visitors per month. Statistical analysis of the data yields the following regression equations and statistics:

	Model	Standard Error of Estimate	R (Adjusted)
1.	$Y = \$7,424 + 3.87X_1$	$2,005	0.71
2.	$Y = \$17,168 + 0.46X_2$	2,712	0.61
3.	$Y = \$13,568 + 5.18X_3$	3,760	0.21
4.	$Y = \$1,120 + 3.71X_1 + 0.47X_2$	1,897	0.73
5.	$Y = \$7,928 + 0.31X_2 + 5.05X_3$	3,118	0.47
6.	$Y = \$1,565 + 3.20X_1 + 5.09X_3$	3,821	0.20
7.	$Y = \$4,442 + 2.19X_1 + 0.31X_2 + 2.12X_3$	1,945	0.72

Correlation Matrix

		Y	X_1	X_2	X_3
Y	(monthly revenue)	1.00	0.71	0.61	0.21
X_1	(passengers carried per month—all cabs)		1.00	0.27	0.70
X_2	(total miles driven per month—all cabs)			1.00	0.34
X_3	(convention visitors per month)				1.00

Based on the information given, which model do you think Rockford should select to forecast its monthly revenues? Explain your choice.

Exercise 3-11. A cost analyst at Hunter Memorial Hospital attempted to use regression analysis to determine the cost behavior of the account Repairs and Maintenance of X-Ray Machines. After gathering data and feeding it into a statistical computer program, the following regression equation was obtained:

$$\text{Cost} = \$12,034 - 0.32X$$

where X is the number of X-ray exposures taken each week.

The analyst was at a loss to explain why repair and maintenance costs should be inversely related to usage.

Consider the following possible explanations and explain why each might lead to the negative value for the explanatory variable:

(1) The company follows a structured preventive maintenance program in which the same maintenance is performed every month. The R^2 for the regression was 0.03.

(2) Because unexpected breakdowns are infrequent, most maintenance is routine and is scheduled during weeks when the X-ray unit is not busy.

(3) Although the machines are generally reliable, they are so complex that, when breakdowns do occur, they are out of operation anywhere from a few days to a week.

(4) Most electrical failures occur when the electric components warm up or cool down after being switched on or off. During busy periods, the X-ray machine is almost continuously left on.

PROBLEMS

Problem 3-1. Revell-Camp Company is a medium-sized producer of molded plastic parts, primarily for sale to the automotive industry. The accountant would like to forecast factory overhead for the next two quarters, October-December and January-March, and has gathered the following overhead cost data for the past four months. Except for those items specifically highlighted, all costs reflect the normal operations of the plant.

	May (4,000 DLH*)	June (4,200 DLH*)	July (4,800 DLH*)	August (5,600 DLH*)
Janitorial department expense	$ 4,000	$ 4,030	$ 4,085	$ 4,240
Maintenance and repair	5,112	3,840	3,888	3,952
Miscellaneous materials	3,000	3,150	3,600	4,200
Light and power	1,815	2,179	2,431	2,767
Heating and cooling	1,370	1,400	1,505	1,487
Factory supervision	6,400	6,400	6,400	6,400
Inspection and quality control	3,200	3,248	3,357	3,520
Depreciation expense—equipment	4,320	4,320	4,320	4,975
Depreciation expense—building	2,720	2,720	2,720	2,720
Lease on factory computer	950	950	950	950
Overtime	2,600	2,725	3,080	3,560
Employee fringe benefits	870	870	870	870
	$36,357	$35,832	$37,206	$39,641

*Direct labor hours.

Maintenance and repair expense is much higher in May because the factory performs most major repairs and overhauls during this month.

During the three summer months, a 20% surcharge is added to the variable portion of light and power costs.

The factory is located in a northern state, where heating costs are significantly higher than summer cooling costs. The accountant, based on past experience, estimates heating costs to average $1,900 per month over the next six months.

Depreciation expense increased in August because fully depreciated equipment was traded in on equipment with a higher basis. No changes in equipment or the building are expected in the next six months. The factory uses straight-line depreciation.

Required (1) Prepare an overhead budget formula for Revell-Camp for use in the next six months. Use the classification of accounts method to identify the cost behavior of various overhead costs. Estimate the variable component of a mixed cost, using the high-low method.

(2) Estimate the overhead costs for October, when 4,800 direct labor hours are scheduled to be used. Use the overhead formula prepared in (1).

Problem 3-2. Gifford Manufacturing Company produces a small line of brass plumbing fittings. The fittings are used primarily in residential houses. Thus, the company's sales and production are tied to the cyclical housing industry and vary greatly. The company's owners have asked its accountants to develop an overhead budget as an initial step toward better control of operating costs. Summarized data for the past six quarters are as follows:

	Quarter					
	I	II	III	IV	V	VI
Indirect labor	$10,710	$21,800	$22,200	$20,400	$30,900	$37,500
Indirect materials	6,930	14,110	14,370	13,200	20,025	24,700
Repair and maintenance	5,490	7,480	7,560	7,200	10,350	12,000
Janitorial services	2,820	3,400	3,400	2,820	3,400	4,500
Heat, light, and power	4,320	6,950	7,050	6,600	9,225	11,260
Inspection	6,750	10,510	10,140	9,600	12,750	16,050
Supervision	11,100	11,100	11,100	11,100	11,100	14,100
Depreciation	7,860	7,860	7,860	7,860	7,860	7,860
Lease expense	5,040	5,040	5,040	5,040	5,040	6,325
	$61,020	$88,250	$88,720	$83,820	$110,650	$134,295
Activity (DLH)	12,600	25,400	25,800	24,000	30,500	36,000

One accountant suggests that a simple, high-low analysis of total overhead would yield a serviceable budget at a minimum cost. Another points out that serious operating inefficiencies occur at outputs outside the relevant production range of 12,000 to 24,000 direct labor hours per quarter. Even fixed costs, such as supervisory costs and lease costs, increase at extreme outputs because of the need for additional supervision and production equipment. The second accountant suggests that the overhead budget line be broken down into several discrete ranges.

Required (1) Prepare a graph of total overhead costs, with total overhead on the vertical axis and direct labor hours on the horizontal axis.

(2) Graph a total overhead budget line, using the high-low method. Mathematical-ly determine the variable and fixed components of total overhead.

(3) Repeat (2), but divide the total production range into three ranges: 12,000-24,000, 24,000-30,000, and 30,000-36,000 direct labor hours per month. Determine the fixed cost component and the variable cost per direct labor hour in each range, using the high-low method for each range.

(4) Project total overhead cost at a production level of 27,000 direct labor hours, using the budgets prepared in (2) and (3).

(5) Which method appears to give the more accurate forecast?

Problem 3-3. As an accountant for Garrett Engineering Company, you have often noticed that the percentage of defective products seems to be related to the number of overtime hours worked during the period. This relationship is under-standable, considering that workers on overtime are tired, less attentive, and more prone to making errors. Because the defective units have no scrap value and incur considerable production costs, you wonder whether this relationship might not warrant consideration when decisions involve filling large orders by using tempo-rary help, overtime, or subcontractors. You have gathered the following data regarding overtime and scrap rates for the past eight months:

	Overtime	Defect Rate
March	275 hours	2.1%
April	200	0.8
May	500	2.7
June	800	2.6
July	850	4.0
August	1,100	4.9
September	600	3.3
October	475	3.5

Required (1) On a graph, plot the product defect rate against overtime hours. Plot the explanatory variable on the horizontal axis. Visually fit a line to the plotted data points.

(2) Calculate a least squares regression equation for the data.

(3) Determine the coefficient of correlation, R, for the regression.

(4) Predict the defect rate for a month in which 650 overtime hours are worked.

Problem 3-4. Asheville Wood Products Company cuts raw lumber into finished boards and beams. Competition in the lumber industry is strong, and Asheville's managers desire more accurate and up-to-date cost information than is currently available in order to make better product pricing decisions and to aid in evaluating special orders. As a preliminary step, Asheville has asked its accountants to measure overhead cost behavior. From the company's internal records, the accountants have gathered the data shown at the top of page 98.

Required (1) Plot the overhead data and visually fit a line to the data points. Determine the equation of the plotted line.

(2) Using the high-low method, calculate the budget for total overhead.

(3) Calculate the least squares regression parameters for the slope and intercept.

(4) (a) Calculate the sum of the squared deviations about the average monthly cost, $\Sigma(Y-\bar{Y})^2$.

	Production	Total Overhead
January	175,000 bd. ft.	$23,200
February	208,000	32,400
March	247,000	33,600
April	235,000	27,400
May	290,000	34,100
June	364,000	42,600
July	380,000	41,800
August	417,000	47,700
September	342,000	36,200
October	299,000	34,300
November	250,000	31,100
December	211,000	30,100

(b) Calculate the sum of the squared deviations from the observations to the lines estimated in (1), (2), and (3).

(c) Divide the values obtained in (b) by the corresponding values from (a). Subtract these ratios of unexplained variation from 1.0, and compare the resulting ratios of explained variation (R^2).

(5) Using each of the three overhead models, estimate total overhead in a month when 275,000 board feet are produced.

Problem 3-5. Olsen-Fiskars is a small metal-working shop which supplies custom-order stainless steel fittings to local yacht builders. The shop is heavily automated, causing monthly overhead costs to vary little. The primary variable overhead item is electricity.

In the past, the company has calculated an average of the past 8 months' overhead costs, and used this amount to budget overhead costs for the next quarter. You feel, however, that with very little additional work, a least squares regression line could be fitted to the data, yielding more accurate cost projections. Overhead cost data for the past eight months are as follows:

	Activity	Total Overhead Cost
August	2,000 dir. mach. hrs.	$ 7,100
September	3,400	9,700
October	3,000	8,700
November	4,100	10,900
December	4,900	9,400
January	5,500	9,800
February	4,900	11,300
March	3,800	8,700

Required (1) Calculate the average monthly overhead for the past eight months and the standard deviation of overhead cost around this average. Calculate the adjusted (sample) standard deviation, using $n - 1$ in the denominator.

(2) Calculate the least squares regression parameters and the standard error of estimate, s_e, using all available data. Calculate the adjusted standard error, using $n - 2$ in the denominator.

(3) Plot the least squares regression line and the average overhead line on the same graph. Construct a 90% confidence interval around each line, using the standard deviations calculated in (1) and (2).

cont.

(4) The standard error of the slope for the data is 0.326. Is the slope coefficient statistically significant at the 95% confidence level?

(5) Assume that in April, when 5,500 machine hours are worked, overhead costs total $12,400. Would this large amount be a cause for alarm under the old budgeting system, if the graph in (3) were used to identify unusually large overhead costs?

Problem 3-6. (*NOTE: This problem assumes access to a computer regression program which will compute multiple regressions with two independent variables. Since the computer output has rounded the original input data, Zawacki's original data are not reproduced exactly, but the results will be adequate.*) Zawacki Corp. manufactures a line of golf carts in its Green Bay plant. These carts are currently sold for $80 each. Because of a business recession, Zawacki anticipates that sales of golf carts will be depressed for at least the next quarter, and wishes to know if next quarter's expected sales (2,800 units) will exceed the break-even point for this product.

Zawacki has a traditional job order cost accounting system. No information concerning the fixed and variable costs of golf carts is directly available from the cost accounting system. A cost analyst at Zawacki was asked to calculate the break-even point for golf carts. Data on the total costs and the number of carts produced for 25 representative weeks were obtained and used as input in a regression analysis. To simplify data entry into the computer, costs were entered in thousands, and volume data were scaled by a factor of 10 before entry. The regression output is reproduced on the following page.

The analyst noted that the constant in the regression output was negative. "Since, for my regression analysis, the intercept represents fixed costs," the analyst observed, "there must be a bug in the program or errors in the data. It makes no sense to have negative fixed costs."

The data and program were reviewed and no errors were found. The analyst then used the regression results to calculate the (weekly) break-even point for golf carts, as follows:

$$
\begin{aligned}
X &= \text{(weekly) break-even volume} \\
80X &= -\$3,890 + 98X \text{ (after rescaling to the original units)} \\
\$3,890 &= 18X \\
X &= 216 \text{ units}
\end{aligned}
$$

Required (1) What interpretation do you believe should be given to the negative fixed costs?

(2) Should Zawacki expect a profit, a loss, or essentially a break-even situation for the next 13-week quarter?

(3) Calculate the t ratio for the slope and intercept parameters of the regression equation. Which parameters are statistically significant?

(4) Calculate a 95% confidence interval about the variable cost coefficient.

(5) Use the regression equation to predict total costs in the coming quarter. Calculate the net income or loss for the quarter. (Round answers to the nearest thousand.)

(6) Fit a regression equation to the data shown in the computer printout, using two explanatory variables. For X_1, use the activity data as given. For X_2, use activity data *squared.* Estimate total costs for the next quarter, based on these

regression results, and compare your answers with those obtained from the one-variable regression.

```
THE REGRESSION EQUATION IS:
Y =  -3.89 + 0.980 X1 (SCALED)
[Y = -3,890 + 98.0 X1 (UNSCALED)]

                                             STAN. DEV.
  CONSTANT       COLUMN     COEFFICIENT       OF. COEF.
                   --         -3.8892          1.9056
  X1               C1          0.9799          0.0778

THE STAN. DEV. OF Y ABOUT REGRESSION LINE IS:
S = 3.22
WITH (25 - 2) = 23 DEGREES OF FREEDOM (D.F.)

R SQUARED = 87.3 PERCENT
R SQUARED = 86.8 PERCENT, ADJUSTED FOR D.F.

             X1        Y       PRED. Y
  ROW        C1       C5        VALUE      RESIDUAL
   1        22.3     15.25      17.94       -2.69
   2        29.0     23.97      24.48       -0.51
   3        31.3     24.99      26.76       -1.78
   4         9.0      6.77       4.94        1.83
   5        13.9      9.89       9.72        0.17
   6        33.4     31.18      28.80        2.37
   7        23.8     15.89      19.39       -3.50
   8        24.9     19.34      20.55       -1.21
   9        25.4     18.14      20.99       -2.85
  10        17.7     13.08      13.44       -0.36
  11        12.8      6.98       8.69       -1.71
  12        24.2     18.00      19.84       -1.84
  13        19.8     14.42      15.52       -1.10
  14        30.6     25.53      26.11       -2.57
  15        24.6     19.55      20.19       -0.64
  16        24.0     18.06      19.66       -1.59
  17        32.7     30.91      28.12        2.78
  18        13.9      9.50       9.71       -0.22
  19        23.8     18.62      19.46       -0.84
  20        24.7     20.06      20.33       -0.27
  21        40.5     44.43      35.80        8.63
  22         3.5      7.80      -0.44        8.23
  23        15.0     12.09      10.85        1.24
  24        32.0     30.30      27.45        2.85
  25        23.5     14.72      19.16       -4.44
```

Problem 3-7 (CMA adapted, 6/79). The Alma Plant manufactures the industrial product line of CJS Industries. Plant management wants to be able to get a good, yet quick, estimate of the manufacturing overhead costs which can be expected to be incurred each month. The easiest and simplest method to accomplish this task appears to be to develop a flexible budget formula for the manufacturing overhead costs.

The plant's accounting staff suggested that simple linear regression be used to determine the cost behavior pattern of the overhead costs. The regression data can provide the basis for the flexible budget formula. Sufficient evidence is available to conclude that manufacturing overhead costs vary with direct labor hours. The actual direct labor hours and the corresponding manufacturing overhead costs for each month of the last three years were used in the linear regression analysis.

The three-year period contained various occurrences not uncommon to many businesses. During two months of the first year, production was severely curtailed due to wildcat strikes. In one month of the second year, production was reduced because of material shortages and, during two months, was materially increased (overtime scheduled) to produce the units required for a one-time sales order. At the end of the second year, employee benefits were raised significantly as the result of a labor agreement. Production during the third year was not affected by any special circumstances.

Various members of Alma's accounting staff raised some issues regarding the historical data collected for the regression analysis. These issues were as follows:

- Some members of the accounting staff believed that the use of data from all 36 months would provide a more accurate portrayal of the cost behavior. While they recognized that any of the monthly data could include efficiencies and inefficiencies, they believed these efficiencies/inefficiencies would tend to balance out over a longer period of time.
- Other members of the accounting staff suggested that only those months which were considered normal should be used, so that the regression would not be distorted.
- Still other members felt that only the most recent 12 months should be used because they were the most current.
- Some members questioned whether historical data should be used at all to form the basis for a flexible budget formula.

The accounting department ran two regression analyses of the data—one using the data from all 36 months and the other using only the data from the last 12 months. The following information was derived from the two linear regressions:

	Data From All 36 Months	Data From Most Recent 12 Months
Coefficients of the regression equation:		
Constant	$123,810	$109,020
Independent variable (DLH)	$1.6003	$4.1977
Coefficient of correlation	.4710	.6891
Standard error of estimate	$13,003	$7,473
Standard error of the regression coefficient for the independent variable	$.9744	$1.3959
Calculated t for the regression coefficient	1.6423	3.0072
t required for a 95% confidence interval:		
34 degrees of freedom (36 − 2) ..	1.960	
10 degrees of freedom (12 − 2) ..		2.228

Required (1) From the results of Alma Plant's regression analysis which used the data from all 36 months:

(a) Formulate the flexible budget equation that can be employed to estimate monthly manufacturing overhead costs.

(b) Calculate the estimate of overhead costs for a month when 25,000 direct labor hours are worked.

(2) Using only the results of the two regression analyses, explain which of the two results (12 months versus 36 months) you would use as a basis for the flexible budget formula.

(3) How could the four specific issues raised by the members of Alma's accounting staff influence your willingness to use the results of the statistical analyses as the basis for the flexible budget formula? Explain your answer.

Problem 3-8. Nutone Paint Company produces a wide variety of exterior and interior latexes and enamels. As a part of its normal preparation for the coming fiscal year, Nutone is updating its comprehensive budgeting system, which includes a budget for administrative costs. Nutone has gathered data for the past 18 months, adjusted for changes in unit costs or abnormal operations, and has performed regression analyses relating monthly administrative costs to monthly sales, monthly cost of goods manufactured, or both. Excerpts from the computer regression printouts are as follows:

```
REGRESSION:  ADMIN. COSTS (Y); COST OF GOODS MANUFACTURED (X1)

THE REGRESSION EQUATION IS: Y = 114,059 + 0.0827 X1

                                  STAN. DEV.      T RATIO =
  CONSTANT       COEFFICIENT      OF. COEF.       COEF./STAN. DEV.
                   114,059          50,048         2.28
  X1                0.0827           0.0274         3.018

THE STAN. DEV. OF Y ABOUT REGRESSION LINE IS:  S = 38,221
WITH (18 - 2) = 16 DEGREES OF FREEDOM (D.F.)

R SQUARED = 63.7 PERCENT

REGRESSION:  ADMIN. COSTS (Y); SALES (X2)

THE REGRESSION EQUATION IS: Y = 151,296 + 0.0432 X2

                                  STAN. DEV.      T RATIO =
  CONSTANT       COEFFICIENT      OF COEF.        COEF./STAN. DEV.
                   151,296          34,622         4.37
  X2                0.0432           0.00799        5.407

THE STAN. DEVIATION OF Y ABOUT REGRESSION LINE IS:  S =  25,660
WITH (18 - 2) = 16 DEGREES OF FREEDOM (D.F.)

R SQUARED = 83.6 PERCENT

REGRESSION:  ADMIN. COSTS (Y); COST OF GOODS MANUFACTURED (X1); SALES (X2)
```

```
THE REGRESSION EQUATION IS: Y = 80,468 + 0.0611 X1 + 0.0586 X2

                                STAN. DEV.      T RATIO =
    CONSTANT     COEFFICIENT      OF COEF.    COEF./STAN. DEV.
                    80,468         11,851        6.790
    X1               0.0611         0.00979       6.241
    X2               0.0586         0.00519      11.291

THE STAN. DEV. OF Y ABOUT THE REGRESSION LINE IS: S = 9,482
WITH (18 - 3) = 15 DEGREES OF FREEDOM (D.F.)

R SQUARED = 97.9 PERCENT
```

The past five month's projections and actual values are as follows:

	Sales		Cost of Goods Manufactured	
	forecast	actual	forecast	actual
August	$ 424,000	$ 905,000	$640,000	$670,000
September	533,000	987,000	704,000	715,000
October	1,875,000	1,115,000	774,000	707,000
November	2,400,000	1,200,000	740,000	742,000
December	775,000	1,384,000	725,000	730,000

Required (1) Assuming that good estimates are available for both X_1 and X_2, which model would you select to forecast monthly overhead? Explain.

(2) In the first month of the new fiscal year, Nutone expects to have sales of $1,525,000 and cost of goods manufactured of $905,000. Project the next month's administrative costs, using each of the three models.

(3) To accurately forecast administrative costs, it is first necessary to project either sales, cost of goods manufactured, or both. Given the projections and the actual results for the 5-month period, which model would you select to predict administrative costs?

(4) To control administrative costs, Nutone has decided to use the simple regression model based on sales. Using this model, construct a schedule of budget allowances for administrative costs for the six sales levels from $500,000 to $1,000,000, in increments of $100,000. Construct a 90% confidence interval for each of these levels, using the standard error of estimate (standard deviation of Y about the regression line).

Problem 3-9. Tennetron Manufacturing Industries is a large plastics manufacturer specializing in the production of plastic parts—trim, knobs, chassis—which are sold primarily to appliance manufacturers. Tennetron's management has requested its accounting staff to use linear regression as a part of an effort to budget manufacturing overhead. The accountants have selected three explanatory variables—direct labor hours per month (X_1), direct labor cost per month (X_2), and direct materials cost per month (X_3)—since these bear an observable relationship to total monthly overhead (Y), and data are easily gathered. The accountants prepared four regression equations. A summary of the results of the analysis, using 19 monthly observations, is as follows (with t values for the regression coefficients in parentheses):

	Model	Stan. Error of Estimate	Adjusted R^2	Unadjusted R^2
1.	$Y = \$20{,}298 + \$5.14X_1$ $(t = 1.05)$	$7,254	0.59	0.61
2.	$Y = \$8{,}837 + .506X_2 + .117X_3$ (4.47) (3.83)	3,693	0.90	0.91
3.	$Y = \$15{,}212 + \$2.16X_1 + .301X_2$ (1.79) (2.21)	6,708	0.67	0.71
4.	$Y = \$14{,}298 + \$1.79X_1 + .165X_2 + .117X_3$ (0.101) (4.12) (2.69)	4,179	0.88	0.93

Correlation Matrix

		Y	X_1	X_2	X_3
Y	(total monthly overhead)	1.00	0.78	0.94	0.86
X_1	(direct labor hours)		1.00	0.96	0.77
X_2	(direct labor cost)			1.00	0.69
X_3	(direct materials cost)				1.00

Required

(1) Based on the correlation matrix alone:

(a) Which single variable should be chosen as a base in applying manufacturing overhead?

(b) Which two variables in combination will probably provide the best results in forecasting monthly overhead? Explain.

(2) Which of the four regression models would you pick to predict monthly overhead cost?

(3) Using the model selected in (2), predict total overhead for the coming month. Input data are forecast as:

> Direct labor hours ...... 12,480 hours
> Direct labor cost $90,355
> Direct materials cost $192,190

(4) For next month's manufacturing overhead, construct a 95% prediction interval around the answer calculated in (3). Use the standard error of estimate given as an estimate of variability in making the prediction.

(5) Why is the prediction interval calculated in (4) an underestimate of the correct prediction interval?

Problem 3-10. Thessalon Company is a privately held, medium-sized producer of ceramic and porcelain products. The company would like to use statistical regression to analyze factory overhead costs. Monthly financial reports have been prepared primarily for internal use, using cash basis accounting. Thessalon's accounting staff has gathered the financial data shown at the top of page 105.

Required   Perform a regression analysis to estimate the fixed and variable components of the overhead cost data. How confident would you be in using these regression estimates?

	Jan.	Feb.	Mar.	April	May	June
Indirect materials	$ 28,800	—	—	$ 46,550	—	—
Factory supplies	2,780	—	$ 3,414	-——	—	$ 1,980
Supervisory expenses	26,200	$26,100	33,700	26,200	$26,400	29,700
Maint. and repair	7,400	8,340	8,100	9,750	10,470	16,900
Heat, light, and power	9,200	9,900	9,300	14,600	14,400	15,100
Janitorial services	5,100	4,960	4,720	4,850	5,400	5,370
Rent—building	72,000					
Depreciation—factory equipment	10,400	10,400	10,400	27,200	10,400	16,100
Property taxes			22,700			22,700
Total	$161,880	$59,700	$92,334	$129,150	$67,070	$107,850
Activity (DLH)	7,200	7,500	7,400	12,000	10,700	10,400

Problem 3-11. Thessalon Company in Problem 3-10 has gathered the following additional information regarding various overhead cost items:

- Indirect materials are ordered quarterly and expensed when ordered. The accountant estimates that usage of indirect materials varies with direct labor hours worked each month. The inventories of indirect materials outstanding prior to each reorder date are as follows:

Date	Indirect Materials Inventory
12/31	$1,400
3/31	590
6/30	2,780

- Factory supplies are reordered and expensed when the current inventory is exhausted. The accountant feels that monthly usage of each batch of supplies purchased is approximately the same. Supplies purchased in June will be exhausted by August 1.
- Supervisors are paid on the 15th and the last day of each month for work performed during the preceding period. A short-term, interest-free advance of $7,500 to the plant superintendent was charged to supervisory expenses in March. The advance was paid off by a monthly $250 deduction in the superintendent's pay, beginning in June. This payment was credited to Supervisory Expenses.
- The factory as well as the company's administrative headquarters are located in the same building. All maintenance and repair expenses are charged to the factory, although the accountant feels that 10% of such costs are applicable to the company's administrative offices.
- All heat, light, and power costs are charged to the factory overhead account. The accountant estimates the monthly amount of this expense applicable to the company's administrative offices to be $750.
- All janitorial and cleaning costs are charged to factory overhead. The company's accountant believes the most reasonable allocation of this cost would be on the basis of floor area. The office occupies 30,600 square feet of the 180,000-square-foot building.
- Rent on the building is paid semiannually. All rent is charged to the factory.

- All factory equipment is depreciated straight-line. On April 1, equipment costing $16,800 was purchased and written off as depreciation expense. The equipment has a 6-year life and no salvage value. The increase in June depreciation expense is the result of new equipment purchased in June, charged to an asset account, and properly depreciated.
- The annual property tax bill is paid in quarterly installments.
- Overtime premium and fringe benefit costs were charged to Wages Expense rather than Factory Overhead. Costs for the past six months were:

	Total Overtime Premium and Fringe Benefit Cost
January	$ 9,200
February	8,700
March	8,900
April	12,300
May	10,800
June	12,500

Required
(1) Using the additional information supplied, recalculate the monthly overhead cost for the factory on an accrual basis. Shared costs should be properly allocated between manufacturing and nonmanufacturing operations.

(2) Based on your adjusted total monthly overhead cost data, as calculated in (1), estimate the fixed and variable components of factory overhead for Thessalon Company, using linear regression.

(3) Comment on the extent to which a regression using the overhead costs for six months and one explanatory variable, direct labor hours, may not be representative of future months.

Problem 3-12. Caron-Meyer Co. produces two electronic control units (a standard and a deluxe model) based on the same patented electronic circuit. The basic circuits are produced in Department 1, and then the control units are assembled in Department 2. Product cost information for the two models is as follows:

Standard Control Unit		Deluxe Control Unit	
Selling price	$150	Selling price	$200
Direct materials	$ 20	Direct materials	$ 25
Direct labor:		Direct labor:	
Dept. 1: 2 hrs.		Dept. 1: 2 hrs.	
@ $10	20	@ $10	20
Dept. 2: 1 hr.		Dept 2: 2 hrs.	
@ $15	15	@ $15	30
Mfg. overhead:		Mfg. overhead:	
3 DLH @ $15	45	4 DLH @ $15	60
Selling and admin. cost*	30	Selling and admin. cost*	40
Total cost	$130	Total cost	$175
Profit per unit	$ 20	Profit per unit	$ 25

*Estimated at 20% of normal selling price.

Next month, Caron-Meyer has sales orders for 1,000 standard units and 2,000 deluxe units and has scheduled production of these quantities. Caron-Meyer's Canadian sales representative has just informed management that it has located in the Klondike a new customer for the control units. The customer is willing to take either 200 standard units at a price of $100 per unit or 150 deluxe units at a price of $150 per unit. Caron-Meyer's initial response is to reject the offer, since the costs shown on its cost sheets are in excess of the offered selling price. The Marketing Department head, whose sales force has again failed to meet its order goal, would like to accept one of the offers and has asked the Accounting Department to perform a quick regression cost analysis in order to identify the variable and fixed costs related to these products. The results of the study are:

Monthly manufacturing overhead (Y_1):

$$Y_1 = \$80,000 + \$6.67 \text{ (Dept. 1 hours)} + \$10 \text{ (Dept. 2 hours)}$$

$$R^2 = 0.93$$

Monthly selling and administrative costs (Y_2):

$$Y_2 = \$91,000 + .02 \text{ (Sales revenue at standard price)}$$

$$R^2 = 0.91$$

Required

(1) Using the standard cost sheets and the results of the regression equations, calculate the unit contribution margin and the contribution margin ratio of each model.
(2) If, with equal effort, Caron-Meyer could sell $10,000 of either the standard or deluxe units to a customer, sales of which model would provide more profit?
(3) Calculate the increase or decrease in profit resulting from acceptance of the order for 200 standard units at $100 per unit and acceptance of the order for 150 deluxe units at $150 per unit.
(4) What factors other than the profit on this order should Caron-Meyer consider before deciding to accept or reject the Klondike customer's order?

Problem 3-13. (*Note: This problem is based in part on Appendix 3.*) Weberware Company markets a line of small home appliances, kitchen utensils, home gifts, and other items, primarily through door-to-door sales in the midwest and northeast. The company's major selling months are June, July, and August, when high school and college students are sent out to sell the company's wares. These salespeople are largely inexperienced and are paid a small amount per sales call in addition to a 20% commission.

The company also maintains a small staff of regular salespeople, who are paid an annual salary and a smaller commission. During the cold winter months, these salespeople perform market research studies and product analyses, set up and staff displays at consumer products shows, and make a small number of sales calls. The number of sales calls increases as the weather improves.

The company's sales director would like to budget total selling expenses on the basis of the number of sales calls made (which heavily influences summer payroll costs). The data at the top of page 108 have been gathered.

A computer printout of a least squares regression based on the scaled data shows that: (a) the regression line is: $Y = -\$2.77 + 2.55X$; (b) the Durbin-Watson statistic for this regression is: $d = 0.81$.

	Sales Calls (X) (in hundreds of thousands)	Monthly Selling Expenses (Y) (in hundreds of thousands)
January	1.00	$ 2.60
February	1.80	2.50
March	3.10	3.00
April	3.40	3.45
May	4.05	5.75
June	4.90	8.10
July	5.60	13.80
August	6.00	14.75

Required

(1) Calculate the coefficient of determination (R^2) for the regression equation. Is the line a good fit?

(2) What does the value of 0.81 for d indicate?

(3) On a graph, plot the value of each residual ($Y - Y'$) against its corresponding X value.

(4) Based on the graph prepared in (3), does the assumption that the residuals have an expected value of zero for any given X value appear to be violated?

(5) What does your analysis of residuals in (4) suggest about the appropriateness of a linear regression model for this application?

Problem 3-14. (*Note: This problem is based in part on Appendix 3.*) Abaco Yachts Inc. builds fiberglass sailing yachts at its plant in southern Florida. Sales have been excellent since the company was founded ten years ago, and the company would now like to develop a model to forecast sales. The company's marketing director feels that annual sales bear an observable relationship to disposable personal income, and would like to construct a linear regression model based on the following data:

	Disposable Personal Income (in billions)	Company Sales (in millions)
19X2	$461	$ 60
19X3	514	69
19X4	542	79
19X5	587	92
19X6	639	108
19X7	699	107
19X8	747	131
19X9	800	143
19Y0	914	198
19Y1	977	201

Required

(1) Calculate the least squares intercept and slope regression parameters for the data.

(2) Calculate the coefficient of determination and the coefficient of correlation for the regression line calculated in (1).

(3) Determine the standard error of estimate for the regression.

(4) Calculate the t ratios for both the slope and intercept parameters.

(5) Project company sales for the coming year, when disposable income is expected to rise to $1,025. Develop a 95% prediction interval for sales, using the standard error of a prediction as the measure of variability.

Four

Cost-Volume-Profit Analysis

Cost-volume-profit (CVP) analysis examines the response of profit to changes in volume. It relies on linear cost analysis and on linear revenue assumptions. This chapter will view profits as resulting from the interaction of costs and revenue, which both vary with volume.

To gain an understanding of CVP analysis, the common example of a firm which produces only a single product will be used. The analysis will then be expanded to cover firms with several products produced by multiple divisions. This analysis will be designed to include the firm's variable costs of order-getting and order-filling.

THE COST-VOLUME-PROFIT MODEL

Cost-volume-profit analysis is based on the concept that profit equals revenue minus costs. The linear cost and revenue assumptions discussed in previous chapters are the basis of the following equation, based on units sold:

Profit = (Selling price per unit × Units) − (Variable cost per unit × Units) − Fixed cost

To illustrate the profit equation, assume the following facts for the saver switch example in Chapter 1:

1. The selling price is $6 per unit. The relevant revenue range is 40,000 to 70,000 units per month.
2. The fixed costs are $90,000 per month, and the variable costs are $4 per unit. The relevant cost range is 35,000 to 65,000 units per month.

The profit equation may be used properly only in the ultimate relevant range which fits within the relevant revenue and cost ranges. In this example, the ultimate relevant range is 40,000 to 65,000 units.

Cost and Revenue Approach to CVP Analysis

One approach to cost-volume-profit analysis is the cost and revenue approach shown in Illustration 4-1. This approach can be used to project estimated profits at various sales volumes. For example, the estimated profit from selling 60,000 units is the vertical distance between the cost and revenue functions, or $30,000. The profit equation below the cost and revenue graph confirms this estimate. The graph also indicates the volume of sales (45,000 units) at which profit will be zero and below which a loss will result.

The zero profit volume that separates the loss and profit zones is referred to as the **break-even point**. The break-even point is calculated, as shown below the cost and revenue graph, by solving the profit equation for the level of sales that produces zero profit.

The terms break-even analysis and cost-volume-profit analysis are sometimes used interchangeably. Break-even analysis is an application of CVP analysis, however, and does not reflect a firm's primary objective.

The break-even point is used as a measure of risk by comparing sales at the break-even point to estimated sales. This comparison yields the **margin of safety**, which is the amount that sales could fall below the estimated sales level before the break-even point is reached. In Illustration 4-1, the margin of safety is 15,000 units (60,000 − 45,000). The margin of safety may also be stated as the percentage by which sales could fall before the break-even point is reached. The margin of safety percentage is computed as follows:

$$\text{Margin of safety percentage} = \frac{\text{Expected sales} - \text{Break-even sales}}{\text{Expected sales}}$$

$$= \frac{60,000 \text{ units} - 45,000 \text{ units}}{60,000 \text{ units}}$$

$$= 25\%$$

Contribution Approach to CVP Analysis

An alternate approach to CVP analysis is based on the contribution margin as a function of volume. The contribution margin of a unit is the net donation each unit makes towards covering fixed costs. It is calculated as follows:

$$\text{Contribution margin per unit} = \text{Selling price per unit} - \text{Variable cost per unit}$$

In the example of the saver switch, the contribution margin of each unit is $2 ($6 selling price − $4 variable cost). The contribution graph in Illustration 4-1 shows that once fixed costs are covered by selling 45,000 units ($90,000 fixed cost ÷ $2 contribution margin), each unit sold in excess of the 45,000-unit break-even point contributes $2 to profit.

Illustration 4-1   Cost-Volume-Profit Analysis

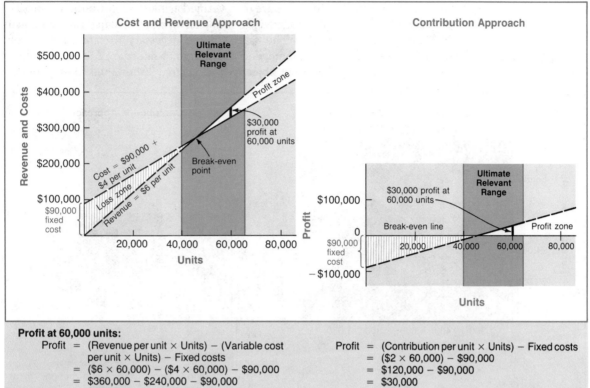

Profit at 60,000 units:

Cost and Revenue Approach:

Profit = (Revenue per unit × Units) − (Variable cost
per unit × Units) − Fixed costs
= ($6 × 60,000) − ($4 × 60,000) − $90,000
= $360,000 − $240,000 − $90,000
= $30,000

Contribution Approach:

Profit = (Contribution per unit × Units) − Fixed costs
= ($2 × 60,000) − $90,000
= $120,000 − $90,000
= $30,000

Break-even point (units at zero profit):

Cost and Revenue Approach:

Profit = (Revenue per unit × Units) − (Variable cost
per unit × Units) − Fixed costs
0 = ($6 × units) − ($4 × units) − $90,000
0 = ($2 × units) − $90,000
$2 × units = $90,000
units = 45,000

Contribution Approach:

Profit = (Contribution per unit × Units) − Fixed costs
0 = ($2 × units) − $90,000
$2 × units = $90,000
units = 45,000

The contribution approach should be used only within the ultimate relevant range, since it nets revenue against cost. To provide maximum information, the analyses in this text will be based primarily on the cost and revenue format.

USING CVP ANALYSIS

Cost-volume-profit analysis can be used to determine the level of sales necessary to achieve a variety of profit objectives. These profit objectives may be either fixed or variable with respect to volume. A fixed profit objective is an absolute desired profit not related to sales, and is commonly expressed as a percentage return on assets. A variable profit objective is stated as a function of sales.

In Illustration 4-2, the use of CVP analysis to analyze profit objectives is demonstrated, based on the following data:

Revenue	$10 per unit	Fixed cost	$2,000 per month
Variable costs	6 per unit	Relevant range	400 to 1,000 units per month

For each objective, the initial solutions are derived by using the cost and revenue approach. The solutions are then verified using the contribution approach. Objective 1 is an example of a fixed profit objective, which is stated as profit equals 10% on assets of $10,000. The sales volume necessary to achieve the profit objective, the break-even volume, and the margin of safety are computed. Objectives 2 and 3 are variable profit objectives. Objective 2 shows the computation of

Illustration 4-2
Using CVP to Analyze
Profit Objectives

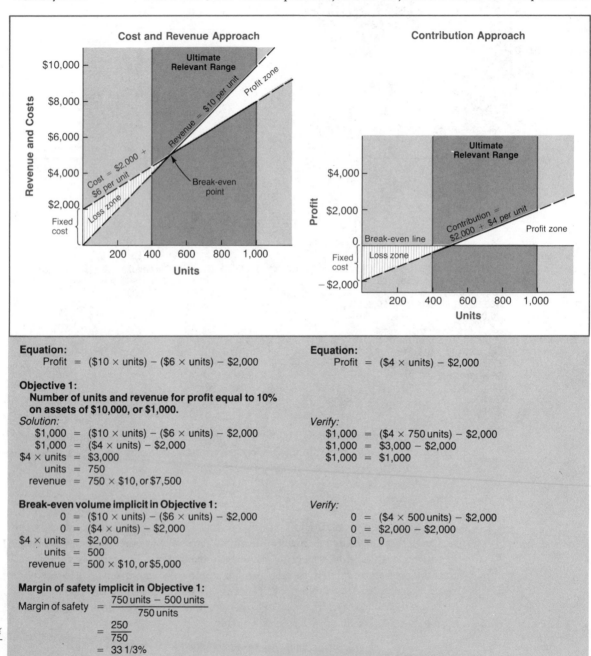

Equation:
   Profit = ($10 × units) − ($6 × units) − $2,000

Objective 1:
  Number of units and revenue for profit equal to 10%
  on assets of $10,000, or $1,000.
Solution:
     $1,000 = ($10 × units) − ($6 × units) − $2,000
     $1,000 = ($4 × units) − $2,000
 $4 × units = $3,000
      units = 750
   revenue = 750 × $10, or $7,500

Equation:
   Profit = ($4 × units) − $2,000

Verify:
   $1,000 = ($4 × 750 units) − $2,000
   $1,000 = $3,000 − $2,000
   $1,000 = $1,000

Break-even volume implicit in Objective 1:
       0 = ($10 × units) − ($6 × units) − $2,000
       0 = ($4 × units) − $2,000
 $4 × units = $2,000
      units = 500
   revenue = 500 × $10, or $5,000

Verify:
   0 = ($4 × 500 units) − $2,000
   0 = $2,000 − $2,000
   0 = 0

Margin of safety implicit in Objective 1:

$$\text{Margin of safety} = \frac{750\ \text{units} - 500\ \text{units}}{750\ \text{units}}$$

$$= \frac{250}{750}$$

$$= 33\,1/3\%$$

Objective 2:

Number of units and revenue for profit equal to 10% of sales.

Solution:

$$.1(\$10 \times \text{units}) = (\$10 \times \text{units}) - (\$6 \times \text{units}) - \$2,000$$
$$\$1 \times \text{units} = (\$4 \times \text{units}) - \$2,000$$
$$\$3 \times \text{units} = \$2,000$$
$$\text{units} = 667$$
$$\text{revenue} = 667 \times \$10, \text{ or } \$6,670$$

Verify:

$$.1(\$10 \times 667 \text{ units}) = (\$4 \times 667 \text{ units}) - \$2,000$$
$$\$667 = \$2,668 - \$2,000$$
$$\$667 = \$668 \text{ (rounding)}$$

Objective 3:

Number of units and revenue for an aftertax profit equal to 10% of sales. Tax rate is 40%.

Solution:

$$\frac{.1}{.6}(\$10 \times \text{units}) = (\$10 \times \text{units}) - (\$6 \times \text{units}) - \$2,000$$
$$.167(\$10 \times \text{units}) = (\$4 \times \text{units}) - \$2,000$$
$$\$1.67 \times \text{units} = (\$4 \times \text{units}) - \$2,000$$
$$\$2.33 \times \text{units} = \$2,000$$
$$\text{units} = 858$$
$$\text{revenue} = 858 \times \$10, \text{ or } \$8,580$$

Verify:

$$\frac{.1}{.6}(\$10 \times 858 \text{ units}) = (\$4 \times 858 \text{ units}) - \$2,000$$
$$.167(\$8,580) = \$3,432 - \$2,000$$
$$\$1,433 = \$1,432 \text{ (rounding)}$$

the units and revenue needed to provide a profit equal to 10% of sales, or $1 per unit. Objective 3 shows the computation of the units and revenue needed for a profit of 10% of sales, after tax. With a tax rate of 40%, this objective means that 10% must be earned on 60% of the profit before tax. For the computation, the objective is restated as 16 2/3% (10% ÷ 60%) of sales, before tax.

CVP Analysis for One Product in a Multiproduct Firm

The concept of CVP analysis has been developed in the context of a single-product firm. Since single-product firms are virtually nonexistent, the analytical technique will be illustrated for a multiproduct firm.

According to the theory of profits discussed in Chapter 1, the primary objective of maximizing a firm's net income is accomplished by maximizing the contributions of the firm's various segments. Net income is a residual figure, determined by subtracting the costs which are first specific at the level of the entire firm from the contributions produced by the various segments of the firm. Each segment's contribution is primarily determined by the contributions of its products, since there are only limited opportunities to maximize a segment's contribution by controlling the segment's costs which are shared in common by two or more products. If the firm's objective is to maximize its net income, the contribution of each of the firm's products should be analyzed by applying the basic procedures of CVP analysis. A profitable mix of the products to be sold by each segment should then be assembled.

Illustration 4-3 shows the application of CVP analysis to one product of a multiproduct division. The product analyzed is a set of car ramps used to elevate cars that are being repaired. The ramps are produced by the Auto Accessory Division of Waukesha Manufacturing Company. The data for the product are as follows:

Revenue	$35 per unit	Specific fixed costs	$15,000 per month
Variable costs	20 per unit	Relevant range	500 to 1,700 units per month

The graphical analysis in Illustration 4-3 parallels that used for a single-product firm, but the analytic meanings are different. The following features of the cost and revenue approach in Illustration 4-3 should be noted:

1. The cost function includes only the specific fixed cost of the product plus its variable costs. A specific fixed cost is one necessitated only by this product, and one which would be eliminated if the product were discontinued.
2. For any projected volume in the relevant range, the analysis estimates product contribution, not profit. Product contribution, which is indicated by the vertical distance between the cost and revenue functions, is the amount provided by the product to cover the common fixed costs of the division. In this example, the estimate of the contribution at a sales level of 1,500 units is $7,500.
3. The intersection of the specific cost and revenue lines could be viewed as a special type of break-even point. It is the **product justification point,** the point at which the product contribution just covers the product's specific fixed costs. The area to the right is the **positive contribution zone,** where a product contributes to the division's fixed costs and to the division's contribution to the firm. The area to the left is the **negative contribution zone,** where a product makes no contribution to the division's fixed costs, but instead consumes the division's contribution.
4. The margin of safety becomes the amount between the projected sales volume and the sales volume that would cause the product to justify its specific fixed costs. In this example, a 33 1/3% fall in sales would cause a zero product contribution.

In the contribution approach shown in Illustration 4-3, $15 per unit is contributed to cover the specific fixed costs of the product. The product justification point occurs at 1,000 units, where all specific fixed costs have been covered and the contribution to the division's fixed costs is zero. At a projected sales level of 1,500 units, the contribution to the division's fixed costs is $7,500.

A firm's ability to manage product contribution can be increased by expanding the previous analysis to consider both **short-run** and **long-run product justification points.** Some fixed costs specific to a product, such as advertising and salaries, could be terminated in the short run. Specifically, these short-run fixed costs could be eliminated before the beginning of the time period being analyzed. Other specific fixed costs are long run in nature. Costs such as rent and machinery depreciation might continue during the period under consideration, even if production ceased. A longer time period is necessary to eliminate these costs, or to put them to an alternate use. In the short run, a product can be justified if it covers only the short-run specific fixed costs, since at least some contribution is being made to the product's long-run specific fixed costs. In the long run, the product can only be continued if its volume is in excess of that necessary to cover both the product's short- and long-run fixed costs.

Illustration 4-4 is a modified version of the cost and revenue graph in Illustration 4-3. The short-run and long-run product justification points are calculated below the graph. Using these product justification points, three contribution zones can be identified. The **negative contribution zone** is the area to the left of the short-run justification point. It indicates that unit sales are so low that specific

Illustration 4-3   CVP for One Product in a Multiproduct Division

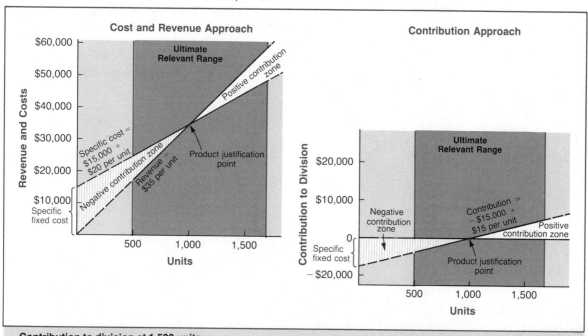

Contribution to division at 1,500 units:

Contribution = (Revenue per unit × Units) − (Variable cost per unit × Units) − Specific fixed costs
  = ($35 × 1,500) − ($20 × 1,500) − 15,000
  = $52,500 − $30,000 − $15,000
  = $7,500

Contribution = (Contribution per unit × Units) − Specific fixed costs
  = ($15 × 1,500) − $15,000
  = $22,500 − $15,000
  = $7,500

Product justification point (zero contribution):

0 = ($35 × units) − ($20 × units) − $15,000
0 = ($15 × units) − $15,000
$15 × units = $15,000
units = 1,000
revenue = 1,000 × $35, or $35,000

0 = ($15 × units) − $15,000
0 = ($15 × 1,000) − $15,000
0 = 0

Margin of safety:

Margin of safety = $\dfrac{1,500 \text{ units} - 1,000 \text{ units}}{1,500 \text{ units}}$

  = 33 1/3%

short-run fixed costs are not covered. It is likely that the segment would save money by discontinuing this product.

The area between the short- and long-run justification points is the **marginal contribution zone**. If unit sales fall in this zone, the segment is justified in continuing production during the next period. In the long run, however, the product must be revitalized to become a positive contributor, or plans for discontinuing production must be made. If the decision is made to discontinue operations, long-run fixed costs must be terminated or redeployed. As a result of this planning and decision making, a significant amount of time will be devoted to marginal products.

The area to the right of the long-run justification point is the positive contribution zone. Products with unit sales in this zone are providing contribution to the segment's common fixed costs, and generally such products will continue to be produced in the long run.

If profits are to be maximized, management will normally emphasize products that are in the positive contribution zone. Exceptional cases will arise, however. For example, a product in the negative contribution zone can sometimes be justified on the basis of its helping to sell more profitable products. A product in the positive contribution zone might be discontinued in favor of an even higher contributing product.

Illustration 4-4
Short- and Long-Run
Analysis of a Single
Product

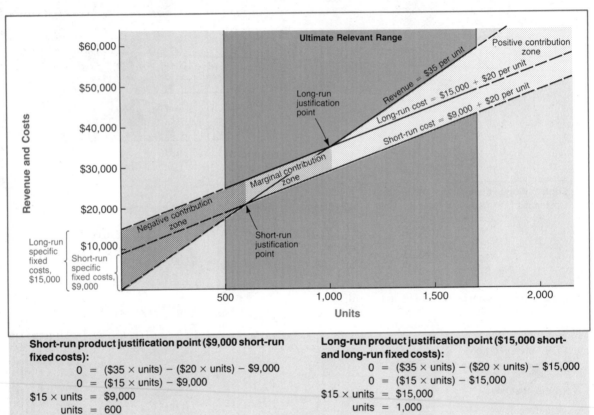

Short-run product justification point ($9,000 short-run fixed costs):

$$0 = (\$35 \times units) - (\$20 \times units) - \$9,000$$
$$0 = (\$15 \times units) - \$9,000$$
$$\$15 \times units = \$9,000$$
$$units = 600$$

Long-run product justification point ($15,000 short- and long-run fixed costs):

$$0 = (\$35 \times units) - (\$20 \times units) - \$15,000$$
$$0 = (\$15 \times units) - \$15,000$$
$$\$15 \times units = \$15,000$$
$$units = 1,000$$

CVP Analysis for Segments

Cost-volume-profit analysis by products is helpful to segment managers in designing the mix of products which will provide the maximum contribution to common fixed costs. When it is likely that a segment will have demand in excess of its capacity, managers will also be concerned with maximizing the contribution per unit of constraining resource. The special procedures used in this situation are discussed in Chapter 5.

Once the optimal product mix has been determined, production and promotional efforts can be planned. For planning purposes, it is usually assumed that within a properly defined relevant range, the proportions in which the various products are produced and sold will remain fairly constant.

To illustrate the application of CVP analysis to a segment of a firm, assume that Division X produces 4 products, A, B, C, and D. Each product's justification point is calculated as follows:

Product	(1) Specific Fixed Cost	(2) Revenue per Product Unit	(3) Variable Cost per Product Unit	(4) Contribution Margin (2) − (3)	(5) Justification Point (1) ÷ (4)
A	$2,000	$10	$ 5	$ 5	400 units
B	3,000	15	6	9	333
C	1,000	16	8	8	125
D	1,000	28	15	13	77

Standard Sales Packs. To apply CVP analysis to the entire division, a standard sales pack will be constructed. A **standard sales pack** is an imaginary set of products that reflects the ratio of units actually sold in the marketplace. For computational purposes, a standard sales pack is the smallest set of whole units sold in the mix ratio. For example, if a men's clothing store typically sells 200 shirts, 100 pairs of pants, and 50 ties in a week, its sales are in a 4:2:1 ratio, and its standard sales pack consists of 4 shirts, 2 pairs of pants, and 1 tie.

The projected sales level and mix of products should not usually include any product whose volume would be less than its individual justification point. Assuming that Products A, B, C, and D meet this test in Division X, the optimal mix of products, in view of market demands, is 5A, 4B, 2C, and 1D. Thus, a standard sales pack would contain 12 units—5A, 4B, 2C, and 1D. The revenue and variable costs of such a pack are calculated as follows:

Product	Mix	Revenue per Standard Sales Pack	Variable Cost per Standard Sales Pack
A	5	$ 50 (5 × $10)	$25 (5 × $5)
B	4	60 (4 × $15)	24 (4 × $6)
C	2	32 (2 × $16)	16 (2 × $8)
D	1	28 (1 × $28)	15 (1 × $15)
Total	12	$170	$80

The total fixed cost of Division X is $12,000, which consists of the sum of the fixed costs specific to the products, $7,000, and fixed cost specific to the division, $5,000. As shown in Illustration 4-5, the intersection of the revenue and cost lines on the standard sales pack graph is the point at which the specific division fixed costs are covered. This point is termed the **division justification point.** When the division contribution is to the left of the division justification point, the division operations should be reviewed, since the fixed costs are not being recouped. When the division contribution is to the right of the division justification point, the division is contributing to the common fixed costs of the firm, as well as to net income, if the sum of all division contributions is sufficient. As was done for individual products, CVP analysis could be used to calculate short- and long-run justification points.

In Illustration 4-5, the projected sales volume is 2,160 total units, or 180 standard sales packs (2,160 ÷ 12 units per pack). The division justification point is converted from standard sales packs to individual product units in order to make the results more meaningful. The conversion is made by multiplying the number of standard sales packs (133.3) at the division justification point by the number of units of each product in each pack. After the conversion, the cost analyst should verify that no units have a projected sales level below their individual justification points.

When products are very similar, an alternate technique may be used to calculate the contribution. This technique is based on the revenue and the variable cost of an average unit. For the division in Illustration 4-5, the contribution on sales of 2,160 average units would be calculated as follows:

$$\text{Revenue per average unit} = \frac{\text{Revenue of standard sales pack}}{\text{Units in standard sales pack}}$$

$$= \frac{\$170}{12}$$

$$= \$14.17$$

$$\text{Variable cost per average unit} = \frac{\text{Variable costs of standard sales pack}}{\text{Units in standard sales pack}}$$

$$= \frac{\$80}{12}$$

$$= \$6.67$$

$$
\begin{aligned}
\text{Contribution} &= (\$14.17 \times 2{,}160 \text{ avg. units}) - (\$6.67 \times 2{,}160 \text{ avg. units}) - \$12{,}000 \\
&= \$30{,}607.20 - \$14{,}407.20 - \$12{,}000 \\
&= \$4{,}200
\end{aligned}
$$

Sales Dollars. It is possible to analyze either the single product or multiple products of a segment by using sales dollars. Once the optimal product mix has been established, the results of the analysis may be easier to communicate if they are stated in sales dollars. This approach may be more logical than the average unit approach when the products differ significantly. It is frequently used to view the performance of segments on a firm-wide basis.

The division contribution formula in terms of sales dollars is derived as follows:

General formula:
   Division contribution = Revenue − Variable costs − Fixed costs
Formula in terms of sales dollars (S):
   Division contribution = S − (Variable cost ratio × S) − Fixed costs

In Illustration 4-5, the variable cost ratio is .4706, which is derived by dividing the variable cost of a standard sales pack, $80, by the sales price of a standard sales pack, $170. Using this variable cost ratio, the division contribution formula for Division X, in sales dollars, would be stated as follows:

Division contribution = S − .4706S − $12,000

The primary differences in using sales dollars and units are the calculations of the division justification point and the margin of safety. As shown in Illustration 4-5, the division justification point is calculated by using the variable cost ratio and solving for the sales dollars (S) at the point of zero contribution. The margin of safety is calculated by using sales dollars to arrive at the same percentage as when units are used.

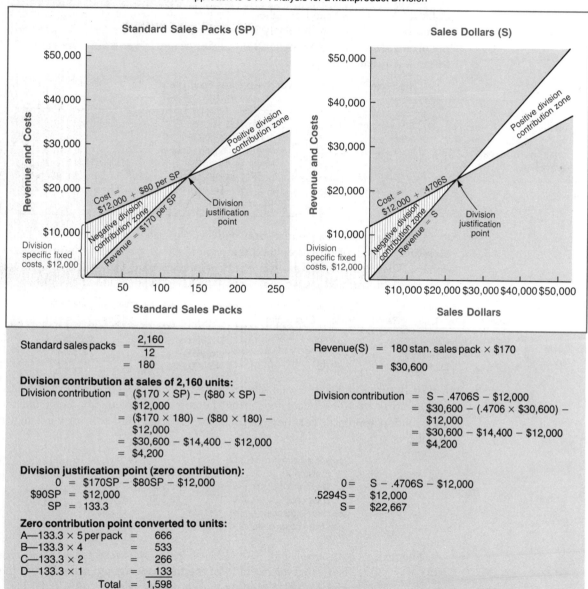

Standard sales packs $= \dfrac{2,160}{12}$

$= 180$

Revenue(S) $= 180$ stan. sales pack $\times \$170$

$= \$30,600$

Division contribution at sales of 2,160 units:

Division contribution $=$ ($\$170 \times$ SP) $-$ ($\$80 \times$ SP) $-$ $\$12,000$

$=$ ($\$170 \times 180$) $-$ ($\$80 \times 180$) $-$ $\$12,000$

$=$ $\$30,600 - \$14,400 - \$12,000$

$=$ $\$4,200$

Division contribution $=$ S $-$ .4706S $-$ \$12,000

$=$ $\$30,600 - (.4706 \times \$30,600) -$ $\$12,000$

$=$ $\$30,600 - \$14,400 - \$12,000$

$=$ $\$4,200$

Division justification point (zero contribution):

$0 =$ $\$170$SP $- \$80$SP $- \$12,000$

$\$90$SP $= \$12,000$

SP $= 133.3$

$0 =$ S $-$ .4706S $- \$12,000$

$.5294$S $=$ $\$12,000$

S $=$ $\$22,667$

Zero contribution point converted to units:

A—133.3×5 per pack $=$ 666

B—133.3×4 $=$ 533

C—133.3×2 $=$ 266

D—133.3×1 $=$ 133

Total $=$ 1,598

Margin of safety:

Margin of safety $= \dfrac{180\text{SP} - 133.3\text{SP}}{180\text{SP}}$

$= \dfrac{46.7\text{SP}}{180\text{SP}}$

$= 26\%$

Margin of safety $= \dfrac{\$30,600 - \$22,667}{\$30,600}$

$= \dfrac{\$7,933}{\$30,600}$

$= 26\%$

CVP Analysis for an Entire Firm

According to the theory of profits within a firm, as discussed in Chapter 1, the contributions of the firm's divisions are viewed as being available to cover the remaining costs of the firm, and any excess is net income for the firm. Using sales dollars, CVP analysis can be applied to the entire firm. All of the firm's fixed costs would be considered in this analysis, including those that can only be attached at the firm-wide level, since they are not specific at any lower level. The basic CVP formula is restated as follows:

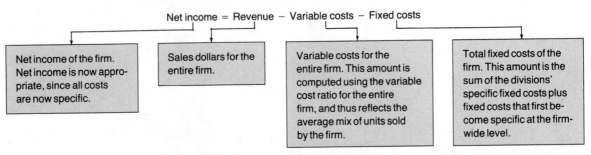

Net income = Revenue − Variable costs − Fixed costs

| Net income of the firm. Net income is now appropriate, since all costs are now specific. | Sales dollars for the entire firm. | Variable costs for the entire firm. This amount is computed using the variable cost ratio for the entire firm, and thus reflects the average mix of units sold by the firm. | Total fixed costs of the firm. This amount is the sum of the divisions' specific fixed costs plus fixed costs that first become specific at the firm-wide level. |

CVP analysis for an entire firm will be illustrated with a firm that has 3 divisions. Each division has defined the parameters of the analysis by using sales dollars. These parameters are the result of the standard sales pack analysis for Division X, illustrated previously, with Divisions Y and Z added as follows:

Division	Variable Cost Ratio	Contribution Ratio (1 − Variable Cost Ratio)	Specific Division Fixed Costs	Division Justification Point (Fixed Costs ÷ Contribution Ratio)
X	.4706	.5294	$12,000	$22,667
Y	.5210	.4790	15,000	31,315
Z	.6324	.3676	12,000	32,644

In Illustration 4-6, the total sales required to earn a target profit of $15,000 and to break even are calculated, using the cost and revenue approach and the contribution approach. For these calculations, the total fixed costs of the firm are as follows:

Specific division fixed costs:		
Division X	$12,000	
Division Y	15,000	
Division Z	12,000	$39,000
Common fixed costs		13,000
Total fixed costs of the firm		$52,000

The firm's contribution rate is .47131 (1 minus the weighted variable cost ratio of .52869). The variable cost ratio of the firm is weighted according to the relative sales of each division. Assuming that the firm's sales are 40% from Division X, 35% from Division Y, and 25% from Division Z, the weighted variable cost ratio is calculated as follows:

Division	(1) Percent of Firm's Sales	(2) Division Variable Cost Ratio	(3) (1) × (2)
X	.40	.4706	.18824
Y	.35	.5210	.18235
Z	.25	.6324	.15810
	1.00		.52869

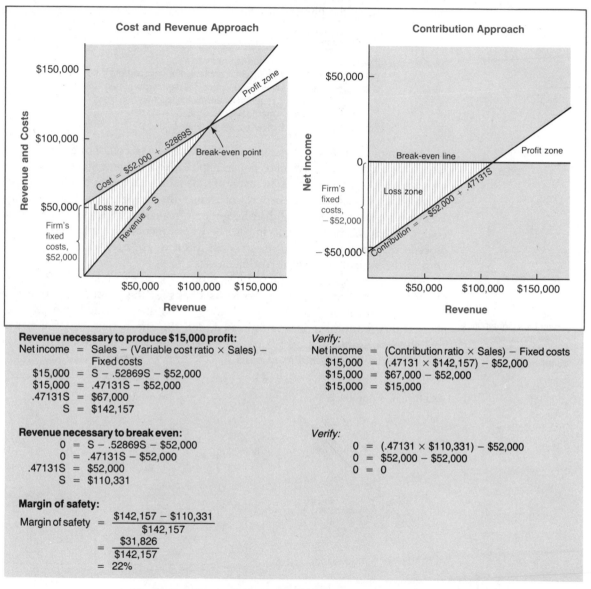

Illustration 4-6   CVP Analysis for an Entire Firm

Revenue necessary to produce $15,000 profit:

Net income = Sales − (Variable cost ratio × Sales) − Fixed costs

$15,000 = S − .52869S − $52,000
$15,000 = .47131S − $52,000
.47131S = $67,000
     S = $142,157

Revenue necessary to break even:

    0 = S − .52869S − $52,000
    0 = .47131S − $52,000
.47131S = $52,000
    S = $110,331

Margin of safety:

$$\text{Margin of safety} = \frac{\$142,157 - \$110,331}{\$142,157}$$

$$= \frac{\$31,826}{\$142,157}$$

$$= 22\%$$

Verify:

Net income = (Contribution ratio × Sales) − Fixed costs
$15,000 = (.47131 × $142,157) − $52,000
$15,000 = $67,000 − $52,000
$15,000 = $15,000

Verify:

0 = (.47131 × $110,331) − $52,000
0 = $52,000 − $52,000
0 = 0

Nonproduction Costs

Thus far, CVP analysis has been used to plan the contribution and the net income in cases where only variable production costs exist. It is also necessary to consider variable nonproduction costs, including variable physical distribution and promotional costs.

Physical Distribution Costs. Physical distribution costs are often budgeted and controlled using a flexible budgeting procedure. There is a complication, however, in that the number of units sold is seldom the sole explanatory variable. Instead, the factors that explain the behavior of physical distribution costs are unique and vary according to the physical distribution functions, as shown in the following table:

Function	Explanatory Variable
Inventory	Average inventory size
Warehousing	Weight, cubic content, number of orders filled
Order processing	Invoice equivalents (all paperwork stated as work required for an invoice, such as one credit memo = .8 invoice)
Transportation	Deliveries, weight times miles

The minimization of physical distribution costs is a complicated task, since suboptimization must be avoided. For example, it is possible to have cost savings in one area, such as a reduction in inventory, be more than offset by cost increases in another area, such as added order processing costs caused by inventory outages. To minimize the total physical distribution cost, managers apply a concept called **trade-off analysis,** by which cost impacts between functions are considered. These procedures, which are beyond the scope of this text, are based on precise definitions of the variable and fixed cost elements.

The cost and revenue graph in Illustration 4-7 is an example of CVP analysis that includes physical distribution costs. As a basis for this graph, the production costs of one level of product sales (10,000 units) are projected, the usage of physical distribution services is estimated, and the appropriate cost function is applied to the estimated usage. The resulting estimate of physical distribution costs includes variable costs and fixed costs specific to a segment.

Illustration 4-7
Product-Line Contribution
Analysis Including
Physical Distribution and
Promotional Costs

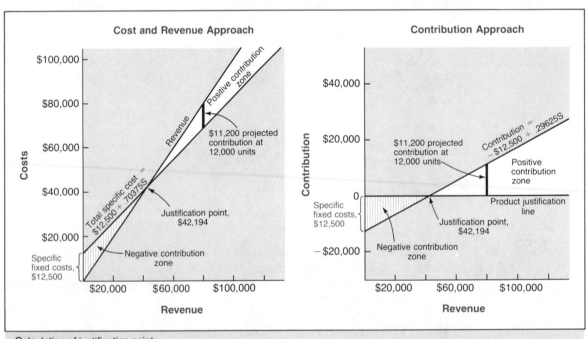

Calculation of justification point:
$$0 = S - .70375S - \$12,500$$
$$.29625S = \$12,500$$
$$S = \$42,194$$

Flexible Monthly Budget for Individual Functions

	Specific Fixed Costs of Function	Function Fixed Costs Specific to Product Line	Variable Cost
Production	$18,000	$8,000	$4 per unit
Inventory	10,000	——	2% of month's production cost
Warehousing	8,000	1,500	$1 per order
Order processing	6,000	——	$1.25 per equivalent invoice
Transportation	5,000	——	$.25 per cwt.-mile
Promotion	24,000	3,000	5% of sales price

Projected Contribution

Sales revenue (10,000 units × $8) $80,000
Less variable costs:

Function	Usage	Unit Variable Cost	Total	
Production	10,000 units	$4.00	$40,000	
Inventory	$40,000 production cost	2%	800	
Warehousing (assume 10 units per order)	$\frac{10,000}{10} = 1,000$ orders	$1.00	1,000	
Order processing (assume 2.4 invoice equivalents per order)	1,000 orders × 2.4, or 2,400 invoice equivalents	$1.25	3,000	
Transportation (assume 100 lbs. per order and an average of 30 miles per order)	1,000 orders × 1 cwt. per order × 30 miles, or 30,000 cwt.-miles	.25	7,500	
Promotion	$80,000 sales	5%	4,000	56,300
Contribution to specific product-line fixed costs				$23,700
Less specific product-line fixed costs:				
Production			$ 8,000	
Warehousing			1,500	
Promotion			3,000	12,500
Contribution to common costs				$11,200

Variable cost rate: $\frac{\$56,300}{\$80,000}$ = .70375

Contribution rate: $\frac{\$23,700}{\$80,000}$ = .29625

Physical distribution costs may also be included in CVP analysis covering a range of unit sales. It is necessary, however, to specify the mix of physical distribution services that is expected to apply at all sales levels within a specified relevant range. In Illustration 4-7, it is assumed that the relative mix of services at the 10,000-unit level will persist at all other levels.

Promotional Costs. Promotional costs require unique consideration in the profit-planning process. These costs include advertising, sales promotions, and sales personnel costs. Promotional costs, with the exception of sales commissions, are typically fixed costs and are thus not a function of unit sales. The level of promotional costs, however, is usually controllable in the short run. These costs may also be shifted among segments. Since management's primary objective is to maximize the contribution by channeling to each segment the amounts necessary, promotional costs must be included in CVP analysis. The cost and revenue graph in Illustration 4-7 includes the specific fixed promotional costs for the product line and the variable promotional costs.

Modification of the Contribution Approach. With the addition of physical distribution and promotional costs, the contribution approach to CVP must be modified. As shown on the contribution graph in Illustration 4-7, the fixed costs on the vertical axis now include fixed nonproduction costs. The contribution margin becomes revenue less all variable costs—production, physical distribution, and promotional.

1. Define cost-volume-profit analysis. Why is the ultimate relevant range important to CVP analysis?

2. What are the implicit assumptions in CVP analysis?

3. Explain the meaning of each of the following terms that are fundamental to CVP analysis:

   (1) Fixed costs
   (2) Variable costs
   (3) Relevant range
   (4) Sales mix

4. Define the break-even point. Why would a company be concerned with the break-even point?

5. What is the margin of safety?

6. Define the contribution margin of a unit. What is the significance of this figure?

7. When performing CVP analysis, how does the cost and revenue approach differ from the contribution approach? What are some advantages of each approach?

8. A manufacturer sells its single product for $20 per unit, estimates its variable costs to be 50% of revenue, and determines that its fixed costs are $80,000. The president of the firm wants to earn an aftertax profit of 15% of sales. Assuming that the firm is in a 40% tax bracket, what sales level will have to be achieved to earn the desired profit?

9. In Question No. 8, what type of profit objective is described? Justify your answer.

10. Is maximizing net income the primary concern of every division within a firm? Why or why not?

11. What are specific fixed costs, and how do they differ from divisional fixed costs?

12. What is a product justification point? How is it calculated?

13. Is there any reason that a firm may choose to continue to manufacture a product that lies in the negative contribution zone of a division?

14. How does contribution analysis help managers decide which products to produce and in what quantity?

15. What is a standard sales pack? Why would it be used?

16. When constructing the hypothetical standard sales pack, is it ever valid to use average revenue and average variable costs?

17. What are the major types of variable costs that should be considered when using CVP analysis? What complication might arise when applying CVP analysis to these costs?

Exercise 1. Fred Forbes would like to rent a booth to sell cream puffs at the state fair. There is only one variable cost, the cost of the cream puffs, which Fred could buy from a local baker for $.75 each. Booth rental is $450 for the ten-day fair. Fred feels he will sell at least 75, but not more than 130, cream puffs per day at his projected selling price of $1.20 per cream puff.

(1) How much profit will Fred earn if he sells 75 cream puffs per day? if he sells 130?
(2) How many cream puffs must Fred sell to break even?

Exercise 2. Wanda Nelson would like to earn money during the summer by selling watermelons from a roadside stand. Wanda can purchase the watermelons from a local farmer for $1.25 each and plans to sell them for $3.45. The cost of a stand, which Wanda can buy from a friend, is estimated to be $880. Finally, Wanda would have to buy a used pickup, at an estimated cost of $1,100, to haul the watermelons. Wanda needs to earn $2,530 over the summer to pay for next year's college tuition.

(1) Using the cost and revenue approach, calculate the number of watermelons Wanda must sell over the summer to meet her profit objective.
(2) What is her margin of safety at this level of sales?
(3) Confirm your answer to (1) using the contribution approach.

Exercise 3 (AICPA adapted, 5/74). High-Flite Company produces plastic golf tees and other golfing accessories. One dozen golf tees sell for $.25 and have variable production costs of $.14. The firm's fixed costs for this product, which total $990 per month, are the lease of the machine which produces the tees and a space in which to house it. High-Flite would like to earn a return on the tees of 16% of sales.

(1) Using the cost and revenue approach, determine how many dozen tees High-Flite must sell each month to meet its profit objective. Confirm your estimate using the contribution approach. Round all numbers to the nearest unit.
(2) Calculate the margin of safety at the desired sales volume.

Exercise 4. In a recent period, Zeron Co. had the following experience:

Sales (10,000 units @ $200)			$2,000,000
Costs:	Fixed	Variable	
Materials	—	$ 200,000	
Direct labor	—	400,000	
Factory overhead	$160,000	600,000	
Administrative expenses	180,000	80,000	
Other expenses	200,000	120,000	
Total cost	$540,000	$1,400,000	1,940,000
Net income			$ 60,000

Consider each of the following items independently, showing your calculations.

(1) Calculate the break-even point for Zeron Co. in terms of units and sales dollars.

(2) What dollar sales volume would be required to generate a net income of $96,000?

(3) What is the break-even point, in sales dollars, if management makes a decision which increases fixed costs by $18,000?

Exercise 5. Millroad Leather Company is investigating a lease of machinery to produce leather work gloves. A cutting machine and a stitching machine would be required; both could be leased for a total of $1,250 per month. The variable costs of producing a pair of gloves are $1.75. The gloves have a selling price of $2.95 per pair. Millroad would like to earn an aftertax profit on the work gloves of 18% of sales and is in the 40% tax bracket.

(1) Use the cost and revenue approach to determine the monthly sales volume (units) necessary to achieve the desired profit. Confirm your answer using the contribution approach. Round your answer to the nearest dollar.

(2) Calculate the margin of safety at the desired sales volume.

Exercise 6. Spartan Company manufactures a line of high strength, galvanized steel flagpoles. The company's longest flagpole, a 45-foot model, is the least popular, and Spartan is investigating discontinuing the line. The 45-foot flagpoles sell for $1,250 each. Variable costs total $975 per flagpole. Spartan estimates it could save $30,250 in fixed production, selling, and administrative costs within one year of discontinuance. By careful cost cutting, an additional $6,875 per year could be saved in later years if the large flagpoles are discontinued. Spartan expects to sell 120 45-foot flagpoles per year.

(1) Calculate the short- and long-run justification points (in unit sales) for the 45-foot line. Does the line justify itself in the short run? in the long run?

(2) After all identifiable fixed costs of the line have been covered, what is the expected yearly contribution of the line in the short run? in the long run?

Exercise 7. Wallace Company manufactures two types of lawn mowers: a basic model, Model A, which sells for $135; and the deluxe, self-propelled Model B, which sells for $275. Past experience has shown that 3 Model As are sold for each Model B. The Model A mower costs $90 to produce. Adding a drive mechanism and a special paint job, which converts a Model A into a Model B, costs an additional $45. Fixed costs common to both mowers total $148,000 per year.

(1) Calculate the company's average contribution percentage per sales dollar.

(2) Assuming that 25% of the total fixed costs could be eliminated in one year if Model A were discontinued, what is the short-run justification point (in units) of the model? (Round to the nearest unit.)

(3) Compute the firm's break-even point in sales dollars. (Round to the nearest dollar.)

Exercise 8. Watercrest Dairies Inc. produces three milk products: whole milk, yogurt, and cream. The sales mix of these products is 8:4:1, respectively. The prices and variable production costs are as follows:

	Price	Variable Production Costs	Other Variable Costs
Whole milk	$1.45 per gallon	$ .70 per gallon	$.20 per gallon
Yogurt	4.50	3.45	.30
Cream	9.00	7.75	.25

(1) Calculate the variable cost ratio of the firm.
(2) Watercrest would like to earn a profit of 10% on sales. Fixed costs for the dairy total $82,600. Calculate the level of sales necessary to meet the profit objective.

Exercise 9. Goliath Cordage Works produces 3 grades of 1/2" diameter rope: championship grade, recreational grade, and super nylon. Prices per foot and variable costs per foot are as follows:

	Revenue	Variable Costs
Championship grade	$.27 per foot	$.21 per foot
Recreational grade	.21	.16
Super nylon	.18	.12

Past experience has shown that the sales mix averages three feet of championship grade, five feet of recreational grade, and two feet of super nylon for every ten feet sold. Goliath expects to incur common fixed costs of $124,750 in the upcoming year and would like to earn a profit of $65,000.

(1) Calculate Goliath's average revenue and variable costs per foot of line.
(2) How many feet of line must Goliath sell in the upcoming year to meet its profit objective?
(3) What is Goliath's margin of safety at this level of sales?

Exercise 10 (AICPA adapted, 5/76). Freedom Inc. management has performed cost studies and projects the following annual costs, based on 40,000 units of production and sales:

	Total Annual Costs	Variable Portion of Total Annual Costs
Materials	$400,000	100%
Direct labor	360,000	75
Manufacturing overhead	300,000	40
Selling, general, and administrative expenses	200,000	25

(1) Compute the unit selling price which will yield a 10% profit on sales of 40,000 units.
(2) Based on the same variable and fixed cost relationships as in (1) and assuming that management selects a selling price of $30 per unit and has sales of 40,000 units, compute Freedom's dollar sales that will yield a projected 10% profit on sales.

PROBLEMS

Problem 4-1. Synchrotron Company would like to expand its product line and begin producing one model of microwave oven. The projected selling price is $500 per unit. The company expects to invest $500,000 in production assets and requires a 10% return on investment to justify production. The cost of producing a unit is estimated as follows:

Materials (all variable)	$110 per unit
Direct labor (all variable)	$80 per unit
Overhead:	
Variable	$90 per unit
Fixed	$105,000
Other variable expenses	$20 per unit
Other fixed expenses	$45,000

The firm expects the above cost relationships to remain unchanged between outputs of 500 and 1,500 units per year.

Required

(1) Prepare a cost-volume-profit graph for Synchrotron.
(2) What volume of sales (in units) is needed to meet the profit objective?
(3) What is the margin of safety at this output?
(4) Confirm the estimates made in (1) by preparing a contribution graph.

Problem 4-2. Delacron Mills operates a small plant which produces cotton denim for sale to blue jeans manufacturers. Results for the current year are given in the following income statement:

Sales (160,000 sq. yards @ $2.40 per sq. yard)		$384,000
Cost of goods sold:		
Variable production costs	$192,000	
Fixed production costs	42,000	234,000
Gross margin		$150,000
Selling, general, and administrative expenses:		
Sales commissions	$ 19,200	
Administrative expenses	76,000	
Sales salaries	9,000	
Shipping expenses	4,800	109,000
Net income		$ 41,000

Sales commissions are paid at the rate of 5% of sales. Shipping expenses are considered variable expenses; $56,000 of the administrative expenses are also variable. There were no beginning or ending inventories.

Delacron would like to increase its net income to 15% of sales in the coming year. All cost relationships will remain unchanged.

Required

(1) What dollar sales volume must Delacron meet in order to reach its profit objective?
(2) Assume that the plant is operating at capacity and cannot increase output. What price would Delacron have to charge to achieve its profit objective? (Round all answers to the nearest unit.)

Problem 4-3. Miller Printing Company specializes in high quality, printed advertising materials. The company's operations are modern and highly automated, resulting in low unit costs. The firm's accountant has developed the following cost structure, based on units of 1,000 pages each:

Direct labor	$ 17 per unit
Materials	12 per unit
Variable overhead	8 per unit
Fixed manufacturing overhead	23,000 per month
Other fixed costs	12,000 per month

Miller Printing's managers expect the industry to go slowly into recession and the number of orders to eventually decrease from the current level of 9,000 units per month to 7,000 units. A severe recession, which Miller's management gives a 15% chance of occurring, could reduce orders to 6,000 units per month. In an effort to reduce costs, the managers are considering replacing their automated process with older, more labor-intensive models. The switch would increase unit labor costs by $2, but would reduce fixed overhead costs by $15,000 because of greatly reduced lease costs. Revenue and materials costs would be unchanged. The average price per unit is $44.

Required (1) Assuming that sales fall to 7,000 units per month, calculate the firm's profit using the older equipment, and the profit using the newer equipment.

(2) Determine the margin of safety for both alternatives, using the sales figure of 7,000 units per month. Which alternative has the greater margin of safety?

(3) At what output is the profit earned under either alternative the same? What generalizations can the managers draw regarding their equipment choice?

Problem 4-4 (CMA adapted, 6/76). All-Day Candy Company is a wholesale distributor of candy. The company services grocery, convenience, and drug stores in a large metropolitan area.

Small but steady growth in sales has been achieved by the company over the past few years, while candy prices have been increasing. The company is formulating its plans for the coming fiscal year. The following data are used to project the current year's aftertax net income of $110,400:

Average selling price	$4.00 per box
Average variable costs:	
Cost of candy	$2.00 per box
Selling expenses	.40
Total	$2.40 per box
Annual fixed costs:	
Selling	$160,000
Administrative	280,000
Total	$440,000
Expected annual sales volume (390,000 boxes)	$1,560,000
Tax rate	40%

Manufacturers of candy anticipate a 15% increase in costs in the coming year, due to increases in materials and direct labor costs. All-Day Candy Company expects that all other costs will remain at the same levels as the current year.

Required (1) What is All-Day Candy Company's break-even point in boxes of candy for the current year, assuming that all revenue and cost projections are unchanged?

(2) What selling price per box must All-Day Candy Company charge to cover the 15 percent increase in the cost of candy and still maintain the current contribution margin ratio?

(3) Assuming that the selling price of candy will remain at $4 per box, and the cost of candy will increase 15 percent, what volume of sales, in dollars, must All-Day Candy Company achieve in the coming year to maintain the same net income after taxes as projected for the current year?

Problem 4-5. Stanek Company is a small chemical processor producing three types of industrial-grade cleaning solutions. In the current year, the company has operated at a loss, as evidenced by the following income statement:

Stanek Company
Income Statement
For Year Ending December 31, 19X2

Sales		$503,125
Cost of goods sold:		
Materials	$140,750	
Direct labor	90,000	
Variable overhead	105,000	
Fixed overhead	75,000	410,750
Gross margin		$ 92,375
Selling expenses		50,000
General and administrative expenses		85,500
Net income (loss)		$ (43,125)

To improve profitability, the company's management has asked you to determine the effect of discontinuing its Bivox cleaner, which accounts for almost 50% of the output but only 32% of the revenues. Additional data gathered in your investigation are as follows:

	Bivox	Triax	Tetra	Total
Materials	$38,905	$47,250	$54,595	$140,750
Direct labor	4,500 hrs.	5,500 hrs.	5,000 hrs.	15,000 hrs.
Gallons sold	80,500	40,250	42,550	163,300
% of total sales dollars	32%	35%	33%	100%

All production is in the same building but on different processing equipment. Fixed overhead costs are expected to fall by only 5% in the first year of closure, but by an additional 20% in the second and subsequent years. Selling expenses include a 2% commission paid on sales of all products. The remainder covers the salaries of two sales representatives, both of whom would be retained even if Bivox production were halted. General and administrative costs are fixed, but could be reduced by 20% within one year and 30% within two years of discontinuance.

The average wage rate in the plant is $6 per hour. Variable overhead is charged to production at the rate of $7 per direct labor hour. There were no beginning or ending inventories.

Required

(1) Prepare a cost-volume-profit graph for Bivox, indicating the short- and long-run product justification points. All cost and revenue estimates will remain unchanged between 20,000 and 180,000 gallons of output.
(2) In spite of intensive marketing efforts, Bivox sales have been falling by roughly 20% per year. Should Stanek continue to produce Bivox?
(3) Stanek requires all products to contribute at least 20% of their sales to the corporation's common costs, after deducting the product's long-run specific fixed costs. What is the minimum sales level necessary for Bivox to meet this goal?

Problem 4-6. Falstaff Company produces three kinds of animal feed: dog nuggets, chicken feed, and pig feed. Falstaff would like to project its earnings for the coming year and has provided the following data:

Historical Sales (000s omitted)

	19X4	19X5	19X6
Dog nuggets	$400	$300	$350
Chicken feed	100	100	150
Pig feed	100	300	300

Cost Projections for 19X7

	Direct Labor per Bag	Materials per Bag	Variable Overhead per Bag	Fixed Overhead	Other Fixed Costs
Dog nuggets	$ .25	$3.00	$.75	$125,000	$35,000
Chicken feed	1.00	4.50	.50	53,000	13,000
Pig feed	.50	5.00	.50	137,000	27,000

Selling costs are 5% of sales. Common fixed costs are $135,000.

Falstaff expects to sell its products for $5.50, $6.50, and $8 per bag, respectively. All cost and revenue projections are expected to be valid between 600,000 and 1,500,000 bags of output per year.

Required (1) Using the historical sales data, calculate the sales mix for the products. The company expects the future mix to mirror the past three-year average.

(2) What profit will Falstaff earn if it sells a total of 900,000 bags in the coming year?

(3) Assuming that all cost and revenue functions remain unchanged, how many bags of feed must Falstaff sell to earn a profit of 15% of sales?

(4) Assuming that the mix changes, so that one less bag of dog nuggets and one more bag of chicken feed per sales pack (6 bags) are sold, how does the profit earned compare with the amount earned in (2) on 900,000 bags?

Problem 4-7 (CMA adapted, 6/77). Hewtex Electronics manufactures two products, tape recorders and electronic calculators, that are sold nationally to wholesalers and retailers. The Hewtex management is very pleased with the company's performance for the current fiscal year. Projections through December 31, 19X7, indicate that 70,000 tape recorders and 140,000 electronic calculators will be sold this year. The projected earnings statement showing that Hewtex will exceed its earnings goal of 9 percent on sales, after taxes, is shown at the top of page 133.

The tape recorder business has been fairly stable the last few years, and the company does not intend to change the tape recorder price. However, the competition among manufacturers of electronic calculators has been increasing. Hewtex's calculators have been very popular with consumers. To sustain this interest in their calculators and to meet the price reductions expected from competitors, management has decided to reduce the wholesale price of its calculator from $22.50 to $20 per unit, effective January 1, 19X8. At the same time, the company plans to spend an additional $57,000 on advertising during 19X8. As a consequence of these actions, management estimates that 80 percent of its total revenue will be derived from calculator sales, compared to 75 percent in 19X7. As in prior years, the sales mix is assumed to apply to all volume levels.

The total fixed overhead costs will not change in 19X8, nor will the variable overhead cost rates (applied on a direct labor hour base). However, the cost of materials and direct labor is expected to change. The cost of solid state electronic components will decrease in 19X8. Hewtex estimates that materials costs will drop

Hewtex Electronics
Projected Earnings Statement
For Year Ending December 31, 19X7

	Tape Recorders		Electronic Calculators		
	Total Amount (000s omitted)	Per Unit	Total Amount (000s omitted)	Per Unit	Total (000s omitted)
Sales	$1,050	$15.00	$3,150	$22.50	$4,200.00
Production costs:					
Materials	$ 280	$ 4.00	$ 630	$ 4.50	$ 910.00
Direct labor	140	2.00	420	3.00	560.00
Variable overhead	140	2.00	280	2.00	420.00
Fixed overhead	70	1.00	210	1.50	280.00
Total production costs	$ 630	$ 9.00	$1,540	$11.00	$2,170.00
Gross margin	$ 420	$ 6.00	1,610	$11.50	$2,030.00
Fixed selling and administrative expenses					1,040.00
Income before income taxes					$ 990.00
Income taxes (55%)					544.50
Net income					$ 445.50

10 percent for the tape recorders and 20 percent for the calculators in 19X8. However, direct labor costs for both products will increase 10 percent in the coming year.

Required

(1) How many tape recorder and electronic calculator units must Hewtex Electronics sell in 19X7 to break even? (Ignore income taxes.)

(2) What volume of sales is required if Hewtex Electronics is to earn a profit in 19X8 equal to 9 percent on sales, after taxes?

(3) What volume of sales must Hewtex achieve if it is to break even in 19X8? (Ignore income taxes.)

Problem 4-8. Natural Harvest Products Inc. specializes in all-natural cereals and snacks. The company's income statement for 19X8, using the absorption method, is as follows:

Natural Harvest Products Inc.
Income Statement
For Year Ended December 31, 19X8

Sales (670,000 lbs. @ $1 per lb.)			$670,000
Cost of goods sold:			
Direct labor (variable)		$ 60,300	
Materials (variable)		234,500	
Overhead		221,500	516,300
Gross margin			$153,700
Selling expenses:			
Commissions (1% of sales)	$ 6,700		
Salaries	43,000		
Advertising	20,000	$ 69,700	
Administrative expenses:			
Salaries and related expenses		80,000	149,700
Net income			$ 4,000

An analysis of the overhead account revealed the following information:

Variable overhead:		
Heat, light, and power	$20,100	
Indirect labor and materials	80,400	$100,500
Fixed overhead:		
Supervisory salaries and related benefits	$46,000	
Plant lease cost	57,500	
Depreciation	17,500	121,000
Total overhead		$221,500

In the selling expense category, both salaries and advertising expense are considered fixed with regard to output. Administrative expenses are also considered to be fixed. Natural Harvest had no beginning or ending inventories in 19X8.

In an effort to improve profitability, the president of the company has asked the marketing department to develop alternate strategies. The following three separate proposals have been developed:

(1) Reduce the product's price by 20%. This is expected to increase unit sales by 25%.
(2) Increase the amount spent on advertising by $40,000. This is expected to increase sales to 850,000 pounds per year.
(3) Improve the product by increasing the quality of the raw materials. This will increase materials costs by $.10 per pound. To partially cover the cost increase, the price will be increased by $.05 per pound. Advertising will increase by $10,000. These changes are expected to yield a volume of 900,000 pounds per year.

Required
(1) Restructure Natural Harvest's 19X8 income statement into the contribution format.
(2) What profit would the firm earn under each of the three marketing proposals?
(3) Assuming that the company selects Proposal 3, by how much would other (nonadvertising) fixed costs have to be reduced for the company to earn a profit of 5% on sales?

Problem 4-9. Dynamic Sound Products Inc. manufactures high quality, consumer electronics. The company is divided into three autonomous divisions: Home Stereo Equipment, Car Stereo Equipment, and Marine Electronics. The sales ratios for the divisions, in terms of sales dollars, are roughly 25%, 60%, and 15%, respectively. The company is planning next year's operations and has asked you to make profit projections for the company. A summary of accounting data for the Marine Electronics Division is presented in the following table:

	Revenue	Total Variable Costs	Mix
Depth sounders	$ 160 per unit	$ 110 per unit	5 units
VHF radios	375	200	4
Radars	4,700	2,850	1

In conversations with the heads of the other divisions, you have learned that the Home Stereo Division has an average variable cost percentage of 80%, which is 36 percentage points higher than that of the Car Stereo Division. The sales and fixed costs of the company are as follows:

	Sales	Specific Fixed Costs
Home Stereo Division	$ 536,812	$178,800
Car Stereo Division	1,288,350	474,000
Marine Electronics		
Division	322,088	142,000
Common to all divisions	—	141,200

Required

(1) Calculate the variable cost percentage of the Marine Electronics Division.

(2) Calculate the justification point in sales dollars for each division.

(3) Determine the variable cost ratio for the entire firm. What amount of sales are required if the firm wishes to earn a 12% aftertax profit (the average tax rate is 40%)?

(4) What is the firm's margin of safety at the current level of sales?

Problem 4-10. Outland Metals Co. consists of two divisions: the Copper Division and the Nickel Division, both of which mine and process raw ore at plants in Australia. Each division has its own production facilities, but both divisions share physical distribution facilities (warehousing, order processing, and transportation) and promotional resources. The company's recent income statement, prepared using absorption costing, is as follows:

Outland Metals Co.
Income Statement
For Year Ending December 31, 19X4

	Copper Division	Nickel Division	Total
Sales	$2,250,000	$1,800,000	$4,050,000
Cost of goods sold	1,750,000	1,125,000	2,875,000
Gross margin	$ 500,000	$ 675,000	$1,175,000
Selling, general, and administrative expenses:			
Administrative expenses	$ 45,200	$ 42,800	$ 88,000
Distribution costs	166,500	156,000	322,500
Selling expenses	65,700	82,800	148,500
Advertising	17,000	24,000	41,000
Total expenses	$ 294,400	$ 284,000	$ 600,000
Net income	$ 205,600	$ 369,400	$ 575,000

For financial reporting purposes, Outland allocates common fixed distribution and selling expenses on the basis of tons shipped.

A detailed analysis of various costs is as follows:

	Copper Division		Nickel Division		Common
	Variable	Fixed	Variable	Fixed	
Production cost	$525 per ton	$175,000	$450 per ton	$225,000	—
Administrative expenses	—	45,200	—	42,800	—
Distribution:					
Warehousing	?	—	1.00 per ton	—	$92,000
Order processing	.30 per ton	—	.50 per ton	—	28,000
Transportation	.20 per ton/mile	—	.35 per ton/mile	—	—
Selling expenses:					
Salaries	—	—	—	—	72,000
Commissions	1% of sales	—	3% of sales	—	—
Advertising	—	17,000	—	24,000	—

During the year, 3,000 tons of copper and 2,000 tons of nickel were processed and sold. There were no beginning or ending inventories. The average order was shipped 150 miles.

Selling expenses include sales salaries. Since the salespeople sell both products, this expense is considered common to both divisions.

Outland Metals expects its sales mix to change from the current 3:2 ratio (tons) to 1:1 next year. Total sales revenue (not tonnage) is forecast to increase by 20%.

Required (1) Calculate the variable warehousing cost per ton for the Copper Division.
(2) Determine the current variable cost percentage of the firm and its break-even point in annual sales.
(3) What profit will the firm earn at next year's forecast level of sales?

Problem 4-11 (CMA adapted, 12/80). Janice Watson was recently appointed executive director of a charitable foundation. The foundation raises money for its activities in a variety of ways, but the most important source of funds is an annual mail campaign.

The annual mail campaign and accompanying public relations efforts are designed to raise the major share of the foundation's annual budget. Although large amounts of money are raised each year from the mail campaign, the year-to-year growth in the amount derived from the mail solicitation has been lower than expected by the foundation's directors. In addition, the directors want the mail campaign to project the image of a well-run, fiscally responsible organization in order to build a base for future contributions. Consequently, the major focus of Watson's efforts in her first year will be devoted to the mail campaign.

The campaign takes place in the spring of each year. The foundation staff makes every effort to secure newspaper, radio, and television coverage of the foundation's activities for several weeks before the mail campaign. In prior years, the foundation has mailed brochures to a large number of people and requested contributions from them. The addresses for the mailing are generated from the foundation's own file of past contributors and from mailing lists purchased from brokers.

The foundation's staff is considering three alternative brochures for use in the upcoming campaign. All three will be 8 1/2″ × 11″ in size. The simplest and the one sure to be available on a timely basis for bulk mailing is a sheet of white paper with a printed explanation of the foundation's program and a request for funds. A more expensive brochure on colored paper stock would contain pictures as well as printed copy. This brochure might not be ready in time to take advantage of bulk postage rates, but there is no doubt that it can be ready in time for mailing at first-class postal rates. The third alternative would be an elegant, multicolored brochure printed on glossy paper, with photographs as well as printed copy. The printer assures the staff that it will be ready in time to meet the first-class mailing schedule, but asks for a delivery date one week later just in case there are production problems.

The foundation staff has assembled the following cost and revenue information for mailing the three alternative brochures to 2,000,000 potential contributors:

	Brochure Costs				Revenue Potential (000s omitted)		
	Design	Type-Setting	Unit Paper Cost	Unit Printing Cost	Bulk Mail	First Class	Late First Class
Plain paper	$ 300	$ 100	$.005	$.003	$1,200	—	—
Colored paper	1,000	800	.008	.010	2,000	$2,200	—
Glossy paper	3,000	2,000	.018	.040	—	2,500	$2,200

The postal rates are $.02 per item for bulk mail and $.13 per item for presorted first-class mail. First-class mail is more likely to be delivered on a timely basis than bulk mail. The charge by outside companies hired to handle the mailing is $.01 per unit for the plain and colored paper brochures and $.02 per unit for the glossy paper brochure.

Required (1) Calculate the net contribution for each brochure for each viable mailing alternative.

(2) Evaluate the three alternative brochures in terms of the three criteria (net revenue raised, image as a well-run organization, and image as a fiscally responsible organization).

Problem 4-12 (CMA adapted, 6/80). Stac Industries is a multiproduct company with several manufacturing plants. The Clinton Plant manufactures and distributes two household cleaning and polishing compounds under the Cleen-Brite label. The forecasted operating results for the first 6 months of 19X2, when 100,000 cases of each compound are expected to be manufactured and sold, are presented in the following statement:

Cleen-Brite Compounds—Clinton Plant
Forecast Results of Operations
For the Six-Month Period Ending June 30, 19X2
(000s omitted)

	Regular	Heavy Duty	Total
Sales	$2,000	$3,000	$5,000
Cost of goods sold	1,600	1,900	3,500
Gross profit	$ 400	$1,100	$1,500
Selling and administrative expenses:			
Variable	$ 400	$ 700	$1,100
Fixed	240	360	600
Total selling and administrative expenses	$ 640	$1,060	$1,700
Income (loss) before taxes	$ (240)	$ 40	$ (200)

The fixed selling and administrative expenses are allocated between the two products on the basis of dollar sales volume on the internal reports.

The regular compound sold for $20 a case, and the heavy-duty compound sold for $30 a case during the first six months of 19X2. Each product is manufactured on a separate production line. Annual normal manufacturing capacity is 200,000 cases of each product. However, the plant is capable of producing 250,000 cases of regular compound and 350,000 cases of heavy-duty compound annually. The manufacturing costs by case of product are as follows:

	Regular	Heavy-Duty
Materials	$7 per case	$8 per case
Direct labor	4 per case	4 per case
Variable manufacturing overhead	1 per case	2 per case
Variable selling and administrative expenses	4 per case	7 per case
Fixed manufacturing overhead	$800,000	$1,000,000

Depreciation charges represent 50% of the fixed manufacturing overhead of each line.

The following schedule reflects the concensus of top management regarding the price/volume alternatives for the Cleen-Brite products for the last six months of 19X2. These alternatives are essentially the same alternatives that management had during the first six months of 19X2.

Regular		Heavy-Duty	
Alternatives	Sales Volume	Alternatives	Sales Volume
$18 per case	120,000 cases	$25 per case	175,000 cases
20	100,000	27	140,000
21	90,000	30	100,000
22	80,000	32	55,000
23	50,000	35	35,000

Top management believes that the loss for the first six months reflects a tight profit margin caused by intense competition. Management also believes that many companies will be forced out of this market by next year and profits should improve.

Required

(1) What unit selling price should Stac Industries select for each of the Cleen-Brite compounds (regular and heavy-duty) for the remaining six months of 19X2. Support your selection with appropriate calculations.

(2) Without prejudice to your answer to (1), assume that the optimum price/ volume alternatives for the last six months were a selling price of $23 and volume of 50,000 cases for the regular compound, and a selling price of $35 and volume of 35,000 cases for the heavy-duty compound.

(a) Should Stac Industries consider closing down its operations until 19X3 in order to minimize its losses? Support your answer with appropriate calculations.

(b) Identify and discuss the qualitative factors which should be considered in deciding whether the Clinton Plant should be closed down during the last six months of 19X2.

Five

Extensions of Cost-Volume-Profit Analysis

The usefulness of cost-volume-profit analysis to a decision maker is increased through the use of two major extensions of basic CVP analytical procedures. The first extension is to use linear programming in applying CVP analysis to firms whose product mix is subject to constraints that limit the sales or production of certain products. The second extension is to consider the risk which surrounds the estimates upon which CVP analysis is built. Rather than ignoring such uncertainties, risk will be explicitly considered in this chapter, using alternate methods which attempt to quantify the uncertainty.

DESIGNING THE OPTIMAL PRODUCT MIX SUBJECT TO CONSTRAINTS

The principal consideration in the design of the product mix is the contribution margin of each potential product. The optimal mix is that set of products which provides the maximum contribution to fixed costs. If there were no constraints on the products that could be manufactured, the final sales plan for any firm could be determined quite easily. Products would be ranked by contribution margin per unit. The firm would plan to sell as many of the most contributing product as the market could absorb and then move down the ranking to less contributing products. When there are constraints, however, designing the mix becomes more difficult. The presence of production constraints, for example, makes it necessary to consider the contribution margin of each product and the product's use of the constraining production resource. To understand this complication, assume that you are the manager of the snowmobile division of a firm. The division produces two models:

1. *Avenger:* a high speed, no frills, competition sled. The reinforced frame requires high welding costs. However, assembly time is minimal due to the lack of accessories.
2. *Trail Smoother:* a luxury, family cruising sled, featuring electric start, handlebar heaters, seat heater, and many other options. Welding of the frame is less time consuming than for the *Avenger,* but assembly time is much greater.

The following revenue and variable cost information is available for the two machines:

	Avenger	Trail Smoother
Sales price	$3,000	$3,800
Variable costs per sled:		
Purchased components	$ 900	$1,100
Materials	200	300
Direct labor	700	900
Variable overhead	400	500
Total variable cost	$2,200	$2,800
Contribution margin per unit	$ 800	$1,000

If you were to design a product mix based on only this information, which does not consider production constraints, the division's contribution would be maximized by selling as many *Trail Smoothers* as the market would accept at the $3,800 price and then as many *Avengers* as possible. Assume, however, that there is one constraint which limits production each month to an amount less than market demand: the current equipment and human resources can make available only 855 hours of assembly time per month. Each *Avenger* requires 3 hours of assembly time, while each *Trail Smoother* requires 4 hours. The question is no longer which product contributes the most per sled, but which sled contributes the most per hour of assembly time. Therefore, you prepare the following table:

	Contribution Margins	Assembly Hours	Contributions per Hour
Avenger	$ 800	3	$267
Trail Smoother	1,000	4	250

Since the *Avenger* produces the greatest contribution per hour of scarce assembly time, you would now give priority to the *Avenger* in the marketing mix. You would produce as many *Avengers* as the market could absorb at the $3,000 price. Remaining product time would be devoted to the *Trail Smoother.*

LINEAR PROGRAMMING

The graphic method will be used to provide a basic understanding of the use of linear programming for maximizing contribution. While this approach can handle any number of constraints, it can only be applied to two products. For more than two products, mathematical approaches that can be solved by standard computer programs may be used. In the appendix to this chapter, a matrix approach to solving a linear programming, product mix problem is illustrated.

Production Constraints

To illustrate the graphic approach when there are two or more production constraints, assume that, in the snowmobile example, there is a limited amount of welding time in addition to the constraint caused by assembly time. Only 640 hours of welding time are available per month. Each *Avenger* requires 4 hours, while each *Trail Smoother* requires 2 hours. The problem, which is to maximize the contribution to fixed costs in view of these two constraints, is expressed as follows:

The objective function is:
Maximize C = $800A + $1,000T
Subject to the following constraints:
Welding: 4A + 2T ≤ 640 hours
Assembly: 3A + 4T ≤ 855 hours

where C is the contribution to the division fixed costs, A is the units of *Avenger,* and T is the units of *Trail Smoother.* The numerical values in the objective function are the contribution margins per unit sold, while the numerical values in the constraints represent each product's use of the scarce resources. Although the linear programming model does not explicitly include fixed costs, it would be wise to consider ceasing production if the maximum contribution possible is not sufficient to cover at least the short-run fixed costs.

Illustration 5-1 shows the graphic solution to the product mix problem.

Illustration 5-1
Linear Programming:
Two Production
Constraints

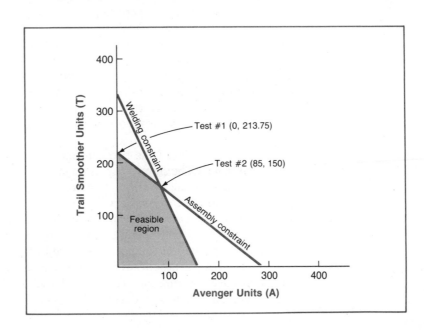

The following steps are involved in preparing the graph:

1. Let the axes represent units of each product being considered. The vertical axis should be used for the product with the greatest contribution margin per unit. In this example, the *Trail Smoother,* with a $1,000 contribution, is shown on the vertical axis, and the *Avenger* is shown on the horizontal axis.

2. Graph the constraints by computing the quantity of each product that could be produced if the constrained resource were used to produce only one product. The slope (rate of change) of the straight line connecting these quantities indicates the substitution that could be made between the two products while still fully using the scarce resource.

   a. Welding time could be used entirely for *Trail Smoothers,* so that 320 units (640 hours ÷ 2 hours per unit) could be built. Welding time could also be devoted only to *Avengers,* so that 160 units (640 hours ÷ 4 hours per unit) could be welded. These two points are connected to form the welding constraint line. The slope of this constraint, −2, is the substitution rate, which means that for each *Avenger* built, two *Trail Smoothers* must be sacrificed. For example, if you as the division manager are willing to give up 100 *Trail Smoothers* and build only 220, the graph shows that you could produce 50 *Avengers.* Any product mix on the welding constraint line would still fully use welding time.

   b. Assembly time could be used entirely for *Trail Smoothers,* so that 213.75 units (855 hours ÷ 4 hours per unit) could be assembled. If all assembly time were used for *Avengers,* however, 285 units (855 hours ÷ 3 hours per unit) could be produced. These two points are connected to form the assembly constraint line. The slope of this constraint, −.75, means that for each *Avenger* you wish to substitute, you must forgo .75 *Trail Smoothers.* For example, if you were to produce 40 more *Avengers,* you would have to give up 30 *Trail Smoothers.*

3. Shade the area below and to the left of both constraint lines. This area is the **feasible region,** in which production may occur without violating either production constraint. The optimal solution will be at one of the corner points of the feasible region. Notice that unless the optimal solution is where the constraint lines intersect, only one constraint will be fully utilized. For example, if it is optimal to produce 160 *Avengers,* you will not fully use assembly time.

4. Compare the slopes of the two constraint lines in order to find the optimal production mix. The slope comparison begins by ignoring the constraints and considering only the contribution margin of the units in order to determine the substitution you would be willing to make. (If the more contributing unit is placed on the vertical axis, substitution will always move from left to right.) Since *Avengers* are contributing only .8 times as much as *Trail Smoothers,* the division's contribution will not be reduced by forgoing .8 or less *Trail Smoothers* for each *Avenger* produced. Substitution at less than the .8 rate will increase the division's contribution. Test 1 on the graph compares substitution rates (slopes) at an assumed production of 213.75 *Trail Smoothers.* Based on contri-

bution, you are willing to give up .8 or less *Trail Smoothers* for each *Avenger*, but the assembly constraint requires that you forgo only .75 *Trail Smoothers* per *Avenger*. Thus, the substitution is made by continuing down the assembly constraint until it intersects with the welding constraint, which now becomes the limiting resource. This point is Test 2 on the graph. No further substitution is warranted, since you would have to give up 2 *Trail Smoothers* per *Avenger*, which exceeds the maximum .8 substitution rate based on contribution. Therefore, the optimal mix is at the intersection of the constraints.

5. Solve for the quantities of each unit at the intersection of the constraints by using simultaneous equations.

   a. State the constraints as equalities.

$$4A + 2T = 640$$
$$3A + 4T = 855$$

   b. Multiply the second equation by .5 and subtract it from the first equation.

$$
\begin{array}{rcr}
4A + 2T &=& 640 \\
-1.5A - 2T &=& -427.5 \\
\hline
2.5A &=& 212.5 \\
A &=& 85
\end{array}
$$

   c. Substitute the value of A into the first equation.

$$
\begin{array}{rcl}
4A + 2T &=& 640 \\
(4 \times 85) + 2T &=& 640 \\
2T &=& 640 - 340 \\
T &=& 150
\end{array}
$$

   d. Verify that the solution fits within the constraints.

$$
\begin{array}{rcl}
4A + 2T &\leq& 640 \\
(4 \times 85) + (2 \times 150) &\leq& 640 \\
640 &=& 640
\end{array}
$$

$$
\begin{array}{rcl}
3A + 4T &\leq& 855 \\
(3 \times 85) + (4 \times 150) &\leq& 855 \\
855 &=& 855
\end{array}
$$

6. Compute the optimal contribution.

	Units	Contribution Margins	Contributions
Avenger	85	$ 800	$ 68,000
Trail Smoother	150	1,000	150,000
Total	235		$218,000

This contribution can be compared with the contribution at the other corner points of the feasible region to make sure the solution is optimal. Producing only *Trail Smoothers* would contribute $213,750 (213.75 × $1,000). Producing only *Avengers* would contribute $128,000 (160 × $800).

7. Make sure that the optimal contribution is sufficient to cover all fixed costs; otherwise, no production is warranted.

Sales Constraints

Although only production constraints have been considered to this point, linear programming can also be applied to sales constraints. To illustrate, assume that market research indicates that the maximum units that can be sold at the established price are 180 *Trail Smoothers* and 60 *Avengers.* Two new constraints would be added, and the problem would be expressed as follows:

Maximize C = $800A + $1,000T
Subject to:
$$4A + 2T \leq 640 \text{ welding hours per month}$$
$$3A + 4T \leq 855 \text{ assembly hours per month}$$
$$T \leq 180 \text{ units per month}$$
$$A \leq 60 \text{ units per month}$$

Illustration 5-2 shows the addition of these constraints to the graph developed in Illustration 5-1. Since one product's sales constraint has no impact on the other product, the sales constraints are straight lines perpendicular to their product axes at the maximum sales level. Substitution (slope) analysis proceeds by assuming production of only *Trail Smoothers* (now limited to 180 units). Test 1 shows that you can gain *Avengers* with no loss of *Trail Smoothers.* Test 2 indicates that you can gain one *Avenger* for each .75 *Trail Smoothers* forgone. This substitution is made, since it is less than the .8 maximum based on contribution. At Test 3, you can gain no more *Avengers,* no matter how many *Trail Smoothers* are forgone. Therefore, you will solve for production at Test 3, as follows:

1. State the constraints as equalities.

$$3A + 4T = 855$$
$$A = 60$$

2. Substitute the second equation into the first equation.

$$(3 \times 60) + 4T = 855$$
$$4T = 855 - 180$$
$$T = 168.75$$

This solution fits within the constraints. Since a partial unit cannot be produced, production would be limited to 168 *Trail Smoothers,* and the optimal contribution would be $216,000 [(60 × $800) + (168 × $1,000)].

Sales Proportion Constraints

It is also possible, but less common, to have a sales proportion constraint. To illustrate, assume that the government required a sales-weighted-average fuel economy of 30 miles per gallon for all snowmobiles sold. If the *Avenger* tests out at 25 mpg and the *Trail Smoother* at 35 mpg, you would have to produce at least one *Trail Smoother* per *Avenger* to comply with the 30-mpg requirement. This constraint could be written: $T \geq A$.

The graph in Illustration 5-3 uses the production constraints from Illustration 5-1 and adds the sales proportion constraint. A new feasible solution is defined, but the optimal solution is unchanged from Illustration 5-1, since that solution contained more *Trail Smoothers* than *Avengers.*

Illustration 5-2
**Linear Programming:
Two Production and
Two Sales Constraints**

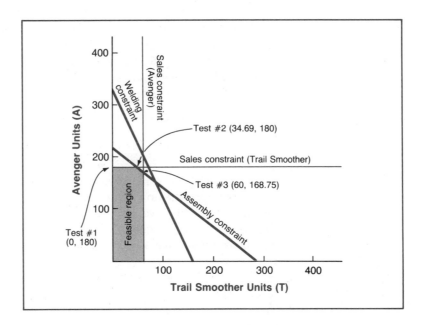

Illustration 5-3
**Linear Programming:
Two Production
Constraints and One
Sales Proportion
Constraint**

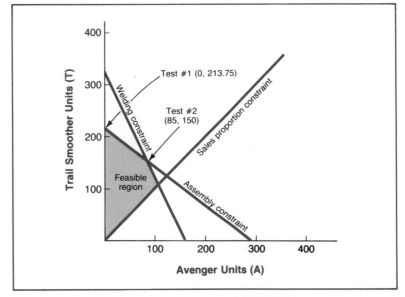

Relaxing a Constraint

There are usually ways of relaxing a constraint if management is willing to
incur additional costs. Before a decision is made, however, the value of expanding
the availability of a resource must be determined by comparing the additional costs
incurred by relaxing the constraint to the incremental contribution. This incremental contribution represents the maximum amount that would be paid for the added
capacity. If a resource is not being used to capacity, it is not a binding constraint,
and there is no value gained by increasing its availability.

Continuing the snowmobile example, assume that you have 50 additional hours of welding time available from a local firm. The variable costs would remain unchanged, but the charge for the use of the equipment would be $700 per month. To determine whether it would pay to spend the $700, the original problem (from Illustration 5-1) must be restated as follows:

Maximize C = $800A + $1,000T
Subject to:
$$4A + 2T \leq 690 \text{ welding hours (50 added) per month}$$
$$3A + 4T \leq 855 \text{ assembly hours (unchanged) per month}$$

A new optimal solution must be calculated. The difference between the contribution of the new and the original optimal solutions is the incremental contribution attributable to the added welding time.

Illustration 5-4 is the graphical solution of the restated problem. The new welding constraint still has a slope, or substitution rate, of -2 ($350 \div -175$).

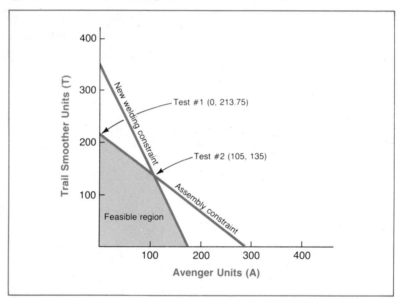

Using the testing procedure, the analysis begins on the vertical axis at 213.75 *Trail Smoothers*. The assembly constraint requires you to give up only .75 *Trail Smoothers* per *Avenger*, which you are willing to do, since the substitution rate based on contribution is .8. At the intersection of the constraints, Test 2 is made. The welding constraint requires giving up 2 *Trail Smoothers* per *Avenger*, which exceeds the maximum .8 rate based on contribution. Therefore, the testing ends, and you will solve for production where the constraint lines intersect. At that point, 135 *Trail Smoothers* and 105 *Avengers* would be produced. The new optimal contribution is computed as follows:

	Units	Contribution Margins	Contributions
Avenger	105	$ 800	$ 84,000
Trail Smoother	135	1,000	135,000
Total	240		$219,000

The excess of the new optimal contribution, $219,000, over the optimal contribution in Illustration 5-1, $218,000, is $1,000. Clearly, you would be willing to pay any amount below $1,000 for the welding equipment. Since $700 is less than $1,000, you would be willing to lease the time on the welding equipment and expand capacity.

Shadow Prices

In Illustration 5-4, each additional hour of welding time contributes $20 ($1,000 ÷ 50 hours). This added contribution of one additional unit of a limited resource is sometimes called the shadow price. In a profit maximization problem, this amount may be called the value of the dual variable. The shadow price is an opportunity cost concept, since it reflects the contribution and not the cost of one more unit of a scarce resource. Resources which are not fully used would have a shadow price of zero.

In addition to being used as an upper limit on what could be paid for additional capacity, shadow prices may also be used as: (1) values for interplant or intracompany transfer pricing purposes, (2) a basis for determining joint cost allocation, (3) charges to current and possible future users of the resources, or (4) substitutes for market-determined prices in allocating resources in a controlled economy, such as the USSR. Shadow prices are computed as part of the algebraic (simplex) solution for linear programming problems. The appendix to this chapter describes one version of the simplex method of solving linear programming problems and shows the computation of the shadow prices for the snowmobile problem.

CONSIDERING THE UNCERTAINTY OF ESTIMATES

Cost-volume-profit analysis relies heavily upon the accuracy of the estimates of costs and revenues as well as the projections of sales volumes. Therefore, the cost analyst must be concerned about the preciseness of these estimates. When these estimates can take on a range of possible values, uncertainty or risk enters into the analysis. The greater the range of possible outcomes about the average, the greater the inherent uncertainty.

The remainder of this chapter will consider uncertainty, using three approaches. First, sensitivity analysis will be used to analyze the possible impact of a likely range of values for each variable in CVP analysis. Then, the likely range of values will be examined by using statistical analysis. Finally, the concept of certainty equivalents will be discussed.

Sensitivity Analysis

Sensitivity analysis tests the impact of an unfavorable change on any of the estimates used in CVP analysis on the decision being considered. An analysis is said to be sensitive if the outcome using the new value significantly reduces the division contribution. A project is not necessarily abandoned, however, if an analysis is sensitive. Instead, the projections would be re-examined to determine the likelihood of the unfavorable change occurring. If the probability of such a change is significant, either the uncertainty must be tolerated or the plan abandoned. Thus, sensitivity analysis alerts management to danger, but it does not indicate that the danger be avoided.

Sensitivity analysis will be illustrated using an example involving one product of a multiproduct division. The original projections for the product, which are shown on the graph in Illustration 5-5(1), are as follows:

> Revenue: $6 per unit
> Variable cost: $4 per unit
> Fixed cost: $20,000 per month
> Sales volume: 12,000 units per month

Sensitivity analysis with respect to sales volume can be applied directly to the graph in (1). The product justification point is calculated to be 10,000 units, and the margin of safety is 16 2/3% [(12,000 − 10,000) ÷ 12,000]. If sales less than 16 2/3% of projected sales are possible, there is a risk of negative contribution. Therefore, management must reassess its decision to determine if the risk is warranted.

In Illustration 5-5(2), (3), and (4), sensitivity analysis is used to evaluate the effects of changes in variable cost, fixed cost, and sales price. In each case, sensitivity analysis tests the effect of the maximum reasonable adverse change in each estimate on the division contribution. The results of these analyses are summarized as follows:

Test	Sensitivity
(2) Statistical analysis predicts, with 95% certainty, that the variable cost will fall in the range of $3.50 to $4.50 per unit. Test for the impact of a variable cost increase to $4.50 per unit.	Very sensitive. A negative contribution would result. Any variable cost over $4.33 will produce a negative contribution.
(3) Fixed costs could increase $1,000 as a result of a possible increase in utilities expense.	Not sensitive. The reduction in contribution is not significant.
(4) Prices may be cut 5% ($.30) in response to competition.	Sensitive. There is still a contribution, but it is near zero, the product justification point.

Statistical Analysis

Statistical analysis may be applied to the cost and price estimates used in CVP analysis. However, the projected sales volume is the variable least subject to management's control and most vulnerable to external influences. In most cases, the projected sales level is, at best, a good estimate, and there is a range of volumes in which the actual volume is likely to fall.

Illustration 5-5   Testing the Sensitivity of CVP Analysis

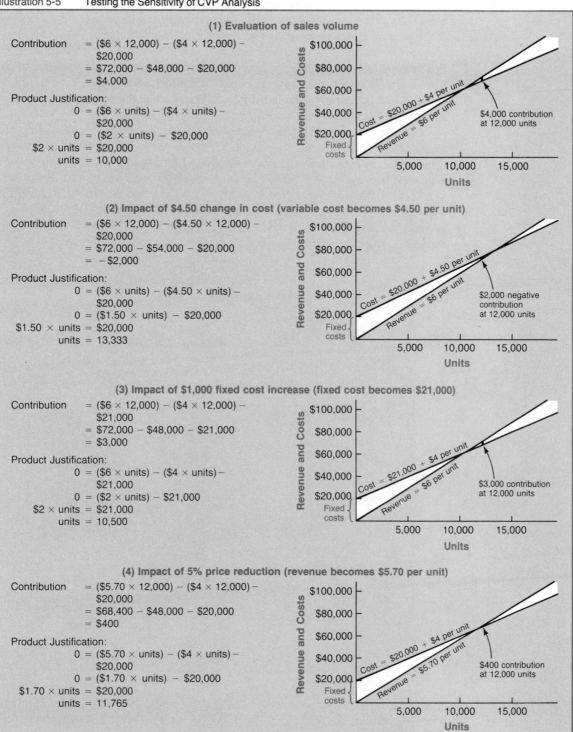

(1) Evaluation of sales volume

Contribution = ($6 × 12,000) − ($4 × 12,000) −
$20,000
= $72,000 − $48,000 − $20,000
= $4,000

Product Justification:
0 = ($6 × units) − ($4 × units) −
$20,000
0 = ($2 × units) − $20,000
$2 × units = $20,000
units = 10,000

$4,000 contribution at 12,000 units

Cost = $20,000 + $4 per unit
Revenue = $6 per unit

(2) Impact of $4.50 change in cost (variable cost becomes $4.50 per unit)

Contribution = ($6 × 12,000) − ($4.50 × 12,000) −
$20,000
= $72,000 − $54,000 − $20,000
= −$2,000

Product Justification:
0 = ($6 × units) − ($4.50 × units) −
$20,000
0 = ($1.50 × units) − $20,000
$1.50 × units = $20,000
units = 13,333

$2,000 negative contribution at 12,000 units

Cost = $20,000 + $4.50 per unit
Revenue = $6 per unit

(3) Impact of $1,000 fixed cost increase (fixed cost becomes $21,000)

Contribution = ($6 × 12,000) − ($4 × 12,000) −
$21,000
= $72,000 − $48,000 − $21,000
= $3,000

Product Justification:
0 = ($6 × units) − ($4 × units) −
$21,000
0 = ($2 × units) − $21,000
$2 × units = $21,000
units = 10,500

$3,000 contribution at 12,000 units

Cost = $21,000 + $4 per unit
Revenue = $6 per unit

(4) Impact of 5% price reduction (revenue becomes $5.70 per unit)

Contribution = ($5.70 × 12,000) − ($4 × 12,000) −
$20,000
= $68,400 − $48,000 − $20,000
= $400

Product Justification:
0 = ($5.70 × units) − ($4 × units) −
$20,000
0 = ($1.70 × units) − $20,000
$1.70 × units = $20,000
units = 11,765

$400 contribution at 12,000 units

Cost = $20,000 + $4 per unit
Revenue = $5.70 per unit

In the context of CVP analysis, risk could be defined as the probability of a sales volume low enough to enter the negative contribution zone (or the loss zone, if the analysis is being applied to an entire firm). Statistical analysis may be used to quantify this risk when the sales estimate is a result of linear regression analysis. For example, sales trend analysis could predict future sales as a continuation of the historical sales pattern; or regional sales of a product, such as snowblowers, could be regressed against some explanatory indicator, such as the year's expected snowfall in each region.

Chapter 3 demonstrated that regression analysis can provide a measure of the standard deviation of a point estimate. To illustrate this use of statistical analysis, assume that the estimated standard deviation in Illustration 5-5 is 2,500 units when estimated sales are 12,000 units. The range that is 95% certain to include the sales would be 7,100 to 16,900 units [12,000 $\pm$ (1.96 standard deviations $\times$ 2,500)].[1] Therefore, there is a reasonable chance that sales could fall below the 10,000-unit product justification level. This situation is shown in Illustration 5-6, Part A, by superimposing the normal distribution of sales over the CVP graph.

Illustration 5-6
CVP Analysis Using
Statistical Analysis

Part A
Projected Profit and
Likelihood of Falling
Below the Product
Justification Point

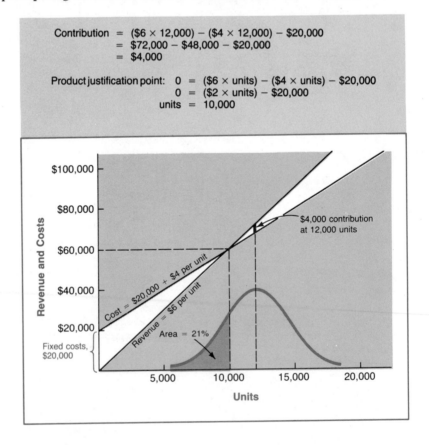

$$\begin{aligned}
\text{Contribution} &= (\$6 \times 12{,}000) - (\$4 \times 12{,}000) - \$20{,}000 \\
&= \$72{,}000 - \$48{,}000 - \$20{,}000 \\
&= \$4{,}000
\end{aligned}$$

$$\begin{aligned}
\text{Product justification point:} \quad 0 &= (\$6 \times \text{units}) - (\$4 \times \text{units}) - \$20{,}000 \\
0 &= (\$2 \times \text{units}) - \$20{,}000 \\
\text{units} &= 10{,}000
\end{aligned}$$

[1] The one-tail value used, based on the *t* table in the appendix of this text, was .025 with infinite degrees of freedom.

The risk of entering the negative product contribution zone can actually be measured by calculating the probability of such an encroachment. The 10,000-unit product justification point is 2,000 units below the projected volume and .8 (2,000 ÷ 2,500) standard deviations from the mean. The area to the left of .8 standard deviations is 21% of the area of the normal curve.[2] Thus, the probability (risk) of entering the negative contribution zone is .21.

A firm will usually choose to maximize contribution. However, a risk-averse firm may occasionally choose to "pay extra" for variable costs, as opposed to fixed costs, and thus sacrifice contribution in order to reduce risk. This may explain why some firms shun technological advances which would increase fixed costs.

Part B of Illustration 5-6 considers an alternate way to meet the 12,000-unit projected demand. Fixed costs should be reduced to $6,000 by eliminating mechanization. As a result, variable costs would escalate to $5.25 per unit. This alternative reduces the projected contribution by $1,000. It also lowers the product justification point and increases the margin of safety, which greatly reduces the risk of entering the negative contribution zone. This zone is now 1.6 (4,000 ÷ 2,500) standard deviations from the mean. The area to the left of 1.6 standard deviations is only 5% of the area of the normal curve.[3]

Illustration 5-6
CVP Analysis Using
Statistical Analysis

Part B
Comparison to
Alternative Cost
Function

$$\text{Contribution} = (\$6 \times 12{,}000) - (\$5.25 \times 12{,}000) - \$6{,}000$$
$$= \$72{,}000 - \$63{,}000 - \$6{,}000$$
$$= \$3{,}000$$

$$\text{Product justification point:} \quad 0 = (\$6 \times \text{units}) - (\$5.25 \times \text{units}) - \$6{,}000$$
$$0 = (\$.75 \times \text{units}) - \$6{,}000$$
$$.75 \times \text{units} = \$6{,}000$$
$$\text{units} = 8{,}000$$

[2] See Table 3 in the appendix at the end of the text.
[3] See Table 3 in the appendix at the end of the text.

A firm may not have the data to apply linear regression or may have found linear regression to be a poor predictor of future performance. In such cases, the firm might predict average sales, estimate the range within which volume may fall, and apply subjective or judgmental probabilities of occurrence to the estimated sales levels. These probabilities can be determined by a variety of means. For sales estimates, sales representatives frequently provide the probabilities. For example, sales representatives might be asked how many months, in the next 20 months, will sales achieve the given levels. If the response were one month out of 20 for the 10,000-unit level, a probability of .05 would be assigned.

For practical purposes, point estimates (also termed discrete estimates) must be used to portray possible outcomes. Therefore, a weighted average, called the expected value, is calculated by using the subjective probabilities as weights, as shown in the following example:

(1) Possible Sales Levels	(2) Subjective Probabilities	(3) Expected Values (1) × (2)
10,000 units	.05	500 units
12,000	.15	1,800
14,000	.30	4,200
16,000	.30	4,800
18,000	.15	2,700
20,000	.05	1,000
Total	1.00	15,000 units

In this example, equal intervals on either side of the mean have identical and declining probabilities. Therefore, the probability distribution can be assumed to be a normal distribution, and the estimate of the standard deviation of the expected value may be computed by using the following equation:

$$\text{Estimate of standard deviation} = \sqrt{\sum_{i}^{n} \left\{ P_i (X_i - \overline{X})^2 \right\}}$$

where n = number of estimates
P_i = probability of each possible sales level
X_i = estimate of unit sales
$\overline{X}$ = expected value (in units)

$$= \sqrt{\begin{array}{l} .05(10,000 - 15,000)^2 + .15(12,000 - 15,000)^2 + \\ .3(14,000 - 15,000)^2 + .3(16,000 - 15,000)^2 + \\ .15(18,000 - 15,000)^2 + .05(20,000 - 15,000)^2 \end{array}}$$

$$= \sqrt{5,800,000}$$
$$= 2,408$$

If the product justification point is 12,500 units, the margin of safety is 17% [(15,000 − 12,500) ÷ 15,000], and the expected value, 15,000 units, is 2,500 units or 1.038 (2,500 ÷ 2,408) standard deviations above that point. The area of the normal curve to the left of 1.038 standard deviations is 15%.[4] Therefore, the risk of entering the negative contribution zone is 15%. Although the measure

[4] See Table 3 in the appendix at the end of the text.

of this risk is more easily determined by observing the original probability distribution, the estimate of the standard deviation is useful in comparing alternate estimates. For example, if two products both have expected values of 15,000 units for estimated sales, but one has an estimated standard deviation of 2,000 and the other 1,000, the range of outcomes for the first product is estimated to be twice that of the second product.

The procedure for calculating an estimate of a standard deviation is only applicable to probability distributions which approximate a normal distribution. For example, assume that the probabilities of the previous example and the expected value are as follows:

Possible Sales Levels	Subjective Probabilities	Expected Values
10,000 units	.10	1,000 units
12,000	.25	3,000
14,000	.30	4,200
16,000	.20	3,200
18,000	.10	1,800
20,000	.05	1,000
Total	1.00	14,200 units

Since the distribution is not normally distributed, no estimate of the standard deviation should be calculated. A measure of the risk of entering the negative contribution zone is indicated, however, by the probability distribution, in which 35% of the outcomes, 10,000 and 12,000 units, are below the product justification point of 12,500 units.

CONSIDERING UNCERTAINTY IN COMPARING ALTERNATIVES

A firm may use expected values to arrive at a decision rule that will best meet continuing uncertainty. A common example is establishing a production schedule to meet varying levels of demand. Production schedules are a special concern when over- or underproduction reduces the profit that would have resulted if demand had been completely predictable. To illustrate, assume that Specialty Cookie Company cannot predict the exact demand for cookies each day, but expects the following random daily demand:

Sales	Probabilities
100 dozen	.3
150 dozen	.4
200 dozen	.3

If the firm bakes more cookies than are sold, the excess cookies are discarded. If demand exceeds the number baked, the firm pays overtime to bake the additional cookies. A dozen cookies sell for $1.50. The cookies cost $1 per dozen to produce in regular time, plus an extra $.20 per dozen if overtime is required.

To help Specialty Cookie Company determine the optimal size of its daily production run, you construct the following **payoff table,** which is based on each of three possible outcomes for each of three actions that could be taken:

Production	Daily Sales		
	100 dozen	150 dozen	200 dozen
100 doz.	100 × $.50 profit = $50	100 × $.50 profit = $50 50 × $.30 profit = 15 Total $65	100 × $.50 profit = $50 100 × $.30 profit = 30 Total $80
150 doz.	100 × $.50 profit = $50 50 × $1 loss = (50) Total 0	150 × $.50 profit = $75	150 × $.50 profit = $75 50 × $.30 profit = 15 Total $90
200 doz.	100 × $.50 profit = $ 50 100 × $1 loss = (100) Total $(50)	150 × $.50 profit = $75 50 × $1 loss = (50) Total $25	200 × $.50 profit = $100

The payoff table identifies nine possible combinations of production and sales. Using these nine outcomes, the expected value of the profit at each production level may be calculated by multiplying each possible outcome by its probability, as follows:

Production		
100 dozen	150 dozen	200 dozen
.3 × $50 = $15	.3 × 0 = 0	.3 × $(50) = $(15)
.4 × 65 = 26	.4 × $75 = $30	.4 × 25 = 10
.3 × 80 = 24	.3 × 90 = 27	.3 × 100 = 30
Expected value $65	$57	$ 25

Without the ability to predict daily demand and given the three choices, daily production of 100 dozen will optimize profits. If, however, exact demand could be predicted, under- or overproduction would be avoided and the optimal profit for each sales level would be realized. With such *perfect information*, the expected value of the average daily profit would be as follows:

Sales of 100 dozen: $50 × .3 .... $15
Sales of 150 dozen: $75 × .4 30
Sales of 200 dozen: $100 × .3 30
Expected value $75

This analysis suggests that the value of the perfect information is the $10 of additional expected value ($75 expected value with perfect information − $65 maximum expected value without perfect information). Although perfect information is not available, its value is a useful guide to what a firm can afford to pay for better information.

SUBJECTIVE CONSIDERATION OF RISK

In previous examples, risk was considered by replacing a single best estimate of sales volume with a mean or expected value, which was derived from a probability distribution of possible outcomes. Statistical analysis was used to consider the risk of sales entering the loss zone.

Implicit in the analyses was the presumption that the mean value is typically the basis for a decision. This assumption may not be true, however, if a large negative outcome is included in the probability distribution of an alternative. For example, one marketing plan may have a mean expected profit of $50,000 while another plan has a mean expected profit of $45,000. Normally, the first plan would be chosen. However, if the first plan included a 10% chance of a $20,000 loss while the second plan had little likelihood of a loss, the decision might be different.

If a loss would endanger the continued existence of the firm, the second plan with its lower expected profit would be chosen because it is worth $5,000 or more to avoid the risk of losing the business. Choosing this plan suggests that **utility theory** has been applied; i.e., the disutility of a loss far exceeds the utility of a profit. Using utility theory, a manager's attitude towards monetary returns can be expressed. For example, if a dollar of normal gain is stated to be worth $1, a manager may view very large gains as worth only $.80, because there may be discomfort with the pressure to repeat the performance or because there is little use for the added wealth. Conversely, $1 of loss may be measured as $2 due to the fear of losing one's job.

Utility theory may be considered explicitly by assigning weights to possible outcomes. For example, assume that you are very adverse to losses and not overly concerned with more than normal profits. You accordingly assign weights to the possible profit or loss outcomes, assume a probability distribution, and calculate an expected value of profits adjusted for the utility of the outcomes, as follows:

(1)	(2)	(3)	(4)	(5)
				Expected Values
Profit (Loss)	Utility Weights	(1) × (2)	Probabilities	(3) × (4)
$(5,000)	3.0	$(15,000)	.1	$(1,500)
(1,000)	3.0	(3,000)	.2	(600)
4,000	1.0	4,000	.2	800
8,000	1.0	8,000	.4	3,200
15,000	.8	12,000	.1	1,200
		Total expected value, adjusted for utility		$3,100

Utility theory may also be applied to cost estimates. It is more common, however, to consider the risk inherent in cost estimates by replacing the mean value of a cost estimate by a **certainty equivalent,** which is the amount one would pay to avoid unknown future expenditures. When there is adversity to risk, this amount may exceed the estimated expected value of the expenditures.

To illustrate the use of certainty equivalents, assume that you are considering the purchase of a maintenance contract on your television set. The maintenance contract costs $49 per year, and you have computed a mean expected repair cost of $35 per year. If you wanted to avoid the risk of a costly repair, such as replacing the picture tube, you would probably be willing to purchase the contract. You would then replace the $35 expected cost with a $49 certainty equivalent. The utility weight for this decision would be 1.4 ($49 ÷ $35). This weight could be used to evaluate other service contracts with expected values of repairs having a similar risk.

Certainty equivalents for a firm may not be so readily available. Instead, a certainty equivalent may be more hypothetical. For example, a firm with an expected value cost estimate of $7,000 for heating might only be able to speculate that it would pay $8,000 to avoid the chance of a higher than normal heating bill.

APPENDIX 5: THE SIMPLEX METHOD OF SOLVING LINEAR PROGRAMMING PROBLEMS

The simplex method is an iterative procedure (i.e., a series of successive approximations) which eventually arrives at an optimum product mix. The graphic method of arriving at a solution is only feasible if there are two products in the problem, since a 3-product problem would require a 3-dimensional graph, and a 4-product problem, a 4-dimensional graph. The simplex method, however, is an algebraic approach which can be applied to problems with any number of products.

The first step is to set up the objective which is to be maximized (or minimized) and the constraints or restrictions on the outputs. While these constraints are usually expressed initially as inequalities, the inequalities are converted to equations through the introduction of **dummy variables,** or **slack variables.** Every variable is included in each equation through the use of zero coefficients.

As a first approximation, a trial solution mix, or product mix, consisting of the maximum amount of the slack variables, is set up in a tabular or matrix form. This initial mix is chosen because it is the simplest possible starting point. As a result,

Simplex Tableau

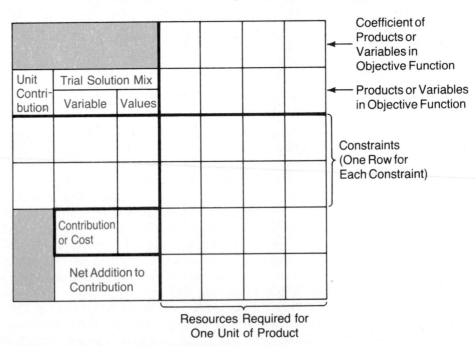

the numbers in the simplex tableau initially represent a statement of a separate restriction on the maximum quantities of the various products which can be utilized without exceeding one scarce resource. The individual values in a given row can thus be interpreted as substitution ratios, since they represent, with reference to some given constraint, the quantities of a product which must be given up for an increase in the quantity of some other product. Each column represents the amount of the various scarce resources required for one unit of a given product.

To move to a more advantageous product mix, one should add to the mix that product, not already in the mix, which would make the largest contribution. The additional contribution added by one unit of a given product is given by the coefficient for that product in the objective function. Introducing one product into the mix, however, means that other products which contribute must be displaced from the mix, because the available quantities of scarce resources limit the total quantities of all products which can be produced. The net contribution of one additional unit of a given product will thus be that product's contribution less the contribution given up by a reduction of the other products.

To determine the contribution of the other products given up, the substitution ratio is multiplied by the contribution margin per unit of scarce resource or alternative product. Initially, the substitution ratio is the ratio of units of scarce resource used per unit of given product. More generally, it is the ratio of units of alternative products sacrificed per unit of given product introduced. Since an attempt to introduce a new product into the mix will displace varying quantities of products already in the mix, the total cost of introducing a new product will include the sum of lost contributions from all products presently in the mix. The product which has the greatest net contribution per unit is selected for introduction into the mix.

Once a product has been selected for introduction into the mix, it is necessary to determine how much of that product is to be introduced. As a result of the computations indicated in the preceding paragraph, a single product which will contribute the most, relative to the products it displaces, has been identified. Without violating one of the constraints, as much of this product as is possible should be introduced. The substitution ratios described in the preceding paragraph are used to determine which one of the constraints will first limit the introduction of additional units of the chosen product into the mix.

In adding the maximum quantity of new product into the mix, one of the variables presently in the mix will be eliminated. The row corresponding to the variable being eliminated may then be dropped from the tableau and replaced by a row corresponding to the new variable being introduced. Since the same constraint which restricted the quantity of the old variable will also restrict the quantity of the new variable being introduced, the new values in the row, representing the substitution ratios in terms of the new product, are simply the old values divided by the coefficient (i.e., the substitution ratio) of the new product. In essence, the same set of substitution ratios, which were originally expressed per unit of one variable, are being expressed in terms of units of the new product.

Each of the remaining rows represents other constraints or other products already in the mix which have been introduced in amounts up to the limits set up by some other scarce resource. The amount of the product mix represented by a row must be reduced to account for the additional quantities of the new product added to the mix. Adding a new product to the mix means that the previous utilization of other scarce resources in terms of previous substitution ratios will be altered. The substitution ratios in each row must be restated in order to account for the exchange just made.

The calculations described in the previous paragraphs will result in a new tableau containing new values for each of the various elements. Once this new tableau has been prepared for the new product mix, calculations are made to determine the possible increases in contribution which could be obtained by adding one unit of each of the products. The most profitable substitution is made, a new tableau constructed, and the contribution of possible substitutions again evaluated. Eventually, a product mix in which the contribution from every possible substitution is negative will be obtained. This solution indicates that any possible change in the product mix will reduce the contribution, and that the optimum product mix has been obtained.

At this point, the change in contribution from the introduction of new products has some interesting characteristics for those hypothetical "products" represented by the slack variables not in the mix. These changes in contribution that would result if one unit less of the scarce resource were available represent the shadow price of that scarce resource.

The simplex method is applied, as follows, to the linear programming problem solved graphically in this chapter:

Objective	Procedure for Achieving Objective	Illustration
1. Determine the relationship between the various products in terms of what is to be maximized or minimized.	Set up the objective function, e.g., maximize marginal contribution.	Maximize contribution: $Z = 800A + 1{,}000T$. (The contribution margin of product A is \$800 per unit and that of product T is \$1,000 per unit.)
2. Determine the relationship between the various products in terms of the existing constraints.	Set up an inequality for each constraint.	Welding time constraint: only 640 hours are available; each unit of A uses 4 hours of welding time; each unit of T uses 2 hours. $4A + 2T \leq 640$ hours. Assembly capacity constraint: only 855 hours are available; each unit of A uses 3 hours of assembly time; each unit of T uses 4 hours. $3A + 4T \leq 855$ hours
	Convert each inequality into an equation by introducing slack variables.	Let U be the unused welding time and V be the unused assembly time. Then, $4A + 2T + U = 640$ $3A + 4T + V = 855$
	Put every variable into every equation by inserting zero coefficients where necessary.	$Z = 800A + 1{,}000B + 0U + 0V$ Subject to: $4A + 2T + 1U + 0V = 640$ $3A + 4T + 0U + 1V = 855$

3. Prepare the initial simplex tableau or matrix.

Insert the appropriate coefficients into the following table by inserting the coefficients of every variable for each equation. Use the slack variables as the initial trial solution product mix.

			800	1,000	0	0
Unit Contri-bution	Trial Solution Mix		A	T	U	V
	Variable	Values				
0	U	640	4	2	1	0
0	V	855	3	4	0	1
	Contribution or Cost					
	Net Addition to Contribution					

4. Determine the contribution of the present product mix and the cost of adding one unit of each possible product to the mix in terms of the other products which would have to be sacrificed.

Multiply the unit contribution of each product in the present mix (given in the far left column) by the value in each cell in every row in the body of the table. Total the amounts for each column. Insert the results in the "Contribution or Cost" row in the table.

Contribution of present mix:
640 units of U: (640) (0) = 0
855 units of V: (855) (0) = 0
Total contribution
of trial solution mix = 0

Cost of adding one unit of A:
(0) (4) + (0) (3) = 0
Cost of adding one unit of T:
(0) (2) + (0) (4) = 0
Cost of adding one unit of U:
(0) (1) + (0) (0) = 0
Cost of adding one unit of V:
(0) (0) + (0) (1) = 0

			800	1,000	0	0
Unit Contri-bution	Trial Solution Mix		A	T	U	V
	Variable	Values				
0	U	640	4	2	1	0
0	V	855	3	4	0	1
	Contribution or Cost	0	0	0	0	0
	Net Addition to Contribution					

5. Determine the contribution which would be added by one unit of each of the products.

Subtract the cost of substituting one unit of product, as just calculated, from the contribution of one unit of product, as shown in the top row. Insert the results in the last row of the table.

Net addition to contribution by adding one unit of:
A: $800 - 0 = 800$
T: $1,000 - 0 = 1,000$
U: $0 - 0 = 0$
V: $0 - 0 = 0$

			800	1,000	0	0
Unit Contri-bution	Trial Solution Mix		A	T	U	V
	Variable	Values				
0	U	640	4	2	1	0
0	V	855	3	4	0	1
	Contribution or Cost	0	0	0	0	0
	Net Addition to Contribution		800	1,000	0	0

6. Identify the product whose introduction into the mix would give the greatest increase in contribution.

Pick out the largest positive value in the "Net Addition to Contribution" row.

Introduce T into the product mix.

			800	1,000	0	0
Unit Contri-bution	Trial Solution Mix		A	T	U	V
	Variable	Values				
0	U	640	4	2	1	0
0	V	855	3	4	0	1
	Contribution or Cost	0	0	0	0	0
	Net Addition to Contribution		800	1,000	0	0

7. Determine how much of the most profitable product can be introduced into the mix without exceeding any of the constraints.

Divide the number of units in the "Trial Solution Mix" column by the corresponding value in the cell under the product which is to be introduced. The lowest

For:
U: $640 \div 2 = 320$
V: $855 \div 4 = 213.75$
Since 213.75 is the smallest of the values, it represents the most T that can be introduced. Put 213.75 units of T in the mix and take out V.

7. continued

resulting value indicates which constraint is the limiting factor, and accordingly, for which variable in the mix the new product is to be substituted.

			800	1,000	0	0
Unit Contri-bution	Trial Solution Mix		A	T	U	V
	Variable	Values				
0	U	640	4	2	1	0
1,000	T	213.75				
	Contribution or Cost					
	Net Addition to Contribution					

8. Insert the new product into the mix, replacing one of the variables in the mix.

Divide each value in the old row being replaced by the value in the cell under the product which is to be introduced.

New value for the amount of T in the product mix (same calculation as in Step 7):
$$855 \div 4 = 213.75$$
New values for remainder of row:
A: $3 \div 4 = 0.75$
T: $4 \div 4 = 1.0$
U: $0 \div 4 = 0$
V: $1 \div 4 = 0.25$

			800	1,000	0	0
Unit Contri-bution	Trial Solution Mix		A	T	U	V
	Variable	Values				
0	U	640	4	2	1	0
1,000	T	213.75	0.75	1	0	0.25
	Contribution or Cost					
	Net Addition to Contribution					

9. Adjust the values of the other products in the mix to compensate for the introduction of the new product.

For each of the other rows, calculate a new value in each cell by subtracting from the original value in that cell the product of:
(a) the value in the new row, as calculated in Step 8, multiplied by

New values for "U" row:
Units in mix: $640 - (213.75)(2)^* = 212.50$
New values for remainder of row:
A: $4 - (0.75)(2) = 2.5$
T: $2 - (1.0)(2) = 0$
U: $1 - (0)(2) = 1$
V: $0 - (0.25)(2) = -0.5$
*Value in old "U" row for the "T" column.

9. continued

(b) the original value in that row for the column corresponding to the new variable being introduced.

			800	1,000	0	0
Unit Contribution	Trial Solution Mix		A	T	U	V
	Variable	Values				
0	U	212.5	2.5	0	1	−0.5
1,000	T	213.75	0.75	1	0	0.25
	Contribution or Cost					
	Net Addition to Contribution					

10. Find the contribution of the present mix and the cost of introducing one unit of each product.

Repeat Step 4.

Contribution of present mix:
$(212.5)(0) + (213.75)(1,000) = 213,750$

Cost of adding one unit of:
A: $(2.5)(0) + (.75)(1,000) = 750$
T: $(0)(0) + (1)(1,000) = 1,000$
U: $(1)(0) + (0)(1,000) = 0$
V: $(-0.5)(0) + (0.25)(1,000) = 250$

11. Find the net addition to contribution by adding one unit of each product.

Repeat Step 5.

Net addition to profit from adding one unit of:
A: $800 - 750 = 50$
T: $1,000 - 1,000 = 0$
U: $0 - 0 = 0$
V: $0 - 250 = -250$

Tableau after first iteration:

			800	1,000	0	0
Unit Contribution	Trial Solution Mix		A	T	U	V
	Variable	Values				
0	U	212.5	2.5	0	1	−0.5
1,000	T	213.75	0.75	1	0	0.25
	Contribution or Cost	213.75	750	1,000	0	250
	Net Addition to Contribution		50	0	0	−250

1. When constructing a product mix, what is a manager's principal consideration?

2. What would a manager be concerned with in designing a product mix that was constrained by a production function?

3. Is it true that the objective function in a linear programming model is always stated as maximizing contribution or some other measure of profit? Explain.

4. Using the graphic method of applying linear programming to multiple production constraints, what do the slopes of the constraint lines indicate?

5. How should one interpret a constraint line perpendicular to its product's axis?

6. What is a shadow price?

7. What are some uses of a shadow price?

8. For what does sensitivity analysis test?

9. A manager is considering a certain project, and using sensitivity analysis, finds that if variable costs increase by $.40, the project will produce a loss. Based on this information, the manager decides not to proceed with the project. Did the manager make a correct decision? Explain.

10. How is the standard deviation of an estimated sales forecast used?

11. Is it true that a firm will always choose the alternative that produces the greatest contribution? Explain.

12. Is it true that contribution may be sacrificed to reduce risk? Explain.

13. Since perfect information is not available, why would a firm ever calculate the expected value of perfect information?

14. What is the importance of considering risk?

15. What is a certainty equivalent?

Exercise 1. Oakridge Furniture Company produces two kinds of upright bookcases: a standard model, and the more ornate, deluxe model. The selling prices of the two models are $75 and $100, respectively. Both models are extremely popular, and demand far exceeds available capacity. Variable costs total $25 for each standard bookcase and $30 for each deluxe bookcase.

Oakridge is located in a small town in which skilled labor is scarce. Until it can train more employees, it is limited to 4,000 hours of assembly time per year. It takes 5 hours to assemble a deluxe bookcase, but only 2 hours to assemble a standard model.

The company is faced with a scarcity of the special veneer it uses on its bookcases. The deluxe model requires 2 square yards of veneer, while the standard model requires only half as much.

(1) Which model should Oakridge produce if there are no production constraints?

(2) If production is subject only to the labor constraint, what model should Oakridge produce?

(3) Taking into consideration both the labor and veneer constraints, what model(s) should Oakridge produce?

Exercise 2 (AICPA adapted, 5/69). The cost accountant of Stangren Corporation wants your opinion of a technique suggested by a young accounting graduate employed as a cost analyst. You were furnished with the following information for the corporation's two products, trinkets and gadgets:

	Daily Capacities in Units		Sales Prices per Unit	Variable Costs per Unit
	Cutting Department	Finishing Department		
Trinkets	400	240	$50	$30
Gadgets	200	320	70	40

The daily capacities of each department represent the maximum production for either trinkets or gadgets. However, any combination of trinkets and gadgets can be produced as long as the maximum capacity of the department is not exceeded. For example, two trinkets can be produced in the Cutting Department for each gadget not produced, and three trinkets can be produced in the Finishing Department for every four gadgets not produced. A materials shortage prohibits the production of more than 180 gadgets per day.

A graph of the linear equations developed from the production information above is as follows:

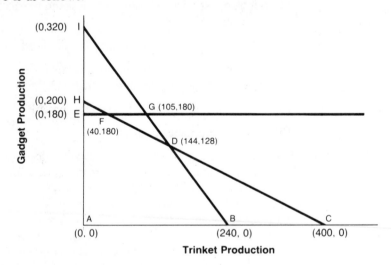

Identify and list the lines or points corresponding with the:

(1) Cutting Department's capacity.
(2) Production limitation for gadgets because of the materials shortage.
(3) Finishing Department's capacity.
(4) Area of feasible production combinations.
(5) Most profitable operating output.

Exercise 3 (CMA adapted, 12/79). Elon Co. manufactures two industrial products: X-10, which sells for $90 a unit, and Y-12, which sells for $85 a unit. The limited availability of labor and equipment capacity has restricted the ability of the firm to meet the demand for its products. The following data are available to the production department:

	X-10	Y-12
Labor (limited to 1,000 hours per week)	1.5 hours	2.0 hours
Machine time (limited to 550 hours per week)	0.5	1.0

Variable costs are $68 for X-10 and $50 for Y-12. In addition to the production constraints, the Marketing Department feels that a minimum of 200 units per week should be produced in order to maintain finished goods inventories. The 200-unit requirement may be satisfied with any combination of X-10 and Y-12.

Prepare the equations necessary to solve the problem using linear programming.

Exercise 4. On separate graphs, plot each of the sets of constraints in the following production situations. Label all axes and intercepts and indicate the feasible regions.

(1) ABC Cannery processes all of its yearly production in the two months following the harvest season. This year, the cannery is processing only peaches in two sizes of cans. A case of the normal, 16-oz. cans requires 1.5 cubic feet of warehousing space, while a case of the 120-oz., institutional-size cans requires 4 cubic feet. The warehouse can store up to 12,000 cubic feet of production per month.

(2) John Davies, a farmer, is deciding what combination of corn and soybeans to plant. The local grain agent has told John that he can store no more than 15,000 bushels of his corn production; no other storage space for corn is available. An unlimited amount of storage space for soybeans is available from a competing agent, however. No consideration is given to losses of planted grains.

(3) Snowden Corporation manufactures rotary lawnmowers. Both the wheels and the lawnmower decks are manufactured in-house, while all other parts are purchased from outside suppliers. Each lawnmower deck requires four wheels, but wheels not used in-house can be easily sold to parts jobbers at a considerable profit. Snowden maintains no inventories of either wheels or decks.

(4) Frieda Hall, an investor, is planning her investment portfolio for the coming year. Frieda invests only in stocks and bonds, and would like to invest a total of $200,000. She will invest no more than 1/3 of the total portfolio in bonds.

Exercise 5. Stratford Electrical Company manufactures and assembles two types of DC electric motors. All component parts are manufactured in-house. Demand is outpacing production capacity, and Stratford's management has asked its Accounting Department to develop a simple linear programming model to optimize its product mix. The computer printout shows the following results:

Variables

Standard electric motor	79 units
Heavy-duty electric motor	368 units
Maximized contribution	$31,550

Constraints	Shadow Prices
Assembly time (hours)	$ 5.26
Machining time (hours)	11.84

The company has been presented with two proposals. An outside contractor is willing to provide machining capacity of 400 hours per month for a fixed rate of $4,240 per month. Stratford could easily utilize the 400 additional hours in producing the existing models. Alternatively, the company could discontinue the heavy-duty motor in favor of a model with a shorter life. The new model would require 4 hours of assembly time and 3 hours of machining time, and would provide a contribution of $52 per unit.

(1) Should the firm purchase the outside assembly time?
(2) Independent of your answer to (1), should the firm begin production of the new model?

Exercise 6. The managers of Birmingham Company have asked you to aid them in an equipment replacement decision. The company can replace its current equipment, which has reached the end of its useful life, with substantially identical production machinery. This equipment is relatively inexpensive to lease, but has a high variable production cost. Automated equipment is more energy-, labor-, and materials-efficient, but is far more expensive to lease. The cost-volume-profit graphs for the plant, using the older and the newer equipment, are as follows:

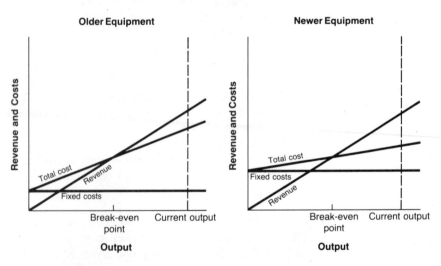

The profit earned by either alternative at the current level of output is the same. Management is confronted by a variety of possible changes in the company's operations:

(1) Unit sales are expected to increase next year by 25%.

(2) There is a slight chance that a new product introduced by a competitor could cause sales to fall by 15%.

(3) Current contract negotiations could increase wage rates for factory employees.

(4) A large reduction in fixed costs could be achieved due to cost-saving measures implemented in the sales and administrative functions.

(5) Legislative action could result in a significant increase in property taxes.

For each of the changes, compare the effect on the company's profits and break-even point, using either the old or the new equipment. Unless otherwise stated, output remains at the current level.

Exercise 7. Zyklon Heating Company delivers fuel oil to residential customers. A gallon of heating oil costs a residential buyer $1.40. Zyklon estimates the total variable cost of a delivered gallon of fuel at $1.05. Zyklon expects to incur fixed costs of $29,750 in its operations this year and projects a mean sales level of 95,000 gallons. The estimated standard deviation of annual oil sales is 6,250 gallons per year.

(1) What profit will Zyklon earn at the projected level of sales?

(2) What is Zyklon's break-even point in gallons of oil?

(3) What is the probability that Zyklon will incur a loss in the coming year?

Exercise 8. Westlane Cinema operates a candy counter in the theater lobby. One of the candy counter's biggest sellers is popcorn. The theater owner would like to estimate popcorn sales in order to better plan popcorn purchases as well as to project the contribution from popcorn sales. To determine the average number of popcorn buyers per week, the following probabilities have been estimated:

Boxes per Week	Probabilities
700	.10
750	.30
800	.40
850	.10
900	.10

The popcorn is sold in three sizes: small (1/10 pound of popcorn), medium (1/5 pound), and large (1/4 pound). The manager estimates that the sales mix is 30%, 50%, and 20% for the small, medium, and large sizes, respectively. Prices and variable costs for the various sizes are as follows:

Sizes	Prices	Variable Costs
Small	$0.75	$0.15
Medium	1.00	0.25
Large	1.20	0.40

The specific fixed costs of the popcorn operation are $400 per month.

(1) Determine the expected value for the number of boxes sold per month, using the manager's sales estimates.

(2) Assuming that the sales mix remains constant, how many pounds are

expected to be used per month?

(3) What is the estimated monthly contribution of the popcorn operation?

Exercise 9. James Jonas has purchased unimproved lakefront property on which he would like to begin constructing his retirement home. One of the decisions he is faced with is the source of water for the home. James can either drill the well, using rented equipment, he can hire an outside contractor to drill for him, or he can connect his home to the local community well. In all cases, the quality of the water and the duration of supply are the same. The cost of each of the alternatives, according to its probable difficulty (indicated in parentheses), is as follows:

	Easy (.10)	Average (.60)	Hard (.30)
Drill well himself	$ 600	$1,000	$1,800
Hire contractor	900	900	1,200
Connect to community well	1,000	1,000	1,000

(1) Determine the expected cost of each alternative. Which alternative should Jonas select?

(2) What is the expected value of perfect information concerning the difficulty of drilling the well?

Exercise 10. As a portfolio manager for a large insurance company, you are confronted daily with the problem of reinvesting the dividends and interest of existing investments and the proceeds of investments which have matured. You are currently confronted with two investment alternatives: one is a slightly speculative land investment; the other, an investment in various types of commercial paper. For each alternative, the possible returns and probabilities are as follows:

Investment in Land		Investment in Commercial Paper	
Returns	Probabilities	Returns	Probabilities
−25%	.10	−5%	.05
−5%	.10	5%	.10
10%	.15	10%	.40
15%	.40	15%	.35
40%	.25	20%	.10

Because your job performance is evaluated on the basis of consistently good returns, you have also developed the following subjective utility weights:

Returns	Utility Weights
loss	3.0
0 – 15%	1.0
> 15%	0.7

(1) Determine the expected value for the return of each of the investments. Which investment offers the higher return?

(2) Determine the expected value of the utility-adjusted return of each investment. Which investment offers the higher utility-adjusted return?

Exercise 11. Janice Dodge has just purchased a used car and has been offered the chance to buy a one-year maintenance agreement for $180. The contract covers the cost of all repairs, major and minor, including parts and labor, for one year from the date of purchase. Janice estimates that her first year's repair costs will be as follows:

	Costs per year	Probabilities
Minor repair	$ 75	.30
Average repair	100	.60
Major repair	675	.10

Janice has also purchased a television set, the annual maintenance cost of which is estimated to be $30. She is offered a service contract by the local dealer for $40 per year.

(1) What is Janice's premium payment to avoid risk, if she purchases the maintenance agreement?
(2) Assume that Janice feels that both the car and television repairs are in the same risk class. Should she purchase the television service contract?

PROBLEMS Problem 5-1. Chinon Laboratories, a small pharmaceutical manufacturer, produces and distributes two kinds of aspirin-free pain reliever: Statril and the new Extra Strength Statril. The primary ingredients in both products are the active ingredient, TLH, and a buffering agent. Chinon has been able to secure only limited supplies of both materials. The following amounts are for a standard production lot of 5,000 vials:

	Statril	Extra Strength Statril
TLH	20 kg	40 kg
Buffer	30 kg	20 kg
Contribution	$1,800	$2,700

Required (1) Assume that Chinon can secure unlimited supplies of both ingredients and can sell all that it produces. Which product should Chinon produce?
(2) Chinon has found access to unlimited amounts of the buffering agent, but can secure only 2 000 kg of TLH each month. On which product should Chinon now concentrate?
(3) In addition to the 2 000-kg limitation on TLH supplies, assume that Chinon can purchase only 1 800 kg of the buffering agent per month. Management has decided that a minimum of 10 lots of Statril should be produced each month in order to maintain the completeness of the company's product line. Develop the constraint functions and the objective function and solve the problem graphically, using linear programming. To prove your answer, calculate the contribution at each intersection.

Problem 5-2 (AICPA adapted, 11/73). Travelise Inc. manufactures two products, Tots and Widgets. Each product is processed on a separate assembly line and then painted in a common painting department. Both assembly lines, the Paint Department, and the general offices are housed in one building.

Travelise could assemble and sell twice as many Tots and Widgets, but production is currently limited by the capacity of the Painting Department and by a shortage of skilled labor. Although the company has studied expansion of the Painting Department, it lacks the financial resources to do so at this time.

In projecting its profits for the coming year, the company has made the following estimates:

- Supervisory costs are charged directly to each department, since there is no supervision interchangeability among the three departments. Supervisory costs are estimated at $2,000 per month, $2,200 per month, and $1,700 per month for the Tot Assembly, Widget Assembly, and Painting Departments, respectively.
- Depreciation falls into three classes: machinery, furniture and fixtures, and building. Machinery depreciation is charged directly to each department, since machinery is used only in a given department. Depreciation on furniture and fixtures is a part of the selling, general, and administrative expenses, while building depreciation is allocated to each department on the basis of floor space. The depreciation per month is as follows:

	Widget Assembly	Tot Assembly	Painting	Offices
Machinery	$1,700	$1,500	$1,500	—
Furniture and fixtures	—	—	—	$1,100
Building	1,250	1,250	1,500	1,000
	(25,000 sq. ft.)	(25,000 sq. ft.)	(30,000 sq. ft.)	(60,000 sq. ft.)

- Utilities costs are measured with meters in each production department and are expected to cost $600 per month for the Tot Assembly Department and $750 per month for the Widget Assembly Department.
- Common janitorial costs will total $20,400 and are allocated to each department on the basis of floor space.
- Painting Department costs not yet mentioned are budgeted at $9,500 per month.
- Officers' salaries, sales salaries, and office expenses are $129,000 per year.

In making its product mix decision, Travelise uses the following constraint data:

	Tots	Widgets	Max. Available per Month
Painting Department	2 hrs.	2 hrs.	15,000 hrs.
Direct labor	4 hrs.	2 hrs.	20,000 hrs.
Revenues	$35 per unit	$27 per unit	
Variable costs	$26 per unit	$20 per unit	

Required
(1) Using the graphic method, calculate the optimal product mix for Travelise. Confirm your answer by calculating the contribution at each intersection.
(2) Travelise decides to produce the optimal mix. Prepare a contribution format income statement for the firm, detailing each product's contribution to the firm's fixed costs and the firm's projected net income.

Problem 5-3 (CMA adapted, 6/78). Excelsion Corporation manufactures and sells two kinds of containers: paperboard and plastic. The company produced and sold 100,000 paperboard containers and 75,000 plastic containers during April. A total of 4,000 and 6,000 direct labor hours were used in producing the paperboard and plastic containers, respectively.

The company has not been able to maintain an inventory of either product, due to the high demand. This situation is expected to continue in the future. Workers can be shifted from the production of paperboard to plastic containers and vice versa, but additional labor is not available in the community. In addition, there will be a shortage of plastic material used in the manufacture of the plastic container in the coming months, due to a labor strike at the facilities of a key supplier. Management has estimated that there will be enough raw materials to produce only 60,000 plastic containers during June. Excelsion's past experience has shown that no more than 3 plastic containers are sold for every 4 paperboard containers. In any case, Excelsion wishes to produce at least 30,000 plastic containers per month to maintain the completeness of its product line.

The income statement for Excelsion Corporation for April is as follows. The costs presented in the statement are representative of prior periods and are expected to continue at the same rates or levels in the future.

Excelsion Corporation
Income Statement
For the Month Ended April 30, 19X8

	Paperboard Containers	Plastic Containers
Sales	$220,800	$222,900
Less: Returns and allowances	$ 6,360	$ 7,200
Discounts	2,440	3,450
	$ 8,800	$ 10,650
Net sales	$212,000	$212,250
Cost of sales:		
Materials	$123,000	$120,750
Direct labor	26,000	28,500
Indirect labor (variable with direct labor hours)	4,000	4,500
Depreciation—machinery	14,000	12,250
Depreciation—building	10,000	10,000
Cost of sales	$177,000	$176,000
Gross profit	$ 35,000	$ 36,250
Selling and general expenses:		
General expenses (variable)	$ 8,000	$ 7,500
General expenses (fixed)	1,000	1,000
Commissions	11,000	15,750
Total operating expenses	$ 20,000	$ 24,250
Income before income taxes	$ 15,000	$ 12,000
Income taxes (40%)	6,000	4,800
Net income	$ 9,000	$ 7,200

Required (1) Formulate and label the objective function and the constraints.
(2) Using the graphic method, determine the optimal production mix for June.

Problem 5-4 (CMA adapted, 6/80). Leastan Company manufactures a line of carpeting which includes a commercial carpet and a residential carpet. Two grades of fiber, heavy-duty and regular, are used in manufacturing both types of carpeting. The mix of the two grades of fiber differs in each type of carpeting, with the commercial grade using a greater amount of heavy-duty fiber.

Leastan will introduce a new line of carpeting in two months to replace the current line. The present fiber in stock will not be used in the new line. Management wants to exhaust the present stock of regular and heavy-duty fiber during the last month of production.

Data regarding the current line of commercial and residential carpeting are as follows:

	Commercial	Residential
Selling price per roll	$1,000	$800
Production specifications per roll of carpet:		
Heavy-duty fiber	80 lbs.	40 lbs.
Regular fiber	20 lbs.	40 lbs.
Direct labor hours	15 hrs.	15 hrs.
Standard cost per roll of carpet:		
Heavy-duty fiber ($3 per lb.)	$ 240	$120
Regular fiber ($2 per lb.)	40	80
Direct labor ($10 per DLH)	150	150
Variable manufacturing overhead (60% of direct labor cost)	90	90
Fixed manufacturing overhead (120% of direct labor cost)	180	180
Total standard cost per roll	$ 700	$620

Leastan has 42,000 pounds of heavy-duty fiber and 24,000 pounds of regular fiber in stock. All fiber not used in the manufacture of the present types of carpeting during the last month of production can be sold as scrap at $.25 a pound.

A maximum of 10,500 direct labor hours are available during the month. The labor force can work on either type of carpeting.

Sufficient demand exists for the present line of carpeting so that all quantities produced can be sold.

Required

(1) Calculate the number of rolls of commercial carpet and residential carpet Leastan Company must manufacture during the last month of production to completely exhaust the heavy-duty and regular fiber still in stock.
(2) Can Leastan Company manufacture these quantities of commercial and residential carpeting during the last month of production? Explain your answer.
(3) Formulate the objective and constraint functions, so that this problem can be solved by linear programming.

Problem 5-5. Frey Company manufactures and sells two products: a toddler bike (B) and a toy high chair (C). Linear programming is used to determine the best production and sales mix of bikes and chairs. This approach allows Frey to speculate on economic changes. For example, management is often interested in knowing how variations in selling prices, resource costs, resource availabilities, and marketing strategies would affect the company's performance.

The demand for bikes and chairs is relatively constant throughout the year. The following economic data pertain to the two products:

	Bike (B)	Chair (C)
Selling price	$12 per unit	$10 per unit
Variable cost	8	7
Contribution margin	$ 4 per unit	$ 3 per unit
Materials required:		
Wood	1 board foot	2 board feet
Plastic	2 pounds	1 pound
Direct labor required	2 hours	2 hours

Estimates of the resource quantities available in a nonvacation month during the year are:

Wood .... 10,000 board feet
Plastic .... 10,000 pounds
Direct labor .... 12,000 hours

During June, July, and August, the total direct labor hours available are reduced from 12,000 to 10,000 hours per month due to vacations. The algebraic formulation of the model for the nonvacation months is as follows:

Objective function: Maximize $Z = 4B + 3C$

Constraints: $B + 2C \le 10{,}000$ board feet
$2B + C \le 10{,}000$ pounds
$2B + 2C \le 12{,}000$ direct labor hours

The results of using the linear programming model indicate that Frey Company can maximize its contribution margin (and thus profits) for a nonvacation month by producing and selling 4,000 toddler bikes and 2,000 toy high chairs. This sales mix will yield a total contribution margin of $22,000 in a month.

Required

(1) Using the graphic method, calculate the best product mix and maximum total contribution when only 10,000 direct labor hours are available during a month.
(2) Using the solution from (1), determine the shadow price for direct labor hours.
(3) If the price of bikes remains constant, by how much must the price of chairs rise or fall to alter the optimal production mix in a vacation month?

Problem 5-6. Dana Smith would like to start a company which would produce automatic phone answering machines. Dana has never before run her own corporation, although she is an expert in electronics. She has projected fixed costs at $30,000 during the first quarter of operations. The machines will sell for $400 each. Variable costs total $125 per unit. Dana expects to sell 180 units during the first quarter, but is concerned with the impact that a number of factors could have on the quarterly profitability of the firm. She has developed the following scenarios:

(1) By leasing automated equipment, labor costs could be reduced by $55 per unit, while fixed costs would increase to $40,000.
(2) Dana could pursue an opposite course, substituting direct labor for equipment. Fixed costs would fall to $20,000, but variable costs would rise to $180 per unit.
(3) Because the manufacturing operation is just starting, inefficiency during the initial stages of production could increase variable costs per unit by 20%.
(4) Dana is uncertain about the level of fixed costs, and fears that actual fixed costs might be 25% higher than projected.
(5) Unit sales in the first quarter might fall 15% below expectations.
(6) Competition might force Dana to cut prices by 15% in order to sell 180 units.

(1) Calculate the firm's quarterly profit, break-even point, and margin of safety, based on Dana's original projections.

(2) For each of the scenarios, calculate the firm's profit, break-even point, and margin of safety.

(3) Assuming that a $5,000 decrease in profits or a 10 percentage point decrease in the margin of safety from the original estimates is considered significant, which scenario requires further investigation?

Problem 5-7. Bolango is a small, tropical island located in the Caribbean basin. The government of Bolango has commissioned the Bolango Utilities Board to build and operate a saltwater desalinization plant to provide fresh water to the island. The board is considering two types of plants. One type relies on pressurized kettles to boil and evaporate the sea water. Although technically advanced, the evaporators require large amounts of energy to heat and boil the sea water. The system's primary advantage is its compactness. Land for the site would have to be leased from private parties at significant cost. The other alternative is a sophisticated, solar-powered desalinization plant. Use of solar power greatly reduces the need for purchased energy, but the system's solar arrays require huge amounts of land, which must also be leased. The board already operates a pressurized water evaporator with an output of 10,000,000 gallons per year. The board has also studied the operation of a solar-powered plant on another island. Operational costs for the two plants are as follows:

	Pressurized Water	Solar Powered
Output	10,000,000 gals. per year	7,000,000 gals. per year
Heat, light, and power (variable)	$350,000	$112,000
Supervision (variable)	60,000	42,000
Maintenance (variable)	40,000	14,000

The board feels that these costs accurately represent the variable costs of the proposed plant, except that heat, light, and power rates are 25% higher on Bolango than on the island studied. The board has also projected the following fixed costs of both operations. These costs are expected to remain fixed for all proposed outputs.

	Pressurized Water	Solar Powered
Maintenance	$47,000	$ 48,000
Administration	75,000	72,000
Depreciation	68,000	113,000
Land lease	85,000	257,000

In preparing its proposals, the board has considered two alternative pricing strategies. One would price the water at $.08 per gallon. At this price, 15 million gallons are expected to be sold per year. Under a second proposal, by which the price of water would be reduced to $.06 per gallon, consumption is expected to rise by 25%. The standard deviation of demand for both outputs is estimated at 2,000,000 gallons.

(1) For each type of plant, calculate the plant's profit and the probability that the plant will operate at a loss for both of the pricing strategies.

(2) Assume that political considerations dictate a maximum price of $.06 per gallon of water. Which plant should be selected?

Problem 5-8. LTD Products Co. is considering producing electrical insulators for use on high-voltage electrical transmission lines. The Marketing Department, on the basis of interviews with utilities and construction companies, has developed the following probability distribution for sales. The probabilities are based on an analysis of potential legislation providing tax credits for utilities, projected energy costs, growth in industrial output, and construction of residential housing, all of which affect demand for electricity and/or the electric utility industry's ability to finance construction.

Sales	Probabilities
50,000 units	.1
80,000	.2
100,000	.4
120,000	.2
150,000	.1

The Production Department has projected the following costs of the insulator operation:

Materials	.$.53 per unit
Direct labor	.$.30 per unit
Variable overhead	.200% of direct labor cost
Fixed overhead	.$29,270
Selling costs (fixed)	.$ 7,600
Administration	.$ 9,870

The insulators will have a selling price of $2 per unit.

Required
(1) Calculate the expected level of insulator sales (in units) and the standard deviation of insulator sales.
(2) What is the probability that the operation generates a profit in its first year of operation?
(3) Assume that the Marketing Department had developed the following probability distribution:

Sales	Probabilities
50,000 units	0.10
80,000	0.10
100,000	0.25
120,000	0.35
150,000	0.20

(a) What is the expected sales volume?
(b) Assuming that all costs and revenue estimates are valid, what is the probability of generating a profit?
(c) How do these values compare with those in (2)?

Problem 5-9 (CMA adapted, 12/78). Jessica Company buys and resells a perishable product. All orders are made at the beginning of the month, since smaller, more frequent purchases considerably increase unit costs and often cannot be filled due to a manufacturer's stockout. Any units of product unsold at the end of the month are worthless and must be discarded. If an insufficient quantity is ordered, additional quantities are usually not available or are of poor quality.

Customer demand is distributed around four discrete volumes: 100,000, 120,000, 140,000, and 180,000 units per month. The firm can order any of these quantities at the standard price of $50,000 + $.50 per unit. The sales manager, on the basis of past sales data, estimates the following sales probabilities for the coming months: 10% for 100,000, 30% for 120,000, 40% for 140,000, and 20% for 180,000. All units sell for $1.25 each.

Required

(1) Calculate the expected volume of sales for the coming month.
(2) Prepare a payoff matrix summarizing the results of the various sales/order-size combinations. On the basis of the payoff matrix, how much should Jessica Company order?
(3) Calculate the expected value of perfect information for the firm.

Problem 5-10 (CMA adapted, 12/77). Stotz Brewery produces and sells nationally a popular premium beer and has enjoyed good profits for many years. In recent years, however, its sales volume has not grown with the general market. This lack of growth is due to the increasing popularity of light beer, a market that Stotz has not entered.

Stotz is now developing its own light beer and is considering potential marketing strategies. Introducing the new light beer nationally would require a large commitment of resources for a full nationwide promotion and distribution campaign. In addition, there is some risk in a nationwide introduction, because Stotz is a late entry into the light beer market. Stotz's advertising agency has helped assess the market risk and has convinced the Stotz management that the following strategies are the only reasonable alternatives to pursue:

- **Strategy 1:** Perform a test advertising and sales campaign in a limited number of states for a six-month period. Stotz would decide whether to introduce the light beer nationally on the basis of the results of the test campaign. If the test is a failure, under no circumstances would the new product be introduced.
- **Strategy 2:** Conduct a nationwide promotion campaign and make the new light beer available in all fifty states immediately, without conducting any test campaign. The nationwide promotion and distribution campaign would be allowed to run for a full two years before a decision would be made to continue the light beer nationally.

Stotz management believes that if Strategy 2 is selected, there is only a 50 percent chance of it being successful. The introduction of light beer nationally will be considered a success if $40 million of revenue is generated while $30 million of variable costs are being incurred during the two-year period in which the nationwide promotion and distribution campaign is in effect. If the two-year nationwide campaign is unsuccessful, revenues are expected to be $16 million and variable costs will be $12 million. Total fixed costs for the two-year period will amount to $6 million, regardless of the result. The cost of a test advertising campaign is estimated at $300,000.

The advertising agency consultants recognize that if Strategy 1 is selected, there is a 20% chance that an introduction would be a failure when the test indicates success. Also, the consultants recognize that there is a chance that the test results will indicate that Stotz should not conduct a nationwide promotion and distribution campaign, when, in fact, a nationwide campaign would be successful.

Required

(1) Prepare a payoff matrix summarizing the outcomes of the above strategies. Which alternative should Stotz select?
(2) Determine the expected value of perfect information for the firm.

Problem 5-11 (AICPA adapted, 5/69). Commercial Products Corporation, an audit client, requested your assistance in determining the potential loss on a binding purchase contract which will be in effect at the end of the corporation's fiscal year. The corporation produces a chemical compound which deteriorates and must be discarded if it is not sold by the end of the month during which it is produced.

The total variable cost of the manufactured compound is $25 per unit, and the compound is sold for $40 per unit. The compound can be purchased from a vertically integrated competitor at $40 per unit plus $5 freight per unit. It is estimated that failure to fill orders would result in the complete loss of 8 out of 10 customers placing orders for the compound.

The corporation has sold the compound for the past 30 months. Demand has been irregular and there is no sales trend. During this period, sales were as follows:

Units Sold per Month	Number of Months (in random sequence)
4,000	6
5,000	15
6,000	9

The cost of the primary ingredient used to manufacture the compound is $12 per unit of compound. Commercial Products has learned that there is a 60% chance that the supplier of this ingredient may be shut down by a strike, and has located an alternate supplier for the compound, but at a considerably higher cost per unit. A firm contract with either the current supplier or the alternate supplier must be signed now in order to ensure adequate supplies of the ingredient for next month's production. If Commercial Products contracts with the existing supplier and a strike occurs, the firm would have to buy finished units from its competitor to meet customer demand. The profit earned under each of the outcomes is estimated as follows:

	Monthly Profit
Ingredient purchased from current supplier	$65,500
Ingredient purchased from alternate supplier	35,000
Finished units purchased from competitor	(25,500)

Required

(1) Prepare a schedule of the probability of sales of 4,000, 5,000, or 6,000 units in any month.
(2) Construct a payoff table which describes the profit earned by the firm at each of the production levels (4,000, 5,000, 6,000 units per month) for all three alternative sales levels.

(3) Calculate the expected monthly profit at each level of production. What production level should the firm select?

(4) Assuming that a local marketing research firm has offered to provide Commercial Products with a sales forecasting computer package which would predict monthly sales with great accuracy, what is the most that Commercial Products should pay per month for the service if it offered complete accuracy (i.e., expected value of perfect information)?

(5) Calculate the expected monthly profit of each of the two alternatives—ordering from existing supplier or ordering from alternate supplier. Which alternative should the firm pursue?

Problem 5-12 (CMA adapted, 12/80). Jon Co. has just agreed to supply Arom Chemical Inc. with a substance critical to one of Arom's manufacturing processes. Due to the critical nature of this substance, Jon Co. has agreed to pay Arom $1,000 for any shipment that is not received by Arom on the day it is required.

Arom established a production schedule which enables it to notify Jon Co. of the necessary quantity 15 days in advance of the required date. Jon can produce the substance in 5 days. However, capacity is not always readily available, which means that Jon may not be able to produce the substance for several days. Therefore, there may be occasions when only one or two days are available to deliver the substance. When the substance is completed by Jon Co., the number of days remaining before Arom Chemical Inc. needs the substance will be known.

Jon Co. has undertaken a review of delivery reliability and costs of alternative shipping methods. The results are presented in the following table:

Shipping Methods	Costs per Shipment	Probabilities of Delivery					
		1 Day	2 Days	3 Days	4 Days	5 Days	6 Days
Motor freight	$100	—	—	.10	.20	.40	.30
Air freight	200	—	.30	.60	.10	—	—
Air express	400	.80	.20	—	—	—	—

Required

Prepare a payoff table which can be used by Jon Co.'s shipping clerk to decide which delivery alternative to select. Use the expected monetary value decision criteria and the following format for constructing the table:

Days Before Due Date	Shipping Methods	Shipment on Time		Shipment Late		Expected Values
		Probabilities	Costs	Probabilities	Costs	
10-6	Motor freight	100%	$100	0	$1,100	$100
	Air freight	100	200	0	1,200	200
	Air express	100	400	0	1,400	400

Problem 5-13. The Kansas City Monarchs, a major baseball team, are negotiating a one-year contract with their star hitter, Homer Whittman. The owner of the Monarchs, Harry Cauldwell, is a classical business manager with a firm belief in the motivating power of incentive pay schemes. To this end, he has proposed the following pay scheme to Homer:

Annual pay = [$400,000(Batting average − 0.150) + $6,000(Home runs − 15) + $2,000(Runs batted in − 25)] + $20,000

Homer, his accountant, and the team statistician developed the following probability distributions of Homer's likely performance:

Batting Averages	Probabilities	Home Runs	Probabilities	Runs Batted In	Probabilities
.230	.05	17	.10	25	.05
.260	.05	24	.20	30	.05
.280	.35	27	.45	40	.30
.320	.30	31	.20	50	.40
.340	.25	35	.05	70	.20

Harry Cauldwell prepared the following similar, but somewhat less optimistic, probability distribution:

Batting Averages	Probabilities	Home Runs	Probabilities	Runs Batted In	Probabilities
.190	.10	12	.10	15	.05
.230	.20	15	.10	20	.25
.270	.30	18	.40	30	.40
.300	.30	24	.25	40	.20
.340	.10	31	.15	60	.10

Required (1) Using both distributions, calculate the expected value of each variable. Then use the expected value of each variable to estimate Homer's pay under each set of assumptions.

(2) Assuming that both parties eventually agree to a fixed sum of $145,000 per year, regardless of performance, calculate Homer's and Harry's certainty equivalent ratios.

Six

Implementing Cost and Revenue Analysis

The purpose of this chapter is to make cost and revenue analysis a practical, usable tool for maximizing the profitability of the segments of a firm as well as the net income of the entire firm. The discussion will be based on the theory of profits in Chapter 1; i.e., only the entire firm has net income, and a segment can only provide a contribution to common costs. It will be assumed that a firm has studied its cost behavior and thus has the ability to predict the response of cost to changes in volume. The basic analytical tool to be used for decision making will be cost-volume-profit analysis.

CVP analysis, however, may not fortify the analyst to meet the ambiguities and realities of cost behavior in the normal business environment. The first issue that must be dealt with in implementing analyses is the lack of clear-cut behavior patterns for many costs, which means that the cost functions used may not materialize as planned. A second issue is that the analytic procedures followed so far have used historically recorded costs, while projections for decision purposes also require a consideration of opportunity costs. Finally, since it is highly unlikely that the cost system used for analytical purposes will comply with generally accepted external and tax accounting methods, it is necessary to understand and to be able to calculate the difference between direct- and full-costing income.

THE REALITY OF COST BEHAVIOR

Cost analysis employing industrial engineering and statistical methods may have an appearance of preciseness that may not materialize in practice. Costs that were analytically viewed as variable may not automatically adjust to volume, but may instead be somewhat unresponsive to sudden volume changes. Costs which were analyzed as fixed may increase or decrease, especially as volumes begin to depart significantly from past levels.

Variable Costs

Variable costs are quoted in a manner that suggests an ability to immediately adjust the consumption of materials, direct labor, and variable overhead in response to changes in output. Such adjustments may not be possible in practice, however. For example, a firm would not retain a skilled labor force for long if it dismissed workers early on any day that sufficient work was not available. Instead, decreases in the labor force are made only when there appears to be a significant, long-lasting shortage of work, since such adjustments may be costly. There are costs of separation, such as unemployment benefits, to consider. In addition, firms must allow for hiring and training costs involved in hiring replacements when workers who are laid off and then recalled have found employment elsewhere. Likewise, increases in the labor force are made only when there is expected to be a continuing need. To avoid the costs and inflexibilities of increasing the full-time labor force, productivity of the existing work force may be increased, overtime may be used, or part-time help may be hired.

While labor cost is the most obvious example of a variable cost that is slow to respond, materials costs, as well as variable overhead, may also be slow to respond. Materials may be used carelessly when a surplus exists, or they may be used very sparingly if a potential shortage exists.

The lack of immediate response of variable costs to changes in output does not lead to treating these costs as fixed. The problem of slow response must be recognized, however, so that management is aware that, in the very short run, costs may not adjust perfectly to output. The failure of costs to so adjust results in cost variances, which are discussed in a later chapter.

The slow response of costs partially explains the random deviation about the estimates, which must be accepted as part of the estimation process. While deviations about the estimate are inevitable, the statement of cost behavior is still valuable for assessing the impact on costs when substantial changes in volume occur.

One possible view of variable costs is shown in Illustration 6-1. The graph indicates that, over a substantial range of volume, variable costs will respond according to line AB. Due to the lack of flexibility of certain costs, AB can be viewed as made up of a series of functions, such as CD, which respond slowly to both increases and decreases in volume, and thus exhibit a lesser slope. Normally, decisions would be insensitive to the difference between the planned variable cost function, AB, and the true, shorter-run cost function, CD.

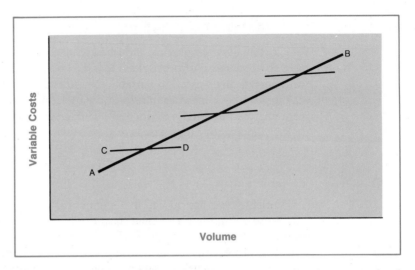

There is evidence that, for some firms, costs may be slow to respond only in a downward sense, and that the very short-run response to an increase in output is a higher variable cost than would result in the longer run as adjustments are made. The graph in Illustration 6-2 can be used to demonstrate such cost behavior in a firm where additional workers, who are untrained and less efficient, are added when volume increases. In this graph, point D is the current planned output. The function CDE is the more immediate response of cost to a change in output. Line DE is the short-run variable cost line. Line AB is the long-run variable cost function, which is possible after the additional workers become efficient and the variable costs decrease.

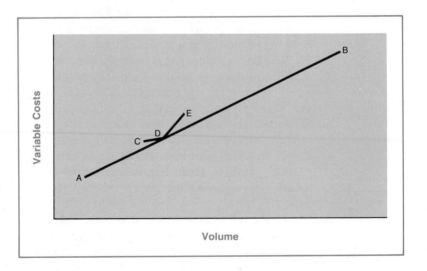

Step Costs

Cost estimates are also made more complicated by the existence of step costs. Step costs do not change proportionally with output, but are viewed as fixed costs which shift upward at specified volumes. The graph in Illustration 6-3 demonstrates the problems involved when step costs are explicitly considered. The graph is based on the following cost and revenue information for a firm that manufactures a single product:

Revenue: $5 per unit
Variable cost: $3 per unit
Step cost: Supervision cost of $1,000 per 2,000 units
Fixed cost: $4,000 at all outputs in the relevant range

Illustration 6-3
CVP Analysis with Step
Costs

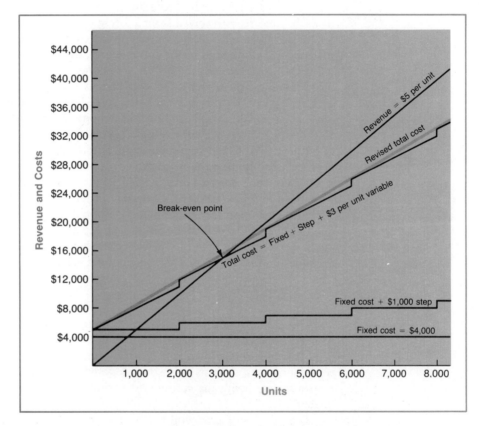

The total cost function includes the fixed cost of $4,000 and the first step cost of $1,000, plus the step cost of $1,000 which is added every 2,000 units. The break-even volume based on this cost function is 3,000 units, and since the firm will not produce less than 3,000 units, the initial required level of supervision is $2,000. If sales beyond 4,000 units are not envisioned when the cost of a unit is being stated, the step cost of $2,000 could be added to the fixed cost of $4,000, and the fixed cost total could be stated as $6,000. If sales up to 10,000 units are envisioned, steps could be specified in the budget, but that would encumber analyses, especially if there are several different step costs with different step-up volumes. A more expedient method is to treat the first step cost as fixed, and to treat increments in the step cost as if they were variable costs. In the example above, $.50 ($1,000 step cost ÷ 2,000 units) would be added to the variable cost.

To make sure that step costs are always adequately covered, the revised cost function would be stated as $5,000 fixed cost, which includes the first $1,000 step, plus $3.50 per unit. This revised cost function is the white line in Illustration 6-3. Management should be aware that the revised cost is overstated, except at each step.

The perceived overstatement of cost caused by the revised cost function may be beneficial, because it offers protection against fixed cost creep. Fixed cost creep is the tendency for fixed costs to edge upward as volume increases. For example, assume that the firm in the preceding example is currently selling 5,000 units at $5 each. An offer is received from a foreign buyer to sell another 1,200 units for $3.40 each, which would not impact on the current demand. If step costs are not specified and not added to the variable cost, the order would be accepted, since the $3.40 price exceeds the $3 variable cost. If the variable cost is increased to $3.50 per unit by treating the step cost as variable, the order would not be accepted. Each unit produced is being forced to carry $.50 of the step cost, and since the firm is currently selling 5,000 units, $2,500 is provided to cover the $2,000 of step costs. As sales increase beyond 5,000 units, $.50 per unit continues to be provided. When step costs increase to $3,000 at 6,000 units, enough has been included in the variable cost to pay for the step. Adding to the variable costs a provision for step costs protects against a creep up in fixed costs, which could wipe out the contribution of a marginal order.

Further support for the per unit allocation of step costs is offered by those who question the preciseness of the traditional step cost function. It has been suggested that a step cost may begin to increase long before the next step is reached.[1] For example, assume that a product cost budget is stated as follows:

$$\text{Total cost} = \$2,000 \text{ fixed cost} + \$2,000 \text{ step cost increments per each 4,000-unit level} + \$1.50 \text{ per unit}$$

The $2,000 step cost represents supervisor salaries. Before each step is reached, total costs may begin to creep up, because a lack of supervision causes productivity and quality to fall. The additional labor and spoilage costs that result would increase total costs above the budgeted cost. Also, there may be unrecorded costs associated with the customer dissatisfaction that results from the decline in quality.

The graph in Illustration 6-4 compares budgeted to total costs, where total costs include both recorded and unrecorded elements. The total cost line may be curvilinear to reflect increasing inefficiency.

The graph reflects the adjustment as a result of the step cost; i.e., the supervision cost is increased at the point at which the $2,000 increment is less costly than the added costs caused by lower productivity and poorer quality. If the total cost increases as suggested, the allocation of step costs on a per unit basis may result in a minor overstatement of the total cost. However, the per unit allocation of the step cost may be a reasonable proxy for the total cost.

The white line in Illustration 6-4 shows the revised budgeted cost, including a $.50 per unit allocation of supervision. If there are alternative combinations of

[1]Jerold L. Zimmerman, "The Costs and Benefits of Cost Allocations," *The Accounting Review*, July, 1979, pp. 504-520.

Illustration 6-4
Analysis of Step Costs

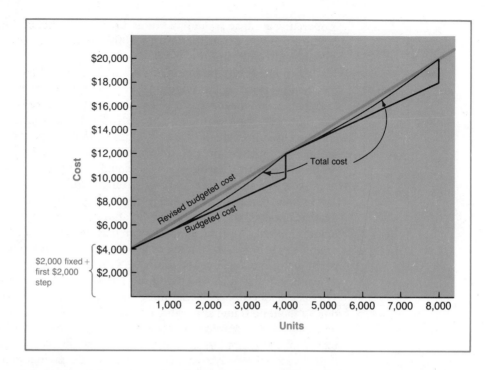

labor, materials, and overhead that may be used to build a product, this allocation procedure provides an added advantage. When a per unit allocation of a step cost results in a good approximation of the total cost, better input decisions may result if the step cost is viewed as variable, so that it may be considered in relevant cost and revenue analysis. Relevant costs and revenues are amounts that will be altered by the decision under consideration, and are thus the only amounts with which the decision maker should be concerned.

OPPORTUNITY COSTS

Chapter 1 defined the opportunity cost of an asset as its value in its best alternative use. This value, which usually differs from the asset's recorded value, is the relevant cost for decision making. Thus far, the assumption has been made that if the decision under consideration did not include the asset, the asset would not be used for any productive purpose by the firm, but would be sold or rented to another firm. Other alternatives may be possible, however. For example, the asset might be used within the firm, but for another purpose. In that case, the opportunity cost of the asset is the contribution it would earn in its alternative use.

When the use of an asset would require displacement of an existing use, the contribution of the displaced use is lost, and that contribution is an opportunity cost. For example, a new product being considered by a firm will produce an incremental contribution of $6,000 if only recorded costs are included in the analysis, and the contribution of the 100 hours of machine time used for the product is ignored. However, the opportunity cost of removing 100 hours of machine time from its existing use must be considered, assuming that the machine is operating at capacity, and that other products are being displaced. If these other products produce a contribution of $8,000, the new product would have a negative incremental contribution of $2,000.

When linear programming is used in situations where capacity is constrained, the shadow price is the additional contribution of one more unit of a scarce resource, which means that it is also the value of the resource time in its current use. Since the shadow price is automatically the opportunity cost, shadow prices are often used in evaluating new proposals. No proposal is considered unless it can produce a contribution per unit which at least covers the shadow price. If a proposal clears this hurdle and is accepted, it displaces some current uses of the resources, and its greater contribution increases the shadow price.

In some cases, the opportunity cost concept may have to be expanded to costs that have not yet been incurred. When the supply of labor, materials, or any other input is limited, the contribution which may be displaced must be considered. For example, a firm may be paying only $10 per hour for labor, but the contribution per hour in the current use could be $15. This higher value should be used in assessing any decision which will use labor.

Special decision analyses must consider which fixed costs can be adjusted during the time frame applicable to the analyses. This consideration is particularly important when contraction decisions might decrease the use of fixed costs. Examples would be dropping products or subcontracting current production processes. In such cases, the analyses depends, in part, on the savings generated by discontinuing current fixed costs. The analyst must be certain to include only savings which can be made to occur by the start of the planning period. In some cases, a firm may continue a product in the short run, since there is some contribution to fixed costs which can only be terminated in the longer run. If there is a short-run opportunity cost (caused by an alternative use) applicable to a long-run, historical-based accounting cost that cannot be terminated immediately, the opportunity cost should be included in the short-run analysis.

When expansion decisions are being considered, such as adding products or providing services which are currently purchased, there should also be a concern for the short-run/long-run fixed cost dichotomy. In the short run, there may be unutilized fixed costs that have no opportunity value. In essence, these costs are "free" for any decision utilizing them in the short run. The problem is that, in the longer run, there may be other uses for the fixed costs or opportunities to terminate these costs. Thus, the decision made now when the cost is free may commit a firm to a decision that, in a later period, cannot cover the longer-run value of the fixed cost. For example, a firm decides to save monthly rent of $2,000 by providing its own warehousing in unused "free" space, rather than using a public warehouse. Later, the firm has an opportunity to use the same space for production which would contribute $5,000 each month. It is then more profitable to return to a public warehouse, but if sufficient space is not available, the firm will sacrifice $3,000 of net contribution each month, because it is committed to its own storage.

TAX IMPACT

Decision analysis should conclude with the *net of tax* impact on the contribution of any decision. When the firm will have an overall net income, there will be an incremental tax expense. Any change in a firm's income, caused by the contribution of a specific decision, will change the tax expense of the firm. When a firm is not expected to have taxable income in the long run, and thus no opportunity to utilize a tax loss carryover, there is no tax consequence of decisions being analyzed. The tax impact of changes in contribution is illustrated in the following matrix:

	Contribution	
	+ $10,000 before tax	− $10,000 before tax
40% tax	$10,000 − $4,000 tax expense = $6,000	− $10,000 + $4,000 tax savings = − $6,000
No tax	+ $10,000	− $10,000

To illustrate the impact of taxes, an expansion situation and a contraction situation will be analyzed. In each case, the impact on only the next planning period will be considered. For any decisions affecting later periods, an interest factor must be used to adjust for the forgone opportunity to use funds alternatively. This problem will be addressed in Chapters 7 and 8, in which capital budgeting procedures apply the concept of the time value of money to relevant cost and revenue analysis.

Expansion Decision: Providing Own Printing Service

Description. Sell-All Inc. spends considerable amounts to print its mailers. This year, the printing bill from the outside printer is expected to be $110,000. It is forecast that the volume of printing will increase 20% each year, and that prices charged by outside printers will increase 10% per year. You have had conversations with a small print shop that is being displaced by a highway project. The owner is reluctant to sell the equipment, but will rent it to you for $25,000 per year. The print shop owner will also manage your print shop for a salary of $20,000. You would be interested in this arrangement as long as there is no loss next year (19X1) and savings of at least $15,000 in the second year (19X2). To analyze the project's impact on 19X1 and 19X2, you have secured the following estimates:

- $20,000 of 19X0's estimated printing bill was for artwork and special printing that your shop could not provide. The percentage of such work will hold constant in the future.
- Materials and supplies constituted 35% of billed costs in 19X0. Materials and supplies will remain at 35% of billed costs in 19X1 and 19X2.
- Fringe benefits for the print shop manager will be 25% of the salary. Should printing be disbanded, the manager will receive $2,000 termination pay.
- An assistant will be hired part-time at a salary of $8,000. Fringe benefits will add 15%.
- Normally, repairs should cost $4,000, but in each year there is a 30% chance of a major component replacement which would cost $3,000.
- Power costs are estimated at $2,500.
- Installation of the machinery costs $1,000 per move.
- Printing can be done in unused office space. Beginning in 19X2, office space will have to be rented for $700 per month to replace the space used.

- The corporate tax rate is 40%.
- Volume will increase 20% per year on a compounded basis.

Analysis. At anticipated volume in 19X1:

Cost saved, outside printing [($110,000 − $20,000) × (1.20 volume increase × 1.10 price increase)]		$118,800
Incremental costs:		
Materials and supplies ($118,800 billed costs × .35)	$41,580	
Print shop manager ($20,000 × 1.25)	25,000	
Assistant ($8,000 × 1.15)	9,200	
Equipment rental	25,000	
Repairs [$4,000 + (.3 × $3,000)]	4,900	
Power	2,500	
Install machinery	1,000	109,180
Added contribution before tax		$ 9,620
Less tax impact (.40 × $9,620)		3,848
Net added contribution		$ 5,772*

*Deduct $1,800 [.6 ($1,000 moving + $2,000 termination pay)], if print shop is discontinued after first year.

At anticipated volume in 19X2:

Cost saved [($118,800 billed costs in 19X1 × 1.20 volume increase × 1.10 price increase)]		$156,816
Incremental costs:		
Materials and supplies ($156,816 × .35)	$54,886	
Print shop manager	25,000	
Assistant	9,200	
Equipment rental	25,000	
Repairs	4,900	
Power	2,500	
Rent ($700 × 12)	8,400	129,886
Added contribution before tax		$ 26,930
Less tax impact (.40 × $26,930)		10,772
Net added contribution		$ 16,158

Conclusion. Print own materials. The short- and long-run contribution objective is met.

Contraction: Dropping a Sales Territory

A common contraction-type decision is the consideration of dropping a marginal sales segment. Typically, a marginal segment is one that operates at a loss when a full-allocation net income approach is used, or one whose contribution towards covering its own specific fixed costs is not adequate. In either case, the analysis that defines the segment as marginal will typically be based on recorded costs. However, a decision to drop the segment must, where appropriate, consider opportunity costs.

Description. The Midwest Sales District of Apex Corporation is a territory in which a variety of products are sold. Management is considering the possibility of dropping the Midwest District, and has collected the territory's data given in the analysis which follows. The question facing management is whether it makes economic sense to keep the territory in operation for another year.

The following income statement is based on a full-allocation net income projection. The net income approach does not include the tax savings generated by the loss, because it is common to allocate tax only to profitable segments. The notes to the statement disclose information that was found during an investigation of the relevant costs.

Net Income Approach

Sales	$1,200,000	Includes sales of inventory on hand at beginning of year. The inventory has a variable cost of $20,000 and a fixed cost of $15,000, and would have been sold for $50,000. A close-out sale would gross $25,000.
Cost of goods sold	820,000	Variable costs are 50% of sales. Some fixed capacity could be utilized to produce a $100,000 net contribution. No fixed production costs would be avoided.
Gross profit	$ 380,000	
Sales commissions	$ 60,000	5% of sales.
Advertising and promotion	50,000	$10,000 is already contracted for and could not be recouped.
Administrative and warehouse salaries	100,000	May be avoided if 3 months' termination pay is paid.
Rent	25,000	Last year of 3-year lease; space could be subleased for $15,000.
Equipment depreciation	20,000	Machinery has little economic value; best plan is to store it for future use.
Shipping	48,000	Averages 4% of sales.
Order processing	70,000	$50,000 of allocated home office salaries could be placed in other use. $20,000 of allocated computer time could be sold externally for a net contribution of $40,000.
Insurance and interest on inventory	35,000	Avoidable.
Supplies	20,000	Avoidable.
Other expenses	60,000	Allocated home office expense. After another year, a retiring manager receiving $25,000 would not be replaced if the segment were dropped.
Total expenses	$ 488,000	
Loss before tax	$ 108,000	
Provision for tax	-0-	Total corporate tax is allocated only to segments with income.
Net loss	$ 108,000	

Analysis. The following income statement includes the costs that are relevant to the decision to continue or discontinue the Midwest Sales District. The relevant cost approach indicates that this district will contribute $67,200, net of tax, if it is retained for another year. The transformation of the loss into a $67,200 contribution is the result of using variable costing instead of full costing, ignoring the allocated fixed costs, considering the opportunity costs, and properly considering the tax impact.

Relevant Cost Approach

Sales		$1,200,000	
Variable cost of goods sold	$600,000		50% of sales.
Sales commissions	60,000		
Shipping	48,000		
Total variable costs		708,000	
Contribution to fixed costs		$ 492,000	
Less contribution from sale of beginning inventory at close-out sale		5,000	
Net incremental contribution to fixed costs		$ 487,000	
Less fixed costs:			
Contribution from redeployment of fixed capacity	$100,000		
Advertising and promotion	40,000		Avoidable.
Administrative and warehouse	75,000		
Rent	15,000		Opportunity cost next period.
Order processing	90,000		$50,000 salaries plus $40,000 opportunity cost for computer time.
Insurance and interest on inventory	35,000		
Supplies	20,000		
Other expenses	-0-		No savings during next year.
Total fixed costs		375,000	
Short-run contribution before tax		$ 112,000	
Tax impact of contribution		44,800	40% corporate tax rate.
Net contribution		$ 67,200	

Conclusion. While continuation is warranted for at least another year, the long-run viability of the segment should be analyzed. If further analysis indicates that the segment will not make a contribution in the long run, plans should be made for its elimination after the current year.

The following factors should be considered in a long-run analysis:

- The sales level and the mix of sales may change.
- $10,000 of contracted advertising would be avoided.
- $25,000 of rent would be saved, which is $10,000 more than the $15,000 opportunity cost included in the short-run analysis.
- The $25,000 salary paid to a manager at the home office would be avoided.
- The $5,000 contribution from the close-out of inventory would not reoccur.
- The opportunity cost of production capacity and computer time would likely change.

DIRECT VERSUS FULL COSTING

Direct costing and full costing are alternative models for calculating the results of operations for a firm and for its segments. Direct costing is a natural companion to CVP analysis, since it focuses on cost behavior. Only variable production costs are inventoried; fixed production costs are treated as period costs. Full costing does not reflect cost behavior, but focuses on the functional classification of costs, primarily manufacturing versus nonmanufacturing costs. All production costs, whether fixed or variable, are unitized. Full costing, while generally not useful for decision making, is required for external and tax reporting purposes. Therefore, full costing and direct costing must be reconciled by considering the difference in the format of the income statements, and the difference in income caused by the beginning and ending inventories of manufactured units.

Format of Income Statements

The following income statement format reveals the basic difference between full- and direct-costing income statements:

Full Costing	Direct Costing

Revenue
− All manufacturing costs,
  variable and fixed (stated as
  cost of goods sold)
	Revenue
	− All variable costs, including the
	  variable manufacturing cost of units
	  sold and all variable nonmanufacturing
	  costs

Gross profit
− All nonmanufacturing costs,
  variable and fixed
	Contribution to fixed costs
	− All fixed costs, including manufacturing
	  and nonmanufacturing costs

Income before tax − Provision for tax	Income before tax − Provision for tax
Net income	Net income

Full costing separates costs by function, with manufacturing costs above the gross profit line and nonmanufacturing costs below. Direct costing separates costs according to their behavior, with variable costs above the contribution to fixed costs line and fixed costs below. As long as there are no beginning or ending inventories of manufactured goods, net income is the same for both approaches. To illustrate, the data and the full costing and direct costing income statements for a single-product firm are as follows:

Sales: 20,000 units at $15 per unit

Manufacturing costs: Variable costs, $8 per unit
                               Fixed costs, $40,000

Nonmanufacturing costs: Sales commissions, 5% of sales
                                   Variable distribution costs, $1 per unit sold
                                   Fixed administrative costs, $50,000

Tax rate: 40%

Full Costing Income Statement			Direct Costing Income Statement			
Sales (20,000 × $15)		$300,000	Sales (20,000 × $15)			$300,000
Less cost of goods sold			Less variable costs:			
[(20,000 × $8) + $40,000)]		200,000	Manufacturing costs			
			(20,000 × $8)	$160,000		
			Sales commissions			
			(5% × $300,000)	15,000		
			Distribution costs			
			(20,000 × $1)	20,000	195,000	
Gross profit		$100,000	Contribution to fixed costs			$105,000
Less nonmanufacturing costs:			Less fixed costs:			
Sales commissions			Manufacturing costs	$40,000		
(5% × $300,000)	$15,000		Administrative costs	50,000		
Distribution costs						
(20,000 × $1)	20,000					
Administrative costs	50,000	85,000				90,000
Income before tax		$15,000	Income before tax			$15,000
Provision for tax (40% × $15,000)		6,000	Provision for tax (40% × $15,000)			6,000
Net income		$ 9,000	Net income			$ 9,000

When applied to segments, the full costing approach usually attempts to calculate the net income of each segment, which implies that all costs have been allocated and the sum of the net incomes of the segments is the net income of the firm. Thus, the full costing approach applied to segments is synonymous with net income analysis.

When direct costing is applied to segments, only the segment's specific costs are deducted. The final amount calculated is not net income, but contribution to common costs. For analyzing segments, this approach is preferred.

Impact on Income Before Tax

As discussed in Chapter 2, direct costing expenses fixed manufacturing costs in the period in which they expire, while full costing converts the fixed manufacturing costs into an asset, as a part of inventory. This fixed cost does not expire until the unit is sold. If all units are sold by the end of the period, as shown in the previous example, there will be no difference between the direct costing and the full costing income. If all units are not sold by the end of the period, there will be a difference between the full costing and direct costing income. The impact of this difference is demonstrated in Illustration 6-5, in which the direct costing and full costing income statements are prepared for the first period of a firm's existence and the subsequent period, assuming a fifo inventory flow.

The net income at the end of the first year being $4,000 higher under full costing is directly traceable to the fact that full costing treats the fixed cost of the ending inventory, 2,000 units at $2 per unit, as an asset. This amount was expensed as a period cost under direct costing. In other words, $4,000 of fixed costs are withheld from the current period and are deferred until the period in which the units are sold.

In the subsequent period, the difference between the direct costing and full costing income is again attributable to the impact of the beginning and ending inventory fixed cost component. The following general formula explains the difference in incomes:

$$\text{Full costing income} = \text{Direct costing income} + EF_E - BF_B$$

where E is the units in the ending inventory, F_E is the fixed manufacturing cost per unit in the ending inventory, B is the beginning inventory units, and F_B is the fixed manufacturing cost per unit in the beginning inventory.

The formula is applied to Part B of Illustration 6-5, as follows:

$$
\begin{aligned}
\text{Full costing income} &= \$41,800 + \left(1,000 \times \frac{\$20,400}{12,000\,\text{units}}\right) - \left(2,000 \times \frac{\$20,000}{10,000\,\text{units}}\right) \\
&= \$41,800 + (1,000 \times \$1.70) - (2,000 \times \$2) \\
&= \$41,800 + \$1,700 - \$4,000 \\
&= \$39,500
\end{aligned}
$$

The general formula will work with any inventory method and with either actual or standard cost systems. When a standard cost system is in use and the standard fixed cost remains unchanged, F_E will equal F_B. The formula can also be expanded to cover any number of products.

The entire difference between direct costing and full costing income is caused by the treatment of fixed manufacturing costs. There is no complication caused by fixed nonmanufacturing costs, which are expensed as period costs under both approaches. For variable manufacturing costs, however, it is important to realize that when a budget is being prepared, units to be produced determine the expenditures for these costs during the period. The number of units sold determines the amount of variable manufacturing cost that will be expensed. In the case of variable nonmanufacturing costs, this distinction is not made, and expenditures equal the expense for the period.

Although taxes were not considered in Illustration 6-5, the calculation of taxes must be based on the full costing income. Tax allocation procedures are applied, however, so that the expense recorded corresponds with the reported income. If direct costing is used, the tax provision is based on direct costing income, and any difference between the tax paid and the tax expensed is recorded as a deferred charge or credit, depending on whether the tax expensed is greater than or less than the tax paid.

Under direct costing, income is a function of sales and is unaffected by the level of production, whereas full costing makes income a function of both sales and production levels. Under full costing, an increase in the level of inventory will tend to increase income, while a decrease in the inventory will tend to lower income. Full costing, therefore, offers management the opportunity to smooth income, which is the practice of eliminating financial peaks and valleys by moving income among periods. If management assumes that shareholders prefer a steadily increasing level of income rather than erratic growth, management may prefer to use full costing for external accounting, even though it is not used internally.

When full costing is used, the amount of fixed costs to be recouped can be increased or decreased by altering inventory levels, since the fixed costs to be covered during a period are not just those which are incurred in the period, as in direct costing. These fixed costs are determined as follows:

$$\text{Period fixed costs} + BF_B - EF_E$$

Illustration 6-5   Impact of Direct Costing and Full Costing on Income

PERIOD 1

Sales: 8,000 units at $12 per unit
Manufacturing costs: Variable costs, $60,000
Fixed costs, $20,000
Nonmanufacturing costs: Sales commissions, 5% of sales
Fixed administrative costs, $7,000

Costs Under Direct Costing

Variable Production
Costs, $60,000

Production Plant
New units, 10,000 × $6 ...... $60,000

10,000
units
at $6
each

Finished Goods
New units, 10,000 × $6 ...... $60,000
End. inv., 2,000 × $6 12,000
Variable cost of goods sold ... $48,000

8,000
units
sold
at $6
each

Variable cost of goods sold	$48,000
Fixed manufacturing costs	20,000
Sales commissions (5% × 8,000 × $12)	4,800
Fixed administrative costs	7,000
Total costs	$79,800

Costs Under Full Costing

Full Production
Costs, $80,000

Production Plant
New units, 10,000 × $8 ...... $80,000

10,000
units
at $8
each

Finished Goods
New units, 10,000 × $8 ...... $80,000
End. inv., 2,000 × $8 16,000
Cost of goods sold $64,000

8,000
units
sold
at $8
each

Cost of goods sold	$64,000
Sales commissions (5% × 8,000 × $12)	4,800
Fixed administrative costs................	7,000
Total costs	$75,800

Direct Costing Income Statement

Sales (8,000 × $12).....................		$96,000
Less variable costs:		
Variable cost of goods sold:		
Variable cost of goods		
manufactured $60,000		
Less ending inventory		
(2,000 × $6) 12,000	$48,000	
Sales commissions		
(5% × $96,000)	4,800	52,800
Contribution to fixed costs..		$43,200
Less fixed costs:		
Manufacturing costs	$20,000	
Administrative costs	7,000	27,000
Income before tax		$16,200

Full Costing Income Statement

Sales (8,000 × $12).....................		$96,000
Less cost of goods sold:		
Full cost of goods manufactured...	$80,000	
Less ending inventory (2,000 × $8) .	16,000	64,000
Gross profit		$32,000
Less nonmanufacturing costs:		
Sales commissions (5% × $96,000).	$ 4,800	
Administrative costs.............	7,000	11,800
Income before tax.................		$20,200

Illustration 6-5 cont.   Impact of Direct Costing and Full Costing on Income

PERIOD 2

Sales: 13,000 units at $12 per unit
Manufacturing costs: Variable costs, $72,000
Fixed costs, $20,000
Nonmanufacturing costs: Sales commissions, 5% of sales
Fixed administrative costs, $8,000

Costs Under Direct Costing

Variable Production
Costs, $72,000

Production Plant
New units, 12,000 × $6 ..... $72,000

12,000
units
at $6
each

Finished Goods

Beg. inv., 2,000 × $6	$12,000
New units, 12,000 × $6	72,000
End. inv., 1,000 × $6	(6,000)
Variable cost of goods sold...	$78,000

Units
sold:
13,000
at $6

Variable cost of goods sold	$ 78,000
Sales commissions (5% × 13,000 × $12) ...	7,800
Fixed manufacturing costs	20,000
Fixed administrative costs...............	8,000
Total costs...........................	$114,200

Costs Under Full Costing

Full Production
Costs, $92,400

Production Plant
New units, 12,000 × $7.70 ... $92,400

12,000
units
at $7.70
each

Finished Goods

Beg. inv., 2,000 × $8	$ 16,000
New units, 12,000 × $7.70 ..	92,400
End. inv., 1,000 × $7.70	(7,700)
Cost of goods sold	$100,700

Units
sold:
2,000
at $8,
11,000
at $7.70

Cost of goods sold	$100,700
Sales commissions (5% × 13,000 × $12) ...	7,800
Fixed administrative costs................	8,000
Total costs...........................	$116,500

Direct Costing Income Statement

Sales (13,000 × $12)....................			$156,000
Less variable costs:			
Variable cost of goods sold:			
Variable cost of goods			
manufactured	$72,000		
Beginning inventory			
(2,000 × $6)	12,000		
Less ending inventory			
(1,000 × $6)	(6,000)	$78,000	
Sales commissions			
(5% × $156,000)		7,800	85,800
Contribution to fixed costs..			$ 70,200
Less fixed costs:			
Manufacturing costs	$20,400		
Administrative costs	8,000	28,400	
Income before tax			$ 41,800

Full Costing Income Statement

Sales (13,000 × $12)....................			$156,000
Less cost of goods sold:			
Full cost of goods manufactured...	$92,400		
Beginning inventory (2,000 × $8)..	16,000		
Less ending inventory			
(1,000 × $7.70)................	(7,700)	100,700	
Gross profit			$ 55,300
Less nonmanufacturing costs:			
Sales commissions			
(5% × $156,000)	$ 7,800		
Administrative costs............	8,000	15,800	
Income before tax			$ 39,500

The formula on the bottom of page 193 can be used to incorporate the full costing impact of inventories on reported income into CVP analysis, as shown in the following example:

Revenue: $20 per unit
Costs: Variable costs, $12 per unit
   Fixed manufacturing costs, $16,000 allocated over
    anticipated production of 8,000 units
   Fixed nonmanufacturing costs of period, $30,000
Production data: Beginning inventory, 1,000 units at $13 ($11 variable, $2 fixed)
       Ending inventory, 2,000 units
       Fifo inventory method

Projected income for anticipated production of 8,000 units (7,000 units projected sales; 1,000 units added to inventory):

$$
\begin{aligned}
\text{Full cost profit} &= \text{Contribution* } - (\text{Period fixed costs} + BF_B - EF_E) \\
&= 1,000(\$20 - \$11) + 6,000(\$20 - \$12) - [\$46,000 + (1,000 \times \$2) - (2,000 \times \$2)] \\
&= \$9,000 + \$48,000 - \$44,000 \\
&= \$13,000
\end{aligned}
$$

---

 *1,000 units from beginning inventory at $11 variable cost; 6,000 units from current production at $12 variable cost.

Break-even point (any portion of the current fixed production cost of $16,000 not absorbed by output is charged to the period):

$$
\begin{aligned}
\text{Full cost profit} &= \text{Contribution* } - (\text{Period fixed costs} + BF_B - EF_E) \\
0 &= 1,000(\$20 - \$11) + x(\$20 - \$12) - [\$46,000 + (1,000 \times \$2) - (2,000 \times \$2)] \\
&= \$9,000 + \$8x - \$44,000 \\
\$8x &= \$35,000 \\
x &= 4,375 \text{ units from current production} \\
\text{Total break-even units} &= 4,375 \text{ units from current production} + 1,000 \text{ units from beginning inventory} \\
&= 5,375 \text{ units}
\end{aligned}
$$

---

*Contribution includes 1,000 units from beginning inventory plus x units from current production.

Although the previous comparisons of direct costing and full costing have considered only the impact of fixed costs on the finished goods inventories, there would also be an impact on the work in process inventories. This complication is easily handled by treating units in process, adjusted for their degree of completion, in a manner similar to finished goods inventories. The procedures for valuing work in process are discussed in Chapter 11.

The Full Costing Versus Direct Costing Controversy

The theoretical propriety of direct costing versus full costing has been argued for decades. The arguments have centered on the desirability of including a portion of the fixed cost in the value assigned to inventory. It is now generally agreed that fixed costs are period costs which expire with the passage of time, and as such, there is no reason to unitize them and include them in the value of a unit.

One could say that incurring variable costs this period saves making the same expenditure next period, and thus, having incurred the cost, an asset exists. On the other hand, incurring a fixed cost last period does not save making the same expenditure next period, and thus no asset exists. The incurrence of fixed costs this period may make available a contribution that would otherwise not be available next period, as in the following situations:[2]

1. Units produced in the past period make possible some sales that could not be made with next period's production, because:
   a. Sales will be made before the units could be produced; i.e., sales can only be made from beginning inventory.
   b. Demand next period will exceed the capacity to produce; thus, units in the inventory allow sales that could otherwise not be made.
2. Variable unit costs will increase in the next period, and having units in the inventory avoids the higher cost that would apply to replacement units.

The value of benefits in such situations may be hard to measure, and if measured, would not be dependable for external reporting, which requires a cost base for inventory value. It could be argued, however, that the allocated fixed cost per unit could serve as a reasonable substitute for this value, which could thereby justify full costing. Nevertheless, direct costing, with its direct link to CVP analysis, is becoming more and more important for internal analytical purposes.

[2]Charles T. Horngren and George H. Sorter, "Asset Recognition and Economic Attributes - The Relevant Costing Approach," *The Accounting Review,* July, 1962, pp. 391-399.

1. In the very short run, according to the CVP model, materials, direct labor, and variable overhead may not adjust perfectly to output. Why is this true?

2. What is a step cost, and why might managers treat a step cost as variable?

3. Is it true that, for decision-making purposes, the sales value or rental value of an asset is considered an opportunity cost of the project, but if the same asset is going to be used for another purpose within the firm, there is no opportunity cost? Explain.

4. What effect will limited inputs, such as labor supply or materials, have on an expansion decision?

5. In decision analysis, does consideration of the net of tax impact on contribution deviate from the concept that only the entire firm has net income, and therefore, tax expense?

6. What are the two basic statement formats for calculating the results of operations for a firm?

7. Briefly describe each of the methods referred to in Question 6.

8. Of the two methods referred to in Question 6, which is more useful for decision making? Why?

9. Under what circumstances will the two basic methods for calculating the results of operations produce the same net income? Different net incomes?

10. Referring to the two methods in Question 6, which method allows income smoothing, and how is it accomplished?

11. Using the full costing approach, how can inventories be incorporated into CVP analysis?

12. Is it true that, in comparing the two formats for reporting the results of operations, one need only be concerned with finished goods inventories? Explain.

13. Why are fixed and variable nonmanufacturing costs not a factor that cause a difference between the two methods of reporting operating results?

14. What argument can be given for including only the variable costs in inventory? Why doesn't this argument apply to fixed costs?

EXERCISES

Exercise 1. Red Barrel Brewers always experiences a significant increase in demand for its beer during the summer months. Traditionally, output and labor hours required increase by roughly 25% during the three-month summer vacation period. For nonsummer months, 6,400 direct labor hours per month is usual. In the past, the brewery has met its summer peak demand by working overtime hours, but the plant manager wonders if it might not be less expensive to hire more full-time workers. Overtime is charged at 150% of the normal rate of $8 per hour. New workers would receive the starting wage of $6 per hour. Because the new workers are untrained, the production manager estimates that the workers are only 70% efficient in the first month and 80% efficient in the second month. The number of workers hired would be based on 160 labor hours per worker per month and 100% efficiency, so some overtime would be worked in the first two months, even if more workers were hired. All workers participate in a company health plan, which has an estimated cost of $40 per month per employee.

(1) Determine the cost of each of the two alternatives over the 3-month summer period. Which alternative is less costly in the short run?
(2) What other issues should the plant manager consider before making a decision?
(3) Assuming that Red Barrel is meeting an overall increase in demand for its beer by working overtime, at what point (in overtime hours) does the increased overtime cost justify hiring a new full-time worker? (Assume that the new full-time worker is 100% efficient immediately.)

Exercise 2. Paul Peters is the manager for a plant producing electronic components. The plant is small and in a highly competitive industry that is subject to erratic swings in production over relatively short periods. The controller for the company is concerned about Paul's poor cost control over the past few months. On the basis of extensive statistical analysis, the controller had prepared the following budget:

Direct labor (2 hrs. @ $5 per hr.) . . . . $10 per unit
Materials . . . . $ 2 per unit
Overhead ($4 per DLH) . . . . $ 8 per unit
Fixed overhead . . . . $10,000 per month

Actual performance data for three recent months are as follows:

	May	June	July
Output	1,000 units	1,500 units	500 units
Direct labor	$9,250	$18,750	$ 6,250
Materials	1,740	3,150	1,000
Variable overhead	7,510	13,200	5,000
Fixed overhead	9,800	9,700	10,000

In explaining the erratic performance, Paul states: "Look, we are doing the best we can. Our volume increases by 50% in one month, and we have to cover almost all those hours with overtime. Not only do those hours cost more, but overtime workers are tired and less efficient, which means that our hours per unit figure increases. The more we push our work force, the higher our spoilage and defective rate, which increases materials costs. On top of all that, our indirect labor and materials costs face the same pressures, and utility rates skyrocket as our peak usage increases.

"On the downside, everything is just the opposite. We may have 10% of the work force idle at one time, but we can't very well lay them off for three weeks, can we?"

(1) Graph both budgeted and actual data on a graph, with units on the horizontal axis and total cost on the vertical axis.
(2) Evaluate Paul's performance for the three-month period. Are his explanations valid?

Exercise 3. Carswell Company produces precision components for electrical generation equipment. Each unit has a normal selling price of $275. Variable costs total

$200 per unit, while fixed costs have a base level of $40,000 per month. Carswell has found that a number of factors combine to increase fixed costs by $4,000 for every 500 additional units of output above 1,000 units per month. Volume commonly fluctuates between 1,000 and 3,000 units.

Carswell is currently operating below full capacity at 1,500 units per month. It has just received a special order from General Power Equipment Company for 600 units. Because of slack capacity, Carswell's plant manager agrees to ship the order at the offered price of $205 per unit, which covers all variable costs and provides a small contribution.

Several months later, while analyzing quarterly statements, Carswell's plant manager notices that the net income for the month in which the special order was received was $67,500, but it was $68,500 for a later month in which only 1,500 units were shipped.

(1) Provide calculations which confirm the two profit figures.
(2) How can Carswell avoid a reoccurence of this problem, while applying consistent accept/reject rules to special orders?

Exercise 4. Electra Printing Co. is considering eliminating its line of high-quality, 4-color advertising materials, and printing illustrated journals and periodicals instead. The press currently used for advertising materials is easily converted to printing periodicals, but the press would have to be moved into a larger building. The annual lease of this new building would cost $15,000, and the old building could be sublet for $12,000 per year.

The result of a detailed linear programming study indicated that press time had a shadow price of $250 per hour. Labor costs $12 per hour. The new printing operation has a projected revenue of $375,000, based on 1,250 press hours and 6,000 direct labor hours. Materials costs are estimated at $115,000 per year. All other costs would remain unchanged between the two alternatives. Should Electra replace its line of advertising materials with journals and periodicals?

Exercise 5. Southwestern Gas Company has just moved into a newly constructed, high-rise office building which it owns. Because of a depressed real estate market, vacancies in the building are high. It is expected that all available space could be leased in roughly 18 months at rentals averaging $15 per square foot per year. Southwestern has always maintained its own Payroll Department, but has received an offer from a medium-sized accounting firm to take over all payroll functions for a flat rate of $9,000 per month. The Payroll Department employs 4 workers, who are each paid $22,000 per year. These workers would be transferred to the Billings Department, which has lost 10 needed employees through retirement. The Payroll Department also consumes roughly 10% of the company's in-house computer capacity, forcing other departments to lease outside time at an annual cost of $5,000. The Payroll Department occupies a 1,500-square-foot office in the new building.

Determine the short-run and the long-run costs of maintaining the Payroll Department. Should Southwestern accept the offer from the outside firm?

Exercise 6. Phyllis Thorn, an accountant, has provided one of her clients, a wealthy doctor, with information about what she feels is an outstanding investment—an apartment complex. The investment is expected to have a life of ten years, after which it would be sold. A projected yearly income statement is as follows:

Rental income		$106,000
Administrative expense	$12,500	
Interest expense	32,600	
Maintenance expense	11,400	
Property taxes	7,500	
Depreciation	60,000	124,000
Income (loss)		$(18,000)

The doctor, who is in the 48% tax bracket, is astonished that the accountant would term a project with an $18,000 yearly loss as "outstanding investment."

Calculate the aftertax cash flow of the project. Any tax losses can be fully used to offset the doctor's other income.

Exercise 7. Redkin Co. produces and manufactures plumbing hardware and supplies which are distributed throughout the eastern half of the United States. The region is divided into three sales territories—Northeastern, Midwestern, and Southeastern. Each territory has its own production plant and is managed autonomously.

Corporate management is concerned with the profit performance of its Northeastern territory, and is considering dropping the territory and closing the idle plant. The territory's most recent income statement is as follows:

Sales			$1,300,000
Cost of goods sold			910,000
Gross profit			$ 390,000
Selling expenses:			
Salaries	$105,000		
Commissions (5% of sales)	65,000		
Warehousing (fixed)	60,000	$230,000	
Administrative cost		190,000	420,000
Income (loss)			$ (30,000)

To aid the analysis, the controller has gathered the following data regarding the cost of goods sold:

Materials		$205,000
Direct labor		68,000
Variable overhead		273,000
Fixed overhead:		
Plant supervision	$187,000	
Heat, light, and power	30,600	
Depreciation—equipment	47,000	
Allocated home office		
expenses	67,000	
Rent—building	32,400	364,000
Total		$910,000

If the sales territory were dropped, production equipment with a value of $279,000 would be transferred to the other production plants. This equipment would replace equipment which is leased by those operations at a cost of $175,000 per year.

Shutdown of the plant would require the payment of $120,000 in severance and termination pay. All production costs would be avoided, except that there would be no decrease in the total amount of allocated home office expenses. All selling costs would also be avoided. Administrative expenses, which primarily involve allocated expenses of the corporate planning department, could be reduced by 30% if the plant were closed.

Determine the impact on the firm in the first year from dropping the sales territory.

Exercise 8 (AICPA adapted, 5/76). The management of Picant Company uses the following costs for the one product it manufactures:

Materials (variable)	$30 per unit
Direct labor (variable)	$19 per unit
Overhead:	
Variable	$ 6 per unit
Fixed	$ 5 per unit
Selling, general, and administrative expenses:	
Variable	$ 4 per unit
Fixed	$28,000 per month

The units sell for $80 each. The fixed costs, which remain fixed within the relevant range of 4,000 to 16,000 units of production, are applied on the basis of a normal volume of 10,000 units. Production data for June, 19X6, are:

Beginning inventory	0
Production during June	10,000 units
Available for sale	10,000 units
Ending inventory	2,000
Units sold	8,000 units

Prepare income statements for June, using (a) full costing and (b) direct costing.

Exercise 9. Faber Manufacturing produces a single product, X-10, at its plant in the Midwest. As a small, privately held company, it does not make its financial statements public; nevertheless, its accountants conform to generally accepted principles in their reports. As part of an effort to introduce contribution analysis into the firm, Faber is considering the preparation of all of its statements on a direct costing basis. However, the company's president is unsure about how the change would affect net income. The company's accounting records show the following data:

	19X1	19X2	19X3
Beginning inventory	1,000 units	2,000 units	1,000 units
Production	5,000	5,000	4,000
Total available for sale	6,000 units	7,000 units	5,000 units
Sales	4,000	6,000	4,000
Ending inventory	2,000 units	1,000 units	1,000 units
Revenue	$12.00 per unit	$12.00 per unit	$13.00 per unit
Manufacturing costs:			
Variable	$ 5.00	$ 6.00	$ 5.50
Fixed	$ 4.00	$ 4.00	$ 4.00
Selling, general, and administrative expense (fixed)	$4,000 per year	$6,000 per year	$6,000 per year

The value of the 19X1 beginning inventory was $9,000 under full costing and $5,000 under direct costing.

Prepare income statements under (a) full costing and (b) direct costing for each of the three years.

Exercise 10 (AICPA adapted, 11/72). Jonesville Company manufactures capacitors used in radios, television sets, and rockets. Some orders are filled from inventory, while others are special orders made to customer specifications as to size, lead wires, voltage, and tolerance.

When manufacturing a custom order, Jonesville intentionally produces more capacitors than are ordered by the customer. These extra capacitors are carried at no value in the inventory, since all costs of the job are charged to cost of goods sold at the time that the order is shipped. The extras are kept (a) to replace any capacitors that may be returned as rejects, which currently constitute 20% of all units sold, and (b) to fill any subsequent orders from the customer for additional units of the same item. Since there is no market for the unused custom-manufactured capacitors, any that remain in inventory for two years are destroyed.

Jonesville warrants the replacement of defective capacitors returned by the purchaser. Often, three to six months elapse between delivery of the order and receipt of the defectives.

Jonesville predicts that its production capacity is adequate, so that no sales would be lost in future periods, even though it did not have the extras on hand to cover subsequent orders of custom-manufactured capacitors.

(1) What are the conceptual merits of Jonesville carrying the custom-manufactured extras held for replacement of defectives at (a) no value? (b) marginal or incremental cost? (c) full cost? Explain.

(2) What are the conceptual merits of Jonesville carrying the custom-manufactured extras held for subsequent sale at (a) no value? (b) marginal or incremental cost? (c) full cost? Explain.

PROBLEMS

Problem 6-1 (CMA adapted, 12/77). Valber Corporation manufactures and distributes toy dollhouses. Business has reached unprecedented levels over the past several months, causing production to jump by over 50%, as shown in the following table:

Month	Output
April	7,000 units
May	8,000
June	9,000
July	11,000
August	12,000
September	13,000

Standard costs are budgeted as follows:

Direct labor (1/2 hour at standard rate of $6 per hour): $3 per unit
Materials: $4 per unit
Variable overhead ($4 per direct labor hour): $2 per unit.
Fixed overhead: $40,000 per month

Due to the increase in output, the applicability of standard costs has been questioned and costs are being reanalyzed. It has been determined that the company's work force is such that only 4,000 direct labor hours are available at straight time. For outputs between 4,000 and 6,000 hours, overtime must be utilized. Overtime is paid at time and a half, but an additional cost of 5% of overtime wages is incurred, due to a slight decrease in efficiency. For all outputs above 6,000 hours, temporary help must be hired. These workers receive the standard hourly rate of $6 per hour, but require 25% more time than regular employees to produce a dollhouse. Materials costs also rise for all outputs above 12,000 units, due to a 25% increase in wastage and defective units.

Regardless of output, at least 3,500 direct labor hours must be paid because of the cyclical nature of the business. The fixed overhead budget includes $2,000 per month for the salary of each inspector. One inspector can handle 8,000 units per month. Management would like to treat this step cost as a variable cost by charging for the step in advance.

Required

Prepare a graph which compares total monthly production cost for various outputs between 6,000 and 13,000 units, using (a) the original budgeted cost estimates and (b) the revised budget estimates.

Problem 6-2 (CMA adapted, 6/72). Anchor Company manufactures several different styles of jewelry cases. During the coming quarter, management estimates that its plant will operate at only 80% of normal capacity, and is willing to consider special orders.

Anchor has received special order inquiries from two companies. The first is from JCP Inc., which would like to sell, under its own label, a case very similar to Anchor's Model 150. JCP is willing to pay $5.75 per case for an order of 15,000 cases. The standard cost for a Model 150 case is:

Materials	$2.50
Direct labor (1/2 hour @ $6 per hour)	3.00
Total overhead (.25 machine hours @ $4 per hour)	1.00
Total standard cost	$6.50

The normal markup on all jewelry cases is 50% of manufacturing cost. According to the specifications provided by JCP, less expensive materials could be substituted for the standard materials at a cost savings of $.25 per case. No shipping costs would be incurred.

The second order, submitted by Krage Co., was for 7,500 cases at $7.50 per case, which would be sold under the Krage brand. The Krage case is completely unlike any of Anchor's other cases. Estimated costs per unit are:

Materials	$3.25
Direct labor (1/2 hour @ $6 per hour)	3.00
Total overhead (.50 machine hours @ $4 per hour)	2.00
Total standard cost	$8.25

In addition to these standard costs, the order would require special design expenses of $1,000 and additional setup costs of $1,500. Anchor deals exclusively with one shipper, to whom it has paid $5,000 in retainer fees per year to ensure priority status for all its orders. Shipping costs for the Krage order are $.30 per unit.

Anchor allocates its overhead on the basis of normal production of 90,000 machine hours per year. The overhead budget for the current year is:

Fixed overhead:		
Supervisory salaries	$76,000	
Insurance	12,400	
Lease of production equipment	51,500	
Taxes	28,000	
Maintenance	37,200	
Other	10,900	$216,000
Variable overhead:		
Indirect materials	$36,000	
Indirect labor	49,500	
Heat, light, and power	58,500	144,000
Total overhead		$360,000

Required

Should Anchor accept either order? Support your answer, and show your calculations.

Problem 6-3 (AICPA adapted, 5/77). As a senior accountant for Arcadia Corporation, you have been asked by management to provide information which would help them make an important plant closure decision. Arcadia operates plants in three states, all of which produce the same product. Projected data for the coming year are as follows:

	Total	Texas	Montana	Maine
Sales (at $25 per unit)	$4,400,000	$2,200,000	$1,400,000	$800,000
Variable costs:				
Production	$1,416,000	$ 616,000	$ 448,000	$352,000
Selling	263,000	132,000	91,000	40,000
Fixed costs:				
Production	866,000	468,000	203,000	195,000
Administration	279,000	164,000	57,000	58,000
Selling	360,000	138,000	130,000	92,000
Allocated home office				
expenses	500,000	225,000	175,000	100,000
Income	$ 716,000	$ 457,000	$ 296,000	$(37,000)

Units sell for $25 each.

Due to the marginal results of the Maine factory, Arcadia is considering ceasing operations at that plant. Arcadia would like to continue serving its customers in the northeast, however, and has developed the following three proposals:

- **Alternative 1:** Maintain the status quo.
- **Alternative 2:** Close the Maine plant and enter into a long-term contract with a competitor who will service the area's customers. The competitor would pay Arcadia a royalty of $4 per unit, based on estimated sales of 30,000 units.
- **Alternative 3:** Close the Maine plant and move the factory's operations to the Montana plant. The Montana plant has 60,000 square feet of

production area which is currently being leased out as warehouse space for $2,000 per month. Utilizing this space for production would increase the Montana plant's fixed production costs by 30%, due to increased maintenance, power, and supervision requirements. The 30% increase does not include depreciation.

All of the Maine plant's sales would be transferred to the Montana plant, but variable costs at that plant would decrease by $1 per unit, due to economies of scale.

One half of the Maine plant's equipment, accounting for 75% of its current depreciation deduction, would be transferred to the Montana plant. The remaining equipment, which is obsolete and has no market value, would be abandoned, as would the building. A member of your staff has prepared the following summary of the depreciation expense:

	Texas	Montana	Maine
Equipment	$ 42,000	$125,000	$28,000
Building	84,000	135,000	17,000
	$126,000	$260,000	$45,000

Selling expenses would be greatly affected by the move. Variable selling expenses consist of a 3% commission paid on sales and a shipping charge whose unit cost varies from plant to plant. Because of the greater shipping distances involved, unit shipping costs for all units shipped to the northeast would be 250% of the Maine plant's current cost.

Fixed selling expenses, which consist of sales salaries and the annual lease cost of the trucks, are as follows:

	Texas	Montana	Maine
Salaries	$ 96,000	$ 86,000	$55,000
Truck lease	42,000	44,000	37,000
	$138,000	$130,000	$92,000

Each plant leases its delivery fleet. Because the trucks would have to be of a heavier, long-distance type, and because of a less competitive lease market, lease costs at the Montana plant would rise by $55,000 per year. The Maine salespeople would be transferred at the current pay level.

All variable production expenses at the Maine plant could be avoided by the payment of $45,000 in termination pay. Moving expenses and setup expenses, incurred only in the year of the move, would total $25,000. Allocated home office expenses would not change from their current level. The Montana plant would be given the Maine plant's home office expense allocation.

Required

To assist management in making the proper decision, calculate:
(1) The contribution of the Maine plant to common corporate costs (Alternative 1).
(2) The increase or decrease in total contribution resulting from subcontracting (Alternative 2).
(3) The increase or decrease in total contribution resulting from a move to Montana (Alternative 3).

Problem 6-4 (CMA adapted, 6/81). Ashley Co. manufactures and sells a household product marketed through direct mail and advertisements in home improvement magazines. The company uses a standard cost system in its manufacturing accounting. The standards, however, have not been reviewed in the past 18 months. The standard costs for a product are as follows:

```
Materials (.75 lbs. @ $1 per lb.) ........ $0.75
Direct labor (.30 hrs. @ $4 per hr.) ......  1.20
Overhead (.30 hrs. @ $4 per hr.) .......  2.10
Standard manufacturing cost per unit .... $4.05
```

The standard for overhead costs was based on the following budgeted costs, using a projected activity level of one million units (300,000 direct labor hours per year):

	Total	Unit Cost
Variable manufacturing overhead	$ 600,000	$0.60
Fixed manufacturing overhead	1,500,000	1.50
Total	$2,100,000	$2.10

The fixed overhead is expected to remain fixed at all production levels between 800,000 and 1,500,000 units per year.

During the current quarter, considered a normal quarter, Ashley incurred the following costs in producing 320,000 units:

Materials	$266,000	
Direct labor	452,000	
Variable overhead	211,000	
Fixed overhead	379,000	
Total manufacturing cost incurred		$1,308,000
Less standard cost of goods (320,000 × $4.05)		1,296,000
Unfavorable variance from standard cost		$ 12,000

Ashley, which is currently operating at well below capacity, has just received a special order from Action Hardware for 200,000 units at $4 each, FOB shipping point. No special selling or administrative costs would be created by the order.

Ashley's production manager feels that the order should not be shipped, since its price is below the standard cost of the units produced. The accounting department head has urged acceptance, however, contending that the fixed manufacturing overhead of $1.50 per unit is not a relevant cost in the decision.

As an outside accountant, you suggest that a thorough review of the standard costs is in order before any decision is made. The accounting department head responds that, in the most recent quarter, the production cost variance was less than 1% of actual cost, so that the standard costs must accurately reflect true production costs.

Required (1) Review the firm's cost control for the most recent quarter. Do the current standard costs reflect true production costs? Explain.
(2) Should the firm accept the special order? Determine your answer, using both standard costs and actual costs for the most recent quarter.

Problem 6-5 (CMA adapted, 6/78). The Scio division of Georgetown Inc. manufactures and sells four related product lines. Each product is produced at one or more of the three manufacturing plants of the division. The following product line profitability statement for the year ended December 31, 19X7, shows a loss for the baseball equipment line. A similar loss is projected for 19X8.

Product Line Profitability—19X7
(000s omitted)

	Football Equipment	Baseball Equipment	Hockey Equipment	Miscellaneous Sports Items	Total
Sales	$2,200	$1,000	$1,500	$500	$5,200
Cost of goods sold:					
Materials	$ 400	$ 175	$ 300	$ 90	$ 965
Labor and variable overhead	800	400	600	60	1,860
Fixed overhead	350	275	100	50	775
Total	$1,550	$ 850	$1,000	$200	$3,600
Gross profit	$ 650	$ 150	$ 500	$300	$1,600
Selling expenses:					
Variable	$ 440	$ 200	$ 300	$100	$1,040
Fixed	100	50	100	50	300
Corporate administration expenses	48	24	36	12	120
Total	$ 588	$ 274	$ 436	$162	$1,460
Contribution to corporation	$ 62	$ (124)	$ 64	$138	$ 140

The baseball equipment is manufactured in the Evanston plant. Some football equipment and all miscellaneous sports items also are processed through this plant. A few of the miscellaneous items are manufactured, and the remainder are purchased for resale. The items purchased for resale are recorded as materials in the records. A separate production line is used to manufacture each product line.

The following schedule presents the costs incurred at the Evanston plant in 19X7. Inventories at the end of the year were substantially identical to those at the beginning of the year.

Evanston Plant Costs—19X7
(000s omitted)

	Football Equipment	Baseball Equipment	Miscellaneous Sports Items	Total
Materials	$100	$175	$ 90	$ 365
Labor	$100	$200	$ 30	$ 330
Variable overhead:				
Supplies	$ 85	$ 60	$ 12	$ 157
Power	50	110	7	167
Other	15	30	11	56
Subtotal	$150	$200	$ 30	$ 380
Fixed overhead:				
Supervision	$ 25	$ 30	$ 21	$ 76
Depreciation	40	115	14	169
Plant rentals	35	105	10	150
Other	20	25	5	50
Subtotal	$120	$275	$ 50	$ 445
Total cost	$470	$850	$200	$1,520

Additional information about the fixed overhead is as follows:

- The supervision costs represents salary and benefit costs of the supervisors in charge of each product line.
- Depreciation cost for machinery and equipment is charged to the product line on which the machinery is used.
- The plant lease rentals are charged to the product lines on the basis of square feet occupied.
- Other fixed overhead costs are the costs of plant administration, which are allocated arbitrarily by management decision.

The management of Georgetown Inc. has requested a profitability study of the baseball equipment line to determine if the line should be discontinued. The marketing department of the Scio division and the Accounting Department at the plant have developed the following additional data to be used in the study:

- If the baseball equipment line is discontinued, the company will lose approximately 10 percent of its sales in each of the other lines.
- The equipment now used in the manufacture of baseball equipment is quite specialized. It has a salvage value of $105,000.
- The plant space now occupied by the baseball equipment line could be closed off from the rest of the plant and sublet for $175,000 per year.
- If the line is discontinued, the supervisor of the baseball equipment line will be released. In keeping with company policy, severance pay of $5,000 would be paid.

Required   (1) Determine the impact of discontinuing the baseball equipment line in (a) the first year and (b) in the second and subsequent years.

(2) Should Georgetown Inc. discontinue the baseball equipment line?

Problem 6-6. Waste Disposal Systems Inc. hauls both residential and commercial/industrial wastes between its customers and waste disposal sites. In addition to its normal trash-hauling activities, the company operates a hazardous waste disposal service as an autonomous division. The hazardous waste operation has not achieved its revenue objectives. In light of the high demand for the firm's trash-hauling service, management feels that the hazardous waste operation should be discontinued and its resources transferred to the more profitable trash-hauling operation. A projected income statement for the hazardous waste operation is as follows:

Revenues ($.62 per ton-mile × 1,050,000 ton-miles)			$651,000
Variable costs:			
Fuel ($.10 per mile × 175,000 miles driven)		$ 17,500	
Fixed costs:			
Drivers' wages (12 @ $22,000 per year)	$264,000		
Trucks—depreciation (12 @ $12,000 per year)	144,000		
Trailers—annual lease costs	60,000		
Maintenance expense	57,000		
Cleaning and washing of trailers	45,000		
Administration and management	49,000	619,000	636,500
Income before tax			$ 14,500
Income taxes (40%)			5,800
Net income			$ 8,700

The trash-hauling service is at or beyond capacity in a number of areas. Five drivers could be immediately utilized in the trash operation. Another two, although not really needed, would be kept on the payroll in anticipation of increased business in roughly one year. The remaining five would be terminated.

The trucks are not appropriate for use in the trash operation. Management is ready to accept an offer to sell 12 trucks to a freight forwarder for $18,500 each. Waste Disposal's management has found that, in the past, the accounting depreciation closely matches the actual decrease in the trucks' market values.

Ten specially designed trailers are leased for $6,000 each. The lease is cancelable, but a penalty of 15% of one year's lease payment would have to be paid (tax deductible).

Maintenance expense includes the cost of truck and trailer parts ($13,000) as well as the wages of two mechanics, each paid $22,000 per year. Both mechanics would be transferred to the trash-hauling operation, which has recently lost two mechanics due to retirement.

Each trailer must be cleaned and washed to remove hazardous chemical residues after each day's use. The cleaning and washing expense includes the wages of three part-time employees and materials costs, and could be fully eliminated if operations were discontinued.

Administration and management of the operation is shared with the trash-hauling service, as is the company's physical plant. A 25% share of the administrative and management expenses is allocated to the hazardous waste operation, but management feels that total costs could be reduced by only 20% if operations were halted. The building area used by the waste operation has no market value, but continuation of the service would force the trash-hauling operation to lease space at a cost of $2,000 per month.

Required

Determine whether Waste Disposal Systems should extend the waste disposal service. The company's other operations are profitable and can fully utilize all tax benefits generated by the waste operation. Ignore the tax effect of gains or losses on the sale of trucks.

Problem 6-7 (AICPA adapted, 5/70). Thrift Shops Inc. operates a chain of three food stores in a state which recently enacted legislation permitting municipalities to levy an income tax on corporations operating within their jurisdiction. The legislation establishes a uniform tax rate and regulations which provide that the tax is to be computed on income derived within the taxing municipality after a reasonable and consistent allocation of general overhead expenses. General overhead expenses which have not been allocated previously to individual stores include warehouse, general office, advertising, and delivery expenses.

Each of the municipalities in which Thrift Shops Inc. operates a store has levied the corporate income tax as provided by state legislation, and management is considering the following two plans for allocating general overhead expenses to the stores:

(1) Allocate all general overhead expenses on the basis of sales volume.
(2) First, allocate central office salaries and other central office expenses evenly to warehouse operations and to each store. Second, allocate the resulting warehouse operations expenses, warehouse depreciation, and

advertising to each store on the basis of sales volume. Third, allocate delivery expenses to each store on the basis of delivery miles multiplied by number of deliveries.

The operating results before general overhead and taxes for each store were as follows:

	Ashville	Burns	Clinton	Total
Net sales	$416,000	$353,600	$270,400	$1,040,000
Less cost of goods sold	215,700	183,300	140,200	539,200
Gross margin	$200,300	$170,300	$130,200	$ 500,800
Less local operating expenses:				
Fixed	$ 60,800	$ 48,750	$ 50,200	$ 159,750
Variable	54,700	64,220	27,448	146,368
Total	$115,550	$112,970	$ 77,648	$ 306,118
Income before general overhead and taxes	$ 84,800	$ 57,330	$ 52,552	$ 194,682

General overhead expenses for the year were as follows:

Warehousing and delivery expenses:		
Warehouse depreciation	$20,000	
Warehouse operations	30,000	
Delivery expenses	40,000	$ 90,000
Central office expenses:		
Advertising	$18,000	
Central office salaries	37,000	
Other central office expenses	28,000	83,000
Total general overhead		$173,000

One fifth of the warehouse space is used to house the central office, and depreciation on this space is included in other central office expenses. Warehouse operating expenses vary with the quantity of merchandise sold.

Delivery expenses vary with distance and number of deliveries. The distances from the warehouse to each store and the number of deliveries made for the year were as follows:

Store	Miles	Number of Deliveries
Ashville	120	140
Burns	200	64
Clinton	100	104

All advertising is prepared by the central office and is distributed in the areas in which stores are located.

As each store is opened, the fixed portion of central office salaries increases $7,000 and other central office expenses increase $2,500. The basic fixed central office salaries amount to $10,000, and the basic fixed other central office expenses amount to $12,000. The remainder of the central office salaries and the remainder of other central office expenses vary with sales.

Required (1) For each of the plans for allocating general overhead expenses, compute the income of each store that would be subject to the municipal levy on corporation income.

(2) Assume that management has decided to expand one of the three stores to increase sales by $50,000. The expansion will increase local fixed operating expenses by $7,500 and require ten additional deliveries from the warehouse. Determine which store management should select for expansion in order to maximize corporate profits.

Problem 6-8 (AICPA adapted, 5/69). Ruidoso Ski Lodge operates a ski shop, restaurant, and lodge during the 120-day ski season, from November 15 to March 15. The proprietor is considering changing operations and keeping the lodge open all year. Results of the operations for the year ended March 15, 19X9, were as follows:

	Ski Shop		Restaurant		Lodge		Total
	Amount	Percent	Amount	Percent	Amount	Percent	
Revenues	$ 189,000	100%	$ 280,000	100%	$756,000	100%	
Variable costs:							
Cost of goods sold	$ 103,950	55%	$ 168,000	60%	—	—	
Supplies	9,450	5	28,000	10	$ 52,920	7%	
Utilities	1,890	1	8,400	3	15,120	2	
Total	$(115,290)	61%	$(204,400)	73%	$(68,040)	9%	
Contribution margin	$ 73,710	39%	$ 75,600	27%	$687,960	91%	
Fixed costs:							
Salaries	$ 11,340	6%	$ 84,000	30%	$189,000	25%	
Insurance	5,670	3%	5,600	2%	22,680	3%	
Property taxes	—	—	—	—			
Depreciation	7,560	4%	—	—	37,800	5%	
Total	$ 24,570	13%	$ 89,600	32%	$249,480	33%	
Contribution to common							
costs	$ 49,140	26%	$ (14,000)	(5%)	$438,480	58%	$473,620
Common fixed costs							202,260
Income before taxes							$271,360

The lodge has 100 rooms, and the rate from November 15 to March 15 is $70 per day for one or two persons. The occupancy rate from November 15 to March 15 is 90 percent. Ski shop and restaurant sales vary in direct proportion to room occupancy.

For the ski shop and restaurant, the cost of goods sold, supplies, and utilities vary in direct proportion to sales. For the lodge, supplies and utilities vary in direct proportion to room occupancy.

Depreciation on specific equipment is charged to each operation. The full cost of restaurant equipment is completely depreciated, but could be sold for $1,200. Depreciation on the building, which houses the lodge, ski shop, and restaurant, is treated as a common cost. All depreciation is calculated using the straight-line method.

Insurance expenses relating only to specific operations, such as casualty and liability policies, are charged to each operation. All insurance expenses related to the entire building are treated as a common cost. Insurance policies are all annual policies.

Salaries are the minimum necessary to keep each operation open and are for the ski season only, except for the salary of a night guard, who is paid $5,400 per year.

The following alternatives are being considered for the future operation of Ruidoso Ski Lodge:

- The proprietor believes that during the ski season the restaurant should be closed, because "it does not have enough revenue to cover its out-of-pocket costs." It is estimated that lodge occupancy would drop to 80 percent of capacity if the restaurant were closed during the ski season. The space utilized by the restaurant would be used as a lounge for lodge guests.
- The proprietor is considering keeping the lodge open from March 15 to November 15. The ski shop would be converted into a gift shop if the lodge operated during this period, with conversion costs of $1,000 in March and $1,000 in November each year. It is estimated that revenues from the gift shop would be the same per room occupied as revenues from the ski shop, that variable costs would be in the same ratio to revenues, and that all other costs would be the same for the gift shop as for the ski shop. The occupancy rate of the lodge, at a room rate of $40 per day, is estimated at 50 percent during the period from March 15 to November 15, whether or not the restaurant is operated.

Required   (1) Prepare a projected income statement for the ski shop and lodge from November 15, 19X9, to March 15, 19X0, assuming that the restaurant is closed during this period and that all facilities are closed during the remainder of the year. (Ignore incomes taxes and use 30 days per month for computational purposes.)

(2) Assuming that all facilities will continue to be operated during the 4-month period from November 15 to March 15 of each year:
 (a) Prepare an analysis which indicates the projected marginal income or loss of operating the gift shop and lodge during the 8-month period from March 15 to November 15. (Ignore income taxes and use 30 days per month for computational purposes.)
 (b) Calculate the minimum rate that must be charged in order to cover the increased costs associated with staying open in the summer, assuming also that neither the restaurant nor the gift shop operate at this time.

Problem 6-9 (AICPA adapted, 11/74). Nubo Manufacturing Inc. is presently operating at 50% of practical capacity, producing annually about 50,000 units of a patented electronic component. Nubo recently received an offer from a company in Yokohama, Japan, to purchase 30,000 components at $6 per unit, FOB Nubo's plant. Nubo has not previously sold components in Japan. Budgeted production costs for 50,000 and 80,000 units of output are as follows:

	50,000 units	80,000 units
Materials	$ 75,000	$120,000
Direct labor	75,000	120,000
Factory overhead	200,000	260,000
Total cost	$350,000	$500,000
Cost per unit	$7.00	$6.25

The sales manager thinks that the order should be accepted, even if it results in a loss of $1 per unit, because sales may build up future markets. The production manager does not wish to have the order accepted, primarily because the order would show a loss of $.25 per unit when computed on the new average unit cost. The treasurer has made a quick computation, indicating that accepting the order will actually increase gross margin.

Required (1) Explain what apparently caused the drop in cost from $7 per unit to $6.25 per unit when budgeted production increased from 50,000 to 80,000 units. Show supporting computations.

(2) (a) Explain whether the production manager, the treasurer, or both are analyzing the problem correctly.

(b) Explain why the conclusions of the production manager and the treasurer differ.

(3) Explain why each of the following may affect the decision to accept or reject the special order:

(a) The likelihood of repeat special sales and/or all sales to be made at $6 per unit.

(b) The sales are made to customers operating in two separate, isolated markets.

(c) The sales are made to customers competing in the same market.

Problem 6-10. Fulton Casteel Inc. specializes in producing a medium-sized, high-strength casting which is used in many types of earth-moving equipment. The company reports its earnings, using full costing, although internal reports are primarily direct costing statements. Summaries of Fulton's production operations for the year just ended (19X4) are as follows:

Beginning inventory (finished goods)	5,000 units
Production during year	50,000
Available for sale	55,000 units
Sales	47,000
Ending inventory (finished goods)	8,000 units

There were no beginning or ending work in process inventories. Fulton uses the fifo method to cost its inventories. This year's beginning inventory was valued using the following costs:

Materials	$8 per unit
Direct labor	7
Variable overhead	7
Fixed overhead	4

During the year, Fulton experienced slight increases in some costs. Costs incurred for the year just ended are:

Direct labor (40,000 hours at $8.75 per hour)	$350,000
Materials	500,000
Variable overhead	420,000
Fixed overhead	205,000
Selling expenses:	
Variable	38,000
Fixed	138,000
General and administrative expenses (fixed)	125,000
Total	$1,776,000

All units sell for $40 each.

Required (1) Prepare income statements for 19X4, using direct costing and full costing.
(2) Reconcile the two income figures calculated in (1), using the formula approach.

Problem 6-11. Haverford Mills Inc. processes lumber stock into a variety of decorative posts and beams, which are then sold primarily to furniture manufacturers. All of the different styles produced incur basically the same production costs.

In reviewing the company's activities for the past year, Haverford's president would like to determine the impact on net income from changing the firm's inventory system from the current lifo method to either fifo, weighted average, or standard cost. The company had a very successful year, selling 57,000 units and producing 51,000 units. The value of the firm's beginning inventory, calculated using the inventory methods under consideration, is as follows:

Method	Beginning Inventory (9,000 units)
Lifo	$17,370
Fifo	18,000
Weighted average	17,820
Standard cost	18,900

Although the firm does not currently use standard costs as the basis for its overall production costing system, standards are developed for cost control and product decision purposes. The standard cost for the past year for a unit of product was:

Direct labor	$0.95
Materials	0.38
Variable overhead	0.57
Fixed overhead*	0.25
	$2.15

*Based on a normal yearly production of 50,000 units.

Actual costs incurred during the year were:

Direct labor	$43,350
Materials	18,870
Variable overhead	30,600
Fixed overhead	11,730
Total	$104,550

Under standard costing, any variance between the standard cost of goods produced and the actual cost is allocated to Cost of Goods Sold. All units have an average selling price of $2.75. There were no beginning or ending work in process inventories.

Required (1) Calculate the firm's gross profit for the current year under each of the four alternative inventory valuation methods. Haverford uses full costing for all its financial reports.
(2) Calculate the firm's gross profit under each of the four inventory valuation methods, assuming that sales were only 45,000 units, but that production remained unchanged at 51,000 units.

Problem 6-12 (CMA adapted, 6/78). Pralina Products is a regional firm which has three major product lines: cereals, breakfast bars, and dog food. Each product is produced at a separate plant with its own plant management. Production data for the coming year are as follows (in thousands of pounds):

	Cereals	Breakfast Bars	Dog Food	Total
Beginning inventory	100 lbs.	0	50 lbs.	150 lbs.
Production	2,500	625 lbs.	825	3,950
Sales	(2,000)	(500)	(500)	(3,000)
Ending inventory	600 lbs.	125 lbs.	375 lbs.	1,100 lbs.

Pralina expects to incur the following costs in the coming year:

	Cereals (2,500 lbs.)	Breakfast Bars (625 lbs.)	Dog Food (825 lbs.)
Production costs:			
Direct labor	$112.50	$ 50.00	$ 33.00
Materials	412.50	200.00	165.00
Variable overhead	37.50	15.00	16.50
Fixed overhead	112.50	75.00	90.75
Total production cost	$675.00	$340.00	$305.25
Nonproduction costs:			
Selling expenses:			
Advertising	$ 50.00	$ 30.00	$ 20.00
Commissions	50.00	40.00	20.00
Salaries and benefits	30.00	20.00	10.00
General and administrative expenses:			
Salaries and benefits	60.00	25.00	15.00
Other (fixed)	25.00	10.00	10.00
Total nonproduction cost	$215.00	$125.00	$ 75.00
Total cost	$890.00	$465.00	$380.25

Pralina uses the fifo inventory method to value its ending inventories. This year's beginning inventory had exactly the same variable cost as the projected units, but had the following somewhat different fixed cost components:

Beginning Inventory	Fixed Overhead
Cereals	$.400 per pound
Dog Food	.105 per pound

Cereal sells for $.50 per pound, breakfast bars for $.80 per pound, and dog food for $.40 per pound.

The company has been unable to determine any causal relationship between advertising and the level of sales. However, because management feels that advertising is necessary, an annual advertising program is implemented for each product line.

Sales commissions are paid to the sales force at the rate of 5% on the cereals and 10% on breakfast bars and dog food.

Sales and general and administrative personnel devote time and effort to all product lines. Their salaries and wages are allocated on the basis of management's estimates of time spent on each product.

Required

(1) Calculate the variable cost ratio for the individual products and for the firm.

(2) Calculate the dollar level of sales necessary to earn a full costing profit of $250,000, given the current sales mix.

Problem 6-13 (CMA adapted, 12/79). The vice president of sales of Huber Corporation has received the following income statement for November, 19X9. The statement has been prepared on the direct costing basis, which the firm has just adopted for internal reporting purposes.

Huber Corporation
Income Statement
For November, 19X9
(000s omitted)

Sales		$2,400
Less variable costs		1,200
Contribution margin		$1,200
Less: Fixed manufacturing costs	$580	
Fixed selling and admin. costs	400	980
Income before taxes		$ 220

The controller attached the following notes to the statement:

· The unit sales price for November averaged $24.
· Production for November was 45,000 units in excess of sales.
· The inventory at November 30 consisted of 80,000 units.
· Production costs in October were substantially the same as those incurred in November.
· Huber values its inventory using fifo.

The vice president of sales is not comfortable with the direct costing basis and wonders what income would be under the full costing basis.

Required

(1) Present the November income statement on a full costing basis.

(2) Reconcile the difference between the direct costing and full costing income figures.

(3) Explain the features which should make direct costing attractive to the vice president of sales.

Seven

Basics of Capital Budgeting

$\mathbf{M}$any business decisions require a significant current investment and produce monetary benefits over several future periods. Evaluation techniques have been developed to measure the financial attractiveness of these multiperiod capital projects. The most commonly accepted methods consider the time value of money, using an interest factor to equate future cash flows to a value today.[1] For example, if a project will return $10,000 in one year and alternative investments will earn 12% per year, 12% interest would be netted out of the return in order to reduce the investment to a value today of $8,929 ($10,000 ÷ 1.12). The adjustment for interest allows flows due at future time periods to be equated with an investment made today.

This chapter describes and illustrates two evaluation techniques that explicitly consider the time value of money: the net present value method and the internal rate of return method. The chapter also describes and illustrates two techniques which ignore the time value of money but are useful in evaluating projects: the payback method and the accounting rate of return method. The tax considerations that apply to capital budgeting, regardless of the evaluation techniques used, are also discussed.

Although the analyses in the chapter are based on annualized cash flows, Appendix 7A at the end of the chapter focuses on the evaluation of projects in which the cash flows are quarterly or monthly. Special issues in capital budgeting

---

[1]Appendix 7B at the end of the chapter reviews basic present value techniques. Present value tables, identified as Table 1 and Table 2, are provided in the appendix at the end of the text.

are considered in Chapter 8. These issues include how to choose among alternative projects, the impact of inflation on project evaluation, and the financial merits of leasing rather than owning long-lived assets.

PROJECT EVALUATION AND THE TIME VALUE OF MONEY

Evaluation techniques which consider the time value of money are based on a comparison of a cash outlay at the inception of a project and the cash flows to be generated in the future. Projects are chosen primarily on the basis of their cash flows, rather than on their effect on accrual accounting measurements of net income. Accrual accounting is used only to report a project's impact on external financial statements. For example, a $10,000 asset might be purchased because it produces a cash flow of $3,950 per year for 5 years and yields a 28% internal rate of return. Using accrual accounting with straight-line depreciation, the project would produce net income of $1,950 per year ($3,950 − $2,000 depreciation).

Before a project can be evaluated, a firm must determine its cutoff rate, which is the minimum acceptable rate that the project must earn to be considered. Some firms use as a cutoff rate the opportunity cost of funds, which is the rate of return that could be earned on alternative investments. The most traditional cutoff rate, however, is the firm's overall cost of capital. The computation of a firm's cost of capital is discussed in a subsequent section of this chapter.

A firm may be tempted to use as a cutoff rate the cost of funds borrowed for a specific project. In the long run, however, the use of this rate is not desirable. A return higher than the cost of borrowed funds is necessary to provide a return to equity investors and to provide a contribution to common costs not specific to any project. Using the borrowing rate might also suggest that all projects should be financed entirely by new debt. As a result, the firm's capital structure may not be optimal, and an overly expensive cost of capital could make the firm less profitable in the long run as well as cause rejection of projects whose cash flows were subjected to such a high cutoff rate.

Net Present Value Method

The net present value technique for evaluating capital projects factors interest out of future payments, using the cutoff rate. To illustrate, assume that a firm is considering a project, A, that would cost $16,761 and would produce cash flows of $5,000 at the end of each of the next 5 years. If the cutoff rate is 10%, the present value (PV) of the project would be determined as follows:

$$
\begin{aligned}
\text{Present value} &= \text{Cash flow} \times \text{Table 2 factor (10\% for 5 years)} \\
&= \$5,000 \times 3.7908 \\
&= \$18,954
\end{aligned}
$$

The present value of $18,954 is the value of future cash flows reduced for the 10% annual compounded interest factor. The present value is compared with the cost of the project in order to determine the net present value (NPV), as follows:

$$
\begin{aligned}
\text{Net present value} &= \text{Present value} - \text{Cost} \\
&= \$18,954 - \$16,761 \\
&= \$2,193
\end{aligned}
$$

Since the net present value exceeds the cost in this example, the profitability of the project is greater than 10%. Although this project clearly meets management's criteria, a **present value index (PVI)** for the project should also be calculated as follows:

$$\text{Present value index} = \frac{\text{Present value}}{\text{Project cost}}$$

The present value index states the dollars of present value per dollar of original investment. The PVI is useful for comparing investments of differing magnitudes, as shown in the following example, which compares Project A with Project B:

Projects	Costs	Present Values	Net Present Values	Present Value Indexes
A	$16,761	$18,954	$2,193	$\frac{\$18,954}{\$16,761} = 1.13$
B	50,000	55,000	5,000	$\frac{\$55,000}{\$50,000} = 1.10$

The greater net present value of Project B would indicate that B is a more profitable project than A. The present value index for B, however, is smaller than for A, which indicates that B is less profitable per dollar of original investment. When a company's dollars for investment are limited, as discussed in Chapter 8, the present value index is therefore a means of ranking alternative investment opportunities.

Internal Rate of Return Method

The **internal rate of return (IRR)** is the interest rate which equates the future cash flows of a project with its initial cost. It is the rate which, if applied to the project, would result in zero net present value.

In the previous example, the positive net present value of Project A indicated that A would earn in excess of the 10% cutoff rate, but did not indicate what that rate would be. To determine the internal rate of return, the present value formula can be used, as follows:

$$\text{Present value} = \text{Cash flow} \times \text{Table 2 factor (for 5 years)}$$
$$\$16,761 = \$5,000 \times \text{Table 2 factor (for 5 years)}$$
$$3.3522 = \text{Table 2 factor (for 5 years)}$$

Table 2 indicates that a 5-year factor of 3.3522 is equivalent to a rate of 15%. Thus, 15% is the internal rate of return which equates the $5,000 annual cash flow to the $16,761 cost of the investment.

In this example, Table 2 contained the exact factor for determining the internal rate of return. When the table does not contain the exact factor, it will be necessary to interpolate between the rates available in the table.

Comparing the Methods

When a single project is being analyzed, the decision should be the same, whether the net present value method or the internal rate of return method is used.

If the cutoff rate is exceeded, the net present value will be positive, and the internal rate of return will exceed the cutoff rate. The method used will therefore depend on the convenience of the method and management's preference. Generally, the net present value method is more convenient than the internal rate of return method, especially when the cash flows are uneven over the life of the project. When the net present value method is used and the cash flows are uneven, the cash flows are discounted at one specified cutoff rate. When the internal rate of return method is used and the cash flows are uneven, repeated trial and error calculations are required until the rate of return is found. This inconvenience in the application of the two methods is shown in Illustration 7-1.

Illustration 7-1
Comparison of Net
Present Value and
Internal Rate of Return
Methods—Uneven Cash
Flows

Project cost: $20,350
Cash flows at end of period 1: $ 4,000
2: 5,000
3: 8,000
4: 10,000
Cutoff rate: 6%

Net Present Value Method

Periods	Cash Flows	Present Value Factors, 6% (from Table 1)	Present Values
1	$ 4,000	.9434	$ 3,773.60
2	5,000	.8900	4,450.00
3	8,000	.8396	6,716.80
4	10,000	.7921	7,921.00
Total present value			$22,861.40
Less project cost			20,350.00
Net present value			$ 2,511.40

Present value index: $\dfrac{\$22,861.40}{\$20,350.00} = 1.12$

Internal Rate of Return Method

Step 1: Pick the first test rate. The net present value method used 6%, and the present value exceeded the cost. Thus, a rate higher than 6% is needed in order to lower the present value to an amount equal to cost. If the test rate produces a present value higher than cost, a higher rate should be used to lower the present value.

Step 2: Try 10%, but allow space for applying other test rates.

Periods	Cash Flows	Present Value Factors at 10%	Present Values at 10%	Present Value Factors at 11%	Present Values at 11%
1	$ 4,000	.9091	$ 3,636.40	.9009	$ 3,603.60
2	5,000	.8264	4,132.00	.8116	4,058.00
3	8,000	.7513	6,010.40	.7312	5,849.60
4	10,000	.6830	6,830.00	.6587	6,587.00
			$20,608.80		$20,098.20

The 10% rate is still too low, since the present value exceeds the $20,350 cost. The higher rate of 11% is too high, since the present value is less than the $20,350 cost. Thus, the internal rate of return is between 10% and 11%.

Step 3: Interpolate to find the internal rate of return.

$\dfrac{\text{PV at 10\% } - \text{ Cost of project}}{\text{PV at 10\% } - \text{ PV at 11\%}} \times (11\% - 10\%) = \dfrac{\$20,608.80 - \$20,350.00}{\$20,608.80 - \$20,098.20} \times 1\% = .506\%$

Internal rate of return: 10% + .506% = 10.506%

(If computed mathematically, the rate is actually 10.5%. The difference is the result of applying interpolation to a non-linear function.)

Management often views the net present value method as being somewhat abstract, since it does not clearly determine the rate of return actually earned. Although textbooks and professional exams tend to use the net present value method because of its relatively simple calculations, the internal rate of return method is being used more frequently in practice, since it can be readily handled with a programmable calculator or a microcomputer. Therefore, the examples in this textbook will provide the internal rate of return, so that those who desire to perform the computations may verify their answers.

The Impact of Taxation on Cash Flows and the Cutoff Rate

Projects which increase the cash flow of a firm will also tend to increase the firm's liability for income taxes. Consequently, the additional tax is a relevant cash flow which should be considered in the analysis. Moreover, the tax impact is complicated by the fact that the additional tax is caused by the annual increase in the accrual basis income rather than simply the increase in cash flows. The difference between the taxable income and the cash flow is caused by depreciation. Although depreciation is not a direct cash outflow, it is deducted in determining taxable income, and thereby affects the cash flow through its impact on the tax liability.

The cash flows net of tax may be computed by using one of three methods. These methods, which are applied in Illustration 7-2, are described as follows:

1. Cash flow approach: The additional tax is subtracted as a cash flow component. The taxable income must be computed separately in order to determine the amount of tax.
2. Net income reconciliation approach: Net income (after tax) is calculated, and the noncash deduction for depreciation is added back to the net income to determine the cash flow.
3. Tax shield approach: All cash flows are initially assumed to be taxable, and the tax on the cash operating flow is calculated. The tax savings, or tax shield, provided by depreciation is added back to the net cash operating flow to determine the net cash flow. This tax shield is the depreciation deduction multiplied by the tax rate.

The tax shield approach is the method preferred in this text, since it permits the comparison of cash flows offered by alternative depreciation methods. As shown in Illustration 7-2, the results of the three approaches are the same.

Since capital projects will now be evaluated on the basis of their cash flow net of tax, the cutoff rate used in the analysis must also be specified net of tax. If the cutoff rate is the cost of capital, the calculation of the cutoff rate net of tax involves some complexity, since the cost of debt is tax deductible and the cost of equity funds is not. The cost of each major capital component, net of tax, is generally computed in finance texts as follows:

$$\text{Cost of debt} = (1 - \text{tax rate}) \times \text{Effective interest rate}$$

$$\text{Cost of preferred stock} = \frac{\text{Dividend per share}}{\text{Net proceeds of issue per share}}$$

$$\text{Cost of common stock} = \frac{\text{Dividend per share}}{\text{Market price per share}} + \text{Expected growth rate}$$

Illustration 7-2
Alternative Methods of
Calculating Cash Flows

Project cost: $12,000
Depreciation: Straight-line
             5 years
             No salvage value
Cash flows: $10,000 revenue per year
            $5,000 operating costs per year
            All cash flows are assumed to occur at year end
Tax rate: 40%

Cash Flow Approach

Annual revenue	$10,000	Revenue	$10,000
Annual cash		Cash costs	(5,000)
operating costs	(5,000)	Depreciation	
Income tax	(1,040)	($12,000 ÷ 5)	(2,400)
Annual cash flow		Income before tax	$ 2,600
(net of tax)	$ 3,960	Tax rate	× .40
		Income tax	$ 1,040

Net Income Reconciliation Approach

Annual revenue	$10,000
Annual cash operating costs	(5,000)
Annual depreciation	
($12,000 ÷ 5)	(2,400)
Income before tax	$ 2,600
Income tax (40% × $2,600)	(1,040)
Net income	$ 1,560
Add noncash deduction	
(depreciation)	2,400
Annual cash flow (net of tax)	$ 3,960

Tax Shield Approach

Annual revenue	$10,000	
Annual cash costs	(5,000)	
Cash operating flow before tax	$ 5,000	
Incremental tax on operating flow (40%)	(2,000)	
Net cash operating flow		$3,000
Annual depreciation ($12,000 ÷ 5)	$ 2,400	
Tax savings on depreciation	40%	960
Annual cash flow (net of tax)		$3,960

The cost of capital is then computed by weighting the cost of each component by the amount of funds provided by that component, as shown in the following example:

Components	(1) Costs of Components			(2) Amount of Funds	(3) Portion of Funds	(4) Weighted Costs (1) × (3)
Debt	(1 − 40%) × 15% interest		= .090	$1,500,000	.375	.03375
Preferred stock	$8 dividend / $98 issue price		= .082	800,000	.200	.01640
Common stock	$7.20 dividend / $60 market price	+ 4% growth	= .160	1,700,000	.425	.06800
				$4,000,000	1.000	.11815

The amount of funds provided by each component is generally an amount that is shown on a firm's balance sheet. The amount for each component is described as follows:

1. Debt: net carrying value, including premium or discount
2. Preferred stock: original issuance proceeds, including premium
3. Common stock: all paid-in capital and retained earnings

ALTERNATIVE METHODS OF PROJECT EVALUATION

In the past, two alternative methods have been used to evaluate capital projects. These methods, which ignore the time value of money, are the payback method and the accounting rate of return method. Although it is not now appropriate to use these methods as primary evaluation techniques, they are useful for providing additional, secondary measures of some of the effects of proposed capital projects. As explained in the following paragraphs, the payback method can be used as a measure of a project's risk. The accounting rate of return method can be used to assess the impact of a project on the financial statements for shareholders and creditors.

Payback Method

The payback method estimates the length of time over which the initial cost of a project will be recouped from the cash flows. The method, which assumes that an investor is willing to forfeit interest but not principal, measures risk from two viewpoints. First, the faster the invested funds are recovered, the lesser the need for reliance on cash flows far into the future. The more distant the flows, the greater the risk of an inaccurate estimate. Second, the faster the invested funds are recovered, the sooner the recovered funds can be redeployed to profitable projects that may be available.

The calculation of the payback period is straightforward. The cash flows are simply accumulated until they equal the original outlay. When the cash flows are equal each period during the life of a project, the payback period is calculated by dividing the original outlay by the periodic cash flow. For example, the payback period for the project in Illustration 7-2 would be calculated as follows:

$$\text{Payback} = \frac{\text{Original outlay}}{\text{Periodic cash flow}} = \frac{\$12,000}{\$3,960} = 3.03 \text{ years}$$

When the cash flows from a project are not equal each period, the periodic cash flows must be accumulated in order to determine the payback period. To illustrate, assume the following cash flows and net cash flows for a project costing $25,000:

Years	Cash Flows	Net Cash Flows to Date	Years	Cash Flows	Net Cash Flows to Date
0	−$25,000	−$25,000	5	$3,500	$ 8,500
1	9,000	− 16,000	6	2,500	11,000
2	9,000	− 7,000	7	2,500	13,500
3	8,000	1,000	8	1,500	15,000
4	4,000	5,000			

For this project, payback occurs during the third year. Since $7,000 is needed after the second year and $8,000 is provided in the third year, the payback period is 2 7/8 years.

The payback method can be made more sophisticated by determining when the cumulative cash flow plus the asset's salvage value are sufficient to repay the initial cost of the asset. This modification of the payback method is called bailout. While the regular payback method suggests that the recovery of the cost of an asset can only be *earned,* the bailout modification suggests that part of the recovery can be *earned* and the balance can result from the *sale* of the asset. To illustrate, the previous example is modified by considering salvage value, as follows:

Years	Cash Flows	Salvage Values	Recoverable Investment to Date (Cumulative Cash Flow + Salvage Value at End of Year)
0	− $25,000	$18,000	− $ 7,000
1	9,000	15,000	− 1,000
2	9,000	12,000	5,000
3	8,000	10,000	11,000
4	4,000	8,000	13,000

Bailout occurs during the second year. Since $1,000 is needed to bail out after the first year and $6,000 ($9,000 cash flow − $3,000 decline in salvage value) is provided in the second year, bailout occurs in 1 1/6 years.

Accounting Rate of Return

Once a capital project is accepted, the future net income of the firm will be influenced, and the assets listed in subsequent balance sheets will be increased. Since an important measure of the performance of a firm is its return on assets, it may be useful to determine the incremental impact of a project on the return on assets. The calculation is a modification of the basic return on assets, which is net income divided by total assets. Although the numerator in this noncash-flow model is the project's annual net income, the denominator may be either the initial investment in the project or the average investment in the project. Using the initial investment is a conservative approach, since the cost of the asset should really be decreased by depreciation by the end of the first reporting period. Using the average investment overstates the project's impact on income in the early years, since the asset base is higher than the average in those years. To illustrate the difference in the two approaches, the accounting rate of return for the project in Illustration 7-2 would be calculated as follows:

$$\text{Accounting rate of return (initial investment)} = \frac{\text{Project's annual net income}}{\text{Project's initial cost}} = \frac{\$\,1,560}{\$12,000} = 13\%$$

$$\text{Accounting rate of return (average investment)} = \frac{\text{Project's annual net income}}{\tfrac{1}{2} \times (\text{Project's initial cost} + \text{Salvage value})} = \frac{\$\,1,560}{\tfrac{1}{2} \times (\$12,000 + 0)} = \frac{\$\,1,560}{\$\,6,000} = 26\%$$

The process of determining the incremental impact of a project on the return on assets can be improved by measuring the rate of return annually. At the end of each year, the net income for the year would be divided by the remaining book value of the asset at the end of the year. This approach is advantageous, since net income need not be equal each year and alternative depreciation methods can be used. For the project in Illustration 7-2, in which the depreciation was $2,400 per year ($12,000 ÷ 5), the annual accounting rates of return would be as follows:

End of year:	(1) Annual Net Income	Book Values			(3) Annual Accounting Rates of Return (1) ÷ (2)
1	$1,560	$12,000 −	$2,400 =	$9,600	16%
2	1,560	9,600 −	2,400 =	7,200	22
3	1,560	7,200 −	2,400 =	4,800	33
4	1,560	4,800 −	2,400 =	2,400	65
5	1,560			−0−	—

Since the asset's book value continues to decrease and there is no drastic decrease in the annual net income, the rate of return improves with the passage of time. In most cases, there will be little concern for the rate of return after the first year, if the rate for the first year is acceptable. If only one rate of return is to be calculated, it should be the rate of return based on the initial investment, since that rate is closer to the rate that could be calculated at the end of the first year (in this case, 13% vs. 16%). The rate based on the initial investment will always be less than the first year's rate, because depreciation is deducted in determining the net income for the numerator, but it is not deducted from the initial cost in the denominator.

TAX CONSIDERATIONS IN CAPITAL BUDGETING

In the preceding discussion, the effects of taxes on capital projects were considered in relation to the tax on additional cash flows and the tax savings provided by depreciation. The following paragraphs will discuss tax depreciation methods, the investment tax credit (ITC), and first-year expensing, all of which are means by which part of an asset's cost can be recovered through tax savings. In addition, the tax effects of disposing of assets will be discussed.

Depreciation

Since 1981, the federal tax laws have generally given taxpayers a choice of only two methods for calculating depreciation for tax purposes: the Accelerated Cost Recovery System (ACRS) and straight-line. The rate of depreciation permitted under ACRS is similar to that which would have been available under the 150%-declining-balance method with a switch to straight-line depreciation at an optimal time. The ACRS percentages are designed to allow automatically for one-half year's depreciation in the first year and none in the year of disposal, regardless of when during the year the asset is purchased or sold. For assets other than real estate, the ACRS percentages and straight-line options are summarized as follows:

Classes of Assets	Types of Assets	ACRS Percentages	Straight-Line Options
3-year	Automobiles, light trucks, research and development equipment	25,38,37	3,5,12 years
5-year	Most other machinery and equipment	15,22,21,21,21	5,12,25 years
10-year	Public utility property	8,14,12,10,10,10, and 9 thereafter	10,25,35 years
15-year	Long-lived public utility property	5,10,9,8,7,7, and 6 thereafter	15,35,45 years

Straight-line options are only attractive when a firm is currently in a low tax bracket and expects to be in higher brackets in later years. When straight-line depreciation is elected, salvage value is ignored, and only one-half year of depreciation is allowed in the year of acquisition and in the year after the regular ACRS recovery period, provided the asset is held for the entire period. For example, an asset with a 5-year recovery period and $10,000 cost would be depreciated $1,000 in year 1, $2,000 in years 2 through 5, and $1,000 in year 6.

For real estate placed in service prior to March 16, 1984, the ACRS percentages are based on a 15-year life, 175%-declining-balance depreciation, and a switch to straight-line depreciation when the straight-line amount exceeds the declining-balance amount. For example, the ACRS depreciation on a $100,000 building would be determined as follows, with the amount deducted each year indicated by the number in color:

Years	175%-Declining-Balance Depreciation			Asset Balances	Straight-Line Depreciation over Remaining Life
1	$11,670	(.1167* ×	$100,000)	$88,330	
2	10,308	(.1167 ×	88,330)	78,022	$6,309 ($88,330 ÷ 14)
3	9,105	(.1167 ×	78,022)	68,917	6,002 (78,022 ÷ 13)
4	8,043	(.1167 ×	68,917)	60,874	5,743 (68,917 ÷ 12)
5	7,104	(.1167 ×	60,874)	53,770	5,534 (60,874 ÷ 11)
6	6,275	(.1167 ×	53,770)	47,495	5,377 (53,770 ÷ 10)
7	5,543	(.1167 ×	47,495)	41,952	5,277 (47,495 ÷ 9)
8	4,896	(.1167 ×	41,952)	36,708	5,244 (41,952 ÷ 8)
9				31,464	5,244
10				26,220	5,244
11				20,976	5,244
12				15,732	5,244
13				10,488	5,244
14				5,244	5,244
15				–0–	5,244

*1.75 × straight-line rate of .0667 $\left(\dfrac{\$100,000}{15} \div \$100,000 \right)$.

ACRS depreciation is highly accelerated and frequently not acceptable for financial reporting purposes. Therefore, when an accounting rate of return is computed, it should be based on the financial net income and financial depreciation, rather than tax depreciation.

Investment Tax Credit

To encourage investment, the federal tax laws permit a taxpayer to receive a credit against a current tax liability for a percentage of the cost of new and used assets other than real estate. This credit is taken in the year of the asset's acquisition, unless the credit exceeds 85% of the tax due, in which case it may be carried forward up to 15 years.

For an asset identified as a 3-year-class asset (automobile, light truck, and equipment used in research and development), the credit is 6% of the cost of the asset. For other assets, the credit is 10% of the cost. When the full 6% or 10% credit is taken, the depreciation base of the asset is reduced by one half of the ITC claimed. For example, a $1,000, 3-year asset would be eligible for a $60 ITC (6% × $1,000), and its depreciable cost would be $970 [$1,000 − (1/2 × $60)]. A $1,000, 5-year asset would be eligible for a $100 ITC (10% × $1,000), and the depreciable cost would be $950 [$1,000 − (1/2 × $100)].

As an alternative to reducing the depreciable base by one half of the ITC, the ITC claimed may be reduced to 4% for 3-year assets and to 8% for other assets. This alternative is generally advantageous only when the taxpayer is in a high tax bracket and has a very low cost of capital. In all other cases, it is advantageous only if the ITC must be carried forward several periods, rather than used currently.

To illustrate the disadvantage of the alternative, assume that a firm purchases a $10,000, 3-year asset and reduces the ITC to 4%. The ITC is reduced by $200 ($600 − $400). Assuming that the firm is subject to a tax rate of 46%, the depreciation deductions over 3 years increase by $138 [46% × (1/2 × $600)]. If the firm had purchased a $10,000, 5-year asset and reduced the ITC to 8%, the ITC would be reduced by $200, and the depreciation deductions gained over 5 years would be $230 [46% × (1/2 × $1,000)]. When converted to present values, the depreciation deductions gained would not likely be greater than the cost of reducing the ITC.

If assets on which the ITC has been taken are sold prior to the end of their life for tax depreciation purposes, the ITC must be recaptured, based on the rate at which it has been "earned." For example, if a 5-year-class asset is sold in the fourth year, the ITC is considered to be earned at the rate of 2% per year for the previous three years and unearned for the remaining two years. Thus, 4% (2 years × 2%) must be repaid during the fourth tax year. The book value of the asset must also be adjusted upward for one half of the ITC recaptured, unless the ITC was discounted and the depreciable cost not reduced. In this latter case, a pro rata portion of the ITC is recaptured, and the asset's book value is not adjusted.

First-Year Expensing

A limited amount of the cost of assets other than real estate may be expensed in the year of acquisition, rather than depreciated. The maximum amount deductible as an expense is $7,500 in 1984 and 1985, and $10,000 thereafter. No ITC may be claimed on the amount expensed. Although electing this option would appear to be advantageous on a present-value basis, the results of the alternatives must be carefully analyzed before a decision is made. For example, it would not be advantageous for a firm subject to a 46% tax rate and an 8% discount rate to expense a 5-year, $10,000 asset in the year of acquisition, since the firm will pay $1,000 (10% × $10,000) to expense $10,000 rather than deduct $9,500 [$10,000 − (1/2 × $1,000 ITC)] over five years. First-year expensing is advantageous only when the tax rate and the discount rate is very high. The high tax rate compensates for the loss of the ITC, and the high discount rate means that the depreciation available in later years will have a low present value.

Comparison of Investment Tax Credit Options and First-Year Expensing

Illustration 7-3 compares the available investment tax credit options and the results of electing first-year expensing. Both 3- and 5-year-class assets are included in the analysis, which uses alternative tax rates and alternative net-of-tax discount rates.

Since the results of the analysis indicate that it is rarely advantageous to elect to reduce the ITC or to expense an asset in the year of acquisition, this textbook will not use examples or assignment materials which include these options, unless otherwise noted. The results verify previous discussion and support the following guidelines:

1. Reducing the ITC is not merited for 3-year assets.
2. Reducing the ITC for 5-year assets is worthwhile only at high tax rates (46%) and low discount rates (6%).
3. First-year expensing is worthwhile only at very high tax rates and very high discount rates.

Gain or Loss on Disposal of an Asset

The final cash flow produced by a capital project is the salvage value of the asset. If the asset is sold after it has been fully depreciated, its book value is zero, and all proceeds from the sale are taxable as a gain. If the asset is sold before it has been fully depreciated, the excess of the selling price over the book value is a taxable gain, while the excess of the book value over the selling price is a deductible loss. If the asset is sold before the investment tax credit is "earned," there may be a recapture of the ITC.

Most gains on disposals of assets are taxed as ordinary income, since the gain is the result of depreciation, which reduced ordinary income. Only a gain in excess of the original cost of an asset is taxable at the more favorable capital gain rates. The gains on certain real estate sales of residential property may also be taxed as capital gains.

To illustrate the cash flows that result from the sale of an asset, assume that a $10,000, 5-year-class asset is (a) sold for $4,500 at the end of the third year, or (b) sold for $1,200 at the end of the fifth year. For each case, the impact of originally taking either a 10% or an 8% ITC is examined. The results are shown at the bottom of page 230.

Illustration 7-3   Comparison of ITC Options with First-Year Expensing

CASE A: Analysis of Tax Savings for a $10,000, 3-Year-Class Asset

		Year 1			Year 2
46% tax rate:	ITC	t(Cost)	t(Depr.)	Total	t(Depr.)
First-year expense		$4,600.00		$4,600.00	
6% ITC; 97% depreciation	$ 600.00		$1,115.50	1,715.50	$1,695.56
4% ITC; 100% depreciation	400.00		1,150.00	1,550.00	1,748.00
30% tax rate:					
First-year expense		3,000.00		3,000.00	
6% ITC; 97% depreciation	600.00		727.50	1,327.50	1,106.00
4% ITC; 100% depreciation	400.00		750.00	1,150.00	1,140.00
16% tax rate:					
First-year expense		1,600.00		1,600.00	
6% ITC; 97% depreciation	600.00		388.00	988.00	590.00
4% ITC; 100% depreciation	400.00		400.00	800.00	608.00

CASE B: Analysis of Tax Savings for a $10,000, 5-Year-Class Asset

		Year 1			Year 2
46% tax rate:	ITC	t(Cost)	t(Depr.)	Total	t(Depr.)
First-year expense		$4,600.00		$4,600.00	
10% ITC; 95% depreciation	$1,000.00		$ 655.50	1,655.50	$ 961.40
8% ITC; 100% depreciation	800.00		690.00	1,490.00	1,012.00
30% tax rate:					
First-year expense		3,000.00		3,000.00	
10% ITC; 95% depreciation	1,000.00		427.50	1,427.50	627.00
8% ITC; 100% depreciation	800.00		450.00	1,250.00	660.00
16% tax rate:					
First-year expense		1,600.00		1,600.00	
10% ITC; 95% depreciation	1,000.00		228.00	1,228.00	334.40
8% ITC; 100% depreciation	800.00		240.00	1,040.00	352.00

* Optimal procedure
**Optimal procedure after first-year expensing option is consumed

	10% ITC; Depreciate 95% of Cost			8% ITC; Depreciate 100% of Cost		
Sale at end of the third year:	Selling price		$4,500.00 $4,500.00	Selling price	$4,500	$4,500
	Book value	$3,990.00[a]		Book value	4,200[c]	
	ITC adjustment	200.00[b]	4,190.00			
	Gain		$ 310.00	Gain	$ 300	
	Tax (46% × $310)		$ 146.60	Tax (46% × $300)	$ 138	
				ITC recapture		
	ITC recapture			(2/5 × .08 ×		
	(4% × $10,000)		400.00 546.60	$10,000)	320	458
	Net proceeds		$3,953.40	Net proceeds		$4,042
Sale at end of the fifth year:	Selling price		$1,200.00 $1,200.00	Selling price	$1,200	$1,200
	Book value		–0–	Book value	–0–	
	Gain		$1,200.00	Gain	$1,200	
	Tax (46% × $1,200)		552.00	Tax (46% × $1,200)		552
	Net proceeds		$ 648.00	Net proceeds		$ 648

[a]$9,500 − [(.15 + .22 + .21) × $9,500]
[b]One half of ITC recaptured: ½(.02 × 2 × $10,000)
[c]$10,000 − [(.15 + .22 + .21) × $10,000]

Year 3 t(Depr.)		6%	8%	10%	12%	14%
				Total Present Value		
		$4,339.62	$4,259.26	$4,181.82	$4,107.14*	$4,035.09*
$1,650.94		4,513.60*	4,352.66*	4,201.21*	4,058.49**	3,923.84**
1,702.00		4,447.01	4,284.92	4,132.46	3,988.87	3,853.48
		2,830.19	2,777.78	2,727.27	2,678.57	2,631.58
1,077.00		3,140.96*	3,032.34*	2,930.03*	2,833.55*	2,742.45*
1,110.00		3,031.48	2,923.33	2,821.56	2,725.66	2,635.18
		1,509.43	1,481.48	1,454.55	1,428.57	1,403.51
574.00		1,939.11*	1,876.30*	1,817.04*	1,761.05*	1,708.09*
592.00		1,792.89	1,731.95	1,674.53	1,620.35	1,569.17

Year 3 t(Depr.)	Year 4 t(Depr.)	Year 5 t(Depr.)	6%	8%	10%	12%	14%
					Total Present Value		
			$4,339.62	$4,259.26	$4,181.82	$4,107.14*	$4,035.09*
$ 917.70	$ 917.70	$ 917.70	4,600.62	4,384.72*	4,185.65*	4,001.69**	3,819.91**
966.00	966.00	966.00	4,604.42*	4,381.58	4,176.28	3,986.74	3,799.62
			2,830.19	2,777.78	2,727.27	2,678.57	2,631.58
598.50	598.50	598.50	3,328.54*	3,181.66*	3,045.98*	2,920.36*	2,795.98*
630.00	630.00	630.00	3,265.39	3,115.20	2,976.63	2,848.50	2,721.80
			1,509.43	1,481.48	1,454.55	1,428.57	1,403.51
319.20	319.20	319.20	2,215.47*	2,128.99*	2,048.76*	1,974.19*	1,900.04*
336.00	336.00	336.00	2,093.75	2,007.12	1,926.93	1,852.53	1,778.71

WORK SHEET FOR EVALUATING CAPITAL PROJECTS

In the following pages, a work sheet for evaluating capital projects is illustrated. This work sheet format will be used in all subsequent examples, and should be used for completing assignment materials when appropriate. It is also usable on microcomputer electronic work sheets. The work sheet, which is based on the tax shield approach, is designed with columns for each type of cash flow and rows for each period's cash flows. The two illustrations use annual cash flows, while Appendix 7A at the end of the chapter applies the same format to quarterly and monthly flows.

In Illustration 7-4, a 5-year, $30,000 capital project is analyzed, using the net present value, internal rate of return, payback, and accounting rate of return methods. The example is based on taking the 10% ITC and depreciating 95% of the asset's cost. As shown in Illustration 7-3, this choice will maximize the present value for an 8% cutoff rate and a 46% tax rate.

Cost: $30,000
ITC: 10%
Depreciation (ACRS on 95% of cost): Year 1 .... 15% × 95% × $30,000 = $4,275
Year 2 .... 22% × 95% × $30,000 = 6,270
Year 3 .... 21% × 95% × $30,000 = 5,985
Year 4 .... 21% × 95% × $30,000 = 5,985
Year 5 .... 21% × 95% × $30,000 = 5,985

Operating flows: $15,000 Revenue − $7,000 Cash expenses = $8,000
Estimated salvage value: $6,000 (0 for tax purposes)
Tax rate: 46%
Cutoff rate: 8%

Years	(1) Cost	(2) ITC	(3) t(Depr.)	(4) Operating Flows	(5) Taxes on Operating Flows
0	− $30,000				
1		$3,000	$1,967	$8,000	− $3,680
2			2,884	8,000	− 3,680
3			2,753	8,000	− 3,680
4			2,753	8,000	− 3,680
5			2,753	8,000	− 3,680

(6) Salvage	(7) Tax on Salvage	(8) Total Flows	(9) PV Factors (8%)	(10) PVs of Total Flows at 8%	(11) Cash Flows to Date	Years
		− $30,000	1.0000	− $30,000	− $30,000	0
		9,287	.9259	8,599	− 20,713	1
		7,204	.8573	6,176	− 13,509	2
		7,073	.7938	5,615	− 6,436	3
		7,073	.7350	5,199	637	4
$6,000	− $2,760	10,313	.6806	7,019	10,950	5
				$ 2,608		

NPV: $2,608
Total PV: $30,000 + $2,608 = $32,608
PVI: $32,608 ÷ $30,000 = 1.087
IRR: 11.21%
Payback: 3 + ($6,436 ÷ $7,073) = 3.91 years
Accounting rate of return (initial investment):
($10,950 ÷ 5) ÷ $30,000 = $2,190 ÷ $30,000 = .0730

(1) Original cost occurring at the start of the first year, designated as occurring in year 0.
(2) The 10% ITC is claimed as a credit against the year-end tax bill.
(3) This amount is 46% of the depreciation deduction each year. It is a year-end savings at the time taxes are paid.
(4) Net cash operating flows before tax.
(5) Tax impact of operating flows.
(6) Sale proceeds of asset at end of useful life.
(7) Tax on gain on salvage. The gain is taxed at ordinary rates, except for gain in excess of original cost, which is taxed at lower capital gain rates.
(8) Summation of all cash flows during year.
(9) PV factor, used for manual computations, is not needed when a microcomputer is used.
(10) Cash flows discounted at the cutoff rate.
(11) Net cash flows to date are not used in present value analysis but are used for payback analysis.

The results of the four evaluation methods, which appear below the work sheet, are explained as follows:

1. Net present value (NPV): In Column 10, the work sheet sums the present value of all flows in Column 8 to provide NPV directly. Total PV is the result of adding the net present value to the original outlay at Period 0. The PVI is the result of dividing the total present value by the original cost.
2. Internal rate of return: The rate of 11.21% is found by trial and error. This rate equates the present value of the cash flows in Column 8 to the original cost. For the trial and error process, an iterative procedure is performed on a microcomputer.
3. Payback: When Column 11 (Cash Flow to Date) produces a positive number, payback has occurred. To determine when payback occurs, interpolation is used. In this illustration, $6,436 (from Column 11) of the period's cash flow of $7,073 (from Column 8), or 91%, is needed. Therefore, the payback is 3.91 years.
4. Accounting rate of return: In this illustration, the initial investment is used to compute the accounting rate of return, although average investment could have been used. The average net income is computed by using a shortcut in which the cumulative cash flow at the end of the fifth year is averaged over the project's life. The cumulative cash flow at the end of the fifth year is the total net income, because it is the total cash flow in excess of cost. Therefore, the shortcut avoids the need to make the following calculation:

Years	(1) Cash Flows	(2) Depreciation		(3) Net Income (1) – (2)
1	$ 9,287	.15 × $30,000 =	$4,500	$ 4,787
2	7,204	.22 × 30,000 =	6,600	604
3	7,073	.21 × 30,000 =	6,300	773
4	7,073	.21 × 30,000 =	6,300	773
5	10,313	.21 × 30,000 =	6,300	4,013
Total				$10,950

The flow through method of accounting for the ITC is used here. This method views the ITC benefit as added income in the year taken, because it reduces the tax provision in that year. It is also acceptable to use the deferral method, which spreads the ITC benefit over the life of the asset, which, in this case, would be 5 years. Under the flow through method, the entire cost of the asset is depreciated for financial reporting purposes.

In Illustration 7-5, the same project is analyzed, using an 8% discounted ITC and depreciation of 100% of the asset's cost. Compared with the analysis in Illustration 7-4, the project's net present value and internal rate of return decrease slightly, and the payback period is lengthened slightly. The accounting rate of return increases, because discounting the ITC produces more cash flow. However, the timing of the cash flows is less favorable, but the timing is not reflected in the accounting rate of return.

Cost: $30,000

ITC: 8%

Depreciation (ACRS on 100% of cost): Year 1 .... 15% × $30,000 = $4,500

Year 2 .... 22% × $30,000 = 6,600

Year 3 .... 21% × $30,000 = 6,300

Year 4 .... 21% × $30,000 = 6,300

Year 5 .... 21% × $30,000 = 6,300

Operating flows: $15,000 Revenue − $7,000 Cash expenses = $8,000

Estimated salvage value: $6,000 (0 for tax purposes)

Tax rate: 46%

Cutoff rate: 8%

Years	(1) Cost	(2) ITC	(3) t(Depr.)	(4) Operating Flows	(5) Taxes on Operating Flows
0	−$30,000				
1		$2,400	$2,070	$8,000	−$3,680
2			3,036	8,000	− 3,680
3			2,898	8,000	− 3,680
4			2,898	8,000	− 3,680
5			2,898	8,000	− 3,680

(6) Salvage	(7) Tax on Salvage	(8) Total Flows	(9) PV Factors (8%)	(10) PVs of Total Flows at 8%	(11) Cash Flows to Date	Years
		−$30,000	1.0000	−$30,000	−$30,000	0
		8,790	.9259	8,139	− 21,210	1
		7,356	.8573	6,306	− 13,854	2
		7,218	.7938	5,730	− 6,636	3
		7,218	.7350	5,305	582	4
$6,000	−$2,760	10,458	.6806	7,118	11,040	5
				$ 2,598		

NPV: $2,598

Total PV: $30,000 + $2,598 = $32,598

PVI: $32,598 ÷ $30,000 = 1.087

IRR: 11.17%

Payback: 3 + ($6,636 ÷ $7,218) = 3.92 years

Accounting rate of return (initial investment):

($11,040 ÷ 5) ÷ $30,000 = $2,208 ÷ $30,000 = .0736

THE IMPACT OF WORKING CAPITAL

The acceptance of a major new capital project may lead to an increase in the working capital needed to support a firm's operations. For example, a chain's opening of another retail outlet will result in increased levels of inventories and receivables, and short-term payables may also increase. In evaluating this project, the net increase in working capital required should be considered.

The investment in working capital may be viewed as a fully returnable investment. The added net investment in inventory and receivables will be liquidated at the end of the project. Since the investment is returnable, it is not depreciable or deductible in any other manner. There is a cost involved, however, since funds which would otherwise earn a return are committed, and the investment is returned in the future at a lower present value.

In Illustration 7-6, a $2,500 working capital investment is added to the analysis of Illustration 7-5. The working capital is a part of the initial cost in year 0 (without any adjustment for tax) and is shown as a return of cost at the end of the fifth year. In more complex situations, working capital may be added and/or removed during interim periods. As the results of the analysis in Illustration 7-6 indicate, the project is made less attractive by the working capital requirement.

Illustration 7-6
Working Capital Impact:
8% ITC; Depreciate
100% of Cost

Cost: $30,000
ITC: 8%
Depreciation (ACRS on 100% of cost):

Year 1 .... 15% × $30,000 =	$4,500
Year 2 .... 22% × $30,000 =	6,600
Year 3 .... 21% × $30,000 =	6,300
Year 4 .... 21% × $30,000 =	6,300
Year 5 .... 21% × $30,000 =	6,300

Operating flows: $15,000 Revenue − $7,000 Cash expenses = $8,000
Estimated salvage value: $6,000 (0 for tax purposes)
Working capital: $2,500 at start; returned at end of fifth year
Tax rate: 46%
Cutoff rate: 8%

Years	(1) Cost	(2) ITC	(3) t(Depr.)	(4) Operating Flows	(5) Taxes on Operating Flows
0	−$32,500				
1		$2,400	$2,070	$8,000	−$3,680
2			3,036	8,000	− 3,680
3			2,898	8,000	− 3,680
4			2,898	8,000	− 3,680
5	2,500		2,898	8,000	− 3,680

(6) Salvage	(7) Tax on Salvage	(8) Total Flows	(9) PV Factors (8%)	(10) PVs of Total Flows at 8%	(11) Cash Flows to Date	Years
		−$32,500	1.0000	−$32,500	−$32,500	0
		8,790	.9259	8,139	− 23,710	1
		7,356	.8573	6,306	− 16,354	2
		7,218	.7938	5,730	− 9,136	3
		7,218	.7350	5,305	− 1,918	4
$6,000	−$2,760	12,958	.6806	8,819	11,040	5
				$ 1,799		

NPV: $1,799
Total PV: $32,500 + $1,799 = $34,299
PVI: $34,299 ÷ $32,500 = 1.0553
IRR: 9.97%
Payback: 4 + ($1,918 ÷ $12,958) = 4.15 years
Accounting rate of return (initial investment):
($11,040 ÷ 5) ÷ $32,500 = $2,208 ÷ $32,500 = .0679

TOWARD MORE REALISTIC CAPITAL PROJECT EVALUATIONS

The use of annual cash flows in analyzing capital projects may lead to correct decisions; but when projects are only marginally profitable, the decision could be sensitive to the preciseness of the analytic model. The use of annual flows tends to understate a project's return for the following reasons:

1. Operating flows occur during the year, not at the end.
2. Tax deductions and ITC credits are realized through a reduction in quarterly tax payments during the year.

Some firms partially correct for the understatement in an analysis based on annual flows by assuming that all flows, other than salvage, occur at midyear, and by discounting those flows with midyear factors. Although these corrections are helpful, the most accurate way to analyze projects is to use quarterly or monthly flows, as discussed in Appendix 7A.

APPENDIX 7A: USING QUARTERLY OR MONTHLY FLOWS IN EVALUATING CAPITAL PROJECTS

The use of annual cash flows is a teaching and problem-solving expediency. In reality, however, flows should be considered on a quarterly or a monthly basis. For projects that earn only slightly more than the cutoff rate, the greater precision that results from using quarterly or monthly flows is especially desirable because:

1. The capital budget is used as a control tool in future periods in order to compare actual to budgeted flows. Better, more precise control is possible when these comparisons are made on a quarterly basis.
2. The sooner that funds become available for reinvestment during each year, the higher the effective yield of a project.
3. Firms must make estimated tax payments on a quarterly basis.

Timing of Flows Within the Year

As mentioned above, the sooner funds become available for reinvestment during the year, the higher their present value or rate of return. When the net present value method is being used, this reinvestment is assumed to be made at the cutoff rate. When the internal rate of return method is being used, the funds are assumed to be reinvested at the project's internal rate of return.

The impact of quarterly and monthly flows is illustrated as follows:

(A) Annual Flow Percentages	(B) Quarterly Flow Percentages (Col. A ÷ 4%)	(C) Effective Annual Percentages $[(100.0\% + \text{Col. B})^4 - 100.0\%]$	(D) Monthly Flow Percentages (Col. A ÷ 12%)	(E) Effective Annual Percentages $[(100.0\% + \text{Col. D})^{12} - 100.0\%]$
8%	2.0%	8.24%	0.67%	8.30%
10	2.5	10.38	0.83	10.43
12	3.0	12.55	1.00	12.68
14	3.5	14.75	1.17	14.98
16	4.0	16.99	1.33	17.18
18	4.5	19.25	1.50	19.56
20	5.0	21.55	1.67	21.99

This analysis shows that a project's return is increased by the frequency of the flows used in its evaluation. For a project which, in fact, has more frequent flows than annually, an annual analysis will negatively bias the project. The significance of this understatement of a project's return is emphasized by considering the following changes in the results from Illustration 7-4 when quarterly and monthly flows are assumed:

	Annually	Quarterly	Monthly
Present value	$2,608 at 8%	$3,509 at 1.9414%	$3,720 at .643%
Internal rate of return	11.21%	3.094%	1.051%
Effective annual internal rate of return	11.21%	12.96%	13.37%

Quarterly Tax Payments

Since a firm pays its tax liability on a quarterly basis, the impact of the ITC, depreciation, operating flows, and any gain on disposal is spread over the quarters.

The complexity of this impact is even greater when a project does not start at the beginning of a quarter.

In Illustration 7A-1, the evaluation results for a $30,000 project are shown, using the beginning of each of the four possible quarters as starting points. The full 10% investment tax credit is taken, and the format of the illustration is identical to previous illustrations. However, the present value factor column is deleted, since it is not likely that a quarterly computation would be done manually.

When the project is started at the beginning of the first quarter, the ITC benefit and the tax benefit of the first year's 15% depreciation are spread over all four quarters of the first tax year. Using ACRS depreciation procedures, 15% of a 5-year asset's cost is deductible the first tax year, regardless of when the acquisition occurs during that year. Subsequent years' depreciation deductions are spread equally over each year's quarters. The salvage value is assumed to be received in the last quarter of the fifth year (the 20th quarter). Therefore, the tax on the gain on disposal is payable in that quarter.

Illustration 7A-1
Evaluation on Quarterly Basis with Project Acquisition in First Quarter

```
Capital Budgeting-Quarterly Flows
First Quarter Acquisition
Cost:  $30000
ITC: 10% (.10 * 30000 = 3000)
Depreciation: ACRS(15/22/21/21/21)
Interest        1 .15 * 28500 = 4275
                2 .22 * 28500 = 6270
                3 .21 * 28500 = 5985
                4              5985
                5              5985
Operating Flow: $15,000 Revenue - $7000 Cash expenses = $8000, $2,000 per quarter
Estimated Actual Salvage Value: $6,000 (0 for tax)
Tax Rate: 46%
Cutoff Rate of Return: 8%      .019414 quarterly
```

Period	Cost	ITC	t(Depr.)	Operating Flows	Tax on Operating Flows	Salvage	Tax on Salvage	Total Flows	Cash Flows to Date
0	-30000							30000.00	30000
1		750	491.63	2000.00	-920.00			2321.63	-27678
2		750	491.63	2000.00	-920.00			2321.63	-25357
3		750	491.63	2000.00	-920.00			2321.63	-23035
4		750	491.63	2000.00	-920.00			2321.63	-20714
5			721.05	2000.00	-920.00			2321.63	-18912
6			721.05	2000.00	-920.00			1801.05	-17111
7			721.05	2000.00	-920.00			1801.05	-15310
8			721.05	2000.00	-920.00			1801.05	-13509
9			688.28	2000.00	-920.00			1768.28	-11741
10			688.28	2000.00	-920.00			1768.28	-9973
11			688.28	2000.00	-920.00			1768.28	-8204
12			688.28	2000.00	-920.00			1768.28	-6436
13			688.28	2000.00	-920.00			1768.28	-4668
14			688.28	2000.00	-920.00			1768.28	-2900
15			688.28	2000.00	-920.00			1768.28	-1131
16			688.28	2000.00	-920.00			1768.28	637
17			688.28	2000.00	-920.00			1768.28	2405
18			688.28	2000.00	-920.00			1768.28	4173
19			688.28	2000.00	-920.00			1768.28	5942
20			688.28	2000.00	-920.00	6000.00	-2760.00	5008.28	10950
21					0.00			0.00	10950
22					0.00			0.00	10950
23					0.00			0.00	10950
24					0.00			0.00	10950

```
NPV = 3509.37
Total PV = 30000 + 3509.37 = 33509.37
PVI = 33509.37/30000 = 1.1117
Internal Rate of Return = .03094 quarterly    .129623 annually
Payback = 15 +(1131/1768.28) = 15.64 quarters, 3.91 years
Accounting Rate of Return = Average Net Income/Initial Investment
                          = (10950/5)/30000
                          = 2190/30000
                          = .073
```

When the project is started at the beginning of the second quarter, the ITC benefit and the first year's depreciation are spread over only the remaining quarters of the first year, and there is no depreciation left for the twenty-first quarter. Since the salvage value flows at the end of the first quarter of the sixth tax year, the gain is spread over that year's quarters. As a result of the faster recovery of the first year's ITC and depreciation and the delay of the gain on the disposal of the asset, the net present value and the internal rate of return for the project increase.

```
Capital Budgeting-Quarterly Flows
Second Quarter Acquisition
Cost:    $ 30000
ITC: 10% (.10 * 30000 = 3000)
Depreciation: ACRS(15/22/21/21/21)
             1 .15 * 28500 = 4275
             2 .22 * 28500 = 6270
             3 .21 * 28500 = 5985
             4              5985
             5              5985
Operating Flow: $15000 Revenue - $7000 Cash expenses =8000, $2000  per quarter
Estimated Actual Salvage Value: $6,000 (0 for tax)
Tax Rate: 46%
Cutoff Rate of Return: 8%     .019414 quarterly
```

Period	Cost	ITC	t(Depr.)	Operating Flows	Tax on Operating Flows	Salvage	Tax on Salvage	Total Flows	Cash Flows to Date
0								0.00	0
1	-30000							-30000.00	-30000
2		1000	655.43	2000.00	-920.00			2735.43	-27265
3		1000	655.43	2000.00	-920.00			2735.43	-24529
4		1000	655.43	2000.00	-920.00			2735.43	-21794
5			721.05	2000.00	-920.00			1801.05	-19993
6			721.05	2000.00	-920.00			1801.05	-18192
7			721.05	2000.00	-920.00			1801.05	-16391
8			721.05	2000.00	-920.00			1801.05	-14589
9			688.28	2000.00	-920.00			1768.28	-12821
10			688.28	2000.00	-920.00			1768.28	-11053
11			688.28	2000.00	-920.00			1768.28	-9285
12			688.28	2000.00	-920.00			1768.28	-7516
13			688.28	2000.00	-920.00			1768.28	-5748
14			688.28	2000.00	-920.00			1768.28	-3980
15			688.28	2000.00	-920.00			1768.28	-2212
16			688.28	2000.00	-920.00			1768.28	-443
17			688.28	2000.00	-920.00			1768.28	1325
18			688.28	2000.00	-920.00			1768.28	3093
19			688.28	2000.00	-920.00			1768.28	4862
20			688.28	2000.00	-920.00			1768.28	6630
21				2000.00	-920.00	6000.00	-690.00	6390.00	13020
22					0.00		-690.00	-690.00	12330
23					0.00		-690.00	-690.00	11640
24					0.00		-690.00	-690.00	10950

```
     NPV = 3778.43
     Total PV = 30000 + 3778.43 = 33778.43
     PVI = 33778.43/30000 = 1.1259
     Internal Rate of Return = .03233 quarterly  .1357276 annually
     Payback = 15 + (443/1768.28) = 15.25 quarters, 3.81 years
     Accounting Rate of Return = Average Net Income/Initial Investment
                              = (10950/5)30000
                              = 2190/30000
                              = .073
```

When the project is started at the beginning of the third quarter, the ITC benefit and the first year's depreciation are spread over only two quarters of the first year, and there is no depreciation left for the twenty-first and twenty-second quarters. The salvage value flows at the end of the second quarter of the sixth tax year, and is spread over the last three quarters of that year. The further acceleration of the first year's deductions is slightly offset by the lessened delay of the salvage gain, but the net present value and internal rate of return for the project are again increased.

Illustration 7A-3
Evaluation on Quarterly
Basis with Project
Acquisition in
Third Quarter

```
Capital Budgeting-Quarterly Flows
Third  Quarter Acquisition
Cost:   $ 30000
ITC: 10% (.10 * 30000 = 3000)
Depreciation: ACRS(15/22/21/21/21)
Interest          1 .15 * 28500 = 4275
                  2 .22 * 28500 = 6270
                  3 .21 * 28500 = 5985
                  4          5985
                  5          5985
Operating Flow: $15000 Revenue - $7000 Cash expenses = $8000, $2000 per quarter
Estimated Actual Salvage Value: $6,000 (0 for tax)
Tax Rate: 46%
Cutoff Rate of Return: 8%     .019414 quarterly
```

Period	Cost	ITC	t(Depr.)	Operating Flows	Tax on Operating Flows	Salvage	Tax on Salvage	Total Flows	Cash Flows to Date
0									
1									
2	-30000							-30000.00	-30000
3		1500	983.25	2000.00	-920.00			3563.25	-26437
4		1500	983.25	2000.00	-920.00			3563.25	-22874
5			721.05	2000.00	-920.00			1801.05	-21072
6			721.05	2000.00	-920.00			1801.05	-19271
7			721.05	2000.00	-920.00			1801.05	-17470
8			721.05	2000.00	-920.00			1801.05	-15669
9			688.28	2000.00	-920.00			1768.28	-13901
10			688.28	2000.00	-920.00			1768.28	-12133
11			688.28	2000.00	-920.00			1768.28	-10364
12			688.28	2000.00	-920.00			1768.28	-8596
13			688.28	2000.00	-920.00			1768.28	-6828
14			688.28	2000.00	-920.00			1768.28	-5060
15			688.28	2000.00	-920.00			1768.28	-3291
16			688.28	2000.00	-920.00			1768.28	-1523
17			688.28	2000.00	-920.00			1768.28	245
18			688.28	2000.00	-920.00			1768.28	2013
19			688.28	2000.00	-920.00			1768.28	3782
20			688.28	2000.00	-920.00			1768.28	5550
21				2000.00	-920.00			1080.00	6630
22				2000.00	-920.00	6000.00	-920.00	6160.00	12790
23					0.00		-920.00	-920.00	11870
24					0.00		-920.00	-920.00	10950

```
     NPV = 3981.32
     Total PV = 30000 + 3981.32 = 33981.32
     PVI = 33981.32/30000 = 1.1327
     Internal Rate of Return = .03352 quarterly   .1409735 annually
     Payback =14 + (1523/1768.28) = 14.86quarters,3.22 years
     Accounting Rate of Return = Average Net Income/Initial Investment
                               = (10950/5)/30000
                               = 2190/30000
                               = .073
```

When the project is started at the beginning of the fourth quarter, all of the ITC benefit and the first year's depreciation flow in the final quarter, and there will be no depreciation left for the twenty-first, twenty-second, and twenty-third quarters. The salvage value is assumed to flow at the end of the third quarter of the sixth tax year and is spread over the last two quarters of that year. Again, the net present value and the internal rate of return increase.

```
Capital Budgeting-Quarterly Flows
Fourth Quarter Acquisition
Cost:    $30000
ITC: 10% (.10 * 30000 = 3000)
Depreciation: ACRS(15/22/21/21/21)
            1 .15 * 28500 = 4275
            2 .22 * 28500 = 6270
            3 .21 * 28500 = 5985
            4            5985
            5            5985
Operating Flow: $15000 Revenue - $7000 Cash expenses = $8000, $2000 per quarter
Estimated Actual Salvage Value: $6,000 (0 for tax)
Tax Rate: 46%
Cutoff Rate of Return: 8%    .019414 quarterly
```

Period	Cost	ITC	t(Depr.)	Operating Flows	Tax on Operating Flows	Salvage	Tax on Salvage	Total Flows	Cash Flows to Date
0								0	0
1								0	0
2								0	0
3	-30000							-30000.00	-30000
4		3000	1966.50	2000.00	-920.00			6046.50	-23954
5			721.05	2000.00	-920.00			1801.05	-22152
6			721.05	2000.00	-920.00			1801.05	-20351
7			721.05	2000.00	-920.00			1801.05	-18550
8			721.05	2000.00	-920.00			1801.05	-16749
9			688.28	2000.00	-920.00			1768.28	-14981
10			688.28	2000.00	-920.00			1768.28	-13213
11			688.28	2000.00	-920.00			1768.28	-11444
12			688.28	2000.00	-920.00			1768.28	-9676
13			688.28	2000.00	-920.00			1768.28	-7908
14			688.28	2000.00	-920.00			1768.28	-6140
15			688.28	2000.00	-920.00			1768.28	-4371
16			688.28	2000.00	-920.00			1768.28	-2603
17			688.28	2000.00	-920.00			1768.28	-833
18			688.28	2000.00	-920.00			1768.28	933
19			688.28	2000.00	-920.00			1768.28	2702
20			688.28	2000.00	-920.00			1768.28	4470
21				2000.00	-920.00			1080.00	5550
22				2000.00	-920.00			1080.00	6630
23				2000.00	-920.00	6000.00	-1380.00	5700.00	12330
24					0.00		-1380.00	-1380.00	10950

```
     NPV = 4187.78
     Total PV = 30000 + 4187.78 = 34187.78
     PVI = 34187.78/30000 = 1.1396
     Internal Rate of Return = .03483 quarterly  .1467693 annually
     Payback =14 + (835/1768.28) = 14.47 quarters, 3.12 years
     Accounting Rate of Return = Average Net Income/Initial Investment
                               = (10950/5)/30000
                               = 2190/30000
                               = .073
```

To demonstrate the greater precision that results when monthly flows are used in evaluating capital projects, the first-quarter acquisition of Illustration 7A-1 is analyzed on a monthly basis in Illustration 7A-2. In this illustration, the taxes are still paid at the end of each quarter, but the pretax operating flows are retained during the quarters. Since the pretax flows can be invested temporarily during the quarter before the tax payment is due, the net present value for the project increases from $3,510 to $3,721, and the internal rate of return increases from 12.96% to 13.37%.

Illustration 7A-5
Evaluation on Monthly Basis

```
Capital Budgeting—Monthly Flows
Cost:   $30000
ITC: 10% (.10 * 30000 = 3,000)
Depreciation: ACRS(15/22/21/21/21)
                    1  .15 * 28500 = 4275
                    2  .22 * 28500 = 6270
                    3  .21 * 28500 = 5985
                    4              5985
                    5              5985
Operating Flow: $15000 Revenue - $7000 Cash expenses = $8000, $667 per month
Estimated Actual Salvage Value: $6,000 (0 for tax)
Tax Rate: 46%
Cutoff Rate of Return: 8%      .00643 monthly
```

Period	Cost	ITC	t(Depr.)	Operating Flows	Tax on Operating Flows	Salvage	Tax on Salvage	Total Flows	Cash Flows to Date
0	-30000							-30000.00	-30000
1				667.00				667.00	-29333
2				667.00				667.00	-28666
3		750	491.63	667.00	-920.46			988.17	-27678
4				667.00				667.00	-27011
5				667.00				667.00	-26344
6		750	491.63	667.00	-920.46			988.17	-25356
12		750	491.63	667.00	-920.46			988.17	-20711
13				667.00				667.00	-20044
14				667.00				667.00	-19377
15			721.05	667.00	-920.46			467.59	-18910
16				667.00				667.00	-18243
26				667.00				667.00	-12171
27			688.28	667.00	-920.46			434.82	-11736
28				667.00				667.00	-11069
29				667.00				667.00	-10402
30			688.28	667.00	-920.46			434.82	-9967
31				667.00				667.00	-9300
57			688.28	667.00	-920.46			434.82	5952
58				667.00				667.00	6619
59				667.00				667.00	7286
60			688.28	667.00	-920.46	6000.00	-2760.00	3674.82	10961

```
NPV = 3730.24
Total PV = 30000 + 3730.24 = 33730.24
PVI = 33730.24/30000 = 1.124
Internal Rate of Return = .01058 monthly   .1336719 annually
Payback = 46 + (456/667) = 46.82 months, 3.90 years
Accounting Rate of Return = Average Net Income/Initial Investment
                          = (11051/5)/30000
                          = 2210/30000
                          = .0737
```

APPENDIX 7B: PRESENT VALUE CONCEPTS

Capital project evaluation techniques that consider the time value of money require one to be familiar with present value concepts. The key concept of present value is that interest charges are removed from future cash flows, so that future flows can be stated at their value today. Frequently, the interest deducted is that rate that could be earned on alternative investments. This process of deducting interest is called **discounting,** and it can proceed in one of two ways:

1. With **present value analysis,** future flows are discounted to their present value. For example, assume that a firm is considering the purchase of a vending machine for $14,000. The vending machine will produce a net cash flow of $4,000 at the end of each of the next five years. If the future flows are discounted at 10% per year (the opportunity cost), the present value of these flows is $15,163. Since the present value exceeds the vending machine's cost, the machine apparently earns more than 10% per year and is therefore a desirable purchase.

2. With **rate of return analysis,** the interest rate is calculated which, when applied to the future flows, produces a present value equal to the cost of the investment. In the preceding example, discounting the $4,000 annual flows at 13.2% produces a present value equal to the $14,000 cost of the vending machine.

Single Payments

To begin the discussion of present value concepts, assume that someone wants to borrow money from you today and promises to repay $1,000 at the end of one year. What amount would you loan? You would first decide what interest rate to charge, say 12%, and then you would make the following calculation:

$$\text{Future value of } \$1,000 = \text{Present value} \times 1.12$$
$$\text{Present value} = \frac{\text{Future value of } \$1,000}{1.12}$$
$$\text{Present value} = \$892.86$$

This calculation indicates that you want $892.86, the amount loaned, to be returned, in addition to 12%. Thus, you multiply the loan by 1.12.

Assume, however, that the loan will not be repaid until the end of 3 years. You would want to earn compound interest; i.e., each year you would add interest due to the loan and determine a new balance which would be the base for the next year's interest charge. The present value of the $1,000 due in three years would be calculated as follows:

$$\text{Future value of } \$1,000 = \text{Present value} \times 1.12 \times 1.12 \times 1.12$$
$$\text{Future value of } \$1,000 = \text{Present value} \times 1.12^3$$
$$\text{Present value} = \frac{\text{Future value of } \$1,000}{1.12^3}$$
$$\text{Present value} = \$711.78$$

This result can be verified as follows:

Years	Interest	Balances	Years	Interest	Balances
0	—	$ 711.78	2	95.66 (.12 × 797.19)	892.85
1	$ 85.41 (.12 × $711.78)	797.19	3	107.15 (.12 × 892.85)	1,000.00

Present value calculations can be performed on a calculator with present value functions, or present value tables may be used. Table 1 in the appendix at the end of the textbook may be used to calculate the value of a single future payment. The factors included in the table show the present value of one payment of $1 due at the end of various periods of time at different interest rates. Using the previous example as an illustration, Table 1 indicates that $1 due at the end of 3 years at 12% interest has a present value of .7118. Therefore, the present value of $1,000 is calculated as follows:

$$\text{Present value} = \text{Table 1 factor for 3 years at 10\%} \times \text{Future value}$$
$$= .7118 \times \$1,000$$
$$= \$711.80$$

Table 1 can also be used to calculate the internal rate of return that equates the future value to a given present value. To illustrate, assume that you were offered $1,000 three years from now in exchange for $600 today. To calculate the rate you would be earning, you would proceed as follows:

$$\text{Present value} = \text{Table 1 factor for 3 years at ?\%} \times \text{Future value}$$
$$\$600 = \text{Table 1 factor for 3 years at ?\%} \times \$1,000$$
$$\$600 \div \$1,000 = \text{Table 1 factor for 3 years at ?\%}$$
$$.6 = \text{Table 1 factor for 3 years at ?\%}$$

In Table 1, .6 on the 3-year line falls between the factors for 18% and 19%. The interest rate can then be derived by interpolation, as follows:

$$\text{Interest rate} = 18\% + \frac{\text{Table 1 value for 18\%} - .6}{\text{Table 1 value for 18\%} - \text{Table 1 value for 19\%}}$$
$$= 18\% + \frac{.6086 - .6}{.6086 - .5934}$$
$$= 18\% + .5658$$
$$= 18.57\%$$

In this example, straight-line interpolation has been applied to a nonlinear function, and some error occurs. The actual rate is 18.56%.

Multiple Future Payments

Present value techniques are also applied to investments offering periodic future payments. These periodic payments, which are called **annuities,** may be equal and occurring at the end of each period, equal and occurring at the start of each period, equal each period except for a final payment, equal but changing after a certain period, or varying each period. These possibilities are discussed in the following paragraphs.

Ordinary Annuities

When periodic payments are equal and flow at the end of each period, the annuity is said to be **ordinary.** The present value of an ordinary annuity can be calculated by adding together the present values of each future payment. For example, the present value of $2,000 at 10%, due at the end of each of the next 6 years, could be calculated as follows:

$$\text{Present value} = (\$2,000 \div 1.10) + (\$2,000 \div 1.10^2) + (\$2,000 \div 1.10^3) +$$
$$(\$2,000 \div 1.10^4) + (\$2,000 \div 1.10^5) + (\$2,000 \div 1.10^6)$$
$$= \$1,818.18 + \$1,652.89 + \$1,502.63 + \$1,366.03 + \$1,241.84 + \$1,128.95$$
$$= \$8,710.52$$

The same calculation can be made more quickly by using Table 2 in the appendix at the end of the textbook. This table provides the present value of $1 due at the end of various periods at different interest rates. To illustrate, Table 2 indicates that $1 due at the end of each year for 6 years, at 10%, has a present value of 4.3553. Therefore, the present value of the $2,000 annuity is calculated as follows:

$$\text{Present value} = \text{Table 2 factor for 6 years at 10\%} \times \text{Payments}$$
$$= 4.3553 \times \$2,000$$
$$= \$8,710.52$$

Table 2 can also be used to compute the internal rate of return which equates the flows of an ordinary annuity with a given present value. For example, assume that the $2,000, 6-year annuity in the previous example could be purchased for $7,500. To determine the rate that it is earning, the following calculation would be made:

$$\text{Present value} = \text{Table 2 factor for 6 years at ?\%} \times \text{Payments}$$
$$\$7,500 = \text{Table 2 factor for 6 years at ?\%} \times \$2,000$$
$$\$7,500 \div \$2,000 = \text{Table 2 factor for 6 years at ?\%}$$
$$3.75 = \text{Table 2 factor for 6 years at ?\%}$$

In Table 2, this factor falls between the factors for 15% and 16%. The rate can then be derived by interpolation, as follows:

$$\text{Interest rate} = 15\% + \frac{3.7845 - 3.7500}{3.7845 - 3.6847}$$
$$= 15\% + \frac{.0345}{.0998}$$
$$= 15\% + .35$$
$$= 15.35\% \text{ (The actual rate is 15.34\%.)}$$

Annuities Due When periodic payments are equal and flow at the start of each period, they are called **annuities due.** Such payment patterns are typical in lease contracts, in which payment is often designed to precede usage. Special tables for annuities due are available but not necessary, since an annuity due is an ordinary annuity with a down payment equal to one periodic payment. For example, assume that a contract with an implied interest rate of 10% requires six payments of $750 each at the beginning of each of the next 6 years. The payments are equivalent to a $750 down payment plus five ordinary annuity payments of $750 each. To calculate the present value of the contract, determine the present value of the 5-year ordinary annuity and add the down payment, as follows:

$$\text{Present value} = (\text{Table 2 factor for 5 years at 10\%} \times \text{Payments}) + \text{Down payment}$$
$$= (3.7908 \times \$750) + \$750$$
$$= \$3,593.10$$

If the present value is known, this formula can be used to compute the internal rate of return, as was done for the ordinary annuity.

Unequal Future Payments An investment may provide equal annual payments plus one final payment. A typical example of this pattern is a lease which requires annual payments plus a final payment to obtain the asset at the end of the lease term. To illustrate the present value procedures in this situation, assume that an investment will provide $5,000 at the end of each of the next 5 years, as well as a salvage value of $2,000 at the end of the fifth year. For calculating the present value, it is helpful to view the investment as two separate payment flows: (1) a 5-year, $5,000 ordinary annuity, and (2) a single $2,000 payment delayed 5 years. If an interest rate of 10% is assumed, the calculations are as follows:

Present value of $5,000, 5-year annuity (3.7908 Table 2 factor for 5 years at 10% × $5,000) $18,950
Present value of $2,000 payment delayed 5 years (.6209 Table 1 factor for 5 years at 10% × $5,000) 1,242
    Total present value $20,192

A lease contract may require large payments during the early years of the lease and smaller payments during the balance of the lease term. This type of contract protects the lessor's equity when the initial depreciation on the leased asset is substantial. To illustrate the present value calculations, assume that a contract requires payments of $2,500 per year for 3 years and $1,500 per year for the remaining 2 years of the lease term. This agreement can be viewed as two contracts: (1) a 3-year, $2,500 ordinary annuity, and (2) a 2-year, $1,500 ordinary annuity delayed 2 years. If an interest rate of 10% is assumed, the calculations are as follows:

Present value of $2,500, 3-year annuity (2.4869 Table 2 factor for 3 years at 10% × $2,500) $6,217
Present value of $1,500, 2-year annuity, delayed 3 years (1.7355 Table 2 factor for 2 years at 10% × $1,500 × .7513 Table 1 factor for 3 years at 10% × $2,603) 1,956
    Total present value $8,173

The calculation of the present value of the $1,500, 2-year annuity that is delayed two years is a two-step process. In the first step, the present value of the annuity is calculated to be $2,603 (1.7355 × $1,500). Since this amount is the value of the annuity at the end of the third year, however, and not the present value, it may be viewed as one $2,603 payment that is delayed 3 years. Therefore, the delayed annuity's present value is then calculated to be $1,956 (.7513 × $2,603), and the total present value of the contract can be determined.

When all of the payments provided by a project are unequal and are therefore not annuities, the present values of all the payments are summed. For example, assume that a project will return $5,200, $4,700, $4,900, $5,000, and $2,500 over 5 years, respectively. The present value of the flow, at 12%, would be calculated as follows:

Years		Flows	Table I Factors (12%)	PV of Flows
0	(date of investment	0	1	0
1		$5,200	.8929	$ 4,643
2		4,700	.7972	3,747
3		4,900	.7118	3,488
4		5,000	.6355	3,178
5		2,500	.5674	1,419
Total present value				$16,475

There is no simple way to calculate the rate of return that equates uneven payments with a given present value. A trial and error iterative process must be used, with all payments discounted at alternative interest rates until the internal rate of return is found. Even computers use such an iterative process to determine the rate of return.

Present Value
Exercises

1. The accounting firm of Fichtel, Sachs, and Bono has agreed to a plan whereby Bono, the retiring partner, would be paid $75,000 at the end of two years, in termination of a partnership interest. Assuming that a 12% interest rate is appropriate under the circumstances, determine the present value of the liquidation payment. Use both the formula and the table methods.

2. Friendly Finance Inc. has arranged a loan for its client, Valerie Rijman. Under the terms of the agreement, Rijman will receive $40,000 today and will pay back $62,436 at the end of three years. What interest rate has Friendly Finance used in calculating the loan repayment?

3. Richard Barton, the happy winner of the Illinois State Lottery, is to receive $125,000 per year, payable at the end of each of the next four years. Assuming that 7% is an appropriate discount rate, what is the present value of the future payments? Use both the formula and the table methods to calculate the present value.

4. The terms of McCurdy's home mortgage require *annual* payments of $10,914 to be made at the end of each of the next 25 years in order to satisfy the $80,000 debt. Determine the interest rate charged by the bank in making the mortgage. What is the total amount of interest McCurdy will pay on the 25-year life of the loan?

5. Dahl Corporation has signed an agreement with Cramer Company to lease 6 computer terminals for the next 3 years. Annual payments of $2,861 are due on the *first* day of each year. The interest rate implicit in the lease is 14%. Calculate the present value of the future lease payments.

6. Under the terms of its agreement with its franchisees, Adam's Ribs Inc. will lend each franchisee any amount up to $175,000 at an interest rate of 8%. Repayment of the loan is deferred for 2 years; i.e., the loan is repaid in equal annual installments made at the end of years 3 through 10. What annual payment would be required to repay a loan of $125,000 under these terms?

7. The terms of the Barber-Klipper Trust require that the following annual payments be made to a charity designated by the trustee:

19X1	$ 8,000
19X2	8,000
19X3	8,000
19X4	8,000
19X5	8,000
19X6	8,000
19X7	52,000
Total	$100,000

Calculate the present value of the above payments, using an 11% discount rate. All payments are made at the end of the designated years.

8. Dan-O Company has sold used equipment to Hawks Inc. on an installment basis. Under the terms of the installment note, Dan-O will pay Hawks $4,000

at the end of years 1 through 4 and $7,500 at the end of years 5 through 7. The interest rate on a similar loan is 15%. If the book value of the equipment on the date of sale was $25,000, what amount of gain (or loss) should Dan-O recognize on the sale?

9. Nick Flatwood has decided to sell his interest in RKO Recording Studios to Century Company, in exchange for a 5% interest in Century's profits over the next 4 years. Profits are to be distributed at the end of each year and are estimated to be as follows: Year 1, $650,000; Year 2, $725,000; Year 3, $950,000; and Year 4, $800,000. Using an 8% rate as the appropriate discount rate, what is the present value of the expected payments to Flatwood?

10. Scott Inc., whose plant is located in the City of Blue River, can elect to pay its property tax bill in one lump sum at the end of the year or in four equal quarterly installments, due on 3/31, 6/30, 9/30, and 12/31. For the year ended 12/31/19X5, Scott estimates its annual property tax bill to total $80,000. Using present value analysis, determine which method of payment is more advantageous to the firm. The firm has a cost of capital of 16%.

1. What is "capital budgeting"?

2. Explain what is meant by the time value of money. Why is the time value of money important to an organization?

3. Describe the two capital project evaluation methods which explicitly consider the time value of money.

4. How does a firm determine the cutoff rate used to evaluate capital investments?

5. Why should a firm *not* use the cost of funds borrowed for a specific project as the cutoff rate in evaluating that project?

6. What is the role of depreciation expense in the calculation of a project's net present value?

7. What two capital project evaluation methods ignore the time value of money? What are the unique advantages of these methods? What are their weaknesses?

8. What is the bailout modification to the regular payback calculation?

9. Assuming that income is constant each year, does a project's accounting rate of return, calculated on a yearly basis, increase or decrease with time?

10. Describe the various ways in which taxes influence capital project evaluation.

11. What combination of discount rates and tax rates makes the 2-point reduction of the investment tax credit desirable?

12. Under what circumstances would first-year expensing of all or part of an asset's cost increase the net present value of a project?

13. How is a firm's incremental investment in working capital associated with a capital project that is being evaluated?

14. Would the use of quarterly or monthly cash flows, as compared to yearly cash flows, increase or decrease the net present value of a project?

EXERCISES

Exercise 1. Don Mondo Company is considering an investment in an $8,000 plastic molding machine, which would be used to produce 1-gallon plastic containers. These containers would broaden the firm's current product line. Cost and revenue estimates for the proposed acquisition are summarized as follows:

	Period				
	0	1	2	3	4
Acquisition cost	$8,000				
Estimated revenue		$12,000	$14,000	$14,000	$15,000
Estimated costs:					
Materials		2,500	2,700	3,000	3,300
Direct labor		1,400	1,700	1,700	1,900
Overhead:					
Depreciation		3,200	2,400	1,600	800
Other		1,500	1,700	1,800	2,000

All Other Overhead costs involve out-of-pocket cash expenditures.

Calculate the net income and cash flow expected to be earned by the project for each of the periods, 0 through 4.

Exercise 2. Sancho Panza Ltd. is evaluating two alternative investment projects. Both projects would have a three-year life. The estimated net cash flows for each project are given in the following table:

	Initial Cost	19X1	19X2	19X3
Project X	($5,000)	$3,000	$3,000	$2,700
Project Y	($8,000)	$4,000	$5,000	$4,000

Sancho Panza's cost of capital is calculated to be 14%.

Calculate the net present value and present value index of each project. Which project would be selected if the net present value criterion is used? Which project would be selected if the present value index is used?

Exercise 3. Raatz in Fashion, an exclusive Beverly Hills boutique, has received an offer from an Argentinian businessperson. In exchange for 5% of the gross sales during the first four years, the businessperson would receive the right to operate a Raatz in Fashion boutique in Buenos Aires and to sell clothes and accessories using the *Raatz in Fashion* trademark. Raatz would bear the boutique's construction cost, 80% of which would be returned at the end of the fourth year. A preliminary analysis has yielded the following projected cash flows:

Years	Cost of Building	5% of Gross Sales
0	($375,000)	—
1	—	$40,000
2	—	50,000
3	—	60,000
4	300,000	70,000

Raatz's financial managers feel that 12% is an appropriate discount rate for the investment. Calculate the project's present value index and its internal rate of return.

Exercise 4. Seger Corporation would like to calculate its weighted average cost of capital to use as a benchmark in evaluating alternative investments. Selected data from the firm's most recent balance sheet are as follows:

Bonds payable (14%, issued at face value) $1,000,000
Preferred stock ($50 par, 12%, 10,000 shares authorized, 8,000 issued and outstanding) 400,000
Common stock ($5 par, 300,000 shares authorized, 240,000 issued and outstanding) 1,200,000
Paid-in capital in excess of par 2,400,000

Dividends declared this year on common stock amounted to $2.20 per share. The firm has increased its annual dividend by 5% per year over the past 7 years, and expects to maintain this growth rate in the future. The current market price per share is $27.50.

Calculate the weighted average cost of capital of the firm. Seger Corporation is in the 30% tax bracket.

Exercise 5. Swartz Trading Company has been approached by a sales representative from a microcomputer firm, who feels that Swartz can improve its efficiency and reduce overhead costs by installing one of the firm's order processing/inventory management systems. Together with several of Swartz's managers, the sales representative has developed the following projections of costs and revenues that would result from installation of the system:

Years	Reduction in Administrative Expenses	Increase in Gross Profit Resulting from Improved Order Processing
1	$ 7,000	$ 3,000
2	8,000	5,000
3	12,000	9,000
4	12,000	15,000
5	12,000	17,000
6–10	12,000	18,000

The system, which would cost $65,000, would be depreciated over 5 years, using ACRS for tax purposes. No investment tax credit is available. The useful life of the machinery is 10 years, with no salvage value. Swartz's marginal tax rate is 40%. Calculate the payback period for the proposed purchase.

Exercise 6. Whitewater Beef Company is considering the purchase of a new slicing machine for $50,000. The new machine would reduce the firm's operating costs, while yielding a better product that could be sold at a higher margin. The combined effect of these changes and the estimated salvage values at the end of each of the next five years are as follows:

	19X1	19X2	19X3	19X4	19X5
Net increase in annual cash flow (includes savings from depreciation)	$18,000	$20,000	$21,000	$20,000	$16,000
Estimated salvage value..	46,750	34,650	23,100	11,500	–0–

The machinery has a five-year useful life and would be scrapped at the end of the fifth year.

Calculate the payback period for the machinery, including the bailout factor for salvage value. Whitewater Beef's marginal tax rate is 46%. Ignore the investment tax credit.

Exercise 7. In its capital budget for the coming year, Excelsior Company has included an investment with the following characteristics:

Cost of machinery	$28,000
Net annual cash inflow	7,000

The machinery will be depreciated over its useful life of 7 years, using the straight-line method for financial reporting purposes. Excelsior Company is in the 46% tax bracket.

Calculate the accounting rate of return on the initial investment.

Exercise 8. McNally Heavy Industries has already decided to purchase new computer-controlled machining equipment. The equipment, which will be depreciated under ACRS, has a cost of $75,000. No salvage value is anticipated at the end of the machinery's six-year useful life. To complete its capital project analysis, McNally must choose between: (a) taking the full 10% investment tax credit and reducing the machinery's depreciable base, or (b) taking an 8% ITC and preserving the entire depreciable base.

Calculate only the net present value of the tax benefits associated with each option and select the more lucrative option. McNally has a 40% incremental tax rate and evaluates all projects by using a 6% aftertax cost of capital.

Exercise 9. Springstein Company has invested in new heating and cooling equipment in an effort to reduce the firm's energy costs. The new, more efficient unit replaces existing equipment which was fully depreciated. The firm must select between 5-year straight-line and 5-year ACRS depreciation methods for tax reporting. Annual cost savings resulting from the purchase are expected to be $15,000 for each of the next five years. The equipment, which cost $45,000, is expected to have no salvage value at the end of its 5-year useful life. The firm is in the 40% tax bracket and evaluates all projects by using a 10% aftertax rate of return.

Calculate the net present value of the project, using each of the depreciation methods. Use the tax shield approach for annual cash flows; ignore the ITC. Note that under the straight-line option, only a half year of depreciation may be taken the first period.

Exercise 10. DB Moving and Cartage would like to purchase a new, medium-duty truck in order to accept business which it must currently refuse for lack of capacity. The truck will cost $17,000 and will be depreciated under the 3-year ACRS method. The truck is expected to be scrapped at the end of the fifth year, with no salvage value. Annual operating revenues and costs generated by the new truck are summarized as follows:

	19X1	19X2	19X3	19X4	19X5
Revenues	$22,000	$23,000	$23,000	$24,000	$24,000
Costs	17,000	18,000	18,000	19,000	19,000

DB uses an 8% aftertax cost of capital in evaluating investment alternatives. The firm is in the 46% tax bracket.

Calculate the net present value of the proposed investment. Ignore the effect of the investment tax credit.

Exercise 11. Brier Patch Natural Foods Ltd. has purchased a new food dehydrater for use in its fruit dehydration operation. The machine, which cost $7,000, qualifies under the first-year expensing election of the tax code. Alternatively, Brier Patch may depreciate the machinery under ACRS and take advantage of a 10% ITC, with a relevant reduction in the equipment's depreciable base. The equipment is not expected to have any salvage value at the end of its 5-year life.

Calculate the net present value of only the tax benefits of the two options, using an 8% cost of capital and a 40% marginal tax rate.

Exercise 12. Vendor Company is evaluating the purchase of an additional delivery truck. The truck would allow the firm to service existing food and beverage vending machines located outside of its current distribution area. The truck is estimated to cost $18,000 and would be depreciated over 3 years, using ACRS. The full 6% ITC would be claimed in the year of purchase. The company estimates an increase of $9,500 in annual cash flow as a result of the purchase. At the end of the third year, the truck would be sold, with negligible salvage value. In addition, the firm estimates that it will need to invest $5,000 in working capital (inventories, supplies, and receivables) as a result of the purchase. Vendor Company's marginal tax rate is 30%, and the firm uses a 12% discount rate in evaluating capital expenditures.

Calculate the net present value of the proposed investment.

PROBLEMS Problem 1. A local service organization is considering the purchase of a computer, which would include word processing software. The organization's management committee feels that the equipment would not only reduce clerical costs, but would increase revenues from contributions by permitting a more efficient fund-raising effort. The committee's best estimate as to the increases in annual cash flow resulting from the purchase are as follows:

Years	Increases in Annual Cash Flow
1	$14,000
2	24,000
3	26,000

The computer would be sold at the end of the third year for $20,000. The cost to purchase the system is $60,000, and it would be depreciated over its useful life by using the sum-of-the-years-digits method for financial reporting purposes. The management committee feels that the project should earn at least 10% to justify its acquisition. The organization pays no taxes.

Required

Calculate the net present value and the internal rate of return of the proposed acquisition. Should the organization purchase the computer?

Problem 2. Eskimo Flavors Inc. needs to replace heating and cooling equipment in its warehouse. The existing system, installed when the warehouse was built, is becoming increasingly unreliable and expensive to maintain. Eskimo has contacted sales representatives from two competing firms to propose replacements for the existing equipment. The sales representative from Viking Heating Products has offered equipment which would cost $22,000, but would reduce annual heating and cooling costs by $5,803 per year. Alternatively, Eskimo can order a system from Braun Company. This system would cost only $12,000, but would reduce annual expenses by only $3,300 per year. Both systems would have five-year lives and negligible salvage values. Eskimo requires a 6% return for all equipment replacement decisions. Taxes are not a factor in the decision.

Required

(1) Calculate the internal rate of return of each alternative. Which proposal should be selected on the basis of this measure?

(2) Calculate the net present value of each alternative. Which alternative has the higher net present value?

(3) Calculate the present value index of each alternative. Which system should be selected on the basis of this measure?

Problem 3. Glenbrook Liquors Inc. is evaluating the purchase of a refrigerated delivery truck for its largest store. The equipment would allow the store to deliver ice blocks and cubes during the warm summer months. The firm already has ice-making equipment, which operates at only 80% of capacity, even in the summer. Glenbrook estimates its annual cash flows from the project as follows:

	19X1	19X2	19X3
Revenue	$6,300	$10,300	$9,900
Operating costs:			
Incremental cost of ice	$ 455	$ 525	$ 570
Maintenance	400	700	650
Fuel	810	1,350	1,400
Other	135	225	280
	$1,800	$ 2,800	$2,900
Net annual cash inflow	$4,500	$ 7,500	$7,000

The truck costs $14,000 and qualifies as 3-year property under ACRS; it will be depreciated using the ACRS rates. The equipment is not expected to have any salvage value at the end of the third year. Glenbrook's marginal tax rate is 40%, and it requires an 8% aftertax return on all investments. No investment tax credit is available.

Required (1) Calculate the annual, aftertax inflow resulting from the purchase, using each of the three methods illustrated in the text: cash flow, net income reconciliation, and tax shield.
(2) Determine the net present value of the project.

Problem 4. ARA Manufacturing Inc. is a manufacturer of industrial switches. The firm currently purchases from outside suppliers the plastic chassis in which the switches are mounted. Its managers, however, are unhappy with the quality of the chassis and the unreliability of their supply, and are considering producing the chassis themselves. This would involve the purchase of a plastic-forming machine and hiring of additional workers. The cost of machinery is $40,000. The units required and the annual cash savings resulting from the purchase are as follows:

	19X1	19X2	19X3	19X4	19X5
Units required	18,000	27,000	30,000	35,000	42,000
Cost to purchase units	$45,000	$67,500	$84,000	$ 98,000	$122,000
Cost to manufacture units:					
Direct labor	$24,000	$25,500	$27,000	$51,000	$ 54,000
Materials	12,500	19,000	22,000	28,000	33,000
Variable overhead	4,000	5,500	6,500	9,000	9,500
Increase in fixed overhead	5,000	5,500	6,000	6,000	6,500
	$45,500	$55,500	$61,500	$94,000	$103,000
Net savings	$ (500)	$12,000	$22,500	$ 4,000	$ 19,000

The machinery would be depreciated over 5 years, using ACRS, and scrapped at the end of the fifth year. Salvage values approximate book values over the life of the investment.

ARA has a simple capital structure. Funds are provided by two sources, debt and common stock. Relevant features of both issues are summarized as follows:

Bonds payable (12%)	$800,000
Common stock ($1 par, 500,000 issued and outstanding) ...	500,000
Paid-in capital in excess of par	204,042

The most recent market price of the common stock was $7.50 per share. Dividends were recently declared in the amount of $.60 per share, and the dividend growth rate is expected to remain near its historical average of 6% per year. ARA has a marginal tax rate of 46%.

Required

(1) Calculate the weighted average cost of capital of the firm.

(2) Calculate the net present value of the project, using the cost of capital calculated in (1). Ignore the investment tax credit.

Problem 5. Eastern Company has invested in new production machinery which is expected to produce the following annual cost savings: Year 1, $8,200; Year 2, $8,800; Year 3, $9,500; Year 4, $9,300; and Year 5, $6,500. The machinery qualifies as 5-year ACRS property, but will be depreciated using the sum-of-the-years-digits method for financial reporting purposes. At the end of its 5-year useful life, the machinery is expected to have a salvage value equal to 5% of its original $25,000 cost. (The sum-of-the-years-digits depreciation will consider this value.) Eastern Company requires all projects to earn 10% after tax to justify acceptance. The firm's marginal tax rate is 46%. No investment tax credit is available.

Required

(1) Calculate the net present value of the investment in machinery.

(2) Determine the accounting rate of return on the project (based on accounting net income):

(a) on an annual basis.

(b) over the life of the project, using average income and the initial investment as a base.

(c) over the life of the project, using average income and the average investment as a base.

Problem 6. The owners of Woodcrest Public Golf Course, in response to the demands of users, are evaluating the purchase of 10 electric golf carts. The golf course is open 12 months each year. For the purpose of projecting revenues, the controller made the following assumptions:

- Each month is 30 days long.
- The carts would be rented an average of 2 hours per day.
- The hourly rental rate is $7. The controller expects the rate to increase by 5% per year over the life of the project.
- Maintenance and repair costs average 15% of gross revenues.
- Other operating costs average 15% of gross revenues.

The golf carts qualify as 5-year ACRS property for depreciation purposes. Each cart costs $4,500 and would have no salvage value at the end of its five-year useful life. Woodcrest Public Golf Course has an incremental tax rate of 46% and requires a 16% aftertax return on all capital investments.

Required

(1) Calculate the net present value of the project under each of the following assumptions:

(a) The full 10% ITC is taken in the year of purchase, with a corresponding reduction in the property's depreciable base.

(b) The discounted, 8% ITC is taken in the year of purchase.

(2) Assume that, as a further alternative to taking a 10% ITC in the year of purchase, the owners may expense $10,000 in the year of purchase and depreciate the residual under ACRS. No ITC is allowed on the portion expensed. Would this option increase or decrease the net present value of the project, and by what amount?

255

Problem 7. In response to the bankruptcy of a rival company, City Veteran Cab Company has decided to add five new taxicabs to its fleet. The five cabs constitute roughly 20% of the capacity of the bankrupt competitor. Under the terms of its agreement with its drivers, City Veteran agrees to purchase the cabs, pay for all maintenance and repair, pay most overhead costs (i.e., insurance, registration fees, etc.), and provide a central dispatching office. The company also agrees to pay all drivers the federal minimum wage of $3.35 per hour. In return, the firm receives 85% of the gross revenues of the cab. The driver receives the remaining 15% in addition to the hourly wage, but must pay for all gasoline. All cabs are in operation 16 hours per day, 360 days per year. The average gross revenue of a cab is $4.75 per hour. Revenues are expected to increase at 6% per year. The firm's accountant has provided you with the following cost data:

	Amount	Expected Rate of Increase per Year
Hourly wage	$3.35 per hour	None
Insurance	$600 per year per cab	10% per year
Registration	$100 per year per cab	None
Maintenance and repair	$350 per year per cab	25% per year
Increase in dispatching		
office costs	$700 per year	10% per year
Other	$200 per year	None

The cabs, which have a 3-year useful life, qualify as 3-year ACRS property for depreciation purposes. Salvage values at the end of the third year are estimated at 20% of the original cost. City Veteran believes it can negotiate a price of $43,500 for the five cabs. The full 6% ITC will be taken in the year of purchase, with a corresponding reduction in the property's depreciable base. City Veteran's incremental tax rate is 40%, and the firm demands a 10% aftertax return on all investments.

Required

(1) Calculate the net annual cash inflow resulting from the project for each year of the project's 3-year useful life.
(2) Calculate the net present value of the project.
(3) Determine the internal rate of return of the proposed investment.

Problem 8. Edward Company sorts and processes scrap steel and other metals. The firm earns most of its revenues by purchasing old cars, crushing them, and then selling the crushed hulks to another scrap processing firm. This firm, in turn, shreds the crushed hulks, separates the ferrous from the nonferrous metals, and sells the ferrous metal, primarily to steel mills. The nonferrous metals are sold to yet another metal processing firm, where they are further sorted, melted, and cast into blocks.

Edward Company is investigating the purchase of a shredder and magnetic separator for its own yard. The firm currently purchases junked cars for roughly $75 each. Usable parts are removed and have a sales value of $25 per car. The stripped car is then sent to the crusher. A crushed car currently sells for $190. Variable costs (primarily direct labor) associated with stripping and crushing a car are $20 per car.

If the shredder/separator is purchased, the crushed car would be shredded rather than sold. The average car hulk weighs 3,500 pounds. Ferrous metals, which comprise 90% of the weight of the car, can be sold to steel mills for $.04 per lb. The remaining nonferrous metals bring a much higher price, roughly $.50 per lb. The costs of operating the shredder/separator are summarized as follows:

Variable costs per car:
Direct labor $3
Variable overhead 3
Fixed overhead (repairs, maintenance, supervision) .... $27,000 per year

In addition to the cost directly associated with owning and operating the shredder, Edward Company expects an increase in working capital as a result of the investment. The change in specific working capital items is summarized in the following table:

	Increase/(Decrease)
Current assets:	
Accounts receivable	($2,500)
Inventory	(6,000)
Current liabilities:	
Accounts payable	700

Edward currently processes 350 cars per year. As shown in the following table, the number is expected to increase modestly over the 5-year life of the equipment.

	19X1	19X2	19X3	19X4	19X5
Cars processed	350	350	370	380	390

The shredding/separating equipment has an installed cost of $50,000. The equipment qualifies as 5-year ACRS property for depreciation purposes. Edward would claim the full 10% ITC in the year of purchase and reduce the machinery's depreciable base accordingly. The equipment is expected to have a salvage value of $7,500 at the end of 19X5. Edward's marginal tax rate is 46%. The firm has an 8% aftertax cost of capital.

Required   (1) Calculate the annual net cash inflow resulting from the acquisition of the equipment.

(2) Calculate the net present value of the proposed acquisition.

Problem 9. The owner of Quick Copy Center is considering the purchase of a sophisticated color-copying machine. The new machine can copy on a wide variety of paper sizes and can handle enlargements as well as reductions. The owner, together with an accountant, has developed the following revenue projections:

		Estimated Revenues				
	Probability	19X1	19X2	19X3	19X4	19X5
Optimistic	.20	$4,900	$5,600	$5,900	$6,300	$6,300
Average	.70	4,100	4,700	5,200	5,500	5,700
Pessimistic	.10	2,800	3,300	3,500	3,800	4,100

Variable costs are estimated at 25% of gross revenues for the life of the project. Fixed costs are expected to increase by $800 the first year as a result of the purchase, and increase by roughly 10% per year over the life of the project.
The cost of the machine is $9,000. In addition, Center's owner expects the following changes in working capital as a result of the investment:

	Increase/(Decrease)
Increase in accounts receivable	$100
Increase in supplies	400
Increase in accounts payable	700

The firm's accountant has urged the owner to expense the entire investment in the year of purchase under the $10,000 first-year expensing election.

Salvage value of the equipment at the end of its five-year useful life is estimated at $700. Center's marginal tax rate is 30%, and its owner demands a 12% aftertax return on all investments.

Required (1) Calculate the expected revenue of the project for each year of its 5-year life.
(2) Determine the annual net cash inflows resulting from the project.
(3) Calculate the net present value of the project.

Problem 10. Canasta Canning Corporation is preparing its capital budget for the coming year. Among the projects selected is the purchase of equipment which will allow Canasta to can food in institutional-size cans, one gallon and up. The anticipated net cash inflows resulting from the investment are summarized as follows:

	19X1	19X2	19X3	19X4	19X5
Increase in annual operating cash flow	$9,800	$10,800	$12,600	$11,500	$10,500

The equipment has a cost of $40,000 and an estimated salvage value of $7,500 at the end of 19X5. The equipment will be depreciated using the 5-year ACRS rates for tax purposes and the 150%-declining-balance method for financial reporting purposes. Canasta will claim the full 10% ITC in the year of purchase, with the appropriate adjustment to the property's depreciable tax basis.

In addition to the investment in equipment, Canasta expects to increase its working capital by $5,000 as a result of the purchase. Canasta's marginal tax rate is 30%, and its aftertax cost of capital is 12%.

Required (1) Calculate the net present value of the 5-year project.
(2) Assume that Canasta sells the equipment at the end of 19X3 for $13,720. Calculate the net present value of the project to the date of sale.

Problem 11. A group of investors have formed Air Atlantic, which will provide scheduled service between Newark and London's Gatwick Airport. The group proposes 5 round trips weekly, using a Boeing 747 aircraft purchased at a bargain price from the creditors of a bankrupt airline.

In estimating the proposed cash flows resulting from the project, the following assumptions were made:

- The year consists of 52 weeks.
- All maintenance and repair will occur during the aircraft's daily 8-hour idle period, or the two days per week when no flights are scheduled.
- The seating capacity of the aircraft will be increased from 361 to 388.
- All tickets will be sold either at the airport ticket counter or at the airline's New York or London offices. Thus, no sophisticated reservation system is needed.
- All ground operations (ticket counter personnel, baggage handling, maintenance, and cleaning) will be subcontracted to other airlines.

On the basis of these assumptions, the following cost/revenue projections were made:

		Estimate	Increase
Revenue:	Ticket price	$179 one way	5% per year
	Load factor	75% of available seats	—
Costs:	Fuel	$28,800 per flight, NYC-LGW	4% per year
	Flight crews:		
	Salary	$68,000 per month	7% per year
	Accommodations	$6,200 per month	5% per year
	Ground operations	$145,000 per month	7% per year
	New York office:		
	Salaries	$5,700 per month	6% per year
	Other	$1,300 per month	None
	London office:		
	Salaries	$5,200 per month	6% per year
	Other	$1,800 per month	None
	Other administrative	$15,000 per month	7% per year

In addition to the above operating cash flows, the following capital expenditures will be made:

Purchase cost of aircraft	$25,000,000
Cost of modifications (repainting, increase in seating capacity, etc.)	270,000
Other	125,000
Total	$25,395,000

All capital expenditures are depreciable over 5 years, using ACRS rates, and all qualify for the investment tax credit. In addition, the investors expect that an investment of $2,000,000 in working capital will be required to sustain the operation. At the end of the fifth year, the aircraft will be sold for an estimated $7,000,000.

Air Atlantic's expected marginal tax rate is 46%. The firm's investors demand an 8% aftertax return before undertaking the investment. The firm will elect to take the full 10% ITC.

Required   (1) Calculate the expected annual net cash inflow resulting from the investment.
(2) Determine the net present value of the investment.

Eight _____

Special Issues in Capital Budgeting

The basic capital project evaluation methods described in Chapter 7 will now be applied to typical investment problems which confront firms. The first issue to be addressed is the problem of choosing the best investment when several alternatives exist. The discussion focuses on the ranking of projects, choosing between two assets when only one can be acquired, and analyzing the profitability of replacing an existing asset with a new one. Although inflation and risk are not always explicitly considered in the analyses currently made by firms, the evaluation procedures will be expanded to include these factors. The chapter concludes by considering the desirability of leasing as an alternative method of financing the acquisition of assets.

CHOOSING AMONG ALTERNATIVES

A firm will often find itself with the dilemma of having many profitable projects from which to choose, but only limited funds to invest. In other cases, a firm may be presented with several alternative proposals for a single project. In both situations, internal rates of return (IRR) or present value indexes (PVI) are used as the primary means of comparing the projects or proposals. These measures, however, may provide differing results.

Conflicting Results of Analyses

The internal rate of return method and the net present value method may produce conflicting results when they are used to evaluate projects with different lives or substantially different patterns of cash flows. The following example illustrates the conflict for two single-payment projects with unequal lives:

Projects	Cash Flows				IRRs	Present Values of Future Flows at 12%	PVIs at 12%
	0	1	2	3			
A	−$1,000	$1,250	0	0	25%	$1,116	1.12
B	− 1,000	0	0	$1,728	20	1,230	1.23

Illustration 8-1 is a graphical explanation of the conflicting results for Projects A and B. The solid horizontal lines represent the rate of return for each project over its life. Project A does earn 25%, but only for one year, while Project B earns 20% for the full three years. When projects are compared by their internal rates of return, it is implicitly assumed that the shorter-lived project (A) will have its proceeds reinvested at its internal rate of return (in this case, 25%) for the remaining period (2 years) in which the longer-lived project's (B's) flows would have been realized. The dashed line on the graph indicates this assumption, which an optimistic management might tolerate, because it would believe that replacement investments could earn at least as much as the original investment.

On the other hand, when projects are compared by their present value indexes, it is implicitly assumed that the shorter-lived project (A) will have its proceeds reinvested at the cutoff rate used in the analysis (in this case, 12%) for the remaining period (2 years) in which the longer-lived project's (B's) flows would have been realized. The dotted line in the graph indicates this assumption, which might be tolerated by a pessimistic or conservative management, because it would believe that replacement investments earning more than the cutoff rate will not exist. In this example, the cutoff rate of 12% is a logical rate of return for the reinvested proceeds of Project A. If any rate above 12% were earned in the

Illustration 8-1
Comparing the Assumptions of IRR and PVI Analysis

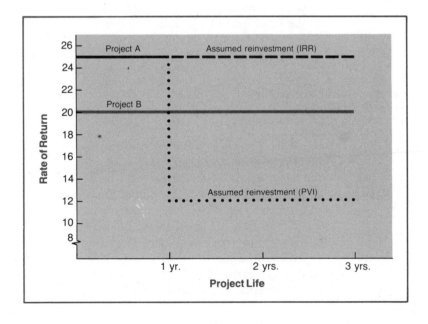

second and third years, the present value of the project would be greater than $1,116. If any rate less than 12% were earned in the second and third years, the present value would be less than $1,116. Only if exactly 12% is earned in the second and third years will the present value be $1,116.

To solve the problem of conflicting analytical results for projects with unequal lives, two alternatives are possible: cut off the longer-lived project by ignoring flows beyond the end of the shorter-lived project; or specify the anticipated reinvestment rate for the shorter-lived project. If the first alternative is used, the longer-lived project's salvage value at the end of the shorter-lived project must be estimated. This estimate may be difficult to make, and it will typically impart a negative bias to the longer-lived project. The negative bias occurs because the asset's premature salvage value is probably far less than the asset's value in continued productive use. The more specific the purpose of the asset, the greater this bias will be.

To illustrate the first alternative applied to the previous example, assume that Project B has an estimated salvage value of $1,150 at the end of one year. Projects A and B would then be analyzed as follows:

| | Cash Flows | | | Present Values of Future | |
Projects	0	1	IRRs	Flows at 12%	PVIs at 12%
A	−$1,000	$1,250	25%	$1,116	1.16
B	− 1,000	1,150	15%	1,027	1.03

When the anticipated reinvestment rate for the shorter-lived project is specified, the future value of the funds reinvested can be determined. The future value of the shorter-lived project and the reinvested funds can then be compared to the value of the longer-lived project. The following table shows the results of applying this alternative to Projects A and B, using an 18% reinvestment rate. The table also shows the results of assuming that the proceeds from Project A are reinvested at the cutoff rate (12%) and the internal rate of return (25%).

| | Amounts of Return at End of Years | | | Overall |
	1	2	3	IRRs
B	-	-	$1,728	20.0%
A (reinvest at estimated future rate of 18%)	$1,250	$1,475 (1.18 × $1,250)	1,741 (1.18 × $1,475)	20.3
A (reinvest at cutoff rate of 12%)	1,250	1,400 (1.12 × $1,250)	1,568 (1.12 × $1,400)	16.2
A (reinvest at internal rate of return of 25%)	1,250	1,562 (1.25 × $1,250)	1,953 (1.25 × $1,562)	25.0

If the proceeds of Project A at the end of year 1, $1,250, are reinvested in other projects during years 2 and 3 and earn 18% per year, the total accumulated funds at the end of three years will be $1,741. This amount exceeds the funds provided by Project B at the end of the third year. If management's objective is to maximize cash flows, this comparison of future values is a sound approach.

As the table indicates, an overall internal rate of return for Project A and its reinvested proceeds can be calculated. This rate equates the single initial payment of $1,000 to a future value. Using Table 1 (in the appendix at the end of the textbook) and the $1,741 accumulated from reinvesting the proceeds at 18%, the overall internal rate of return is determined as follows:

$$\text{Overall IRR} = 20.0\% + \frac{\text{Table 1 factor for 3 years at 20.0\%} - .5744^*}{\text{Table 1 factor for 3 years at 20.0\%} - \text{Table 1 factor, 3 years at 21.0\%}}$$

$$= 20.0\% + \frac{.5787 - .5744}{.5787 - .5645}$$

$$= 20.0\% + .3028$$

$$= 20.3\%$$

$*$Present value factor $\times \$1,741 = \$1,000$

$$\text{Present value factor} = \frac{\$1,000}{\$1,741}$$

$$\text{Present value factor} = .5744$$

The internal rate of return method and the net present value method may also produce conflicting evaluations of annuities with different lives and different initial costs, as shown in the following example:

Projects	0	1	2	3	4	5	IRRs	Present Values of Future Flows at 12%	PVIs at 12%
			Cash Flows						
C	−$5,000	$2,374	$2,374	$2,374	0	0	20%	$5,702	1.14
D	− 8,000	2,558	2,558	2,558	$2,558	$2,558	18	9,221	1.15

For resolving these conflicts, the procedures used to evaluate single-payment projects with different lives or different cash flows are applicable. Illustration 8-2 shows the impact on the evaluation of Projects C and D when the proceeds from these projects are reinvested at four different rates—a 15% estimated future rate, the 12% cutoff rate, the 20% IRR for Project C, and the 18% IRR for Project D. In this illustration of evaluating the two annuities, a future value (FV) and a future value index (FVI) are determined. The future value index is the ratio of dollars of future value per dollar of original investment.

When the proceeds from Projects C and D are reinvested at the 12% cutoff rate, Project D is the more profitable project, as was suggested by the comparison of the projects' present value indexes. When the proceeds are reinvested at the

Illustration 8-2
Comparison of
Reinvestment
Assumptions for Capital
Projects with Unequal
Lives

	C	D
Reinvest at estimated future rate of 15%:		
FV	$10,903	$17,427
FVI	2.18	2.16
Overall IRR	16.87%	16.61%
Reinvest at cutoff rate of 12%:		
FV	$10,049	$16,251
FVI	2.01	2.03
Overall IRR	14.98%	15.23%
Reinvest at IRR for Project C, 20%:		
FV	$12,444	$19,035
FVI	2.49	2.38
Overall IRR	20.00%	18.93%
Reinvest at IRR for Project D, 18%:		
FV	$11,809	$18,300
FVI	2.36	2.29
Overall IRR	18.75%	18.00%

20% IRR of Project C, the shorter-lived project, the analysis indicates that Project C is the more profitable project.

Another example of conflicting evaluations will occur when projects have equal lives but different cash flow patterns. The following table shows the internal rates of return and the present value indexes for two projects, E and F, that have these characteristics:

Projects	Cash Flows				IRRs	Present Values of Future Flows at 12%	PVIs at 12%
	0	1	2	3			
E	−$ 6,000	0	0	$9,858	18%	$ 7,017	1.17
F	− 10,000	$4,747	$4,747	4,747	20	11,401	1.14

When the net present value method is used, the proceeds of Project F are assumed to be reinvested at 12%. Under this assumption, Project E is the more profitable project. When the internal rate of return method is used, however, the proceeds of Project F are assumed to be reinvested at 20%, which makes Project F more attractive. In general, the net present value method favors later flows, while the internal rate of return method favors earlier flows. The impact of these evaluation methods is verified in Illustration 8-3, in which the proceeds from Projects E and F are reinvested at three different rates—a 15% estimated future rate, the 12% cutoff rate, and the 20% IRR for Project F.

Illustration 8-3
Comparison of Reinvestment Assumptions for Capital Projects with Different Cash Flow Patterns

	E	F
Reinvest at estimated future rate of 15%:		
FV	$9,858	$16,484
FVI	1.64	1.72
Overall IRR	18.00%	18.13%
Reinvest at cutoff rate of 12%:		
FV	$9,858	$16,019
FVI	1.64	1.60
Overall IRR	18.00%	17.01%
Reinvest at IRR for Project F, 20%:		
FV	$9,858	$17,279
FVI	1.64	1.73
Overall IRR	18.00%	20.00%

Most firms have exhibited a willingness to tolerate the differing reinvestment assumptions inherent in the net present value and internal rate of return methods. If a firm desires to further refine capital project evaluations, however, the procedures described in the preceding paragraphs may be used.

Ranking Investment Opportunities

Frequently, a decision maker will be confronted with mutually exclusive alternatives; i.e., only one project from a given set may be chosen. For example, a firm may need one milling machine; but several models are available, and each provides a different return. It is also typical for a firm to have more investment opportunities than it has available funds. In this situation, the firm should use a ranking procedure for identifying the set of investments which will maximize the return on available funds.

Mutually Exclusive Projects. Mutually exclusive projects can be classified as one of two common types. The first type is the situation in which it is necessary to choose the best asset from a set of possible assets, e.g., choosing the best factory, the best computer system, or the best delivery truck. The other type is the situation in which it is necessary to choose the proper scale of a project, e.g., choosing to build either a 4-, 8-, 12-, or 16-unit building on land zoned for multifamily dwellings.

Since funds usually are limited, it is most common to begin with the lowest cost alternative and then progress to more expensive options. For example, assume that you are considering alternative computer system configurations, each of which offers cash savings when compared to the current manual system. To avoid conflicting reinvestment assumptions, you assume that each system has a 5-year life with negligible salvage value. To determine which system is the most profitable, you measure the return of each system, as shown in the following table:

Systems	Costs	Annual Cash Savings	IRRs	Present Values of Cash Savings at 10%	PVIs at 10%
A	$ 5,000	$1,250	7.93%	$ 4,738	.95
B	8,000	2,165	11.03	8,208	1.03
C	12,000	3,600	15.26	13,647	1.14
D	15,000	4,312	13.47	16,347	1.09
E	18,000	5,270	14.21	19,979	1.11
F	20,000	5,780	13.69	21,912	1.10

The calculations would seem to indicate that the most profitable project is System C. Assume, however, that the firm's opportunity cost of funds is 10%, and that any project exceeding that rate should be undertaken. Thus, System F would appear to be the project to choose, since it would involve more funds being invested at more than 10%. To determine if System F is the best project under this assumption, **incremental analysis** is needed. Incremental analysis is applied, as shown in Illustration 8-4, by proceeding according to the following steps:

1. Arrange projects in the order of increasing initial cost.
2. Find the first level that exceeds the cutoff rate and consider it the base level. For the next level of investment above the base level, compare the incremental initial cost and the incremental cash savings. Accept the increment if its IRR exceeds the cutoff rate; reject it if its IRR is less than the cutoff rate.
3. Once an increment is accepted, proceed to the next highest initial cost alternative. Compare the incremental initial cost and the incremental cash savings, as in Step 2, and accept or reject the increment.

In Illustration 8-4, incremental analysis indicates that System E will employ the maximum funds at a rate of return that exceeds the cutoff rate of 10%. Although System C is the most profitable, System E produces an additional return. Unless funds are limited and other projects earn more than 12.13%, System E is the best choice.

Incremental analysis becomes more difficult when projects have unequal cash flows and/or unequal lives. The approach remains the same, however, except for the consideration of differing reinvestment assumptions.

Illustration 8-4   Incremental Analysis

Systems	Costs	Annual Cash Savings	Incremental Initial Costs	Incremental Annual Cash Savings	Incremental IRRs	Incremental PVs at 10%	Incremental PVIs at 10%	Decisions
A	$ 5,000	$1,250	$5,000	$1,250	7.93%	$4,738	.95	Do not accept. Analyze B as base level.
B	8,000	2,165	8,000[a]	2,165	11.03	8,208	1.03	Accept B as base level. Consider next increment.
C	12,000	3,600	4,000[b]	1,435	23.27[c]	5,440	1.36[d]	Replace B with C. Consider next increment.
D	15,000	4,312	3,000	712	6.01	2,699	.90	Stay with C. Consider increment to E.
E	18,000	5,270	6,000[e]	1,670	12.13	6,331	1.06	Replace C with E, since increment exceeds cutoff rate.
F	20,000	5,780	2,000	510	8.70	1,933	.97	Stay with E.

[a] Analysis starts from zero, since A was rejected.
[b] System C is compared to System B.
[c] Rate that equates incremental annual cash savings, $1,435, with incremental cost, $4,000.
[d] Incremental PV of $5,440 ÷ incremental cost of $4,000.
[e] System E is compared to System C, since D was rejected.

Project Selection with Limited Funds. When projects are ranked by their profitability measures, it would seem reasonable to proceed down the ranking until all funds are exhausted. This process is not usually possible, however, because most investments cannot be divided when the last funds available are not sufficient for a complete project. Therefore, a firm must select a **portfolio** or set of projects which will maximize the return for the entire portfolio. This selection is accomplished through an iterative process which computes the present value index or the internal rate of return for each possible portfolio.[1]

In Illustration 8-5, several projects are analyzed for the purpose of selecting a portfolio. Included in the list of possible projects are Computer Systems C and E from Illustration 8-4. Although these two projects are mutually exclusive, System E is ranked as "Computer System E>C" in order to show that it is the increment of E over C and that it can only be accepted if C has met the criteria for being included in the portfolio.

The amount of available funds for the portfolio is $40,000. If all the funds are not spent because some of the investments are indivisible, the remaining funds are assumed to be invested in the market at the cutoff rate of 10%. This rate is assumed to reflect the opportunity value of other available investments, such as publicly traded securities.

[1]Portfolio selection can be designed as an integer programming problem that involves maximizing the combined net present value or the interest earnings of the portfolio, subject to the constraint that the total cost of the portfolio cannot exceed the funds available.

The investment alternatives included in Illustration 8-5 are first ranked, in (1), according to their present value indexes. In Iteration 1, projects with the highest present value indexes are selected for the portfolio, using as much of the $40,000 as possible without dividing an investment. In Iteration 2, the portfolio's present value index was increased by substituting the furnace for the phone system, the office copier, and the investment in the market.

Substitution should be attempted whenever a project preempted by a lack of funds results in including in the portfolio small, "filler" projects that offer a lower PVI. In Illustration 8-5, the $15,000 furnace, with a PVI of 1.12, was initially preempted, and the phone system, the office copier, and the market investment were included, even though their PVIs were lower. If the furnace is to be included in the portfolio, other projects with higher PVIs must be sacrificed, so that $15,000 is made available. By making this substitution, the present value of the portfolio can be increased by $16,733. To maximize profits, the projects sacrificed should be those which have the least effect on profits. Therefore, the following alternatives should be considered:

	Costs	PVIs at 10%	PVs at 10%
1. Drop phone system	$ 3,000	1.16	$ 3,486
Drop office copier	8,000	1.10	8,763
Drop investment in market	4,000	1.00	4,000
	$15,000		$16,249
2. Drop Computer System C	$12,000	1.14	$13,647
Drop investment in market	3,000	1.00	3,000
	$15,000		$16,647

Iteration 2 of Illustration 8-5 (1) uses the first substitution. Substitution then ceases, since there are no other preempted projects which would provide a higher return and which have not been considered.

In Illustration 8-5 (2), the investment alternatives are ranked according to their internal rates of return. To assemble the most profitable portfolio under this ranking, it is necessary to compute the interest earnings for the first year. These earnings should be maximized, since it is assumed that the funds from each project are reinvested at that project's internal rate of return.

As in Illustration 8-5 (1), substitution is attempted when a preempted project offers a higher IRR than the small, "filler" projects. In this illustration, the furnace offers an IRR of 11.98%, which exceeds the rates offered by the soft drink machine and the market investment. Therefore, the following alternatives should be considered in order to determine which projects could be sacrificed without reducing profits more than the $1,797 ($15,000 × 11.98%) of first-year interest that would be gained by including the furnace in the portfolio:

	(1) Costs	(2) IRRs	(3) First-Year Interest (1) × (2)
1. Drop materials handler	$12,000	14.00%	$1,680
Drop investment in market	3,000	10.00	300
	$15,000		$1,980

		(1)	(2)	(3) First-Year Interest
		Costs	IRRs	(1) × (2)
2.	Drop phone system	$ 3,000	17.31	$ 519
	Drop office copier	8,000	12.87	1,030
	Drop investment in market	4,000	10.00	400
		$15,000		$1,949

Illustration 8-5
Portfolio Analysis

In this illustration, both substitutions require a sacrifice in excess of the earnings offered by the new furnace. Thus, the initial portfolio of (2) is retained. However, the final portfolios of (1) and (2) are different, since the projects being considered have different lives.

Investment Alternatives	Life	Cost	Annual Cash Flows	IRRs	Present Values of Cash Flows at 10%	PVIs at 10%
Computer System C	5 yrs.	$12,000	$3,600	15.26%	$13,647	1.14
Computer System E > C	5	6,000	1,670	12.14	6,331	1.06
Office copier	7	8,000	1,800	12.87	8,762	1.10
Materials handler	10	12,000	2,300	14.00	14,134	1.18
Phone system	4	3,000	1,100	17.31	3,487	1.16
New furnace	15	15,000	2,200	11.98	16,733	1.12
Soft drink machine	10	1,000	170	11.06	1,045	1.05

(1) Portfolio Selection Using PVI

Iteration 1

Portfolio	Cost	PVs of Cash Flows at 10%	PVIs at 10%
Materials handler	$12,000	$14,334	1.18
Phone system	3,000	3,487	1.16
Computer System C	12,000	13,647	1.14
Office copier	8,000	8,762	1.10
Soft drink machine	1,000	1,045	1.05
Investment in market	4,000	4,000	1.00
	$40,000	$45,075	1.127 ($45,075 ÷ $40,000)

Comment: Try substituting furnace, with PVI of 1.12, for phone system, office copier, and investment in market.

Iteration 2

Portfolio	Cost	PVs of Cash Flows at 10%	PVIs at 10%
Materials handler	$12,000	$14,334	1.18
Computer System C	12,000	13,647	1.14
New furnace	15,000	16,733	1.12
Soft drink machine	1,000	1,045	1.05
	$40,000	$45,558	1.139 ($45,558 ÷ $40,000)

Comment: This set of investments is the most profitable.

(2) Portfolio Selection Using IRR

<u>Iteration 1</u>

Portfolio	(1) Cost	(2) IRRs	(3) First-Year Interest (1) × (2)
Phone system	$ 3,000	17.31%	$ 519
Computer System C	12,000	15.26	1,831
Materials handler	12,000	14.00	1,680
Office copier	8,000	12.87	1,030
Soft drink machine	1,000	11.06	111
Investment in market	4,000	10.00	400
	$40,000	13.93 ($5,571 ÷ $40,000)	$5,571

Replacing an Existing Asset

Replacing an existing asset with a new asset involves a unique, mutually exclusive type of decision. The question to be answered is whether the added savings or profit contributions of the new asset, as compared to the old asset, justify the added cost.

One of the special considerations of a replacement decision is that the remaining cash flows for the existing asset, as well as the cash flows for the new asset, must be projected. These cash flows should be projected separately, and their differences should then be compared.

Another special consideration is the problem of the differing lives of the existing asset and the new asset. For example, if the existing asset has a remaining life of 5 years and the replacement asset has a 10-year life, there is no basis for comparison of the cash flows during the last 5 years of the replacement asset's life. One possible solution for this problem is to base the comparison on the first 5 years of the new asset's life, specifying a salvage value at the end of the fifth year. Although the value of the asset in its productive use may exceed its market value, as mentioned previously, basing the comparison on the first five years may not distort the analysis, since the present value of flows that are five or more years away is usually not significant.

Another possible solution to the problem of the differing lives is to construct a replacement chain. In the previous example, the asset that would replace the existing asset at the end of its 5-year life could be specified, along with the replacement asset's projected cash flows. These flows would then be compared with the flows that would result from replacing the existing asset now. However, if the life of the asset acquired five years hence exceeds the life of the asset acquired currently, the chain would need to be expanded, as shown in the following diagram:

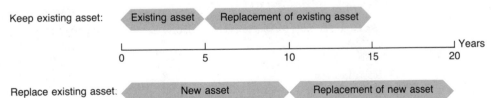

Although a replacement chain could be constructed for infinite future periods, it would be reasonable to end the comparison at 10 years, since the present value of distant flows is low at any reasonable cutoff rate. The replacement chain also involves the problem of specifying an early salvage value for the asset that replaces the existing asset; but since that value is discounted 10 years, its effect will not be significant. For simplicity, the text will project cash flows over the life of the existing asset and will assume an early salvage value for the replacement asset.

The analytic technique for a replacement decision is demonstrated in Illustration 8-6. In this illustration, the cash flows offered by the new asset and the old asset are analyzed separately, and the differences between the cash flows each period are then calculated. In (1), the cash flows used in the analysis of the new asset include the proceeds from the sale of the old asset as well as the tax loss on the sale. Cash flows applicable to the old asset's sale are included because the current salvage value of the old asset is only realized *if the new asset is purchased.* In (2), the analysis of the old asset is based on the assumption that the old asset is retained; therefore, the salvage value included is that which is estimated for 5 years later.

The comparison of the net flows in (3) identifies clearly the incremental flows made available by the new asset. Illustration 8-6 (3) resembles the typical evaluation of a new capital asset acquisition, and includes all four measures discussed in Chapter 7.

Illustration 8-6
Evaluation of Proposal To
Replace Existing Asset

Facts as of January 1, 19X3:

Current asset . . . . Asset was purchased on January 1, 19X1, for $15,000. The investment tax credit of $1,500 (10%) was taken. ACRS depreciation has been applied to 95% of the asset's cost, as follows: 19X1, $2,137.50; 19X2, $3,135; 19X3-19X5, $2,992.50.

Asset would be sold on January 1, 19X3, for $5,000. As a result, $900 (3 years × 2% × $15,000) of the ITC would be recaptured. The loss on the sale would be:

Price		$5,000
Book value:		
Undepreciated basis (.63 × $14,250)	$8,978	
One half of ITC recaptured (1/2 × $900)	450	9,428
Loss on sale		$4,428

Operating costs per year were $15,000.

Salvage value after 5 years (if asset is retained) is $2,000, which would be entirely gain.

New asset . . . . . . The cost of the asset would be $30,000. The 10% investment tax credit of $3,000 would be taken. ACRS depreciation would be applied to 95% of the asset's cost, as follows: 19X3, $4,275; 19X4, $6,270; 19X5-19X7, $5,985.

Operating costs per year will be $7,000.

Salvage value after 5 years would be $6,000, which would be entirely gain.

Tax rate 46%

Cutoff rate 10%

(1) Analysis of New Asset

	Cost	ITC	t(Depr.)	Operating Flows	Taxes on Operating Flows	Salvage	Cash Flows on Salvage	Net Flows
Jan. 1, 19X3	−$30,000					$5,000		−$25,000[a]
Dec. 31, 19X3		$2,100[b]	$1,966[c]	−$7,000	$3,220		$2,037[d]	2,323
Dec. 31, 19X4			2,884	− 7,000	3,220			− 896
Dec. 31, 19X5			2,753	− 7,000	3,220			− 1,027
Dec. 31, 19X6			2,753	− 7,000	3,220			− 1,027
Dec. 31, 19X7			2,753	− 7,000	3,220	6,000	− 2,760[e]	2,213

[a] $30,000 cost − $5,000 sale of old asset
[b] $3,000 on new asset − $900 (3 × 2% × $15,000) recaptured on old asset
[c] 46% × $4,275 depreciation
[d] $4,428 tax loss on sale × 46% = $2,037 cash provided
[e] 46% × $6,000 salvage = $2,760 cash outflow

(2) Analysis of Old Asset

	Cost	ITC	t(Depr.)	Operating Flows	Taxes on Operating Flows	Salvage	Cash Flows on Salvage	Net Flows
Jan. 1, 19X3								-0-
Dec. 31, 19X3			$1,377[a]	−$15,000	$6,900			−$ 6,723
Dec. 31, 19X4			1,377	− 15,000	6,900			− 6,723
Dec. 31, 19X5			1,377	− 15,000	6,900			− 6,723
Dec. 31, 19X6				− 15,000	6,900			− 8,100
Dec. 31, 19X7				− 15,000	6,900	$2,000	−$ 920[b]	− 7,020

[a] 46% × $2,992.50 depreciation
[b] 46% × $2,000 salvage

(3) Comparison of Net Flows

	Net Flows New Asset	Net Flows Old Asset	Differences	PV Factors (10%)	PVs of Differences	Cash Flows to Date
Jan. 1, 19X3	−$25,000	-0-	−$25,000	1.0000	−$25,000	−$25,000
Dec. 31, 19X3	2,323	−$6,723	9,046	.9091	8,224	− 15,954
Dec. 31, 19X4	− 896	− 6,723	5,827	.8264	4,815	− 10,127
Dec. 31, 19X5	− 1,027	− 6,723	5,696	.7513	4,219	− 4,431
Dec. 31, 19X6	− 1,027	− 8,100	7,073	.6830	4,831	2,642
Dec. 31, 19X7	2,213	− 7,020	9,233	.6209	5,733	11,875
					$ 2,822	

NPV: $2,822
Total PV: $25,000 + $2,822 = $27,822
PVI: $27,822 ÷ $25,000 = 1.113
IRR: 14.411%
Payback: 3 + ($4,431 ÷ $7,073) = 3.6 years
Accounting rate of return (initial investment):
($11,875 ÷ 5) ÷ $25,000 = $2,375 ÷ $25,000 = .095

A possible complication that may arise in determining cash flows when assets are traded is the result of the federal tax provision for like-kind exchanges. Under this provision, no gain or loss is recognized on the trade of assets of "like kind." Instead, the cost of the new asset is the book value of the old asset plus the cash difference paid. Thus, the gain (loss) on the old asset is spread over the depreciable life of the new asset by increasing (decreasing) the depreciation deduction.

THE IMPACT OF INFLATION ON CAPITAL PROJECT EVALUATIONS

Since the focus of capital project evaluations is the analysis of future cash flows, the impact of inflation on those flows must be considered. In the discussion thus far, it has been assumed that there would be no inflationary impact and that future flows could be expressed in today's dollars. However, the erosion of the dollar's purchasing power is likely to continue; therefore, the evaluation of capital projects should not overlook the impact of inflation. The alternatives that firms use in considering inflation range from ignoring it to adjusting the cutoff rate to adjusting cash flows. These alternatives are described and illustrated in the following paragraphs.

Ignoring Inflation

Illustration 8-7 is a typical capital project analysis that includes no adjustment for inflation, since it is assumed that no changes in price levels will occur. It is also assumed that the full 10% ITC will be taken, that ACRS depreciation will be applied to 95% of the asset's cost, and that the operating flows are uneven over the project's life.

When inflation is ignored, all projections are in today's dollars. This approach is sometimes defended on the basis that the same values would result if all flows were inflated to their future dollar values and then deflated to today's dollars. For example, if the first-year flows in Illustration 8-7 were inflated by 6% to $20,222.15 ($19,077.50 × 1.06) and then deflated to today's dollars by dividing $20,222.15 by 1.06, the result would be the same as if inflation had been ignored. However, this procedure for considering inflation is based on the assumption that all operating flows will change exactly according to the general inflation rate, which is an average rate applicable to an assumed mix of goods. Furthermore, the cash flows provided by the depreciation tax shield and ITC will not change at all, since they are based on the original cost of the asset. Thus, the failure to adjust for inflation is simplistic and not theoretically justified.

Illustration 8-7
Capital Project Evaluation
When Inflation Is Ignored

Cost: $50,000
ITC: 10%
Depreciation (ACRS on 95% of cost): Year 1 .... 15% × 95% × $50,000 = $ 7,125
                                      Year 2 .... 22% × 95% × $50,000 = 10,450
                                      Year 3 .... 21% × 95% × $50,000 =   9,975
                                      Year 4 .... 21% × 95% × $50,000 =   9,975
                                      Year 5 .... 21% × 95% × $50,000 =   9,975

Operating flows:
  Revenue: Year 1-3 .... $50,000   Expenses: Year 1-3 .... $30,000
            Year 4   40,000   Year 4 20,000
            Year 5   30,000   Year 5 15,000
Salvage value: $15,000
Tax rate: 46%
Cutoff rate: 8%

Years	Cost	ITC	Revenue	Expenses	Net Flows	Taxes on Operating Flows	t(Depr.)
0	−$50,000						
1		$5,000	$50,000	−$30,000	$20,000	−$9,200	$3,277.50
2			50,000	− 30,000	20,000	− 9,200	4,807.00
3			50,000	− 30,000	20,000	− 9,200	4,588.50
4			40,000	− 20,000	20,000	− 9,200	4,588.50
5			30,000	− 15,000	15,000	− 6,900	4,588.50

Salvage	Tax on Salvage	Total Flows	PV Factors (8%)	PVs of Total Flows at 8%	Cash Flows to Date	Years
		−$50,000.00	1.0000	−$50,000.00	−$50,000.00	0
		19,077.50	.9259	17,663.86	− 30,922.50	1
		15,607.00	.8573	13,379.88	− 15,315.50	2
		15,388.50	.7938	12,215.39	73.00	3
		15,388.50	.7350	11,310.55	15,461.50	4
$15,000	−$6,900	20,788.50	.6806	14,148.65	36,250.00	5
				$18,718.33		

NPV: $18,718.33
Total PV: $50,000 + $18,718.33 = $68,718.33
PVI: $68,718.33 ÷ $50,000 = 1.374
IRR: 21.28%
Payback: 3 + ($15,315.50 ÷ $15,388.50) = 4 years
Accounting rate of return (initial investment):
($36,250 ÷ 5) ÷ $50,000 = $7,250 ÷ $50,000 = .145

Adjusting the Cutoff Rate

Decision makers commonly consider inflation by adding the assumed inflation rate to the cutoff rate. For example, if the cutoff rate is 8% and the inflation rate is 6%, the adjusted cutoff rate would be 14%. This adjusted rate is then applied to noninflation-adjusted returns.

When this approach is used, as shown in Illustration 8-8, the net present value and the present value index are much lower than they were when inflation was ignored in Illustration 8-7. The net present value has fallen from $18,718.33 to $9,040.69, and the present value index has fallen from 1.374 to 1.181. The internal rate of return is still 21.28%, but it is now compared to the adjusted cutoff rate of 14%. The payback and accounting rate of return do not change.

Illustration 8-8
Capital Project Evaluation
When Inflation Is
Considered by Adjusting
the Cutoff Rate

Cost: $50,000
ITC: 10%
Depreciation (ACRS on 95% of cost):
Year 1 .... 15% × 95% × $50,000 = $ 7,125
Year 2 .... 22% × 95% × $50,000 = 10,450
Year 3 .... 21% × 95% × $50,000 = 9,975
Year 4 .... 21% × 95% × $50,000 = 9,975
Year 5 .... 21% × 95% × $50,000 = 9,975

Operating flows:
Revenue: Year 1-3 ... $50,000   Expenses: Year 1-3 .... $30,000
           Year 4   40,000   Year 4   20,000
           Year 5   30,000   Year 5   15,000
Salvage value: $15,000
Tax rate: 46%
Cutoff rate: 8%
General inflation rate: 6%

Years	Cost	ITC	Revenue	Expenses	Net Flows	Taxes on Operating Flows	t(Depr.)
0	− $50,000						
1		$5,000	$50,000	− $30,000	$20,000	− $9,200	$3,277.50
2			50,000	− 30,000	20,000	− 9,200	4,807.00
3			50,000	− 30,000	20,000	− 9,200	4,588.50
4			40,000	− 20,000	20,000	− 9,200	4,588.50
5			30,000	− 15,000	15,000	− 6,900	4,588.50

Salvage	Tax on Salvage	Total Flows	PV Factors (14%)	PVs of Total Flows at 4%	Cash Flows to Date	Years
		− $50,000.00	1.0000	− $50,000.00	− $50,000.00	0
		19,077.50	.8772	16,374.78	− 30,922.50	1
		15,607.00	.7695	12,009.59	− 15,315.50	2
		15,388.50	.6750	10,387.24	73.00	3
		15,388.50	.5921	9,111.53	15,461.50	4
$15,000	− $6,900	20,788.50	.5194	10,797.55	36,250.00	5
				$ 9,040.69		

NPV: $9,040.69
Total PV: $50,000 + $9,040.69 = $59,040.69
PVI: $59,040.69 ÷ $50,000 = 1.181
IRR: 21.28%
Payback: 3 + ($15,315.50 ÷ $15,388.50) = 4 years
Accounting rate of return (initial investment):
  ($36,250 ÷ 5) ÷ $50,000 = $7,250 ÷ $50,000 = .145

Adjusting Cash Flows

The difficulty with adjusting only the cutoff rate for inflation is that the results of a project evaluation become overly conservative. To overcome this deficiency, the future cash flows should be adjusted for inflation.

In Illustration 8-9, the specific rates of inflation are estimated for the revenue, cash expenses, and the salvage value, and the cash flows for each year are increased by these percentages. The cash flows provided by depreciation and ITC are not inflated, however, since the future tax dollars are fixed (based on the original cost of the asset). The total flows, including the cash flows provided by depreciation and ITC, are then deflated at the general inflation rate of 6%. After the total flows are converted to today's dollars, they are discounted at the cutoff rate of 8%. The

Cost: $50,000
ITC: 10%
Depreciation (ACRS on 95% of cost): Year 1 .... 15% × 95% × $50,000 = $ 7,125
Year 2 .... 22% × 95% × $50,000 = 10,450
Year 3 .... 21% × 95% × $50,000 = 9,975
Year 4 .... 21% × 95% × $50,000 = 9,975
Year 5 .... 21% × 95% × $50,000 = 9,975

Operating flows:
Revenue: Year 1-3 ... $50,000   Expenses: Year 1-3 .... $30,000
          Year 4 40,000   Year 4 20,000
          Year 5 30,000   Year 5 15,000
Salvage value: $15,000
Tax rate: 46%
Cutoff rate: 8%
General inflation rate: 6%
Specific inflation rates: Revenue 9%
                           Expenses 5%
                           Salvage 6%

Years	Cost	ITC	Revenue	Expenses	Net Flows	Taxes on Operating Flows	t(Depr.)	Salvage
0	−$50,000							
1		$5,000	$54,500.00	−$31,500.00	$23,000.00	−$10,580.00	$3,277.50	
2			59,405.00	− 33,075.00	26,330.00	− 12,111.80	4,807.00	
3			64,751.45	− 34,728.75	30,022.70	− 13,810.40	4,588.50	
4			56,463.26	− 24,310.13	32,153.16	− 14,790.50	4,588.50	
5			46,158.72	− 19,144.22	27,014.50	− 12,426.70	4,588.50	$20,073.38

Tax on Salvage	Total Flows (In Future Dollars)	PV Factors (6%)	Total Flows (In Today's Dollars)	PV Factors (8%)	PVs of Total Flows at 8%	Cash Flows to Date (In Today's Dollars)	Years
	−$50,000.00	1.0000	−$50,000.00	1.0000	−$50,000.00	−$50,000.00	0
	20,697.50	.9434	19,526.02	.9259	18,079.14	− 30,473.98	1
	19,025.20	.8900	16,932.43	.8573	14,516.17	− 13,541.55	2
	20,800.80	.8396	17,464.35	.7938	13,863.20	3,922.80	3
	21,951.16	.7921	17,387.51	.7350	12,779.82	21,310.31	4
−$9,233.76	30,015.92	.7473	22,430.90	.6806	15,266.44	43,741.21	5
					$24,504.77		

NPV: $24,504.77
Total PV: $50,000 + $24,504.77 = $74,504.77
PVI: $74,504.77 ÷ $50,000 = 1.490
IRR: ₋ 24.87%
Payback: 2 + ($13,541.55 ÷ $17,464.35) = 2.78 years (based on today's dollars)
Accounting rate of return (initial investment):
  ($43,741.21 ÷ 5) ÷ $50,000 = $8,748 ÷ $50,000 = .175 (based on today's dollars)

results of the analysis, compared to the noninflation-adjusted results in Illustration 8-7, show a higher profitability for the project, since the revenue inflation rate was higher than the cost inflation rate.

The procedures used to adjust the cash flows for inflation may vary. Quite often, a firm will apply the general inflation rate to all flows except depreciation, because the specific price-level increases cannot be ascertained. Another variation which may be used as a shortcut is to discount only once at a combined adjusted cutoff rate, rather than discounting in two steps, first at the general inflation rate and then at the cutoff rate. If this procedure were followed in Illustration 8-9, the present values would change as indicated in the following table:

	Present Values of Total Flows, Year 1	NPVs	Total PVs	PVIs
Discount at 14%	$18,155.85 ($20,697.50 × .8772)	$25,421	$75,421	1.51
Discount at 6%, then 8% (as in Illus. 8-9) . . .	18,079.14 ($20,697.50 × .9434 × .9259)	24,505	74,505	1.49

Although the present values do not differ significantly, it is preferable to use the double discounting procedure if the remaining measures (IRR, payback, and accounting rate of return) are to be calculated. These measures should be calculated on a basis consistent with that used for the present values.

THE IMPACT OF UNCERTAINTY ON CAPITAL PROJECT EVALUATIONS

Uncertainty refers to the likelihood that actual future costs and revenues will not comply with the original estimates in the capital budgeting model. Since evaluations of capital asset proposals involve projecting amounts into future periods, uncertainty is inherent in the evaluations. The alternatives that firms use in considering uncertainty, and the risk that results from it, range from adjusting the cutoff rate to incorporating an adjustment factor into the estimates to identifying other possible outcomes. These alternatives are discussed in the following paragraphs.

Adjusting the Cutoff Rate

Perhaps the simplest and most common procedure for including risk in the evaluation of capital projects is to adjust the cutoff rate. For example, a firm may use its average cost of capital as the aftertax cutoff rate for "safe" proposals, such as machine replacements. If that rate is 10%, the firm may add 2 percentage points and require an aftertax rate of 12% on projects which it considers to be moderately risky, such as automation of its plants. An even higher rate of 15% may be required for high-risk projects, such as new products.

Adjusting the cutoff rate is a very subjective procedure, since the decision maker must decide whether a proposal is "safe," "moderately risky," or "highly risky," as well as the amount of the adjustment. Furthermore, only the overall risk of the project is estimated, and the specific projections which create the uncertainty are not analyzed in terms of risk.

Adjusting the Estimates

A more effective method of dealing with uncertainty is to focus on the projections which are subject to errors in estimation. In the examples thus far, single "best estimates" for projections have been used. These estimates, however, can be replaced by estimates that incorporate risk, using two methods which were discussed in Chapter 5.

One method of incorporating risk into capital project evaluations is to use estimates based on probability distributions. These estimates then become the expected value (weighted average) of the distribution. This method is especially valid for estimates of future sales and operating costs. It also is beneficial because, in the process of preparing probability distributions, the cost analyst is required to focus on the risk caused by the array of possible outcomes.

Another method of adjusting for risk is to use certainty equivalents, which incorporate risk aversion into projections. This method is quite often used by financial institutions that act as lessors, contracting with a third party (not the lessee) to purchase the asset at the end of the lease term. The certainty equivalent of the asset's salvage value replaces a "risky" estimate of that value in a project evaluation.

Sensitivity Analysis

In the evaluation of capital projects, sensitivity analysis determines which projections have alternative outcomes which, if they occurred, would make the investment undesirable. The basic steps in sensitivity analysis are as follows:

1. Specify which estimates in the analysis may take on values other than those used.
2. For the estimates which may take alternative values, determine the likely range in which these values may fall.
3. For each estimate which may change, separately recalculate all the analytical measures in order to avoid compounding the risk. Use the value at the undesirable boundary of the range of estimates. This amount is the value with unfavorable effects on the analysis; i.e., the low volume projection and the high cost estimate for a new product, and the low cost savings and the low salvage value for a machine replacement.
4. Determine the projections to which the analysis is sensitive. An analysis is sensitive to a projection when the maximum unfavorable change in the projection makes the project unprofitable or marginally profitable.
5. For each sensitive projection, analyze the *most likely* (as opposed to *most*) unfavorable outcome, which is the largest unfavorable outcome that has a reasonable probability of occurring. (The *most* unfavorable outcome was used in Step 4 to discover sensitivity.)
6. Incorporate the revised, unfavorable estimates into a final project evaluation in order to determine if the project is still desirable.

Illustration 8-10 is an example of the application of sensitivity analysis. In Illustration 8-10 (1), the original estimates are presented, and the four basic measures of profitability are calculated. In (2), the *most* unfavorable outcomes for each variable are analyzed. The following four independent tests are used to discover the estimates to which the analysis is sensitive:

	Estimates Tested	Most Unfavorable Outcomes	Results of Test
Test 1	Revenue	Falls 10% below original estimate	*Very Sensitive* (makes project marginal). Almost eliminates NPV. IRR falls close to cutoff rate.
Test 2	Expenses	Increase 15% over original estimate	*Quite Sensitive* (eliminates most profit). Very little NPV. IRR is only 1.3 percentage points above cutoff rate.
Test 3	Salvage value	Falls 50% below estimate	*Moderately Sensitive* (significant reduction of profit). NPV falls 39%. IRR falls almost 2 percentage points. Project is still safe.
Test 4	Tax rate	Firm income declines, so that marginal tax rate is 30%	*Insensitive.*

The impact of a tax rate change is difficult to predict, since a lower rate increases the net-of-tax operating flows and lowers the depreciation tax shield, while a higher rate has the opposite effects. Therefore, both increases and decreases in the tax rate must be tested. In Illustration 8-10, only a decrease in the tax rate was tested, because the firm was already at the maximum tax rate.

After the estimates to which the analysis is sensitive are identified, new estimates based on the most likely unfavorable outcomes for revenue, expenses, and salvage value are used to reevaluate the project in Illustration 8-10 (3). The results of this evaluation indicate that, although it is less profitable than in the original evaluation in (1), the project can still be described as profitable.

Sensitivity analysis is the most sophisticated means of considering the risk in estimates. Although it is very time consuming if it is performed manually, a microcomputer can quickly recalculate the results of a change in any estimate.

Illustration 8-10
Capital Project Evaluation with Sensitivity Analysis

Cost: $40,000
ITC: 10%
Depreciation (ACRS on 95% of cost):

Year 1	15% × 95% × $40,000 =	$ 5,700
Year 2	22% × 95% × $40,000 =	8,360
Year 3	21% × 95% × $40,000 =	7,980
Year 4	21% × 95% × $40,000 =	7,980
Year 5	21% × 95% × $40,000 =	7,980

Operating flows:
  Revenue: Years 1-5 ... $24,000   Expenses: Years 1-5 ... $13,000
Salvage value: $12,000
Tax rate: 46%
Cutoff rate: 8%

(1) Evaluation Without Consideration of Risk

Years	Cost	ITC	Revenue	Expenses	Net Flows	Taxes on Operating Flows	t(Depr.)
0	−$40,000						
1		$4,000	$24,000	−$13,000	$11,000	−$5,060	$2,622.00
2			24,000	− 13,000	11,000	− 5,060	3,845.60
3			24,000	− 13,000	11,000	− 5,060	3,670.80
4			24,000	− 13,000	11,000	− 5,060	3,670.80
5			24,000	− 13,000	11,000	− 5,060	3,670.80

Salvage	Tax on Salvage	Total Flows	PV Factors (8%)	PVs of Total Flows at 8%	Cash Flows to Date	Years
		−$40,000.00	1.0000	−$40,000.00	−$40,000.00	0
		12,562.00	.9259	11,631.16	− 27,438.00	1
		9,785.60	.8573	8,389.19	− 17,652.40	2
		9,610.80	.7938	7,629.05	− 8,041.60	3
		9,610.80	.7350	7,063.94	1,569.20	4
$12,000	− $5,520	16,090.80	.6806	10,951.40	17,660.00	5
				$ 5,664.74		

NPV: $5,664.74
Total PV: $40,000 + $5,664.74 = $45,664.74
PVI: $45,664.74 ÷ $40,000 = 1.142
IRR: 13.07%
Payback: 3 + ($8,041.60 ÷ $9,610.80) = 3.84 years
Accounting rate of return (initial investment):
  ($17,660 ÷ 5) ÷ $40,000 = $3,532 ÷ $40,000 = .088

(2) Sensitivity Testing of the Most Unfavorable Outcomes

Test 1: Reduce Revenue 10% per Year to $21,600

Years	Cost	ITC	Revenue	Expenses	Net Flows	Taxes on Operating Flows	t(Depr.)
0	− $40,000						
1		$4,000	$21,600	−$13,000	$8,600	−$3,956	$2,622.00
2			21,600	− 13,000	8,600	− 3,956	3,845.60
3			21,600	− 13,000	8,600	− 3,956	3,670.80
4			21,600	− 13,000	8,600	− 3,956	3,670.80
5			21,600	− 13,000	8,600	− 3,956	3,670.80

Salvage	Tax on Salvage	Total Flows	PV Factors (8%)	PVs of Total Flows at 8%	Cash Flows to Date	Years
		−$40,000.00	1.0000	−$40,000.00	−$40,000.00	0
		11,266.00	.9259	10,431.19	− 28,734.00	1
		8,489.60	.8573	7,278.13	− 20,244.40	2
		8,314.80	.7938	6,600.29	− 11,929.60	3
		8,314.80	.7350	6,111.38	− 3,614.80	4
$12,000	− $5,520	14,704.80	.6806	10,069.34	11,180.00	5
				$ 490.33		

NPV: $490.33
Total PV: $40,000 + $490.33 = $40,490.33
PVI: $40,490.33 ÷ $40,000 = 1.012
IRR: 8.45%
Payback: 4 + ($3,614.80 ÷ $14,794.80) = 4.24 years
Accounting rate of return (initial investment):
  ($11,180 ÷ 5) ÷ $40,000 = $2,236 ÷ $40,000 = .056

Test 2: Increase Expenses 15% per Year to $14,950

Years	Cost	ITC	Revenue	Expenses	Net Flows	Taxes on Operating Flows	t(Depr.)
0	−$40,000						
1		$4,000	$24,000	−$14,950	$9,050	−$4,163	$2,622.00
2			24,000	− 14,950	9,050	− 4,163	3,845.60
3			24,000	− 14,950	9,050	− 4,163	3,670.80
4			24,000	− 14,950	9,050	− 4,163	3,670.80
5			24,000	− 14,950	9,050	− 4,163	3,670.80

Salvage	Tax on Salvage	Total Flows	PV Factors (8%)	PVs of Total Flows at 8%	Cash Flows to Date	Years
		−$40,000.00	1.0000	−$40,000.00	−$40,000.00	0
		11,509.00	.9259	10,656.18	− 28,491.00	1
		8,732.60	.8573	7,486.46	− 19,758.40	2
		8,557.80	.7938	6,793.18	− 11,200.60	3
		8,557.80	.7350	6,289.98	− 2,642.80	4
$12,000	−$5,520	15,037.80	.6806	10,234.73	12,395.00	5
				$ 1,460.53		

NPV: $1,460.53
Total PV: $40,000 + $1,460.53 = $41,460.53
PVI: $41,460.53 ÷ $40,000 = 1.036
IRR: 9.33%
Payback: 4 + ($2,642.80 ÷ $15,037.80) = 4.18 years
Accounting rate of return (initial investment):
  ($12,395 ÷ 5) ÷ $40,000 = $2,479 ÷ $40,000 = .062

Test 3: Decrease Salvage Value by 50% to $6,000

Years	Cost	ITC	Revenue	Expenses	Net Flows	Taxes on Operating Flows	t(Depr.)
0	−$40,000						
1		$4,000	$24,000	−$13,000	$11,000	−$5,060	$2,622.00
2			24,000	− 13,000	11,000	− 5,060	3,845.60
3			24,000	− 13,000	11,000	− 5,060	3,670.80
4			24,000	− 13,000	11,000	− 5,060	3,670.80
5			24,000	− 13,000	11,000	− 5,060	3,670.80

Salvage	Tax on Salvage	Total Flows	PV Factors (8%)	PVs of Total Flows at 8%	Cash Flows to Date	Years
		−$40,000.00	1.0000	−$40,000.00	−$40,000.00	0
		12,562.00	.9259	11,631.16	− 27,438.00	1
		9,785.60	.8573	8,389.19	− 17,652.40	2
		9,610.80	.7938	7,629.05	− 8,041.60	3
		9,610.80	.7350	7,063.94	1,569.20	4
$6,000	−$2,760	12,850.80	.6806	8,746.25	14,420.00	5
				$ 3,459.59		

NPV: $3,459.59
Total PV: $40,000 + $3,459.59 = $43,459.59
PVI: $43,459.59 ÷ $40,000 = 1.087
IRR: 11.24%
Payback: 3 + ($8,041.60 ÷ $9,610.80) = 3.84 years
Accounting rate of return (initial investment):
  ($14,420 ÷ 5) ÷ $40,000 = $2,884 ÷ $40,000 = .072

Test 4: Decrease Tax Rate to 30%

Years	Cost	ITC	Revenue	Expenses	Net Flows	Taxes on Operating Flows	t(Depr.)
0	−$40,000						
1		$4,000	$24,000	−$13,000	$11,000	−$3,300	$1,710
2			24,000	− 13,000	11,000	− 3,300	2,508
3			24,000	− 13,000	11,000	− 3,300	2,394
4			24,000	− 13,000	11,000	− 3,300	2,394
5			24,000	− 13,000	11,000	− 3,300	2,394

Salvage	Tax on Salvage	Total Flows	PV Factors (8%)	PVs of Total Flows at 8%	Cash Flows to Date	Years
		−$40,000	1.0000	−$40,000.00	−$40,000	0
		13,410	.9259	12,416.32	− 26,590	1
		10,208	.8573	8,571.32	− 16,382	2
		10,094	.7938	8,012.62	− 6,288	3
		10,094	.7350	7,419.09	3,806	4
$12,000	−$3,600	18,494	.6806	12,587.02	22,300	5
				$ 9,186.37		

NPV: $9,186.37
Total PV: $40,000 + $9,186.37 = $49,186.37
PVI: $49,186.37 ÷ $40,000 = 1.23
IRR: 15.99%
Payback: 3 + ($6,288 ÷ $10,094) = 3.62 years
Accounting rate of return (initial investment):
  ($22,300 ÷ 5) ÷ $40,000 = $4,460 ÷ $40,000 = .112

(3) New Analysis with Most Likely Unfavorable Outcomes
Reduce revenue 3% to $23,280
Increase expenses 5% to $13,650
Decrease salvage value to $10,000

Years	Cost	ITC	Revenue	Expenses	Net Flows	Taxes on Operating Flows	t(Depr.)
0	−$40,000						
1		$4,000	$23,380	−$13,650	$9,630	−$4,429.80	$2,622.00
2			23,380	− 13,650	9,630	− 4,429.80	3,845.60
3			23,380	− 13,650	9,630	− 4,429.80	3,670.80
4			23,380	− 13,650	9,630	− 4,429.80	3,670.80
5			23,380	− 13,650	9,630	− 4,429.80	3,670.80

Salvage	Tax on Salvage	Total Flows	PV Factors (8%)	PVs of Total Flows at 8%	Cash Flows to Date	Years
		−$40,000.00	1.0000	−$40,000.00	−$40,000.00	0
		11,822.20	.9259	10,946.17	− 28,177.80	1
		9,045.80	.8573	7,754.96	− 19,132.00	2
		8,871.00	.7938	7,041.80	− 10,261.00	3
		8,871.00	.7350	6,520.19	− 1,390.00	4
$10,000	−$4,600	14,271.00	.6806	9,712.84	12,881.00	5
				$ 1,975.96		

NPV: $1,975.96
Total PV: $40,000 + $1,975.96 = $41,975.96
PVI: $41,975.96 ÷ $40,000 = 1.049
IRR: 9.82%
Payback: 4 + ($1,390 ÷ $14,271) = 4.1 years
Accounting rate of return (initial investment):
  ($12,881 ÷ 5) ÷ $40,000 = $2,576 ÷ $40,000 = .064

PERFORMANCE EVALUATION

After a capital budgeting decision has been made and implemented, the resulting cash flows should be compared with those originally projected. Such analyses should encourage accountability on the part of those who make the estimates, and should provide insight into how estimates on future projects may be made more accurately. Also, the continual monitoring of existing projects should make it possible to improve the estimates applicable to the remaining life of these projects, with consideration given to altering, discontinuing, or replacing them.

Although evaluation of a project's performance is desirable, the accounting records may not be designed to provide the necessary data. The source of the original data used in making the decision is an analysis that is not part of the accounting records. Also, once the project is accepted, the results may not be accounted for separately. For example, a firm has installed robot welders on its production line, based on projected cost savings; but the actual costs related to the welders are commingled with other costs in the accounting records. To compare the actual costs with the projected costs, a special cost analysis would be required. Since costs were not originally captured specifically for the welders, arbitrary allocations may be needed, which reduces the value of the performance evaluation.

LEASING: AN ALTERNATIVE FINANCING METHOD

Many assets being considered for purchase may also be acquired through a long-term lease, which typically conveys the use of the asset to the user/lessee for most of the asset's economic life. When leasing is a possible alternative, lease-buy analysis should be used to evaluate its profitability. The term "lease-buy analysis" should really be "lease-borrow analysis," since the analysis begins after the decision to buy has been made. Long-term leasing is a means of financing the acquisition of an asset, and the analysis of the leasing alternative determines whether it is more profitable to lease or to borrow with a conventional loan.

The analyses of leases as financing options depend on their status for tax purposes. When the sale of an asset is structured as a lease in order to provide tax advantages to the lessee and/or the lessor, the Internal Revenue Service views such a lease as a sale/loan. With some exceptions provided by the *Tax Equity and Fiscal Responsibility Act of 1982*, such as bargain-purchase options and/or leases of specific-purpose equipment, a lease will be viewed as a sale/loan when the following conditions are present:[2]

1. The rent is unreasonably high in the initial periods. Rent in excess of market suggests that the lessee is paying for the right to later acquire the asset.
2. The lessee is being granted the right to own the asset, either by specifying that a portion of the payments is a reduction in the principal, by providing for a transfer of title, or by providing an option to buy at a bargain price.
3. The lessor appears to be assured of cost recovery through the lessee's payments, which include interest at a reasonable rate and any bargain purchase option.
4. The asset is specifically tailored to the needs of the lessee, and therefore has little value to others.

Analysis of a Lease Deemed To Be a Sale/Loan

When a lease is deemed by the IRS to be a sale/loan, the lessee is the buyer under a long-term debt obligation and, as the owner of the asset, receives the investment tax credit and the deductions for depreciation and for interest on the implied loan. The only analysis needed is to determine if the interest rate offered under the lease is more favorable than the available borrowing rate.

The payments required under a sale/loan lease, which must be carefully determined, include the following:

1. A required initial deposit, if any, which is returned at the end of the lease term.
2. The rent payments, which are now considered to be payments of principal and interest. These payments should be net of any operating costs ("executory costs") which are paid by the lessor but which would otherwise be paid by the lessee, such as maintenance and property taxes.
3. Any payment which is required at the end of the lease term and which is necessary to secure title to the asset. This condition would be the bargain purchase option, if one exists; otherwise, the payment would be the estimated fair market value of the asset at the end of the lease term. Even if the lessee does not intend to purchase the asset, this payment is still an economic sacrifice that is a result of leasing rather than buying the asset.

Once the payments have been defined, they can be analyzed using one of the following methods:

1. Present value approach: The payments are discounted at the firm's borrowing rate applicable to a loan which uses the acquired asset as collateral. If the

---

[2]Revenue Ruling 55-540 and Revenue Procedure 75-21.

present value of the payments exceeds the cost of buying, the lease is not financially attractive.

2. Implicit lease rate approach: This method identifies the interest rate which equates the payments under the lease to the cost of buying. If this rate is higher than the borrowing rate, the lease is not financially attractive.

In Illustration 8-11, the two evaluation methods are applied to alternative lease terms, and the results of the evaluation are shown. Under the present value approach for Lease 1, for example, the lease costs $947 more than buying. Under the implicit lease rate approach for the same lease, the lease rate of 13.5% exceeds the 12% borrowing rate. Therefore, Lease 1 is not a financially attractive alternative.

The calculations for the implicit lease rate method are not shown in Illustration 8-11 because they involve successive iterations at alternative test rates. For convenience, the flows in the illustration are annual flows rather than the more typical monthly flows. To avoid the need to compute interest deductions, the rates used are pretax rates. However, they can be converted to an aftertax basis by multiplying by the reciprocal of the tax rate $(1 - t)$.

Illustration 8-11
Evaluation of a Lease
Deemed To Be a
Sale/Loan

General assumptions:
  Borrowing rate is 12%
  Lease payments are in advance.
  Lease term is 5 years.
  Cost to buy asset is $40,000.
  Fair market value of asset after 5 years is $15,000.

Lease 1

Terms:
  Deposit, $0.
  Annual rent, $10,142.
  Title transfers to lessee at end of lease term.

Analysis:
  1. Determine the present value:

     PV = $10,142 × (4-year Table 2 factor + 1) = $10,142 × (3.0373 + 1) = $40,946

  2. Determine the added lease cost or savings:

     PV $40,946
     Asset cash cost 40,000
     Added lease cost .... $ 946

  3. Determine the implicit lease rate: The rate that equates the lease payments to the asset's $40,000 cost is 13.5%.

Conclusion: Do not lease.

Lease 2

Terms:
  Deposit, $5,000.
  Annual rent, $8,242.
  Bargain purchase price, $7,000.

Analysis:
1. Determine the present value:

   PV = $5,000 + [$8,242 × (4-year Table 2 factor + 1)] + ($7,000 × 5-year Table 1 factor) − ($5,000 × 5-year Table 1 factor)
   = $5,000 + [$8,242 × (3.0373 + 1)] + ($7,000 × .5674) − ($5,000 × .5674)
   = $5,000 + $33,275 + $3,972 − $2,837
   = $39,410

2. Determine the added lease cost or savings:

   PV $39,410
   Asset cash cost 40,000
   Savings by leasing .... $ 590

3. Determine the implicit lease rate: The rate that equates the lease payments to the asset's $40,000 cost is 11%.

Conclusion: Lease.

Lease 3

Terms:
   Deposit, $5,000.
   Annual rent, $7,616.
   Asset reverts to lessor at end of lease term.

Analysis:
1. Determine the present value:

   PV = $5,000 + [$7,616 × (4-year Table 2 factor + 1)] + ($15,000 × 5-year Table 1 factor) − ($5,000 × 5-year Table 1 factor)
   = $5,000 + [$7,616 × (3.0373 + 1)] + ($15,000 × .5674) − ($5,000 × .5674)
   = $5,000 + $30,748 + $8,511 − $2,837
   = $41,422

2. Determine the added lease cost or savings:

   PV $41,422
   Asset cash cost 40,000
   Added lease cost .... $ 1,422

3. Determine the implicit lease rate: The rate that equates the lease payments to the asset's $40,000 cost is 14%.

Conclusion: Do not lease.

Analysis of an Operating Lease

The analysis of a lease that is considered to be an operating lease for tax purposes is more complicated than the analysis of a sale/loan lease. Under an operating lease, the lessee is not considered to be the owner. Thus, the tax shelter provided by depreciation and any salvage value, which very likely influenced the decision to acquire the asset, are lost. However, the lessee is partially compensated for these losses, since the entire rent payment, rather than just the interest portion of loan payments, becomes deductible for tax purposes.

The following components of an operating lease are discounted to arrive at the present value of the lease payments:

+ Deposit:	The deposit due at the beginning of the term and returned at the end.
+ Rent:	The rent net of costs which are paid by the lessor but which would otherwise be paid by the lessee.
− t(Rent):	The tax deduction provided by the rent. The tax rate is t.
+ t(Depreciation):	The tax shield provided by the depreciation that is lost by leasing.
+ ITC:	The ITC available to the lessor, who is the owner of the asset. If the lessor agrees to pass the ITC to the lessee, it is deleted from the analysis.
+ Residual:	The asset's fair market value to the lessor, or the option price, at the end of the lease term. If the asset is worth more than the option price, it is assumed that it would be purchased, and the lessee would not forfeit the excess of the market value.
− t(Residual):	The tax gain on the residual. Normally, the asset would be fully depreciated, so that the entire residual value is gain that is taxed as ordinary income. If there is an option price below the market value, it is again assumed that the option will be exercised. The gain that would have occurred had the asset been purchased is then reduced by the option price paid.

The following methods are available for analyzing an operating lease:

1. **Present value approach:** The payments are discounted at the lessee's aftertax, incremental borrowing rate. The aftertax rate is used because the payments are calculated net of tax.
2. **Implicit lease rate approach:** This method identifies the interest rate which equates the present value of the payments to the asset's cash purchase cost.

In addition to the quantifiable factors which these methods consider, the following nonquantifiable factors favor leasing and may be worth the additional cost which an analysis may ascribe to leasing:

1. The service provided in acquiring and disposing of assets.
2. Guidance in the choice of the most economical assets. For example, auto lessors encourage lessees to choose cars which have a maximum resale value.
3. Preferential treatment when service is required.
4. The ability to acquire assets with little or no down payment.
5. The possible advantage of not listing on the balance sheet the debt that results from the asset's acquisition.[3]
6. Simplified recordkeeping. It is only necessary to maintain a record of rent paid. There is no need to record depreciation or interest expense on a loan.

In Illustration 8-12, various operating leases are analyzed, using the same facts as in Illustration 8-11. Due to the difference in the tax attributes, the results of the two illustrations differ.

For each lease analyzed in Illustration 8-12, the difference in present values between leasing and purchasing is calculated. For example, the net present value of the payments and the tax attributes of Lease 1 is $3,328.11 greater than the cost of purchasing the asset. Also, the aftertax implicit interest rate for each lease is shown. For Lease 1, this rate is 12.23%.

---

[3]The obligation under the lease is disclosed in the footnotes to the financial statements. See *Statement of Financial Accounting Standards, No. 13,* "Accounting for Leases," (Stamford: Financial Accounting Standards Board, 1976).

Lease 2 in the illustration includes an option price, which represents the portion of the asset's value that is forfeited when the asset is leased. This forfeited value reduces the taxable gain. Lease 2 is also an example of a lease in which the lessee retains the ITC, and thus no ITC is shown as a forfeited payment.

Under the terms of Lease 3, the asset reverts to the lessor at the end of the lease term. Although the entire value is sacrificed, it is again offset by the reduction in tax, since the asset is not owned by the lessee and there is no gain on which the lessee would be taxed.

Illustration 8-12
Evaluation of an
Operating Lease

General assumptions:
  The lessee's tax rate is 46%.
  The lessee's borrowing rate is 13% before tax and 7% (1 − 46%) (13%) after tax.
  Lease payments are due in advance.
  The lease term is 5 years.
  The cost to buy the asset is $40,000.
  The 10% ITC would be available.
  If the asset were purchased, ACRS depreciation would be applied to 95% of the asset's cost, as follows:

  Year 1 . . . . . $5,700
       2 8,360
       3 7,980
       4 7,980
       5 7,980

  The fair market value at the end of 5 years is $15,000.

Lease 1

Terms:
  Deposit, $0.
  Annual rent, $10,142.
  The ITC is retained by the lessor.
  Asset title transfers to the lessee at the end of the term.

Years	Deposit	Rents	t(Rent)	t(Depr.)	ITC	Residual	t(Resid.)	Net Payments	PV Factors (7%)	NPVs
0	$0	$10,142						$10,142.00	1.0000	$10,142.00
1		10,142	− $4,665.32	$2,622.00	$4,000			12,098.68	.9346	11,307.43
2		10,142	− 4,665.32	3,845.60				9,322.28	.8734	8,142.08
3		10,142	− 4,665.32	3,670.80				9,147.48	.8163	7,467.09
4		10,142	− 4,665.32	3,670.80				9,147.48	.7629	6,978.61
5	0		− 4,665.32	3,670.80		$0	$0	− 994.52	.7130	− 709.09

Present value of lease payments at aftertax borrowing rate $43,328.12
Asset cash cost 40,000.00
Added lease cost . . . . $ 3,328.12
Aftertax implicit interest rate 12.23%

Lease 2

Terms:
  Deposit, $5,000.
  Annual rent, $8,242.
  The ITC is passed to the lessee.
  Option price, $7,000.

Years	Deposit	Rents	t(Rent)	t(Depr.)	ITC	Residual	t(Resid.)	Net Payments	PV Factors (7%)	NPVs
0	$5,000	$8,242						$13,242.00	1.0000	$13,242.00
1		8,242	−$3,791.32	$2,622.00	$0			7,072.68	.9346	6,610.13
2		8,242	− 3,791.32	3,845.60				8,296.28	.8734	7,245.97
3		8,242	− 3,791.32	3,670.80				8,121.48	.8163	6,629.56
4		8,242	− 3,791.32	3,670.80				8,121.48	.7629	6,195.88
5	− 5,000		− 3,791.32	3,670.80		$7,000	−$3,220	− 1,340.52	.7130	− 955.79

Present value of lease payments at aftertax borrowing rate $38,967.75
Asset cash cost 40,000.00
Savings by leasing . . . . $ 1,032.25
Aftertax implicit interest rate 5.25%

Lease 3

Terms:
Deposit, $5,000.
Annual rent, $8,242.
The ITC is retained by the lessor.
Residual value, $15,000, reverts to lessor.

Years	Deposit	Rents	t(Rent)	t(Depr.)	ITC	Residual	t(Resid.)	Net Payments	PV Factors (7%)	NPVs
0	$5,000	$7,616						$12,616.00	1.0000	$12,616.00
1		7,616	−$3,503.36	$2,622.00	$4,000			10,734.64	.9346	10,032.59
2		7,616	− 3,503.36	3,845.60				7,958.24	.8734	6,950.72
3		7,616	− 3,503.36	3,670.80				7,783.44	.8163	6,353.62
4		7,616	− 3,503.36	3,670.80				7,783.44	.7629	5,937.99
5	− 5,000		− 3,503.36	3,670.80		$15,000	−$6,900	3,267.44	.7130	2,239.68

Present value of lease payments at aftertax borrowing rate $44,220.60
Asset cash cost 40,000.00
Added lease cost . . . . $ 4,220.60
Aftertax implicit interest rate 13.5%

A more precise analysis of leasing requires the consideration of monthly and quarterly cash flows. Such an analysis, which can be quickly performed by a microcomputer, is shown for a 3-year car lease in Illustration 8-13. In this illustration, the rent is paid monthly, and the tax deduction for the rent is taken at the end of each quarter. Also, the sacrifice of depreciation and the ITC occurs on a quarterly basis.

Illustration 8-13
Monthly Evaluation of a
Car Lease

General assumptions:
The lessee's tax rate is 46%.
The lessee's borrowing rate is 11.9% before tax.
Lease payments are due in advance. The tax deduction is taken quarterly.
The cost to buy the car is $9,343.
The 6% ITC would be available if the asset were purchased.
If the asset were purchased, 3-year ACRS depreciation would be applied to 97% of the asset's cost, as follows:

Year 1 . . . . . $2,266
     2 3,444
     3 3,352

The fair market value at the end of the lease term is estimated to be $4,100.

Terms:
Deposit, $0.
Monthly rent, $211.56.
The ITC is retained by the lessor.
The asset reverts to the lessor at the end of the lease term.

Month	Deposit	Rent	t(Rent)	t(Depr.)	ITC	Salvage	Tax on Salvage	Net Payment
0	0	211.56						211.56
1		211.56						211.56
2		211.56						211.56
3		211.56	−291.95	260.55	140.15			320.31
4		211.56						211.56
5		211.56						211.56
6		211.56	−291.95	260.55	140.15			320.31
7		211.56						211.56
8		211.56						211.56
9		211.56	−291.95	260.55	140.15			320.31
10		211.56						211.56
11		211.56						211.56
12		211.56	−291.95	260.55	140.15			320.31
13		211.56						211.56
14		211.56						211.56
15		211.56	−291.95	396.04				315.65
16		211.56						211.56
17		211.56						211.56
18		211.56	−291.95	396.04				315.65
19		211.56						211.56
20		211.56						211.56
21		211.56	−291.95	396.04				315.65
22		211.56						211.56
23		211.56						211.56
24		211.56	−291.95	396.04				315.65
25		211.56						211.56
26		211.56						211.56
27		211.56	−291.95	385.62				305.23
28		211.56						211.56
29		211.56						211.56
30		211.56	−291.95	385.62				305.23
31		211.56						211.56
32		211.56						211.56
33		211.56	−291.95	385.62				305.23
34		211.56						211.56
35		211.56						211.56
36			−291.95	385.62		4100.00	−1886.00	2307.67

```
Present value of lease payments at aftertax borrowing rate     9883.91
Asset cash cost                                                9343.00

Added lease cost                                                540.91

Aftertax implicit lease rate: monthly                            .0081
                              annually                           .1016
```

1. Describe the conditions under which the net present value method and the internal rate of return method would give conflicting project rankings.

2. How can a firm resolve the dilemma posed by a conflict in project ranking under the NPV and IRR methods?

3. How does a firm select the optimal project from a list of mutually exclusive alternatives?

4. Explain the method by which a firm creates a portfolio of investment projects, given a limitation on funds available for investment.

5. What are the methods by which a decision maker can include the effects of inflation in a capital project analysis?

6. How can the impact of risk or uncertainty be incorporated in a capital project analysis?

7. Describe the use of sensitivity analysis to evaluate the risk inherent in an investment project.

8. Summarize the tax status of a lessee who has acquired an asset through a lease which the IRS has deemed to be a sale/loan.

9. How does a lessee evaluate a lease which the IRS has classified as a sale/loan?

10. In general terms, explain how a lessee evaluates a lease that the IRS views as an operating lease.

Exercise 1. Fordham Company has before it two alternative investment proposals, A and B. Both investments are shares in limited partnerships and involve roughly the same risk. The cash flows expected to be generated by the investments are as follows:

			Years			
	0	1	2	3	4	5
Investment A	−$5,000	$2,226	$2,226	$2,226	—	—
Investment B	− 5,000	1,456	1,456	1,456	$1,456	$1,456

(1) Calculate (to the nearest whole percentage) the internal rate of return of each investment. Which proposal has the higher internal rate of return?

(2) Calculate the net present value of each investment, using an 8% aftertax cutoff rate. Which proposal should be selected on the basis of the net present values?

(3) Graph the reinvestment rate assumptions implicit in the two methods.

Exercise 2. Altman Inc. has before it proposals to invest in two separate projects. Project S requires only a two-year investment, while Project V would have an economic life of four years. Both projects have roughly the same risk. Projected cash flows from the two projects are summarized as follows:

			Years		
	0	1	2	3	4
Project S	−$50,000	$29,584	$29,584	—	—
Project V	− 50,000	16,116	16,116	$16,116	$16,116

Altman uses a cutoff rate of 8%.

On the basis of these data, the following project evaluation measures were prepared:

	IRRs	NPVs	PVIs
Project S	12%	$2,757	1.055
Project V	11	3,377	1.068

Altman is concerned about the conflicting rankings and decides to reanalyze the projects by cutting off Project V at the end of two years. Altman assumes that it can liquidate Project V at the end of year 2 for an estimated $22,000.

Calculate the internal rate of return and the net present value for Project V at the end of year 2. Based on this analysis, which project would Altman select?

Exercise 3. Peckinpaugh Ltd. would like to produce precision bearings under license from SCF Industries. The firm may select either a two-year or a four-year licensing agreement. It estimates the following cash flows as a result of the investment:

	Years				
	0	1	2	3	4
K (2-year agreement)	−$35,000	$19,626	$19,626	—	—
T (4-year agreement)	− 35,000	10,333	10,333	$10,333	$10,333

The internal rates of return, net present values (at Peckinpaugh's 4% cutoff rate), and present value indexes of the above investments are summarized as follows:

	IRRs	NPVs	PVIs
K	8%	$2,017	1.058
T	7	2,508	1.072

Peckinpaugh reasonably expects to earn 5% on all funds provided by the investments.

Calculate the future value of both investments and their future value indexes.

Exercise 4. Rally Arcade Company would like to open a video game arcade in a new shopping mall. The issue confronting the company is the size of the arcade. Although the cost per square foot of leased space decreases as the leased area increases, the total monthly lease cost and most other overhead items increase as the leased area increases. Revenues increase with the area leased, although the relationship is not proportional. The following table summarizes the anticipated construction costs, the expected annual net cash flows, and the evaluation measures for each possible size:

Area	Construction and Other Initial Costs	Annual Cash Flows	IRRs	PVs of Annual Cash Flows at 10%	PVIs at 10%
3,200 sq. ft.	$407,457	$115,000	12.70%	$435,942	1.070 ($435,942 ÷ $407,457)
3,600	484,163	131,000	11.00	496,595	1.026 (496,595 ÷ 484,163)
4,000	525,586	144,000	11.50	545,875	1.039 (545,875 ÷ 525,586)
4,500	548,486	159,000	13.80	602,737	1.099 (602,737 ÷ 548,486)
5,000	565,725	163,497	13.67	619,784	1.096 (619,784 ÷ 565,725)

Present values and internal rates of return were calculated on the basis of an expected five-year project life and a 10% cutoff rate. The analysis shows that a 3,200-sq.-ft. size is acceptable.

Based on present value analysis, should the firm consider a larger size, and if so, what size?

Exercise 5. Tannenberg Minerals has approved investments for possible inclusion in its capital budget. Tannenberg has funds of $350,000 to invest in capital projects during the coming fiscal year. A summary of the projects approved for consideration is as follows:

	Life	Cost	Annual Cash Flows	IRRs	NPVs at 8%	PVIs at 8%
Materials handling equip.	5 years	$110,000	$29,018	10%	$5,860	1.0533
Excavating equip.	9	225,000	37,530	9	9,446	1.0420
Air conditioning	3	60,000	26,279	15	7,724	1.1287
Power generator—A	4	50,000	17,160	14	6,836	1.1367
Power generator—B > A	4	25,000	8,058	11	1,689	1.0676

The power generator A involves the purchase of a new direct generating system. Generator B involves additional equipment which becomes practical only if A is installed first.

Use the present value indexes as the criteria to select the optimal portfolio. Assume that all excess funds can be invested at Tannenberg's cutoff rate of 8%.

Exercise 6. Use internal rates of return to select the optimal investment portfolio for the available $350,000 for Tannenberg Minerals (described in Exercise 5), based on the first year's return. Assume that any excess funds can be invested at Tannenberg's cutoff rate of 8%.

Exercise 7. Catskill Distillers Inc. would like to replace its 5-year-old corporate car with a newer model. The cost of a new car is estimated by the firm's purchasing manager to be $9,800. The new car would be depreciated using the 3-year ACRS rates and disposed of at the end of the third year. The existing car is fully depreciated. Salvage values and related gains and losses on disposal are as follows:

	Salvage Values	Taxes on Salvage Values
New asset (end of third year)	$3,920	$1,568
Old asset (current)	2,700	1,080
Old asset (end of third year)	1,200	480

One of the firm's accountants has prepared the following analysis of annual operating costs for years 1, 2, and 3:

	Old Asset	New Asset
Fuel	$2,000	$1,500
Insurance	500	700
Repairs and maintenance	600	200
Taxes and licenses	50	50
	$3,150	$2,450

Prepare tables summarizing the aftertax cash flows associated with the new asset, the old asset, and the difference between the two. Catskill's marginal tax rate is 40%. Ignore the effects of the investment tax credit. You need not calculate the present value of the replacement decision.

Exercise 8. Pied Piper Pipe Company would like to purchase a new, computer-controlled lathe to replace an existing lathe. The old lathe has reached the end of its 5-year useful life and has no book, tax, or salvage value. The capital project analysis prepared for the new equipment is as follows:

Years	Cost	ITC	t(Depr.)	Reduction in Operating Costs	Taxes on Operating Flows	Salvage	Tax on Salvage	Total Flows	PV Factors (8%)	PVs of Total Flows at 8%
0	−$32,500*							−$32,500	1.0000	−$32,500
1		$2,400	$2,070	$8,000	−$3,680			8,790	.9259	8,139
2			3,036	8,000	− 3,680			7,356	.8573	6,306
3			2,898	8,000	− 3,680			7,218	.7938	5,730
4			2,898	8,000	− 3,680			7,218	.7350	5,305
5	2,500		2,898	8,000	− 3,680	$6,000	−$2,760	12,958	.6806	8,819
										$ 1,799

*Includes $2,500 investment in working capital

The firm's senior accountant feels that the analysis is unrealistic because it fails to incorporate the effects of inflation. The senior accountant believes that the firm will face a 7% per year average increase in costs over the life of the project, while the general rate of inflation is expected to average 6% per year. The equipment's salvage value and the investment in working capital will inflate at only a 4% rate.

Determine the effects of inflation on the fifth year's cash flows *only,* using the method that adjusts cash flows.

Exercise 9. Sun Valley Florists Inc. has decided to purchase a delivery van, which would allow the firm to deliver flowers to weddings and other social events. The decision to purchase the van was made on the basis of the following analysis:

Years	Cost	ITC	t(Depr.)	Operating Flows	Taxes on Operating Flows	Salvage Value	Tax on Salvage Value	Total Flows	PV Factors (10%)	PVs of Total Flows at 10%
0	−$11,500ª							−$11,500	1.0000	−$11,500
1		$570ᵇ	$ 691	$4,000	−$1,200			4,061	.9091	3,692
2			1,051	4,000	− 1,200			3,851	.8264	3,182
3	2,000		1,023	4,000	− 1,200	$1,500	−$450	6,873	.7513	5,164
										$ 538

ª Includes $9,500 cost of van + $2,000 investment in working capital
ᵇ $9,500 × 6% = $570

The depreciable base is $9,215 ($9,500 × 97%). The depreciation tax shield was calculated using the following ACRS depreciation rates:

Years	ACRS Rates	Depreciation Expense	Tax Rates	t(Depr.)
1	.25	$2,304	.30	$ 691
2	.38	3,502	.30	1,051
3	.37	3,410	.30	1,023

Sun Valley's owner is concerned that the assumptions under which the analysis was prepared may later prove to be incorrect.

Evaluate the impact on the net present value of the project if operating flows are 20% less than originally expected. It is not necessary to recalculate the entire table presented above. Simply determine the impact of the change on each year's total cash flows, and calculate the present value of the revised flows.

Exercise 10. The owner of Sun Valley Florists in Exercise 9 feels that the salvage value of the van may be only $500 rather than the $1,500 anticipated.

Determine the impact of this change on the project's net present value. It is not necessary to recalculate the entire table. Simply determine the impact of the change on the third year's total cash flow and calculate the present value of the revised flows.

Exercise 11. The owner of Sun Valley Florists in Exercise 9 feels that the estimate of the firm's tax rate could increase from 30% to 46% as a result of profitable operations.

Determine the impact of the change in tax rate on the project's net present value. Since taxes affect almost every cash flow, simply recalculate the analysis using the new tax rate.

Exercise 12. Boston Motors leases cars to firms and individuals for extended periods, usually three years. The leases qualify as sales for tax purposes. A typical 3-year lease of a $12,000 car involves annual payments of $4,360, payable on the first day of the year. At the end of the third year, the lessee has the option to purchase the car for $1,000, which is significantly below the market value. Syntac Corp. is evaluating the lease of a car from Boston under these terms. Syntac has a pretax interest rate of 15%.

Using the present value approach, should the corporation lease the car?

Exercise 13. Horizon Corp., in addition to other financial services, leases automobiles for 3-year periods. The leases qualify as operating leases under the Internal Revenue Code. Progressive Securities Inc. would like to arrange a lease and has been offered the following terms: annual payments of $4,680, due on the first day of each of the next three years.

Progressive Securities' aftertax borrowing rate is 8%, and it has a 46% tax rate. The firm could purchase a comparable car for $12,000. If the asset is purchased, Progressive will take the full investment tax credit in the year of purchase and reduce the asset's depreciable base. The lessor will retain the ITC, however. The asset, with an estimated market value of $3,200, would become the property of the lessor at the end of the lease term.

Calculate the savings or extra cost associated with the lease, using the present value method.

PROBLEMS

Problem 1. Friedan Corporation has funds which it would like to invest in one of several available limited partnerships that are involved in mineral exploration projects in South America. Friedan has selected two acceptable partnership ventures and must now choose between them. The initial investment and the anticipated future cash flows resulting from each investment are summarized as follows:

	Years					
Investment	0	1	2	3	4	5
ABC Partnership	−$75,000	$29,102	$29,102	$29,102	—	—
XYZ Partnership	− 75,000	− 15,000	28,123	28,123	$28,123	$28,123

Required (1) Calculate the net present value, the present value index, and the internal rate of return of each investment opportunity. Friedan applies a 5% cutoff rate to all investments. Which venture should be selected?

(2) Assume that the firm's interest in the XYZ Partnership could be sold back to the partnership for $51,000 at the end of year 3. If this option were taken, which investment should be selected? Calculate the net present value, the present value index, and the internal rate of return of each investment.

(3) Friedan's management is confident that all funds yielded by either investment can be reinvested at 6%. Calculate the future value index and the overall internal rate of return for each investment, using the original cash flows. Which project should be selected on the basis of these measures?

Problem 2. Jarvis Company has the option to invest in two alternative projects. Both projects have the same 5-year life, but the timing of their returns is very different. A summary of the project's cash flows is as follows:

	Years					
	0	1	2	3	4	5
Investment A	−$40,000	$ 1,000	$1,000	$1,000	$1,000	$78,138
Investment B	− 40,000	44,508	1,000	1,000	1,000	1,000

Required (1) Calculate the internal rate of return of both projects.

(2) Calculate the net present value of each project, using Jarvis' required aftertax return of 8%.

(3) Calculate the present value index for each investment.

(4) On the basis of the above calculations, which investment would you select?

(5) Assuming that funds can be reinvested at 11%, calculate the future value and the future value index for both projects. Also, determine each project's overall internal rate of return. On the basis of these new data, which project would you select?

Problem 3. Varsity Company's various division heads have submitted the following projects for possible inclusion in the coming year's capital budget. Project E involves the purchase of a computer system with varying levels of capability. Before E2 can be selected, E1 must first be selected. Before E3 can be chosen, E2 must be accepted. All other projects are independent.

	Years							
Investments	0	1	2	3	4	5	6-9	10
A	−$ 60,000	$ 10,619	$10,619	$10,619	$10,619	$10,619	$10,619	$10,619
B	− 60,000	17,059	17,059	17,059	17,059	17,059	—	—
C	− 100,000	115,000	—	—	—	—	—	—
D	− 90,000	—	—	—	—	—	—	255,548
E1	− 50,000	12,854	12,854	12,854	12,854	12,854	—	—
E2	− 70,000	12,900	12,900	12,900	12,900	12,900	12,900	12,900
E3	− 80,000	15,337	15,337	15,337	15,337	15,337	15,337	15,337

(1) Calculate the internal rate of return of each project, and rank the projects in descending order according to the internal rates of return.

(2) Determine the net present value and the present value index of each project. Varsity uses a 10% cutoff rate in evaluating all capital investments. Rank the projects according to their present value indexes.

(3) Assume that Varsity has $250,000 available for investment. Determine the optimal portfolio, using both the internal rates of return and present value index criteria. All excess funds are invested at the firm's 10% cutoff rate.

Problem 4. Goodman Sausage Company is evaluating the replacement of one of its grinding/packing machines with a newer model. The old machine was purchased 2 years ago for $13,000. The equipment was depreciated using the straight-line method for tax purposes over its 7-year useful life. It had no salvage value. If replaced, the equipment could be sold for its current book value. The grinding/packing machine under consideration has a cost of $18,000 and would be depreciated using the 5-year ACRS rates. The new equipment is expected to have a negligible salvage value at the end of its useful life. The new machine is not eligible for the investment tax credit; no ITC was taken on the old equipment. Goodman's plant manager estimates that operating costs will fall from $27,000 to $22,000 per year as a result of the replacement. The firm has a marginal tax rate of 30% and requires an 11% aftertax return on all equipment replacements.

Calculate the net present value of the equipment replacement.

Problem 5. Family Photo would like to replace its existing photo processing machine with a more sophisticated model. The newer equipment would reduce processing time, improve picture quality, and could handle enlargements and reductions. The current machine was purchased 3 years ago for $17,500. The firm's bookkeeper has assembled the following data:

> Old equipment:
> Depreciated using 5-year ACRS rates
> 10% ITC was taken in the year of purchase
> Current market value: $5,500
> Estimated market value in 5 years: $400
> Annual operating inflow: $4,000
>
> New equipment:
> Purchase price: $30,000
> Depreciated using 5-year ACRS rates
> 10% ITC will be taken in the year of acquisition
> Estimated market value in 5 years: $2,000
> Annual operating inflow: $10,000

Family Photo is in the 40% marginal tax bracket and has a 10% aftertax cutoff rate.

Calculate the net present value and the present value index of the equipment replacement. Assume that the old machine is sold and that a taxable gain or loss arises.

Problem 6. Lucas Company is evaluating the purchase of a wind-driven electrical generator to supply power to its small manufacturing operation. Lucas estimates that the windmill will supply 60% of the firm's total electricity. Currently, its annual electricity bill is $18,000 per year. The windmill will have an estimated cost of $125,000; 70% of the cost will be borne by the federal government as a result of an energy research grant. The portion of the cost paid by Lucas is fully available for depreciation and the investment tax credit. Lucas will take the full 10% ITC and reduce the asset's depreciable base. The asset qualifies as 5-year ACRS property for depreciation purposes. At the end of the project's 7-year economic life, it will be scrapped at a salvage value of $11,000. The entire salvage proceeds will accrue to Lucas. Lucas estimates that maintenance and repair expenses related to the wind generator will total $3,500 per year.

(1) Determine the net present value of the project, using a 10% aftertax cutoff rate and a marginal tax rate of 46%.

(2) One of Lucas' accounting staff feels that the analysis is flawed because it ignores the effects of inflation. The accountant suggests that the cutoff rate should be increased to roughly 18% to include the impact of general inflation. Discuss the merits and flaws of this approach, and the validity of the accountant's assertion.

(3) Assume that all cash flows are expected to increase at an average rate of 7%. Prepare a project analysis which includes the effects of inflation. Compare your answer using both the shortcut method (combined discount and inflation rate) and the double discount method.

Problem 7. Fiske Corporation manufactures high-strength steel castings and extrusions for the aircraft industry. The company is considering an offer from the Fairchild Company to supply turbine blades for that firm's gas turbine engines. Acceptance of the offer would require the purchase of extruding equipment with an estimated cost of $100,000. The offer requires Fiske to supply Fairchild with all the blades it may require for a period of 5 years, but not to exceed 12,000 blades per year. On the basis of Fairchild's estimates for sales of its gas turbine engines, Fiske has prepared the following sales probability distributions:

Annual Sales	Probabilities (Years 1-3)	Probabilities (Years 4-5)
4,000 units	.10	.05
5,000	.30	.10
7,000	.30	.30
9,000	.25	.40
12,000	.05	.15

Fiske's accountants have prepared the following cost projections related to the contract:

Items	Fixed	Variable
Direct materials	—	$10.00 per unit
Direct labor	—	3.75
Factory overhead (excluding depreciation)	$148,000 per year	9.75
General and administrative expenses	10,000	.50
Selling expenses	15,000	4.00

Fiske has negotiated a clause with Fairchild to guarantee a $20,000 salvage value for the extruding equipment at the end of the 5-year contract period.

Ch. 8
297

The offer from Fairchild calls for a unit selling price of $55 per blade. This price is scheduled to rise by 7% per year over the life of the agreement. On the basis of past experience, Fiske expects its manufacturing costs to rise by 6% per year. General, administrative, and selling expenses, however, will increase at a 9% annual rate. The general rate of price increases is expected to be 7% per year.

Fiske will depreciate the equipment using the 5-year ACRS rates, and will claim a 10% ITC in the year of purchase. The firm uses an 8% cutoff rate in all investment decisions and a marginal tax rate of 46%.

Required (1) Using the sales probability distributions, calculate the expected annual sales, in units, of turbine blades.

(2) Using the estimate calculated in (1), determine the pretax operating cash flows generated by the contract. Adjust these flows for inflation, using the specific rates supplied.

(3) Prepare a project evaluation, using present value analysis. Use the shortcut method to adjust the nominal flows for inflation.

Problem 8. Flemming Inc. is planning to acquire a new machine at a cost of $36,000. The estimated useful life of the machine is 5 years, with a salvage value of $2,000. Flemming estimates that the new machine will provide annual revenues of $21,000 and have operating costs of $12,000 over each of the next 6 years. The machine will be depreciated using the 5-year ACRS rates, and Flemming will elect to take the full 10% ITC. Flemming's cutoff rate is 8%, and its marginal tax rate is 40%. On the basis of these data, the following project analysis was prepared:

Years	Cost	ITC	t(Depr.)	Operating Flows	Taxes on Operating Flows	Salvage	Tax on Salvage	Total Flows	PV Factors (8%)	PVs of Total Flows at 8%
0	−$36,000							−$36,000	1.0000	−$36,000
1		$3,600	$2,052	$9,000	−$3,600			11,052	0.9259	10,233
2			3,010	9,000	− 3,600			8,410	0.8573	7,210
3			2,873	9,000	− 3,600			8,273	0.7938	6,567
4			2,873	9,000	− 3,600			8,273	0.7350	6,081
5			2,873	9,000	− 3,600	$2,000	−$800	9,473	0.6806	6,447
										$ 538

Before acquiring the asset, Flemming's managers would like to determine how sensitive the analysis is to changes in the underlying assumptions. Management feels that four variables are critical to the analysis, and their best estimates as to the most likely unfavorable outcomes are summarized in the following table:

Variables	Ranges	Most Likely Unfavorable Outcomes
Revenue	$18,000-$22,000	$20,000
Salvage value	0-$2,500	$ 1,000
Tax rate	40%-46%	46%
Project life	2-5 yrs.	3 yrs.

Insofar as project life is concerned, Flemming fears that the product produced by the machine may be a fad item, and that the market for the product may disappear earlier than anticipated. The machine could be sold at the end of year 2 for $25,000.

(1) Using the most unfavorable outcome, determine to which of the four decision variables the analysis is sensitive. "Sensitive" would be any change which would cause the project's net present value to decrease by more than 70%. It is not usually necessary to recalculate the entire analysis. Simply determine the effect of the change on each year's cash flows and determine the net present value of the revised flows.

(2) Having determined the "sensitive" variables, recalculate the project's net present value, using the most likely unfavorable outcomes for all sensitive variables.

Problem 9. Energy Company is considering the lease of a fleet of light trucks from Pacifico Leasing Company. The company may lease the trucks under one of two leasing options. Pertinent terms of the lease agreements are as follows:

Lease A: Sale/Loan

a. Annual lease payment of $55,492, due on the first day of each of the next 3 years.
b. Option to purchase fleet of trucks for $5,000 at the end of the lease term.
c. Lessor agrees to pay for all ordinary and extraordinary repairs and replacements. Energy estimates that the market value of these services will be $7,500 per year.

Lease B: Operating Lease

a. Annual lease payment of $36,000, due on the first day of each of the next 3 years.
b. If purchased, the trucks would have been depreciated using the 3-year ACRS rates. The full 6% ITC would have been taken in the year of purchase.
c. At the end of year 3, the trucks, with an estimated market value of $40,000, revert to the lessor.

In evaluating the leases, Energy Company applies a 15% pretax cutoff rate and a 9% aftertax rate. If purchased, the trucks would cost $125,000. Energy Company's marginal tax rate is 40%.

Required

Determine whether Energy Company is better off leasing the fleet of trucks under Lease A or Lease B, or purchasing the trucks outright.

Problem 10. California Financial Services has investigated leasing a computer system from Comdata Corp. In response to California Financial Services' inquiry, Comdata has made the following proposal for an operating lease:

• 5-year lease.
• Annual payments of $18,000 are due at the beginning of each year.
• Computer system, with an estimated fair market value of $14,000, reverts to lessor at the end of the lease term.
• Deposit of $20,000 is required at the inception of the lease and is returned at the end of the lease term.
• Lessor agrees to pay all maintenance and repair costs.
• Lessor retains ITC.

The computer system, if purchased, would cost $60,000 and be depreciable over 5 years using the ACRS rates. A 10% ITC would be taken in the year of purchase. California Financial Services estimates that the value of the annual repair and maintenance costs will be $5,000 per year.

California Financial Services is worried about the impact of the initial deposit and first lease payment on its cash position, and has asked Comdata to develop an alternative proposal. In response, Comdata has offered the following revisions:

a. No deposit required.

b. Payments due at the beginning of each year, as follows:

Years	Payments
1	$ 5,000
2	5,000
3	10,000
4	20,000
5	30,000

c. Cost of all maintenance and repairs is borne by the lessee.

California Financial Services is in the 46% marginal tax bracket and evaluates all projects using an 8% aftertax cutoff rate.

Required Determine which lease proposal, if either, California Financial Services should accept.

Problem 11. Brike Apparel Company would like to introduce a line of women's robes to enhance its line of women's clothing. The firm expects sales of 100,000 robes the first year. Unit sales are expected to increase by 4% per year over the life of the project. A projected annual cash flow analysis for the line is as follows:

	Per Unit	Totals
Sales	$12.50	$1,250,000
Manufacturing costs—variable	$ 6.25	$ 625,000
Manufacturing costs—fixed	1.75	175,000
Gross profit	$ 8.00	$ 800,000
Selling expenses—variable	$ 4.50	$ 450,000
Selling expenses—fixed	(1.80)	(180,000)
	(1.45)	(145,000)
Cash flow before tax	$ 1.25	$ 125,000

Introduction of the line would require the purchase of machinery and equipment costing $850,000. In addition, working capital is expected to increase by $125,000 as a result of the acquisition. Brike would depreciate the asset over 5 years using the ACRS rates, and would claim the full 10% ITC in the year of acquisition. At the end of its 5-year life, the equipment could be sold for 15% of its original cost.

As an alternative to purchasing the equipment, Brike has discussed a leasing arrangement with Century Trust Company. The lease, which would qualify as an operating lease, would require annual payments of $230,000 at the beginning of each of the next five years. At the inception of the lease, Brike would be required to deposit with Century Trust 20% of the cost of the machine. The deposit would be returned in two parts: 20% at the end of year 3 and 80% at the end of year 5. The lessee would be responsible for all repairs, maintenance, and incidental costs.

Brike has a marginal tax rate of 46% and a cutoff rate of 8%.

Required (1) Prepare a present value analysis for the purchase of the asset.
(2) Analyze the lease, using present value analysis. Should Brike lease the asset or purchase it?

Nine

Standard Costs

Standard costs are formal estimates of the costs of materials, labor, and overhead on a per-unit-of-output basis. Separate standard costs are developed for each production process and become modular costs for building the standard unit cost of a product. These cost modules are used to account for the units produced, to compare budgeted to actual costs, and to implement cost-volume-profit analysis.

A standard cost system that is properly designed may be viewed as a cafeteria of carefully predetermined costs. The cafeteria line is composed of a series of processes, from which various standard costs for materials, labor, and overhead are served. The processes are often termed cost centers, since they are usually well-defined units for management purposes and are the focal point for comparing budgeted and actual costs.

As each product moves down the cafeteria line, it accumulates the necessary inputs of materials, labor, and overhead. The product is charged for the standard cost of these inputs, and each process, or cost center, is credited for the inputs served. Thus, the cost of each unit produced is a standard cost, and the actual cost of the unit is not known. However, the actual costs of the inputs are accumulated in each cost center, where they are later compared to the standard costs that have been charged to the units produced.

A standard cost system offers several advantages. First, bookkeeping costs can be significantly reduced, since all cost accounting entries for the units moving from work in process to finished goods to goods sold are made at the predetermined standard costs. This advantage is especially beneficial when inventories are maintained on a perpetual basis and actual costs could not be determined in time to update the inventories. Second, the opportunity for cost control is greater in a standard cost system. In each cost center, actual costs are compared to budgeted costs for each period. The budgeted costs are determined by multiplying the actual units produced by the standard unit cost. The differences between the actual costs and the budgeted standard costs can be separated into spending variances, which analyze the amount paid for production inputs, and usage variances, which analyze the quantity of inputs used in the production process.

Standard costs are also helpful in decision making, where they are used to derive the costs associated with alternative plans. Once alternatives are evaluated and selected, the standard unit costs become the costs needed for constructing the master budget.

TYPES OF STANDARDS

Standard costs are sometimes classified as basic standards, theoretical standards, or currently attainable standards. The difference in each type of standard is the degree to which it approximates the anticipated actual cost of a unit produced. Obviously, the degree to which the standard cost relates to the estimated actual cost is one of management's prime concerns if standards are to be used for planning, control, and reporting purposes.

A basic standard cost is one that may have been accurate in the past, but it has not been updated to reflect changes in prices and technology. Since basic standards are not an accurate estimate of actual costs, they are not directly useful for planning or control purposes. Their primary use is in providing a benchmark for identifying the trend of actual costs over a period of time.

Theoretical standards are ideal standards which represent the very minimum possible costs. Such standards are not useful for planning and control purposes, since they make no allowance for waste, spoilage, mechanical breakdowns, or human factors. The use of an unrealistic standard in planning would require the budgeting of variances. If used for control purposes, an unattainable, theoretical standard would have a negative motivational impact.

Currently attainable standards are reasonable estimates of what costs should be. These standards may be based on theoretical standards which were derived by industrial engineering methods and then factored for expected inefficiencies. Although they may be optimistic, they are definitely possible to attain. Since these standards are reasonable and attainable, they are useful for planning and control purposes. They provide meaningful product costs which can be used to approximate the work in process inventories, the finished goods inventories, and the cost of goods sold. Accounting Research Bulletin No. 43 provides that standard costs are acceptable for reporting inventories, if the standards are adjusted at reasonable intervals to reflect current conditions and thus approximate costs.

Since production is charged with standard costs and actual costs are incurred by cost centers, variances will exist in each cost center. When currently attainable standards are being used, it is common for these variances to represent an additional expense as a result of the actual costs exceeding the standard costs. The net variance, whether an added expense or a cost savings, commonly becomes an adjustment to the cost of goods sold.[1]

---

[1]Alternative methods of disposing of variances are described in Chapter 10.

STANDARDS FOR MATERIALS

Setting materials standards begins with the specification of an estimated standard quantity of each material input for a given product. This quantity should include an allowance for unavoidable waste, such as the scrap lumber that would result from cutting circular shapes from rectangular stock. Once they are stated in physical terms, materials standards are easily converted to standard costs by multiplying the physical quantities by anticipated materials prices.

The difference between the standard and actual cost of materials in any period is attributed to spending and usage variances. A materials spending variance is the result of a difference between the actual unit cost and the standard unit cost of the materials, while a materials usage variance is the result of a difference between the actual quantity and the budgeted standard quantity of materials used, based on the units produced.

Materials Spending Variance

Materials spending variances are generally the responsibility of the purchasing agent. They may be the result of either judicious buying or careless buying, or the result of price changes over which the firm has no control. Thus, spending variances may be influenced more by the quality of the predictions than by the shrewdness of buying. Occasionally, spending variances may be caused by rush orders or by uneconomical-sized orders placed by production management. In such cases, production management should be responsible for the spending variances.

To assure timely control over spending, most firms isolate spending variances at the time materials are purchased. Materials are charged to inventory at standard cost, and any variance from actual cost is recorded in a separate spending variance account. For example, if 1,000 board feet of lumber with a standard cost of $1.20 per board foot are purchased for $1,400, the following entry would be made:

Materials (1,000 × $1.20)	1,200	
Materials Spending Variance	200	
Accounts Payable		1,400

If a lesser degree of control can be tolerated, the spending variance may be calculated and recorded when the materials are issued. Under this procedure, materials inventories are recorded at actual cost. Continuing the previous example, if 800 board feet of lumber are issued to production, the purchase and issuance entries would be as follows:

Materials (actual cost)	1,400	
Accounts Payable		1,400
To record purchase at actual cost.		

Work in Process (800 × $1.20)	960	
Materials Spending Variance	160	
Materials (800 × $1.40)		1,120
To record issuance at standard cost.		

The materials spending variance is $40 less than it was when it was calculated at the time of purchase. The difference is the amount of the variance applicable to the materials inventory, and it remains in the inventory until the materials are issued.

Regardless of when the spending variance is calculated, the cost of the materials issued, which is debited to Work in Process, is the standard cost. This procedure reflects the basics of responsibility accounting, since production management is not generally responsible for the actual prices paid for materials.

The calculation of the materials spending variance can be summarized as follows:

Calculated at time of purchase: $P_A Q_P$ vs. $P_S Q_P$

Calculated at time of issuance: $P_A Q_A$ vs. $P_S Q_A$

where P_A is the actual materials price per unit, P_S is the standard materials price per unit, Q_P is the quantity of materials purchased, and Q_A is the actual quantity of materials used. To emphasize the logic in the calculation, rather than memorization, "vs." (versus) is used instead of a minus sign. The variance can be described as favorable when P_A is less than P_S, and unfavorable when P_A is greater than P_S.

Materials Usage Variance

The control of materials used is clearly the responsibility of production management in each cost center. The calculation of the materials usage variance requires that the actual usage of materials be compared to budgeted standard usage each period. The budgeted standard usage is derived by multiplying the standard amount of materials per unit of product by the number of units produced. For most production management purposes, calculating the quantity difference between the actual and budgeted usage is sufficient. To show the dollar importance of the usage variance, however, and to provide for accounting entries, the quantity difference is multiplied by the standard unit cost. The standard cost is used, rather than the actual cost, because production managers base their plans on standard costs, and they seldom have control over the actual unit cost of materials.

The calculation of the materials usage variance can be summarized as follows:

$$(Q_A \text{ vs. } Q_S) \times P_S$$

where Q_A is the actual quantity of materials used per unit, Q_S is the standard quantity of materials used per unit, and P_S is the standard price per unit of material. When Q_A is greater than Q_S, the variance can be described as unfavorable, and when Q_A is less than Q_S, the variance is favorable.

Summary Illustration of Materials Variances

To illustrate the materials variances, assume that a product requires two materials, A and B, and that the spending variance is calculated when the materials are purchased. The following facts are available:

Materials standard for one unit of product:
Material A .... 5 lbs. @ $2.00 per lb.
Material B .... 2 lbs. @ 3.20 per lb.

Actual results for January:

Material A .... 6,500 lbs. purchased for $12,500
6,200 lbs. issued to production
Material B .... 3,000 lbs. purchased for $10,200
2,500 lbs. issued to production
1,200 units of product were completed in January

The variances are calculated as follows:

Spending Variances ($P_A Q_P$ vs. $P_S Q_P$)

Material A: $12,500* vs. ($2 × 6,500 lbs.) = $12,500 vs. $13,000 = $500 F
Material B: $10,200 vs. ($3.20 × 3,000 lbs.) = $10,200 vs. $9,600 = $600 U

*Since $12,500 is the product of P_A and Q_P, there is no need to calculate P_A and Q_P separately.

Usage Variances [(Q_A vs. Q_S^*) × P_S]

Material A: 6,200 lbs. vs. (1,200 × 5 lbs.) × $2 = 200 lbs. U × $2 = $400 U
Material B: 2,500 lbs. vs. (1,200 × 2 lbs.) × $3.20 = 100 lbs. U × $3.20 = $320 U

*The quantity standard, Q_S, is the budgeted use of materials based on actual production. It is derived by multiplying units produced by the standard quantity of materials per unit.

In this example, the favorable spending variance for Material A was accompanied by an unfavorable usage variance. Although spending and usage variances typically reflect separate responsibilities and are interpreted separately, the Material A variances could be the result of a purchase of inferior materials at a bargain price, which created more scrap or shrinkage. In this situation, there would be a dilemma for responsibility accounting, since the purchase price and the spending variance are the responsibility of the purchasing agent, while the usage variance is the responsibility of the production manager.

STANDARDS FOR DIRECT LABOR

It is particularly important that labor standards be set carefully, since they have behavioral implications. The labor standard must be reasonably attainable if labor and production management are to attempt to achieve it. Therefore, the labor standard is currently attainable and allows for normal deviations from the minimum theoretical time which might be established by using industrial engineering methods.

For a given cost center, the standard hours allowed for a unit of output are the total number of hours of direct labor for various labor classifications at different rates of pay. The standard labor cost per hour is a weighted average rate based on a given mix of labor classifications. Thus, for the unit in the previous example, the direct labor standard might be derived as follows:

Labor Classifications	Hours Required per Unit	Pay Rates	Totals
A	2.0	$4 per hr.	$ 8.00
B	.5	5	2.50
C	1.0	7	7.00
	3.5		$17.50

Average rate: $17.50 ÷ 3.5 hrs. = $5 per hr.
Standard labor per unit: 3.5 hrs. at $5 per hr.

Variance analysis for direct labor is based on two possible deviations from the standard. First, there may be a difference between the actual cost of the hours used and the standard (weighted average) cost of the hours used. Generally, this spending (or rate) variance for labor is really a labor mix variance, since it results from a mix of labor classifications that differs from the mix used in determining the standard. The labor spending variance should not result from a change in the pay rate for a given classification, since the standard cost per hour should be adjusted immediately for such changes. Although the spending variance may result from premium pay for overtime, most firms charge overtime premiums to a separate overhead account in order to provide better control of overtime.

The second labor variance is a usage or efficiency variance, which results from a difference between the actual hours used during a given period and the total budgeted hours based on the units produced. The quantity difference in hours is multiplied by the standard (weighted average) cost per hour, since the variance between the actual cost and the standard cost per hour has already been isolated in the calculation of the labor spending variance. Unlike the situation for materials, responsibility for the labor spending and labor usage variances is often vested in the same person—the cost center supervisor, who is responsible for the labor classifications and quantity used.

To illustrate the labor variances, assume the following facts for the unit in the previous example:

Direct labor standard for one unit of product: 3.5 hours at an average cost of $5 per hour
Actual results for January: 4,300 direct labor hours used at a cost of $22,600
1,200 units produced

The variances are calculated as follows:

Spending Variance ($P_A Q_A$ vs. $P_S Q_A$)

$22,600* vs. ($5 × 4,300 hrs.) = $22,600 vs. $21,500 = $1,100 U

*Since $22,600 is the product of P_A and Q_A, there is no need to calculate separately P_A and Q_A.

Usage Variance [(Q_A vs. Q_S*) × P_S]

(4,300 actual hrs. vs. 4,200 budgeted hrs.) × $5 = 100 hrs. U × $5 = $500 U

*The quantity standard, Q_S, is the budgeted use of labor based on actual production. It is derived by multiplying units produced by the standard number of labor hours per unit.

STANDARDS FOR OVERHEAD

Overhead has been previously defined as a set of production costs which are analyzed in the aggregate as to their behavior with respect to output. The total overhead cost with respect to output is estimated, and a flexible budget for overhead can then be stated, as follows:

Total overhead = Fixed cost per period + Variable cost per unit of activity

In theory, the unit of activity used in the flexible budget should be that unit which best explains cost behavior. As indicated in Chapter 2, it is most common to use direct labor hours as the unit of activity, since information on labor hours must be compiled in order to compute labor variances. Machine hours may also be used as a unit of activity when the level of overhead varies more closely with this activity than with labor hours.

Traditional, 3-Way Analysis of Overhead

For control purposes, overhead variance analysis focuses on the actual cost of overhead compared to the budget, and the difference between the actual and budgeted use of overhead support activities. The overhead spending variance is the difference between the actual cost of overhead and the flexible budget amount for the actual hours of labor supported (or machine hours if they are used as the unit of activity). Actual hours of direct labor are used because it is necessary for overhead services to support all direct labor hours, whether or not the labor hours are budgeted. For example, the performance of a janitorial staff should be analyzed by comparing the actual janitorial cost with the cost budgeted according to all direct labor hours actually supported.

To illustrate the overhead spending variance, assume that the unit in the previous example is the only unit built in a given cost center, and that the overhead flexible budget for that cost center is stated as follows:

Total estimated overhead = $6,000 per period + $1.50 per direct labor hour (DLH)

Since 4,300 direct labor hours were worked in January, the budgeted cost is $12,450 [$6,000 + ($1.50 × 4,300)]. If $13,000 was actually spent for overhead in that period, the overhead spending variance would be $550 unfavorable.

The variable overhead usage or efficiency variance is the difference between the actual and budgeted use of overhead. In the example of labor variance calculations, 100 hours of labor were used in excess of the hours budgeted. Since the variable cost of overhead is $1.50 per direct labor hour, $150 of additional overhead was incurred to support the extra direct labor hours.

The overhead usage variance is directly linked to the labor usage variance. It has the same base (100 hours unfavorable) and the same explanation of its cause. Thus, the real standard cost of an hour of labor is $6.50 ($5 labor standard + $1.50 variable overhead). Unfortunately, accounting practice continues to separate the usage variances for labor and overhead, even though the overhead cost caused by extra labor hours is the responsibility of the supervisor of the direct labor force, rather than the provider of the overhead services, assuming that separate responsibilities exist.

If a firm were to use direct costing, its analysis of overhead would be complete with just the spending and usage variances. Firms using full costing need one more variance, however, in order to reconcile their overhead account. In full costing, fixed overhead must be applied to each unit produced during a period. Before the period begins, therefore, the standard fixed overhead cost per unit must be derived, usually by allocating the budgeted fixed overhead on the same basis as the variable overhead. This basis is typically direct labor hours, since overhead can then be applied to a variety of products, with differing labor contents.

To avoid variations in the fixed overhead rate from one period to another, due to changes in production levels, it is common to use a long-run average production level, called **normal production.** In the previous example, if normal production is 5,000 direct labor hours, the standard fixed overhead rate would be $1.20 per direct labor hour ($6,000 fixed overhead ÷ 5,000 DLH). Since 3.5 labor hours are required, each unit is allocated $4.20 (3.5 hours × $1.20) of fixed overhead, and this amount is applied to each unit as it is produced.

The total budgeted amount of fixed overhead can only be exactly applied if actual production equals the normal production in terms of the direct labor hours. If production is above or below normal, there will be overapplied or underapplied fixed overhead. The difference between the budgeted and the applied fixed overhead is called a **volume variance.** In the example, the volume variance is $960 [(5,000 normal DLH − 4,200 budgeted hours necessary to produce 1,200 units) × $1.20 standard fixed overhead rate]. Note that fixed overhead is applied to the budgeted hours, rather than actual hours, since only budgeted hours are unitized in a standard cost system.

The volume variance is described as favorable when the fixed overhead is overapplied, i.e., when the actual production exceeds normal production. The variance is unfavorable when the fixed overhead is underapplied. The use of the terms "favorable" and "unfavorable" is more traditional than logical. For example, it is likely that fewer Chevrolet Vegas were produced in the car's final production years than in normal production years. The below-normal production should not be described as unfavorable, since a normal output of cars would not sell.

Since the volume variance is dependent on unit sales, it is usually not controllable by production management, unless it stems from an inability to meet production schedules. The variance could also be the result of not meeting sales quotas.

To summarize the overhead variances presented in the preceding paragraphs, the facts of the example are as follows:

Flexible budget for overhead: $6,000 per period + $1.50 per DLH
Fixed overhead application rate: $6,000 ÷ 5,000 normal DLH = $1.20 per DLH
Labor standard: 3.5 DLH per unit
Actual results for January: $13,000 spent to support 4,300 direct labor hours
                                              1,200 units produced

The variances are calculated as follows:

Spending Variance
(Actual total overhead vs. Flexible budget for DLH)

$13,000 vs. $6,000 + ($1.50 × 4,300 DLH) = $13,000 vs. $12,450 = $550 U

Usage Variance
[(Q_A vs. Q_S) × Variable overhead per DLH]

(4,300 DLH vs. 4,200 DLH*) × $1.50 = 100 DLH U × $1.50 = $150 U

---

*Based on budgeted DLH (1,200 units × 3.5 DLH per unit).

Volume Variance
[(Budgeted DLH vs. Normal DLH) × Fixed overhead per DLH]

(4,200 DLH vs. 5,000 DLH) × $1.20 = 800 DLH U × $1.20 = $960 U

Variations of Overhead Analysis

There are two variations of the 3-way analysis of overhead described in the preceding section. The first variation is a 4-way analysis, which differs from a 3-way analysis by dividing the spending variance into fixed and variable portions. To illustrate, if the actual total overhead of $13,000 consisted of $5,700 fixed overhead and $7,300 variable overhead, the unfavorable spending variance of $550 could be analyzed as follows:

Fixed Spending Variance
(Actual fixed overhead vs. Budgeted fixed overhead)

$5,700 vs. $6,000 = $300 F

Variable Spending Variance
[Actual variable overhead vs. (Actual DLH × Variable overhead per DLH)]

$7,300 vs. (4,300 DLH × $1.50) = $7,300 vs. $6,450 = $850 U

This subdivision of the overhead spending variance is only possible when the actual fixed and variable overhead can be and actually are separated in the accounts. This separation is seldom feasible, since many overhead costs are mixed costs.

The second variation of the 3-way overhead analysis is a 2-way analysis. This approach is haphazard and tends to commingle responsibilities between service and production departments by lumping the overhead spending and usage variances into a single budget, or controllable, variance. There is no justification for the use of 2-way analysis, unless a firm does not measure standard labor hours and thus has no measure of budgeted hours. Unlike the spending variance, which uses actual direct labor hours, the budget variance is the result of comparing the actual total overhead with the flexible budget for the budgeted direct labor hours. The budget variance in the example is calculated as follows:

Budget Variance
(Actual total overhead vs. Flexible budget for budgeted DLH)

$13,000 vs. [$6,000 + ($1.50 × 4,200 DLH)] = $13,000 vs. $12,300 = $700 U

Summary Comparison of 2-Way, 3-Way, and 4-Way Analyses of Overhead

The three methods of analyzing overhead variances are summarized in Illustration 9-1, using the facts of the preceding example. The center column is the 3-way analysis, which is the most frequently used method. The column on the left shows the 4-way analysis, which subdivides the single spending variance of the 3-way analysis into fixed and variable components. The column on the right shows the 2-way analysis, which merges the spending and usage variances of the 3-way analysis into a single budget variance.

Illustration 9-1
Comparison of 2-Way, 3-Way, and 4-Way Analysis of Overhead

Summary of Facts

Flexible budget for overhead: $6,000 + $1.50 per DLH
Fixed overhead application rate: $6,000 ÷ 5,000 normal DLH = $1.20 per standard DLH
Labor standard: 3.5 DLH per unit
Actual results for January: $5,700 fixed overhead and $7,300 variable overhead spent to support 4,300 hours of labor
1,200 units produced

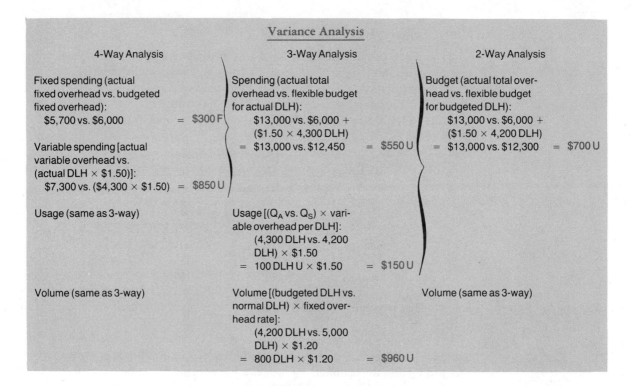

Variance Analysis

4-Way Analysis	3-Way Analysis	2-Way Analysis
Fixed spending (actual fixed overhead vs. budgeted fixed overhead): $5,700 vs. $6,000 = $300 F	Spending (actual total overhead vs. flexible budget for actual DLH): $13,000 vs. $6,000 + ($1.50 × 4,300 DLH) = $13,000 vs. $12,450 = $550 U	Budget (actual total overhead vs. flexible budget for budgeted DLH): $13,000 vs. $6,000 + ($1.50 × 4,200 DLH) = $13,000 vs. $12,300 = $700 U
Variable spending [actual variable overhead vs. (actual DLH × $1.50)]: $7,300 vs. ($4,300 × $1.50) = $850 U		
Usage (same as 3-way)	Usage [(Q$_A$ vs. Q$_S$) × variable overhead per DLH]: (4,300 DLH vs. 4,200 DLH) × $1.50 = 100 DLH U × $1.50 = $150 U	
Volume (same as 3-way)	Volume [(budgeted DLH vs. normal DLH) × fixed overhead rate]: (4,200 DLH vs. 5,000 DLH) × $1.20 = 800 DLH × $1.20 = $960 U	Volume (same as 3-way)

COMPREHENSIVE ILLUSTRATION OF VARIANCE ANALYSIS

Variance analysis procedures are reviewed in Illustration 9-2, which is divided into two parts. In the Summary of Facts (Part A), the standard cost of a unit of production, the actual operating results for December, and the overhead information are presented. In the Variance Analysis (Part B), all the variances are calculated, based on the facts and the analyses in Part A.

The facts necessary for a variance analysis may be available in diverse forms, but they should be organized in a format similar to that of Part A before the analysis is begun. Variance analyses should never be attempted while data are being gathered. Likewise, the overhead variance analysis should not be attempted until the flexible budget for total overhead and the fixed overhead application rate have been derived, as shown in Part A. Errors in variance analysis are usually traceable to failures in these areas.

The following features of the variance analysis in Part B should be noted:

1. The materials spending variances are based on purchases, rather than issuances.
2. A single set of calculation formats for the spending and usage variances is used for all materials and direct labor.
3. The flexible budget for total overhead is a direct component of the overhead spending variance under the 3-way analysis of overhead, and a component of the budget variance under the 2-way analysis. The budget is applied to actual hours of direct labor under the 3-way analysis, and to budgeted hours under the 2-way analysis.

4. Under the 3-way analysis of overhead, the overhead usage variance is the change in overhead cost traceable to the difference between the actual and the budgeted direct labor hours. This difference is multiplied by only the variable overhead rate, since the fixed overhead is constant and the only change in cost is the variable cost.
5. The quantity base for the overhead volume variance is direct labor hours. Budgeted direct labor hours are used to calculate this variance.

Standard production costs:

1 lb. of Afex at $.80 per lb.	$ .80
3 lbs. of Bevos at $.50 per lb.	1.50
2 hrs. of direct labor at average rate of $5 per hr.	10.00
Variable overhead ($1.50 per DLH)	3.00
Fixed overhead ($1 per DLH, based on 4,000 normal DLH)	2.00
Total	$17.30

Results for December:
Afex, 2,500 lbs. purchased for $2,450; 1,900 lbs. issued
Bevos, 5,800 lbs. purchased for $2,800; 5,550 lbs. issued
Labor, 3,725 hours used at a cost of $18,065
Actual overhead, $9,100
1,800 units produced
1,600 units sold

Flexible budget, total overhead: $4,000 fixed + $1.50 per DLH
Fixed overhead application rate: $4,000 fixed overhead ÷ (2,000 units × 2 DLH)
                                   = $4,000 fixed overhead ÷ 4,000 normal DLH
                                   = $1 per standard DLH

Materials and Direct Labor

Afex Spending ($P_A Q_P$ vs. $P_S Q_P$):
  $2,450 vs. ($.80 × 2,500 lbs.)
= $2,450 vs. $2,000
= $450 U

Afex Usage [(Q_A vs. Q_S) × P_S]:
  [1,900 lbs. vs. (1,800 × 1 lb.)] × $.80
= 100 lbs. U × $.80
= $80 U

Bevos Spending:
  $2,800 vs. ($.50 × 5,800 lbs.)
= $2,800 vs. $2,900
= $100 F

Bevos Usage:
  [5,550 lbs. vs. (1,800 × 1 lb.)] × $.50
= 150 lbs. U × $.50
= $75 U

Direct Labor Spending ($P_A Q_A$ vs. $P_S Q_A$):
  $18,065 vs. ($5 × 3,725 DLH)
= $18,065 vs. $18,625
= $560 F

Direct Labor Usage:
  (3,725 actual DLH vs. 3,600* budgeted DLH) × $5
= 125 DLH U × $5
= $625 U

Overhead—3-Way Analysis

Spending (Actual total overhead vs. Flexible budget for actual DLH):
  $9,100 vs. [$4,000 + ($1.50 × 3,725 actual DLH)]
= $9,100 vs. $9,587.50
= $487.50 F

Usage [(Q_A vs. Q_S) × Variable overhead per DLH]:
  (3,725 DLH vs. 3,600 DLH*) × $1.50
= 125 DLH U × $1.50
= $187.50 U

Volume [(Budgeted DLH vs. Normal DLH) × Fixed overhead application rate]:
(3,600 DLH* vs. 4,000 DLH) × $1
= 400 DLH U × $1
= $400 U

Overhead—2-Way Analysis

Budget Variance (Actual total overhead vs. Flexible budget for budgeted DLH):
$9,100 vs. [$4,000 + ($1.50 × 3,600* budgeted DLH)]
= $9,100 vs. $9,400
= $300 F

---

*1,800 units time 2 standard DLH per unit.

ACCOUNTING FOR VARIANCES

A variety of methods are available for recording production activities in a standard cost system. The differences in these methods, which are related to the recording of the actual and the standard costs, are demonstrated in Illustration 9-3 and Illustration 9-4. In Illustration 9-3, which is based on the example in Illustration 9-2, the entries and ledger accounts are designed as follows:

1. Materials spending variances are recorded in the variance summary account at the time of purchase. This procedure allows the materials inventory ledger to be maintained at standard cost.
2. All variances for which production management is usually responsible are contained in the work in process ledger account. These variances include the materials usage, labor spending, labor usage, and overhead usage variances. These variances are isolated at the end of the period and are closed to the variance summary account.
3. Overhead variances for which production management may not be responsible are contained in the overhead control account. These variances include the overhead spending and volume variances, which are calculated at the end of the period and are closed to the variance summary account.
4. All variances of the period will thus be aggregated in one account, Variance Summary. This nominal (income statement) account must be closed at the end of the period. In this illustration, the net variances of the period are closed to Cost of Goods Sold.

Illustration 9-3
Accounting Procedures
for Standard Costs

Entry No.	Entry		
1.	Materials—Afex (2,500 lbs. × $.80)	2,000.00	
	Variance Summary (Afex spending)	450.00	
	Payables		2,450.00
2.	Materials—Bevos (5,800 lbs. × $.50)	2,900.00	
	Variance Summary (Bevos spending)		100.00
	Payables		2,800.00
3.	Work in Process	1,520.00	
	Materials—Afex (1,900 lbs. × $.80)		1,520.00

Entry No.	Entry		
4.	Work in Process	2,775.00	
	Materials—Bevos (5,550 lbs. × $.50)		2,775.00
5.	Work in Process	18,065.00	
	Payables (actual cost of labor)		18,065.00
6.	Overhead Control (actual cost of overhead)	9,100.00	
	Payables		9,100.00
7.	Work in Process	5,587.50	
	Overhead Control (variable overhead, 3,725 actual DLH × $1.50)		5,587.50
8.	Work in Process	3,600.00	
	Overhead Control (fixed overhead, 1,800 units × 2 DLH × $1)		3,600.00
9.	Finished Goods Inventory	31,140.00	
	Work in Process (1,800 units × $17.30 standard cost)		31,140.00
10.	Cost of Goods Sold	27,680.00	
	Finished Goods Inventory (1,600 units × $17.30 standard cost)		27,680.00
11.	Variance Summary	407.50	
	Work in Process		407.50

Net unfavorable production variances:

Afex usage	80.00	U
Bevos usage	75.00	U
Direct labor usage	625.00	U
Overhead usage	187.50	U
Direct labor spending	560.00	F
Total	407.50	U

Entry No.	Entry		
12.	Overhead Control	487.50	
	Variance Summary (overhead spending)		487.50
13.	Variance Summary (volume variance)	400.00	
	Overhead Control		400.00
14.	Cost of Goods Sold	670.00	
	Variance Summary		670.00

Ledger

Materials—Afex				Materials—Bevos			
Beg. inventory, 200 lbs. × $.80	160.00	(3) Issuances, 1,900 actual lbs. × $.80	1,520.00	Beg. inventory, 300 lbs. × $.50	150.00	(4) Issuances, 5,550 actual lbs. × $.50	2,775.00
(1) Purchases, 2,500 lbs. × $.80 stan. cost	2,000.00			(2) Purchases, 5,800 lbs. × $.50 stan. cost	2,900.00		
Balance, 800 lbs. × $.80	640.00			Balance, 550 lbs. at $.50	275.00		

Work in Process

(3) Afex, 1,900 lbs. × $.80	1,520.00	(9) Transferred out 1,800 units × $17.30 stan. cost	31,140.00
(4) Bevos, 5,550 lbs. × $.50	2,775.00	(11) Net unfavorable production variances (controllable by production management)	407.50
(5) Labor, 3,725 DLH × actual cost	18,065.00		
(7) Variable overhead, 3,725 DLH (actual) × $1.50	5,587.50		
(8) Fixed overhead, 1,800 units × 2 DLH × $1	3,600.00		

Finished Goods Inventory

(9) 1,800 units received × $17.30 stan. cost	31,140.00	(10) 1,600 units sold × $17.30 stan. cost	27,680.00
Balance, 200 units × $17.30 stan. cost	3,460.00		

Overhead Control

(6) Actual cost	9,100.00	(7) Applied variable overhead, 3,725 DLH × $1.50	5,587.50
(12) Overhead spending var.	487.50	(8) Applied fixed overhead, 1,800 units × 2 DLH × $1	3,600.00
		(13) Overhead volume variance	400.00

Cost of Goods Sold

(10) 1,600 units sold × $17.30 stan. cost	27,680.00
(14) Close variances	670.00
Total	28,350.00

Variance Summary

(1) Afex spending	450.00 U	(2) Bevos spending	100.00 F
(11) Afex usage	80.00 U	(11) Labor spending	560.00 F
(11) Bevos usage	75.00 U	(12) Overhead spending	487.50 F
(11) Labor usage	625.00 U		
(11) Overhead usage	187.50 U		
(13) Overhead volume	400.00 U		
		(14) Close variances	670.00

In Illustration 9-3, only the materials spending variances are recorded when they are incurred. Other variances are not recorded until the end of the period. Illustration 9-4 is an example of a method which offers a tighter control of costs by recording variances on a perpetual basis. For example, materials are controlled by initially issuing to production only the standard quantity of materials. Any requisitions in excess of the standard quantity are recorded on a special variance requisition. In a similar manner, direct labor is debited to work in process at standard hours and the standard rate. Any difference between actual labor costs and standard labor costs is recorded in a variance account as the labor hours are used. When labor is recorded in this manner, overhead is debited to work in process on the basis of standard labor hours. All overhead variances are therefore contained in the overhead control account.

The accounting procedures contained in Illustrations 9-3 and 9-4 tend to be two extremes, with other possible variations between these extremes. The calculation of the amount of the variances is not generally affected by the accounting techniques used, except when materials spending variances are calculated at the time of issuance rather than at the time of purchase. A common feature of all methods is that units always leave work in process and enter finished goods at the standard cost.

Illustration 9-4
Alternative Accounting Procedures for Standard Costs

Entry No.	Entry		
1.	Materials—Afex (2,500 lbs. × $.80)	2,000.00	
	Variance Summary (Afex spending)	450.00	
	Payables		2,450.00
2.	Materials—Bevos (5,800 lbs. × $.50)	2,900.00	
	Variance Summary (Bevos spending)		100.00
	Payables		2,800.00
3.	Work in Process (1,800 lbs. × $.80)	1,440.00	
	Variance Summary (Afex usage)	80.00	
	Materials—Afex (1,900 lbs. × $.80)		1,520.00
4.	Work in Process (5,400 lbs. × $.50)	2,700.00	
	Variance Summary (Bevos usage)	75.00	
	Materials—Bevos		2,775.00
5.	Work in Process (3,600 DLH × $5)	18,000.00	
	Variance Summary (labor usage)	625.00	
	Variance Summary (labor spending)		560.00
	Payables (actual cost of labor)		18,065.00
6.	Overhead Control (actual cost of overhead)	9,100.00	
	Payables		9,100.00
7.	Work in Process	5,400.00	
	Overhead Control (variable overhead, 3,600 standard DLH × $1.50)		5,400.00
8.	Work in Process	3,600.00	
	Overhead Control (fixed overhead, 1,800 units × 2 DLH × $1)		3,600.00
9.	Finished Goods Inventory	31,140.00	
	Work in Process (1,800 units × $17.30 stan. cost)		31,140.00
10.	Cost of Goods Sold	27,680.00	
	Finished Goods Inventory (1,600 units × $17.30 stan. cost)		27,680.00
11.	Variance Summary (overhead usage)	187.50	
	Overhead Control		187.50

Entry No.	Entry		
12.	Overhead Control	487.50	
	Variance Summary (overhead spending)		487.50
13.	Variance Summary (overhead volume)	400.00	
	Overhead Control		400.00
14.	Cost of Goods Sold	670.00	
	Variance Summary		670.00
	To close variances to Cost of Goods Sold.		

Ledger

Materials—Afex

Beg. inventory, 200 lbs. × $.80	160.00	(3) Issuances, 1,900 actual lbs. × $.80	1,520.00
(1) Purchases, 2,500 lbs. × $.80 stan. cost	2,000.00		
Balance, 800 lbs. × $.80	640.00		

Materials—Bevos

Beg. inventory, 300 lbs. × $.50	150.00	(4) Issuances, 5,550 actual lbs. × $.50	2,775.00
(2) Purchases, 5,800 lbs. × $.50 stan. cost	2,900.00		
Balance, 550 lbs. × $.50	275.00		

Work in Process

(3) Afex, 1,800 lbs. × $.80	1,440.00	(9) Transferred out, 1,800 units × $17.30 stan. cost	31,140.00
(4) Bevos, 5,400 lbs. × $.50	2,700.00		
(5) Labor, 3,600 DLH × $5	18,000.00		
(7) Variable overhead, 3,600 stan. DLH × $1.50	5,400.00		
(8) Fixed overhead, 1,800 units × $2	3,600.00		

Finished Goods Inventory

(9) 1,800 units received × $17.30 stan. cost	31,140.00	(10) 1,600 units sold × $17.30 stan. cost	27,680.00
Balance, 200 units × $17.30 stan. cost	3,460.00		

Overhead Control

(6) Actual cost	9,100.00	(7) Applied variable overhead, 3,600 stan. DLH × $1.50	5,400.00
(12) Overhead spending variance	487.50	(8) Applied fixed overhead, 1,800 units × 2 DLH × $1	3,600.00
		(11) Overhead usage variance	187.50
		(13) Overhead volume variance	400.00

Cost of Goods Sold

(10) 1,600 units sold × $17.30 stan. cost	27,680.00		
(14) Close variances	670.00		
Total	28,350.00		

IMPLEMENTING STANDARD COST SYSTEMS

Standard costs may be used in both process and job order cost systems. The same attributes that favor the use of standards—routine and standardized operations—are also attributes of process cost systems. In such systems, standards are calculated for each process, and variance analysis is performed individually for each process. Although used less frequently in job order shops, standard cost concepts may be used to allocate overhead to individual jobs, and variance analysis may aid the control of job costs.

Process Cost Applications

A process is usually designed to be a major control point for the use of materials and labor. Therefore, a process is a logical focal point for variance analysis. Variance analysis may proceed by processes to the degree that responsibility has been assigned, which differs according to the cost being analyzed.

Materials. Since materials usage is normally a prime responsibility of the process manager, materials usage variances are calculated for each process. Spending variances, however, are usually the responsibility of a management level higher than the process, because materials are typically purchased in common for all processes. Although spending variances are not the responsibility of the process manager, they may be allocated to each process when they reflect a somewhat permanent price change, which process managers should consider if it is possible to alter the use of the materials.

Direct Labor. As discussed previously, the labor spending variance represents the change in cost which results from using a mix of labor classifications and pay levels different from those included in the budget. In most cases, the process manager is responsible for the mix used and should be accountable for the process's labor spending variance.

Control of the amount of labor used will usually be the most important responsibility of a process manager. It is therefore imperative that the actual and the budgeted labor usage be compared for each process. This comparison is the basis of the labor usage variance which is calculated for each process.

Overhead. In many firms, overhead is a central support function provided by a service department and shared by several processes. In such cases, the overhead budget is prepared for the service department, which is responsible for the spending variance. There is therefore no benefit in calculating an overhead spending variance for each process.

The volume variance tends to be a plant-wide responsibility, since it is caused by the aggregate use of overhead services by all processes. It is possible to allocate the volume variance to each process by comparing actual and planned production for each process. This allocation should be made only when a process manager has some degree of control over output, such as scheduling production. For example, if fewer units are produced than had been planned, due to errors in scheduling, the process manager could be held accountable for the volume variance.

In most firms, the overhead usage variance is a direct result of the labor usage variance. Since the labor usage variance is a process responsibility, the overhead usage variance is also a process responsibility and is analyzed for each process. If these two variances are not linked together, the full dollar impact of deviating from the planned usage of labor would not be known to the process. This lack of control is a weakness of the 2-way method of analysis.

Processes may have responsibility for incurring major amounts of their own overhead. In these situations, overhead may be classified as internally supplied and externally supplied. Overhead supplied by the production department itself, such as cleaning costs, is the complete responsibility of the process manager, who should be charged with the spending and usage variances. The 2-way analysis of variances may be used, since both the price and the use of the overhead is the process manager's responsibility. Externally supplied overhead is supplied to a process by a service department. Therefore, only the usage variance is chargeable to the process. The spending variance is separately calculated and is the responsibility of the service department.

Job Order Cost Applications

The majority of job shops do not have sufficiently standardized operations to make the use of standard costing beneficial. There are job shops, however, that produce large batches of special-order products, using various combinations of standardized operations. An example would be firms that manufacture canvas bags for promotional purposes. Different sizes, grades of canvas, and printing are offered, but each order of bags requires some combination of routine operations. By applying standard cost procedures and analyzing variances, such a firm could better control production costs and have a basis for improving future cost estimates. If production cost control were the only concern, the guidelines for calculating variances by the job would parallel those discussed for processes. If there is also some concern for future cost estimates, some variances not controllable at the job level, such as the materials spending variance, may be allocated to jobs in order to be considered in future estimates.

Job shops that cannot use standard costs for materials and labor may use standard costs for overhead. Since overhead cannot be identified with specific jobs, it is applied according to some measure of usage, such as direct labor hours. The use of a predetermined overhead rate is an application of standard cost procedures. In Chapter 2, an **overhead application variance** was computed by comparing actual and applied overhead. This variance can now be separated into a **budget variance** and a **modified volume variance**. An overhead usage variance is not calculable, since there is no measure of standard direct labor hours upon which to base the variance.

To illustrate overhead variance analysis in a job order shop, assume that the following flexible budget was derived:

$$\text{Total overhead} = \$54,000 + \$2 \text{ per DLH}$$

To arrive at the full cost of units produced, the fixed overhead must be spread over some number of hours. Therefore, assume that 90,000 hours are used, which results in a fixed overhead application rate of $.60 per DLH ($54,000 ÷ 90,000

DLH). The total overhead application rate is $2.60 per DLH. If $230,000 was incurred for overhead in support of 87,000 direct labor hours, the overhead application variance would be computed as follows:

Application Variance
(Actual total overhead vs. Applied overhead)

$230,000 vs. (87,000 DLH $\times$ $2.60) = $230,000 vs. $226,200 = $3,800 U

The budget variance portion of the application variance is computed as follows:

Budget Variance
(Actual total overhead vs. Flexible budget for actual DLH)

$230,000 vs. [$54,000 + ($2 $\times$ 87,000 DLH)] = $230,000 vs. $228,000 = $2,000 U

In previous analyses, the overhead volume variance has resulted from comparing the planned and budgeted usage of direct labor hours when a variety of products utilizes the overhead. In a job shop, fixed overhead cannot be applied to budgeted direct labor hours, since there is no record of standard direct labor hours. Thus, fixed overhead must be applied to actual direct labor hours, which leads to the calculation of the modified volume variance, as follows:

Modified Volume Variance
(Actual DLH vs. Planned DLH) $\times$ Fixed overhead rate

(87,000 DLH vs. 90,000 DLH) $\times$ $.60 = 3,000 DLH U $\times$ $.60 = $1,800 U

This variance is unfavorable because the deficiency of hours worked compared to planned hours leaves 3,000 hours of fixed overhead unapplied. Although fewer hours might mean greater efficiency, such a conclusion is not possible, since a record of budgeted hours is not maintained.

1. What are standard costs? What are some advantages to using them?

2. What are three types of standards? Describe each.

3. What creates a variance?

4. What are the differences in isolating a materials spending variance at the time of purchase and isolating it at issuance?

5. Which of the two methods referred to in Question 4 offers better control of costs? Why?

6. Logically, when is a spending variance considered unfavorable? favorable?

7. If various classifications of skilled labor work on a product, how can a standard labor rate be set?

8. Why is fixed overhead applied to budgeted direct labor hours and not actual hours?

9. How does 4-way overhead variance analysis differ from 3-way analysis? Why is it not widely used?

10. What is a budget variance? Why is it not widely used?

11. Before any overhead variances are calculated, what information should be gathered? Why?

12. List all variances one would normally be concerned with when doing variance analysis. Which of these variances would be contained in work in process inventory, and what does their inclusion imply?

13. What is a common feature of all standard cost systems?

14. How can standards be used in a process cost system? Is this practical?

15. Why might it be impractical to use standard costs in a job order cost system?

EXERCISES

Exercise 1. During a recent period, Avery Asphalt Company purchased 100,000 barrels of oil for $25.30 per barrel. The standard cost of each barrel is $25. Production used 95,000 barrels during the period.

Calculate the spending variance (1) at the time of purchase, (2) at the time of issuance.

Exercise 2. For Avery Asphalt Company in Exercise 1, prepare the journal entries to record the purchase of materials and their issuance to production, isolating the materials spending variance (1) at the time of purchase, (2) at the time of issuance.

Exercise 3. Cole Construction Company has a standard cost system for their prefab decks. The materials standard for a deck is 1,600 board feet of pretreated 2" × 8" lumber at $2.10 per 8-ft. board. The records show that 10,500 8-ft. boards were purchased for $21,420. Fifty decks were built, using 81,200 feet of lumber.

(1) Calculate the materials spending variance (a) at the time of purchase, (b) at the time of issuance.
(2) Calculate the materials usage variance.

Exercise 4. Morecredit Company specializes in analyzing credit applications and making recommendations for small firms without a full credit department. To process applications efficiently, each one passes through three departments. On the average, 10 applications can be processed in Department 1 in 1 hour. The wage rate in that department is $3.50 per hour. Department 2 handles 4 applications per hour at $6 per hour. The final department handles 5 applications per hour at $6.50 per hour.

Determine the average rate of labor per hour for the entire company.

Exercise 5. Allen Manufacturing Company produces a single product. The standard labor rate is $6.50 per hour. Each unit is allowed 2.5 hours of labor. During the period, labor actually cost $6.60 per hour for 3,950 hours, and 1,500 units were produced.

Calculate the labor spending and usage variances.

Exercise 6. Brownfield Company's outboard motor division spent $30,420 for 4,680 hours of labor to build 1,200 10-horsepower motors. The labor standard to manufacture this motor is 3.7 hours at $6.70 per hour.

Calculate the labor spending and usage variances for the division.

Exercise 7. Meyer Manufacturing Company produces transistor radios. After careful study, the flexible overhead budget was determined to be $8,500 + $2.75 per direct labor hour. The labor standard per unit is 1.2 direct labor hours. In producing 2,000 radios last period, 2,500 direct labor hours were used. The total expenditure for overhead was $15,500. Overhead services are provided by a separate service department.

Calculate the overhead spending and usage variances. Who should be held responsible for each of these variances? Why?

Exercise 8. ATC Company needs to determine the level of normal output to use for allocating the fixed overhead cost of $12,000 to units produced. If sales remain high, 10,000 units would be a reasonable allocation base. If sales decline, 7,500 units would better approximate average output. Each unit requires 2.5 direct labor hours to produce, and overhead is allocated to units on the basis of standard direct labor hours.

Calculate the overhead volume variance for a period in which 9,000 units are produced, and explain the meaning of the variance, using both possible normal outputs of 10,000 units and 7,500 units.

Exercise 9. Hanna Ltd.'s overhead budget is $13,000 + $2 per direct labor hour. The actual expenditures were $12,825 fixed overhead and $7,400 variable overhead to support 3,500 direct labor hours.

(1) Calculate the overhead spending variance, using the 3-way method of variance analysis.
(2) Divide the spending variance between the variances due to the fixed overhead and the variable overhead.

Exercise 10. Turbin Light Company has a normal production of 120,000 light fixtures per year. Its overhead budget is $105,000 + $1.10 per direct labor hour. For each fixture, .7 hours of direct labor is needed. Actual results for the year were:

84,700 direct labor hours were worked, total overhead was $197,325, and 120,500 fixtures were produced.

(1) Calculate all the overhead variances, using the 3-way method.
(2) What would be different about your analysis if the 2-way method were used? What are the shortcomings of this method?

Exercise 11. Hanan Manufacturing Group produces special metal castings for local industries on a job order basis. Because of the diversity of products manufactured, Hanan's management has found it impossible to implement standards for labor and materials, but the firm does set standards to control overhead cost. In 19X7, the firm's casting department incurred the following costs:

Incurred by Jobs	Materials	Labor	Other	Totals
No. 1376	$ 1,000	$ 7,000	—	$ 8,000
No. 1377	26,000	53,000	—	79,000
No. 1378	12,000	9,000	—	21,000
No. 1379	4,000	1,000	—	5,000
Not Incurred by Jobs				
Indirect materials and supplies	15,000	—	—	15,000
Indirect labor	—	53,000	—	53,000
Employee benefits	—	—	$23,000	23,000
Depreciation	—	—	12,000	12,000
Supervision	—	20,000	—	20,000
Total	$58,000	$143,000	$35,000	$236,000

The Casting Department's overhead rate for 19X7 was determined as follows:

Budgeted overhead:
Variable:
Indirect materials	$ 16,000
Indirect labor	56,000
Employee benefits	24,000

Fixed:
Supervision	20,000
Depreciation	12,000
Total	$128,000

$128,000 ÷ 8,000 budgeted direct labor hours = $16 per direct labor hour

In 19X7, actual direct labor hours incurred in the Casting Department totaled 14,000.

Calculate the overhead application variance, the overhead budget variance, and the modified volume variance for the job order shop.

Problem 9-1. Hill Company manufactures hard hats worn by construction workers. The hats are made of a heavy-duty plastic. During 19X5, 500,000 of the hats were produced. The standard cost of a pound of plastic is $2.25. It takes .75 pounds to make each hat. The amount of plastic purchased and used is as follows:

Purchased: 400,000 pounds at $2.30 per pound
Issued: 382,000 pounds

Required (1) Calculate the materials spending and usage variances, assuming that the spending variance is determined (a) at the time of purchase, (b) at the time of issuance. Explain any differences you find.
(2) Prepare the appropriate journal entries to record the purchase and issuance of the materials and all variances, using both methods.

Problem 9-2. Gulliver's Publishing Inc. uses two grades of paper in printing its soft-cover books. The standards for the books using these papers are:

Books	Grade Nos.	Costs	Quantities
Series A	50	$24 per 100 lbs.	.5 lbs. per book
Series B	200	30 per 100 lbs.	.7 lbs. per book

During the period, the following purchases were made:

Grade Nos.	Quantities	Total Costs
50	100,000 lbs.	$24,000
200	130,000	38,350
50	20,000	5,700

The second purchase of Grade 50 was due to a rush order when the supervisor forgot to place a requisition on time. No inventories of paper are maintained.

A total of 229,000 Series A and 175,000 Series B books were published during the period.

Required Calculate the materials spending and usage variances. How would you explain the Grade 50 spending variance to management?

Problem 9-3. Binkowski Company employs a standard cost system. Three classifications of skilled labor are involved in the manufacture of each unit of its product, as follows:

Classifications	Hours per Unit	Rates
1	4	$ 6.00 per hour
2	3	7.50
3	1	11.50

To manufacture 45,000 units during 19X2, Binkowski Company spent $2,697,300 for 364,500 direct labor hours. The overhead flexible budget is $450,000 + $3 per direct labor hour.

Required (1) Calculate the standard average labor rate per hour.
(2) Calculate the following variances:
   (a) labor spending variance,
   (b) labor usage variance, and
   (c) overhead usage variance.
(3) Explain why the overhead usage variance is important to consider in conjunction with the labor variances.

Problem 9-4. Miller Mirror Manufacturing Company is ready to determine the overhead variances for the period. According to the controller, the actual overhead for the year was $36,150, of which $23,500 was fixed. At the beginning of the period, a standard overhead budget was set as $24,000 + $3 per direct labor hour. Normal production is 15,000 units. A standard mirror uses .25 direct labor hours in production. During the period, 16,000 mirrors were produced, using 4,200 direct labor hours.

Required (1) Calculate the overhead variances, using the 3-way method.
(2) Calculate the overhead variances, using the 2-way and 4-way methods. Show only those variances that differ from that of the 3-way analysis.
(3) Reconcile the variances determined under each of the three methods. (Consider using a 3-column reconciliation.)

Problem 9-5. Wilcox Company purchases medium- and large-sized trucks, which the company then modifies by adding outriggers, hoists, cranes, power-generating units, and other equipment specified by its customers. Although the firm does not set standards for materials and labor costs, such standards are set for overhead. Production data for the quarter just ended are summarized as follows:

Job Nos.	Customers	Contract Selling Prices	Materials	Labor Hours	Labor Costs
117	Northwest Electric	$ 72,000	$23,400	1,343	$10,880
118	Pacific Coast Gas	114,500	40,075	2,970	23,760
119	City of Long Beach	107,100	32,100	1,710	13,250
120	Wisc. Dept. of Trans.	179,000	53,700	3,100	24,800
121	Trans-Western Airlines	88,000	21,600	1,070	8,850

There was no beginning work in process inventory. The ending work in process consisted entirely of Job 121. All other jobs were delivered to customers.

For cost control purposes, the firm has calculated a quarterly overhead budget of $24,000 + $3.45 per direct labor hour. This budget yields a combined overhead application rate of $5.45 on the basis of a normal quarterly activity of 12,000 direct labor hours. Actual overhead for the period totaled $65,440.

Required (1) Prepare journal entries and T accounts summarizing the firm's production activities for the quarter. Overhead is applied to jobs at the end of each quarter. All variances are closed into Cost of Goods Sold.
(2) Calculate the firm's gross profit for the quarter.

Problem 9-6 (AICPA adapted, 5/81). Vogue Fashions Inc. manufactures ladies' blouses of one quality, produced in lots to fill each special order from its customers, which are department stores located in various cities. Vogue sews the particular store's labels on the blouses. The standard costs for a dozen blouses are:

Material (24 yards @ $1.10)	$26.40
Direct labor (3 hours @ $4.90)	14.70
Overhead (3 hours @ $4.00)	12.00
Total standard cost per dozen	$53.10

During June, Vogue worked on three orders, for which the month's job cost records disclose the following:

Lot Nos.	Units in Lot	Material Used	Hours Worked
22	1,000 dozen	24,100 yards	2,980
23	1,700	40,440	5,130
24	1,200	28,825	3,570

The following information is also available:

- Vogue purchased 95,000 yards of material during June at a cost of $106,400. The materials price variance is recorded when goods are purchased. All inventories are carried at standard cost.
- Direct labor during June amounted to $55,000. According to payroll records, production employees were paid $5 per hour.
- Overhead during June amounted to $45,600.
- A total of $576,000 was budgeted for overhead for the year, based on estimated production at the plant's normal capacity of 48,000 dozen blouses annually. Overhead at this level of production is 40% fixed and 60% variable. Overhead is applied on the basis of direct labor hours.
- There was no work in process on June 1. During June, Lots 22, 23, and 24 were completed.

Required (1) Prepare a schedule showing the computation of the standard cost of Lots 22, 23, and 24 for June.

(2) Prepare a schedule showing the computation of the materials price variance for June. Indicate whether the variance is favorable or unfavorable.

(3) For each lot produced during June, prepare a schedule showing computations of the (a) materials quantity variance in yards, (b) labor efficiency variance in hours, and (c) labor rate variance in dollars. Indicate whether each variance is favorable or unfavorable.

(4) Prepare a schedule showing computations of the total controllable (budget) and noncontrollable (volume) overhead variances for June (2-way analysis). Indicate whether the variances are favorable or unfavorable.

Problem 9-7 (AICPA adapted, 11/75). Milner Manufacturing Company uses a standard cost system. It manufactures one product whose standard costs are as follows:

Materials (20 yards at $.90 per yard)	$18
Direct labor (4 hours at $6 per hour)	24
Total factory overhead, applied at 5/6 of direct labor (the ratio of variable costs to fixed costs is 3 to 1)	20
Variable selling, general, and administrative expense	12
Fixed selling, general, and administrative expense	7
Total unit cost	$81

The standards are based on normal activity of 2,400 direct labor hours. Actual activity for October is as follows:

Materials purchased: 18,000 yards at $.92 per yard
Materials used: 9,500 yards
Direct labor: 2,100 hours at $6.10 per hour
Total factory overhead (500 units produced): $11,100

Required (1) Compute the inventoriable unit cost using direct costing.

(2) Based on direct costing, compute the selling price per unit and the number of units which will yield an operating profit of $5,200. (Increasing this selling price by 4% will increase operating profit to $6,800, with all costs and the number of units remaining unchanged.)

(3) Compute all variances, using 2-way analysis for overhead. Develop the flexible budget for overhead and the fixed overhead application rate.

Problem 9-8 (AICPA adapted, 5/63). Jones Furniture Company uses a standard cost system in accounting for its production costs. The standard cost of a unit of furniture is as follows:

Lumber (100 ft. @ $150 per 1,000 ft.)		$15
Direct labor (4 hrs. @ $2.50 per hour)		10
Manufacturing overhead:		
Fixed (30% of direct labor)	$3	
Variable (60% of direct labor)	6	9
Total unit cost		$34

The following flexible monthly overhead budget is in effect:

Direct Labor Hours	Estimated Overhead
5,200	$10,800
4,800	10,200
4,400	9,600
4,000 (normal capacity)	9,000
3,600	8,400

The actual unit costs for December were as follows:

Lumber used (110 ft. @ $120 per 1,000 ft.)	$13.20
Direct labor (4 1/4 hours @ $2.60 per hour)	11.05
Manufacturing overhead ($10,560 for 1,200 units)	8.80
Total actual unit cost	$33.05

Required   Prepare a schedule which shows an analysis of each element of the total variance from standard cost for December. Use 2- and 3-way analysis of the overhead variances.

Problem 9-9 (AICPA adapted, 11/77). Terry Company manufactures a commercial solvent that is used for industrial maintenance. This solvent is sold by the drum and generally has a stable selling price. Due to a decrease in demand for this product, Terry produced and sold 60,000 drums in December. The following information is available regarding Terry's operations for December:

• Standard costs per drum of product manufactured were as follows:

Materials:		
10 gallons of raw materials		$20
1 empty drum		1
Total materials cost		$21
Direct labor (1 hour)		$7
Fixed factory overhead (per direct labor hour)		4
Variable factory overhead (per direct labor hour)		6

• Costs incurred during December were as follows:

Raw materials: 600,000 gallons were purchased at a cost of $1,150,000.
700,000 gallons were used.

Empty drums: 85,000 drums were purchased at a cost of $85,000.
60,000 drums were used.

Direct labor: 65,000 hours were worked at a cost of $470,000.

Factory overhead:

Depreciation of building and machinery	$230,000
Supervision and indirect labor	360,000
Other factory overhead	76,500
Total factory overhead	$666,500

- The fixed overhead budget for the December level of production was $275,000.
- Normal capacity is 68,750 direct labor hours.

Required

Prepare a schedule computing the following variances for December:

(1) Materials price variance (computed at time of purchase).
(2) Materials usage variance.
(3) Labor rate variance.
(4) Labor usage (efficiency) variance.
(5) Factory overhead, using the three-way method.

Indicate whether each variance is favorable or unfavorable.

Problem 9-10 (CMA adapted, 12/72). Carberg Corporation manufactures and sells a single product. The company uses a standard cost system. The standard cost per unit of product is as follows:

Materials (1 lb. of plastic @ $2)	$ 2.00
Direct labor (1.6 hours @ $4)	6.40
Variable overhead cost	3.00
Fixed overhead cost	1.45
Total	$12.85

The overhead cost per unit was calculated from the following annual overhead cost budget for a 60,000-unit output:

Variable overhead cost:	
Indirect labor (30,000 hours @ $4)	$120,000
Supplies—oil (60,000 gallons @ $.50)	30,000
Allocated variable service department costs	30,000
Total variable overhead cost	$180,000
Fixed overhead cost:	
Supervision	$ 27,000
Depreciation	45,000
Other fixed costs	15,000
Total fixed overhead cost	$ 87,000
Total budgeted annual overhead cost for 60,000 units	$267,000

The charges to the Manufacturing Department for November, when 5,000 units were produced, are as shown at the top of page 328.

The Purchasing Department normally buys about the same quantity as is used in production during a month. In November, 5,200 pounds were purchased at a price of $2.10 per pound.

Materials (5,300 pounds @ $2)	$10,600
Direct labor (8,200 hours @ $4.10)	33,620
Indirect labor (2,400 hours @ $4.10)	9,840
Supplies—oil	3,300
Allocated variable service department costs	3,200
Supervision	2,475
Depreciation	3,750
Other costs	1,250
Total	$68,035

Required
(1) Calculate the following variances from standard costs for the data given:
    (a) Materials price variance
    (b) Materials quantity variance
    (c) Direct labor rate variance
    (d) Direct labor efficiency variance
    (e) Overhead variances (3-way analysis)
(2) The company has divided its responsibilities such that the Purchasing Department is responsible for the prices at which materials and supplies are purchased. The Manufacturing Department is responsible for the quantities of materials used. Does this division of responsibilities solve the conflict between price and quantity variances? Explain your answer.

Problem 9-11 (CMA adapted, 12/77). Eastern Company manufactures special electrical equipment and parts. Eastern employs a standard cost accounting system with separate standards established for each product.

A special transformer is manufactured in the Transformer Department. Production volume is measured by direct labor hours in this department, and a flexible budget system is used to plan and control departmental overhead.

Standard costs for the special transformer are determined annually in September for the coming year. The standard cost of a transformer for 19X7 was computed as follows:

Materials:	
Iron (5 sheets @ $2)	$10
Copper (3 spools @ $3)	9
Direct labor (4 hours @ $7)	28
Variable overhead (4 hours @ $3)	12
Fixed overhead (4 hours @ $2)	8
Total	$67

Overhead rates were based upon normal and expected monthly capacity for 19X7, both of which were 4,000 direct labor hours. Practical capacity for the department is 5,000 direct labor hours per month. Variable overhead costs are expected to vary with the number of direct labor hours actually used.

During October, 19X7, 800 transformers were produced. This amount was below expectations because a work stoppage occurred during contract negotiations with the labor force. Once the contract was settled, the department scheduled overtime in an attempt to catch up to expected production levels.

The following costs were incurred in October, 19X7:

Materials:

    Iron: 5,000 sheets purchased @ $2.00 per sheet; 3,900 sheets used

    Copper: 2,200 spools purchased @ $3.10 per spool; 2,600 spools used

Direct labor:

    Regular time: 2,000 hours @ $7.00; 1,400 hours @ $7.20

    Overtime: 600 of the 1,400 hours were subject to overtime premium.

                 The total overtime premium of $2,160 is included in vari-

                 able overhead in accordance with company accounting practices.

Variable overhead: $10,000

Fixed overhead: $8,800

Required

Calculate all production variances, including a 4-way analysis of overhead. Materials spending variances are isolated at the time of purchase.

Problem 9-12 (AICPA adapted, 11/76). On May 1, Bovar Company began the manufacture of a new mechanical device known as *Dandy.* The company installed a standard cost system in accounting for manufacturing costs. The standard costs for a unit of *Dandy* are as follows:

Materials (6 lbs. at $1 per lb.)	$ 6
Direct labor (1 hour at $4 per hour)	4
Overhead (75% of direct labor cost)	3
	$13

The following data were obtained from Bovar's records for May:

Actual production of *Dandy* :   4,000 units

	Debit	Credit
Sales (2,500 units)		$50,000
Purchases (26,000 pounds)	$27,300	
Materials price variance	1,300	
Materials quantity variance	1,000	
Direct labor rate variance	760	
Direct labor efficiency variance		800
Total overhead variance	500	

The amount of the materials price variance is applicable to materials purchased during May.

Required

Compute each of the following items for Bovar for May. Show computations in good form.

(1) Standard quantity of materials allowed (in pounds).

(2) Actual quantity of materials used (in pounds).

(3) Standard hours allowed.

(4) Actual hours worked.

(5) Actual direct labor rate.

(6) Actual total overhead.

Problem 9-13. Ettner Manufacturing Company produces 1 product. The standard production costs are:

Materials: Beno, 2 lbs. at $1.20 per lb.

Direct labor: 1.5 hrs. at $6 per hr. average labor rate

Variable overhead (to support 3,000 direct labor hours):
    Indirect labor $2,010
    General overhead   1,500
Fixed overhead (normal production is 8,250 hours per period): $11,055

During October, the following activities were observed:

Materials: 9,500 lbs. of Beno were purchased for $12,350.
                    9,800 lbs. of Beno were issued.
Direct labor: 7,700 hours were used; cost, $47,740.
Actual overhead: $25,500
Units produced: 5,000

The beginning inventory, priced at standard cost, is 575 lbs. Spending variances for materials are separated at the time of purchase. The variances controllable by the process supervision are recorded initially in the work in process account. There were no beginning or ending inventories of work in process or finished goods.

Required (1) Calculate all variances, using 3-way analysis for overhead.
          (2) Establish T accounts for Materials, Work in Process, Overhead Control, and Variance Summary. Post entries to record all purchases and issuances of materials and the closing of all variances to Variance Summary.

Problem 9-14. Maxwell Tire Company has developed a new process for manufacturing tires for compact cars. The firm has installed a standard cost system for the production costs. The standard costs for one tire are:

Materials (2 lbs. at $8 per lb.)	$16.00
Direct labor (1 hr. at $9 per hr.)	9.00
Variable overhead (30% of direct labor cost)	2.70
Fixed overhead (25% of direct labor cost based on production of 30,000 tires)	2.25
Standard cost per unit	$29.95

Actual production data are:

Materials: 59,500 lbs. purchased at $8.05 per lb.; 59,500 lbs. issued.
                      The price variance is isolated upon purchase.
Direct labor: $8.90 for 30,000 hours
Total overhead: $148,000

The records show that 29,500 tires were produced and 29,000 were sold at $50 per tire. Variable selling expenses are 5% of the sales price. Fixed selling expenses amounted to $57,500. The company's other nonproduction costs were $160,000, and the corporate tax rate is 45%.

There are no beginning inventories of work in process or finished goods.

Required (1) Calculate all variances, using 3-way analysis for overhead.
          (2) Prepare all journal entries for production costs, including the transfer of variances to a variance summary account and closing variances to Cost of Goods Sold.
          (3) Prepare an income statement in good form. All variances are adjustments to Cost of Goods Sold.

Ten

Special Issues in Standard Costing

There are several complexities that may need to be considered when variances are analyzed in a standard cost system. For example, variance analysis must accommodate situations in which several materials are used in varying proportions. Also, complexities may arise when manufacturing inputs do not result in salable units, or when there is an expected shrinkage in the quantity of outputs resulting from a given amount of inputs. These complexities are discussed in this chapter, along with the alternatives for disposing of variances at the end of an accounting period and the decision rules for investigating variances.

MIX AND YIELD VARIANCES

When production processes combine several materials in varying proportions, there will normally be a predetermined range of substitutions allowable in combining the materials. This range of substitutions may be limited by such factors as the availability of materials or their relative prices. For example, a sausage manufacturer who uses a mix of meats will need to determine an optimal mix of meats, based on the market prices of the meats as well as the expected yield resulting from various meat mixes.

To illustrate the complications that arise in analyzing variances when several materials are used in varying proportions and a shrinkage in production is also anticipated, assume that 100 gallons of materials X, Y, and Z are put into a process to produce *Super Car Cleaner*. The specified mix of materials X, Y, and Z, based on their current prices, is in the ratio of 35:45:20. The anticipated yield for the input is 95%. The standard cost of a gallon of *Super Car Cleaner* is computed as follows:

```
Materials:
    X (35 gallons @ $.80 per gallon) . . . . . . . . . .    $28.00
    Y (45 gallons @ $1.30 per gallon) . . . . . . . .       58.50
    Z (20 gallons @ $1.50 per gallon) . . . . . . . .       30.00     $116.50
Direct labor (4 hours @ $5 per hour) . . . . . . . .                   20.00
Overhead:*
    Variable ($2 per DLH × 4 DLH) . . . . . . . . . .    $ 8.00
    Fixed [($6,000 ÷ 4,000 DLH) × 4 DLH] . . . .          6.00         14.00
Total cost of batch  . . . . . . . . . . . . . . . . . . . . . . .              $150.50
Yield (95% × 100 gallons) . . . . . . . . . . . . . . .                        ÷    95
Cost per gallon of output . . . . . . . . . . . . . . . .                       $  1.584
```

*Flexible budget: $6,000 ÷ $2 per direct labor hour (DLH)

The 5% loss of quantity is accounted for by dividing the cost of a batch by 95 gallons of completed output, rather than the 100 gallons of input. Thus, the materials lost, along with the labor and overhead incurred in processing them, are embodied in the final unit cost.

Materials Variances

When several materials are used in manufacturing one product, the calculation of the materials spending variance is the same as when one materials input is used. However, two new variances—a **materials mix variance** and a **materials yield variance**—are calculated. The materials mix variance is the difference between the standard cost of the actual mix of materials used and the budgeted (planned) mix. The materials yield variance is the difference between the actual and budgeted use of inputs. This variance is the materials usage variance, modified to accommodate a budgeted loss of output based on the specified yield.

To illustrate these variances, assume the following facts which relate to the production of 97,500 gallons of *Super Car Cleaner* during a given month:

```
Materials (102,000 gallons):
    X (34,680 gallons @ $.82 per gallon)  . . . . .    $28,437.60
    Y (44,880 gallons @ $1.35 per gallon)  . . . .      60,588.00
    Z (22,440 gallons @ $1.30 per gallon)  . . . .      29,172.00    $118,197.60
Direct labor (4,150 hours) . . . . . . . . . . . . . . .                21,165.00
Overhead . . . . . . . . . . . . . . . . . . . . . . . . . . .          14,500.00
Total cost of 97,500 gallons of output . . . . . . .                  $153,862.60
```

The materials spending variance in this example is calculated when the materials are issued. It is the difference between the actual and standard costs of units issued. The calculation is based on the actual mix and yield, as follows:

Materials	Actual Costs	Actual Gallons	Standard Costs per Gallon	Standard Costs of Actual Gallons	Spending Variances	
X	$ 28,437.60	34,680	$ .80	$ 27,744	$ 693.60	U
Y	60,588.00	44,880	1.30	58,344	2,244.00	U
Z	29,172.00	22,440	1.50	33,660	4,488.00	F
	$118,197.60	102,000		$119,748	$1,550.40	F

After the spending variance has been isolated, the amount of the variance caused by the difference in the mix of materials used, stated at standard cost, can be determined. The materials mix variance is calculated as the difference between the standard cost of the actual mix of materials used and the standard cost of the budgeted mix. As shown in the following calculation of the mix variance for *Super Car Cleaner,* the net unit variance will always be zero.

Materials	Actual Gallons	Actual Gallons in Standard Mix	Unit Variances	Standard Costs per Unit	Mix Variance
X	34,680	35,700 (.35 × 102,000)	1,020 F	$ .80	$ 816 F
Y	44,880	45,900 (.45 × 102,000)	1,020 F	1.30	1,326 F
Z	22,440	20,400 (.20 × 102,000)	2,040 U	1.50	3,060 U
	102,000	102,000	-0-		$ 918 U

Once the variances caused by price and mix have been isolated, the materials yield variance is calculated, using the standard mix at the standard cost. The calculation compares the actual usage of materials with the materials that should have been used, based on the budgeted yield, which allows for a specified percentage of loss. In the example, the total difference in gallons of materials is first calculated. Since 97,500 gallons were produced, 102,362 gallons (97,500 gallons of output ÷ .95 budgeted yield) are allowed by the budget. The materials yield variance is then calculated as follows:

Materials Yield Variance

$$[Q_A \text{ vs. (Actual yield } \div \text{ Standard yield)} \times P_S]$$

102,000 gals. vs. (97,500 gals. ÷ .95) × $116.50 per 100 gallons of standard mix
= 102,000 gals. vs. 102,632 gals. × $116.50 per 100 gallons of standard mix
= 632 gals. F × $116.50 per 100 gallons of standard mix
= $736.28 F

Note that the original budget, based on standard costs and the standard mix of 35:45:20, provides the budgeted materials cost of $116.50 per 100 gallons of input. Using this information is a shortcut alternative to determining the 35:45:20 mix of materials X, Y, and Z in the 632 gallons and then extending the cost of each of the materials.

It may be expected that some relationship exists between the materials variances. In the example, the materials costs were less than the amounts budgeted. This savings could have been offset by a more costly mix. It is also possible that the more expensive mix produced a better yield.

As implied in the example, the key to the materials variances is to calculate them in the correct order. To help achieve the proper order, each variance might be viewed as a strainer through which the spending, mix, and yield variances are successively removed, as shown in Illustration 10-1. This illustration should make it clear that the mix variance must be calculated at the standard cost, since the actual cost impurity has been removed. The yield variance must be stated at the standard mix and standard cost, since the actual mix and cost impurities have been removed.

Illustration 10-1
Sequence of Determining
Materials Variances

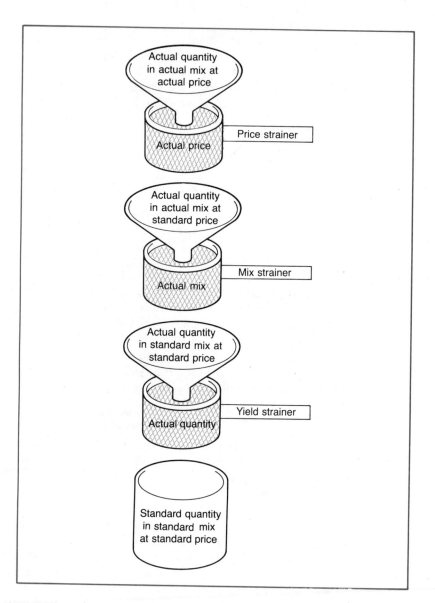

Total Yield Variance

The materials yield variance, when stated in physical terms, represents the materials input saved (favorable) or lost (unfavorable). The total savings or loss, however, may not be determined if only the materials yield is considered. For example, an unfavorable materials yield variance could also involve a loss of labor and overhead costs, since labor and overhead are usually a function of input into the process. In the *Super Car Cleaner* example, in which there is a favorable materials yield variance of 632 gallons, the total savings should include the savings in labor and overhead that would have been used in processing the 632 gallons. Therefore, the total yield variance is calculated as follows:

Materials (632 gals. F × $116.50 per 100 gals. of standard mix) . . . $736.28
Labor (632 gals. F × $20 per 100 gals. of standard mix) 126.40
Overhead (632 gals. F × $14 per 100 gals. of standard mix) 88.48
Total yield variance . . . . $951.16 F

A change in yield would not influence costs that are not a function of input. Therefore, if there are any labor or overhead costs that are a function of output, such as packaging costs, those elements of labor or overhead would not be included in the total yield variance.

Labor and Overhead Variances

The computations of the usual labor and overhead variances are not affected by yield, since the cost variances due to the yield have already been accounted for in the total yield variance. However, the usage variances for labor and overhead will be based on the actual *inputs* of materials, rather than output, since labor is a function of inputs. Labor variances for the production of *Super Car Cleaner* would be calculated as follows:

Labor Spending Variance ($P_A Q_A$ vs. $P_S Q_A$)

$21,165 vs. ($5 × 4,150 DLH) = $21,165 vs. $20,750 = $415 U

Labor Usage Variance [(Q_A vs. Q_S^*) × P_S]

[4,150 DLH vs. (102,000 × 4 DLH per 100 gals.)] × $5 = (4,150 DLH vs. 4,080 DLH) × $5 = 70 DLH × $5 = $350 U

*Q_S is a function of materials input.

The overhead variances would be calculated as follows, using 3-way analysis:

Overhead Spending Variance
(Actual total overhead vs. Flexible budget for actual DLH)

$14,500 vs. [$6,000 + ($2 × 4,150 DLH)] = $14,500 vs. $14,300 = $200 U

Overhead Usage Variance
[(Q_A vs. Q_S^*) × Variable overhead per DLH]

(4,150 DLH vs. 4,080 DLH) × $2 = 70 DLH U × $2 = $140 U

*Q_S is a function of materials input.

Overhead Volume Variance
[(Budgeted DLH vs. Normal DLH) × Fixed overhead per DLH]

(4,080 DLH vs. 4,000 DLH) × $1.50 = 80 DLH F × $1.50 = $120 F

SCRAP

Materials that are consumed in order to produce units of output, but which are never physically a part of a unit of output, are called scrap. Scrap may be unavoidable excess materials resulting from the production process, such as the stock that remains after round table tops are cut from rectangular stock, or the excess plastic from the trimming of molded parts. Scrap may also include materials which are not usable because they are damaged or have imperfections.

Normal scrap that is expected in the production process should be included in the standard materials cost. If scrap varies from that which is budgeted, the difference should be reflected in the materials usage variance, along with the difference between the actual and planned amount of materials used.

Some firms may be able to sell scrap for a nominal amount and thereby recoup some of the cost. Although the recovery may be recorded as "other revenue," it is more appropriate to reduce the production costs of the period by the amount of the revenue. Scrap recovery is usually treated as a reduction of the cost of goods sold. This procedure is preferable to reducing the cost of goods manufactured, which would technically require an adjustment of the ending finished goods inventory. It is also possible to use the scrap recovery as a reduction of the actual materials cost for the period. If this procedure is followed, the scrap recovery would be reflected in the materials spending variance.

SPOILAGE

Units which were intended to become good units of output but are rejected as a result of errors in the production process are described as spoiled units. While scrap is limited to a loss of materials, **spoilage** involves a loss of labor and overhead as well as materials.

The cost of spoiled units depends on when the units are removed from the production process, rather than on when spoilage actually occurs. For example, a unit might be spoiled at the beginning of a process, but the cost of disrupting the process to remove the unit might exceed the additional costs of processing the spoiled unit. Thus, if the spoiled unit is not removed until it is inspected at the end of the process, the unit cost of the spoiled unit is equal to the cost of a good unit. If inspection and removal of a spoiled unit occur earlier in the process, the cost of the spoiled unit is less.

Inspection points are usually arranged to minimize the disruption to production as well as to provide a means of detecting spoilage as soon as possible after it occurs. It is quite common to inspect units just prior to a major addition of new materials. Although there may be several inspection points, the examples in this text will be based on only one inspection point in a given process.

To illustrate the cost impact of the timing of inspection and the removal of spoiled units, assume the following standard cost for a good unit of a fiberglass table:

Materials:	
A (5 lbs. @ $2.20 per lb.)	$11
B (1 lb. @ $3 per lb.)	3
Labor (2 hrs. @ $7 per hr.)	14
Overhead:	
Variable ($2 per DLH)	4
Fixed ($1.50 per DLH)	3
Standard cost of a good unit	$35

If inspection occurs at the end of the production process, the cost of a spoiled unit is also $35, since it includes the same inputs as a good unit. However, if all spoilage occurs in the first half of the process and inspection occurs at the midpoint of the process, just prior to the addition of material B, the cost of a spoiled unit would include only material A and one half of the labor and overhead, as follows:

Material A (5 lbs. @ $2.20 per lb.)	$11.00
Labor (1 hr. @ $7 per hr.)	7.00
Overhead:	
Variable ($2 per DLH)	2.00
Fixed ($1.50 per DLH)	1.50
Standard cost of a spoiled unit	$21.50

It is a common mistake to assume that if a unit is inspected at the midpoint of a process, the cost should be half that of a completed unit. However, a full share of the materials entering in the first half of the process is embodied in a spoiled unit.

Typically, some level of spoilage is anticipated and included in the production budget as a part of the standard cost of a good unit, since the cost of avoiding all spoilage is usually unreasonably expensive. Therefore, the cost of quality controls designed to reduce spoilage must be weighed against the cost of spoiled units. In the example of the fiberglass table, if it is anticipated that one spoiled unit will be produced for each 20 good units, the cost of the one spoiled unit should be spread over the 20 good units. The spoilage rate of 5% is stated as a function of good units in order to expedite the allocation of the spoilage cost to the good units. If inspection occurs at the end of the process, the standard cost of a good unit transferred to finished goods would include 5% of the cost of a spoiled unit, as follows:

Standard cost of good unit	$35.00
Spoilage allowance (5% × $35 cost of completed spoiled unit)	1.75
Standard cost of a unit manufactured	$36.75

If inspection occurred at the midpoint of the process, however, the standard cost of a unit manufactured and transferred out would be calculated as follows:

Standard cost of good unit	$35.00
Spoilage allowance (5% × $21.50 standard cost of half-converted spoiled unit)	1.08
Standard cost of unit manufactured	$36.08

When spoilage is built into the standard product cost, there are potentially three standard costs: the cost of a good unit (before a spoilage allowance), the cost of a spoiled unit, and the cost of a unit manufactured and transferred out (which includes a spoilage allowance). There is also a spoilage variance, which is the difference between budgeted and actual spoilage levels. If inspection occurs at the midpoint of the process in the fiberglass table example, and 40,000 good units and 2,600 spoiled units are produced, the spoilage variance would be calculated as follows:

Spoilage Variance
[(Actual spoiled units vs. Budgeted spoiled units) × Standard cost of spoiled units]

2,600 spoiled units vs. (.05 × 40,000 units) × $21.50
= (2,600 units vs. 2,000 units) × $21.50
= 600 units U × $21.50
= $12,900 U

If inspection had occurred at the end of the process, the unfavorable spoilage variance would be $21,000 (600 spoiled units × $35).

The procedures for calculating the materials, labor, and overhead variances are unaffected by spoilage. However, spoiled units represent production and must be counted. Therefore, it is necessary to include spoiled units when the budgeted usage of materials, labor, and overhead is determined. Budgeted usage is based on **equivalent production units (EPUs)**, which are the units completed plus the spoiled units adjusted for their degree of completion. These calculations are shown in Illustration 10-2.

Illustration 10-2
Variance Analysis with Spoilage

Production Process

Material C enters production at the beginning of the process. Material D is added at the 60% conversion point. Inspection occurs immediately before material D is added. A spoilage rate of 4% of good output is expected.

Standard Costs

Standard cost of good unit:

Material C (3 lbs. @ $1.20 per lb.)	$ 3.60
Material D (2 lbs. @ $1.50 per lb.)	3.00
Direct labor (2 hrs. @ $6 per hr.)	12.00
Variable overhead ($2.50 per DLH × 2 DLH)	5.00
Fixed overhead ($1 per DLH × 2 DLH, based on 30,000 units and 60,000 direct labor hours)	2.00
Total	$25.60

Standard cost of spoiled unit:

Material C	$ 3.60
60% of labor for good unit	7.20
60% of overhead for good unit	4.20
Total	$15.00

Standard cost of unit manufactured and transferred out:

Cost of good unit	$25.60
Spoilage allowance, 4% × $15 cost of spoiled unit	.60
Total	$26.20

Actual Results

Production: 25,000 good units; 1,200 spoiled units
Materials:
    C: 90,000 lbs. purchased for $112,500; 83,000 lbs. used
    D: 55,000 lbs. purchased for $79,750; 51,000 lbs. used
Labor: 53,000 hours used at a cost of $320,000
Overhead: $185,000

Supplemental Overhead Analysis

Flexible budget (total overhead): $60,000 + $2.50 per DLH
Fixed overhead application rate: $60,000 ÷ 60,000 normal DLH = $1 per DLH

Calculation of Equivalent Production Units

	Material C	Material D	Conversion
Good units	25,000	25,000	25,000
Spoilage (all material C, no material D, 60% conversion)	1,200	-0-	720
Total production in equivalent whole units	26,200	25,000	25,720

Material C spending variance (P_AQ_P vs. P_SQ_P):
$112,500 vs. ($1.20 × 90,000)
= $112,500 vs. $108,000
= $4,500 U

Material C usage variance [(Q_A vs. Q_S) × P_S]:
[83,000 lbs. vs. (26,200 lbs. × 3)] × $1.20
= 4,400 lbs. U × $1.20
= $5,280 U

Material D spending variance:
$79,750 vs. ($1.50 × 55,000)
= $79,750 vs. $82,500
= $2,750 F

Material D usage variance:
[51,000 lbs. vs. (25,000 lbs. × 2)] × $1.50
= 1,000 lbs. U × $1.50
= $1,500 U

Labor spending variance:
$320,000 vs. (53,000 × $6)
= $320,000 vs. $318,000
= $2,000 U

Labor usage variance:
[53,000 hrs. vs. (25,720 hrs. × 2)] × $6
= 1,560 hrs. U × $6
= $9,360 U

Overhead (3-way analysis):
Overhead spending variance (actual total overhead vs. flexible budget for actual DLH):
$185,000 vs. $60,000 + ($2.50 × 53,000 actual hours)
= $185,000 vs. $192,500
= $7,500 F

Overhead usage variance [(Q_A vs. Q_S) × variable overhead per DLH]:
[53,000 hrs. vs. (25,720 hrs. × 2)] × $2.50
= 1,560 hrs. U × $2.50
= $3,900 U

Overhead volume variance [(budgeted DLH vs. normal DLH) × fixed overhead application rate]:
(51,440 vs. 60,000) × $1 per DLH
= 8,560 DLH U × $1 per DLH
= $8,560 U

Spoilage variance:
[1,200 spoiled units vs. (.04 × 25,000 good units)] × $15
= 200 units U × $15
= $3,000 U

DISPOSITION OF VARIANCES

When a standard cost system is in use, the flow of units through the factory into finished goods and on to the cost of goods sold is recorded at standard cost. Any difference between the actual and standard costs of production during a period remain in variance accounts awaiting disposition. These accounts are nominal accounts that must be closed to either income or balance sheet accounts.

Some accountants, who might be labeled loss theorists, claim that the standard cost of a unit is a more valid measure of value than the actual cost, since it represents what the cost should be. Any unfavorable variance, then, is a loss (or revenue, if favorable) for the period. Loss theorists would hold that the cost of goods manufactured, the cost of goods sold, and all inventories should remain at standard cost. The net unfavorable production variances would be shown at the bottom of the income statement as "other gains and losses." Although this approach may be appropriate in internal statements, it is not popular for external statements, since it would seem to emphasize inefficiencies which might not be entirely avoidable.

A more common approach is to treat net unfavorable variances as a reasonable expense of production and net favorable variances as a reduction in costs. According to this view, the traditional income statement would include the variances above the gross profit line, since variances are by nature a manufacturing cost. Typically, the net variances would be shown as follows:

Zable Incorporated
Income Statement
For Year Ended December 31, 19X1

Sales		$942,000
Cost of goods sold:		
Standard cost of goods manufactured	$630,000	
Finished goods inventory, January 1, at standard cost	78,000	
Finished goods inventory, December 31, at standard cost	(92,000)	
Cost of goods sold, at standard	$616,000	
Net unfavorable cost variances	4,700	
Adjusted cost of goods sold		620,700
Gross profit		$321,300
Selling expenses	$ 84,000	
General and administrative expenses	123,000	207,000
Net income		$114,300

Although this method of disposing of variances is convenient, it has an inconsistency. If variances are an additional production expense, the adjustment should really be made to the cost of goods *manufactured,* rather than the cost of goods *sold,* which includes units produced in a previous period and excludes some units produced during the current period. This inconsistency is tolerated, because adjusting the cost of goods manufactured would require adjusting the ending finished goods inventory, which conflicts with the loss theorists' intent to charge all variances to the period in which they occur.

At the other end of the variance disposition argument are the allocation theorists, who hold that standards are good estimates, at best, and that the costs shown on at least externally prepared statements should be actual costs, not estimated costs. According to these accountants, all inventories, as well as the cost of goods manufactured and the cost of goods sold, should be restated at actual costs. Since it is unreasonable and uneconomical to undo all the period's entries made at standard cost and recast them at actual cost, the variances are systematically allocated to those accounts which contain standard costs at the end of the period. These accounts and the variances which should be allocated to them may be summarized as follows:

Accounts	Variances To Be Allocated	Notes
Materials	Materials spending variance	Allocation is needed only when the variance is isolated at purchase and the inventory is recorded at standard cost.
Work in process	All variances	Spoilage variance would be included in the allocation if the ending work in process has been inspected and thus includes only good units.
Finished goods	All variances	
Cost of goods sold	All variances	Variances should be allocated only to units produced in the current period. Units from a previous period would already include variances.

In many firms, the majority of units are sold in the period in which they are produced. For example, the ending inventories of a bakery might consist of only .02% of the units produced during the period. If variances were allocated, the amounts allocated to inventories would be immaterial. Thus, based on materiality, it often occurs that all variances are closed to the cost of goods sold. Ironically, the results are the same as those which would occur when the loss theorists' approach is used.

Generally accepted accounting principles require that if standard costs are used for external reports, they should be a reasonable approximation of actual costs. When the test of reasonableness is met, either theory for the disposition of variances may be used. When the test of reasonableness is not met, allocation procedures should be followed.

Methods of Allocating Variances

If variances are to be allocated, the allocation base must be established. The bases which may be used and comments on their appropriateness are as follows:

Base	Comments on Results
Production units	• Requires special procedures for materials inventory if materials are recorded at standard cost. It is necessary to equate materials to sets of material sufficient to produce a given quantity of units.
	• Tends to overallocate labor and overhead variances to work in process. These units are only partially complete and should not receive the same spoilage charge as complete units.
	• Requires separate allocation for each product line.
Production units factored for degree of completion	• Requires same special procedures for materials as the production units base.
	• Allows a more reasonable allocation to work in process, since units are factored for degree of completion.
	• Requires separate allocation for each product line.
Total standard dollars in each account	• If an allocation is necessary for materials inventory, it will be understated, since inclusion of labor and overhead in other accounts will result in a disproportionate allocation of materials variances to other accounts.
	• The allocation of labor and overhead variances to work in process may be overstated. The typical higher degree of completion for materials as compared to conversion will cause the total dollars to be disproportionate to conversion dollars.
Relevant standard component costs (e.g., allocate materials variances according to the standard materials in each account)	• Solves problem of allocation to materials inventory.
	• Results in fair allocation to work in process.
	• Has the same final results as allocation by production units factored for degree of completion, but can be used by multiple products.

Clearly, the most defensible bases of allocation are relevant standard component costs and production units factored for degree of completion, since they are the fairest methods and may be used for a wide range of product lines. Illustration 10-3 is a complete example of allocating variances by relevant standard component costs. In the illustration, the standard cost of goods sold, prior to the allocation, already reflects the variances allocated to the last period's ending inventories. The beginning inventories are therefore already an approximation of actual cost. Notice that Step 1 of the allocation addresses this problem by allocating variances only to that portion of the cost of goods sold that comes from the current period's production, the *new costs in the cost of goods sold.* Step 1 will not be needed when there are no beginning inventories.

After the distribution of new costs has been calculated, the allocation percentages are constructed in Step 2. In Step 3, these percentages are applied to the variances. Two sets of allocation percentages are needed for materials. The materials spending variance is spread over four accounts, since the materials inventory is at standard cost. If the materials inventory had been at actual cost (i.e., the spending variance had been isolated at issuance), the spending and usage variances for materials could have used the same allocation percentages. All conversion variances can be allocated using one set of percentages, since overhead is proportionate to the labor cost.

Illustration 10-3
Allocation of Variances
by Relevant Standard
Component Costs

Standard Cost of Goods Sold
For Year Ended December 31, 19X1

Materials issued (standard cost)	$260,000
Materials inventory, Jan. 1 (adjusted cost*)	56,000
Materials inventory, Dec. 31 (standard cost)	(50,000)
Materials used	$266,000
Direct labor (standard cost), 30,000 hours	180,000
Overhead applied (variable, $3 per DLH; fixed, $2 per DLH)	150,000
Total manufacturing cost (new production at standard cost)	$596,000
Work in process, Jan. 1 (adjusted cost*)	94,000
Work in process, Dec. 31 (standard cost of materials, $68,000; labor, $24,000; and overhead, $20,000)	(112,000)
Cost of goods manufactured (new production at standard cost)	$578,000
Finished goods, Jan. 1 (adjusted cost*)	110,000
Finished goods, Dec. 31 (standard cost of materials, $35,000; labor, $30,000; and overhead, $25,000)	(90,000)
Cost of goods sold (new production at standard cost)	$598,000

*Beginning inventories are stated at last year's standard cost plus an allocated share of variances.

Summary of Variances for 19X1

	Spending	Usage	Volume	Totals
Materials	$22,500 U	$12,600 U	—	$35,100 U
Conversion:				
Labor	3,400 F	6,000 U	—	$ 2,600 U
Variable overhead	3,800 F	5,000 U	—	
Fixed overhead	1,300 U	—	$13,000 U	15,500 U
Total conversion variances				$18,100 U
Total variances				$53,200 U

<u>Allocation of Variances</u>

Step 1: Distribution of current period's standard costs:

	Materials	Labor	Overhead	Total
Standard costs entering production	$260,000	$180,000	$150,000	$590,000
New costs in ending inventory, using fifo flow for variances:				
Materials	(50,000)			(50,000)
Work in process	(68,000)	(24,000)	(20,000)	(112,000)
Finished goods	(35,000)	(30,000)	(25,000)	(90,000)
New costs in the cost of goods sold	$107,000	$126,000	$105,000	$338,000

Step 2: Computation of allocation percentages according to standard cost account balances:

Accounts	Materials Costs (for Spending Variance Allocation)	%	Materials Costs (for Usage Variance Allocation)	%	Labor Costs	%	Overhead Costs	%
Materials	$ 50,000	19%						
Work in Process	68,000	26	$ 68,000	32%	$ 24,000	13%	$ 20,000	13%
Finished Goods	35,000	13	35,000	17	30,000	17	25,000	17
Cost of Goods Sold	107,000	42	107,000	51	126,000	70	105,000	70
Totals	$260,000	100%	$210,000	100%	$180,000	100%	$150,000	100%

Step 3: Allocation of variances:

Accounts	Materials Spending Variance	%	Materials Usage Variance	%	Conversion (Labor and Overhead Variances)	%	Total Allocation
Materials	$ 4,275 U	19%					$ 4,275 U
Work in Process	5,850 U	26	$ 4,032 U	32%	$ 2,353 U	13%	12,235 U
Finished Goods	2,925 U	13	2,142 U	17	3,077 U	17	8,144 U
Cost of Goods Sold	9,450 U	42	6,426 U	51	12,670 U	70	28,546 U
Totals	$22,500 U	100%	$12,600 U	100%	$18,100 U	100%	$53,200 U

Step 4: Preparation of statement:

Cost of Goods Sold, Including Allocations
For Year Ended December 31, 19X1

Materials purchased ($260,000 standard cost plus $22,500 spending variance plus $12,600 usage variance)	$295,100	
Materials inventory, Jan. 1 (actual cost)	56,000	
Materials inventory, Dec. 31 ($50,000 standard cost plus $4,275 allocated variance)	(54,275)	
Materials used		$296,825
Direct labor ($180,000 standard cost plus $2,600 net unfavorable labor variance)		182,600
Overhead ($150,000 standard cost plus $15,500 net unfavorable overhead variance)		165,500
Total manufacturing cost		$644,925
Work in process inventory, Jan. 1 (actual cost)		94,000
Work in process inventory, Dec. 31 ($112,000 standard cost plus $12,235 allocated variances)		(124,235)
Cost of goods manufactured		$614,690
Finished goods inventory, Jan. 1 (actual cost)		110,000
Finished goods inventory, Dec.31 ($90,000 standard cost plus $8,144 allocated variances)		(98,144)
Cost of goods sold (approximation of actual cost)		$626,546*

*Verification:	Original standard cost	$598,000
	Variances allocated to cost of goods sold	28,546
	Total	$626,546

Variance Allocation and Direct Costing

A firm that uses direct costing for internal analysis purposes computes all variances from standards in the same way as a firm that uses full costing. Since fixed overhead is not allocated on a unit-of-production basis for internal reports, there is no unitization of fixed overhead and thus no overhead volume variance. However, a firm that uses direct costing must convert to full costing for external reporting purposes. Therefore, the firm must allocate fixed overhead to units.

One method of allocating fixed overhead to units is to simply allocate the actual fixed costs by production to arrive at an actual fixed cost per unit. To avoid wide fluctuations in unit costs, however, it is more common to allocate fixed overhead to units by using a standard fixed overhead cost per unit. When this procedure is followed, there will be a volume variance for external reporting purposes.

The procedures for disposing of variances on internal, direct costing reports are similar to those discussed for full costing reports. However, loss theorists might prefer to adjust the variable cost of goods sold for the variable cost variances and to report fixed overhead at actual cost (budgeted overhead plus or minus the fixed overhead spending variance). To achieve this objective, the actual fixed overhead cost must be known, so that a separate spending variance for fixed overhead may be computed, using the 4-way analysis as described in Chapter 9. When actual costs are approximated by allocating variances, only the variable cost variances are allocated for internal reports. The fixed overhead variances become part of the actual fixed costs deducted from the contribution to fixed costs.

INVESTIGATION OF VARIANCES

A variance is a signal that the actual cost has deviated from the budget. Once a variance has been determined, the question to answer is whether the cause of the variance should be investigated, so that corrective action might be taken. It is not reasonable to investigate all variances, since many variances are simply expected deviations around the standard. At best, the standard is a type of average. Very often, firms do not investigate favorable variances, because opportunities for cost reductions that could be perpetuated would not likely be revealed. Only unfavorable variances that are large enough that they are not likely to be random deviations from the standard are investigated. Examples in this chapter will follow the common practice of investigating only unfavorable variances.

To illustrate the most common models for guiding the decision to investigate a variance, assume that the standard time for direct labor in an assembly process is 12 hours. Since the approaches to be considered are based on deviations about a mean, the 12 hours is assumed to be the expected mean time as well as the standard time. If the firm uses an optimistic standard time which is below the mean, the portion of a variance equal to this difference between the mean and the standard time is expected, and only variances in excess of the mean time would be subject to investigation.

The answer to the question of what deviation from 12 hours per unit is large enough to warrant investigation could be based on management's general experience. For example, a supervisor might state that it is not common for the average time of a sample of 5 units to exceed 12.5 hours. If a sample with a mean greater than 12.5 hours were found, the variance would likely be investigated. The supervisor's decision model might be quantified by defining what is "not common" in this situation. In other words, given 100 samples, how often would the average be expected to equal or exceed 12.5 hours? The supervisor might estimate that 20 times out of 100, the average would be 12.5 hours or greater, resulting in a 20% estimated probability of an unfavorable random deviation of one-half hour. This estimate could also be interpreted to mean that there is an 80% (100% − 20%) probability that the variance reflects a *real (nonrandom)* change in the mean time, such that the process is out of control, with a mean time exceeding the standard.

Cost-Benefit Analysis

In the previous example, the decision to investigate an unfavorable variance was based only on an estimated probability of 80% that a sample mean as great as 12.5 hours would not come from a population with a mean of 12 hours. To test the correctness of this decision rule, cost-benefit analysis should be used. **Cost-benefit analysis** compares the cost of investigating a variance and correcting the process (if a change in standard has occurred) with the loss that would occur if the standard has changed and no corrective action is taken.

To illustrate the application of cost-benefit analysis to the previous example, the following estimates are assumed:

Probability (P) that the observation is not random and that a sample mean
    of a given size or larger would not occur (1 − the probability of a random deviation) 80%
Cost of investigating the variance (C) . . . . $ 10
Cost of adjusting the process back to the standard cost (A)   25
Loss resulting from the failure to investigate the variance (L)   120

The loss is a function of the size of the variance. In this example, 30 more units would be built prior to the next sample being measured. If the conversion cost is $8 per unit per hour, the cost per hour of variance is $240 (30 × $8), and the loss is $120 ($240 × .5 hours).

The payoffs of the decision to investigate or not to investigate may be shown in a decision tree, as follows:

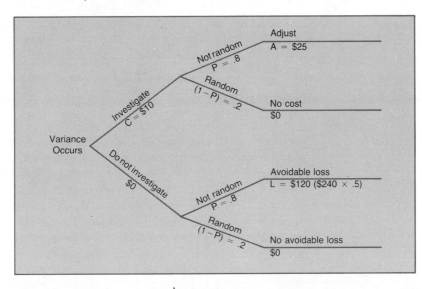

From this decision tree, the following costs may be calculated:

Cost of decision to investigate:
$$C + PA + [(1 - P) \times \$0] = C + PA$$
$$= \$10 + (.8 \times \$25)$$
$$= \$30$$

Loss through failure to investigate:
$$\$0 + PL + [(1 - P) \times \$0] = PL$$
$$= .8 \times \$120$$
$$= \$96$$

With a variance of .5 hours and a probability of 80% that a variance of .5 or more hours will not be observed if the mean time is 12 hours, it is wise to investigate the variance in this example. The expected value of the failure to investigate, $96, far exceeds the expected value of the cost of investigation and adjustment, $30.

The investigation decision may be sensitive to the correctness of the estimated probability. To analyze this sensitivity, the critical probability (Pc) could be determined. This critical probability is the probability at which the expected value of a decision to investigate a variance is equal to the expected value of the loss through a failure to investigate. The critical probability in the example is determined as follows:

$$\text{Cost of decision to investigate} = \text{Loss if no investigation}$$
$$C + P_CA = P_CL$$
$$P_CA - P_CL = -C$$
$$P_CL - P_CA = C$$
$$P_C(L - A) = C$$
$$P_C = \frac{C}{L - A}$$
$$= \frac{\$10}{\$120 - \$25}$$
$$= \frac{\$10}{\$95}$$
$$= .105$$

If the probability of not observing a variance as large as .5 hours is greater than .105, an investigation is warranted. Since the estimate of P is .8, which far exceeds the P_C of .105, the preciseness of the estimated probability is not an important consideration.

Statistical Analysis

A more sophisticated model for estimating the probability of not observing a sample mean of a given size is based on statistical analysis. To illustrate, assume that 12 hours is the estimated mean $(\overline{X})$ of the entire population of all 30-unit production runs. Assume also that the estimate of the standard deviation about the mean (σ_x) is .25 hours. The observed sample mean of 12.5 hours would therefore be 2σ (.5 ÷ .25) from the mean, as shown in Illustration 10-4. Table 3 in the appendix at the end of the text indicates that only .0228, or 2.28%, of all random observations are 2 or more standard deviations from the mean. Thus, there is only a 2.28% chance that a time of 12.5 hours comes from a sample whose population mean is 12 hours. Since only unfavorable variances are to be investigated, the Table 3 probability should be divided by .5, which means that the likelihood of a random deviation of .5 hours (2σ) from samples including only unfavorable variances is 4.56% (.0228 ÷ .5). When the probability of a random deviation is 4.56%, there is a 95.44% (100% − 4.56%) probability that the observation is a real (nonrandom) change and does not come from a population with a mean of 12. Since this probability exceeds the required critical probability, investigation is still warranted, using the more sophisticated statistical calculation of the probability.

Illustration 10-4
Applying the Normal Curve to Variances

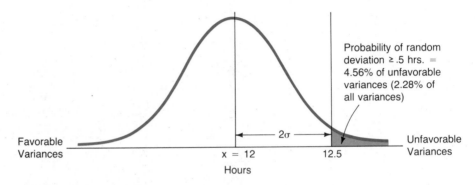

Probability of random deviation ≥ .5 hrs. = 4.56% of unfavorable variances (2.28% of all variances)

Favorable Variances

2σ

x = 12   12.5

Unfavorable Variances

Hours

Control Graphs

Using the formula for the critical probability, a **control graph** showing the critical probability for various unfavorable deviations from the mean can be constructed, as shown in Illustration 10-5. Critical probabilities can be computed for a range of unfavorable variances. Since the cost of investigation plus adjustment (C + A) is $35, no variance of less than $35 would ever be investigated. The critical probabilities, P_C, are calculated as shown previously, and the probabilities that variances are nonrandom variations are calculated by dividing 1 minus the normal table value by .5. The results for the selected range of variances are as follows:

Variances	L ($240 × Variance)	P_C	Probabilities of Nonrandom Variations
.15 hrs.	$ 36	.909	.46
.20	48	.435	.58
.30	72	.213	.78
.40	96	.141	.89
.50	120	.105	.95
.60	144	.084	.98
.70	168	.070	.99

From this information, the decision control graph in Illustration 10-5 is prepared. For each observation, the critical probability is entered. The critical probabilities are connected with a brown line. The statistical probabilities of nonrandomness are also entered on the graph and connected with the white line.

For each variance, the statistical probability of a nonrandom occurrence, based on Table 3, may be compared with P_C in order to arrive at a decision. For example, the graph shows that the P_C for a variance of .5 hours is .105. By asserting the statistical probability of .9544, as previously calculated, it is clear that investigation of the variance is warranted. In the control graph in Illustration 10-5, the probability of nonrandomness overtakes the critical probability at a variance just below .2 hours, which means that any larger variance warrants investigation.

Illustration 10-5
Control Graph for
Investigation of Labor
Variance

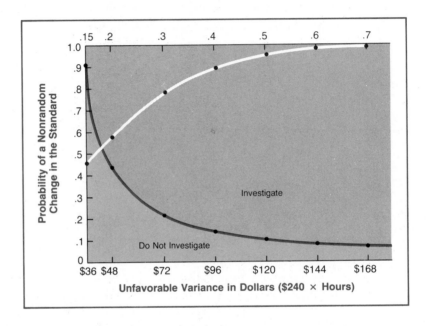

1. If it is expected that some shrinkage will occur in the production process, how is this handled when standard costs are being set?

2. When several materials are combined in the production process, what new variance arises? What causes the variance? How is the variance calculated?

3. Why is it important to calculate the materials spending variance first?

4. What is a yield variance? How is it calculated?

5. What does the yield variance represent?

6. When are labor and overhead included in the total yield variance? What is the logic behind the inclusion of labor and overhead?

7. Labor and overhead usage variances are calculated on the basis of actual inputs of materials. Is this true? Why? Why not?

8. How does scrap differ from spoilage? Which should be included in the standard cost of a unit?

9. How is the standard cost of a spoiled unit determined?

10. How is spoilage allocated over good units?

11. What is an EPU schedule and what is its use?

12. If you are an allocation theorist, what is the best way to allocate variances?

13. Why do many allocation theorists end up with the same income statement as loss theorists?

14. Why does a firm which uses direct costing not calculate a volume variance?

15. How can a firm that is experiencing unfavorable variances decide whether to investigate the variances?

EXERCISES

Exercise 1. Amax Company manufactures laundry detergent. The preferred ratio of materials D, E, and F is 2:5:3. The standard costs per gallon of D, E, and F are $1.10, $.75, and $.90, respectively. For each 100 gallons of input, 3 hours of direct labor are needed at $5.50 per hour. Overhead standards are: variable, $2.10 per DLH; fixed, $8,000 for a normal production of 2,000 batches of 100 gallons each. The normal yield is 90% of total input.

Calculate the standard full cost per gallon of laundry detergent. Round your answer to the nearest cent.

Exercise 2. The results of the production of 1,755 batches (175,500 gallons) of laundry detergent (discussed in Exercise 1) were:

Materials	Actual Gallons
D	37,550
E	97,000
F	63,450
Total	198,000

Calculate the (a) materials mix variance, and (b) materials yield variance. Assume that the spending variances for materials have already been isolated.

Exercise 3. Murphy Co. manufactures a product with the following standards for 100 lbs. of mix:

> Material Q: 35 lbs. @ $2.75 per lb.
> Material S: 65 lbs. @ $1.80 per lb.
> Direct labor: 2 hrs. per 100 lbs. @ $4.50 per hr.
> Variable overhead: $3 per DLH
> Fixed overhead: $1.75 per DLH (based on 1,000 batches of 100 lbs.)
> Yield: 95% of input

All conversion costs are incurred as a function of input. During the period, 100,000 lbs. of materials were used, producing 94,525 lbs. of output.

Calculate the (a) materials yield variance and (b) total yield variance.

Exercise 4. Farrah Company manufactures a product that requires the following two materials:

> BAC: 1.5 lbs. @ $3 per lb.
> MAC: 2 lbs. @ $1.60 per lb.

The direct labor standard is 1.1 hours per unit at $6 per DLH. Total overhead is applied at $4 per DLH. Inspection of a unit occurs halfway through the production process, just before MAC is added. The standard spoilage allowance is 5% of good units.

The results for the month just ended showed that 12,000 good units were produced and that 750 were imperfect and removed from production.

(1) Calculate the standard cost of a good unit, including the spoilage allowance.

(2) Calculate the spoilage variance.

Exercise 5. The production data of Beckett Company are as follows:

> Standards:
> Material J: 1 lb. added at beginning of process
> Material K: 2 lbs. added at 40% through processing, immediately
>   after inspection and removal of spoilage
> Direct labor: 1.5 hours at $6.50 per DLH
> Total overhead: applied at $2.50 per DLH
> Spoilage allowance: 5% of good units
>
> Actual:
> 30,000 good units produced and transferred to Finished Goods
> 1,800 units spoiled
> 46,500 DLH used at a cost of $303,250
> No beginning or ending work in process inventories

(1) Prepare a schedule of EPUs for the current period. Include schedules for both materials and conversion.

(2) Calculate the labor spending and usage variances.

Exercise 6. The management of M & J Block Inc. are loss theorists and report net production variances as an addition to (deduction from) the cost of goods sold. The records show the following information for the year ended December 31, 19X5:

Standards:
    Materials: 3 lbs. @ $1.25 per lb.
    Direct labor: 2 hrs. @ $5.50 per hr.
    Variable overhead: $1 per DLH
    Fixed overhead: $2 per DLH

Actual:
    104,000 units produced
    102,500 units sold
    $28 selling price per unit
    $225,000 selling expenses
    $140,000 administrative expenses
    No work in process or materials inventories

Variances:
    $2,550 U Materials spending
      700 F Materials usage
    3,200 U Labor spending
      800 U Labor usage
    1,200 F Overhead volume

Prepare an income statement for M & J Block. Variances are to be adjustments to Cost of Goods Sold.

Exercise 7. T and J Merkel Inc. uses the standard component cost method to allocate production variances. For the period ended December 31, 19X5, the firm's accountant has prepared the following standard cost income statement:

T and J Merkel Inc.
Income Statement (Standard Cost)
For the Year Ended December 31, 19X5

Sales (26,900 units @ $12.50)		$336,250
Cost of goods sold (standard):		
Materials used in production (standard)	$114,000	
Direct labor (standard)	90,000	
Overhead applied (standard)	105,000	
Total manufacturing cost	$309,000	
Work in process (Jan. 1, 19X5)	-0-	
Work in process (Dec. 31, 19X5)	(56,000)	
Cost of goods manufactured	$253,000	
Finished goods (Jan. 1, 19X5)	-0-	
Finished goods (Dec. 31, 19X5)	(48,500)	
Cost of goods sold		204,500
Gross profit		$131,750
Selling and administrative expense		68,200
Net income		$ 63,550

During the year, the following variances were incurred:

	Materials	Labor	Overhead
Spending	$10,000 U	$4,400 U	$2,800 U
Usage	8,500 U	5,300 U	2,200 U
Volume			1,300 F

As a preliminary step in allocating the variances by standard component cost, the firm's accountant has prepared the following allocation percentage matrix:

Variance	Materials	Work in Process	Finished Goods	Cost of Goods Sold
Materials Spending	5%	25.0%	13.3%	56.7%
Materials Usage		26.0	14.0	60.0
Labor		13.3	16.7	70.0
Overhead		13.3	16.7	70.0

Allocate all variances, using the standard component cost method, and calculate the cost of goods sold as adjusted for variances. (A complete statement is not required.)

Exercise 8. Turner Industrial Company manufactures a single product in high production volumes. Production costs are accounted for using standard costs. The company's accountants are in the process of preparing the firm's year-end financial statements and are developing the allocation ratios necessary to allocate year-end cost variances to the various inventory accounts. These ratios are determined on the basis of EPUs.

Relevant production data for the year are summarized as follows:

	Materials EPUs	Conversion EPUs	Units in Beginning Inventory
Beginning inventories:			
Materials	—	—	None
Work in process	—	—	None
Finished goods	—	—	None
EPUs entering production	84,000	80,400	84,000

There was no ending materials inventory. In work in process, 9,000 units remained, 100% complete as to materials and 60% complete as to conversion costs. Sales during the year totaled 63,000 units.

Calculate allocation ratios for materials and conversion variances.

Exercise 9. Energetics Inc. manufactures sophisticated ceramic parts which are used primarily in military and space applications. The ceramic parts are fired in a special furnace, whose operations are controlled by a microprocessor, since time and temperature limits are critical to producing defect-free parts.

Energetics' managers have recently seen the defect rate rise from 3% to 8%, and suspect that the furnace microprocessor may be faulty. The microprocessor costs $375 to remove and inspect. If the microprocessor is defective, replacement costs an additional $400, including installation charges. The current microprocessor, which is 2,000 hours old, would be replaced at 5,000 hours. If a new microprocessor were installed, it would be removed after 3,000 hours in order to preserve the existing maintenance schedule. The furnace can fire 5 units per hour. Each unit incurs a manufacturing cost of $7 prior to firing. The defectives have no salvage value.

Energetics' managers, in consultation with the furnace's designers, estimate that there is only a 15% chance that the increase in the defect rate is a random occurrence.

Use a decision tree to determine whether Energetics' managers should replace the microprocessor.

Exercise 10. Milner Corp. manufactures a line of high-speed, carbide twist drills. The company has recently purchased fully automated production equipment because of energy-saving features. The equipment is designed to produce 1,800 drill bits per hour, using 2.647 kilowatt-hours of electricity (standard deviation, 0.2954). The company's managers have determined the actual energy use of the equipment to be 3.018 kilowatt-hours at the 1,800-drill-bits-per-hour level of production. The machine's designers believe that the excessive energy use is caused by a defective hydraulic pump which regulates much of the machine's activity. Removal and testing of the pump would cost $375, while replacement and reinstallation of the pump is estimated to cost $800 if the pump is defective, and $300 if it is not. The pump is currently scheduled to be removed and rebuilt in 480 hours. Electricity cost averages $8.50 per kilowatt-hour.

Calculate the critical probability of observing a variance, and the probability of observing the given energy consumption. Should the managers investigate the variance?

PROBLEMS

Problem 10-1 (CMA adapted, 6/79). Lonn Manufacturing Co. produces two primary chemical products to be used as base ingredients for a variety of products. The 19X8 budget for the two products was (000s omitted):

	X-4	Z-8	Total
Production output in gallons	600	600	1,200
Materials (gallons)	625	625	1,250
Materials	$1,500	$1,875	$3,375
Direct labor (function of output)	900	900	1,800
Total	$2,400	$2,775	$5,175

The budgeted direct labor rate was $6 per hour.
The actual materials and labor costs for 19X8 were (000s omitted):

	X-4	Z-8	Total
Production output in gallons	570.0	658.0	1,228.0
Materials (gallons)	600.0	700.0	1,300.0
Materials	$1,368.0	$2,138.5	$3,506.5
Direct labor (function of output)	936.0	1,092.0	2,028.0
Total	$2,304.0	$3,230.5	$5,534.5

The direct labor cost per hour for both products was $6.50.

Required

(1) For product X-4, calculate (a) the materials price variance, and (b) the materials efficiency (yield) variance.
(2) For product Z-8, calculate (a) the direct labor rate variance, and (b) the direct labor efficiency variance.

Problem 10-2. Norwich Chemicals Inc. produces a wide variety of agricultural fertilizers and pesticides. The standard materials data for a 25-gallon batch of the company's popular pesticide, Centec, are as follows:

Di-methyl tropazine (DMT) (8 gals. @ $.45 per gal.)	$ 3.60
Monohydrate-dichloride (MHD) (15 gals. @ $1.05 per gal.) ...	15.75
DEFT-7 (2 gals. @ $3.45 per gal.)	6.90

During a recent month, the following materials purchases were made:

Materials	Quantity	Price
DMT	15,000 gal.	$ 6,450
MHD	22,000	24,200
DEFT-7	3,000	10,350
Total		$41,000

During the month 36,763 gallons of Centec were produced with the following quantities of materials:

DMT	12,075	gals.
MHD	24,210	
DEFT-7	3,515	
Total	39,800	gals.

The average production yield is 97% of input materials.

Required
(1) Calculate the materials cost per gallon of finished pesticide.
(2) For each material, calculate the materials price variance. The variance is isolated at the time of purchase.
(3) Calculate the materials mix variance.
(4) Calculate the materials yield variance.

Problem 10-3. Winston Manufacturing Co. produces a chemical product with two ingredients. The company has a standard cost system. The standard and actual production data for March are as follows:

Standard	Actual
Materials:	
H-2, 55 gals. at $2.40 per gal.	H-2: 26,900 gals.
P-4, 45 gals. at $2.00 per gal.	P-4: 24,100 gals.
Direct labor: 1.5 hours per 100 gals. at $6 per DLH	Direct labor: 790 hours, $4,937.50
Overhead:	Overhead: $3,250
Variable: $1.80 per DLH	
Fixed: $2.50 per 100 gals. (based on 60,000 gals. per period)	
Yield: 85%	

The total inputs for the month were 51,000 gallons, producing 44,150 gallons of output. Labor and overhead use are a function of materials input.

Required
(1) Calculate the materials yield variance.
(2) Calculate the total yield variance.
(3) Calculate the labor spending and usage variances.
(4) Calculate the overhead variances, using 2-way analysis.

Problem 10-4. Ferris Company is designing a production line for a sophisticated electronic thermostat. Preliminary cost data for the new product are as follows:

Materials:
Plastic: 4 ozs. @ $.30 per oz.
Aluminum: 7 ozs. @ $.15 per oz.
Circuit components: $7.25 per unit
Miscellaneous hardware: $1.65 per unit
Labor: .10 hrs. @ $6.40 per hour
Variable overhead: .10 hrs. @ $8 per hr.
Fixed overhead: $2.70 per unit (based on estimated production of 5,000 units per month)

In designing the production line, the firm has the alternative of placing the inspection station at either the 50% completion point or the 100% completion point. All materials enter at the start of production, except for plastic, which enters when the units are 60% complete. Labor and overhead costs are incurred evenly throughout the production process. The anticipated spoilage rate is 4%.

Required   Calculate the standard cost of a completed unit, including the spoilage allowance, when inspection occurs (a) at the 50% completion point, and (b) the 100% completion point. Round all answers to the nearest cent.

Problem 10-5. The Automotive Division of Kennecott Industries manufactures automotive carburetors, following the design specifications of the major automakers. In preparing its quarterly financial reports, the firm's accountants have gathered the following production data for its Model 5001 carburetor:

Standard		Actual
Materials:		
Aluminum (30 ozs. @ $.35 per oz.)	$10.50	Aluminum purchases: 21,000 lbs. @ $114,660
		Aluminum issued to production: 15,700 lbs.
Steel (6 ozs. @ $.15 per oz.)	.90	Steel purchases: 3,100 lbs. @ $7,595
		Steel issued to production: 3,250 lbs.
Labor (1.2 hours @ $5.10 per hr.)	6.12	Labor: 10,100 hours @ $51,914
Variable overhead (1.2 hrs. @ $16 per hr.)	19.20	Overhead: $227,500
Fixed overhead (based on a quarterly production of 7,500 units)	7.18	
Total	$43.90	

During the quarter, 8,200 units were completed and transferred to Finished Goods; 425 units were found to be defective. The average standard spoilage rate is 7%. All materials enter at the start of production. Labor and overhead are incurred evenly throughout the production process. Inspection occurs when the units are fully completed.

Required   (1) Prepare an EPU schedule summarizing the quarter's production activities.
(2) Calculate all production variances for the firm for the quarter just ended, including a spoilage variance. Use the three-way method to calculate overhead variances. Materials price variances are isolated at the time of purchase. (Round all answers to the nearest dollar.)

Problem 10-6. Sandove Inc. builds a product in a single process. Sandove has developed the following standard cost for a good unit of output:

Material A: 4 lbs. at $2.20 per lb.		$ 8.80
Material B: 2 gals. at $.80 per gal.		1.60
Labor: 2 hrs. at $5 per DLH		10.00
Overhead:		
Variable: $2 per DLH	$4.00	
Fixed (based on 3,000 units per mo.)	2.00	6.00
Total		$26.40

At the 60% conversion point, Sandove adds Material B to only good units that have passed inspection. It is expected that the spoilage rate will be 5% of good output. All spoilage occurs prior to inspection at the 60% conversion point. Actual results for a past month were as follows:

Production: 3,500 good units; 250 spoiled units
Materials:
A: 18,000 lbs. purchased for $40,000; 16,000 lbs. used
B: 7,500 gals. purchased for $7,000; 7,200 gals. used
Labor: 7,200 hours used at a cost of $36,500
Actual overhead: $19,000

Required (1) Calculate the standard cost of a good unit transferred out.
(2) Calculate all variances, including a spending and usage variance for overhead.

Problem 10-7. Saxon-Weber Company is preparing its financial statements for the end of the current fiscal year. The company's accountants have already completed a calculation of the standard cost of goods sold, production variances for the year, and a preliminary variance allocation schedule (all variances are allocated using the standard component cost method). These items are as follows:

Saxon-Weber Company
Standard Cost of Goods Sold
For the Year Ended December 31, 19X4

Materials purchases (standard cost)	$151,000		
Materials inventory, Dec. 31	(18,120)		
Materials issued to production (standard cost)		$132,880	
Materials usage variance (unfavorable)		(10,500)	
Materials entering production (budgeted usage)			$122,380
Direct labor (standard cost)			210,000
Applied overhead			198,000
Total manufacturing cost			$530,380
Work in process (12/31/19X4) (standard cost)			(94,243)
Cost of goods manufactured			$436,137
Finished goods, Dec. 31 (standard cost)			(105,260)
Cost of goods sold at standard			$330,877

Schedule of Variance and Allocation Percentages

Variances		Materials	Work in Process	Finished Goods	Cost of Goods Sold
Materials Spending	$ 7,400 U	12%	24%	14%	50%
Materials Usage	10,500 U		27	16	57
Labor (net)	9,000 U		15	21	64
Overhead (net)	11,000 U		15	21	64

Required (1) Using the allocation percentages given, allocate the production variances.
(2) Calculate the actual cost of goods sold, using the income statement format. Verify your answer.

Problem 10-8. Graf Company has calculated the following variances for the 19X3 fiscal year:

	Favorable	Unfavorable
Materials price (based on purchases)		$23,500
Materials usage	$6,700	
Labor price		35,600
Labor usage		7,800
Overhead budget		27,400
Overhead volume		64,000

Your audit has revealed the following amounts in accounts using standard costs:

	Materials	Work in Process	Finished Goods	Cost of Goods Sold
Materials	$15,000	$ 7,000	$10,000	$168,000
Labor		6,400	16,000	297,600
Overhead		5,120	12,800	238,080
Total	$15,000	$18,520	$38,800	$703,680

There were no beginning inventories of any type.

The following income statement includes only standard costs. No adjustment has been made for variances.

Sales	$950,000
Less cost of goods sold	703,680
Gross profit	$246,320
Less selling and administrative expenses	163,500
Net income	$ 82,820

Required

(1) Prepare an adjusted income statement, using the loss theory of variance disposition.

(2) Prepare an adjusted income statement, using the allocation theory of variance disposition. Use the most preferred of all available allocation procedures.

Problem 10-9. Metal Box Inc. is a large manufacturer of steel and aluminum cans and containers. To prepare its end-of-year financial statements, the firm's accountants must first allocate all production variances. The firm uses the standard component cost method for allocation purposes. Relevant information for the year is as follows:

Beginning inventories (adjusted cost):
Materials	$87,000
Work in process	$205,000
Finished goods	$300,000

An examination of the firm's ending work in process, finished goods, and materials inventories revealed the following component costs:

Inventories	Materials	Labor	Overhead
Work in Process	$ 74,000	$ 97,125	$69,375
Finished Goods	111,000	129,500	92,500
Materials	148,000		

Manufacturing costs incurred during the year (at standard) were as follows:

New materials issued to production	$ 679,000
Direct labor	647,500
Applied overhead	462,500
Total	$1,789,000

The materials issued to production includes this period's purchases at standard cost plus the beginning inventory of materials at adjusted cost.

The firm has calculated the following production variances for the current year:

Materials spending	$34,000	U
Material usage	9,000	F
Labor spending	18,000	F
Labor usage	24,000	F
Overhead (net)	44,000	U
Spoilage	25,000	U

The spoilage variance arose because of an unusually high defective rate in the third quarter. All units are inspected after production is complete, just prior to being transferred to Finished Goods.

Required (1) Allocate all variances, using the standard component cost method.
(2) Calculate the firm's standard and adjusted cost of goods sold.

Problem 10-10. The standard for a particular cost is $1,000, which represents the mean or average amount expected. Based on prior observations of this cost, it is determined that the normal curve may be used to describe its frequency distribution. The standard deviation for the item is $75.

An unfavorable variance of $85 is observed. The benefits obtained from an investigation of this variance would consist of an adjustment in performance equal to about 50% of the variance. The cost to investigate a variance is $35. The cost to correct the process is 0.

Required (1) You are asked to give your advice on whether this variance should be investigated. Set up a decision chart to indicate the appropriate response to a variance, given a final cost of investigation of $35 and assumed probabilities of finding nonrandom causes of the variance.
(2) Use these data to prepare a control graph, using variances in $20 increments.

Eleven

Process Costing

$\mathbf{P}$rocess costing is typically used by firms that produce a large number of identical units. The volume and speed of production in such firms usually makes it uneconomical and infeasible to determine the actual cost of each unit produced. Costing is therefore accomplished by using a predetermined standard cost or by computing an average cost for all units produced during a time period.

In previous chapters, the units produced were equated with the productivity of a given time period. However, this approach is overly simplistic, since it does not consider work in process inventories and spoilage. Regardless of whether a process cost system uses standard costs or actual costs, the output for any period must be measured in equivalent production units (EPUs). In this chapter, an EPU schedule will be designed and used in both standard and actual process cost applications.

MEASURING OUTPUT WITH EPUs

Equivalent production units (EPUs) are defined as the equivalent number of complete units that could be produced from the quantity of inputs used. For example, the labor content of 100 units that are 50% complete could be expressed as 50 EPUs. EPUs include not only the units produced in a given period, but also spoilage and the changes in work in process inventories.

In an actual process cost system, the total EPUs for a period are divided into the period's costs in order to determine the average per unit cost for the period. In a standard process cost system, EPUs are used to determine the budgeted usage of materials, labor, and overhead. They are also used to calculate the quantity standard (Q_S) for usage variances and are used as the base for computing volume variances. EPUs are never needed for calculating spending variances, however, since spending variances are calculated on the basis of actual rather than budgeted inputs.

Since EPUs will differ for various materials and conversion costs (labor and overhead), separate EPU measurements will be needed for each input. For any cost element, the EPUs can be determined as follows:

Units transferred out (complete units)
+ Ending work in process EPUs (units adjusted for degree of completion)
+ Spoilage EPUs (units adjusted for degree of completion)
Maximum EPUs for the period
− Beginning work in process EPUs (units adjusted for degree of completion)
EPUs completed in the current period

Degree of Completion

The EPU concept is used to convert units counted in the inventories of work in process and units counted as spoiled into a measure of work that is equivalent to the amount that would be embodied in a complete unit. To accomplish this conversion, the degree of completion for work in process inventories and for spoiled units must be specified for each raw material, for labor, and for overhead. Since overhead is most often applied on the basis of direct labor hours, a common degree of completion may be specified for labor and overhead.

The following statements are generally applicable to the process of specifying the degree of completion for EPU calculations:

1. Some materials typically enter the process at the beginning of the process. Thus, even though a unit is only 20% processed, it is 100% complete as to these initial raw materials. Other materials may be added during the process. Most often, these added materials enter at discrete points in the conversion process. For example, if materials are added at the 50% stage of conversion, a unit 40% converted would have no added materials, but a unit 55% converted would have 100% of added materials.

2. **Prior department cost** is the cost assigned to production units received from the process immediately preceding the process being costed. In essence, a prior department cost is the cost of one unit of an internally procured material. EPUs of prior department costs are measured in the same manner as materials. Most commonly, prior department costs enter at the beginning of the receiving department's process and would be considered 100% complete.

3. Conversion costs typically enter uniformly throughout a process. Thus, if a unit is 70% converted, it will contain 70% of the conversion cost.

4. Degree of completion may have two meanings when applied to work in process inventories. For example, if 100 units of work in process are 60% complete, either all of the units are 60% complete, or the average state of completion is 60%. The meaning of degree of completion will not matter for conversion costs, prior department costs, or raw materials costs that enter at the beginning of the process; but it will matter for an added raw material that enters at a given point during the process. For example, if materials are added

at the 50% stage of processing and if all 100 units of work in process are 60% converted, the 100 units are complete as to materials and would be stated at 100 EPUs. If, however, the average degree of completion is 60%, the number of units that have passed the 50%-converted stage would need to be determined. Thus, if 50 of the 100 units were 40% converted and 50 units were 80% converted, the 100 units would be stated as 50 EPUs. Unless otherwise stated, it may be assumed that the percentage of conversion means that all units are at that stage of conversion.

5. The degree of completion for spoiled units is the investment of inputs at the time that the spoiled units are removed from the process. Thus, if a spoiled unit becomes defective when it is 20% converted but is not removed prior to the end of the process, it is counted as 100% complete.

All product unit quantities should be available for the calculation of EPUs. It may occur, however, that the units spoiled or the units in one of the inventories will not be known. In such cases, the unit quantities will need to be imputed from the known information.

EPU Schedule

The calculation of EPUs can be aided by the preparation of schedules showing the work performed in each process during a period. To illustrate such a schedule, assume that a unit is produced in two departments, with the following procedures:

- **Process A:** Materials enter at the beginning of the process, and conversion costs enter uniformly during the process. Inspection for possible spoilage does not occur until the end of the process.
- **Process B:** Prior department costs enter at the beginning of the process, and additional materials are added immediately after spoiled units are removed. Inspection occurs when the units are 50% converted. Conversion costs enter uniformly during the period.

Production information for the period is as follows:

	Process A	Process B
Beginning inventory	200 units (50% converted)	100 units (20% converted)
Transferred out	900 units	600 units
Ending inventory	300 units (60% converted)	320 units (75% converted)
Spoilage	-0-	80 units (50% converted)

From this information, the following EPU schedules can be constructed:

EPU Schedule—Process A

	Product Units	Percent Converted	Materials EPUs (Enter at 0%)	Conversion EPUs
Transferred out	900		900	900
Ending inventory	300	60%	300	180
Maximum EPUs	1,200		1,200	1,080
Beginning inventory	200	50	200	100
Current output	1,000		1,000	980

EPU Schedule—Process B

	Product Units	Percent Converted	Prior Depart-ment EPUs (Enter at 0%)	Materials EPUs (Enter Good Units at 50%)	Conver-sion EPUs
Transferred out	600		600	600	600
Ending inventory	320	75%	320	320	240
Spoilage	80	50	80		40
Maximum EPUs	1,000		1,000	920	880
Beginning inventory	100	20	100		20
Current output	900		900	920	860

There should always be a direct link between the units transferred out of a prior department and the units started in the next department. In the example, the 900 units transferred out of Process A are the 900 units of current output started in Process B during the period. This relationship may not always be one to one, however. For example, if 1,200 lawnmowers enter production in the assembly process, it would be expected that 1,200 cutting decks would be transferred out of the cutting deck stamping process, and that 4,800 (4 $\times$ 1,200) wheels would be transferred out of the wheel forging process. A one-to-one relationship between wheels and lawnmowers could be created, however, by redefining an EPU in the wheel process as a set of 4 wheels.

STANDARD PROCESS COSTING

When a standard cost system uses process costing procedures, EPUs must be used as the definition of work accomplished. Although variance analysis and book-keeping procedures are not changed, it is necessary to prepare an EPU schedule before the usage and volume variances are calculated.

In the following paragraphs, two examples of standard process costing are analyzed. The first example focuses on the role of EPUs in variance analysis, while the second example focuses on the complications caused by spoilage.

Variance Analysis and EPUs

Illustration 11-1 is a summary of variance analysis procedures in a molding process. The analysis parallels Illustration 9-2, except that an EPU schedule is prepared before the variances are calculated.

Illustration 11-1
Summary of Variance
Analysis Procedures in
a Process Cost Shop

Part A
Summary of Facts

Production process:
Alnex enters at the beginning of the process. Betros enters when the unit is 50% complete. Conversion costs enter uniformly.

Standard production costs:
Alnex (2 lbs. @ $3.60 per lb.)	$ 7.20
Betros (3 lbs. @ $1 per lb.)	3.00
Direct labor (2 hrs. @ an average rate of $8 per hr.)	16.00
Variable overhead ($2 per DLH)	4.00
Fixed overhead ($.75 per DLH, based on 24,000 normal DLH)	1.50
Total	$31.70

Results for January:
  Beginning inventory, 2,000 units, all 40% converted
  Ending inventory, 3,500 units, all 70% converted
  Transferred out, 11,000 units
  Alnex, 26,000 lbs. purchased for $96,200; 25,200 lbs. issued
  Betros, 45,000 lbs. purchased for $42,360; 44,000 lbs. issued
  Labor, 25,800 hours used at a cost of $210,300
  Actual overhead, $64,250

Supplemental overhead analysis:

  Flexible budget, total overhead: $18,000 fixed + $2 per DLH
  Fixed overhead application rate: $18,000 fixed overhead ÷ 24,000 normal DLH = $.75 per DLH

Illustration 11-1   Summary of Variance Analysis Procedures in a Process Cost Shop
Part B   EPU Schedule

	Product Units	Percent Converted	Alnex EPUs (Enter at 0%)	Betros EPUs (Enter at 50%)	Conver- sion EPUs
Transferred out	11,000		11,000	11,000	11,000
Ending inventory	3,500	70%	3,500	3,500	2,450
Maximum EPUs	14,500		14,500	14,500	13,450
Beginning inventory	2,000	40	2,000		800
Current output	12,500		12,500	14,500	12,650

Illustration 11-1   Summary of Variance Analysis Procedures in a Process Cost Shop
Part C   Variance Analysis

Materials and Direct Labor

Alnex Spending ($P_A Q_P$ vs. $P_S Q_P$):
  $96,200 vs. ($3.60 × 26,000 lbs.)
  = $96,200 vs. $93,600
  = $2,600 U

Alnex Usage [(Q_A vs. Q_S) × P_S]:
  [25,200 lbs. vs. (12,500 EPUs × 2 lbs.)] × $3.60
  = 200 lbs. U × $3.60
  = $720 U

Betros Spending:
  $42,360 vs. ($1 × 45,000 lbs.)
  = $42,360 vs. $45,000
  = $2,640 F

Betros Usage:
  [44,000 lbs. vs. (14,500 EPUs × 3 lbs.)] × $1
  = 500 lbs. U × $1
  = $500 U

Direct Labor Spending ($P_A Q_A$ vs. $P_S Q_A$):
  $210,300 vs. ($8 × 25,800 DLH)
  = $210,300 vs. $206,400
  = $3,900 U

Direct Labor Usage:
  [25,800 actual DLH vs. (12,650 EPUs × 2 DLH)] × $8
  = 500 DLH U × $8
  = $4,000 U

Overhead—3-Way Analysis

Spending (Actual total overhead vs. Flexible budget for actual DLH):
  $64,250 vs. [$18,000 + ($2 × 25,800 actual DLH)]
  = $64,250 vs. $69,600
  = $5,350 F

Usage [(Q_A vs. Q_S) × Variable overhead per DLH]:
  [25,800 DLH vs. (12,650 EPUs × 2 DLH)] × $2
  = 500 DLH U × $2
  = $1,000 U

Volume [(Budgeted DLH vs. Normal DLH) × Fixed overhead application rate]:
(25,300 DLH vs. 24,000 DLH) × $.75
= 1,300 DLH F × $.75
= $975 F

A review of the variance computations in Illustration 11-1 reveals that:

1. Materials usage variance calculations use the current materials EPUs as the basis for the budgeted usage of materials.
2. Labor and variable overhead usage variance calculations use the current conversion EPUs as the basis for the budgeted usage of labor hours.
3. The basis for applying fixed overhead is budgeted labor hours, which are based on current conversion EPUs.
4. EPUs have no effect on the calculation of spending variances.

When the two-way analysis of overhead variances is used, conversion EPUs are also used to compute the budgeted usage of direct labor hours. For Illustration 11-1, the budget variance would be calculated as follows:

Budget Variance (Actual total overhead vs. Flexible budget for budgeted DLH)

$64,250 vs. $18,000 + ($2 × 12,650 EPUs × 2 DLH) = $64,250 vs. $68,600 = $4,350 F

As was explained in Chapter 9, the budget variance is the sum of the overhead spending and usage variances. If 4-way analysis of overhead had been used, the overhead spending variance would have been subdivided into its fixed and variable components.

Spoilage

The impact of spoilage on variance analysis is demonstrated in Illustration 11-2. In this illustration, a cleaning compound is produced in a mixing process, using two raw materials, Cram and Deltrex. Inspection for spoilage occurs when the conversion is 50% complete and just before Deltrex is added to good units of output. The budgeting of normal spoilage at 10% of good production affects Illustration 11-2 as follows:

1. In Part A, the standard cost of both a good and a spoiled unit must be derived, and the cost of a unit transferred out, including the spoilage allowance, must be calculated.
2. In Part C, spoiled units factored for their degree of completion must be counted in the calculation of current EPUs in the EPU schedule.
3. In Part D, a spoilage variance comparing the actual and budgeted level of spoilage must be calculated.

Illustration 11-2 demonstrates that the calculations of the materials, labor, and overhead variances are unaffected by spoilage if the spoiled units are counted in the current EPUs of output. However, a spoilage variance is calculated, as it was in Chapter 10, by comparing actual spoilage with budgeted spoilage. In the illustration, this budgeted spoilage is determined by applying the normal spoilage rate (10%) to the units passing inspection (13,000), which are simply the units to which Deltrex was added.

Production process:
Cram enters at the beginning of the process. Deltrex is added to only good units that pass inspection at the 50% conversion stage. Conversion costs enter uniformly.

Standard production costs:

Cram (3 gals. @ $2 per gal.)	$ 6.00
Deltrex (1 lb. @ $3 per lb.)	3.00
Direct labor (1.5 hrs. @ $6 per hr.)	9.00
Variable overhead ($2.50 per DLH)	3.75
Fixed overhead ($1.50 per DLH, based on 30,000 normal DLH)	2.25
Standard cost of good unit	$24.00

Standard cost of spoiled unit:

Cram (3 gals. @ $2 per gal.)	$ 6.00	
One half of direct labor for good unit	4.50	
One half of variable and fixed overhead for good unit	3.00	
Total	$13.50	
Spoilage allowance	10%	1.35
Standard cost of unit, including spoilage		$25.35

Results for January:
Beginning inventory, 3,000 units, all 60% converted
Ending inventory, 4,000 units, all 40% converted
Transferred out, 16,000 units
Spoilage, 2,000 units, all 50% converted
Cram, 60,000 gals. purchased for $1.96 per gal.; 58,000 gals. issued
Deltrex, 14,000 lbs. purchased for $43,200; 13,200 lbs. issued
Labor, 26,000 hours used at a cost of $147,420
Actual overhead, $98,000

Supplemental overhead analysis:

Flexible budget, total overhead: $45,000 fixed + $2.50 per DLH
Fixed overhead application rate: $45,000 fixed overhead ÷ 30,000 normal DLH = $1.50 per DLH

	Product Units	Percent Converted	Cram EPUs (Enter at 0%)	Deltrex EPUs (Enter at 50%)	Conversion EPUs
Transferred out	16,000		16,000	16,000	16,000
Ending inventory	4,000	40%	4,000		1,600
Spoilage	2,000	50	2,000		1,000
Maximum EPUs	22,000		22,000	16,000	18,600
Beginning inventory	3,000	60	3,000	3,000	1,800
Current output	19,000		19,000	13,000	16,800

Materials and Direct Labor

Cram Spending ($P_A Q_P$ vs. $P_S Q_P$):
  (60,000 vs. $1.96) vs. (60,000 × $2)
 = $117,600 vs. $120,000
 = $2,400 F

Cram Usage [(Q_A vs. Q_S) × P_S]:
  [58,000 gals. vs. (19,000 EPUs × 3 gals.)] × $2
 = 1,000 gals. U × $2
 = $2,000 U

Deltrex Spending:
$43,200 vs. ($3 × 14,000 lbs.)
= $43,200 vs. $42,000
= $1,200 U

Deltrex Usage:
[13,200 lbs. vs. (13,000 EPUs × 1 lb.)] × $3
= 200 lbs. U × $3
= $600 U

Direct Labor Spending ($P_A Q_A$ vs. $P_S Q_S$):
$147,420 vs. ($6 × 26,000 DLH)
= $147,420 vs. $156,000
= $8,580 F

Direct Labor Usage:
[26,000 actual DLH vs. (16,800 EPUs × 1.5 DLH)] × $6
= 800 DLH U × $6
= $4,800 U

Overhead—3-Way Analysis

Spending (Actual total overhead vs. Flexible budget for actual DLH):
$98,000 vs. [$45,000 + ($2.50 × 26,000 actual DLH)]
= $98,000 vs. $110,000
= $12,000 F

Usage [(Q_A vs. Q_S) × Variable overhead per DLH]:
[26,000 DLH vs. (16,800 EPUs × 1.5 DLH)] × $2.50
= 800 DLH U × $2.50
= $2,000 F

Volume [(Budgeted DLH vs. Normal DLH) × Fixed overhead application rate]:
(25,200 DLH vs. 30,000 DLH) × $1.50
= 4,800 DLH U × $1.50
= $7,200 U

Spoilage [(Actual spoilage vs. Budgeted spoilage) × Cost of spoiled unit]

[2,000 units vs. (10% × 13,000 units*)] × $13.50
= (2,000 units vs. 1,300 units) × $13.50
= 700 units U × $13.50
= $9,450 U

---

* Units passing inspection, which are the units to which Deltrex was added.

Production Flow Diagram. The number of units passing inspection may not always be as easily determined as it was in Illustration 11-2. In more complicated situations, a **production flow diagram** may aid in the analysis of the number of good units and spoiled units. To illustrate, the following diagram is constructed, using the quantity information from Illustration 11-2:

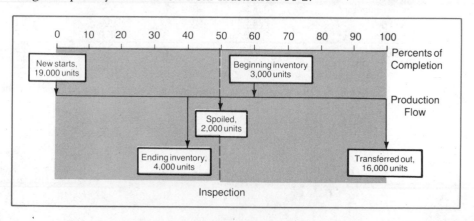

The steps used in constructing the diagram may be summarized as follows:

1. Draw a horizontal line with a scale for percents of completion, and draw a horizontal line to indicate the flow of units from their starting point to their completion point.
2. Draw a broken vertical line from the point on the horizontal scale at which inspection occurs, and draw a vertical line indicating the percent of completion of units involved in the production flow.
3. Insert the number of new units started at the beginning of the production flow line, and the number of units in the beginning inventory and the ending inventory at their respective degrees of completion.
4. Insert the number of units spoiled at the point where the spoilage is discovered, and the number of units transferred out of the process at the end of the production flow line.

To further illustrate the use of the production flow diagram, assume that the inventories in the previous diagram are reversed with respect to inspection; i.e., the beginning inventory has not been inspected, but the ending inventory has been inspected. This change in the example is reflected in the following facts:

	Product Units	Percent Converted
Transferred out	16,000	
Ending inventory	4,000	70%
Spoilage	2,000	50
Maximum EPUs	22,000	
Beginning inventory	3,000	30
Current output	19,000	

A production flow diagram prepared on the basis of these facts would appear as follows:

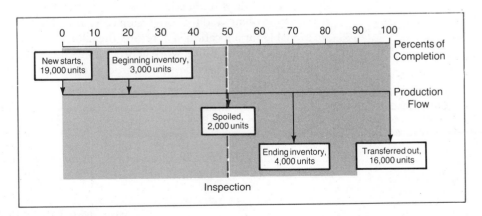

Disposing of the Spoilage Variance. A spoilage variance that arises in a standard cost system must be disposed of at year end. One means of disposing of the variance is to treat it as a loss that should not be inventoried and charge it entirely to the current period, usually by adjusting the cost of goods sold. Another means of disposal is to allocate the variance to the good units which passed inspection in the current period. If this procedure is followed, the production flow diagram is useful for determining which units should receive an allocation of the spoilage variance. In Illustration 11-2, for example, the $9,450 unfavorable spoilage variance would be allocated to the 13,000 units that had passed inspection. Thus, the cost of each good unit produced in the current period would be increased by $.73 ($9,450 ÷ 13,000). Since none of the 13,000 good units remain in the work in process inventory, all the spoilage variance would be included in the ending finished goods inventory and in the cost of goods sold.

ACTUAL PROCESS COSTING

In a process cost system that uses actual costs, rather than standard costs, units are accounted for only at their average actual cost for the period in which they were produced. This average unit cost is derived by dividing the period's costs by the EPUs produced. The period's costs are then allocated to the ending work in process inventory and to the units transferred out of the process. Assuming that there is no spoilage during a period, the cost allocation process can be viewed as follows:

$$
\begin{array}{l}
\text{Cost of beginning work in process EPUs} \\
+ \quad \text{Cost of EPUs produced during the period} \\
\hline
\text{Cost to account for} \\
- \quad \text{Cost allocated to ending work in process EPUs} \\
\hline
\text{Cost allocated to EPUs transferred out}
\end{array}
$$

Cost Allocation Schedules

Since the EPUs for materials and conversion costs are different, separate allocation schedules are needed for each raw material (or sets of materials entering at a common point) and for conversion costs. As indicated above, three sets of costs are available for allocation. Therefore, the allocation of the set of costs determines the valuation of the ending work in process inventory and the units transferred out of the process, and may be summarized as follows:

Costs assigned to beginning inventory	÷ Beginning inventory EPUs	= Lifo unit cost
Costs added during period	÷ New EPUs of current output	= Fifo unit cost
Costs to account for (beginning inventory plus costs added)	÷ Beginning inventory EPUs + New EPUs of current output	= Weighted average unit cost

To illustrate the cost allocation process, using conversion costs, assume that the following facts are known:

Beginning work in process	2,000 EPUs
	$6,000 conversion cost from the previous period
Current output	10,000 EPUs
	$36,000 conversion cost added in the current period
Ending work in process	1,500 EPUs (3,000 units, 50% converted)
Transferred out	10,500 units

Using each of the three inventory valuation methods—lifo, fifo, and weighted average—the following cost allocation schedules (or cost of production reports) are prepared. In each schedule, the line used to derive the ending work in process unit cost is shown in brown.

Cost Allocation Schedules

	EPUs	Cost per EPU	Total Costs
Lifo			
Beginning work in process	2,000	$3.00	$ 6,000
Current output	10,000		36,000
EPUs to account for	12,000		$42,000
Ending work in process	1,500	3.00	4,500
Transferred out	10,500		$37,500
Fifo			
Beginning work in process	2,000		$ 6,000
Current output	10,000	3.60	36,000
EPUs to account for	12,000		$42,000
Ending work in process	1,500	3.60	5,400
Transferred out	10,500		$36,600
Weighted Average			
Beginning work in process	2,000		$ 6,000
Current output	10,000		36,000
EPUs to account for	12,000	3.50	$42,000
Ending work in process	1,500	3.50	5,250
Transferred out	10,500		$36,750

The cost allocation schedules indicate that:

1. All EPUs in the first column of each schedule can be taken from the EPU schedules that have been prepared. The inventory valuation method has no effect on the EPUs.
2. The total costs for the beginning work in process and the current production must be provided by the accounting records.
3. The only unit cost that usually needs to be calculated is the cost required according to the inventory valuation method being used. A second unit cost could be required under lifo or fifo if the following circumstances exist:
   a. Under lifo, if the ending work in process exceeds the beginning work in process, the excess units are priced at the cost of the current production.
   b. Under fifo, if the ending work in process exceeds the current production, the excess units are priced at the cost of the current production.
4. The cost allocated to the units transferred out is the cost not allocated to the ending work in process. However, the cost allocated to the units transferred out can be verified. In the lifo case, for example, the cost of the units transferred out is verified as follows:

Current output (10,000 units)	$36,000
From beginning work in process (500 units @ $3)	1,500
Cost transferred out	$37,500

In practice, the fifo and weighted average methods are most commonly used. Very few lifo cost systems are used to value work in process inventories, since lifo applied over a period of years will result in meaningless, undervalued inventories. When work in process inventories are undervalued, the management of these inventories and working capital is difficult. Also, lifo does not offer great tax savings for most production firms, since work in process inventories are usually not a large asset investment, as compared to finished goods inventories. Therefore, the use of lifo is commonly confined to finished goods inventories.

Illustration 11-3 is a summary of the cost allocation procedures for a process cost shop that uses actual costs. The EPU schedules for Departments A and B are shown in Part B. Parts C through E illustrate the three alternative inventory valuation methods, which impact upon the cost allocation schedules as follows:

- **Lifo:** Uses beginning inventory cost; units in excess of beginning inventory priced at new unit cost.
- **Fifo:** New unit cost.
- **Weighted average:** Total cost of units to account for.

In the cost allocation schedules, the costs transferred out of Department A become the prior department costs assigned to the new units started in Department B. A cost summary column in the cost allocation schedules for each department aids the transfer of costs to successive departments and to the finished goods inventory.

Cost allocation schedules provide the data needed for journalizing the production costs during a period. In Illustration 11-4, the entries for the example used in Illustration 11-3 are recorded, based on the weighted average method, and the T accounts for the two departmental work in process accounts are shown.

Illustration 11-3
Actual Process Costing
with Alternative Inventory
Valuation Methods

Part A
Summary of Facts

Production process:
In Department A, Elcho enters at the beginning of the process, and conversion costs enter uniformly. In Department B, units from the prior department enter at the beginning of the process, and another material, Falfex, is added at the 50% point. Conversion costs enter uniformly.

Production quantities and costs:

Department A	Units	% Converted	Prior Dept.	Materials	Conversion
Beginning work in process	4,000	50%	—	$12,480	$ 9,480
New units started	20,000		—	66,000	104,960
Units to account for	24,000				
Ending work in process	5,000	70			
Transferred out	19,000				
Department B					
Beginning work in process	3,000	60	$21,600	6,300	11,070
New units started	19,000*		?**	33,750	119,260
Units to account for	22,000				
Ending work in process	4,000	40			
Transferred out	18,000				

* New units started should agree with the units transferred out of the previous department.
** Cost of new units started is cost transferred out from Department A for the current period.

Illustration 11-3   Actual Process Costing with Alternative Inventory Valuation Methods
Part B   EPU Schedules

Department A	Product Units	Percent Converted	Elcho EPUs (Enter at 0%)	Conversion EPUs
Transferred out	19,000		19,000	19,000
Ending inventory	5,000	70%	5,000	3,500
Maximum EPUs	24,000		24,000	22,500
Beginning inventory	4,000	50	4,000	2,000
Current output	20,000		20,000	20,500

Department B	Product Units	Percent Converted	Prior Dept. EPUs (Enter at 0%)	Falfex EPUs (Enter at 50%)	Conversion EPUs
Transferred out	18,000		18,000	18,000	18,000
Ending inventory	4,000	40%	4,000	—	1,600
Maximum EPUs	22,000		22,000	18,000	19,600
Beginning inventory	3,000	60	3,000	3,000	1,800
Current output	19,000		19,000	15,000	17,800

Illustration 11-3   Actual Process Costing with Alternative Inventory Valuation Methods
Part C   Cost Allocation Schedules—Lifo

Department A		Elcho				Conversion			
	EPUs	Unit Cost	Total Costs		EPUs	Unit Cost	Total Costs		Cost Summary
LIFO Beginning inventory	4,000	$3.12	$12,480		2,000	$4.74	$ 9,480		$ 21,960
Current output	20,000		66,000		20,500	5.12*	104,960		170,960
Units to account for	24,000		$78,480		22,500		$114,440		$192,920
Ending inventory	5,000	4,000 × $3.12 1,000 × 3.30	15,780		3,500	2,000 × $4.74 1,500 × 5.12	17,160		32,940
Transferred out	19,000		$62,700		19,000		$ 97,280		$159,980

Department B		Prior Department	
	EPUs	Unit Cost	Total Costs
LIFO Beginning inventory	3,000	$7.20	$ 21,600
Current output	19,000	8.42*	159,980**
Units to account for	22,000		$181,580
Ending inventory	4,000	3,000 × $7.20 1,000 × 8.42	30,020
Transferred out	18,000		$151,560

*Needed because ending inventory exceeds beginning inventory.
**Total cost transferred out of Department A.

	Falfex			Conversion			
EPUs	Unit Cost	Total Costs	EPUs	Unit Cost	Total Costs	Cost Summary
3,000	$2.10	$ 6,300	1,800	$6.15	$ 11,070	$ 38,970
15,000		33,750	17,800		119,260	312,990
18,000		$40,050	19,600		$130,330	$351,960
—	—	—	1,600	6.15	9,840	39,860
18,000		$40,050	18,000		$120,490	$312,100

Illustration 11-3   Actual Process Costing with Alternative Inventory Valuation Methods
Part D   Cost Allocation Schedules—Fifo

Department A	EPUs	Unit Cost	Total Costs	EPUs	Unit Cost	Total Costs	Cost Summary
		Elcho			Conversion		
Beginning inventory	4,000		$12,480	2,000		$ 9,480	$ 21,960
FIFO Current output	20,000	$3.30	66,000	20,500	$5.12	104,960	170,960
EPUs to account for	24,000		$78,480	22,500		$114,440	$192,920
Ending inventory	5,000	3.30	16,500	3,500	5.12	17,920	34,420
Transferred out	19,000		$61,980	19,000		$ 96,520	$158,500

Department B	EPUs	Unit Cost	Total Costs
		Prior Department	
Beginning inventory	3,000		$ 21,600
FIFO Current output	19,000	$8.34	158,500
EPUs to account for	22,000		$180,100
Ending inventory	4,000	8.34	33,360
Transferred out	18,000		$146,740

EPUs	Unit Cost	Total Costs	EPUs	Unit Cost	Total Costs	Cost Summary
	Falfex			Conversion		
3,000		$ 6,300	1,800		$ 11,070	$ 38,970
15,000	$2.25	33,750	17,800	$6.70	119,260	311,510
18,000		$40,050	19,600		$130,330	$350,480
—			1,600	6.70	10,720	44,080
18,000		$40,050	18,000		$119,610	$306,400

Illustration 11-3   Actual Process Costing with Alternative Inventory Valuation Methods
Part E   Cost Allocation Schedules—Weighted Average

Department A	EPUs	Unit Cost	Total Costs	EPUs	Unit Cost	Total Costs	Cost Summary
		Elcho			Conversion		
Beginning inventory	4,000		$12,480	2,000		$ 9,480	$ 21,960
Current output	20,000		66,000	20,500		104,960	170,960
WEIGHTED AVERAGE EPUs							
to account for	24,000	$3.27	$78,480	22,500	$5.09	$114,440	$192,920
Ending inventory	5,000	3.27	16,350	3,500	5.09	17,815	34,165
Transferred out	19,000		$62,130	19,000		$ 96,625	$158,755

Department B	EPUs	Unit Cost	Total Costs
		Prior Department	
Beginning inventory	3,000		$ 21,600
Current output	19,000		158,755
WEIGHTED AVERAGE EPUs to account for	22,000	$8.20	$180,355
Ending inventory	4,000	8.20	32,800
Transferred out	18,000		$147,555

| Falfex | | | Conversion | | | |
EPUs	Unit Cost	Total Costs	EPUs	Unit Cost	Total Costs	Cost Summary
3,000		$ 6,300	1,800		$ 11,070	$ 38,970
15,000		33,750	17,800		119,260	311,765
18,000	$2.225	$40,050	19,600	$6.65	$130,330	$350,735
—		—	1,600	6.65	10,640	43,440
18,000		$40,050	18,000		$119,690	$307,295

Illustration 11-4
Journal Entries and T Accounts for Actual Process Costing (Weighted Average Method)

Entry No	Entry		
1.	Work in Process—Dept. A .... Materials—Elcho .... To charge work in process for Elcho used.	66,000	66,000
2.	Work in Process—Dept. A .... Miscellaneous Payables .... To charge work in process for labor and overhead.	104,960	104,960
3.	Work in Process—Dept. B .... Work in Process—Dept. A .... To transfer finished output of Dept. A to Dept. B.	158,755	158,755
4.	Work in Process—Dept. B .... Materials—Falfex .... To charge work in process for Falfex used.	33,750	33,750
5.	Work in Process—Dept. B .... Payables .... To charge work in process for labor and overhead.	119,260	119,260

6.	Finished Goods Inventory ....
	    Work in Process—Dept. B ....
	To transfer finished output of Dept. B to the
	    finished goods inventory.
		307,295	307,295

Ledger

Work in Process—Dept. A

Beginning
  inventory,
  4,000 units
	$ 21,960	Transferred
		out, 19,000
		units
			$158,755

Elcho usage	66,000		
Conversion cost	104,960		

Ending
  inventory,
  5,000 units
	$ 34,165		

Work in Process—Dept. B

Beginning
  inventory,
  3,000 units
	$ 38,970	Transferred
		out, 18,000
		units
			$307,295

Transferred in
  from Dept.
  A, 19,000
  units
	158,755		

Falfex usage	33,750		
Conversion cost	119,260		

Ending
  inventory,
  4,000 units
	$ 43,440		

Spoilage

An actual process cost system should allocate the cost of normal, expected spoilage to good output, just as a standard cost system includes an allowance for spoilage in the cost of good output. For controlling spoilage costs, it is preferable to include spoiled units in the EPU schedule for the period and, in the cost allocation schedule, to allocate a portion of the period's cost to the spoiled units. The accumulated spoilage cost of the period is reduced by the sales value, if any, of the spoiled units. To better match the costs and the output of the period, this sales value is commonly the net realizable value of the spoiled units as they are produced.

Spoilage Counted and Priced. The following procedures summarize the approach used to account for spoilage in an actual process cost system:

1. Include spoiled units in the EPU schedule. The spoilage EPUs should reflect the degree of completion at the point where the spoiled units are removed from the process.
   a. If the number of spoiled units is not known, the following calculation will be necessary:

Units in beginning inventory of work in process
+ New units started
Units to account for
− Units of ending inventory of work in process
− Units transferred out
Units spoiled

   b. Units of normal and abnormal spoilage should be separated in the EPU schedule and in the cost allocation schedule.
2. In the cost allocation schedule, allocate the total costs to account for during the period to spoiled EPUs, as follows:
   a. Price spoiled units at cost of new EPUs if all the spoiled units were started this period; i.e., the spoiled units do not include units from the beginning work in process.
   b. Price spoiled units at a weighted average cost (beginning work in process plus new EPUs) if spoiled units came from both units started this period and units in the beginning work in process inventory. Technically, the average cost should be based on only new EPUs that have passed inspection and exclude those that have not yet been inspected. Since following this procedure does not make a material difference in the outcome, however, the average cost will generally be based on all new EPUs.

   The spoilage pricing rules can be illustrated by referring to the production flow diagrams on pages 366 and 367. In the first diagram, all units coming forward to inspection came from new starts and thus would be priced at the new unit cost. In the second diagram, the units coming forward to inspection came from both the beginning inventory and new starts, and thus a weighted average cost would be used to price spoilage. *The pricing of spoilage is independent of the inventory valuation method being used.*

3. That portion of the net spoilage cost (reduced for recovery) which is considered abnormal spoilage should be accounted for separately and charged to the period as a loss.

4. That portion of the net spoilage cost which is considered normal should be allocated to units transferred out and to units in the ending work in process inventory if the ending inventory has passed inspection. Allocation is by potential whole units, not conversion EPUs, since the spoilage charge per unit is applicable once a unit is inspected, and the charge will not change as the unit moves from inspection to completion. The production flow diagrams on pages 366 and 367 again illustrate the application of this rule. In the first diagram, the ending inventory has not been inspected, and thus no spoilage cost is allocated. In the second diagram, the ending inventory has been inspected, and thus spoilage cost has been allocated to it.

Illustration 11-5 applies the various rules for counting and pricing spoilage to the production of a product that flows through two processes in an actual cost system.

Illustration 11-5   Actual Process Costing, with Spoilage Counted and Priced
Part A   Summary of Facts

Production process:
 In Department A, Gello enters at the start of the process, and conversion costs enter uniformly. Inspection for spoilage occurs at the end of the process, just before the good units are transferred out. In Department B, units from the prior department enter at the beginning of the process. Inspection occurs, and all spoiled units are removed when the units are 50% converted. Hapex is added to the good units immediately after the spoiled units are removed. Conversion costs enter uniformly.

Production quantities and costs (Inventory valuation method: Fifo):

Department A	Units	% Converted	Prior Dept.	Materials	Conversion
				Costs	
Beginning work in process	3,000	60%	—	$ 5,800	$ 6,015
New units started	34,000			74,120	140,610
Units to account for	37,000				
Ending work in process	(5,000)	50			
Units spoiled (all normal)	(2,000)	100			
Transferred out	30,000				

Department B	Units	% Converted	Prior Dept.	Materials	Conversion
Beginning work in process	4,000	60	$26,305	13,000	12,600
New units started	30,000		?	99,125	146,575
Units to account for	34,000				
Ending work in process	(8,000)	60			
Units spoiled, normal	(2,500)	50			
Units spoiled, abnormal	(1,000)	50			
Transferred out	22,500				

Illustration 11-5   Actual Process Costing, with Spoilage Counted and Priced
Part B   EPU Schedules

Department A	Product Units	Percent Converted	Gello EPUs (Enter at 0%)	Conversion EPUs
Transferred out	30,000		30,000	30,000
Ending inventory	5,000	50%	5,000	2,500
Spoilage, normal	2,000	100	2,000	2,000
Maximum EPUs	37,000		37,000	34,500
Beginning inventory	3,000	60	3,000	1,800
Current output	34,000		34,000	32,700

Department B	Product Units	Percent Converted	Prior Dept. EPUs (Enter at 0%)	Hapex EPUs (Enter at 50%)	Conversion EPUs
Transferred out	22,500		22,500	22,500	22,500
Ending inventory	8,000	60%	8,000	8,000	4,800
Spoilage, normal	2,500	50	2,500	—	1,250
Spoilage, abnormal	1,000	50	1,000	—	500
Maximum EPUs	34,000		34,000	30,500	29,050
Beginning inventory	4,000	60	4,000	4,000	2,400
Current output	30,000		30,000	26,500	26,650

Illustration 11-5   Actual Process Costing, with Spoilage Counted and Priced
Part C   Cost Allocation Schedules—Fifo

Department A	Gello EPUs	Unit Cost	Total Costs
Beginning inventory	3,000		$ 5,800
FIFO Current output	34,000	$2.18	74,120
WEIGHTED AVERAGE EPUs to account for	37,000	2.16	$79,920
Ending inventory	(5,000)	2.18	(10,900)
Spoilage	(2,000)	2.16*	(4,320)
Transferred out	30,000		$64,700

Conversion EPUs	Unit Cost	Total Costs	Cost Summary	Spoilage Allocation	Cost Including Spoilage
1,800		$ 6,015	$ 11,815		$ 11,815
32,700	$4.30	140,610	214,730		214,730
34,500	4.25	$146,625	$226,545		$226,545
(2,500)	4.30	(10,750)	(21,650)		(21,650)
(2,000)	4.25*	(8,500)	(12,820)	$(12,820)	—
30,000		$127,375	$192,075	$ 12,820	$204,895

*Average price used, since units spoiled include units from beginning inventory and new units started. All new EPUs are included in the average. Units of ending inventory which have not been inspected have not been subtracted.

Department B	Prior Department		
	EPUs	Unit Cost	Total Costs
Beginning inventory	4,000		$ 26,305
FIFO Current output	30,000	$6.83	204,895
EPUs to account for	34,000		$231,200
Ending inventory	(8,000)	6.83	(54,640)
Spoilage, normal	(2,500)	6.83	(17,075)
Spoilage, abnormal	(1,000)	6.83	(6,830)
Transferred out	22,500		$152,655

Hapex			Conversion			Cost Summary	Normal Spoilage Allocation*	Adjusted Costs
EPUs	Unit Cost	Total Costs	EPUs	Unit Cost	Total Costs			
4,000		$ 13,000	2,400		$ 12,600	$ 51,905		$ 51,905
26,500	$3.74	99,125	26,650	$5.50	146,575	450,595		450,595
30,500		$112,125	29,050		$159,175	$502,500		$502,500
8,000	3.74	29,924	(4,800)	5.50	(26,400)	(110,964)	$ (7,230)	(118,194)
			(1,250)	5.50	(6,875)	(23,950)	23,950	
			(500)	5.50	(2,750)	(9,580)		(9,580)
22,500		$ 82,201	22,500		$123,150	$358,006	$ 16,720	$374,726

*Schedule to allocate normal spoilage:

Account	Units	Allocation	
Ending inventory	8,000	$ 7,230	[(8,000 ÷ 26,500) × $23,950]
Transferred out	18,500[a]	16,720	[(18,500 ÷ 26,500) × $23,950]
	26,500	$23,950	

[a] 22,500 units transferred out − 4,000 units from beginning inventory which were inspected in the previous period.

Illustration 11-5
Actual Process Costing, with Spoilage Counted and Priced

Part D
Production Flow Diagrams

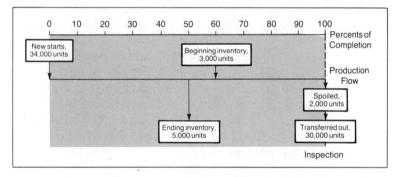

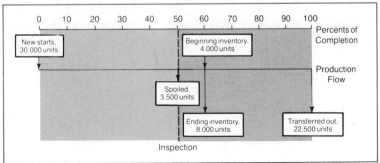

The following journal entries highlight the treatment of spoilage in this illustration:

Entry No	Entry		
1.	Work in Process—Department B	204,895	
	Work in Process—Department A		204,895
	To record the cost of units transferred out of Dept. A to Dept. B.		
2.	Finished Goods	374,726	
	Work in Process—Department B		374,726
	To record the transfer of completed production to finished goods.		
3.	Spoilage Loss	9,580	
	Work in Process—Department B		9,580
	To record the abnormal spoilage in Dept. B as a loss for the period.		

The most convenient method of carrying the spoilage allowance applicable to the previous period's ending work in process to the succeeding period is to add the spoilage cost to the conversion cost component. For the example in Illustration 11-5, the total cost of the next period's beginning work in process inventory is calculated as follows:

Total conversion cost of ending inventory from previous period for Department B	$26,400
Spoilage allocated to previous period's ending inventory	7,230
Total	$33,630

Spoilage Neglected. A shortcut method of allocating the cost of spoilage to good units is sometimes encountered in practice. This method, which might be called the "method of neglect," deletes spoiled units from the EPU schedules and the cost allocation schedules. Since the materials and conversion costs embodied in the spoiled units are still in the cost allocation schedules, but the spoiled units are not, the normal and abnormal spoilage costs are allocated automatically to the good units in the ending work in process and to the units transferred out of the process. In Illustration 11-6, in which the "method of neglect" is applied to the data from Illustration 11-5, the unit costs of current production are higher than the unit costs that resulted when spoilage was counted and priced.

Illustration 11-6
Actual Process Costing, with "Method of Neglect" for Spoilage

Part A
EPU Schedules

	Department A			
	Product Units	Percent Converted	Gello EPUs (Enter at 0%)	Conversion EPUs
Transferred out	30,000		30,000	30,000
Spoilage	2,000	NA	—	—
Ending inventory	5,000	50%	5,000	2,500
Maximum EPUs	37,000		35,000	32,500
Beginning inventory	3,000	60	3,000	1,800
Current output	34,000		32,000	30,700

Department B					
	Product Units	Percent Converted	Prior Dept. EPUs (Enter at 0%)	Hapex EPUs (Enter at 50%)	Conversion EPUs
Transferred out	22,500		22,500	22,500	22,500
Spoilage	3,500	NA	—	—	—
Ending inventory	8,000	60%	8,000	8,000	4,800
Maximum EPUs	34,000		30,500	30,500	27,300
Beginning inventory	4,000	60	4,000	4,000	2,400
Current output	30,000		26,500	26,500	24,900

Illustration 11-6   Actual Process Costing, with "Method of Neglect" for Spoilage
Part B   Cost Allocation Schedules—Fifo

Department A	Gello			Conversion			Cost Summary
	EPUs	Unit Cost	Total Costs	EPUs	Unit Cost	Total Costs	
Beginning inventory	3,000		$ 5,800	1,800		$ 6,015	$ 11,815
FIFO Current output	32,000	$2.32	74,120	30,700	$4.58	140,610	214,730
EPUs to account for	35,000		$79,920	32,500		$146,625	$226,545
Ending inventory	5,000	2.32	11,600	2,500	4.58	11,450	23,050
Transferred out	30,000		$68,320	30,000		$135,175	$203,495

Department B	Prior Department		
	EPUs	Unit Cost	Total Costs
Beginning inventory	4,000		$ 26,305
FIFO Current output	26,500	$7.68	203,495
EPUs to account for	30,500		$229,800
Ending inventory	8,000	7.68	61,440
Transferred out	22,500		$168,360

Hapex			Conversion			Cost Summary
EPUs	Unit Cost	Total Costs	EPUs	Unit Cost	Total Costs	
4,000		$ 13,000	2,400		$ 12,600	$ 51,905
26,500	$3.74	99,125	24,900	$5.89	146,575	449,195
30,500		$112,125	27,300		$159,175	$501,100
8,000	3.74	29,924	4,800	5.89	28,272	119,636
22,500		$ 82,201	22,500		$130,903	$381,464

In many cases, the automatic allocation of spoilage may not be accurate. For example, assume that the spoiled units are removed at the 50% conversion point and that the ending work in process is 40% converted. Under the "method of neglect," some spoilage costs will be included in the ending work in process inventory, even though the units have not yet been inspected.

Another example of the inaccuracy of this method is the case in which the spoiled units are removed at the 50% conversion point and the ending work in process is 60% converted. In the conversion cost allocation schedule, all costs, including the unquantified spoilage costs of the period, will be allocated according to the EPUs in the ending inventory and in production transferred out of the process. Thus, the ending work in process is charged with less spoilage cost if it is 60% converted than if it were 100% converted. However, the spoilage charge does not change as the unit proceeds down the production line. Therefore, the spoilage cost per unit should be equal for both units transferred out and units in the ending work in process inventory.

The "method of neglect" can be justified only because its inaccuracies are immaterial or because there is no better alternative. In some processes, spoiled units may be removed when they are spotted, rather than at some discrete point. In such cases, the degree of completion of the spoiled units may not be feasibly calculated, and the "method of neglect" may be logically used.

SUMMARY: USE OF EPUs

The use of EPUs in process costing is summarized in the following diagram:

EPU Schedule
includes EPUs of spoilage[1]

Standard Cost System

Use EPUs as allowable use of inputs to calculate usage and volume variances

Actual Cost System

Allocate input costs to EPUs using cost allocation schedules

---

[1] Except for "method of neglect" in actual cost system which does not count EPUs of spoilage.

1. What is the role of equivalent production units in variance analysis?

2. Assume that the units from process 1 are put immediately into the following process. What correspondence will there be in the EPU schedules for the two processes?

3. What complications in the analytic process are caused by spoilage in a standard process cost system?

4. When actual spoilage is compared with budgeted spoilage in a standard process cost system, how is budgeted spoilage determined?

5. Describe two methods of disposing of a spoilage variance at the end of the year.

6. Describe three ways of pricing the ending inventory in an actual process cost system.

7. (a) In pricing the ending inventory using fifo, what complications arise if the ending inventory EPUs exceed the new EPUs?
   (b) In pricing the ending inventory using lifo, what complications arise if the ending inventory EPUs exceed the beginning inventory EPUs?

8. How is spoilage accounted for in an actual process cost system?

9. What unit cost is used to price spoilage in an actual process cost system?

10. What units will have normal spoilage costs allocated to them?

11. Assume that inspection occurs at 50% completion, at which time 2,000 spoiled units are removed from the process. The beginning inventory consists of 5,000 units, 40% complete; current production is 25,000 units; and 8,000 units, 60% complete, are in the ending inventory. At what unit cost will spoilage be priced? Why?

12. Referring to the information given in Question 11, which units will have spoilage costs allocated to them? Why?

13. How does the "method of neglect" deal with spoiled units?

Exercise 1. Pearson Co. manufactures a single type of ceramic brick which has found wide application because of its attractive finish and resistance to high temperatures. The main material used in production, a special clay, enters at the beginning of production. A second material, a glazing compound, enters when the units are 75% complete as to labor and overhead. Labor and overhead costs enter uniformly throughout processing. At the beginning of December, the firm had an inventory of 4,000 bricks, 30% complete as to labor and overhead. During the month, 75,000 bricks were completed and transferred to finished goods. The inventory on December 31 consisted of 6,500 bricks, 80% complete. There were no spoiled units during December.

Prepare an EPU schedule summarizing the firm's production operations during December, and calculate the number of EPUs entering production for each material, labor, and overhead.

Exercise 2. Xantec Chemical Company manufactures a chemical catalyst known as *Dennarol. Dennarol* is produced in two departments: the Mixing Department and the Refining Department. In the Mixing Department, 3 materials—A, B, and C—are combined to produce an intermediate product. A and B enter at the beginning of the process, while C is added at the 60% stage of completion. The intermediate product is sent to the Refining Department, where it undergoes distillation and purification. A final material, D, is added at the 40% point of completion in the Refining Department. Labor and overhead are incurred uniformly in both production departments. The finished catalyst is sent from the Refining Department to the finished goods inventory.

During the month, an electronic temperature regulator failed in the Refining Department, ruining 800 gallons of work in process. The production manager estimates that the units were 70% complete at the time of the equipment failure.

A summary of relevant production statistics for the month is as follows:

	Mixing Dept.	Refining Dept.
Beginning work in process	3,200 gals., 70% complete	2,400 gals., 50% complete
Ending work in process	1,200 gals., 40% complete	1,900 gals., 70% complete
Units transferred to finished goods:	36,000 gals.	

Prepare EPU schedules for both departments for the month.

Exercise 3 (AICPA adapted, 11/74). Poole Inc. produces a chemical compound by a unique chemical process which Poole has divided into two departments, A and B, for accounting purposes. The process functions as follows:

- The formula for the chemical compound requires one pound of Chemical X and 2 gallons of Chemical Y. In the simplest sense, one pound of Chemical X is processed in Department A and transferred to Department B for further processing, where 2 gallons of Chemical Y are added at the beginning of the process. When the processing is complete in Department B, the finished chemical compound is transferred to finished goods. The process is continuous, operating twenty-four hours a day. The addition of Chemical Y yields 2 gallons of final product.
- Normal spoilage occurs in Department A. Five percent of Chemical X is lost in the first few seconds of processing.
- No spoilage occurs in Department B.
- At roughly the 80% point of processing in Department B, the volume of chemical compound (gals.) is reduced by 20% due to evaporation.
- Poole's unit of measure is pounds for the work in process in Department A, and gallons for Department B and the finished goods inventory.

The following data are available for October, 19X4:

	Dept. A	Dept. B
Work in process, October 1	8,000 pounds	10,000 gals.
Stage of completion of beginning inventory (one batch per dept.)	3/4	6/10
Started or transferred in	50,000 pounds	?
Transferred out	46,500 good lbs.	75,200 gals.
Work in process, October 31	9,000 pounds	7,200 gals.
Stage of completion of ending inventory (one batch per dept.)	1/3	9/10
Total equivalent gals. of material added in Dept. B	—	93,000 gals.

Prepare schedules computing equivalent production units (materials and conversion costs) for Department A and for Department B for October, 19X4.

Exercise 4. Dolence Boat Co. manufactures a limited number of *Dragon* sailboats, a medium-sized sailing dinghy. *Dragons* are an Olympic-class boat, and the hulls manufactured by the firm are built to exacting standards of size and weight. Production begins in the Molding Department, where the boat hulls are laid up in molds, using fiberglass cloth and resin. These materials enter uniformly throughout production in the Molding Department. Standards for materials per hull are as follows:

Fiberglass cloth (1,650 sq. ft. @ $.70 per sq. ft.)	$1,155
Fiberglass resin (50 gals. @ $12 per gal.)	600
	$1,755

In February, the Molding Department completed and transferred 18 hulls to the next department, Finishing. On February 1, 5 hulls, 35% complete as to materials, were in process. The ending work in process inventory for the Molding Department consisted of 4 hulls, 70% complete as to materials.

Materials purchases and usage during the month are summarized as follows:

	Purchased	Issued to Production
Fiberglass cloth	35,000 sq. ft. for $25,550	34,570 sq. ft.
Fiberglass resin	875 gals. for $11,200	980 gals.

Prepare an EPU schedule for materials, and use it to calculate materials price and usage variances. Materials price variances are isolated at the time of purchase.

Exercise 5. The Assembly Department of Guarantee Lock Company assembles padlocks, using components manufactured in other departments of the firm. A consulting firm, recently engaged to do a time-motion study for the company, has reported that a reasonable time standard for the assembly of one lock is 18 minutes. All assembly workers are paid a uniform wage of $5.25 per hour, as specified in the latest union contract. Variable overhead is charged to Work in Process at the rate of $3.40 per DLH. Budgeted fixed overhead of $3,000 per month is applied to production on the basis of 750 normal DLHs per month. Production statistics for April are summarized as follows (1 unit = 1 lock):

Work in process:
April 1:   225 units, 20% complete as to labor and overhead
April 30: 480 units, 40% complete as to labor and overhead
Units transferred out: 2,310 units

Payroll records for April show that the Assembly Department had 766 direct labor hours at a cost of $4,136. Overhead costs for the month totaled $5,470.

Prepare an EPU schedule for labor for the Assembly Department. Use the schedule to calculate both a labor rate variance and a labor efficiency variance for the department. Also calculate overhead variances, using the 3-way method.

Exercise 6. Jennerson Supply Co. produces clay flower pots at a small plant in the eastern United States. The only material, red clay, is introduced at the start of production. At the 70% point of completion, just after firing, the units are inspected and the defective pots discarded. The remaining good pots are then glazed. Glazing compound is relatively inexpensive and is accounted for as an indirect material (overhead). After glazing, the pots are sent on to finished goods inventory. The standard costs of a spoiled pot and a good pot, including a spoilage allowance, are as follows:

Standard Cost of a Spoiled Pot		Standard Cost of a Good Pot	
Direct materials—Clay (1.7 lbs. @ $.30 per lb.)	$0.510	Direct materials—Clay	$0.510
Direct labor (.035 hrs. @ $5 per DLH)	0.175	Direct labor (.05 hrs. @ $5)	0.250
Overhead (.035 hrs. @ $4 per DLH)	0.140	Overhead (.05 hrs. @ $4)	0.200
	$0.825	Spoilage allowance—4% of good units	0.033
			$0.993

During the current month, 7,250 pots were transferred from work in process to finished goods. The beginning inventory consisted of 880 units, 80% complete as to labor and overhead. The ending work in process consists of 450 units, 90% complete as to conversion. During the month, 423 units were found defective and removed from production.

Prepare a production flow diagram. Use the information in the diagram to calculate the spoilage variance for the month.

Exercise 7. Deleware Paper Products manufactures grocery bags in one division of its New Jersey plant. The operation is fully automated—there is no direct labor. All labor is either indirect labor or supervisory. Paper is led off large, 500-lb. rolls and fed into the production machinery. The equipment cuts the paper into an appropriate size, folds it, glues the edges shut, prints the client's name on the bag, and bundles the bags in plastic for shipping. The bundles are moved along a conveyor to a warehouse for storage and eventual shipment.

At the beginning of May, the firm had an in process inventory of 7,400 lbs. of paper bags, 40% complete as to conversion. Inventory records give this inventory a materials value of $88.80 and a conversion cost of $370. During the month, 950,000 lbs. of bags were transferred to the warehouse. The ending work in process inventory consisted of 12,400 lbs. of bags, 20% complete. There were no spoiled units. Production costs incurred during the month were as follows:

Materials	$ 13,370.00
Conversion	123,437.60

Calculate the value of the ending work in process inventory and the units transferred out. Deleware uses the fifo method to cost all inventories.

Exercise 8. The Home Products Division of Eaton Corp. manufactures plexiglass skylights for use in commercial and residential buildings. In the Assembly Department, a plexiglass dome, an aluminum frame, and a worm-and-sector opening/

closing mechanism are jointed together to produce a finished skylight. The component parts are produced in other departments of the division.

The divisional accountant is trying to determine the value of the ending work in process inventory in order to prepare monthly financial statements. October production data for the Assembly Department, relating to materials, is summarized as follows:

Beginning work in process	1,000 units, 40% complete
Ending work in process	940 units, 70% complete
Units transferred out	4,300 units
Materials costs incurred:	
Plexiglass domes	$ 78,016
Aluminum frames	169,600
Opening/closing mechanism	42,444

The plexiglass dome and the aluminum frame enter production at the beginning of assembly. The opening/closing mechanism enters when the units are 60% complete. The cost of materials in the beginning work in process inventory was broken down as follows:

Aluminum frames	$38,690
Plexiglass domes	16,304
	$54,994

Calculate the value of the materials component of the ending work in process inventory. All inventories are costed using the weighted average method.

Exercise 9. Pearson Corporation manufactures aluminum master brake cylinders as a subcontractor to an American farm equipment manufacturer. In the firm's Machining Department, the rough-cast aluminum cylinder (produced in the Casting Department) is first bored to accept a piston and then tapped in five places where brake lines will later be connected. The machined cylinders are then sent on to the Assembly Department for completion. At the beginning of the month, there were 400 aluminum cylinders, 30% complete, in the Machining Department. The ending work in process inventory in the Machining Department consists of 650 cylinders, 70% complete. During the month, 3,700 cylinders were transferred into the Machining Department from the Casting Department. There were no spoiled units in the Machining Department. Labor and overhead costs are incurred uniformly in the Machining Department. Relevant costs incurred during the month are summarized below:

	Materials (Prior Dept.)	Conversion
Cost in beginning inventory	$ 8,800	$ 1,680
Cost incurred during the month	89,725	53,747

Calculate the value of the units transferred out of the Machining Department, using the lifo and weighted average methods.

Exercise 10. Technical Design Ltd.'s primary product is a ceramic heat-reflecting tile which is used to shield delicate electronics from high temperatures. The product is used primarily in space-related and military hardware. All production is accounted for using actual process costing. At the beginning cf March, the firm had 625 tiles in process, 40% complete as to labor and overhead. Materials sufficient to produce 2,900 tiles were introduced to production during the month. The ending inventory consisted of 470 tiles, 80% complete. All tiles are inspected at the 70% point of completion. Defective units have no salvage value and are discarded. During the month, 580 tiles were tested and found to be defective, about average for the process. The cost of the spoiled units, calculated by the firm's accountant, was $12,760.

(1) Prepare a production flow diagram, and use the diagram to answer the following questions:
    (a) Did the spoiled units originate from the beginning work in process inventory, from new units started in March, or both?
    (b) Which units (units transferred out, units in ending inventory, or both) receive a share of the current period's spoilage costs?
(2) Allocate the period's spoilage costs to the proper units.

Exercise 11. Assume the same facts as in Exercise 10, except that the beginning work in process inventory was 75% complete as to conversion costs.

(1) Prepare a production flow diagram, and use the diagram to answer the following questions:
    (a) Did the spoiled units originate from the beginning work in process inventory, from new units started in March, or both?
    (b) Which units (units transferred out, units in ending inventory, or both) receive a share of the current period's spoilage cost?
(2) Allocate the period's spoilage costs to the proper units.

Exercise 12. Essex Paint Co. produces paint in several production departments at its Ohio manufacturing facility. In the Finishing Department, paint which is substantially complete is received in bulk quantities from a prior department. The paint undergoes further processing before it is inspected at the 80% point of completion, just prior to packaging. Defective batches are disposed of, while good batches are packaged in cans and transferred to the finished goods inventory. Labor and overhead costs enter uniformly.

To prepare the firm's end-of-month financial statements, one of the firm's accountants has begun preparation of an inventory cost schedule for the Finishing Department. The partially complete schedule is reproduced as follows (all amounts are correct as calculated):

	% Completed	Prior Dept. Cost			Packaging Materials			Conversion			
		Units	Unit Cost	Cost	Units	Unit Cost	Cost	Units	Unit Cost	Cost	Totals
Beginning inventory	85%	500	$4.000	$ 2,000	500	$1.400	$ 700	425	$1.800	$ 765	$ 3,465
Units started		7,680	4.250	32,640	6,600	1.350	8,910	7,219	2.000	14,438	55,988
To account for		8,180	4.235	$34,640	7,100	1.354	$9,610	7,644	1.989	$15,203	$59,453
Ending inventory	40	(800)			—			(320)			
Spoilage	80	(280)			—			(224)			
Transferred out		7,100			7,100			7,100			

Essex uses the weighted average method to cost its ending work in process inventory. All spoilage was considered normal spoilage.

Complete the schedule and allocate the cost of spoiled units to the proper inventories. It may be helpful to construct a production flow diagram.

PROBLEMS

Problem 11-1 (AICPA adapted, 5/69). To prepare its 19X8 year-end financial statements, Norwood Corporation is calculating its production variances for the year. The firm employs a process cost system.

The corporation manufactures Gink, which is sold for $20 per unit. Marsh is added before processing starts, and labor and overhead are added evenly during the manufacturing process. Production capacity is budgeted at 110,000 units of Gink annually. The standard costs per unit of Gink are:

Marsh, 2 pounds	$3.00
Labor (1.25 hrs. @ $4.80 per hr.)	6.00
Variable manufacturing overhead (1.25 hrs. @ $.80 per hr.)	1.00
Fixed manufacturing overhead	1.10

Inventory data for 19X8 are as follows:

	January 1	December 31
Marsh	50,000 lbs.	21,600 lbs.
Work in process:		
2/5 processed	10,000 units	
1/3 processed		15,000 units
Finished goods	20,000 units	12,000 units

During 19X8, 220,000 pounds of Marsh were purchased for $310,200, and 248,400 pounds were transferred to work in process. Materials price variances are isolated at the time of purchase. Also, 110,000 units of Gink were transferred to finished goods.

Direct labor hours worked totaled 134,590 at a cost of $659,491. Overhead costs totaled $237,820.

Required

(1) Prepare a schedule of equivalent production units for materials, labor, and overhead.

(2) Calculate all production variances, including a three-way analysis of overhead.

Problem 11-2. Sanjawa Manufacturing Ltd. manufactures steel and aluminum gas tanks to the specifications of the major Japanese automobile and truck manufacturers. In the Stamping Department, the material for each tank is cut and stamped into the appropriate shape. In the Assembly Department, a pair of metal stampings, each constituting the upper and lower halves of a completed tank, are fitted with a filler tube, a gas gauge unit, and 4 plastic baffles, before being welded together into the final product. The company employs a process cost system based on standard costs. Standard cost sheets for both departments are as shown on page 388.

Materials enter the Stamping Department at the beginning of processing. In the Assembly Department, materials enter at the following points: tank halves—beginning of process; filler tube—10%; gas gauge—30%; baffles—60%. Conversion costs enter uniformly in both departments.

Stamping Department

Materials:

Steel (9 sq. ft. @ $.55 per sq. ft.)	$4.95
Labor (.02 hrs. @ $9 per hr.)	0.18
Overhead:	
Variable (.02 hrs. @ $7 per hr.)	0.14
Fixed (.02 hrs. @ $27 per hr.)*	0.54
Standard cost per half tank	$5.81

*Based on a normal monthly output of 5,120 DLH per month.

Assembly Department

Materials:

2 tank halves (@ $5.81 each)	$11.62	
Filler tube (1 @ $.40)	0.40	
Gas gauge (1 @ $1.75)	1.75	
Baffles (4 @ $.12 each)	0.48	$14.25
Labor (.25 hrs. @ $6 per hr.)		1.50
Overhead:		
Variable (.25 hrs. @ $3 per hr.)		0.75
Fixed (.25 hrs. @ $6 per hr.)*		1.50
Standard cost per tank		$18.00

*Based on a normal output of 30,000 DLH per month.

In the Stamping Department, 1 tank half equals 1 EPU. In the Assembly Department, 2 tank halves equal 1 EPU. Inventory levels during January in both departments are summarized as follows:

Stamping Department

Work in process:

Beginning inventory (70% complete)	27,000 units
Ending inventory (30% complete)	21,000
Transferred out	240,000

Assembly Department

Work in process:

Beginning inventory (70% complete)	19,000 units
Ending inventory (40% complete)	25,000
Transferred out	234,000

Cost reports from the firm's three departments (Purchasing, Stamping, and Assembly) are as follows:

Purchasing Department—Cost Report

	Quantity	Unit Price	Total
Steel	1,980,000 sq. ft.	$0.52 per sq. ft.	$1,029,600
Filler tubes	110,000 tubes	0.393 ea.	43,230
Gas gauges	140,000 gauges	1.754 ea.	245,560
Baffles	468,000 baffles	0.128 ea.	59,904
Total cost			$1,378,294

	Quantity	Unit Price	Total
Steel	2,169,180 sq. ft.		
Labor	4,458 hours		$ 40,345
Overhead			159,180

Assembly Department—Cost Report

	Quantity	Unit Price	Total
Filler tubes	120,480 tubes		
Gas gauges	120,200 gauges		
Baffles	460,100 baffles		
Tank halves	240,000 halves		
Labor	27,684 hours		$170,100
Overhead			251,751

Sanjawa management isolates materials price variances at the time of purchase.

Required (1) Prepare a schedule of equivalent production units for each production department.

(2) Calculate all variances for each department, using three-way analysis to isolate overhead variances.

Problem 11-3. The Lens Division of Centron Corp. produces precision-ground optical lenses and reflecting surfaces. These products are then transferred to other divisions, which assemble camera lenses, binoculars, telescopic sights, and other products. Among the production departments in the Lens Division is the Grinding Department, where standardized pieces of optical glass (produced in another department or purchased from outside suppliers) are ground into the desired shape. The majority of this department's output consists of a 60mm lens, Model 2-60CL. The standard cost sheet for this lens is as follows (excluding spoilage allowance):

Standard Cost Sheet—Model 2-60CL

Materials (1 flat disc, Model 1-60P)	$3.30
Direct Labor (0.15 DLH @ $7 per DLH)	1.05
Overhead:	
Variable (0.15 DLH @ $12 per DLH)	1.80
Fixed* (0.15 DLH @ $8 per DLH)	1.20
Standard cost per unit	$7.35

*Based on a monthly output of 12,800 DLH per month.

All lenses produced by the Grinding Department are tested using laser equipment for clarity and precision just prior to being transferred to the firm's other divisions. The average spoilage rate is 3.5% of the good units. Spoiled lenses have no salvage value and are discarded.

Production data for the Grinding Department for the month of May are summarized as follows:

Materials (77,900 discs, Model 1-60P)	$254,733
Direct labor (11,460 DLH)	80,793
Overhead: Variable	143,021
Fixed	99,740

Work in process inventory (May 1)	7,200 units, 15% complete
Work in process inventory (May 31)	3,400 units, 30% complete
Transferred out	78,000 units
Spoiled	2,820 units

All materials are added at the beginning of processing; labor and overhead are incurred uniformly. Materials price variances are isolated at the time of issuance to production.

Required

(1) Prepare an EPU schedule summarizing the Grinding Department's activities during May.

(2) Calculate all variances, including a spoilage variance and a 4-way analysis of overhead.

Problem 11-4. Stellar Plastics Inc. manufactures a patented plastic drafting template used widely in electronic circuit design. The template is produced in the firm's single production department. Standard costs per 100 units, exclusive of spoilage allowance, are as follows:

Plastic (12.5 lbs. @ $3 per lb.)	$37.50
Printed stencil (100 @ $.18 each)	18.00
Direct labor (1.7 hours @ $5.80 per DLH)	9.86
Variable overhead (1.7 hours @ $4.50 per DLH)	7.65
Fixed overhead (1.7 hours @ $7.20 per DLH)*	12.24
Total	$85.25

*Based on a normal activity of 5,610 DLH per month.

The plastic enters at the beginning of the process. After initial processing, the units are inspected at the 50% stage of completion, when defective units are removed. The remaining good units are imprinted with the stencil, and are then transferred to finished goods. Labor and overhead costs are incurred uniformly throughout the process. Normal spoilage amounts to 5% of all good units.

During February, the following quantities were produced:

Transferred to finished goods	320,000 units
Work in process (February 1)	24,000 units, 40% complete
Work in process (February 28)	28,000 units, 60% complete
Spoiled	16,000 units

Cost data for February were as follows:

Materials purchased:
    Plastic: 51,850 lbs. for $157,624
    Stencils: 452,000 stencils for $80,456
Materials issued:
    Plastic: 41,950 lbs.
    Stencils: 354,900 stencils
Direct labor: 5,920 hrs. @ $34,040
Variable overhead: $29,520
Fixed overhead: $44,400

Required

(1) Calculate the standard cost per template, including an allowance for spoilage.

(2) Prepare an equivalent production unit schedule, summarizing production activities during February.

cont.

(3) Prepare a production flow diagram, and calculate all variances, including a 2-way analysis of overhead and a spoilage variance. Materials price variances are isolated at the time of materials purchases.

Problem 11-5 (AICPA adapted, 11/69). Ross Shirts Inc. manufactures short- and long-sleeve men's shirts for large stores. Ross produces a single quality shirt in lots to each customer's order and attaches the store's label to each. The standard costs for a dozen long-sleeve shirts are:

Direct materials (24 yards @ $1.55)	$37.20
Direct labor (3 hours @ $4.45)	13.35
Manufacturing overhead (3 hours @ $4.00)	12.00
Standard cost per dozen	$62.55

During October, 19X9, Ross worked on three orders for long-sleeve shirts. Job cost records for the month disclose the following:

Lot	Units in Lot	Material Used	Hours Worked
30	1,000 dozen	24,100 yards	2,980
31	1,700 dozen	40,440 yards	5,130
32	1,200 dozen	28,825 yards	2,890

The following information is also available:

- Ross purchased 95,000 yards of material during the month at a cost of $150,000. The materials price variance is recorded when goods are purchased, and all inventories are carried at standard cost.
- Direct labor incurred amounted to $50,050 during October. According to payroll records, production employees were paid $4.55 per hour.
- Overhead is applied on the basis of direct labor hours. Manufacturing overhead totaling $48,600 was incurred during October.
- A total of $576,000 was budgeted for overhead for the year 19X9, based on estimated production at the plant's normal capacity of 48,000 dozen shirts per year. Overhead is 40% fixed and 60% variable at this level of production.
- There was no work in process at October 1. During October, lots 30 and 31 were completed, and all material was issued for lot 32, which was 80% complete as to labor and overhead.

Required

(1) Prepare a schedule computing the standard cost of lots 30, 31, and 32 for October.
(2) Prepare a schedule computing the materials price variance for October, and indicate whether the variance is favorable or unfavorable.
(3) For each lot produced during October, prepare schedules computing the (a) materials quantity variance in dollars, (b) labor efficiency variance in dollars, and (c) labor rate variance in dollars. (Indicate whether the variances are favorable or unfavorable.)
(4) Prepare a schedule computing the total controllable and noncontrollable (capacity) manufacturing overhead variances for October, and indicate whether the variances are favorable or unfavorable.

Problem 11-6 (AICPA adapted, 5/79). You are engaged in the audit of the December 31, 19X8 financial statements of Spirit Corporation, a manufacturer of a digital watch. You are attempting to verify the costing of the ending inventory of work in process and finished goods which were recorded on Spirit's books, as follows:

	Units	Cost
Work in process (50% complete as to labor and overhead)	300,000	$ 660,960
Finished goods	200,000	1,009,800

Materials are added to production at the beginning of the manufacturing process, and overhead is applied to each product at the rate of 60% of direct labor costs. There was no finished goods inventory on January 1, 19X8. A review of Spirit's inventory cost records disclosed the following information:

		Costs	
	Units	Materials	Labor
Work in process, January 1, 19X8 (80% complete as to labor and overhead)	200,000	$ 200,000	$ 315,000
Units started in production	1,000,000	1,300,000	1,995,000
Units completed and transferred out	900,000		

Required (1) Prepare an EPU schedule for the firm for 19X8.
(2) Calculate the cost of the ending work in process and ending finished goods inventories, using (a) the weighted average method, (b) lifo, and (c) fifo.

Problem 11-7 (AICPA adapted, 5/78). Melody Corporation is a manufacturing company that produces a single product known as *Jupiter*. Melody uses the fifo process costing method for both financial statements and internal management reporting. In analyzing production results, standard costs are used, whereas actual costs are used for financial statements. The standards, which are based on equivalent production units, are as follows:

Materials per unit: 1 pound at $10 per pound
Direct labor per unit: 2 hours at $4 per hour
Factory overhead per unit (all fixed): 2 hours at $1.25 per hour

Budgeted factory overhead for estimated April production is $30,000.

The April beginning inventory consisted of 2,500 units which were 100% complete as to materials and 40% complete as to direct labor and factory overhead. An additional 10,000 units were started during the month. The ending inventory consisted of 2,000 units which were 100% complete as to materials and 40% complete as to direct labor and factory overhead.

Costs applicable to April production are as follows:

	Actual Cost	Standard Cost
Materials used (11,000 pounds)	$121,000	$100,000
Direct labor (25,000 hours actually worked)	105,575	82,400
Factory overhead	31,930	25,750

Required (1) For each element of production for April (materials, direct labor, and factory overhead), compute the following:
(a) Equivalent production units.

(b) Cost per equivalent production unit at actual and at standard.
(2) Prepare a schedule analyzing, for April production, the following variances as either favorable or unfavorable:
   (a) Total materials.
   (b) Materials price.
   (c) Materials usage.
   (d) Total labor.
   (e) Labor rate.
   (f) Labor efficiency.
   (g) Total factory overhead.
   (h) Factory overhead volume.
   (i) Factory overhead budget.

Problem 11-8. Cane Corporation produces a single product and has two departments, A and B. All materials enter at the beginning of Department A. One unit of material is required for each unit of finished product. The materials emerge from Department A as semifinished products, which are transferred to Department B and completed. Both Department A and Department B use average cost. Finished goods inventory is accounted for using the lifo method, however. Labor and overhead costs enter uniformly in both departments.

Cane Corporation had the following data for the month ended March 31:*

	Department A	Department B
Good units transferred out	12,000	10,000
Final inventories (units)	15,400	3,000
Initial inventories (units)	1,200	?
Materials started (26,200 units)	21,484	—
Conversion costs:		
Labor costs incurred	$24,906	$ 7,600
Overhead costs incurred	16,604	3,258
Cost of initial inventories:		
Materials	436	-0-
Conversion	1,050	302
Prior department	-0-	2,290
Percent complete as to conversion costs:		
Initial inventories	50%	20%
Final inventories	80%	80%

Beginning finished goods inventory (4,000 units): $13,080
Sales: 12,000 units @ $4.75
Selling expenses: $5,990
General and administrative expenses: $7,370

---

*Planned overhauls of equipment in Department A during April led management to build up stocks of work in process in Department A during March.

Required (1) Prepare EPU schedules for both departments, summarizing production activities during March.
(2) Prepare inventory valuation schedules for both departments.
(3) Prepare journal entries to record Cane Corporation's production operations during March.
(4) Prepare an income statement in good form for the month ended March 31.

Problem 11-9. Berndt Chemical Company manufactures a special type of pliable foam rubber which has found use in a wide variety of products, including furniture, automobile seats and dashboards, and mattresses. Production takes place in two departments: the Delta Department and the Caravelle Department.

In the Delta Department, two materials, A and B, enter at the beginning of the process. The materials undergo various mixing and refining processes. After processing, the primary product, *Delta,* is ready for shipment to the second department. For each Caravelle Department EPU, 3.15 Delta Department EPUs are required. EPUs are defined as follows:

Delta Department: 1 EPU = 1 gal. of *Delta*
Caravelle Department: 1 EPU = 1 50-cubic-foot bat of completed foam

In the second department, the liquid *Delta* is immediately combined with material C, yielding a basic foam rubber. At the 80% point of conversion, the addition of a catalyst, material D, causes the foam to increase in volume by roughly 25%. After a small amount of additional processing, the foam is ready for transfer to finished goods in 50-cubic-foot bats. The finished foam bats are sold under the *Caravelle* brand name.

The following costs were incurred during the month:

	Delta Department	Caravelle Department
Material A	$ 6,000.00	—
Material B	32,000.00	—
Material C	—	$ 1,032.00
Material D	—	10,500.00
Labor	1,861.20	2,849.60
Overhead	3,722.40	2,212.00
	$43,583.60	$16,593.60

At the beginning of the month, Berndt held the following amounts in its work in process inventories:

Delta Department	Material A	Material B	Conversion
Beginning inventory (802 gals., 80% complete)	$569	$3,047	$470
Ending inventory (675 gals., 40% complete)	?	?	?

Caravelle Department	Prior Dept.	Material C	Material D	Conversion
Ending inventory (10,000 cubic ft., 90%)	?	?	?	?
Beginning inventory (16,800 cubic ft., 40%)	$7,098	$164	-0-	$307

During the month, materials sufficient for 8,000 gals. of *Delta* were started into production in the Delta Department. Both departments use the fifo method to value ending inventory. Labor and overhead enter both departments uniformly.

Required

(1) Prepare equivalent production unit schedules for both departments.
(2) Prepare inventory valuation schedules for both departments. Calculate the value and quantity of foam bats transferred to finished goods.

Problem 11-10 (AICPA adapted, 11/76). Dexter Production Company manufactures a single product. Its operations are a continuing process carried on in two departments - machining and finishing. In the production process, materials are added to the product in each department without increasing the number of units produced. Dexter uses the fifo method to value ending work in process inventories in both departments.

For June, 19X5, the company records indicated the following production data for each department:

	Machining Department	Finishing Department
Units in process, June 1, 19X5	-0-	-0-
Units transferred from preceding department	-0-	60,000
Units started in production	80,000	-0-
Units completed and transferred out	60,000	50,000
Units in process, June 30, 19X5*	20,000	8,000
Units spoiled in production (normal)	-0-	2,000

*Percent of completion of units in process at June 30, 19X5:

	Machining Department	Finishing Department
Materials	100%	100%
Labor	50%	70%
Overhead	25%	70%

The units spoiled in production had no scrap value and were 50% complete as to materials, labor, and overhead. The company's policy is to treat the cost of spoiled units in production as a separate element of cost in the department in which the spoilage occurs.

Cost records showed the following charges for June:

	Machining Department	Finishing Department
Materials	$240,000	$ 88,500
Labor	140,000	141,500
Overhead	65,000	25,470

Required

(1) For both the Machining and Finishing Departments, prepare in good form the following reports for June:
(a) EPU schedules.
(b) Production flow diagrams, if applicable.
(c) Cost allocation schedules, in good form.
(2) Prepare journal entries to record production activities in both departments during June.

Problem 11-11 (AICPA adapted, 5/64). Mantis Manufacturing Company manufactures a single product that passes through two departments: Extruding and Finishing-Packing. The product is shipped at the end of the day in which it is packed. The production in the Extruding and Finishing-Packing Departments does not increase the number of units started.

The cost and production data for January are as follows:

	Extruding Department	Finishing-Packing Department
Work in process, January 1:		
Cost from prior department		$60,200
Materials	$ 5,900	—
Labor	1,900	1,500
Overhead	1,400	2,000
Costs added during January:		
Materials	20,100	4,400
Labor	10,700	7,720
Overhead	8,680	11,830
Percentage of completion of work in process:		
January 1:		
Materials	70%	0%
Labor	50%	30%
Overhead	50%	30%
January 31:		
Materials	50%	0%
Labor	40%	35%
Overhead	40%	35%
January production data:		
Units in process, January 1	10,000	29,000
Units in process, January 31	8,000	6,000
Units started	20,000	22,000
Units transferred out	22,000	44,000

In the Extruding Department, materials are added at various phases of the process. All spoiled units are removed when inspection takes place at the end of the process.

In the Finishing-Packing Department, the materials added consist only of packing supplies. These materials are added at the midpoint of the process, when the packing operation begins. Cost studies have disclosed that one half of the labor and overhead costs apply to the finishing operation and one half to the packing operation. All spoiled units are removed when the product is inspected at the end of the finishing operation. All the work in process in this department at January 1 and January 31 was in the finishing operation phase of the manufacturing process.

The company uses the average costing method in its accounting system.

Required (1) Prepare EPU schedules for both departments.
(2) Prepare production flow diagrams for both departments, if applicable.
(3) Prepare a cost allocation schedule for each department for January.
(4) Record journal entries summarizing production activities in both departments during January.

Problem 11-12 (AICPA adapted, 11/58). King Company manufactures one product through two processes. For each unit of Process 1 output, 2 units of Material X are put in *at the beginning* of processing. For each unit of Process 2 output, 3 cans of Material Y are put in *at the end* of processing. For each unit of finished goods, two pounds of Process 1 output are placed in process at the beginning of Process 2. Normal spoilage occurs in Process 2, when processing is approximately 50% complete.

In process accounts are maintained for materials, conversion costs, and prior department costs. The company uses the fifo basis for inventory valuation for Process 1 and finished goods, and average cost for inventory valuation for Process 2.

The following data are available for March:

- Units transferred: From Process 1 to Process 2 .... 2,200 lbs.
  From Process 2 to finished goods .... 900 gals.
  From finished goods to cost of goods sold 600 gals.
- Units spoiled in Process 2: 100 gals.
- Materials unit costs: X .... $1.51 per unit
  Y .... $2 per can
- Conversion costs: Process 1 .... $3,344
  Process 2 .... $4,010
- Spoilage recovery: $100 (normal; treated as cost reduction)
- Inventory data:

	Process 1		Process 2		Finished Goods	
	Initial	Final	Initial	Final	Initial	Final
Units	200	300	200	300	700	1,000
Fraction complete as to conversion costs	1/2	1/3	1/2*	2/3		
Valuation of units:						
Materials	$560		0			
Conversion costs	108		$ 390			
Prior department costs			2,200			
Completed units					$13,300	

*All units inspected.

Required Journalize March entries to record the transfer of costs from Process 1 to Process 2 to finished goods, and from finished goods to cost of goods sold. Prepare schedules of computations to support entries.

Problem 11-13. Mark Manufacturing Company produces one product in two departments. Materials are placed in production at the beginning of processing in Department 1 and uniformly throughout Department 2. The materials placed in production in Department 2 do not increase the number of accountable units. Inventories are priced on a fifo basis in both Department 1 and Department 2. Inspection occurs at the 80% point of completion in Department 1 and at the 60% completion point in Department 2.

The following data are available:

	Department 1		Department 2	
	Initial	Final	Initial	Final
Units	400	250	700	1,200
% of completion:				
Materials	100%	100%	70%	30%
Conversion	60%	80%	70%	30%
Valuation:				
Prior department cost	—	—	$4,697	?
Materials	$960	?	275	?
Conversion	912	?	1,813	?

New units started in Department 1 were 11,400.

Units spoiled in Department 1 totaled 150, and in Department 2, 550. The spoiled units had no salvage value. In addition to the units discovered during normal inspection, a small fire destroyed 300 units of in process inventory in Department 1 during the month. The production supervisor estimates that these units were 20% complete at the time of the fire. Insurance will cover 80% of the value of the lost units. The loss will be treated as abnormal spoilage.

Costs incurred during the current period were:

	Department 1	Department 2
Materials purchased and issued	$27,816	$ 7,175 (excluding prior department cost)
Conversion costs	49,566	39,975

Finished goods inventory at the beginning of the month was 1,000 units, costing $11,430. Sales totaled 8,400 units of finished goods, priced on a lifo basis.

Required

(1) Prepare EPU schedules for both departments for the month.

(2) Prepare a production flow diagram for each department. (Pay particular attention to the cost of the units lost in the fire in Department 1.)

(3) Calculate the value of the Department 2 ending work in process inventory and the cost of goods sold for the month, using appropriate schedules. Carry unit costs to three decimal places and inventory values to the nearest dollar.

Problem 11-14 (AICPA adapted, 11/67). Crews Company produces a chemical agent for commercial use. The company accounts for production in two cost centers: (1) Cooking and (2) Mix-Pack. In the first cost center, liquid substances are combined in large cookers and boiled. The boiling causes a normal decrease in volume from evaporation. After the "batch" is cooked, it is transferred to Mix-Pack. A quantity of alcohol equal to the liquid measure of the "batch" is added. The "batch" is then mixed and bottled in one-gallon containers.

Materials are added at the beginning of production in each cost center, and labor is added during production in each cost center. Overhead is applied on the basis of 80% of labor cost. The "method of neglect" is used in accounting for spoiled units (that is, all costs are allocated only to equivalent good units). The process is "in control" as long as the yield ratio for the first department is not less than 78%.

The fifo method is used to cost work in process inventories, and transfers are at an average unit cost; i.e., the total cost transferred divided by the total number of units transferred.

The following information is available for October, 19X7:

	Cooking	Mix-Pack
Work in process, October 1, 19X7:		
Materials	$ 990	$ 120
Labor	100	60
Prior department cost		426
Month of October:		
Materials	39,600	15,276
Labor	10,050	16,000

Inventory and production records show that Cooking had 1,000 gallons, 40% processed on October 1, and 800 gallons, 50% processed on October 31. Mix-Pack had 600 gallons, 50% processed on October 1, and 1,000 gallons, 30% processed on October 31.

Production reports for October show that Cooking started 50,000 gallons into production and completed and transferred 40,200 gallons to Mix-Pack. Mix-Pack completed and transferred 80,000, one-gallon containers of the finished product to the distribution warehouse.

Required Prepare EPU schedules and cost allocation schedules for both cost centers, using the "method of neglect" to account for spoilage.

Problem 11-15 (AICPA adapted, 5/72). In the course of your examination of the financial statements of Zeus Company, for the year ended December 31, 19X1, you have gathered the following information about its manufacturing operations:

- Zeus had two production departments (Fabricating and Finishing) and a service department. In the Fabricating Department, polyplast is prepared from miracle mix and bypro. In the Finishing Department, each unit of polyplast is converted into six tetraplexes and three uniplexes. The service department provides services to both production departments.
- The Fabrication and Finishing Departments use process cost accounting systems. Actual production costs, including overhead, are allocated monthly. Spoilage is accounted for using the "method of neglect".
- Service department expenses are allocated to production departments, as follows:

Expense	Allocation Base
Building maintenance	Space occupied
Timekeeping and personnel	Number of employees
Other	1/2 to fabricating, 1/2 to finishing

- Materials inventory and work in process are priced on a fifo basis.
- The following data were taken from the Fabricating Department's records for December, 19X1:

Quantities (units of polyplast):

In process, December 1	3,000
Started in process during month	25,000
Total units to be accounted for	28,000
Transferred to Finishing Department	19,000
In process, December 31	6,000
Spoilage	3,000
Total units to be accounted for	28,000

Cost of work in process, December 1:

Materials	$13,000
Labor	17,500
Overhead	21,500
Total	$52,000
Direct labor costs, December	$154,000
Departmental overhead, December	$132,000

- Polyplast work in process at the beginning and at the end of the month was partially completed, as follows:

	Materials	Labor and Overhead
December 1	66 2/3%	50%
December 31	100 %	75%

- The following data were taken from materials inventory records for December:

	Miracle Mix		Bypro	
	Quantity	Amount	Quantity	Amount
Balance, December 1	62,000	$62,000	265,000	$18,550
Purchases:				
December 12	39,500	49,375		
December 20	28,500	34,200		
Fabricating Department				
usage	83,200		50,000	

- Service department expenses for December (not included in departmental overhead above) were:

Building maintenance	$ 45,000
Timekeeping and personnel	27,500
Other	39,000
Total	$111,500

- Other information for December, 19X1, is as follows:

	Square Feet of Space Occupied	Number of Employees
Fabricating	75,000	180
Finishing	37,500	120
	112,500	300

Required (1) Compute the equivalent number of units of polyplast manufactured during December, with separate calculations for materials and conversion costs (direct labor plus overhead).

(2) Prepare a cost allocation schedule for the Fabricating Department for December.

Twelve

Allocation of Joint Costs and Common Costs

Previous chapters of this text have shown how managers use cost accounting data for decision making, planning, and control. This chapter will examine how managers can deal with the special problems which are caused by joint costs (those costs arising from processing a single raw material which simultaneously yields several outputs) and common costs (those costs of a facility or activity whose services are simultaneously shared by several users). Although special emphasis will be given to decision-making implications, the traditional procedures used by accountants to allocate such costs to individual products will also be examined. A discussion of linear programming applications to joint products and joint costs is contained in Appendix 12A at the end of this chapter.

For most external accounting reports, it is necessary to assign all the manufacturing costs incurred by a firm (or a division or other organizational segment of a firm) to all goods produced, so that the inventories of unsold goods and the cost of goods sold are properly computed. In statements which are being prepared in accordance with generally accepted accounting principles, all manufacturing costs —whether direct or indirect, fixed or variable—must be assigned to the products manufactured. The Securities and Exchange Commission (SEC), the Internal Revenue Service (IRS), and other governmental agencies also impose similar requirements relating to reports and forms which they require.

For pricing and for informational purposes, management may also wish to allocate costs other than manufacturing costs (e.g., engineering, selling, and administrative costs) to product lines. When costs have been properly allocated, the performance of different segments may be compared in terms of their relative profitability, the operating performance of a division manager may be evaluated, or the profitability of a product may be determined by comparing its unit cost with its selling price.

ALLOCATION OF JOINT PRODUCTION COSTS

A significant allocation problem occurs when several products are created from a single source. In processing raw materials which occur naturally, several distinct and different products may be separated. In mining, for example, the same mineral lode which contains copper may also contain sizable amounts of silver. Processing ore from such a lode will produce both metals. Similarly, refining crude oil will yield fuel oil, gasoline, kerosene, and a variety of other petroleum products. In processing agricultural products or in slaughtering animals, multiple products will occur. At some point in the processing, called the split-off point, several different products emerge. The one or more products which have significant value are called the main products. Those which have negligible value are called by-products. If there are several main products, they are usually called joint products.

Although terminology differs somewhat from industry to industry and from one firm to another, the combined cost of the raw materials plus the costs of processing these materials up to the point of split-off will be referred to as joint costs. To illustrate how accountants deal with joint costs, assume that the seeds of a special flower variety are processed by Madison Corporation in a series of operations which ultimately yield both a refined, high-grade oil and a ground meal. The flower oil is used as a cooking oil, and the meal is used as a protein supplement in animal foods.

A diagram of Madison's operations is shown in Illustration 12-1. The flower seeds, purchased from area farmers at $100 per ton, are pressed in Department 1. Department 1's output per ton of seeds is two joint products: 12.5 gallons of raw oil weighing 200 pounds, and 1,800 pounds of seed cake. The split-off point is at the conclusion of the processing in Department 1, where the two joint products are first identifiable.

The raw oil is transferred to Department 2, where it is refined to remove certain impurities and bottled. The seed cake is transferred to Department 3, where it is ground and packaged in ten-pound boxes. A small amount of waste occurs in Department 3.

The cost accounting problem which this production process poses is how to divide or allocate the raw material and processing costs incurred in Department 1 prior to the split-off point. Separate costs for the oil and cake are required primarily in order to provide a basis for valuing work in process and finished goods inventories of oil, seed cake, and ground meal. The final costs of the joint products are also used to determine the amount to be charged to the cost of goods sold.

Illustration 12-1   Madison Corporation Manufacturing Operations

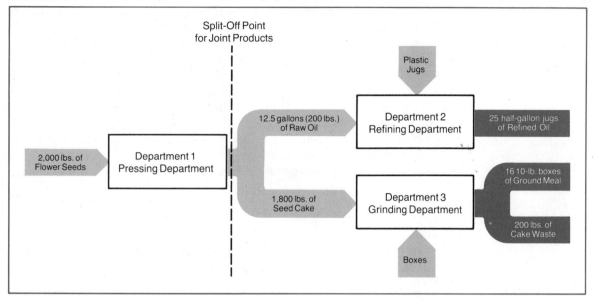

Management Decisions Involving Joint Products

The identifiable contribution margin is the relevant starting point for making rational economic decisions involving joint products. Because the allocation of joint costs among the joint products is arbitrary to a large extent, the allocations are of little value for most managerial applications and may lead to incorrect conclusions. Also, joint cost allocations are not required for most managerial applications if the joint products are produced in fixed proportions, as is the case for Madison Corporation. At best, using cost data which incorporate arbitrary allocations is cumbersome, since the data must be carefully evaluated in order to understand what effect the particular allocation method had on the analysis. In the following paragraphs, effective cost control in departments which produce joint products, and the approach to decision making involving joint products, will be examined.

Cost Control and Performance Evaluation. The only production department at Madison Corporation in which the existence of joint costs needs to be considered is Department 1. Both Departments 2 and 3 process a single input and produce a single output. To evaluate how well the manager in Department 1 keeps costs under control, the unit processing cost per ton of seed can be tracked on a daily, weekly, or monthly basis. This procedure is just as useful as monitoring the separate output costs per unit of cake and oil. Moreover, it is a simpler cost control system to operate.

Poor cost control may be the result of overspending, even though the amount of output from the production process is at the standard level for the amount of inputs processed. Excessive costs may also result from technical production inefficiencies in converting inputs to outputs, i.e., low yields. An increase in the current period's unit cost of outputs may be the result of either one or both of these factors, which most firms measure and report separately. To control overspending, the dollar cost per unit of input is reported. To monitor production efficiency, physical yield statistics (the ratio of outputs to inputs) are calculated and reported.

Cost reports designed to highlight overspending are usually adequate if they are prepared on a monthly basis, but production yields should be monitored on a weekly or daily basis. In line with this practice, Madison Corporation's Department 1 prepares monthly cost reports which show the cost per ton of seed processed, and daily production reports which show the yield of raw oil and seed cake per ton of seed. These actual yields are compared to the standard yields of 200 pounds of raw oil per ton and 1,800 pounds of seed cake per ton. Corrective action is taken when there are significant differences between the actual and standard yields.

Cost-Volume-Profit Analysis. In making decisions involving processes which produce joint products, it is important to know the effect on profit of changes in the scale or level of operations. Such cost-volume-profit analysis should be carried out using the combined revenues generated by all the joint products and the combined total costs. This analysis is similar to the CVP analysis for an entire firm, as described in Chapter 4.

The calculation of the break-even point is one means of analyzing the effect of a change in the level of operations. To calculate the break-even point for Madison Corporation, the variable costs and the fixed costs must be known. The analysis of Madison's cost structure is shown in Part A of Illustration 12-2. After this cost analysis has been completed, each product's identifiable contribution margin is computed, as shown in Part B, by subtracting the separable variable costs from that product's selling price. Separable costs are costs incurred after split-off that are identifiable with a single product.

Once the identifiable contribution margins are calculated, they are combined in order to obtain the amounts which are generated by processing one unit (i.e., one ton) of flower seed. The joint variable processing costs per ton of seed incurred in Department 1, along with any joint variable selling and administrative costs, are then subtracted from the combined contribution margin at split-off. The resulting value is the overall contribution margin achieved from processing one ton of seed and finishing and selling the resulting refined oil and ground meal. This overall contribution margin corresponds exactly to the concept of the contribution margin of a standard sales pack, which was developed in Chapter 4 for multiproduct situations.

Madison Corporation's break-even point is calculated, as shown in Part C of Illustration 12-2, by dividing the combined fixed costs of $129,500 per month by the combined contribution margin of $350 per ton. Madison Corporation must process 370 tons of flower seed per month and sell the resulting 9,250 jugs of refined oil and 59,200 boxes of ground meal in order to break even. The same variable and fixed cost information used to calculate Madison's break-even point can also be used in other cost-volume-profit calculations, such as determining the profits which would result from processing other volumes of flower seed or determining the activity level necessary to provide a specific amount of profit.

	Variable Costs	Fixed Costs
Department 1	$115.00 per ton of seed processed	$ 59,500 per month
Department 2	.50 per jug of oil processed	8,750
Department 3	.35 per box of meal processed	16,800
Selling and administrative costs	{ .20 per jug of oil sold .15 per box of meal sold }	44,450
Total		$129,500 per month

Illustration 12-2
Break-Even Analysis Involving Joint Products

Part A
Cost Structure

Illustration 12-2
Break-Even Analysis Involving Joint Products

Part B
Contribution Margin from Processing and Selling Oil and Meal

	Refined Oil	Ground Meal
Selling price	$6.50 per jug	$2.50 per box
Less identifiable variable costs:		
Department 2 costs	$ .50 per jug	—
Department 3 costs	—	$ .35 per box
Selling and administrative costs	.20	.15
Total	$ .70 per jug	$ .50 per box
Identifiable product contribution margin	$5.80 per jug	$2.00 per box

Total identifiable product contribution margin:

25 jugs per ton of seed × $5.80 per jug	$145	per ton of seed
160 boxes per ton of seed × $2 per box	320	
Less variable joint costs in Department 1	(115)	
Combined total contribution margin	$350	per ton of seed

---

Illustration 12-2
Break-Even Analysis Involving Joint Products

Part C
Combined Break-Even Point

$$\text{Break-even point} = \frac{\$129,500 \text{ per month combined fixed costs}}{\$350 \text{ per ton contribution margin}} = 370 \text{ tons per month}$$

Since each ton of seed produces 25 jugs of refined oil and 160 boxes of meal, this break-even level of activity corresponds to sales of 9,250 jugs (25 jugs × 370) of refined oil and 59,200 boxes (160 boxes × 370) of ground meal.

Processing a Joint Product Beyond the Split-Off Point. Although management cannot choose which joint products it will produce up to the split-off point, it can decide whether or not to process each joint product further. This decision should be based on a comparison of the identifiable product contribution margin at split-off, if the product is processed further, with the contribution margin generated by disposing of that joint product at split-off. The allocation of joint costs is irrelevant for this decision. The contribution margin that results from disposing of the joint product at split-off may be positive (if there is a strong market for the unprocessed joint product), zero (if the product can be dumped at zero cost), or negative (if the disposal costs exceed any revenues that might be generated).

In a regular monthly management meeting, Madison Corporation's president raised the question of whether its current practice of processing both joint products further was justified. In responding to this question, the controller commented that Madison's costs and selling prices (as shown in Illustration 12-2) reflected current conditions. In the marketing manager's opinion, the raw oil could probably be sold in bulk quantities for $1.75 per pound. However, no market is readily available for the seed cake. Madison's plant manager stated that if the seed cake was not processed into salable meal, it would be used as landfill for the rear of the acreage on which Madison's plant is located.

In deciding whether to process the raw oil further, Madison's controller compared the identifiable product contribution margin for the refined oil at split-off, $5.80 per half-gallon jug or 8 pounds of oil, with the contribution margin from selling 4 pounds of raw oil at $1.75 per pound. In this case, the contribution margin is the sales revenue of $7, since the additional costs of bulk sales of the raw oil would be negligible. Based on these data, Madison's profit could be increased by selling the raw oil in bulk at the split-off point, rather than processing it further and selling it as refined oil.

The controller also noted that a decision not to process the raw oil further would involve either shutting down the refining operations in Department 2 or converting this facility to other uses. Therefore, additional studies should be made in order to answer such questions as whether all the costs initially classified as variable could be eliminated, whether all the fixed costs would remain, what the net-of-tax impact from the sale of the equipment in Department 2 would be, and what alternative use might be found for the space and the employees currently involved in refining operations. The results of these studies indicated that further processing of the raw oil was desirable.

The discussion then turned to evaluating the further processing of the seed cake. It was clear that as long as the fixed costs did not change and as long as there was any identifiable contribution margin for ground meal, Madison would be better off processing the seed cake further. Since the current identifiable contribution margin is $2 per box, the sales price could drop from $2.50 per box to $.50 per box, or the variable costs after split-off could increase from $.50 to $2 per box before dumping the seed cake should be considered.

Joint Cost Allocations for Product Costing

As discussed in the previous section, the allocation of joint costs is not necessary for most managerial applications. For financial reporting purposes, however, such allocations are required in order to provide an acceptable product cost that includes both fixed and variable manufacturing costs.

The allocation methods commonly used by firms will be illustrated with the Madison Corporation data from Department 1, given in Illustration 12-2. The combined variable and fixed costs of $200 per ton will be allocated. The $115 per ton variable cost includes materials ($100 per ton), direct labor ($10 per ton), and variable manufacturing overhead ($5 per ton). The unit fixed cost ($85 per ton) results from dividing the monthly fixed costs of Department 1, $59,500, by the normal monthly production activity, 700 tons. Although the variable costs and the fixed costs could be allocated separately to each joint product, very little useful information would be provided in this instance.

Physical Units Method. One way of allocating the joint costs incurred prior to split-off is to calculate a single unit cost which would apply to the joint products. For Madison Corporation, the average cost per pound of output in Department 1 (raw oil and seed cake) is $.10 ($200 per ton joint cost ÷ 2,000 pounds). Therefore, 10% of the Department 1 costs will be assigned to the raw oil, since the 200 pounds of raw oil represent 10% of the total output from a ton of flower seeds. Similarly, 90% of the joint costs will be assigned to the seed cake.

Although the physical units method is simple, it allocates the same cost to each unit. Since a pound of raw oil is much more valuable than a pound of seed cake, for example, it may be more reasonable to allocate more of the joint cost to the oil and less to the seed cake. Moreover, when an average cost is assigned to a joint product with little commercial value, the cost of the product may exceed the net realizable value. The generally accepted accounting principle that inventories must be valued at the lower of cost or market would rule out such a cost allocation.

Weighted Physical Units Method. A way of assigning more cost to the raw oil is to use a weighted average cost, rather than a simple average. The weights can be chosen in such a way that the more valuable products are given larger weights. Such weighted physical unit allocations are used in the oil refining industry, where the relative BTUs (energy content) of the joint products are used as the weighting factors.

Since a higher caloric content is one factor that makes Madison Corporation's raw oil more valuable than the seed cake, the controller was asked to give consideration to the differing number of calories per pound in the two products. Using the weighted physical units method, Madison Corporation's joint cost of $200 would be allocated as shown in Illustration 12-3. The physical quantities of raw oil and seed cake are first multiplied by the caloric content of each product. The weighted quantities are then summed, and the proportion of the total accounted for by each product is determined. Since raw oil accounts for 31.87% of the total caloric content, $63.74 (31.87% × $200), or $.3187 per pound ($63.74 ÷ 200 pounds), is allocated to the oil. A similar calculation for the seed cake results in an allocation of $.0757 per pound. Thus, a pound of raw oil, which has more than four times the caloric content of a pound of seed cake, is allocated a joint cost that is also more than four times as large as the amount allocated per pound to the seed cake.

Illustration 12-3
Weighted Physical Units
Method of Joint Cost
Allocation

Joint Products	(1) Quantities Produced per Ton of Seed	(2) Joint Product Caloric Contents	(3) Weighted Quantities [(1) × (2)]	(4) Percent of Total	(5) Total Joint Cost Allocation [$200 × (4)]	(6) Joint Cost Allocations per Pound [(5) ÷ (1)]
Raw oil	200 lbs.	4,000 calories per lb.	800,000	31.87%	$ 63.74	
Seed cake	1,800	950	1,710,000	68.13	136.26	
Total	2,000 lbs.		2,510,000	100.00%	$200.00	

Relative Sales Value Method. While the caloric content is one important factor which influences the relative value of Madison Corporation's joint products, other factors are also important. A direct way of insuring that the unit costs assigned to the two joint products are proportional to their market value is to use the unit selling prices at split-off as the weights. This relative sales value method of joint cost allocation is one of the most commonly used allocation methods.

To illustrate the relative sales value method, assume that Madison could sell the raw oil in bulk for $.50 per pound and the seed cake for $.11 per pound. The total relative value accounted for by each of the joint products at the split-off point is calculated as shown in Illustration 12-4. This value is then used to allocate the $200 joint cost. The amount allocated to the raw oil, $.3356 per pound, reflects exactly the proportionately higher selling price of the oil.

Joint Products	(1) Quantities Produced per Ton of Seed	(2) Unit Selling Prices	(3) Total Sales Value [(1) × (2)]	(4) Percent of Total	(5) Total Joint Cost Allocation [$200 × (4)]	(6) Joint Cost Allocations per Pound [(5) ÷ (1)]
Raw oil	200 lbs.	$.50 per lb.	$100	33.56%	$ 67.12	
Seed cake	1,800	.11	198	66.44	132.88	
Total	2,000 lbs.		$298	100.00%	$200.00	

A consequence of using the relative sales value method is that each product will show the same gross profit percentage. For Madison Corporation, the gross profit is 33% of the selling price, as shown in the following calculation:

Products	(1) Selling Prices	(2) Unit Costs	(3) Gross Profit	(4) Gross Profit as a Percentage of Selling Price [(3) ÷ (1)]
Raw oil	$.50	$.3356	$.1644	33%
Seed cake	.11	.0738	.0362	33

If the joint products are always produced from the raw materials in fixed proportions, which is the case at Madison Corporation, management has no other choice but to accept this mix of output. In such situations, it is reasonable to allocate the joint costs in such a way as to make the joint gross profit percentage for each product equal to the overall gross profit percentage realized on the sale of all products.

Relative Net Realizable Value Method. For the relative sales value method, it was assumed that a market existed for the joint products at the point of split-off. However, there is often no readily available market for partially processed items. If Madison Corporation is unable to find a buyer for its semiprocessed products, it can approximate a selling price at split-off by computing the net realizable value of each product at the split-off point. The net realizable value is the sales revenue from the finished product, less the additional identifiable variable and fixed manufacturing, selling, and administrative costs incurred between the split-off point and the sale.

To calculate the net realizable value for Madison Corporation, the manufacturing costs incurred in Departments 2 and 3, as well as the selling and administrative expenses which relate to the refined oil and the ground meal, must be known. Part A of Illustration 12-5 shows the separate costs incurred after the split-off point for each product. Deducting these costs per unit incurred after split-off from the selling price gives the net realizable value per unit for each product: $5 per jug for refined oil and $1.50 per box for ground meal. Since each 200-pound batch of raw oil yields 25 jugs of refined oil, the total net realizable value of the oil is $125 (25 jugs × $5) per ton of seed processed. Similarly, since each 1,800-pound batch of seed cake yields 160 ten-pound boxes of ground meal, the total net realizable value of the meal is $240 (160 boxes × $1.50) per ton of seed processed. (Two hundred pounds of cake waste per ton of seed are also generated in the grinding operation, but this cake waste has no commercial value.)

Part B of Illustration 12-5 shows the allocation of the joint cost, using the relative net realizable values of the two joint products. Compared to the values computed using the relative sales value method, the net realizable value method allocates slightly more cost to the raw oil and slightly less to the seed cake.

The use of net realizable values in the allocation of joint costs represents the hypothetical sales values of the joint products at split-off when there is no ready market for the unprocessed products at that point. Although the products appear to be equally profitable when profits are computed as a percent of the net realizable value at split-off (column 8 in Part C of Illustration 12-5), the various joint products will typically not show the same percentages when profits are more commonly expressed as a percentage of selling price. If the same gross profit as a percent of sales were desired, the overall gross profit percentage for all products would be determined. An amount of joint cost would then be assigned to each product, so that in combination with that product's identifiable separable cost, the desired average gross profit percentage would result.

Costing By-Products

If a product manufactured jointly with others has little or no value, it is usually referred to as a **by-product**. By-products are similar to scrap, and are accounted for with procedures similar to those used for scrap.

If the cake waste produced in Department 3 of Madison Corporation can be sold for some small amount, such as 10% of the ground meal revenue, Madison will probably treat the cake waste as a by-product. If the waste can be sold for much more than 10% of the meal revenue, Madison will account for the waste as a joint product. If the waste can be sold for only a nominal amount or not at all, Madison will treat it as scrap, crediting Manufacturing Overhead for the cash received at the time the cake waste is sold.

Since the amount of revenue realized from the sale of by-products is not significant, firms devote little attention to developing elaborate or theoretically correct accounting procedures for dealing with them. As a result, a wide variety of accounting procedures are used for by-products.

Entries relating to by-products may be recorded at the time the by-products are produced, or deferred until the by-products are sold. In the latter case, no inventories of unsold by-products would appear on the books. A by-product may be valued at its sales price, at its net realizable value (if there are identifiable separable costs associated with disposing of it), at its disposal value reduced by a profit margin, or at the replacement cost of a comparable substitute (if the by-product is used internally). Some firms credit the cost of a by-product to the main product (often by crediting Manufacturing Overhead). Others credit By-Product Revenue or Other Income—By-Product Sales.

Illustration 12-6 shows two common methods of accounting for by-products, *Ch. 12* using data for the 200 pounds of cake waste produced by Madison Corporation's

Illustration 12-5   Relative Net Realizable Value Method of Joint Cost Allocation, Using Net Realizable Values at Split-Off
Part A   Unit Net Realizable Value of Joint Products at Split-Off

	Refined Oil	Ground Meal
Selling price	$6.50 per half-gallon (4-lb.) jug	$2.50 per 10-lb. box
Less unit costs incurred subsequent to split-off:		
Department 2 processing costs	$1.00 per jug	—
Department 3 processing costs	—	$ .50 per box
Selling and administrative costs	.50	.50
Total separable costs	$1.50 per jug	$1.00 per box
Net realizable value	$5.00 per jug	$1.50 per box
Total net realizable value from processing 1 ton of flower seed:		
25 jugs of oil @ $5 per jug	$125	
160 boxes of meal @ $1.50 per box		$240

Illustration 12-5   Relative Net Realizable Value Method of Joint Cost Allocation, Using Net Realizable Values at Split-Off
Part B   Joint Cost Allocation

Unprocessed Joint Products	(1) Quantity of Unprocessed Joint Products per Ton of Seed	(2) Net Realizable Values of Unprocessed Joint Products	(3) Percent of Total	(4) Total Joint Cost Allocation [$200 × (3)]	(5) Unit Joint Cost Allocation [(4) ÷ (1)]
Raw oil	200 lbs.	$125	34.25%	$ 68.50	$.3425 per lb.
Seed cake	1,800	240	65.75	131.50	.0731
	2,000	$365	100.00%	$200.00	

Illustration 12-5   Relative Net Realizable Value Method of Joint Cost Allocation, Using Net Realizable Values at Split-Off
Part C   Relative Profitability of Finished Joint Products

Finished Joint Products	(1) Selling Prices	(2) Dept. 1 Joint Costs	(3) Dept. 2 Unit Costs	(4) Dept. 3 Unit Costs
Refined oil	$6.50 per jug	$2.7400 per jug[a]	$1 per jug	—
Ground meal	2.50 per box	.8224 per box[b]	—	$.50 per box

(5) Unit Selling and Administrative Expenses	(6) Total Unit Costs	(7) Unit Net Profit	(8) Profit as a Percent of Net Realizable Value	(9) Profit as a % of Selling Price [(7) ÷ (1)]
$.50 per jug	$4.2400	$2.2600 per jug	45.2%[c]	34.8%
$.50 per box	$1.8224	.6776 per box	45.2 [d]	27.1

[a] $\frac{200 \text{ lbs. of oil @ \$.3425 per lb.}}{25 \text{ jugs of refined oil}} = \frac{\$68.50}{25} = \$2.7400 \text{ per jug}$

[b] $\frac{1,800 \text{ lbs. of cake @ \$.0731 per lb.}}{160 \text{ boxes of ground meal}} = \frac{\$131.58}{160} = \$.8224 \text{ per box}$

[c] $\frac{\$2.26}{\$5.00} = 45.2\%$

[d] $\frac{\$.6776}{\$1.50} = 45.2\%$

manufacturing process. It is assumed that one half of the product was sold at $.05 per pound in the week it was produced, and the remainder was sold in the following week. Both methods credit the net sales value of the by-product to Manufacturing Overhead. In Method A, however, no entry is made until the by-product is sold, while in Method B, the inventory of by-product is recorded at its sales value when it is produced. Since no profit results from the sale of the by-product, the sale in Method B is credited directly to the inventory account to simplify the bookkeeping, rather than using special revenue and cost of goods sold accounts for the by-products.

Illustration 12-6
Accounting for
By-Products

	Method A		Method B	
Week 1				
Production of 200 lbs. of by-product	No entry		By-Product Inventory	10
			Manufacturing Overhead—Dept. 3		10
Sale of 100 lbs. of				
by-product	Cash	5	Cash	5
	Manufacturing Overhead—Dept. 3	5	By-Product Inventory		5
Week 2				
Sale of 100 lbs. of				
by-product	Cash	5	Cash	5
	Manufacturing Overhead—Dept. 3	5	By-Product Inventory		5

ALLOCATION OF SERVICE DEPARTMENT COSTS

Prior chapters have emphasized the accounting for production department costs, since these costs are used to determine the costs of the products and services which an organization provides to its customers or clients. For management purposes, however, it is usually desirable to organize a firm in such a way that there are service departments as well as production departments. Service departments provide their output to other production and/or service departments within the organization. The output of service departments is typically a service and not a physical product.

Nonmanufacturing firms have the equivalent of production and service departments, although the terminology used is often different. Hospital wards in a general hospital are analogous to production departments in a manufacturing firm, while the hospital's accounting department is a service department.

Madison Corporation has three service departments in its plant, in addition to its three production departments. Department R maintains and repairs factory equipment in the three production departments, Department A is the accounting department, and Department P is the personnel office. A diagram of Madison's departmental structure is shown in Illustration 12-7.

The cost accounting procedures for production departments and service departments are essentially the same. For control purposes, costs should be accumulated in departmental accounts, so that each department manager can be held responsible for the department's costs. For product costing purposes, however, the costs of service departments in the plant must be treated as manufacturing overhead, and the total manufacturing overhead for all departments must be allocated

Illustration 12-7
Madison Corporation's
Departmental Structure

to production departments. Such allocations are necessary in order to establish the cost of each product for valuing work in process and finished goods inventories and for computing the cost of goods sold for the period.

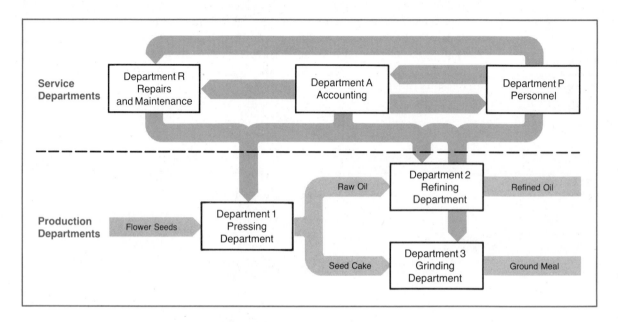

Allocation of Variable Service Department Overhead Costs

For most managerial purposes, the costs that are variable must be distinguished from those that are fixed. Therefore, it is important to adopt accounting procedures which will keep the two types of costs separate. Since variable costs are most often needed in managerial decision making, more elaborate procedures can be justified in accounting for variable costs, while simpler procedures will suffice for fixed costs. The following paragraphs develop accounting procedures for dealing with variable costs. These procedures, or simple modifications of them, can then be used in accounting for fixed overhead costs.

Plantwide Variable Overhead Rate. The simplest procedure for developing the variable overhead component of a product's cost is to accumulate the total variable manufacturing overhead for the year in a single variable overhead cost pool. This total can then be used to establish a single plantwide overhead rate based on plantwide direct labor or some other appropriate allocation base. To illustrate, assume that Madison Corporation's total variable manufacturing overhead is estimated to be $394,800 for the coming year, as shown in Illustration 12-8. When this amount is divided by the total direct labor cost in all three production departments, $218,400, a plantwide rate of 180.77% of direct labor cost is obtained. This rate is used in costing the work in process inventories in the three production departments, as well as in arriving at the costs of producing the refined oil and ground meal.

Illustration 12-8   Annual Manufacturing Overhead Costs and Allocation Bases*

	Service Departments			Production Departments			Total Plant
	Dept. R	Dept. A	Dept. P	Dept. 1	Dept. 2	Dept. 3	
Variable overhead cost directly incurred in each department	$ 30,000	$ 25,000	$ 45,000	$ 44,662	$ 17,724	$232,414	$ 394,800
Fixed overhead cost directly incurred in each department	100,000	80,000	50,000	597,122	55,557	137,921	1,020,600
Total manufacturing overhead	$130,000	$105,000	$ 95,000	$641,784	$ 73,281	$370,335	$1,415,400
Direct labor cost	—	—	—	$ 42,000	$ 42,000	$134,400	$ 218,400
Statistical information:							
Hours spent by repair crews	—	—	—	1,000	600	400	2,000
Factory vouchers processed by the Accounting Department	1,000	400	900	4,000	1,500	2,600	10,400
Number of employees	20	30	15	45	45	110	265
Plant equipment costs				$2,000,000	$1,040,000	$960,000	$4,000,000

* Data based on processing 8,400 tons of flower seed and finishing the resulting 210,000 jugs of oil and 1,344,000 boxes of ground meal.

. While the use of a plantwide variable overhead rate satisfies the minimum accounting objective of charging all variable manufacturing overhead costs to production, it is deficient with respect to controlling costs. This method does not require the accumulation of overhead costs by department. Even if a departmental accumulation procedure were used, the control of service department overhead costs would still pose a special problem. As long as no service department overhead is charged to the other departments using the services, the managers of the other departments will tend to use excessive amounts of these "free" services. Excessive demands can result in soaring service department costs, and if the plant manager tries to limit the total amount of service department costs which can be incurred, formal rationing schemes (quotas) or informal rationing schemes (such as filling requests on a first-come, first-serve basis) will need to be devised. These rationing schemes may result in unfair and/or suboptimal provisions of services to the user departments as well as long delays in providing services.

The use of plantwide overhead rates is also deficient with respect to decision making. If the marketing managers at Madison Corporation set product prices on the basis of product costs that reflect the overall average plantwide overhead rate, some products may be underpriced and others may be overpriced. The products which are manufactured in departments that have a high ratio of variable overhead cost to labor cost (such as ground meal in Department 3) will tend to be underpriced, while products requiring small amounts of variable overhead in their processing (such as refined oil in Department 2) will be overpriced. The overpriced oil would likely cause some customers to purchase from firms that determine their product costs more accurately.

The Direct Method. To avoid the problems associated with the use of a single plantwide overhead rate, individual production department overhead rates can be used. Individual rates provide more accurate costs because each production department's activity measure (the denominator in the overhead rate calculation) can be selected so that the overhead base (such as labor hours, machine hours, or materials weight) is the one most closely associated with variations in overhead in that department.

The simplest method of establishing separate overhead rates for production departments is called the direct method. With this method, the overhead of each service department is allocated directly to the various production departments, ignoring any services which one service department might provide to other service departments. An overhead base is chosen for each service department according to the workload caused by, and the services rendered to, the other departments.

Illustration 12-9 shows the allocation of service department overhead for Madison Corporation, using the direct method. Since the major activity of Department R is to repair and maintain the production equipment in the factory, the number of hours spent by repair crews in each department is chosen as the overhead base for Department R. The number of factory vouchers processed for each department is chosen as a reasonable measure of the workload for Department A, and the number of employees is the overhead base used for Department P. The resulting service department overhead allocation rates are $15 per hour of repair time for Department R, $3.08642 per voucher processed for Department A, and $225 per employee for Department P. When these rates are used to allocate the costs of the three service departments to the production departments, the overhead allocated represents 195.55%, 98.76%, and 201.78% of the direct labor costs for Departments 1, 2, and 3, respectively. These percentages are in sharp contrast to the 180.77% plantwide variable overhead rate.

Illustration 12-9
Direct Method of Allocating Service Department Overhead Costs

	Service Departments			Production Departments			Total Plant
	Dept. R	Dept. A	Dept. P	Dept. 1	Dept. 2	Dept. 3	
Variable overhead cost directly incurred in each department	$30,000	$25,000	$45,000	$ 44,662	$17,724	$232,414	$394,800
Allocation of R[a]	(30,000)	—	—	15,000	9,000	6,000	—
Allocation of A[b]	—	(25,000)		12,345	4,630	8,025	—
Allocation of P[c]	—		(45,000)	10,125	10,125	24,750	—
Total variable overhead after allocation of service departments	–0–	–0–	–0–	$ 82,132	$41,479	$271,189	$394,800
Total direct labor cost				$ 42,000	$42,000	$134,400	$218,400
Production department variable overhead rates based on direct labor cost				195.55%	98.76%	201.78%	

[a] Department R overhead rate: $30,000 ÷ 2,000 hours = $15 per hour
[b] Department A overhead rate: $25,000 ÷ 8,100 vouchers = $3.08642 per voucher
[c] Department P overhead rate: $45,000 ÷ 200 employees = $225 per employee

The Step Method. Although the direct method is an improvement on the crude costing that results from a single plantwide rate, it is deficient from a cost control standpoint. No service department manager has any incentive to limit demands for the services of other service departments. To deal with this problem, the step, or

step-down, method is commonly used. The step method is so named because the allocation proceeds in a series of steps. In each step, one service department's costs are closed out by allocating its accumulated overhead to production departments and to other service departments whose costs have not yet been closed.

Since no overhead is allocated to a service department whose costs have been closed out in a prior step, the order in which the service departments are closed out is important. A service department's costs allocated in the first step will be allocated to all other service departments, while a service department's costs allocated in the last step will not be allocated to any other service department. Since different sequences will give different production department overhead rates, simple rules of thumb are often used to sequence the departments in such a way that those departments which provide the most services to other departments, relative to the amounts they receive, are allocated first.

A popular method of allocating service department overhead is by relative size, with the largest department's cost allocated first. If this method is applied to Madison Corporation, however, there is still a problem of determining which department's costs to allocate first. Department P incurs the largest amount of variable overhead costs, but Department R incurs the largest amount of total manufacturing overhead. To avoid this problem, Madison sequences the steps to give consideration to the relative amount of net services provided by each service department to the others. When this procedure is followed, Department R's costs should clearly be allocated in the last step, since it provides no services to the other service departments. Both Department A and Department P service each other, but considering the relative amount of P's directly incurred variable costs, more of P's cost will be allocated to A than vice versa. Accordingly, P's costs will be allocated in Step 1, A's costs in Step 2, and then R's costs in Step 3.

Illustration 12-10 shows the detailed computations involved in the allocation of service department overhead for Madison Corporation, using the step method. To highlight the mechanics of the allocation process, the service departments are listed in columns from left to right in the order in which their costs are allocated. In each step, an overhead rate is computed for the service department whose costs are to be closed out in that step. The numerator for that rate consists of the overhead costs directly incurred by that department, plus all the overhead costs allocated to that department in previous steps. To determine the denominator, the portions of the overhead base which relate to itself as well as to departments closed out in previous steps are eliminated from the total base.

In Step 1 in Illustration 12-10, only Department P's own overhead costs appear in the numerator, and only Department P's employees are eliminated from the base. In Step 2, the $5,400 allocated from Department P to Department A is added to the $25,000 of overhead directly incurred in Department A to give a total cost pool of $30,400. This cost pool is then allocated to Departments R, 1, 2, and 3, using an overhead rate based on the 9,100 vouchers from those four departments. In the third step, the total cost pool of Department R, which now includes allocations from Departments P and A, is allocated to the three production departments. After the third step has been completed, all the service department overhead will have been assigned to the production departments. The departmental overhead rates for the production departments are then calculated.

	Service Departments			Production Departments			Total Plant
	Dept. P	Dept. A	Dept. R	Dept. 1	Dept. 2	Dept. 3	
Variable overhead cost directly incurred in each department	$45,000	$25,000	$30,000	$44,662	$17,724	$232,414	$394,800
Allocation of P[a]	(45,000)	5,400	3,600	8,100	8,100	19,800	—
Allocation of A[b]	—	(30,400)	3,340	13,363	5,011	8,686	—
Allocation of R[c]	—	—	(36,940)	18,470	11,082	7,388	—
Total variable overhead after allocation of service departments	–0–	–0–	–0–	$84,595	$41,917	$268,288	$394,800
Total direct labor cost				$42,000	$42,000	$134,400	$218,400
Production department variable overhead rates based on direct labor cost				201.42%	99.80%	199.62%	

[a] Department P overhead rate: $45,000 ÷ 250 employees = $180 per employee
[b] Department A overhead rate: ($25,000 + 5,400) ÷ 9,100 vouchers = $3.34066 per voucher
[c] Department R overhead rate: ($30,000 + $3,600 + $3,340) ÷ 2,000 hours = $18.47 per repair hour

For Madison Corporation, the rates obtained with the step method (201.42%, 99.80%, and 199.62% for Departments 1, 2, and 3, respectively) correspond more closely to the correct production department rates than do the rates calculated by the direct method. The step method may not produce more accurate rates in every case, however. Since both the direct method and the step method systematically ignore some or all of the services provided by service departments to each other, neither method should be relied upon to provide accurate, detailed information for decision-making purposes. If the differences between the production department rates which result from using the direct method and the step method are not large, the choice between the two methods may not be critical. For inventory costing purposes, either method is satisfactory.

The Reciprocal Services Method. To obtain the most useful service department rates and the most accurate production department overhead rates for decision-making purposes, the reciprocal services, or simultaneous equation, method of overhead allocation should be used. With this method, the overhead costs of each service department are expressed in equation form, and then the complete set of equations is solved simultaneously. The solution provides the amount of each department's overhead costs after all relevant service department costs have been allocated. Although a few equations can be solved manually without much difficulty, practical applications involving a large number of service departments normally require the use of a computer. With standard program packages for solving linear equations, the accountant needs only to set up the allocation problem in equation form. A discussion of the use of matrix algebra and computer programs to solve overhead allocation problems is contained in Appendix 12B at the end of this chapter.

Although there are six departments at Madison Corporation, only two departments, P and A, provide services to and receive services from each other. Accordingly, equations will be needed only for these two departments. These equations, which describe the costs after allocation of the other service department, are as follows:

$$P = \frac{900}{10,000} A + \$45,000 \qquad A = \frac{30}{250} P + \$25,000$$

Part A of Illustration 12-11 shows the solution of these two equations. Part B uses these values (P = \$47,766 and A = \$30,732) in the allocation of service department costs to the other service department and to the three production departments. The sequence of the allocation is immaterial, since the simultaneous equation solutions insure that the resulting overhead allocations are mutually consistent.

$$P = \frac{9}{100} A + 45,000 = .09A + 45,000 \qquad (1)$$

$$A = \frac{30}{250} P + 25,000 = .12P + 25,000 \qquad (2)$$

Substituting equation (2) into equation (1):
$$P = .09(.12P + 25,000) + 45,000 \qquad (3)$$

Simplifying and solving for P:
$$P = 47,766 \qquad (4)$$

Substituting this value for P into equation (2):
$$A = .12(47,766) + 25,000 = 30,732 \qquad (5)$$

Illustration 12-11   Reciprocal Services Method of Allocating Service Department Overhead Costs
Part B   Allocation of Service Department Variable Overhead, Using Simultaneous Equation Solutions

	Service Departments			Production Departments			Total Plant
	Dept. P	Dept. A	Dept. R	Dept. 1	Dept. 2	Dept. 3	
Variable overhead cost directly incurred in each department	\$45,000	\$25,000	\$30,000	\$44,662	\$17,724	\$232,414	\$394,800
Allocation of Dept. P[a]	(47,766)	5,732	3,821	8,598	8,598	21,017	—
Allocation of Dept. A[b]	2,766	(30,732)	3,073	12,293	4,610	7,990	—
Allocation of Dept. R[c]	—	—	(36,894)	18,447	11,068	7,379	—
Total variable overhead after allocation of service departments	–0–	–0–	–0–	\$84,000	\$42,000	\$268,800	\$394,800
Total direct labor cost				\$42,000	\$42,000	\$134,400	\$218,400
Production department variable overhead rates based on direct labor cost				200%	100%	200%	

[a] Department P variable overhead rate: \$47,766 ÷ 250 employees = \$191.064 per employee
[b] Department A variable overhead rate: \$30,732 ÷ 10,000 vouchers = \$3.0732 per voucher
[c] Department R variable overhead rate: \$36,894 ÷ 2,000 hours = \$18.447 per repair hour

The equations constructed to show the total overhead after allocation of Departments P and A follow the common practice of ignoring the services provided by a service department to itself. Likewise, the portion of the overhead base which applies to Department A, 400 vouchers, is ignored in computing the total overhead base, leaving 10,000 vouchers as the denominator for allocating Department A costs to other departments. Also, the 15 employees in Department P are not *Ch. 12* included in the 250-employee base used in allocating Department P costs to other departments.

If the portion of the overhead base relating to itself were to be included, the costs after allocation of each service department which provides some services to itself would be larger than if no costs were associated with such self-service. Although the numerator (the total costs to be allocated) used in computing the overhead rate of a service department increases, the denominator (which is a measure of the total amount of services provided) increases in exactly the same proportion, leaving the overhead rate the same as it would be if self-service were to be ignored. Thus, the overhead rates for the production departments, as well as the product costs based on those rates, will be the same. To illustrate, if Madison does not ignore self-service, the equations, solutions, and overhead rates for P and A will be as follows:

$$P = \frac{900}{10,400}A + \frac{15}{265}P + \$45,000; \ P = \$50,631.79$$

$$A = \frac{30}{265}P + \frac{400}{10,400}A + \$25,000; \ A = \$31,961.22$$

Department P variable overhead rate: $\dfrac{\$50,631.79}{265\,\text{employees}} = \$191.064\,\text{per employee}$

Department A variable overhead rate: $\dfrac{\$31,961.22}{10,400\,\text{vouchers}} = \$3.0732\,\text{per voucher}$

Since the overhead rates are the same, the inclusion of self-service is not important for most decision-making and product-costing purposes. For cost control in a service department, however, self-service should be included in order to give the manager of the service department an incentive to economize on the use of the department's own services.

Managerial Implications of Service Department Cost Allocations

In many cases, needed services can either be provided by a service department internally or acquired from an outside firm. If management decides to acquire the services from an outside firm, the service department may no longer be needed. The effect of service department cost allocations on these decisions is discussed in the following paragraphs.

Purchasing Services or Providing Them Internally. Although many factors need to be considered before deciding whether to purchase services or provide them internally, the relative costs of the two sources of services are of major importance. The first step in the decision process is to compare the total variable costs of the two alternatives. To illustrate, assume that Madison Corporation is considering the offer of a local accounting firm to perform certain portions of Madison's accounting. Transactions involving 3,060 vouchers in the three production departments would be processed by the outside firm. The accounting firm agrees that the number of vouchers processed is a satisfactory measure of the workload volume, and offers to do the work for a fee of $3.25 per voucher. If the offer is accepted, microcomputers will be placed in Madison's factory office and operated by employees of the accounting firm. Data on magnetic disks compatible with Madison's computer system, as well as hard-copy reports, will be provided.

When the reciprocal services method of allocation is used, a direct comparison can be made between the variable overhead rate calculated in Illustration 12-11, $3.0732 per voucher, and the charge proposed by the outside firm, $3.25 per voucher. A direct comparison of the outside charge with the rates determined by the direct method or the step method would not be useful, since the rates derived by these methods are incorrect. The direct method ignores all of the work done by both the personnel and the accounting departments for all three service departments. The step method gives an incorrect rate for Department A, since the allocation of Department P's costs to A includes only costs directly incurred by Department P.

In addition to determining whether variable cost savings would occur, Madison Corporation should consider whether fixed costs would remain unchanged. Other factors not quantified in dollar terms, such as quality, speed of processing, and flexibility, should also be considered. If the fixed costs will not change and if there are no significant qualitative benefits to offset the increased variable costs of performing the accounting service externally, Madison should reject the outside firm's offer.

Discontinuing the Operations of a Service Department. In evaluating the consequences of eliminating a service department, the following steps are involved:

1. Compare the variable costs which would be eliminated with the charge for acquiring the service outside the firm.
2. Determine the reduction in fixed costs which would occur if the service department were to be eliminated.
3. Evaluate the impact of qualitative factors.

These steps are identical to those involved in the decision to purchase the service externally. However, the analysis of discontinuing a service department must be much more detailed, because the cost function for the service department is, in effect, being evaluated at a zero volume level. This level is well outside the relevant range for the usual linear cost function.

To illustrate the analysis, assume that Madison Corporation is considering a plan to eliminate Department A. As a first approximation, the variable cost which would be eliminated is the $25,000 cost now incurred directly by Department A. To this amount would be added the variable cost savings generated by reducing the size of Department P, because that department will discontinue service to Department A. Of the 250 employees outside of Department P, 30 are in Department A. Eliminating these 30 employees would reduce the personnel demands by 12% (30 ÷ 250). Accordingly, the total reduction in variable costs would be $30,400 [$25,000 + (12% × $45,000)]. This initial approximation must be reviewed carefully, since Madison may not be able to eliminate these variable costs completely. For instance, the variable labor costs in Department A will probably not drop to zero, since termination costs may be incurred if employees are laid off, and retraining costs may be incurred if these employees are transferred to other duties.

The $30,400 reduction in variable costs from eliminating Department A would be compared to the additional variable costs for purchasing the accounting services externally at $3.25 per voucher. Because Department P would need to be only 88% of its former size, it could be assumed that P will also generate proportionately fewer vouchers. The elimination of 108 Department P vouchers (12% of 900 vouchers), along with the elimination of 400 Department A vouchers, reduces the total number of vouchers to be processed from 10,400 to 9,892. The cost of 9,892 vouchers at $3.25 per voucher is $32,149, which is $1,749 more than the $30,400 in variable costs that were generated by the existence of Department A.

The next step in the analysis is to consider fixed costs. Although a reduction in the size of a service department may not change the fixed costs, the elimination of an entire department will undoubtedly free up fixed resources, including floor space, equipment, and supervisory personnel. If the equipment is sold or leased, if personnel are laid off, or if some of the resources are put to alternative uses, additional cash inflows or reductions in cash outflows will add to the variable cost savings. The qualitative factors which have not been directly incorporated in the analysis should then be considered, as discussed previously.

Allocation of Fixed Service Department Overhead Costs

Fixed service department costs can be allocated to products, departments, and activities, using the same procedures as were used in allocating variable costs. A single plantwide overhead rate for fixed costs can be established, or separate fixed overhead departmental rates can be calculated for each production department. If departmental rates are desired, then fixed costs of service departments can be allocated to the individual production departments, using the direct method, the step method, or the reciprocal services method. Although fixed costs need to be allocated for product costing purposes, such an allocation accomplishes little with respect to providing decision-making information.

Although the basic procedures for allocating fixed service department overhead costs are the same as for allocating variable costs, the specific fixed overhead base may be different from the variable overhead base. The variable overhead of a department for a given period represents the cost of resources consumed in providing the actual amount of services demanded in that period. Budgeted (or actual) variable costs for a period would be allocated in proportion to the actual demands expected (or realized) during that period. The fixed overhead of a department, on the other hand, usually represents the cost of the physical and organizational capability to provide certain services, up to some peak capacity limit. Some firms, therefore, allocate the fixed costs of service departments in proportion to the maximum demands which different users might place on the department. Presumably, management considers these peak demands when it provides floor space and acquires machinery and other fixed resources for a service department.

To illustrate this approach, assume that Madison Corporation chooses to allocate the fixed costs of Department R by using the direct method, with the total cost of the equipment in the production departments as the fixed overhead base. Since Madison set up its repair department to service this equipment, the overall size of Department R is presumably a reflection of the total amount of equipment to be serviced.

Illustration 12-12 shows the allocation of the fixed costs incurred in each of Madison Corporation's service departments. In addition to Department R's fixed costs, the fixed costs of Departments A and P are allocated to the production departments, using as the bases the vouchers processed and the number of employees, respectively. The direct method is used to allocate the service department costs because it is the simplest method and it provides reasonably accurate final product costs for inventory valuation purposes and for use in reviewing product prices.

Illustration 12-12
Allocation of Service Department Fixed Overhead Costs, Using the Direct Method

	Service Departments			Production Departments			Total Plant
	Dept. R	Dept. A	Dept. P	Dept. 1	Dept. 2	Dept. 3	
Fixed overhead cost directly incurred in each department	$100,000	$80,000	$50,000	$597,122	$ 55,557	$137,921	$1,020,600
Allocation of Dept. R[a]	(100,000)			50,000	26,000	24,000	—
Allocation of Dept. A[b]		(80,000)		39,506	14,815	25,679	—
Allocation of Dept. P[c]			(50,000)	11,250	11,250	27,500	—
Total fixed overhead after allocation of service departments	0	0	0	$697,878	$107,622	$215,100	$1,020,600
Total direct labor cost				$ 42,000	$ 42,000	$134,400	$ 218,400
Production department fixed overhead rates based on direct labor cost . .				1,661.61%	256.24%	160.04%	

[a] Department R fixed overhead rate: $100,000 ÷ $4,000,000 plant equipment costs = 2.5%.
[b] Department A fixed overhead rate: $80,000 ÷ 8,100 vouchers = $9.87654 per voucher.
[c] Department P fixed overhead rate: $50,000 ÷ 200 employees = $250 per employee.

RELEVANT COSTS AND RESPONSIBILITY ACCOUNTING

When accounting procedures do not provide for a distinction between variable and fixed costs, costs over which a manager has some control are combined with costs that are not controllable by that manager. Since a manager's cost control efforts need to be monitored, however, accountants have developed special reporting systems, called **responsibility accounting systems,** to assist managers in controlling costs.

In responsibility accounting systems, the cost report for a given segment of a company includes only those costs for which the manager is responsible, and omits allocations and other costs which that manager cannot control. In general, a manager is usually held responsible for the labor costs of the segment's employees, the raw materials on which those employees work, the supplies they use, the variable overhead related to their activities, and the fixed, discretionary costs of assets and services which are acquired on the basis of the manager's recommendations. In most firms, however, operating managers do not negotiate the wage rates of the employees they supervise, they do not choose the source of supply for raw materials, nor do they actually purchase inventoriable items, plant assets, or outside services. Therefore, responsibility cost reports for a production manager should reflect excess amounts of resources used but not cost variations due to increases or decreases in the prices paid for these resources. On the other hand, the responsibility reports for purchasing agents should reflect price variances but not usage variances.

The February responsibility accounting report for the supervisor of Madison Corporation's Department 1 is shown in Illustration 12-13. Portions of the responsibility reports for the vice-president of production and the president of the corporation are also shown in this illustration. In addition to figures for February, the reports contain year-to-date totals. The year-to-date totals help put the individual month's results in a broader perspective. Minor month-to-month fluctuations will tend to smooth out, and continuing problem areas will tend to be highlighted.

The totals in the Department 1 cost report, along with the results of all the other departments in the plant, are carried to the cost performance report of the vice-president of production. In addition to the department totals, the controllable costs of the production vice-president's own staff are shown in the report. Although the production vice-president receives a copy of the detailed cost report of each of the department supervisors, these reports will probably not be referred to unless the total variance for a department appears to be excessive.

The controllable costs for which the vice-president of production has ultimate responsibility are carried forward to the next higher level of responsibility in the firm, the president. The president's cost report shows the results from all the vice-president's reports as well as the costs incurred by the president's staff.

Firms which have instituted responsibility accounting systems are careful that cost variances over which a manager has no control do not distort the cost reports. If the firm has a standard cost system, the report should emphasize the usage (efficiency) and mix variances for the prime costs. The spending variances (i.e., the unit price and hourly rate variances) for raw materials and direct labor may not be shown at all. If they are included in the report, they should clearly be identified as uncontrollable. Similarly, a firm using absorption costing would not show the fixed overhead volume variance among the controllable cost variances.

Allocations of variable overhead costs from service departments should be included among the controllable costs in a production department, since these costs can be influenced through control over the portion of the overhead base in that department. When service department costs are charged at predetermined budget rates, poor cost control by service department supervisors will not be passed along to the departments that use those services. Allocations of fixed service department costs, however, should either not be made, be made each month in fixed amounts equal to the budget (and will thus generate no variances), or be segregated into a separate category clearly identified as uncontrollable costs.

Cost Performance Report
Department 1, Pressing Department
February, 19X2

	Flexible Budget		Cost Variances	
	February	Year-to-Date	February	Year-to-Date
Raw materials (seed)	$50,000	$104,000	$2,000 U	$2,500 U
Direct labor	10,000	23,000	1,000 F	250 F
Supplies	5,000	8,000	200 F	1,000 F
Indirect labor	25,000	43,000	800 U	1,600 F
Allocated variable costs of service departments:				
Department R	2,000	4,000	—	—
Department A	1,500	3,000	100 F	150 F
Department P	700	1,500	70 F	100 F
Total controllable costs	$94,200	$186,500	$1,830 U	$ 600 F

Cost Performance Report
Vice-President of Production
February, 19X2

	Flexible Budget		Cost Variances	
	February	Year-to-Date	February	Year-to-Date
Office of the vice-president of production:				
Salaries and wages	$ 20,000	$ 43,000	$1,000 U	$1,000 F
Department 1, Pressing Department	94,200	186,500	1,830 U	600 F
Department P, Personnel Department				
Total controllable costs	$305,000	$600,000	$5,000 U	$8,000 U

Cost Performance Report
President
February, 19X2

	Flexible Budget		Cost Variances	
	February	Year-to-Date	February	Year-to-Date
Office of the president:				
Supplies	$ 1,000	$ 1,500	$ 200 U	$ 100 F
Vice-president of production	305,000	600,000	5,000 U	8,000 U
Vice-president of sales				1,500 F
Vice-president of finance .				
Total controllable costs	$400,000	$820,000	$10,000 U	$2,000 F

APPENDIX 12A: LINEAR PROGRAMMING APPLICATIONS TO JOINT PRODUCTS AND JOINT COSTS

In Chapter 4, the use of linear programming to formulate a firm's optimum production and sales mix was discussed. Linear programming can also be used by firms producing joint products, although the flexibility of altering the mix of production outputs is not available if the joint products are produced in fixed proportions. To illustrate the use of linear programming for planning production and sales of joint products, assume that the following data reflect next month's production and sales opportunities for Madison Corporation:

1. Only 850 tons of flower seed can be purchased on the seed market next month.
2. At the established selling prices of $6.50 per jug of oil and $2.50 per box of meal, only 20,000 jugs of oil and 100,000 boxes of meal can be sold.
3. There is no market for either joint product at split-off, and any quantities produced which are in excess of demand can be disposed of at no cost.
4. Inventories of seed, oil, and meal at the end of the month are to be equal to inventories at the beginning of the month. (Since inventories will not change, they are ignored in this linear programming problem.)

To formulate the linear programming problem, the following notation is used:

$$X_1 = \text{jugs of refined oil sold}$$
$$X_2 = \text{boxes of ground meal sold}$$
$$X_3 = \text{production output of oil at split-off (1 unit = 1 jug)}$$
$$X_4 = \text{production output of seed cake at split-off (1 unit = 1 box)}$$
$$X_5 = \text{tons of seed processed}$$

The identifiable contribution margins of refined oil ($5.80 per jug) and ground meal ($2 per box) at split-off, along with the variable costs of operations in Department 1 ($115 per ton of seed), are used to construct the objective function. This function shows the total contribution margin of next month's production and sales to be maximized, as follows:

$$\text{Maximize } Z = 5.8X_1 + 2X_2 - 115X_5$$

The first two constraints for this problem require that sales of each product cannot exceed the quantity produced, as follows:

For oil: $X_1 \leq X_3$, or $X_1 - X_3 \leq 0$ **(Constraint 1)**

For meal: $X_2 - X_4 \leq 0$ **(Constraint 2)**

The next two constraints show the fixed proportions in which oil and seed cake are produced from one ton of seed. Since one ton of seed (X_5) produces 25 jugs of oil (X_3):

$$.04X_3 - X_5 = 0 \qquad \textbf{(Constraint 3)}$$

Similarly, for seed cake:

$$.00625X_4 - X_5 = 0 \qquad \textbf{(Constraint 4)}$$

The fifth constraint expresses the maximum amount of seed available for processing, as follows:

$$X_5 \leq 850 \qquad \text{(Constraint 5)}$$

Finally, the market demand for oil and seed cake are specified:

$$X_1 \leq 20,000 \qquad \text{(Constraint 6)}$$

$$X_2 \leq 100,000 \qquad \text{(Constraint 7)}$$

A more complete description of Madison Corporation would incorporate other factors. For example, production capacity constraints in each department could be added, and any inventory changes which are desired could be incorporated in the first two constraints. These elaborations, however, would not change the basic nature of the problem.

When this linear programming problem is solved, the following information is obtained:

Value of objective function: Z = $224,000
Solution values:

X_1	20,000	jugs
X_2	100,000	boxes
X_3	20,000	units
X_4	128,000	units
X_5	800	tons

Shadow prices:

Constraint 1	$4.60 per jug
Constraint 2	–0–
Constraint 3	– 115.00 per ton
Constraint 4	–0–
Constraint 5	–0–
Constraint 6	1.20 per jug
Constraint 7	2.00 per box

The value of the objective function is the total contribution margin earned by processing 800 tons of seed (X_5) at a variable cost of $115 per ton, and selling 20,000 jugs of oil (X_1) and 100,000 boxes of meal (X_2). All of the oil which is produced is sold, but 28,000 potential boxes of meal (128,000 X_4 − 100,000 X_2) remain unsold. This quantity of seed cake is disposed of at split-off, since there is no market for it.

Each shadow price reflects the value of an additional unit of the economic resource reflected in that particular constraint. The shadow price of $2 per box for the last constraint, for example, reflects the value of increasing the market demand for meal by one additional unit. This value is equal to the identifiable product contribution margin which would be earned by selling one additional box of meal.

Although the object of formulating the linear programming problem was to develop an optimal operating plan, the shadow prices associated with the joint product proportions (constraints 3 and 4) provide an allocation of the total variable joint cost among the various joint products. Since the shadow price for the oil (constraint 3) is −$115, and the shadow price for the seed cake (constraint 4) is zero, all of the $115 variable joint cost should be allocated to oil and none to the seed cake. Even though the 100,000 boxes of meal provide $200,000, or more than 63%, of the total net realizable value at split-off, management might not regard the meal as a joint product in this situation, because so much more of it is produced than can be sold profitably.

Linear programming allocations are seldom seen in practice, partly because few firms use linear programming to develop comprehensive production and sales plans. Also, management may object to a procedure which can assign no joint costs to products that contribute substantial revenues to the firm. Another drawback is that if the seed availability constraint (constraint 5) or a Department 1 capacity constraint had been binding (which was not the case in this situation), an opportunity cost for these scarce resources would have been added to the $115 per ton variable joint cost. The resulting joint cost allocations to oil and seed cake would then have been equal to this larger sum and would have exceeded the actual variable costs.

Exercise   The Dubai Central Utilities Board operates several desalinization plants which convert seawater into fresh water and salt. For each 100,000 gallons of seawater that enter the Evaporation Department, 72,000 gallons of fresh water and 14,000 pounds of raw salt are produced. The 14,000 pounds of raw salt is cleaned and packaged in the Refining Department, yielding 12,000 pounds of processed salt and 1,000 pounds of other minerals.

The costs incurred in the various departments are summarized as follows:

	Variable Costs	Fixed Costs
Evaporation	$.0085 per gallon processed	$24,000 per month
Refining	.0750 per pound processed	19,000 per month

The revenues of the three end-products are as follows:

Fresh water	$.0175 per gallon
Minerals	.1800 per pound
Processed salt	.0800 per pound

To optimize its production operations, the directors of the Dubai Central Utilities Board have asked you to develop a linear programming model for sales and production.

The plant can process a maximum of 4.0 million gallons of seawater each month. The Board's Marketing Department further estimates that a maximum of 425,000 pounds of processed salt can be sold each month at the current market price.

Formulate the linear programming equations, using the following notations:

S	=	number of gallons of seawater processed
F_1	=	production output of fresh water at split-off, in gallons
F_2	=	sales of fresh water, in gallons
L	=	production output of raw salt at split-off, in pounds
M_1	=	production output of minerals at split-off, in pounds
P_1	=	production output of processed salt at split-off, in pounds
M_2	=	sales of minerals, in pounds
P_2	=	sales of processed salt, in pounds

APPENDIX 12B: OVERHEAD ALLOCATION USING MATRIX ALGEBRA

If there are cost centers or departments in an organization which provide services to each other, a correct allocation of costs involving these departments requires the solution of a set of simultaneous equations. The use of matrix algebra to arrive at a solution is advantageous for several reasons. From a conceptual standpoint, using matrix algebra is desirable because, in addition to the actual solution values, the inverse matrix is obtained. The inverse contains economic information that is useful in answering some questions related to the allocation of costs from one department to another. From a practical standpoint, a matrix algebra solution for very large problems is easy to implement, since matrix algebra routines are standard software for most computers.

To illustrate the use of matrix algebra in allocating Madison Corporation's personnel and accounting departmental costs to Departments P and A, the following notations will be used:

$[X]$ = the 2×1 vector of unknowns, $\begin{bmatrix} P \\ A \end{bmatrix}$ (the overhead costs of Departments P and A after allocation of the other service department)

$[C]$ = the 2×2 matrix of coefficients in which c_{ij} is the proportion of cost center j's costs to be allocated to department i

$[E]$ = the 2×1 vector of expenses directly incurred by the departments

$[I]$ = the 2×2 identity matrix

Assuming that self-service is not considered, the following equations, which were given on page 417, show the relationships between the costs of Departments P and A:

$$P = 0P + .09A + 45,000$$
$$A = .12P + 0A + 25,000$$

Using matrix notation, these equations can be expressed as follows:

$$[X] = [C][X] + [E], \text{ or } \begin{bmatrix} P \\ A \end{bmatrix} = \begin{bmatrix} 0.00 & 0.09 \\ 0.12 & 0.00 \end{bmatrix} \times \begin{bmatrix} P \\ A \end{bmatrix} + \begin{bmatrix} 45,000 \\ 25,000 \end{bmatrix}$$

Rearranging the matrix expression:

$$[X] - [C][X] = [E]$$
$$[I - C][X] = [E]$$

*Pre*multiplying both sides by $[I - C]^{-1}$:

$$[I-C]^{-1}[I-C][X] = [I-C]^{-1}[E]$$
$$[I][X] = [I-C]^{-1}[E]$$
$$[X] = [I-C]^{-1}[E]$$

The following inverse matrix is provided by the computer program:

$$[I-C]^{-1} = \begin{bmatrix} 1.010918 & 0.090983 \\ 0.121310 & 1.010918 \end{bmatrix}$$

When the inverse is *post*multiplied by the two-element vector, E, as follows, the resulting values for P and A are the same values as shown on page 417:

$$\begin{bmatrix} P \\ A \end{bmatrix} = \begin{bmatrix} 1.010918 & 0.090983 \\ 0.121310 & 1.010918 \end{bmatrix} \times \begin{bmatrix} 45,000 \\ 25,000 \end{bmatrix} = \begin{bmatrix} 47,766 \\ 30,732 \end{bmatrix}$$

The inverse may be viewed as giving a general solution to the allocation of $1 of overhead cost in each department. Each element in the inverse shows how much of $1 of costs incurred in a given department (column j) ultimately flows through the allocation process to the department in row i. Such information is useful in exploring the impact of cost changes in one department on the costs of other departments. For example, the value of 0.121310 in row 2, column 1 of the inverse indicates that, for every dollar of cost incurred in Department P, 12.131 cents is eventually allocated to Department A. If supply costs in Department P were to increase by $1,000, the allocated costs in Department A would increase by $121.31.

In some cases, the allocation bases do not change from period to period, although the costs to be allocated are constantly changing. If this situation prevails, using matrix algebra to allocate costs simplifies the computations. If the allocation bases, [C], do not change, then the inverse, $[I-C]^{-1}$, will not change either, so that this inverse need only be calculated once. The allocation of each new set of costs can be accomplished by simply postmultiplying the same inverse matrix by the vector of new costs.

If the set of simultaneous equations representing the overhead allocation of service departments is solved manually, it is desirable to limit the size of the problem by including only those service departments that service each other. Manually solving sets of more than three or four equations is extremely time consuming. If matrix algebra routines are used on a computer, however, the size of the problem can be much larger, and the entire cost allocation problem may be solved at once by setting up a separate equation for every service and production department.

In the case of Madison Corporation, there are six departments, so there will be six equations. The allocation bases for all three service departments are shown in Part A of Illustration 12B-1. When expressed in percentage form, these bases form the first three columns of the coefficient matrix, [C]. Part B shows the $[I-C]$ matrix and the values of $[I-C]^{-1}$. Part C shows the matrix multiplication of $[I-C]^{-1}$ by the vector of costs, [E], to give the total overhead costs of all six departments after service department allocations, [X]. These values are the same as the results of the overhead allocation shown in Illustration 12-11.

Illustration 12B-1
Matrix Algebra Allocation of Service Department Overhead

Part A
Overhead Bases and Allocation Proportions (Self-Service Ignored)

	Dept. P (Number of Employees)	Dept. A (Number of Vouchers)	Dept. R (Repair Crew Hours)	Department Bases as a Proportion of the Total Dept. P	Dept. A	Dept. R
Dept. P	—	900	—	—	.09	—
Dept. A	30	—	—	.12	—	—
Dept. R	20	1,000	—	.08	.10	—
Dept. 1	45	4,000	1,000	.18	.40	.50
Dept. 2	45	1,500	600	.18	.15	.30
Dept. 3	110	2,600	400	.44	.26	.20
Total	250	10,000	2,000	1.00	1.00	1.00

Illustration 12B-1   Matrix Algebra Allocation of Service Department Overhead
Part B   Matrices Used for Allocation

	Coefficient Matrix [C]							[I−C]							[I−C]⁻¹					
	P	A	R	1	2	3		P	A	R	1	2	3		P	A	R	1	2	3
P	.00	.09	0.0	0	0	0		1.00	−.09	0.0	0	0	0		1.011	0.091	0.0	0	0	0
A	.12	.00	0.0	0	0	0		−.12	1.00	0.0	0	0	0		0.121	1.011	0.0	0	0	0
R	.08	.10	0.0	0	0	0		−.08	−.10	1.0	0	0	0		0.093	0.108	1.0	0	0	0
1	.18	.40	0.5	0	0	0		−.18	−.40	−0.5	1	0	0		0.277	0.475	0.5	1	0	0
2	.18	.15	0.3	0	0	0		−.18	−.15	−0.3	0	1	0		0.228	0.201	0.3	0	1	0
3	.44	.26	0.2	0	0	0		−.44	−.26	−0.2	0	0	1		0.495	0.325	0.2	0	0	1

Illustration 12B-1   Matrix Algebra Allocation of Service Department Overhead
Part C   Overhead Allocation

		[I−C]⁻¹[E] = [X]								
	P	A	R	1	2	3				
P	1.010918	0.090983	0.0	0	0	0		45,000		47,766
A	0.121310	1.010918	0.0	0	0	0		25,000		30,732
R	0.093004	0.108370	1.0	0	0	0		30,000		36,894
1	0.276992	0.474929	0.5	1	0	0	×	44,662	=	84,000
2	0.228063	0.200526	0.3	0	1	0		17,724		42,000
3	0.494945	0.324545	0.2	0	0	1		232,414		268,800

The 2×2 upper left partition of the larger 6×6 coefficient matrix and the inverse matrix contain the same values as the 2×2 matrices used when the smaller, two-equation overhead allocation problem was formulated at the beginning of this appendix. Similarly, the discussion of the smaller, two-equation problem applies to the complete, 6-equation problem. For example, the element in the 4th row and the 2nd column of the 6×6 inverse, 0.475, shows that for every $1,000 incurred directly by Department A, $475 will eventually be allocated to Department 1.

An added benefit of using matrix algebra is that each diagonal element of the $[I-C]^{-1}$ matrix can be used to determine the amount of services which must be acquired outside the firm if that service department were to be eliminated. The analysis which involved discontinuing Department A showed that 9,892 vouchers would have to be processed by the outside accounting firm, and the variable costs would increase by $1,749. The same numbers can be calculated by using the data from Illustration 12B-1.

The number of vouchers to be processed if accounting services are performed by an external accounting firm, 9,892, can be determined by dividing the present voucher volume, 10,000, by the second diagonal element in the inverse matrix, 1.010918, which refers to Department A. The additional costs can be calculated by multiplying the difference in unit variable costs by this voucher volume, as follows:

Unit cost of processing vouchers externally	$	3.2500
Unit cost of processing vouchers internally ($30,732 ÷ 10,000 vouchers)		3.0732
Additional unit cost	$	.1768
Additional total cost ($.1768 × 9,892 vouchers)		$1,749.9056

Exercises   1. Cincinnati Paint Company has three service departments, A, B, and C. These three departments provide services to each other and to two production departments, X and Y. Service department costs are allocated using the reciprocal services method.

The firm's accounting staff has developed the following equations to calculate each service department's cost after allocations:

$$A = .2C + \$29,000$$
$$B = .1A + .2C + \$55,000$$
$$C = .3A + .2B + \$47,000$$

(1) Restate the equations in matrix form.
(2) Calculate the total cost for each service department, after allocations, using the following inverse matrix:

$$[I-C]^{-1} = \begin{bmatrix} 1.071429 & 0.044643 & 0.223214 \\ 0.178571 & 1.049107 & 0.245536 \\ 0.357143 & 0.223214 & 1.116071 \end{bmatrix}$$

    (3) What is the economic significance of each of the following values contained in the middle column of the inverse matrix: 0.044643 and 0.223214?

2. Corporate Financial Services operates two divisions, Management Consulting and Tax Advisory, which provide financial consulting to clients. These two divisions draw upon the services of two service departments, Data Processing and Econometric Forecasting. For budgetary control purposes, the cost of the two service departments is allocated to the operating divisions on the basis of usage, using the reciprocal services method. Relative usage and direct costs are summarized in the following table:

	Data Processing	Econometric Forecasting	Management Consulting	Tax Advisory	Total
From Data Processing	—	0.20	0.30	0.50	1.00
From Econometric Forecasting	0.15	—	0.65	0.20	1.00
Direct costs	$108,000	$71,000	$225,000	$307,000	$711,000

(1) Formulate the two equations for showing the total overhead after allocations of the two service departments.
(2) Express the equations developed in (1) in matrix form.
(3) Calculate the total service department cost after allocations for each of the two service departments, using the following inverse matrix:

$$[I-C]^{-1} = \begin{bmatrix} 1.03093 & 0.15464 \\ 0.20619 & 1.03093 \end{bmatrix}$$

(4) Calculate the total cost of the Tax Advisory Division after allocations.

3. Dennison Wood Products Company operates a largely self-contained wood-cutting and processing operation in Brazil. Two production departments, Milling and Finishing, are served by three service departments, Power, Maintenance, and Administration. The following table shows the allocation percentages for service department costs and the total costs directly incurred by departments during the quarter just ended:

	Power	Maintenance	Administration	Milling	Finishing
From Power	—	5%	15%	55%	25%
From Maintenance	25%	—	5	40	30
From Administration	15	20	—	40	25
Direct costs	$70,000	$45,000	$62,000	$172,000	$145,000

(1) Formulate the three equations showing the total overhead costs after allocation of the three service departments.

(2) Express the equations formulated in (1) in matrix form.

(3) Determine the total cost of the three service departments after allocation, using the following inverse matrix:

$$\begin{array}{c} \\ P \\ M \\ A \end{array} \begin{array}{ccc} P & M & A \\ \left[\begin{array}{ccc} 1.045269 & 0.271875 & 0.211165 \\ 0.084466 & 1.032071 & 0.219084 \\ 0.161014 & 0.092385 & 1.042629 \end{array}\right] \end{array}$$

(4) Allocate the service department costs to the two production departments.

4. Sea-Air Lines is a freight carrier which operates three semi-independent transportation divisions. AirLink, one of the divisions, operates a fleet of wide-bodied aircraft which have been modified to carry overseas freight. SeaLink, the firm's second division, maintains a fleet of bulk-goods and container ships in the Pacific basin. LandLink arranges land transportation for the goods carried by SeaLink and AirLink. All three operating divisions draw upon the resources of three centralized service divisions: the Marketing Division, which schedules all fleet movements, maintains a central reservations center, and handles promotion; the Accounting Division; and a Data Processing Division. For cost accounting purposes, the costs of these service divisions are allocated to the operating divisions on the basis of usage, using the reciprocal services method. The following table summarizes the relative usage and costs (in 000s) before allocation for the current month:

	Service Divisions			Operating Divisions		
	Marktg.	Acctg.	Data Proc.	SeaLink	AirLink	LandLink
From Marketing	—	—	5%	40%	30%	25%
From Accounting	15%	—	5%	25%	25%	30%
From Data Processing	40%	20%	—	20%	15%	5%
Direct costs	$475	$495	$300	$2,000	$2,900	$1,750

(1) Formulate the six equations which describe the cost after allocations of the six service and operating divisions.

(2) Restate the equations formulated in (1) in matrix form.

(3) Calculate the monthly cost of each operating division after service department cost allocations, using the following inverse matrix. Round your answers to the nearest thousand.

$$[I-C]^{-1} = \begin{array}{c} M \\ A \\ D \\ SL \\ AL \\ LL \end{array} \begin{array}{cccccc} M & A & D & SL & AL & LL \\ \left[\begin{array}{cccccc} 1.022199 & 0.175529 & 0.443986 & 0 & 0 & 0 \\ 0.010325 & 1.011874 & 0.206505 & 0 & 0 & 0 \\ 0.051626 & 0.059370 & 1.032524 & 0 & 0 & 0 \\ 0.421786 & 0.335054 & 0.435725 & 1 & 0 & 0 \\ 0.316985 & 0.314533 & 0.339701 & 0 & 1 & 0 \\ 0.261229 & 0.350413 & 0.224574 & 0 & 0 & 1 \end{array}\right] \end{array}$$

1. What is the distinguishing characteristic of a joint product?

2. What kinds of costs are included in joint costs?

3. Describe the two broad causes of excessive costs in a department where joint products emerge as output.

4. In what way does cost-volume-profit analysis in the joint product situation differ from that in a single product situation?

5. Give the reasons for allocating joint costs to products and the major methods used to allocate joint costs.

6. Discuss two potential problems arising from allocating costs to joint products using the physical units method.

7. Contrast the relative sales value method and the relative net realizable value method for allocating joint costs.

8. Why are elaborate accounting procedures not usually applied to by-products?

9. What are the disadvantages of allocating service department overhead costs using a plantwide overhead rate?

10. What factors should be considered in selecting an overhead base for service departments?

11. Rank the direct method, the step method, and the reciprocal services method of allocating service department overhead in terms of the degree to which each takes into account the service provided to other service departments.

12. What factors should be considered in making the decision to eliminate a service department and acquire the output of that department from outside firms?

13. Compare the allocation of fixed service department costs with the allocation of variable service department costs.

14. Should all variable costs be included and all fixed costs be excluded from a manager's responsibility accounting report?

Exercise 1. A. J. Ayers Company recycles waste motor and industrial oil into two products: a highly refined, light machine oil and a tar-like sludge used in making asphalt. Initially, 1,000-gallon batches of waste oils enter the Distilling Department, where the oil is separated into 400 gallons of light oil and 600 gallons of sludge. The light oil is sent to the Processing Department, where it is refined, filtered, and packaged, yielding 400 gallons of salable machine oil. The sludge is also piped to the Processing Department, where it is packaged in 50-gallon drums, yielding 12 drums of salable sludge.

Statistical cost analysis performed last quarter yielded the following departmental costs:

	Variable Costs	Fixed Costs
Distilling	$ .18 per gallon processed	$22,500 per month
Processing	1.25 per gallon of light oil	24,000
	5.00 per drum of sludge	
Selling and Administration	.13 per gallon of machine oil	17,500
	1.25 per sludge drum	

Waste oil can generally be obtained without cost, but delivery to the plant costs an average of $.14 per gallon of oil. A gallon of machine oil sells for $3 and a drum of sludge sells for $28.

Calculate the amount of machine oil and sludge the firm must sell each month in order to break even.

Exercise 2. (*Note: Exercise 1 in Appendix 12A applies linear programming techniques to this enterprise.*)

The Dubai Central Utilities Board operates several desalinization plants which convert seawater into fresh water and salt. The following flowchart depicts the utility's operations:

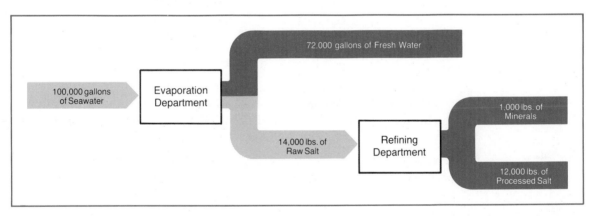

Seawater is converted to fresh water and raw salt in the Evaporation Department. The raw salt is cleaned and packaged in the Refining Department, yielding processed salt and an assortment of other minerals. The costs incurred in the various departments are summarized as follows:

	Variable Costs	Fixed Costs
Evaporation	$.0085 per gallon processed	$24,000 per month
Refining	.0750 per pound processed	19,000 per month

The revenues of the three end-products are as follows:

Fresh water	$.0175 per gallon
Minerals	.1800 per pound
Processed salt	.0800 per pound

Calculate the break-even point of the operation in units of input, and indicate the quantities of output that would be produced at that level of activity.

Exercise 3. The Dubai Central Utilities Board in Exercise 2 has received an offer from a private chemical processor to purchase its entire production of raw salt for

$.075 per pound. The Refining Department, which operates at high unit costs because of its relatively small scale, would be shut down. The Board's management expects monthly fixed costs to decrease by $16,500 as a result of the closure. The Board also expects to process 3.7 million gallons of seawater per month over the foreseeable future.

Calculate the monthly profit (loss) from current operations. Calculate the monthly profit (loss) from the alternative operating plan. Should Dubai accept the offer from the private chemical processor?

Exercise 4. Diversified Oil Refineries Inc. operates a small oil refinery. Crude oil is refined into gasoline, kerosene, and heavy fuel oil in the Refining Department. During a recent month, the Refining Department incurred variable and fixed conversion costs of $182,000 in processing 850,000 barrels of crude oil. Normal output is 925,000 barrels per month. Fixed conversion costs totaled $148,000. A barrel of crude oil (31.5 gallons) yields the following quantities of finished products:

	Quantity	BTUs per Gallon
Gasoline	12 gals.	95,000
Kerosene	8	87,000
Fuel oil	9	85,000
	29 gals.	

The average price of the crude oil is $28 per barrel.

Calculate the inventoriable cost of a gallon of output for each product leaving the Refining Department. Use (a) the physical units method and (b) the weighted physical units method, with BTUs as weights.

Exercise 5. Davidson Food Processing Company produces its popular brand of boneless canned chicken at its plant in Iowa. A schematic of the plant's operations is as follows:

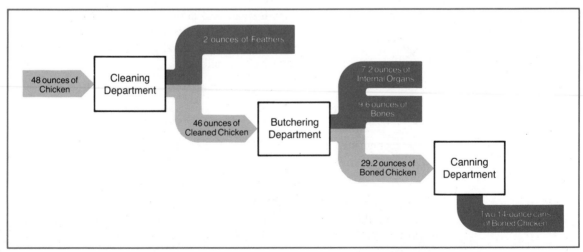

Budgeted cost data for each department are as follows:

	Fixed Costs	Variable Costs
Cleaning	$18,000 per month	$.02 per lb.
Butchering	22,500	.07 per lb. processed
Canning	14,000	.54 per lb. processed

The processed food market is competitive, and market prices are available for both final and intermediate products. A list of current market prices is given in the following table:

	Prices	Customers
Feathers	No market value	None
Cleaned chicken	$.24 per lb.	Food processors
Internal organs	.40 per lb.	Cat and dog food manufacturers
Bones	.25 per lb.	Animal feed producers
Boned chicken	.45 per lb.	Food processors
14-oz. can of boned chicken	1.15 per can	Food wholesalers

On the average, 3-pound chickens can be purchased by the firm for $.60 per chicken. Normal production for the firm is 240,000 chickens per month.

Calculate the inventoriable cost per can of boned chicken. Davidson uses the relative sales value method to allocate joint production costs. Round your answer to the nearest tenth of a cent.

Exercise 6. Davidson Food Processing Company, described in Exercise 5, has three service departments which serve all of the production departments: a Computing Department, a Repair and Maintenance Department, and an Accounting Department. During a recent month, the following costs were incurred within each department:

	Variable Overhead Costs	Fixed Overhead Costs
Computing	$ 1,230	$ 8,500
Repair and Maintenance	9,600	2,500
Accounting	1,170	10,000
Cleaning	11,500	18,000
Butchering	33,800	22,500
Canning	212,700	14,000

During the month, the following activity levels were measured within each department. The measures were chosen because of their explanatory value in calculating variable costs.

	Activity Measure	Computing Dept.	Repair and Maint. Dept.	Accounting Dept.	Cleaning Dept.	Butchering Dept.	Canning Dept.	Total Usage or Activity
Computing	Hours of computer time	—	—	20	40	80	280	420
Maintenance	Hours of maintenance time	30	—	20	300	450	400	1,200
Accounting	Forms processed	500	100	300	600	350	1,150	3,000
Production	Direct machine hours	—	—	—	12,000	31,000	29,000	72,000

(1) Allocate all variable service department costs to the production departments, using a single plantwide variable overhead rate based on direct machine hours.

(2) Allocate the variable service department costs to the production departments, using the direct method, with departmental activity measures as the allocation base.

Exercise 7. Precision Molding Corporation produces a variety of molded plastic parts to the engineering specifications of its customers, primarily consumer electronics manufacturers. The firm has two production departments, Molding and Packaging, which are served by three service departments, Personnel, Accounting, and Maintenance. Variable overhead costs incurred within each department for a typical month of normal operations are summarized as follows:

Personnel	$ 9,500
Accounting	7,500
Maintenance	12,000
Molding	85,000
Packaging	27,000
Total	$141,000

Variable service department costs are allocated to production departments, using the following activity measures:

	Activity Measure	Personnel	Accounting	Maintenance	Molding	Packaging	Total Usage or Activity
Personnel	Employees	12	14	7	55	12	100
Accounting	Forms processed	700	600	—	550	150	2,000
Maintenance	Hours worked	—	70	50	655	225	1,000

(1) Allocate the variable service department costs to each production department, using the step method of allocation. The order of allocation should be determined by the size of each service department's variable cost, allocating the service department with the largest variable cost first.

(2) Calculate the variable overhead rate, after allocations, for the Molding Department, which has a normal operating level of 10,000 machine hours per month.

Exercise 8. In an effort to increase the accuracy of their financial statements, the managers of Precision Molding Corporation in Exercise 7 would like to use the reciprocal services method to allocate service department costs.

(1) Allocate the total variable overhead costs to each production department. Ignore self-service in the three service departments.

(2) The allocation base used to allocate manufacturing overhead in each production department and the total variable overhead after service department allocations are as follows:

	Allocation Base	Total Hours for a Normal Month	Total Variable Overhead After Allocations
Molding	Machine hours	10,000 machine hrs.	$107,680
Packaging	Labor hours	10,000 labor hrs.	33,320

If Job #1202 required 100 machine hours of molding time and 10 hours of packaging time, how much manufacturing overhead (to the nearest dollar) would be allocated to this job?

PROBLEMS

Problem 12-1. Texhoma Industries, a large refiner of crude oil, has a single production department, the Refining Department, in which a barrel of crude oil (31.5 gallons) is refined into three products: gasoline, kerosene, and fuel oil. The relative quantities and market prices of the three products are as follows:

	Quantity	Price
Gasoline	12 gals.	$1.15 per gal.
Kerosene	8	.98
Fuel oil	9	.95
	29 gals.	

Gasoline and fuel oil are sold through the Consumer Sales Department, while kerosene is sold through the Industrial Sales Department. During a recent month, the firm's various departments incurred the following costs:

	Total Costs	Variable	Fixed	Quantities Sold and Processed
Refining	$6,468,750*	80%	20%	225,000 bbls.
Consumer Sales	354,375	40	60	4,725,000 gals.
Industrial Sales	121,500	20	80	2,025,000 gals.

*Includes materials cost

In planning its production for the coming quarter, Texhoma's managers are considering changing the product mix. Because the firm is the dominant producer in the area which it serves, the Marketing Department anticipates that this change in product mix will result in price changes. The new product mix and the changes in price are as follows:

	Product Mix	New Prices
Gasoline	14 gals.	$1.10
Kerosene	4	1.08
Fuel oil	11	0.90
	29 gals.	

Fixed costs and unit variable costs within the various departments would not change as a result of the revised product mix.

Required (1) Calculate the break-even point of the firm, in barrels processed, using the current product mix.
(2) Calculate the firm's break-even point, in barrels processed, using the revised product mix.
(3) Assuming that the next month's output is 25% greater than the current month's, which product mix yields the larger profit (smaller loss)?

Problem 12-2. Rio Brava Zinc Ltd. operates mines in Africa, South America, and Australia. The firm's largest mine is a silver mine located in Western Australia. *Ch. 12* Low-grade silver ore is mined from an open-pit mine and pulverized in the Crush- 437 ing Department. Silver, trace amounts of gold, and sulphur are extracted from the ore in the Extraction Department. The two metals are then chemically refined in the Refining Department, yielding base metals which are 99.9% pure. A schematic of the mine's operations is as follows:

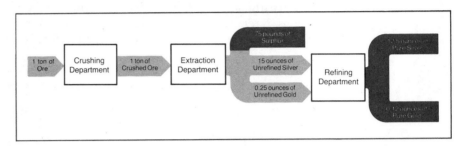

Costs incurred within each of the three departments during a recent month are summarized as follows:

	Crushing Department	Extraction Department	Refining Department	
Materials	$720,000[a]	—	—	
Direct labor	31,500	$ 72,000	Silver	$ 18,000
			Gold	5,400
Variable overhead:				
Indirect materials	—	486,000	Silver	33,250
			Gold	8,600
Other	79,200	126,000	Silver	168,000
			Gold	23,000
Fixed overhead:				
Supervision	4,500 per mo.	9,000 per mo.	9,000 per mo.[b]	
Maintenance	1,800 per mo.	700 per mo.	1,200 per mo.[b]	
Other	7,700 per mo.	16,000 per mo.	21,300 per mo.[b]	

[a] Represents the cost of extracting and transporting the ore to the processing departments.
[b] Fixed Refining Department costs are presumed to be incurred equally for each product and are to be allocated one half to each.

Required (1) Allocate the joint product costs of the Crushing and Extraction Departments to the final products, using the physical units method based on the products generated at the split-off point.

(2) Calculate the inventoriable cost per ounce of silver and of gold.

(3) Comment on the reasonableness of the inventoriable unit costs produced by the physical units method in this company's operations.

Problem 12-3 (AICPA adapted, 11/74). Harrison Corporation produces three products: Alpha, Beta, and Gamma. Alpha and Gamma are joint products, while Beta is a by-product of Alpha. No joint cost is to be allocated to the by-product. The production processes for the current year are as follows:

• In Department 1, 110,000 pounds of raw material, Rho, were processed at a total cost of $120,000. After processing in Department 1, 60% of the units were transferred to Department 2 and 40% of the units (now Gamma) were transferred to Department 3.

- In Department 2, the material was further processed at a total additional cost of $38,000. Seventy percent of the units (now Alpha) were transferred to Department 4 and 30% emerged as Beta, the by-product, to be sold at $1.20 per pound. Selling expenses related to disposing of Beta were $8,100.
- In Department 4, Alpha was processed at an additional cost of $23,660. After this processing, Alpha was sold at $5 per pound.
- In Department 3, Gamma was processed at an additional cost of $165,000. In this department, a normal loss of 10% of the good output of Gamma occurred. The good output of Gamma was then sold for $12 per pound.

During the year, the firm expects to sell 41,000 pounds, 19,800 pounds, and 41,000 pounds of Alpha, Beta, and Gamma, respectively.

Beginning inventories consisted of 2,400 pounds of Alpha, valued at $4,416, and 1,950 pounds of Gamma, valued at $10,530. No beginning or ending inventory records are maintained for the by-product Beta. Revenue from Beta sales is treated as a reduction of Alpha's cost of goods manufactured, while the costs incurred in selling Beta are an expense of the period. Harrison Corporation values all inventories using the lifo method. There were no beginning or ending in-process inventories.

Required (1) Prepare a schedule showing the allocation of the $120,000 joint cost between Alpha and Gamma, using the relative sales value method. The net realizable value of Beta should be treated as an addition to the sales value of Alpha.

(2) Calculate the anticipated gross profit for the current year.

Problem 12-4. Northern Scrap Processors Inc. operates a large automobile salvage yard. Junked cars are purchased at an average cost of $125 each. The cars are then stripped of parts having a resale value. After removal of such parts, which have an average value of $100 per car, the car is crushed and shredded. The shredded metal is then sent to a magnetic separator, where the ferrous and nonferrous metals are separated. A schematic of the firm's operations is as follows:

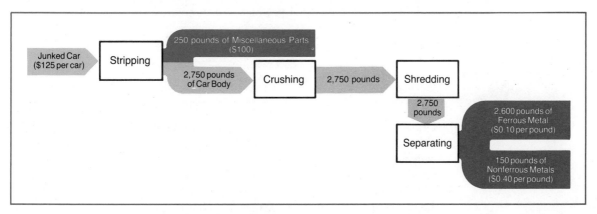

During the month just ended, Northern Scrap incurred the following costs while processing 250 cars.

	Variable Costs	Fixed Costs
Stripping	$46.00 per car	$1,800
Crushing	12.00 per car	800
Shredding	22.00 per car	2,400
Separating	.01 per lb. separated	400

Required (1) Calculate the total costs incurred for the month.

(2) Allocate the total joint costs and calculate the inventoriable cost per pound of ferrous metal, using (a) the physical units method based on weight, and (b) the relative net realizable value method.

(3) Calculate the gross profit percentage of ferrous and nonferrous metals under each of the above methods.

Problem 12-5. Telerand Corporation operates a division which reprocesses used photographic fixer chemicals. In the Processing Department, 100 gallons of used fixer are combined with 8 pounds of the agent T-12. The output of this process is 10 pounds of silver precipitate and 80 gallons of Product Q.

The silver precipitate is processed further in the Refining Department, yielding 8 ounces of pure silver. Product Q is sent to the Distillation Department, where it is distilled into 40 gallons of Product T and 30 gallons of Product W. Product W is further refined in the Finishing Department, yielding 25 gallons of Product Y.

Costs incurred in the various departments during the current month are summarized as follows:

	Processing Department	Refining Department	Distillation Department	Finishing Department
Materials:				
Used fixer	$.10 per gal. of input	—	—	—
T-12..............	.35 per lb.	—	—	—
Packaging	—	$.25 per oz. of silver	—	$.10 per gal. of Y
Direct labor	.10 per gal. of fixer	.13 per lb. of precipitate	$.07 per gal. of Q	.09 per gal. of W
Variable overhead		150% of direct labor cost in each department		
Fixed overhead	$1,368 per month	$1,330 per month	$2,128 per month	$1,938 per month

Selling prices for the final products are summarized in the following table:

Silver	$6.00 per oz.
Product T	.45 per gal.
Product Y	.50 per gal.

During the month, 76,000 gallons of used photographic chemicals were processed by the firm.

Required (1) Draw a diagram of Telerand's production process.

(2) Calculate the net realizable values of the silver precipitate and Product Q which result from processing 100 gallons of used fixer chemical in the Processing Department.

(3) Allocate the joint costs in the Processing Department and Distillation Department, using the relative net realizable value method.

(4) Calculate the inventoriable cost per unit of silver, Product T, and Product Y.

Problem 12-6. Surral Juice Company produces lemon juice at a plant in California. The lemons are processed in 500-pound batches. The lemons enter production in the Peeling Department, where 500 pounds of fresh lemons, costing an average of $.07 per pound, yield 450 pounds of peeled lemons and 50 pounds of peels. During a normal month, Surral processes 350,000 pounds of lemons.

The peels are sent to the Grinding Department, where they are dried and ground into 35 pounds of fine meal. The meal is sent on to the Packaging Department, where it is boxed for sale to food processors.

The peeled lemons are sent to the Pressing Department, where they are pressed to yield 70 gallons of juice. A further output of the Pressing Department is 100 pounds of pressed pulp, which is sold as a by-product to animal feedlots. The value of the by-product is credited to the cost of production in the Pressing Department. The juice is concentrated and packaged in the Packaging Department, yielding 10 gallons of lemon juice concentrate.

The standard costs for each production department are as follows:

	Variable Costs	Fixed Costs
Peeling	$.025 per lb. processed[a]	$6,860 per month
Pressing	.015 per lb. processed[b]	1,190
Grinding	.03 per lb. processed	3,780
Packaging:		
Meal	.20 per lb. processed	3,675
Concentrate	.25 per gal. processed	3,675

[a] Excludes cost of lemons
[b] Excludes credit for by-product

As in most of the food processing industry, final and intermediate product prices are readily available. These prices are listed as follows:

Ground meal	$1.00 per lb. (after packaging)
	.75 per lb. (before packaging)
Lemon concentrate	9.00 per gal.
Pulp	.05 per lb.
Lemon juice	.95 per gal.
Peeled lemons	.13 per lb.
Lemon peels	.20 per lb.

Required
(1) Draw a diagram of Surral's lemon processing operations.
(2) Allocate the joint costs of purchasing and peeling a 500-pound batch of lemons, using the relative sales value method.
(3) Calculate the inventoriable unit costs of meal and juice concentrate, using the joint cost allocations determined in (2).
(4) Calculate the unit identifiable contribution margins for packaged meal and concentrate and the unit variable joint cost per pound of lemons processed.
(5) Calculate the firm's total profit at a production level of 350,000 pounds of lemons per month.
(6) Analyze each department, using incremental analysis. Should any of the four departments now in operation be discontinued, assuming that the fixed costs of the department would continue?
(7) Would your answer to (6) change if the fixed costs in a department could be eliminated by discontinuing operations in that department?

Problem 12-7 (*Note: This problem is based on the solution to Problem 12-6 and on Appendix 12A.*) The managers of Surral Juice Company would like to introduce linear programming techniques to their production planning. The company, which is located in a small town, has a limited supply of direct labor. The firm estimates that no more than 4,100 direct labor hours can be worked next month; however, workers can be assigned to any department, as needed. The firm can sell as much pressed pulp or lemon juice concentrate as it can produce, but the demand for ground meal next month is limited to 30,000 pounds. The current year's lemon crop is poor, and the firm can secure a maximum supply of 440,000 pounds of lemons next month. Surral has decided that no intermediate products will be sold next month, and all products will be processed to completion. No beginning inventories will be on hand at the beginning of next month.

Direct labor hours required in each department are as follows:

Peeling Department	.003 hrs. per lb. processed
Pressing Department	.002 hrs. per lb. processed
Grinding Department	.004 hrs. per lb. processed
Packaging Department:	
Meal	.015 hrs. per lb. processed
Concentrate	.020 hrs. per gal. processed

The team assigned to develop the model has selected the following symbols:

LM	=	pounds of lemons processed
M	=	pounds of packaged meal produced
J	=	gallons of lemon juice concentrate produced
MS	=	pounds of packaged meal sold
JS	=	gallons of lemon juice concentrate sold

Required

Develop the objective function and all the constraints necessary to formulate the linear programming model of next month's operations.

Problem 12-8 (AICPA adapted, 11/73). Parker Manufacturing Company has two production departments, Fabrication and Assembly, and three service departments, General Factory Administration, Factory Maintenance, and Factory Cafeteria. A summary of costs and other data for each department, prior to allocation of service department costs for the year ended June 30, 19X3, is as follows:

	Fabrication Department	Assembly Department	General Factory Administration Department	Factory Maintenance Department	Factory Cafeteria
Direct labor hours	562,000	437,500	31,000	27,000	42,000
Number of employees	280	200	12	8	20
Square footage occupied	88,000	72,000	1,750	2,000	4,800
Direct labor	$1,950,000	$2,050,000	$90,000	$82,100	$87,000
Materials	3,130,000	950,000	—	65,000	91,000
Manufacturing overhead	1,650,000	1,850,000	70,000	56,100	62,000

The costs of the General Factory Administration Department, Factory Maintenance Department, and Factory Cafeteria are allocated on the basis of direct labor hours, square footage occupied, and number of employees, respectively. There are no manufacturing overhead variances.

(1) Calculate the total production cost for each production department, using the direct method of cost allocation. Round all final calculations to the nearest ten dollars.

(2) Calculate the total production cost for each production department, using the step method to allocate service department costs. Begin with the service department having the greatest total cost.

Problem 12-9. Anglo-American Minerals Ltd. operates mines in many parts of South America. Among the company's holdings is a copper mine in northern Chile. The mine is located in a part of the country which is rugged and has no cities, forcing the firm to provide its labor force with all essential services. The mining operation is divided into two production departments, Mining and Refining, and three service departments, Accomodation (which provides meals and sleeping quarters for all mine employees), Power (which provides heat and electricity to all production and service departments), and Mine Administration (which handles all the administrative functions necessary to operate the mine).

Management allocates variable service department costs, using the following bases: Accomodation Department—number of employees; Power Department—kilowatt-hours used; Mine Administration Department—total labor hours worked (including overtime). Fixed service department costs are allocated using the same explanatory variables, but using estimated peak usage, rather than actual usage. Tables summarizing relevant data are as follows:

Quarterly Actual Usage

	Accomodation Department	Power Department	Mine Administration Department	Mining Department	Refining Department
Number of employees	209	38	57	1197	399
Kilowatt-hours used (000s)	22.5	15.0	7.5	232.5	472.5
Total labor hours (000s)	148.4	31.8	42.4	593.6	243.8

Quarterly Peak Demand

	Accomodation Department	Power Department	Mine Administration Department	Mining Department	Refining Department
Number of employees	252	56	168	1,848	476
Kilowatt-hours used (000s)	40.0	17.5	9.0	340.0	593.5
Total labor hours (000s)	288.0	32.0	96.0	832.0	352.0

Expenditures for each of the service departments during the quarter were as shown at the top of page 444.

(1) Allocate the service department costs, using the step method of cost allocation. Actual usage should be used as the allocation base to allocate variable costs, and peak usage should be used to allocate fixed costs. Allocate the department with the greatest total cost first.

(2) Allocate the fixed service department costs by the reciprocal services method, using peak usage as the allocation base.

Accomodation Department

Variable expenses:	
Food	$1,134,000
Facilities:	
Repair and maintenance	72,500
Miscellaneous supplies	102,040
Labor	356,160
Total variable expenses	$1,664,700
Fixed expenses:	
Supervision	148,400
Total overhead	$1,813,100

Power Department

Variable expenses:	
Oil, including transportation	$ 342,000
Labor	89,040
Repair parts	14,800
Miscellaneous supplies	9,240
Total variable expenses	$ 455,080
Fixed expenses:	
Supervision	66,320
Total overhead	$ 521,400

Mine Administration Department

Variable expenses:	
Supplies	$ 35,660
Clerical personnel	118,720
Total variable expenses	$ 154,380
Fixed expenses:	
Supervisory personnel	76,320
Total overhead	$ 230,700

Problem 12-10. Cutler-Davis Mills Inc. produces a wide range of natural and synthetic fiber carpeting at their manufacturing facility. The firm is organized into three service departments, Maintenance, Data Processing, and Power, and three production departments, Weaving, Dyeing, and Cutting. Service department costs are allocated to the various production departments, using the following bases: Maintenance Department - maintenance hours incurred; Data Processing Department - computing hours incurred; Power Department - kilowatt-hours demanded. Budgeted costs for the actual usage, rather than actual costs, are allocated to the various user departments, with the difference charged to the service departments as a budget variance.

The flexible budget for each service department is as follows:

	Variable Costs	Fixed Costs
Maintenance	$7.50 per maintenance hour	$4,800 per month
Data Processing	2.00 per computer hour	5,160
Power	.20 per kilowatt-hour	8,060

During the quarter just ended, the actual usage of the service departments was as follows:

	Maint. Dept.	Data Proc.	Power	Weaving	Dyeing	Cutting	Total
Maintenance hours	—	—	840	1,008	336	1,176	3,360
Computing hours	24	—	—	216	96	144	480
Kilowatt-hours (000s)	—	28.8	—	76.8	38.4	48.0	192

Actual costs incurred in each service department during the quarter were $43,560, $17,200, and $61,035 for the Maintenance, Computing, and Power Departments, respectively.

Cutler-Davis allocates budgeted total service department costs for each quarter, using the reciprocal method of cost allocation and actual usage as the allocation base. In the past, the firm has found relative peak usage to correspond closely to actual usage, and thus allocates budgeted fixed service department costs as well as variable costs, using actual usage as the allocation base.

Cutler-Davis has received an offer from a local power-generating cooperative to provide all of its power needs at a cost of $.33 per kilowatt-hour. Elimination of the Power Department would result in an 80% reduction in the Power Department's fixed costs, but would have no effect on the other departments' fixed costs.

Required

(1) Calculate the budget variance for each service department.
(2) Allocate service department costs to each production department, using the reciprocal services method.
(3) Should the firm accept the offer from the cooperative?

Problem 12-11. The Baseball Products Division of T.A.K. Industries produces baseball bats at its plant in Georgia. The factory consists of two production departments, the Cutting Department and the Finishing Department. Each production department has a supervisor who is responsible for the usage variances, but not the price variances. All price variances, the overhead spending (budget) variances, and the fixed overhead volume variances are the responsibility of the vice-president of production, who oversees the two production supervisors, and the firm's purchasing agents. The vice-president of production reports to the divisional president, along with the vice-presidents of sales, finance, personnel, and data processing.

During June, 19X3, the Cutting Department completed and transferred 70,000 units to the Finishing Department. All materials enter at the beginning of the process; conversion costs enter uniformly. The beginning and ending work in process inventories were 9,000 units and 8,500 units, respectively. Both the beginning and ending work in process inventories were 40% complete with respect to conversion costs. There was no spoilage during June. Normal production, used to determine unit standard fixed costs, is 75,000 units a month.

The standard cost sheet for a unit passing through the Cutting Department is as follows:

Materials (35 oz. of wood @ $.02 per oz.)	$ .70
Direct labor (.03 hrs. @ $5 per hr.)	.15
Overhead:	
Variable (.03 hrs. @ $4 per hr.)	.12
Fixed	.60
	$1.57

In the Finishing Department, 65,000 units were completed and sent to finished goods. The beginning inventory totaled 6,000 units, 50% complete. The ending inventory was 11,000 units, 60% complete. As in the Cutting Department, materials enter at the start of production, while conversion costs enter uniformly. There were no spoiled units. The standard cost sheet for a unit passing through the Finishing Department is as follows:

Materials (.10 gals. of varnish @ $3.40 per gal.)	$ .34
Direct labor (.05 hrs. @ $5 per hr.)	.25
Overhead:	
Variable (.05 hrs. @ $7 per hr.)	.35
Fixed*	.30
	$1.24

*Based on a normal monthly production of 75,000 units.

Relevant cost data for the month are summarized as follows:

	Cutting Dept.	Finishing Dept.
Materials purchased	190,000 lbs. of wood for $59,888	8,280 gals. of varnish for $27,324
Materials issued	168,600 lbs.	6,820 gals.
Direct labors hours incurred	2,200 DLH for $10,780	3,510 DLH for $17,550
Overhead (actual)	$57,500	$43,390

	Personnel Department	Data Processing Department
Budgeted cost, based on actual usage	$47,200	$23,500
Actual cost	51,100	22,900

	Sales Department	Finance Department	Office of the Vice-President of Production	Office of the Divisional President
Budgeted cost	$63,600	$29,100	$14,700	$27,200
Actual cost	65,800	34,000	16,100	25,900

Required   (1) For each production department, calculate the spending and usage variances for materials and labor. Also calculate the overhead spending, usage, and volume variances.

(2) Prepare cost performance reports for (a) the Cutting Department supervisor, (b) the Finishing Department supervisor, (c) the vice-president of production, and (d) the divisional president.

Thirteen

Project Planning and Budgeting

In previous chapters, detailed product cost data were developed, models for management planning were studied, and various procedures for exercising better management control were discussed. Chapter 9 focused on how standard cost systems incorporate detailed information on materials, direct labor, and manufacturing overhead into the cost system. In Chapters 7 and 8, planning issues involving which capital project investments the firm should make were discussed. In this chapter, many of these ideas on operational cost reporting, planning, and performance evaluation and control will be integrated into a comprehensive budgeting system for planning and control.

Budgeting is a powerful management tool which is used to accomplish four major objectives: (1) planning, (2) coordination, (3) motivation, and (4) control. The budget is a planning tool that represents the expected results of operations for the coming year, and thus it is a way of formulating and expressing in dollar terms the objectives of an organization and the operational plans for achieving these objectives. The budget is a coordinating tool that is summarized in the form of pro forma financial statements for an entire organization, and thus it ties together the financial, marketing, and production activities of all of the departments and divisions which make up the organization. Budgeting is used to motivate managers by providing explicit goals, by involving managers in the planning and goal-setting process through which the budget is developed, and by providing rewards (and/or penalties) for the achievement of (or the failure to achieve) the goals. Finally, the budget is a control tool because it provides a yardstick for comparing actual results with the organization's planned objectives, and thus it is a basis for taking corrective actions when the actual results are unsatisfactory.

BUDGETING AND ORGANIZATIONAL PLANNING

The basic time horizon chosen for budgeting is usually one year. However, firms may find it useful to break down annual budgets into monthly or quarterly time periods, or to build annual budgets from budgets constructed for shorter time periods. The basic time horizon is usually one year because it is long enough to smooth out minor week-to-week fluctuations and seasonal variations. It is also long enough that the operational details of purchasing individual components for specific products, scheduling the work force, and servicing individual customer demands will not be overwhelming. These operational plans will be developed after the overall budget for the year has been constructed. On the other hand, a year is short enough to allow the necessary quantitative data to be estimated with reasonable accuracy.

Budgeting should be accompanied by other forms of planning which address both longer and shorter time frames. Longer-run analyses take the form of **strategic planning,** which typically has a 3- to 5-year time horizon. In strategic planning, the overall goals and objectives of the organization are established. Many of these broad goals and objectives are stated in general terms, and are not quantified in numerical terms. For example, an oil company may state that its objective is to become an energy company, encompassing nuclear, solar, and plant-derived energy sources, rather than limiting itself to the production, refining, and distribution of petroleum products.

Strategic planning is carried out by a firm's top executives. In some organizations, strategic planning is conducted informally at executive conferences which are held whenever it is recognized that the organization will need to make major changes to remain viable. Such organizations do not engage in strategic planning until forced to do so by a crisis situation. Other organizations have a more formal strategic planning process. Meetings are held at regularly scheduled intervals, and formalized planning is carried out under the direction of a top-level executive, often given the title of Vice-President—Planning.

For time periods shorter than one year, **operational planning** focuses on decisions which need to be made daily or weekly in order to keep the organization running smoothly. Since operational planning is concerned with day-to-day operations, it deals with individual products, workers, suppliers, and customers at a detailed level. Operational planning is usually carried out by the operational managers or special planning groups in each functional area. For example, the purchasing agent who issues the purchase order, or the production and inventory planning section in a firm, may decide when to order a specific component.

The differences that have developed between budgeting and strategic planning and operational planning in practice are summarized in the following table. The basic difference is that budgeting is an integrated planning process specifically incorporating all the functional areas—manufacturing, marketing, finance, and personnel—into one master plan.

	Operational Planning	Budgeting	Strategic Planning
Typical planning horizon	Short-term (1 day, 1 week, or 1 month)	Intermediate (1 year)	Long-term (3 to 5 years or longer)
Level of managers involved	Primarily lower-level operating managers	All levels	Primarily top-level management
Degree of structure to planning models	Often well-defined models	Semi-structured models	Often unstructured
Type of information which predominates	Physical data	Financial data	Physical and/or financial data
Level of detail involved	Very detailed (individual machine, product, customer, etc.)	Some detail (department or division level)	Usually at the level of the organization as a whole
Example of planning decision	Scheduling machines for the next day's production in a job shop	Developing the firm's profit plan for the next year	Deciding on a corporate acquisition or merger

An Overview of the Budgeting Process

Although budgeting procedures may vary considerably from firm to firm, the individual steps in the budgeting process are similar for most firms. The steps described in the following paragraphs and in Illustration 13-1 are typical of those used by medium-sized manufacturing organizations. In most cases, budgets (or profit plans, as they are often called) begin with a set of overall corporate goals established by top management. These goals are based on what the organization has been able to accomplish in the past and the economic climate in which the organization must operate during the coming year.

The specific planning usually begins with a sales forecast. For most organizations, the demand for their products (or services) is the factor or variable which activates the planning process. Accordingly, a schedule of prices and a sales promotion strategy need to be established concurrently with the sales forecasts, since sales volume is dependent on both the prices charged and the sales promotion.

Two general approaches can be used to derive demand forecasts: a "bottom-up" approach and a "top-down" approach. The bottom-up approach is often used by firms with a decentralized organizational structure, and the top-down approach is used by centralized firms.

In the bottom-up approach, the sales force's estimates of the probable demand for all products by individual customers are aggregated to provide total product-line demands for the firm. One of the advantages of this approach is that the experience and judgment of sales personnel, who have the closest contact with customers, are utilized. Another potential advantage is that the salespeople play a part in the formulation of the projected sales volumes by which their performance will be evaluated. This behavioral consideration is important, since the sales force will consider their sales targets to be reasonable and will be more committed to achieving them.

In the top-down approach, the initial forecasts come from upper-level management or from analyses provided by staff groups who advise the upper-level managers and have particular expertise in market forecasting. The forecasts may be based on past periods' demand, with past trends extrapolated into the future, or the

Illustration 13-1
**An Overview of the
Budget Planning Process**

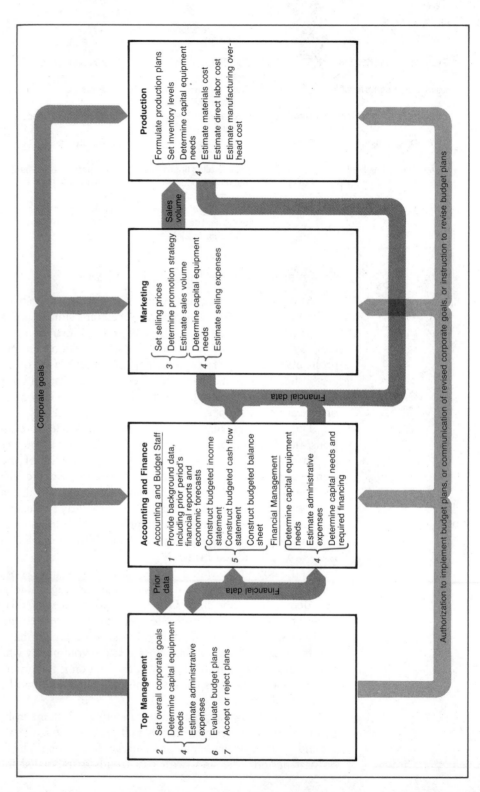

forecast demand for the firms' product may be related to factors that are expected to influence the demand, such as customers' disposable income (for consumer products) or gross national product (for industrial sales). From these sales forecasts, the upper-level managers set sales volume goals at a level that is both desirable from the firm's standpoint and also achievable by the sales force.

Once the sales forecast has been completed, the existing and the desired finished goods inventory levels can be determined, and production plans can be developed. From the production plans, the materials and direct labor requirements can be determined. Based on the planned production and sales activity levels, flexible budgets for manufacturing overhead and marketing and administrative expenses can be established.

Preparation of a Master Budget

A company's overall goals to be achieved for the coming year are contained in a **master budget,** which is the set of annual budgets approved by top management. The basic components of a master budget are a projected, or pro forma, income statement, which is the firm's profit plan for the coming year; a projected cash flow statement for the year; and a year-end, pro forma balance sheet, which combines information from the budgeted income and cash flow statements with the beginning-of-year balance sheet information.

As the basis for formulating detailed operating plans to achieve a firm's goals, the master budget is usually broken down into monthly or quarterly budgets. Monthly reports that compare the monthly budget with actual performance for the month and for the year-to-date can then be used to signal the need to revise operating plans and goals, to motivate managers to exert greater effort in the event the goals are not achieved, and to determine financial and other rewards for goal achievement.

To illustrate the preparation of a master budget, assume that a small manufacturing firm, Chemco Inc., produces a chemical fertilizer. Chemco uses a standard cost accounting system, and values its inventories on an absorption basis, using the lifo method. The 19X1 current standard costs and the 19X2 projected standard costs are shown in Illustration 13-2. The current standard costs are the same as the costs used in Chapter 9, page 311, to illustrate variance analysis procedures.

Illustration 13-2
Current and Projected Standard Costs for Chemco Inc.

19X1 Current Standards	Current Standard Cost	Expected Change	19X2 Standard Cost
Materials:	•		
1 lb. of Afex @ $.80 per lb.	$ .80	+10%	$ .88
3 lbs. of Bevos @ $.50 per lb.	1.50	+10%	1.65
Direct labor (2 hrs. @ $5 per hr.)	10.00	+12%	11.20
Variable overhead (2 hrs. @ $1.50 per hr.)	3.00	+10%*	3.30
Fixed overhead (2 hrs. @ $1 per hr.)	2.00	+ 8%*	2.16
Total	$17.30		$19.19

* See Illustration 13-3.

The first step in preparing the master budget for Chemco Inc. is to determine the general state of the economy which is likely to prevail in the coming year, and the prospects for any inflationary or deflationary price changes. Because of inflationary factors, Chemco expects materials and supply prices to increase by 10% in the coming year, and labor rates to increase by 12%. The marketing managers at Chemco have established a selling price of $27 per carton, and they expect to sell 25,000 cartons in 19X2.

The required production of fertilizer is determined by adjusting the expected sales level for any desired changes in inventory levels. If inventory levels are excessive, some of the demand will be met by depleting existing inventories. If strong customer demand has depleted inventories, or if unexpected orders have resulted in stockouts or rush production jobs, then production will be increased over forecasted sales levels in order to provide for the establishment of adequate inventories.

The production schedules must also be consistent with the firm's operating capabilities. If capacity limits are reached, plans must be made to add capacity, to increase operating efficiency, to alter product design, or to scale down the initial projections of operating levels.

The production and inventory control managers at Chemco believe that the current inventory of finished fertilizer on hand (3,000 cartons) is too small. They plan to gradually increase the finished goods inventory to a level of 5,000 cartons by year end. Thus, 27,000 cartons (expected sales of 25,000 + desired ending inventory of 5,000 − beginning inventory of 3,000) are scheduled for production during the coming year. Inventories of work in process at Chemco are negligible and are ignored in the budgeting process.

Once the level of production has been established, Chemco determines its materials requirements. Since the present inventory of Bevos (6,000 pounds) is at a satisfactory level, Chemco needs to purchase 81,000 pounds of Bevos (27,000 cartons × 3 pounds per carton) in 19X2. In regard to Afex, however, Chemco has been plagued with delays in deliveries. To deal with this situation, Chemco plans to increase its Afex inventories from 2,000 pounds to 3,000 pounds. Required purchases of Afex will be based on production requirements of 27,000 pounds (production volume of 27,000 cartons × 1 pound per carton). To this amount will be added the 1,000-pound desired increase in inventory, so that 28,000 pounds of Afex must be purchased.

The manufacturing overhead costs projected for 19X2 are shown in Illustration 13-3. Chemco begins with its 19X1 budget as its starting point, rather than its actual 19X1 costs, since the actual costs incurred in 19X1 include the effect of some spending, excess usage, and labor efficiency variances which it plans to eliminate in 19X2. The proposed 19X2 overhead budget incorporates the effect of an expected inflationary increase in prices as well as the increase in expected production volume. Chemco uses normal production volume to arrive at its fixed overhead rate in order to avoid changes in the unit costs due to variations in production from period to period.

The selling and administrative expenses budget for 19X2 is shown in Illustration 13-4. The sales commissions are entirely variable, while $275 of the supplies expense is fixed and the remainder is variable. All other selling and administrative expenses are entirely discretionary fixed expenses.

Illustration 13-3
Manufacturing Overhead Budget for 19X2 for Chemco Inc.

	19X1 Flexible Budget for Actual Production (21,600 Units)	19X2 Flexible Budget for Expected Production (27,000 Units)
Variable overhead expenses:		
Supplies	$ 20,000	$ 27,500
Indirect labor	24,000	33,600
Other variable expenses	20,800	28,000
Total variable expenses	$ 64,800	$ 89,100
Fixed overhead expenses:		
Depreciation	$ 12,000	$ 12,000
Supervision	15,000	16,800
Factory, rent, and insurance	12,000	13,320
Other fixed expenses	9,000	9,720
Total fixed expenses	$ 48,000	$ 51,840
Total manufacturing overhead	$112,800	$140,940

	19X1	19X2	Increase
Variable overhead rate:			
Production	21,600 units	27,000 units	
Standard labor hours per unit	× 2 hours	× 2 hours	
Total standard labor hours for production	43,200 hours	54,000 hours	
Standard variable overhead per hour	$\frac{\$64,800}{43,200} = \$1.50$	$\frac{\$89,100}{54,000} = \$1.65$	$.15 (10\%)
Fixed overhead rate:			
Normal production	24,000 units	24,000 units	
Standard labor hours per unit	× 2 hours	× 2 hours	
Total standard labor hours for normal volume	48,000 hours	48,000 hours	
Standard fixed overhead per hour	$\frac{\$48,000}{48,000} = \$1$	$\frac{\$51,840}{48,000} = \$1.08$	$.08 (8\%)

Illustration 13-4
Selling and Administrative Expenses Budget for 19X2 for Chemco Inc.

Selling expenses:		
Sales commissions ($.40 per carton × 25,000 cartons)	$10,000	
Sales salaries	15,000	
Advertising	5,000	
Sales administration	20,000	
Total selling expenses		$ 50,000
Administrative expenses:		
Clerical wages	$20,000	
Supplies [$275 + (.7% × $675,000)]	5,000	
Executive salaries	30,000	
Depreciation of computer	10,000	
Total administrative expenses		65,000
Total selling and administrative expenses		$115,000

The information developed up to this point is used in the preparation of Chemco's budgeted income statement, which is shown in Illustration 13-5. In the budgeted income statement, the standard cost of goods sold for 19X2 is computed as $479,750 ($19.19 per carton × 25,000 cartons expected to be sold). The expected volume variance of $6,480 is deducted from this amount, giving an expected net cost of goods sold of $473,270. The expected volume variance is the difference between the expected production volume of 27,000 units and the normal production volume of 24,000 units, multiplied by the fixed overhead rate of $2.16 per unit.

The budgeted operating income of $86,730 would then be evaluated with reference to a desired target return on sales or return on investment. If the budgeted operating income does not meet the target, then either marketing strategies must be changed in order to provide greater revenues, or costs must be reduced. If the budgeted operating income meets management's goals, then the budgeting process can continue to the next stage.

Sales (25,000 cartons @ $27 per carton)			$675,000
Less cost of goods sold (lifo):			
Beginning inventory (3,000 cartons @ $17.30)		$ 51,900	
Cost of goods manufactured (27,000 @ $19.19)		518,130	
Available for sale		$570,030	
Ending inventory:			
3,000 cartons @ $17.30	$51,900		
2,000 cartons @ $19.19	38,380	90,280	
Cost of goods sold at standard cost		$479,750	
Less expected favorable volume variance		6,480[a]	473,270
Gross margin			$201,730
Less selling and administrative expenses			115,000
Operating income			$ 86,730
Less interest expense			4,420
Income before taxes			$ 82,310
Less state and federal income taxes (50%)			41,155
Net income			$ 41,155

[a] Expected production units, 27,000 − normal volume, 24,000, or 3,000 units @ $2.16 per unit.

Although the revenues and operating expenses provide the logical starting point for the income statement, the statement cannot be completed until the interest expense and income taxes, for which the interest is deductible, are known. Thus, after the budgeted operating income is determined, the income statement is temporarily put aside, and the cash flows are analyzed.

As shown in Illustration 13-6, the usual starting point in estimating cash flows is to convert the budgeted income statement, which was prepared on an accrual basis, to a cash-basis statement. Sales revenues are converted to cash collections from customers by adding the beginning-of-the-period receivables to the revenues and subtracting the portion of the receivables which are not expected to be collected by the end of the period. Since accounts receivable on January 1 total $23,000, and two weeks' sales (1/26 of $675,000, or $25,962) are not expected to be collected by December 31, Chemco's cash collections from customers will total $672,038 ($675,000 + $23,000 − $25,962). Any portion of the sales represented by cash sales requires no adjustment for accruals, and if a portion of the sales are not expected to be collected at all but are to be written off, the uncollectible sales should not be included in cash collections.

On the average, cash is disbursed for most of Chemco's materials purchases one month after receipt of the item, leaving one month's purchases unpaid at year end. In addition, there are two weeks' wages not yet paid to employees at the end of the year. The cash disbursements for purchases and labor are computed by adding to the appropriate costs shown in the income statement the beginning-of-the-period accruals and subtracting the amounts unpaid at year end.

Chemco pays its factory rent and insurance 6 months in advance. Accordingly, the cash outlays for factory rent and insurance for the current year are the expense for the current year, $13,320, less the December 31, 19X1 prepayment of $6,120, plus the December 31, 19X2 prepayment of $7,200 for the first half of the next year.

Some expenses, such as depreciation, do not represent current cash flows and should not be included in the budgeted cash flow statement. However, any cash outlays for purchases of plant assets should be included. Since Chemco is replacing a rental computer with a purchased minicomputer costing $55,000, this amount is included in the 19X2 cash flow statement.

Illustration 13-6
Work Sheet for Preparing a Cash Flow Statement for Chemco Inc.

Income Statement		Additions[a]	Deductions[b]	Budgeted Cash Flow Statement	
				Receipts	Disbursements
Sales	$675,000	$23,000	$25,962	$672,038	
Materials purchases	69,190[c]	4,600	5,766		$ 68,024
Direct labor	302,400[d]	8,308	11,631		299,077
Manufacturing overhead:[e]					
Supplies	27,500	1,667	2,292		26,875
Indirect labor	33,600	923	1,292		33,231
Other variable expenses	28,000	1,733	2,333		27,400
Supervision	16,800	500	646		16,654
Factory rent and insurance	13,320	7,200	6,120		14,400
Other fixed expenses	9,720	750	810		9,660
Selling and administrative expenses:[f]					
Sales commissions and salaries	25,000	800	962		24,838
Advertising	5,000	400	417		4,983
Sales administration	20,000	600	769		19,831
Clerical wages and executive salaries	50,000	1,500	1,923		49,577
Supplies	5,000	500	417		5,083
Total 19X2 operating cash flows				$672,038	$599,633
Net cash flow from operations ($672,038 − $599,633)				$ 72,405	
Expenditures for capital equipment (minicomputer)					$ 55,000
Borrowing on 4-year term loan				40,000	
Borrowing and retirement of short-term bank loan				24,000	24,420
Cash payments for income taxes[g]					40,866
January 1, 19X2 cash balance				25,000	
Total cash available, receipts, and disbursements				$161,405	$120,286
Budgeted December 31, 19X2 cash balance ($161,405 − $120,286)				$ 41,119	

[a] Except for factory rent and insurance, additions are the beginning-of-year balances for receivables (for cash collections from customers) or liabilities (for cash disbursements for expenses). Since rent and insurance are prepaid, the addition for this item is the end-of-year asset balance.

[b] Except for factory rent and insurance, deductions are the year-end uncollected sales (1/26 of $675,000), unpaid purchases of materials, supplies, and other expenses (1/12 of annual costs), and the unpaid wages and salaries for factory labor and office staff (1/26 of annual costs). The deduction for rent and insurance is the beginning-of-year prepaid balance for this item.

[c] 28,000 lbs. of Afex @ $.88 per lb., plus 81,000 lbs. of Bevos @ $.55 per lb.

[d] 27,000 units @ $11.20 per unit.

[e] See manufacturing overhead budget for source of individual items.

[f] See selling and administrative expenses budget for individual items.

[g] $41,155 income taxes for 19X2, per income statement, plus beginning-of-year accrual, $10,000, less end-of-year accrual, $10,289 (1/4 of $41,155).

After the cash impact of operating revenues and expenses has been incorporated in the budgeted cash flow statement, it is necessary to consider cash flows that result from financing transactions. Temporary investments may be purchased or sold, payments may be made on existing loans, or additional cash may be borrowed. Changes in the long-term debt structure or in common and preferred stock outstanding may also be made. Although a cash flow statement covering the entire year may be adequate to plan for major changes in the firm's financial position, short-term adjustments in temporary investments and short-term borrowing within the year typically make it necessary for cash flows to be projected on a monthly or even weekly basis. These short-term projections capture the important seasonal variations that are not observed in the annual statements.

Although the 19X2 income subject to tax will contain a deduction for interest expense, the amount of interest is unknown at this stage of the budgeting process. However, a satisfactory approximation of the tax can be obtained by ignoring the interest deduction and the tax accrual and multiplying Chemco's operating income by 50% (the effective combined federal and state income tax rate). The resulting preliminary tax estimate is $43,365 (50% × $86,730), and the preliminary estimate of cash available is $54,040 ($72,405 net cash from operations + $25,000 January cash balance − $43,365 preliminary tax estimate).

The preliminary estimate of cash available is not adequate to pay for the computer ($55,000) and provide for a desired $25,000 cash balance. Accordingly, the treasurer decides to secure a 4-year term loan for $40,000 from the bank at an interest rate of 10%. Chemco's bank requires the loan to be paid off in four equal installments of $12,619 each, covering interest and principal. The first installment, due in January, 19X3, will consist of the first year's interest of $4,000 (10% × $40,000), and a principal repayment of $8,619 ($12,619 − $4,000).

Chemco's treasurer has also prepared a monthly cash flow analysis which reveals that seasonal variations in sales and production will produce a temporary need for cash of $20,000 during the second quarter of 19X2 in order to carry a temporary increase in inventories and receivables. This cash will be provided through short-term bank credit. For this type of loan, the interest rate will be 7%, and the bank will require that Chemco maintain a compensating balance. To insure that the compensating balance requirement will be met, Chemco will arrange for a 3-month loan of $24,000. The monthly analysis indicates that the normal collection of receivables will enable Chemco to retire this short-term loan on schedule. Therefore, $24,000 is added to the year's cash receipts, and $24,420 [$24,000 principal + ($24,000 × 7% × 1/4 year)] is added to the disbursements.

At this point, the income statement can be completed. The cash flow calculations have given the amount borrowed, which in turn provides the interest expense for the year, $4,420 ($4,000 on the 4-year term loan + $420 on the 3-month loan). The year's income tax expense can now be calculated, and the budgeted net income for 19X2 can be determined. The income tax expense for the year is carried to the cash flow work sheet and adjusted for beginning and ending accruals in order to compute the end-of-year cash balance. The resulting amount, $41,119, will be adequate to cover the January 2, 19X3 payment on the term loan, $12,619, and still leave Chemco with a cash balance ($28,500) which approximates the treasurer's cash balance goal. The cash flows are then summarized in the statement of budgeted cash receipts and disbursements, shown in Illustration 13-7.

Illustration 13-7   Statement of Budgeted Cash Receipts and Disbursements for 19X2 for Chemco Inc.

Cash balance, January 1, 19X2			$ 25,000
Add operating receipts (cash collections from customers)	$672,038		
Less disbursements for operating expenses	599,633		
Net cash flow from operations, before taxes		$ 72,405	
Add:			
Borrowing on 4-year term loan	$ 40,000		
Borrowing on short-term bank loan	24,000		
Cash receipts from borrowing	$ 64,000		
Less repayment of principal and interest on short-term bank loan	24,420		
Net cash flow from financing transactions		39,580	111,985
Less:			$136,985
Cash disbursements for income taxes			
Cash disbursements for purchase of capital equipment		$ 40,866	
Budgeted cash balance, December 31, 19X2		55,000	95,866
			$ 41,119

In Illustration 13-8, the information used in preparing the income statement and cash flow statement are combined with the January 1, 19X2 balance sheet information to provide the December 31, 19X2 budgeted balance sheet. The end-of-year accruals and deferrals used in calculating the year's cash flow will appear also on the year-end balance sheet. The specific source of the individual items on the balance sheet is given in the notes to the budgeted balance sheet.

TECHNIQUES FOR MAKING BUDGETING MORE EFFECTIVE

The preceding section concentrated on the mechanics of constructing budgets. A successful budgeting program, however, involves much more than simply putting together pro forma financial statements. Unless the managers responsible for carrying out the organization's plans actively strive to maximize output and minimize costs, the goals reflected in those plans will not be achieved. Some of the techniques which have been utilized by firms which have had successful budgeting programs are described in the following paragraphs.

Continuous Budgets

In a dynamic environment, the assumptions on which a budget is based may become unrealistic later in the year. At that point, a firm may revise its budget to reflect more current conditions. Some firms establish procedures for updating their budgets on a regular schedule in order to incorporate management's latest planning and control decisions. These updated budgets are often referred to as **continuous budgets** or **rolling budgets.**

In a continuous budgeting process, the budget for the quarter (or month or half year) just ended is dropped from the annual budget at the end of the quarter, and a budget for the quarter a year hence is added. For example, on March 31, 19X2, the first quarter of the 19X2 budget would be dropped, and a budget for the first quarter of 19X3 would be added to the remaining three quarters of the original 19X2 budget. Any necessary adjustments for those three quarters would also be made at this time. In this way, the firm is always operating with an up-to-date budget for the next twelve months.

Illustration 13-8
Beginning and Ending
Balance Sheets for
Chemco Inc.

	Jan. 1, 19X2 Balance Sheet	Dec. 31, 19X2 Balance Sheet
Cash	$ 25,000	$ 41,119[b]
Accounts receivable	23,000	25,962[c]
Inventories	57,000[a]	96,260[d]
Prepaid rent and insurance	6,120	7,200[e]
Equipment (net)	84,000	117,000[f]
Total assets	$195,120	$287,541
Accounts payable	$ 9,650	$ 12,035[g]
Accrued payroll	12,631	17,223[h]
Taxes payable	10,000	10,289[i]
Bank loan payable (current portion)	—	12,619[j]
Term bank loan payable	—	31,381[k]
Common stock	50,000	50,000
Retained earnings	112,839	153,994[l]
Total equities	$195,120	$287,541

[a] Beginning inventory of materials:

Afex (2,000 lbs. @ .80)	$1,600	
Bevos (6,000 lbs. @ .50)	3,000	$ 4,600
Beginning inventory of work in process		500
Beginning inventory of finished goods		51,900
Total inventories, January 1, 19X2		$57,000

[b] See Illustration 13-7.

[c] 1/26 of annual sales ($675,000).

[d] Materials:

Afex: 2,000 lbs. @ $.80	$1,600		
1,000 lbs. @ .88	880	$ 2,480	
Bevos: 6,000 lbs. @ .50		3,000	$ 5,480
Work in process			500
Finished goods: 3,000 units @ $17.30 ...	$51,900		
2,000 units @ 19.19 ...	38,380	90,280	
Total December 31, 19X2 inventories			$96,260

[e] Prepaid portion (1/2 year) of rent and insurance.

[f] Beginning balance ($84,000) plus purchase of computer ($55,000) less depreciation ($12,000 factory and $10,000 administrative).

[g] 1/12 of annual purchases of materials ($69,190), supplies ($32,500), advertising ($5,000), and other variable and fixed expenses ($37,720).

[h] 1/26 of annual wages and salaries ($447,800).

[i] 1/4 of annual taxes ($41,155).

[j] First-year's payment, due January 2, 19X3.

[k] Remaining principal on term loan ($40,000 − $8,619).

[l]

January 1, 19X2 balance	$112,839
Budgeted net income	41,155
Retained earnings, December 31, 19X2 ...	$153,994

Some firms, however, do not use continuous budgets, because budgets that are automatically revised downward to accommodate some unfavorable set of external circumstances may weaken employees' motivation. Once the budget for a department or a division in the firm has been discussed and agreement on the budget has been reached, the manager of that department is deemed to have made a commitment to achieve the results reflected in the budget. If conditions change, the manager is expected to exert extra effort and develop new strategies to achieve the expected results.

Participative Budgeting

Behavioral studies of the budgeting process indicate that managers generally feel a greater commitment to achieving the budget goals if they have played a part in constructing the budget. The participative approach to budgeting emphasizes the active involvement of the managers who will subsequently be evaluated on the basis of the budgeted goals.

Depending on the management philosophy of the firm, the specific role played by the upper-level managers and subordinates will differ. Subordinates may participate by providing information and forecasts about the operating environment, such as customer demands and materials and labor prices and availability. This information may then be used by upper-level managers and staff groups in constructing the budgeted operating plans for the next period.

Subordinates may participate to a greater extent by becoming involved in selecting the particular operating strategies to be followed in the next period in order to achieve upper-level management's goals. For example, the sales force may be asked to help decide whether a cut in prices or additional advertising should be used to achieve an increase in sales volume. In some cases, participation may even extend to joint decision making involving the determination of what the goals for the next period should be. In the marketing area, for example, the level of budgeted sales (sales quotas) would be determined jointly by sales management and the sales force.

One approach to participative budgeting is to give the subordinate the opportunity to construct the first-round, initial budget, which is then reviewed and modified by the subordinate's superior. This approach gives the lower-level manager a larger creative role; however, if the subordinate's budget requests are subsequently rejected, it risks generating the attitude that upper-level management is only encouraging pseudo-participation. Widespread negative feelings can lead to an informal banding together of subordinates and a rejection of upper-level management's goals.

Another approach is to include the subordinate in a group which collectively arrives at a final budget decision through a consensus. Effective use of this approach requires special skills on the part of the superior who manages the group decision-making process. Also, the subordinates must bring to the process a broad understanding of how their sphere of operations meshes with other aspects of the firm's activities, and they must be willing to make necessary compromises in order to achieve overall organization goals.

This approach could be viewed as conflicting with a traditional organization structure that is based on a well-defined organization chart and clear limits to authority and responsibility at each level. However, the productivity and concern for quality exhibited by Japanese firms is a consequence of this style of management, which has been called Theory Z.[1] Examples of this approach to decision making can also be found in the United States in such organizations as IBM, Hewlett-Packard, Eastman Kodak, and Procter & Gamble. The budgeting process in these Type Z organizations is likely to emphasize communication, participation,

---

[1]William Ouchi, *Theory Z* (Reading, Mass.: Addison-Wesley Publishing Company, 1981), p. 69.

motivation, and commitment to long-run, companywide goals as the primary mechanisms for achieving good performance.

Although greater participation is generally believed to be desirable, the expected benefits are not always realized. Many of the empirical studies of the effects of participation on budgeting find that while greater participation often leads to better attitudes or feelings, significant improvement in performance is difficult to document.

Zero-Base Budgeting

In constructing budgets, it is quite common to start with last year's operating results as a base. Adjustments are then made to reflect anticipated price and volume changes which are expected for the coming period. A disadvantage of this approach is that any inefficiencies in existing operations may be carried forward into the new budget. To deal with this problem, a technique called zero-base budgeting has received widespread attention. Rather than beginning with the present year's results or budget, zero-base budgeting begins with a base of zero and forces the entire proposed set of activities to be justified. Zero-base budgeting was first introduced in governmental budgeting. It then spread into the private sector, after early users reported significant benefits.

A typical zero-base budgeting program involves the following steps:

1. Each organizational decision unit develops decision packages (programs). In constructing these decision packages, each different activity presently carried out or proposed must be represented by a separate decision package. One package is developed for minimum or business-as-usual operations. Additional packages are then prepared by adding to the base package an incremental or expanded level of activity.
2. The various packages are ranked, on a cost-benefit basis, by the manager who has constructed them. For each decision package, the benefits associated with an activity, along with its costs, are identified. Benefits may be measured in both financial and nonfinancial terms. Typically, nonprofit organizations concentrate on nonfinancial objectives.
3. The collection of packages of all units at a given organizational level is reviewed and ranked by one or more managers at the next higher level, and a subset of this collection is selected. Consideration is given to the consequences of not approving lower-ranked packages. A cutoff which becomes more stringent at each higher level is imposed, and only those packages which exceed the cutoff criterion are reviewed in detail at the next higher level.
4. At each higher organizational level, the packages chosen by lower-level managers are evaluated until, at the top level, the available resources are allocated among the chosen packages.

Firms that have used zero-base budgeting cite two major difficulties in implementing this approach. First, since zero-base budgeting involves a different approach to budgeting, significant costs may be incurred in developing new forms and procedures and in communicating and explaining these new procedures throughout the organization. Secondly, both the construction and the review of the large number of zero-base decision packages require much more time and effort than traditional approaches. Organizations using zero-base budgeting have dealt with this problem in one of the following ways: (1) by applying zero-base budgeting on a rotating basis, involving only selected departments or divisions within the firm in a given year; (2) by using a modified approach in which plans based on 10% or 20% variations from current levels are used; or (3) by applying zero-base budgeting only to those units which are in financial trouble or those in which major management changes have occurred.

FINANCIAL SIMULATION MODELS

As the use of computers for accounting applications increased, firms began to store their detailed budget data in computer processible form. Computer programs were written to compare budgeted revenues, costs, and income with actual results. Since the budget is a quantitative and financial expression of the organization's operating plans for the future, management then began to explore how the computer could be used in conjunction with a mathematical model of the firm's activities to generate pro forma financial statements.

Computerized financial simulation models were first constructed in the 1960s. At that time, the most advanced formal mathematical models were those of the economy which were being constructed by macroeconomists, and business operations problems that were too large and complex to solve analytically were being studied by operations researchers through computer simulations. Thus, the early budget modeling efforts relied on the technical expertise of these groups.

Typically, the larger mathematical models consisted of numerous equations or mathematical relationships which could be characterized as falling into one of the following major categories:

1. Identities or definitional statements (often referred to as accounting identities): The term identity is used to describe a relationship which is true by definition in these formal models. For example, in a macroeconomic model of the economy, national income (the net product of the economy) is defined as consumption plus net investment plus government expenditures ($NI = C + I + G$). In a financial model of the firm, the equation Assets = Liabilities + Owner's Equity, or $A = L + OE$, is an accounting identity that equates the firm's resources with the claims against those resources. Since most models incorporate both stocks and flows, those models would also contain equations such as beginning inventory + acquisitions = ending inventory + usage (i.e., transfers out).

2. Policy relationships: Models often contain equations expressing desired relationships which management attempts to maintain. For example, management may wish to establish an inventory policy that the materials inventory be maintained at a level at least equal to one month's anticipated usage.

3. Behavioral relationships: Behavioral relationships in models attempt to capture observed regularities in the behavior of customers, employees, or other groups. For example, a firm selling goods on terms of 2/10, n/30 may observe that 60% of its credit customers pay within the 10-day discount period, another 30% pay in the next 20 days, 7% take up to 3 months to pay, and the remaining accounts are written off as uncollectible. This payment pattern is

reflected in an equation for cash receipts from customers. The coefficients in behavioral equations, such as the percentage of customers who take discounts, may be estimated by calculating the average proportion observed in the past, as shown in the accounting records. These values may also be obtained by using statistical regression procedures to obtain the parameter estimates.

4. Technological relationships: Technological relationships are equations which are a consequence of the product design, the production technology in place at a particular time, or other engineering design applications. A simulation model of a manufacturing firm, for example, might show the technological relationships among components of a given product or among the various stages in a production process.

Design of Financial Simulation Models

To illustrate the designing of a financial simulation model, the description of the master budgets for Chemco Inc., given in the first part of this chapter, will be used. For each of the relationships, the written description will be accompanied by an equation and a numerical illustration.

Often the first step in designing a financial simulation model is the formulation of a series of identities or definitional statements which will generate financial statements or reports from input data. For Chemco, an accounting identity in the financial simulation model is the equation which determines production quantities as a function of beginning inventory, units sold, and desired ending inventory. This equation is stated as follows:[2]

$$\frac{\text{Production}}{\text{units}} = \frac{\text{Sales}}{\text{units}} + \frac{\text{Ending finished goods}}{\text{inventory units}} - \frac{\text{Beginning finished goods}}{\text{inventory units}}$$

If Chemco's January sales have been forecasted at 2,000 units, if it desires to have 3,500 units of finished product on hand at the end of January, and if its beginning inventory is 3,000 units, its January production should be:[3]

$$\begin{array}{ccccccc} PU_t & = & SU_t & + & FGIU_t & - & FGIU_{t-1} \\ 2,500 & = & 2,000 & + & 3,500 & - & 3,000 \end{array}$$

An entire financial simulation model consisting entirely of identities could be built. Such a model might be referred to as a **report generator,** since the only function performed by the model is to summarize the detailed accounting transaction data and display the results in meaningful financial statement form. A disadvantage of a report generator model is that it requires too much detailed data input. To reduce the amount of inputs required, policy, behavioral, and technological relationships can be introduced into the model. These relationships would then be used to generate much of the data which would otherwise have to be estimated separately outside the model.

---

[2] Subscripts refer to months. Month t refers to the current (or any) month. For cash flow, income, and expense variables, month $t - 1$ refers to flows of the previous month and month $t + 1$ refers to the following month. For balance sheet (stock) variables, balances for month t refer to the balance at the end of that month.

[3] Since the model is formulated in terms of monthly activities, the individual values, while consistent with the annual master budget developed earlier in the chapter, cannot necessarily be derived from the annual data.

An example of a policy relationship at Chemco is the one which determines inventory levels. Chemco's production planning and inventory control managers have decided that, to meet customer demand, finished goods inventory levels should be maintained at an amount equal to the next one and one-half month's expected sales. Once monthly sales forecasts have been made, this inventory policy will enable month-end finished goods inventory levels to be established. This inventory policy relationship is stated as follows:

$$\text{Finished goods inventory units at the end of the current month} = \text{Expected sales units for the next 1-1/2 months}$$

If the current month's sales are expected to be 2,000 units and sales units are expected to grow 10% per month, the ending inventory for the current month should be:

$$FGIU_t = SU_{t+1} + 1/2\,SU_{t+2}$$
$$3,410 = 2,200 + 1/2(2,420)$$

An example of a behavioral equation is the one describing the cash payment pattern of customers. If 75% of the customers typically pay their bills in the month in which the sale is made and the remainder pay in the following month, this payment pattern can be expressed as follows:

$$\text{Cash collections on account in the current month} = \text{75\% of current month's sales} + \text{25\% of sales in the preceding month}$$

If the current month's sales are $60,000 and the prior month's sales were $80,000, cash collections in the current month would be:

$$CCA_t = .75S_t + .25S_{t-1}$$
$$\$65,000 = .75(\$60,000) + .25(\$80,000)$$

The buildup of the manufacturing cost of Chemco's fertilizer reflects the chemical technology used to formulate the product and the production technology used to produce it (as well as the prices of materials, labor, and services). This technological relationship could be formulated as follows:

$$\text{Unit standard cost} = \text{Cost of 1 lb. of Afex} + \text{Cost of 3 lbs. of Bevos} + \text{Labor and overhead costs for 2 hours of direct labor}$$

If the cost of Afex (CA) is $.88 per pound, the cost of Bevos (CB) is $.55 per pound, and the combined labor and overhead rate (CL) is $8.33 per hour, the unit standard cost of the fertilizer (USC) will be:

$$USC = 1\,CA + 3\,CB + 2\,CL$$
$$\$19.19 = (1)(\$.88) + (3)(\$.55) + (2)(\$8.33)$$

More Complex Financial Simulation Models

Most existing financial simulation models are the type illustrated in the preceding paragraphs. This type of model could be described as a deterministic, descriptive model. The model is deterministic, since each unknown variable is given only a single point estimate.

A more elaborate probabilistic or stochastic model would represent each uncertain variable by an entire probability distribution. Stochastic models require more input data, since the entire distribution, or all the parameters for a specified statistical distribution, must be provided, rather than just the most likely value (mode) or the expected value (mean). Stochastic models also generate entire probability distributions for each uncertain output variable.

The parameters for a statistical distribution may be derived mathematically, or an approximation of the entire distribution may be generated using Monte Carlo simulation techniques. In Monte Carlo simulations, hundreds of individual trials or iterations are performed, and the results are summarized in terms of frequency distributions. These frequency distributions, for a large number of trials, closely approximate the desired statistical probability distribution. Since the mathematics involved in deriving the parameters analytically are often quite complex, and Monte Carlo simulations are difficult to program and are expensive to run, only a few financial simulation models are constructed as stochastic models.

The Chemco simulation model can be characterized as a descriptive model, since the output describes what would result for the given input data. There is no claim that the budgeted statements reflect the *best* that could be done, although several different sets of input data may be tested, and the manager may subjectively select one as superior to the others. A financial manager at Chemco, for example, could use the financial simulation model to answer "what if" questions, such as: "What would be the effect on cash flow if the inventory policy were changed?"

If a single objective for the firm can be constructed or if a set of objectives can be prioritized, it would be possible to construct an optimizing model. The primary objective of the firm, for example, may be specified as maximizing the firm's net profit after taxes for the year. A linear programming financial model could then be constructed, with aftertax profit as the objective function to be maximized. The various accounting identities, policy relationships, and behavioral relationships would appear as constraints in such a model. Since it is usually difficult to specify precisely what the objectives should be, and since very large linear programming problems are difficult to construct and solve, few financial simulation models currently take the form of optimizing models.

Management Uses of Financial Simulation Models

Applications of financial modeling fall into the following three categories:

1. Improving planning and decision making. An important planning use for financial simulation models is to evaluate the impact of environmental changes and business problems. If changes in the government's economic policy are expected to increase interest rates, for example, the effect of the higher interest rates can be modeled by substituting the new rates for the present rates in the input data. An integrated financial simulation model will then show the increased interest expense, the reduced income taxes due to a greater interest deduction, and the resulting lower earnings after taxes. In addition, the impact on cash flows, on the firm's cash position, and on the entire balance sheet can be seen. If the impact is severe, alternative management strategies can then be evaluated. Alternatives involving changing the product prices, reducing operating costs, increasing operating efficiency, and obtaining funds from different debt or equity sources can all be explored by providing different input data

to the model or by making changes in the relationships that constitute the model. Because computer models make it easier and quicker to explore many different alternatives, it is more likely that a better solution will be found.

2. Facilitating the evaluation of operating performance. Financial simulation models can also be used to improve performance evaluations. It is generally agreed that a manager should not be held accountable for the effect of uncontrollable factors. For example, the supervisor of a production department is not usually free to determine what the volume of production should be in a given period. Accordingly, it is necessary to distinguish the controllable portion of the overhead variance from the uncontrollable, or volume, variance. Since financial simulation models incorporate dozens of variables, it is possible to modify financial plans (budgets) to give effect to changes in values of all of the uncontrollable factors.

3. Expediting the budgeting process. Many firms use their financial simulation model as a supplement to the budgeting process. Since models are usually computerized, while the budget preparation process may not be computerized, a firm may find it useful to use its computerized model to develop and evaluate a number of alternative budgets before deciding on its final master budget and profit plan for the year. Once into the next year, the firm can also use its financial simulation model to prepare a revised financial plan when a major, unanticipated change occurs.

Management must decide which of the many potential uses will be emphasized, since the uses will influence the design and construction of the model. A model constructed at the firm level, for example, would enable top management to carry out planning at the corporate level, but would not be suitable for generating financial reports for evaluating performance at the divisional level. Similarly, a very detailed financial simulation model of activities at the department level can be used for departmental decision making and performance evaluation, but may generate far too much detailed output to be useful to top managers engaged in overall planning for the firm.

1. Describe the objectives of budgeting.

2. Compare and contrast strategic planning, budgeting, and operational planning.

3. Briefly describe the major steps involved in developing a master budget.

4. Describe two methods commonly used to develop a sales budget for the firm.

5. Briefly describe the steps involved in preparing a cash budget.

6. What is the primary purpose of a cash budget?

7. Explain how continuous budgets are prepared.

8. What are the major advantages and disadvantages of continuous budgets, as compared to static budgets?

9. What is the objective of participative budgeting? How are participative budgets prepared?

10. What is meant by zero-base budgeting? How are zero-base budgets prepared?

11. Identify four different types of quantitative relationships found in financial simulation models. Give an example of each.

12. Explain how a descriptive financial simulation model differs from an optimizing model.

Exercise 1. ABC Block Company manufactures a standard line of cement blocks for use in residential and commercial construction projects. Sales for the next five quarters are forecast as follows, using a multiple regression sales forecasting model:

Year	Quarter	Sales (in Thousands of Pounds)
19X4	I	47,700
	II	67,000
	III	69,300
	IV	54,700
19X5	I	57,500

To insure rapid delivery of orders, ABC would like to maintain an ending inventory equal to 1/4 of the following quarter's projected sales. Inventory on hand on January 1, 19X4, is 27,200,000 pounds.

Prepare a quarterly production schedule for 19X4.

Exercise 2 (CMA adapted, 12/80). George Mai invented a special valve for application in the paper manufacturing industry. At the time of its development, he could not find a company willing to manufacture the valve. As a result, he formed Maiton Co. to manufacture and sell the valve. George Mai's business experience is limited, since prior to forming Maiton Co., he was an engineer for a large company.

Maiton Co. grew quite slowly because George Mai found it difficult to persuade paper companies to try a new valve designed and manufactured by an unknown company. However, the company has prospered and now has a number of smaller companies as regular customers. There is also increasing interest by a number of large paper companies because of the very good results experienced by the smaller paper companies. The size of the potential new customers and their probable needs over the next several years will dramatically increase the sales of the valve.

Explain to George why it is important to introduce business planning and budgeting activities into his company at this time. Identify major problem areas that likely would be disclosed as a result of Maiton Co.'s long-range budgeting process.

Exercise 3. Lauder Pharmaceutical Company has developed the following production budget for its primary product, Siatril, based on sales forecasts for the next four months:

| April .... | 164,200 lbs. | June .... | 195,000 lbs. |
| May ..... | 165,700 | July ..... | 184,600 |

Each pound of Siatril requires 0.47 pounds of DTZ-12 and 0.38 pounds of Thyoxin. The remainder consists of water and a minor amount of a binding agent. On April 1, inventories of DTZ-12 and Thyoxin were 12,200 pounds and 24,100 pounds, respectively. Lauder has reliable suppliers of both ingredients and maintains ending inventories of 15% of the next month's production requirement when possible.

One direct labor hour is required to process 28 pounds of final product. Currently, 6,000 regular direct labor hours are available per month. All additional labor requirements will require overtime.

(1) Prepare a schedule of materials purchases for both materials for April, May, and June.
(2) Prepare a schedule of direct labor requirements, detailing both regular and overtime hours.

Exercise 4. Melbourne-Rand Company produces steel snowplows for use on pickup and 4×4 trucks. In preparation for the coming fiscal year, 19X6, beginning in March, Melbourne-Rand would like to update its fixed and variable overhead cost budgets. Last year's budget, based on production of 82,000 hours, is as follows:

Variable overhead:		
Indirect labor	$ 84,870	
Indirect materials	192,700	
Blueprint and copy costs	17,220	$294,790
Fixed overhead:		
Plant supervision	$207,500	
Other administrative costs	39,400	
Depreciation	29,650	
Insurance expense	9,800	
Property taxes	8,075	
Lease expense—equipment	14,000	308,425
Total overhead		$603,215

As a result of contract negotiations, indirect labor costs will increase by $.05 per direct labor hour. Indirect materials costs per direct labor hour should remain unchanged, but blueprint and copy charges will increase by 8% (consumption per direct labor hour will remain the same).

Plant supervision costs and administrative costs are expected to decrease by 5%, due to staff cutbacks. Equipment which was previously leased for $14,000 per year will be purchased in March, increasing depreciation expense by $7,500 per year. No other change is expected in depreciation expense. Insurance costs will remain the same, but property taxes will increase by 15%.

Melbourne-Rand expects 96,000 direct labor hours to be worked in the coming year. Both variable and fixed overhead rates are established on the basis of expected direct labor hours.

Calculate the fixed and variable overhead application rates for Melbourne-Rand for the coming year.

Exercise 5. The owner of Old Oake Beverage Mart is performing some simple cash flow analysis to determine the cash position at the end of April, when a major remodeling project is scheduled to begin. The owner, on the basis of past experience, feels that sales are roughly 70% cash and 30% credit sales. On the average, 25% of the credit sales are collected in the month of sale, while the remaining 75% are collected in the following month. Sales data, based on a forecast of historical trends and a simple linear regression model, are as follows:

December, 19X7	$28,200 (actual)	March, 19X8	$37,500
January, 19X8	35,100	April, 19X8	39,000
February, 19X8	33,400		

The main expense of the business is the cost of goods sold, which averages 60% of sales. Other expenses, primarily fixed in nature, total $3,500 per month. All expenses are paid in the month of incurrence, and no changes in inventory are forecast for the 4-month period. On December 31, 19X7, the business had a cash balance of $7,970.

Prepare a cash budget for Old Oake Beverage Mart and calculate the expected cash balance on April 30, 19X8.

Exercise 6. Arcor Company produces a special, plastic-based marine paint from a petroleum residue. The paint is durable and color-fast and has an unusually long life. Production, in units of final output, is scheduled for the next four months as follows:

| August .... | 62,000 gals. | October ...... | 81,000 gals. |
| September .... | 74,000 | November .... | 67,000 |

Each gallon of paint produced requires 2-1/2 gallons of petroleum residue as an input. The difference is lost as a waste product or through evaporation.

On August 1, the inventory of petroleum residue on hand totals 15,500 gallons. To maintain adequate materials inventories for production, Arcor desires to have an ending materials inventory equal to 25% of the next month's scheduled production requirement. The petroleum residue costs $.97 per gallon. All purchases are paid for in the month of purchase.

One hour of direct labor is required for every 20 gallons of output. The average wage rate in the factory is $7.70 per hour. The overhead budget for the firm is $12,250 plus $2.79 per direct labor hour. This budget closely approximates actual monthly overhead costs incurred. All wages and overhead expenses are paid in the month of incurrence, except for depreciation, which totals $6,700 per month.

(1) Determine a materials purchases budget for August, September, and October.

(2) Calculate the total cash disbursements for production for each of the three months and for the three-month period, August through October.

Exercise 7. Carlisle Glassworks has just recently begun producing stemmed glassware, which is sold primarily to restaurants. On the basis of the marketing manager's sales forecasts, the following projected income statement for June has been prepared:

Sales (7,500 cases @ $7.75 per case)		$58,125
Cost of goods sold (lifo):		
Beginning finished goods inventory (1,150 cases @ $4)	$ 4,600	
Cost of goods manufactured (7,190 cases @ $4.20)	30,198	
Ending finished goods inventory (840 cases @ $4)	(3,360)	31,438
Gross profit		$26,687
Selling expenses	$ 7,220	
General and administrative expenses	8,005	
Shipping expenses	2,330	17,555
Income before taxes		$ 9,132
Income tax (40%)		3,653
Net income		$ 5,479

The beginning work in process inventory had a value of $4,565. Work in process on June 30, 19X4, is forecast to be $3,117. Carlisle is a process shop which uses actual cost as the basis for its cost accounting records.

Cash sales are 75% of total sales; the remainder are credit sales, with roughly 50% of the collections occurring in the month of sale and 50% in the month thereafter. All manufacturing costs are paid in the month of incurrence, except for depreciation, which totals $7,100 per month. Of the selling, general, and administrative expenses, 75% are paid in the month of incurrence and 25% are paid in the month thereafter. Shipping costs and income taxes are paid when incurred.

In May, 19X4, Carlisle experienced the following results:

Sales	$40,200
Selling expenses	7,420
General and administrative expenses	8,008

Prepare a schedule of cash receipts and disbursements for June. Round all amounts to the nearest dollar.

Exercise 8. Harlowe's of Bayshore is a small boutique selling high-fashion women's apparel. As in many retail stores, sales are quite seasonal. The proprietor of the store and the store's accountant have prepared the following semiannual schedule of cash receipts and disbursements:

	January	February	March	April	May	June
Cash collections	$27,200	$17,650	$12,190	$15,600	$18,420	$21,880
Cash disbursements:						
Purchases	12,290	19,400	21,630	17,340	16,700	13,270
Wages and salaries	1,875	1,320	1,475	1,470	1,515	1,660
Rent	600	600	600	675	675	675
Other	415	405	310	370	390	405

The cash balance on January 1 is $9,880. The owner feels that a minimum cash balance of $7,500 should be on hand at the beginning of each month to cover normal operating expenses, and any borrowings should be repaid as soon as funds are available. All borrowings and repayments occur at the end of the month, in increments of $1,000. Interest is charged at the rate of 18% per year, or 1-1/2% per month. Interest is to be paid when a repayment of principal is made, and is calculated on the amount of the principal repayment.

(1) Determine the borrowing and repayments required during the first six months.
(2) Calculate the interest expense that should appear on Harlowe's income statement for the 6-month period.

Exercise 9. Farber Pharmacy has recently acquired a minicomputer. The computer has a forecasting package which the proprietor has used with excellent results. The income statement forecast for February is as follows:

Sales		$22,270
Cost of goods sold:		
Beginning inventory	$ 6,450	
Purchases	15,160	
Ending inventory	(9,700)	11,910
Gross profit		$10,360
Wages expense	$ 1,872	
Utilities expense	220	
Rent expense	470	
Depreciation expense	515	3,077
Income before taxes		$ 7,283

Wages are paid on the 15th and the last day of each month. The payroll paid on the 15th is for wages earned in the last half of the prior month. The payroll paid on the last day of the month is for wages earned in the first half of the month. Purchases are paid with a lag of about one week, so that 75% of a given month's purchases are paid for in the month of purchase, and the remainder are paid for in the following month. All other expenses are paid in the month in which they are incurred.

One half of the firm's sales are for cash and the remainder are on account. All credit sales are collected in the month following the sale. All accounts receivable on the firm's books relate to sales of merchandise on account.

On the basis of the relationships described above and the data for January, the following schedule of cash receipts and disbursements for February has been prepared:

Cash receipts		$21,015
Cash disbursements:		
Purchases	$15,490	
Wages	1,904	
Utilities	220	
Rent	470	18,084
Net increase in cash		$ 2,931

On January 31, 19X0, the pharmacy's balance sheet appeared as follows:

Assets		Liabilities		
Cash	$12,315	Wages payable	$ 968	
Accounts receivable	9,880	Accounts payable	4,120	$ 5,088
Inventory	6,450	Owner's Equity		
Equipment (net)	4,740	Farber, capital		28,297
Total assets	$33,385	Total liabilities and capital		$33,385

Prepare a pro forma balance sheet for the pharmacy as of February 28, 19X0. Ignore the impact of taxes.

Exercise 10. Mitchell-Krause, a team of management consultants, is developing a simple financial simulation model for a client. Selected items reflecting the firm's operations are described as follows:

1. Unit sales for a month are projected as a simple average of the past three months' sales, increased by a growth factor of 0.5%.
2. The client desires an ending merchandise inventory, in units, equal to 30% of an average of the current month's and the next month's sales, in units.
3. Purchases, in units, for any month will equal the ending merchandise inventory plus sales for the month less the beginning inventory of merchandise.
4. Total revenues reflect sales of products whose average selling price is $40 per unit.
5. Selling and administrative costs equal $2 per unit sold plus $57,000 per month in fixed costs.
6. On the average, 70% of the current month's dollar sales are collected in the current month, 25% in the following month, and 5% are never collected.
7. Cash disbursements equal 20% of the current month's purchases plus 80% of the preceding month's purchases plus 25% of the current month's revenues. On the average, the client pays $20 per unit for the merchandise sold.

8. The net cash flow from operations equals cash receipts from customers less cash disbursements.

(1) For each of the above items, prepare an appropriate equation which could be incorporated in the financial simulation model. Use the following symbols:

S_m = sales in units during month
I_m = merchandise inventory in units at the end of month
P_m = purchases in units during month
R_m = revenues for month
SA_m = selling and administrative expenses for month
CR_m = cash receipts from customers during month
CD_m = cash disbursements during month
CF_m = net cash flow from operations during month

(2) For each of the first three equations developed in (1), specify whether that equation represents an identity, a policy relationship, a behavioral relationship, or a technological relationship.

PROBLEMS

Problem 13-1. Bannistar Corporation produces a popular kettle-type outdoor grill. The firm's various models are minor variations of one standard design. In preparation for the company's peak selling period, May through August, Bannistar's accountants are preparing a sales forecast, production schedule, and various other budgets.

The company uses historical, time-series analysis to forecast sales. On the basis of past experience and current market trends, Bannistar's sales department has developed the following index numbers for relative forecast sales volumes:

February	62	July	139
March	87	August	117
April	100	September	84
May	122	October	75
June	149		

Actual sales in February were 9,000 units. There were 7,200 finished units on hand at the beginning of February.

To maintain adequate stocks to fill all orders, Bannistar would like to maintain an ending finished goods inventory equal to 25% of the average monthly sales for the next two months.

The materials required for each grill and the beginning inventories and desired ending inventories of materials are as follows:

	Inventory (February 1)	Desired Inventory (% of Next Month's Production)
Rolled steel (36 sq. ft. @ $.17 per sq. ft.)	105,400 sq. ft.	20%
Aluminum tubing (14 ft. @ $.03 per ft.)	62,790 ft.	25
Enamel (26 oz. @ $5.85 per gallon)	607 gals.	10

All materials are purchased on account. Roughly 1/3 is paid for within the month of purchase. The remaining 2/3 is paid for in the next month.

Required
(1) On the basis of the sales forecast, prepare a monthly sales budget, in units, for the 9-month period February through October.

(2) Prepare a monthly production budget, in units, for the period February through August.

(3) Prepare a monthly schedule of materials purchases for the 6-month period February through July.

(4) Calculate the monthly cash disbursements associated with the materials purchased for the months February through July. Total purchases of materials in January were $37,232.

Problem 13-2 (AICPA adapted, 11/78). Scarborough Corporation, a medium-sized metalworking firm, produces two types of high-performance camshafts for automobile engines: one for 4-cylinder engines and one for 8-cylinder engines. In July, 19X7, Scarborough's budget department gathered the following data in order to project sales and budget requirements for 19X8:

19X8 Projected Sales

	Model No.	Units	Price
4-cylinder camshaft	400	60,000	$ 70
8-cylinder camshaft	800	40,000	100

19X8 Inventories (In Units)

Model No.	Expected Inventory, January 1, 19X8	Desired Inventory, December 31, 19X8
400	20,000	25,000
800	8,000	9,000

The materials used to produce one unit of either model and the projected data for 19X8 with respect to materials are as follows:

	Amount Used per unit #400	#800	Anticipated Purchase Price	Expected Inventories, January 1, 19X8	Desired Inventories December 31, 19X8
Steel—Type 1224	4 lbs.	5 lbs.	$8 per lb.	32,000 lbs.	36,000 lbs.
Steel—Type 703	2 lbs.	3 lbs.	5 per lb.	29,000 lbs.	32,000 lbs.
Graphite		1 oz.	3 per oz.	6,000 oz.	7,000 oz.

Projected direct labor requirements for 19X8 and rates are as follows:

Model No.	Hours per Unit	Rate per Hour
400	2	$3
800	3	4

Overhead is applied at the rate of $2 per direct labor hour.

Required
Prepare the following budgets for 19X8:

(1) Sales budget (in dollars).

(2) Production budget (in units).

(3) Materials purchases budget (in quantities).

(4) Materials purchases budget (in dollars).

(5) Direct labor budget (in dollars).

(6) Budgeted finished goods inventory at December 31, 19X8 (in dollars).

Problem 13-3 (CMA adapted, 12/77). The Wyoming Division of Reid Corporation produces an intricate component part used in Reid's major product line. The division manager, who has recently been concerned by a lack of coordination between purchasing and production personnel, believes that a monthly budgeting system would be better than the present system. Therefore, the division manager has decided to develop budget information for the third quarter of the current year on a trial basis, before the budget system is implemented for an entire fiscal year. In response to the division manager's request for data which could be used to develop budget information, the division controller accumulated the following data:

- Wyoming Division expects to sell 60,000 units during 19X7. Sales through June 30, 19X7, total 24,000 units. Actual sales in units for May and June and estimated unit sales for the next four months are as follows:

May (actual)	4,000	August (estimated)	6,000
June (actual)	4,000	September (estimated)	7,000
July (estimated)	5,000	October (estimated)	7,000

- The monthly ending inventory goal for all materials is to have sufficient materials on hand to produce the next month's estimated sales. Data regarding the materials used in the component are shown in the following schedule:

Materials	Units of Materials per Finished Component	Cost per Unit	Inventories, June 30, 19X7
#101	6	$2.40	35,000 units
#211	4	3.60	30,000
#242	2	1.20	14,000

- Each component must pass through three different processes to be completed. Data regarding the direct labor in each process are as follows:

	Direct Labor Hours per Finished Component	Cost per Direct Labor Hour
Forming	.80	$8.00
Assembly	2.00	5.50
Finishing	.25	6.00

- The division produced 27,000 components and worked 82,350 hours during the six-month period ended June 30, 19X7. The actual variable overhead costs incurred during this six-month period are as follows. The division controller believes that the variable overhead costs will be incurred at the same rate during the last six months of 19X7.

Supplies	$ 59,400
Electricity	27,000
Indirect labor	54,000
Other	8,100
Total variable overhead	$148,500

- The fixed overhead costs incurred during the first six months of 19X7 amounted to $93,500. Fixed overhead costs budgeted for the full year are as follows:

Supervision	$ 60,000
Taxes	7,200
Depreciation	86,400
Other	32,400
Total fixed overhead	$186,000

- The desired monthly ending inventory in units of completed components is 80 percent of the next month's estimated sales. There are 5,000 finished units in the inventory on June 30, 19X7.

Required

(1) Prepare a monthly production budget, in units, for the Wyoming Division for the third quarter ending September 30, 19X7.

(2) Prepare a monthly materials purchases budget, in units and dollars, for the third quarter.

(3) Prepare a monthly direct labor budget, in hours and dollars, for the third quarter.

(4) Prepare a monthly factory overhead budget for the third quarter. Assume that any remaining fixed overhead cost is incurred evenly throughout the year.

Problem 13-4 (CMA adapted, 6/81). Rein Company, a compressor manufacturer, is developing a budgeted income statement for the calendar year, 19X2. The president is generally satisfied with the 19X1 projected net income of $700,000, which will provide earnings per share of $2.80. However, the president would like the earnings per share in 19X2 to increase to at least $3.

Rein Company uses a standard absorption cost system. Inflation necessitates an annual revision in the standards. The total standard manufacturing cost for 19X1 is $72 per unit produced, and the 19X2 standards will be appropriately increased.

Rein expects to sell 100,000 compressors at $110 each in the current year, 19X1. Forecasts from the sales department project an annual increase of 10% in unit sales in 19X2, and another 10% increase in 19X3. This increase in sales volume is expected in spite of a $15 increase in the selling price for 19X2. This increase is expected to compensate for the increase in production costs and operating expenses. Any additional sales price increase, however, would probably curtail the desired growth in volume.

Standard production costs are developed for the compressor's two primary metals (brass and a steel alloy), the direct labor, and the manufacturing overhead. The 19X2 standard quantities and rates for materials and labor for one compressor are as follows:

Brass (4 pounds @ $5.35 per pound)	$21.40
Steel alloy (5 pounds @ $3.16 per pound)	15.80
Direct labor (4 hours @ $7 per hour)	28.00
Total prime costs	$65.20

The materials content of the compressor has been reduced slightly. This minor reduction will not change product quality. Improved labor productivity and some increase in automation have decreased the labor hours per unit from 4.4 to 4.0. The manufacturing overhead cost per unit has yet to be determined. Preliminary data on overhead are as follows:

	Activity Level (Units)		
	100,000	110,000	120,000
Supplies	$ 475,000	$ 522,500	$ 570,000
Indirect labor	530,000	583,000	636,000
Utilities	170,000	187,000	204,000
Maintenance	363,000	377,500	392,000
Taxes and insurance	87,000	87,000	87,000
Depreciation	421,000	421,000	421,000
Total overhead	$2,046,000	$2,178,000	$2,310,000

The standard overhead rate, based on direct labor hours, is computed by dividing the total overhead cost from the above schedule by the activity level closest to planned production.

In developing the standards for the manufacturing costs, the following two assumptions were made:

(1) The purchasing manager expects the price of the brass, which is currently $5.65 per pound, to drop to the predetermined standard early in 19X2.

(2) Several new employees will be hired for the production line in 19X2. The employees will be unskilled. If the training programs are not effective and the improved labor productivity does not materialize, then the production time will increase by 15 minutes per unit over the 19X2 standards.

Rein uses the lifo inventory method for costing its finished goods. Its inventory policy for finished goods is to have 15% of the expected annual unit sales for the coming year in finished goods inventory at the end of the prior year. The finished goods inventory at December 31, 19X1, is expected to consist of 16,500 units, at a total carrying cost of $1,006,500. Work in process inventories are negligible.

Operating expenses are classified as selling, which are variable, and administrative, which are fixed. The budgeted selling expenses are expected to average 12% of sales revenue in 19X2, which is consistent with the performance in 19X1. The administrative expenses in 19X2 are expected to be 20% higher than the budgeted 19X1 amount of $907,850.

Management accepts the cost standards developed by the production and accounting departments. However, management is concerned about the possible effect on net income if the price of brass does not decrease and/or the labor efficiency does not improve as expected. Management has asked that the budgeted income statement be prepared using the standards as developed but considering the worst possible situation for 19X2. Rein is subject to a 45% income tax rate.

(1) Prepare a budgeted income statement for 19X2, as specified by management. Each manufacturing variance should be separately identified and added to or subtracted from the standard gross margin to show the actual gross margin.

(2) Review the 19X2 budgeted income statement prepared for Rein Company and discuss whether the president's objectives can be achieved. No capital stock or other financing transactions will occur in 19X2.

Problem 13-5. Sno-Cat Company produces and sells a line of snowmobiles at its plant in Minnesota. The firm's managers are planning production for the company's best-selling model, the Lynx, for the peak selling months of August to February. The following sales forecast was prepared by the firm's marketing department:

August, 19X4	1,100 units
September, 19X4	1,650
October, 19X4	1,976
November, 19X4	2,100
December, 19X4	1,720
January, 19X5	1,240
February, 19X5	750
Total	10,536 units

In preparing a production budget for the coming six-month period ending January 31, 19X5, the firm's managers are faced with two alternatives. Under one alternative, the firm can vary production with sales, producing only sufficient units to meet that month's sales requirement and the desired ending inventory of 10% of the next month's forecast sales. Under the second alternative, the firm could produce the average of the 6 months' sales, or 1,631 units per month. Under this "steady state" production schedule, the firm would eliminate overtime costs, but would increase inventory holding costs. The inventory of finished goods on August 1, 19X4, is 75 units.

The standard cost of a Lynx snowmobile is as follows:

Materials	$ 974.00
Direct labor (25 hrs. @ $9 per hr.)	225.00
Variable overhead (25 hrs. @ $7.50 per hr.)	187.50
Fixed overhead (25 hrs. @ $8.75 per hr.*)	218.75
Total standard cost	$1,605.25

*Based on normal production of 1,600 units (40,000 hours) per month.

During a month, 40,000 hours of direct labor time are available at straight-time rates. For production rates between 40,000 and 50,000 hours per month, time and one half must be paid on the excess. All hours beyond 50,000 per month are paid at double time.

Sno-Cat's managers have determined that monthly inventory holding costs average $28.90 per unit. This figure includes the opportunity cost of funds, the cost of warehouse space, and insurance costs. The inventory holding cost is applied to each month's average inventory. Under the "steady state" production plan, orders in excess of available supply are filled as soon as the units become available.

Sno-Cat's management estimates that the cost to the company of a late order is $120 per month in terms of lost sales, customer goodwill, and harm to dealer-manufacturer relations.

Required (1) Prepare a production budget, in units, for each alternative, detailing each month's beginning inventory, ending inventory, and production.
(2) Calculate the incremental labor cost of the first alternative.
(3) Calculate the incremental inventory holding cost for the second alternative.
(4) Calculate the cost of late shipments.
(5) Under which alternative is total production cost minimized?

Problem 13-6. The Laredo Division of Futima Electronics Ltd. produces a remote control unit for the firm's color television sets. The division's accounting department is preparing a schedule of cash receipts and disbursements for the third quarter in order to determine the firm's short-term financing needs.

The Sales Department projects the following monthly sales for 19X7. The units have a standard selling price of $30 each.

May (actual)	2,300 units	September (forecast)	3,600 units
June (actual)	2,500	October (forecast)	3,100
July (forecast)	2,400	November (forecast)	3,000
August (forecast)	3,800		

The standard cost sheet for the unit is as follows:

Materials:	
Electronic chip—Model 1717 (1 @ $.45)	$ 0.450
Plastic (7 oz. @ $.15 per oz.)	1.050
Direct labor:	
Molding Dept. (1/2 hr. @ $6.25 per hr.)	3.125
Assembly Dept. (1/2 hr. @ $5.80 per hr.)	2.900
Overhead (1 hr. @ $14.05 per hr.*)	14.050
	$21.575

*Based on an overhead budget of $7,360 plus $11.75 per direct labor hour and 3,200 normal hours per month.

Sales consist of 80% credit sales and 20% cash sales. On the average, 20% of the credit sales are collected in the month of sale, 50% in the following month, and 30% in the second month.

The company has the following payments policy:

Materials	Materials are paid for, on the average, 1/2 in the month of purchase and 1/2 in the following month.
Direct labor	All labor costs are paid in the month of incurrence.
Overhead	Overhead items are paid, on the average, 1/3 in the month of incurrence and 2/3 in the following month. The noncash overhead items total $8,400 per month.
Selling and administrative expenses	These expenses, which are all fixed, total $18,700 per month and are paid when incurred.

In July, the company plans to perform major overhaul work on its building and equipment. The additional cost associated with this work is estimated at $21,900 and will be paid in August. This cost will be capitalized.

In February, 19X7, the company ordered a small computer for its manufacturing operations, with an expected delivery date in September. The $9,900 cost of the equipment is due in the month of delivery.

Materials purchased in June totaled $3,300. Overhead incurred in June totaled $31,500.

The balance of the company's cash account on July 1, 19X7, was $15,700. The division's managers feel a beginning monthly balance of $15,000 is necessary to meet monthly expenses. All borrowing or repayments are made in increments of $1,000 at the end of the month. The monthly interest rate is 1.5%.

Inventories on June 30, 19X2, consist of the following:

Finished goods	750 units
Materials:	
Electronic chips—Model 1712	480 units
Plastic	4,540 oz.

The firm's management seeks to maintain ending inventories equal to 25% of the next month's sales requirements for finished goods and 10% of next month's production requirements for materials.

Required (1) Prepare a sales budget, in dollars, for the period May through November, 19X7.

(2) Prepare a monthly production budget, in units, for July through October, 19X7.

(3) Prepare a monthly schedule of materials purchases, in units and dollars, and monthly schedules of direct labor and overhead expenses for the third quarter, July through September, 19X7.

(4) Prepare a monthly schedule of cash receipts and disbursements, including borrowing and repayments, for July through September, 19X7.

(5) What is the Laredo Division's projected cash balance on September 30, 19X7?

Problem 13-7. Gronstaal Co. is a producer of collector's edition plates and figurines. The company's managers are preparing budgeted statements for the fourth quarter, which is the company's peak selling period. The sales forecast and actual data are as follows. All units sell for $70 each.

	Units	Revenues
August (actual)	1,100	$ 77,000
September (actual)	1,400	98,000
October (forecast)	1,900	133,000
November (forecast)	2,600	182,000
December (forecast)	2,100	147,000
January (forecast)	1,100	77,000

All sales are on account. The company collects 25% of its sales in the month of sale and 75% in the month thereafter.

The firm is currently producing 1,400 units per month. This production rate will be maintained through December. In January, only 1,200 units will be produced. The current inventory of finished plates on October 1 is 2,400 units.

The company uses the following standard costs in order to budget materials purchases and labor requirements:

Materials: Clay (2 lbs. @ $6.40 per lb.)	$12.80
Direct labor (4 hrs. @ $7 per hr.)	28.00
Variable overhead (4 hrs. @ $1.20 per hr.)	4.80
Fixed overhead (4 hrs. @ $1.60 per hr.)	6.40
	$52.00

Overhead is applied on the basis of direct labor hours, using a base of 8,000 normal hours per month. The overhead budget, which very closely approximates actual overhead expenses, is $12,800 plus $1.20 per DLH. All overhead expenses require cash expenditures; all equipment is leased.

The company had an inventory of clay of 1,900 pounds on October 1. The firm's policy is to purchase enough clay to leave an ending inventory equal to 90% of next month's production requirement. All labor costs and selling and administrative costs are paid in the month of incurrence. Selling and administrative costs normally total $21,300 per month. All materials purchases and overhead expenses are recorded as accounts payable, and are paid, on the average, 2/3 in the month of incurrence and 1/3 in the following month. Materials purchases in September totaled $12,700. September overhead expenses were $18,550.

In October, the company plans to participate in a special art fair in Cologne, West Germany. The October payments estimated for the art fair total $19,500 and will be treated as a selling expense.

The company wishes to begin each month with a minimum cash balance of $10,000. All borrowings and repayments are made at the end of the month, in increments of $1,000. Interest is charged at 1-1/2% per month.

The firm's balance sheet on September 30, 19X3, is as follows:

Cash	$ 11,700	Accounts payable	$ 10,417
Accounts receivable	73,500	E. Gronstaal, capital	211,743
Inventories:			
·Finished goods	124,800		
Materials	12,160		
Total assets	$222,160	Total liabilities and capital	$222,160

Required (1) Prepare a production budget, in units, detailing monthly production, beginning inventories, and ending inventories for the fourth quarter.

(2) Prepare a monthly schedule of materials purchases for the fourth quarter, in pounds and dollars.

(3) Prepare a monthly schedule of direct labor, in hours and dollars, for the fourth quarter.

(4) Prepare a monthly schedule of overhead expenses, using the overhead budget.

(5) Calculate a schedule of monthly cash receipts and disbursements.

(6) Prepare an income statement summarizing the fourth quarter's forecast activities.

(7) Prepare a pro forma balance sheet for the firm on December 31, 19X3.

Problem 13-8 (AICPA adapted, 5/71). The administrator of Wright Hospital has presented you with a number of service projections for the year ending June 30, 19X2. Estimated room requirements for inpatients by type of service are:

Type of Patient	Total Patients Expected	Average Number of Days in Hospital		Percent of Regular Patients Selecting Types of Service		
		Regular	Medicare	Private	Semi-Private	Ward
Medical	2,100	7	17	10%	60%	30%
Surgical	2,400	10	15	15	75	10

Of the patients served by the hospital, 10% are expected to be Medicare patients, all of whom are expected to select semi-private rooms. Both the number and proportion of Medicare patients have increased over the past five years. Daily rentals per patient are: $40 for a private room, $35 for a semi-private room, and $25 for a ward.

Operating room charges are based on personnel-minutes (number of minutes the operating room is in use multiplied by the number of personnel assisting in the operation). The personnel-minute charges are $.13 for inpatients and $.22 for outpatients. Studies for the current year show that operations on inpatients are divided as follows:

Type of Operation	Number of Operations	Average Number of Minutes per Operation	Average Number of Personnel Required
A	800	30	4
B	700	45	5
C	300	90	6
D	200	120	8
	2,000		

The same proportion of inpatient operations is expected for the next fiscal year, and 180 outpatients are expected to use the operating room. Outpatient operations average 20 minutes and require the assistance of three persons.

The budget for the year ending June 30, 19X2, by departments, is:

General services:	
Maintenance of plant	$ 50,000
Operation of plant	27,500
Administration	97,500
All others	192,000
Revenue producing services:	
Operating room	68,440
All others	700,000
	$1,135,440

The following information is provided for cost allocation purposes:

	Square Feet	Salaries	Basis of Allocation
General services:			
Maintenance of plant	12,000	$ 40,000	Salaries
Operation of plant	28,000	25,000	Square feet
Administration	10,000	55,000	Salaries
All others	36,250	102,500	8% to operating room
Revenue producing services:			
Operating room	17,500	15,000	Not allocated
All others	86,250	302,500	Not allocated
	190,000	$540,000	

Prepare a schedule showing the computation of:

(1) The number of patient days expected (number of patients multiplied by average stay in hospital) by type of patient and service.

(2) The total number of personnel-minutes expected for operating room services for inpatients and outpatients. For inpatients, show the breakdown of total operating room personnel-minutes by type of operation.

(3) Expected gross revenue from routine services.

(4) Expected gross revenue from operating room services.

(5) Cost per personnel-minute for operating room services, assuming that the total personnel-minutes computed in (2) is 800,000 and that the step-down method of cost allocation is used (i.e., costs of the general services departments are allocated in the sequence listed, first to the general services departments that they serve and then finally to the revenue producing departments).

Problem 13-9 (AICPA adapted, 5/72). In June, 19X0, after ten years with a large CPA firm, Jill Johnson, CPA, opened an office as a sole practitioner.

In 19X2, Walter Smith, CPA, joined Johnson as a senior accountant. The partnership of Johnson and Smith was organized July 1, 19X7, and a fiscal year ending June 30 was adopted and approved by the Internal Revenue Service.

Continued growth of the firm has required additional personnel. The current complement, including approved salaries for the fiscal year ending June 30, 19X3, is as follows:

	Annual Salary
Partners:	
Jill Johnson, CPA	$24,000
Walter Smith, CPA	18,000
Professional staff:	
Supervisor:	
Harold Vickers, CPA	17,500
Senior accountant:	
Duane Lowe, CPA	12,500
Assistants:	
James Kennedy	10,500
Viola Quinn	10,500
Secretaries:	
Mary Lyons	7,800
John Hammond	6,864
Livia Garcia	6,864

A severe illness kept Johnson away from the office for over four months in late 19X1. The firm suffered during this period, mainly because other personnel lacked knowledge about the practice.

After Johnson's illness, a plan was developed for delegation of administrative authority and responsibility and for standardization of procedures.

The goals of the plan included (1) income objectives, (2) standardized billing procedures (with flexibility for adjustments by the partners), and (3) assignment schedules to eliminate overtime and to allow for nonchargeable time, such as vacations and illnesses. The firm plans a 52-week year, with five-day, forty-hour weeks.

The budget for fiscal year 19X3 is 700 hours of chargeable time at $45 per hour for Johnson and 1,100 hours at $40 per hour for Smith. Johnson and Smith are to devote all other available time, except as specified below, to administration. The billing rates for all other employees, including secretaries, are to be set at a level to recover their salaries plus the following overhead items: fringe benefits of $15,230, other operating expenses of $49,380, and a contribution of $20,500 to target income.

The partners agree that salary levels are fair bases for allocating overhead in setting billing rates, with the exception that the portion of the secretaries' salaries relating to nonchargeable time is to be added to overhead to arrive at total overhead to be allocated. (Thus, the billing rate for each secretary will be based on the salary costs of the chargeable time plus a share of the total overhead.) No portion of total overhead is to be allocated to partners' salaries.

The following information is available for nonchargeable time:

- Because of her recent illness, Johnson expects to be away an additional week. Smith expects no loss of time from illness. All other employees are to be allowed one illness day per month.
- Allowable vacations are as follows:

> Johnson: 1 month
> Smith: 1 month
> Vickers: 3 weeks
> Lyons: 3 weeks
> All other employees: 2 weeks

- The firm observes seven holidays annually. If the holiday falls on a weekend, the office is closed the preceding Friday or the following Monday.
- Kennedy and Quinn should each be allotted three days to sit for the November, 19X2, CPA examination.
- Hours are budgeted for other miscellaneous activities of the personnel as follows:

	Johnson	Smith	Vickers	Lowe	Kennedy	Quinn	Lyons	Hammond	Garcia
Firm projects		100	40	40	40		200		
Professional development	80	80	56	40	40	50	24	16	24
Professional meetings	184	120	40	40	16	16	24	8	8
Firm meetings	48	48	48	24	24	24	48	8	8
Community activities	80	40	40	24	16	16	12		
Office time other than firm administration			84	72			1,000	716	808
Total other miscellaneous	392	388	308	240	136	106	1,308	748	848

- Unassigned time should be budgeted for Lowe, Kennedy, and Quinn as 8, 38, and 78 hours, respectively.

Required (1) Prepare a time allocation budget for Johnson, Smith, and each employee for the year ending June 30, 19X3. Begin your schedule with total available hours per year, then deduct nonchargeable activities to yield budgeted chargeable time.

(2) Independent of your solution to (1), prepare a schedule computing billing rates by employee for the year ending June 30, 19X3. The schedule should show the proper allocation of appropriate expenses and target income contribution to salaries. (Round allocation calculations to one decimal place. Round billing rate calculations to the nearest dollar.) Assume that the following data are budgeted chargeable hours:

Vickers	1,600 hours
Lowe	1,650
Kennedy	1,550
Quinn	1,450
Lyons	500
Hammond	1,150
Garcia	1,200

(3) Independent of your solutions to (1) and (2), and assuming the following data are budgeted chargeable hours and billing rates, prepare a condensed statement of budgeted income for the year ending June 30, 19X3.

	Budgeted Chargeable Hours	Budgeted Hourly Billing Rate
Johnson	700	$45
Smith	1,100	40
Vickers	1,600	32
Lowe	1,650	25
Kennedy	1,550	15
Quinn	1,450	17
Lyons	500	5
Hammond	1,150	7
Garcia	1,200	7

Problem 13-10. Condor Games Company has recently introduced two games: *The Snake,* a plastic, puzzle-type game; and *Fantasy,* an electronic chase game. Market research indicates that the games should sell quite well over the coming holiday season, with increasing monthly sales followed by lower January sales. Sales projections for the critical four-month holiday season are as follows:

	The Snake	Fantasy
September	120,000 units	70,000 units
October	126,000	73,000
November	132,000	77,000
December	139,000	81,000
January	83,000	49,000

On the basis of these projections, the production manager developed the production schedules shown at the top of page 485. Company policy is to maintain ending inventories of finished goods at 25% of next month's projected sales.

Actual sales of *The Snake* and *Fantasy* were the same in September as projected sales, but October sales were 144,000 units and 84,000 units, respectively. Sales orders in November were also significantly above forecast levels, at 173,000 and 100,800 units respectively. Alarmed by the sudden depletion of inventories in

	The Snake				Fantasy			
	Sept.	Oct.	Nov.	Dec.	Sept.	Oct.	Nov.	Dec.
Desired Ending Inventory	31,500	33,000	34,750	20,750	18,250	19,250	20,250	12,250
Projected Sales	120,000	126,000	132,000	139,000	70,000	73,000	77,000	81,000
Beginning Inventory	(30,000)*	(31,500)	(33,000)	(34,750)	(17,500)*	(18,250)	(19,250)	(20,250)
Production	121,500	127,500	133,750	125,000	70,750	74,000	78,000	73,000

*Actual inventories

October, Condor's managers increased November production to full capacity output of 150,000 units of *The Snake* and 78,000 units of *Fantasy*. Nevertheless, large numbers of November sales orders went unfilled.

Demand for the two products is expected to exceed the original forecast by a significant margin again in December. The firm's Marketing Department forecasts that December sales orders will total 207,000 units for *The Snake* and 121,000 for *Fantasy*. Condor's managers realize that they cannot possibly fill all sales orders, even at full capacity. The company has available to it only 56,000 direct labor hours each month. Furthermore, Condor's materials suppliers have set a month-end ceiling of $400,000 on Condor's outstanding accounts payable because of certain collection difficulties under the firm's former management. Condor reached this ceiling at the end of November. Condor expects to have cash receipts available in December just sufficient to pay for the November purchases. A short-term financing agreement will also put an additional $200,000 for materials at the company's disposal. Materials inventories on December 1, which are critically low, are as follows:

Product	Materials Inventories
The Snake	$10,500
Fantasy	$44,400

The standard cost sheets for the two products are as follows:

The Snake

Selling price		$5.25
Materials	$1.00	
Direct labor		
(.20 hrs. @ $6 per hr.)	1.20	
Variable overhead		
(.20 hrs. @ $1.20 per hr.)	.24	
Fixed overhead		
(.20 hrs. @ $3 per hr.)	.60	
Total manufacturing cost		3.04
Gross margin		$2.21

Fantasy

Selling price		$16.00
Materials	$5.60	
Direct labor		
(1/3 hr. @ $6 per hr.)	2.00	
Variable overhead		
(1/3 hr. @ $1.20 per hr.)	.40	
Fixed overhead		
(1/3 hr. @ $3 per hr.)	1.00	
Total manufacturing cost		9.00
Gross margin		$ 7.00

One of Condor's accountants suggests that linear programming could be used to plan production for December. In formulating the production plan, there is some disagreement on whether the materials purchase constraint should include a provision for an ending inventory of materials. The production manager feels that such an inventory is essential, but the marketing manager thinks it is foolish to build an inventory of materials when the firm cannot even meet its current sales orders.

Required (1) Use the information provided to develop a monthly schedule detailing beginning inventory, ending inventory, production, and sales amounts in units for both products for the months of September, October, and November.

(2) Formulate Condor's December profit-planning problem as a linear programming problem.

    (a) Develop the direct labor constraint.

    (b) Develop two materials purchase constraints: one which incorporates an allowance for the ending materials inventory equal to $40,000 for *The Snake* materials and $30,000 for *Fantasy* materials, and an alternative constraint which has no ending inventory of materials.

    (c) Develop the objective function which would maximize Condor's December profits.

(3) Graph this problem and determine the optimum production under both inventory assumptions.

(4) What is the cost, in terms of lost profit, of building the inventory?

Problem 13-11. The owner of Bay View Liquor Store would like to institute a credit arrangement for the store's customers. Currently, all sales are for cash.

On the basis of past experience and industry sales projections, the proprietor has prepared the following monthly sales forecast, assuming only cash sales would be made:

January	$37,500	April	$29,200
February	29,700	May	31,000
March	28,800	June	37,400

According to industry analyses, total sales increase by roughly 10% when credit is available. Typically, 20% of the customers are expected to buy on credit, and the remaining 80% of sales will be for cash. The owner feels that under the terms offered, 10% of the credit sales would be collected in the month of sale, 65% in the next month, 20% in the second month following the sale, and 5% would be uncollectible.

The store owner expects to carry roughly 120 credit accounts. The monthly cost of servicing an account, including postage, paper, and office time, is estimated at $4 per account.

Required (1) Calculate the present value of the net cash collections for January through June sales under the cash-only and the cash-and-credit policies. Assume that all cash flows occur at the end of the month. The store's cost of capital is 1.25% per month. The present value factors for $1 at 1.25% per period are:

Period 1	.9877	Period 5	.9398
Period 2	.9755	Period 6	.9282
Period 3	.9634	Period 7	.9167
Period 4	.9515	Period 8	.9054

(2) Which policy maximizes the present value of the cash collections?

Problem 13-12. Kressey Company is a manufacturer of a household product which sells for $12 a unit. The company's management would like to develop a financial simulation model which could be used to forecast net income and cash flow. The firm will initially develop a simple model and move progressively to more sophisticated models. A rough outline of the model, along with other data, is as follows:

- Sales units equal the past month's sales plus 50% of the difference between the past month's sales and the month prior to that.

- Units manufactured equal the desired ending finished goods inventory, in units, plus the sales forecasted for the month, less any beginning finished goods inventory.

- Finished goods inventory equals 4,000 units plus 25% of the next month's forecasted sales units.

- Cost of goods sold equals units sold times $8 per unit production cost.

- Cost of goods manufactured equals units manufactured times the $8 per unit production cost.

- Revenue equals unit sales times the $12 per unit selling price.

- Selling and administrative costs equal $10,000 per month plus 15% of revenues.

- Cash receipts equal 50% of the current month's revenues plus 50% of the prior month's revenues.

- Cash disbursements equal one third of the current month's cost of goods manufactured plus two thirds of the prior month's cost of goods manufactured plus the current month's selling and administrative costs. This sum is then reduced by 10% to allow for noncash expenses.

- Net income before taxes equals revenue less cost of goods sold less selling and administrative costs.

- Cash flow from operations equals cash receipts less cash disbursements.

Required
(1) Prepare a formula which describes each of the above items.
(2) Using the formulas prepared in (1), forecast income before taxes and cash flow from operations for July. (May sales were 12,000 units, and June sales were 14,000 units.)

Problem 13-13 (AICPA adapted, 11/71). Department A is one of 15 departments in Thomas Company's plant. It is involved in the production of all six products that Thomas manufactures. The department is highly mechanized, and as a result, its activity and output are measured in direct machine hours. Flexible budgets are utilized throughout the factory in planning and controlling costs, but here the focus is on the application of flexible budgets in Department A. The following data covering a time span of approximately six months were taken from the various budgets, accounting records, and performance reports in Thomas Company:

- On March 15, 19X8, the following flexible budget was approved for the department. It will be used throughout the 19X9 fiscal year, which begins on July 1, 19X8. This budget was developed through the cooperative efforts of the department manager, division vice-president, and the staff of the budgeting department.

Department A 19X9 Flexible Budget—Prime Costs

	Product					
	1	2	3	4	5	6
Materials, per unit[1]	2 lbs.	3 lbs.	2 lbs.	2 lbs.	4 lbs.	6 lbs.
Direct labor, per unit[2]	0.1 hrs.	0.1 hrs.	0.2 hrs.	0.3 hrs.	0.4 hrs.	0.4 hrs.
Machine hours required, per unit[3]	0.3 hrs.	0.4 hrs.	0.6 hrs.	0.8 hrs.	1.0 hr.	1.1 hrs.

[1] The estimated cost of materials in 19X8-19X9 is $2 per pound. All materials for products 1 - 6 are added in Department A. Roughly equal amounts of all products are produced.

[2] The 19X8 labor contract specifies that direct labor in Department A will be paid an average wage of $8 per hour.

[3] One production line employee operates several machines simultaneously.

Department A 19X9 Flexible Budget for Manufacturing Overhead

	Fixed Amount per Month	Variable Rate per Machine Hour
Controllable costs:		
Employee salaries	$ 9,000	—
Indirect wages	?	?
Indirect materials	—	$.09
Other controllable costs	6,000	.03
Other costs:		
Supervisors' salaries	1,500	—
Depreciation—Equipment	10,000	—
Allocated plant overhead	10,000	—

- Indirect wages for the period November, 19X7, to February, 19X8, are as follows. The union contract for the 19X9 fiscal year specifies that indirect labor will receive a 10% wage increase.

	Machine Hours	Indirect Wages
November, 19X7	28,000	$18,172
December, 19X7	30,000	18,273
January, 19X8	25,000	18,091
February, 19X8	20,000	17,636

- On May 5, 19X8, the annual sales plan and production budget were completed. The production budget was then translated into monthly activity levels for each factory department. The planned activity for Department A for the 12 months ending June 30, 19X9, is shown at the top of page 489.
- On August 31, 19X8, the manager of Department A was informed that planned output for September had been raised to 34,000 direct machine hours. The manager expressed some doubt as to whether this volume could be attained on such short notice.

July	22,000	machine hrs.
August	25,000	
September	29,000	
October	32,000	
November	34,000	
December	31,000	
January	29,000	
February	26,000	
March	25,000	
April	25,000	
May	24,000	
June	23,000	
Total	325,000	machine hrs.

- At the end of September, 19X8, accounting records provided the following actual data for the department for the month:

Standard machine hours allowed	31,200	hours
Standard quantity of materials allowed	141,400	pounds
Standard direct labor hours allowed	11,785	hours
Actual activity in machine hours	33,000	hours
Actual direct material costs (140,000 lbs. @ $2.10 per lb.)	$294,000	
Actual direct labor costs (12,000 hours)	$ 96,000	
Actual overhead costs incurred:		
Employee salaries	$ 9,600	
Indirect wages	20,500	
Indirect materials	2,850	
Other controllable costs	7,510	
Supervisors' salaries	1,500	
Depreciation—equipment	10,000	
Allocated plant overhead	11,000	
Total September overhead costs	$ 62,960	

Required

(1) Calculate the 19X8/19X9 flexible budget allowance for indirect labor. Thomas Company uses the high-low method of cost estimation.

(2) What other methods might be used to estimate the budget allowance for indirect labor? What are the advantages and disadvantages of the other methods as compared to the high-low method?

(3) Thomas Co. wishes to maintain ending materials inventories equal to the next two months' production needs. Purchase orders are placed on the 10th of each month, and delivery of materials occurs by the 15th of that month, with payment terms of net 10 days. How much should be budgeted for July, 19X8 cash disbursements for materials?

(4) Assuming that the estimates of the May 5 budget will be substantially correct through August 31, 19X8, what will be the August 31 forecast of the September 30 materials inventory, in pounds, given the revised production target for September?

(5) On August 31, Thomas Company's managers revise the materials purchases budget for the expected level of production in September. What additional amount, if any, will Thomas Company have to order in September to meet its desired ending inventory target?

Fourteen

Segmental Analysis and Transfer Pricing

The profitability of a firm is dependent on its ability to successfully market its products and services. The marketplace is the ultimate test for the firm's combination of production, physical distribution, and promotional efforts. The success of these efforts may be measured by the firm's net income. For planning and control purposes, however, it is also necessary to measure performance by market segments. **Market segments** are analytic units based on categories of customers, geographical location, or product lines. Although firms vary in the extent to which they divide their markets, almost all firms measure the performance of major product lines or divisions.

This chapter will provide the analytic means by which segment performance may be measured. The tools of contribution analysis developed in preceding chapters will be applied, and methods of considering performance with respect to a segment's investment in assets will be discussed. Since it is common for segments to transfer units and services to other segments, a means of accounting for transfers will also be developed. Transfer prices will be discussed in terms of their impact on decision making within a firm.

SEGMENTAL ANALYSIS

The profitability of a segment is measured by its contribution. Therefore, the prime ingredient for market segment analysis is the appropriate attachment of revenues and costs to the segment. Revenues are automatically traceable to segments, and product costs are easily identified with segments by matching the usually well-defined variable unit costs with sales. The more difficult task involves attaching nonmanufacturing costs, such as physical distribution costs and promotional costs, which are discussed in this chapter.

As mentioned in previous chapters, a cost is specific to a segment only when it is believed that the cost would cease if the segment were eliminated. While variable costs are specific at all levels of analysis, fixed costs that are not specific to small segments will become specific as higher levels of aggregation are reached. For example, fixed warehousing costs cannot be specific to individual sales territories within a district, but may be specific to the entire district. Generally, the higher the level of aggregation, the more specific the fixed costs become.

Control and Analysis of Physical Distribution Costs

As manufactured products have become more standardized, improved customer service has become an increasing part of a firm's marketing strategy. As a result, physical distribution costs, or order-filling costs, have become a greater percentage of the total costs in many firms.

In controlling physical distribution costs, there are two major concerns: the cost of providing the service and the usage of the services by the segments of a firm. Although cost data should be provided in a form which satisfies both objectives, accounting for distribution costs is an undeveloped area in many firms. Frequently, these costs are scattered among differing responsibilities, with very little attempt made to budget and control them. In such firms, the first step must be to regroup costs and responsibilities by well-defined functions, such as warehousing, shipping, and order-processing. Once the functions are defined, a flexible budget should be established for each activity.

As indicated in Chapter 2, the factors of variability which explain the behavior of nonmanufacturing costs are more elusive and varied than for manufacturing costs. Nevertheless, the following formula may be used to create a flexible budget for each of the physical distribution functions:

Function cost = Fixed cost + (Variable cost × Factor of variability)

Frequently, the amounts of the fixed and variable costs will be derived through statistical estimates, and more than one factor of variability may be identified for a function. For example, warehousing cost might be stated as follows:

Warehousing = $17,500 per month + ($.05 × Cost of units stored per month) + ($3 × Number of orders filled)

The choice of the factors of cost variability, some of which are listed on page 122, should be based primarily on their power to explain variability. The following guidelines will also be useful in choosing the variability factors:

1. Costs should be in a form that allows cost comparisons to be made between functions, so that the total cost of physical distribution may be quantified and minimized. These cost comparisons are often termed **trade-off analysis**. For example, if a proposal to reduce the number of field warehouses is being considered, cost data must be available to compare reduced inventory holding costs against higher shipping costs.

2. Costs should be in a form that allows them to be attached to the segments making use of the services. Although variable costs will be attached in proportion to usage, the factor that defines usage may not always be readily measurable. For example, ton-miles delivered may be the best explanatory factor for shipping costs, but it may not be feasible to maintain a record of weight and distance for each sale. Therefore, some sacrifice of accuracy may be made for the sake of expediency.

3. Costs should be in a form that allows a firm to defend its practice of charging different prices to competing customers. If a firm is charged with price discrimination under the Robinson-Patman Act, it can generally cite the factor of variability used for decision-making purposes to defend its pricing structure.

The Modular Data Base. If accounting input data are properly coded, the objectives of the above guidelines can be achieved. Such coding of data can be described as a modular data base, which can be used for three primary purposes: (1) external accounting; (2) cost control by function, which includes the production, physical distribution, and promotion functions; and (3) analysis of market segments, which is accomplished by comparing each segment's revenues to its specific costs. These uses are shown in the following diagram:[1]

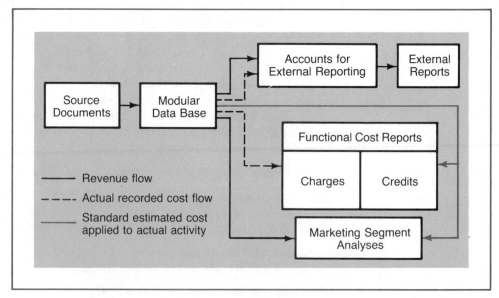

[1] Frank J. Mossman, W. J. E. Crissy, and Paul M. Fischer, *Financial Dimensions of Marketing Management* (New York: John Wiley & Sons, 1978), p. 38. Reprinted by permission of John Wiley & Sons, Inc.

The following features are characteristic of a modular data base:

1. Actual revenues are aggregated for external reports, but are also assigned to market segments.

2. Actual costs of both production and nonproduction activities are aggregated into accounts for external reporting and are also assigned to appropriate functional cost centers. In a functional cost center, identifiable activities fall under one manager's responsibility. Actual costs are compared by function to standard costs. The actual costs are not charged to sales segments, based on the principle that the segments are responsible for the use of the services at only the budgeted costs and are not responsible for variances between actual and budgeted costs of the functions.

3. The budgeted cost is applied to the market segments. The budgeted cost is also credited to the appropriate cost function. Variance analysis by function can then be used to compare standard and/or budgeted costs to actual costs. In addition, sales segments are charged with only budgeted costs. Variable costs are attached according to each segment's usage. Fixed costs are attached at the first level of analysis to which the costs are specific.

In Illustration 14-1, the modular data base concept of analysis is applied to a firm with three market territories. There is one production department and three distribution cost functions: warehousing, shipping, and order-processing. The following features of Illustration 14-1 should be noted:

1. Only actual revenues and costs are directed from the chart of accounts to the external statements.

2. Actual costs flow to the functional cost centers, where they are compared to the budget.

3. The modular data base facilitates crediting the cost centers for the standard variable cost of units produced or services provided. Fixed costs flow only to segments where they specifically attach. No fixed manufacturing costs are attached to segments, while all fixed warehousing costs are attached.

4. The attachment of revenues and specific budgeted costs to sales segments allows the calculation of each segment's contribution to the firm's nonspecific fixed costs.

5. The difference between actual and applied cost is the cost variance for each functional cost center. This variance is viewed as a cost attachable only at the firm-wide level.

The data base should be designed so that cost information can be attached to as many different analyses as possible. For example, order-handling costs should be attachable to both product-line and customer analyses. Although the modular data base may be difficult to implement in a manual accounting system, it is easily handled by a computerized system.

Illustration 14-1   Modular Data Base for January, 19X1

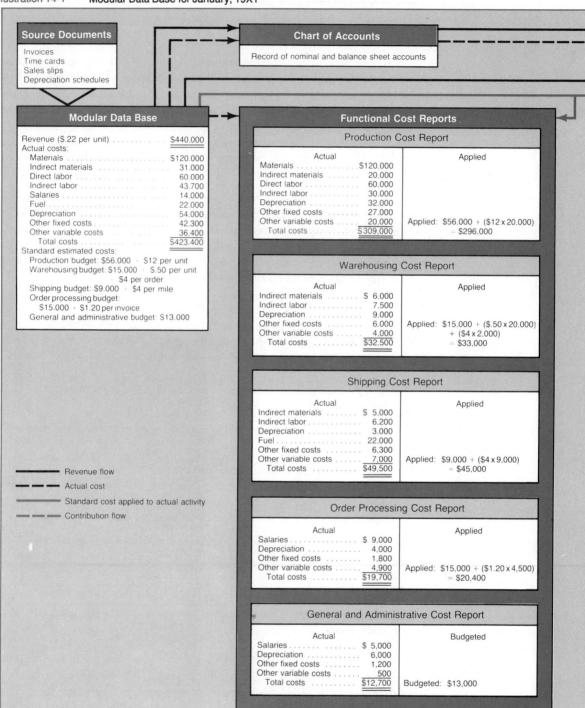

Source Documents

Invoices
Time cards
Sales slips
Depreciation schedules

Chart of Accounts

Record of nominal and balance sheet accounts

Modular Data Base

Revenue ($.22 per unit)	$440.000
Actual costs:	
Materials	$120.000
Indirect materials	31.000
Direct labor	60.000
Indirect labor	43.700
Salaries	14.000
Fuel	22.000
Depreciation	54.000
Other fixed costs	42.300
Other variable costs	36.400
Total costs	$423.400

Standard estimated costs:
Production budget: $56.000 · $12 per unit
Warehousing budget: $15.000 · $.50 per unit
· $4 per order
Shipping budget: $9.000 · $4 per mile
Order processing budget:
$15.000 · $1.20 per invoice
General and administrative budget: $13.000

——— Revenue flow

– – – Actual cost

——— Standard cost applied to actual activity

– – – Contribution flow

Functional Cost Reports

Production Cost Report

Actual		Applied
Materials	$120.000	
Indirect materials	20.000	
Direct labor	60.000	
Indirect labor	30.000	
Depreciation	32.000	
Other fixed costs	27.000	
Other variable costs	20.000	Applied: $56.000 + ($12 x 20.000)
Total costs	$309.000	= $296.000

Warehousing Cost Report

Actual		Applied
Indirect materials	$ 6.000	
Indirect labor	7.500	
Depreciation	9.000	
Other fixed costs	6.000	Applied: $15.000 + ($.50 x 20.000)
Other variable costs	4.000	+ ($4 x 2.000)
Total costs	$32.500	= $33.000

Shipping Cost Report

Actual		Applied
Indirect materials	$ 5.000	
Indirect labor	6.200	
Depreciation	3.000	
Fuel	22.000	
Other fixed costs	6.300	
Other variable costs	7.000	Applied: $9.000 + ($4 x 9.000)
Total costs	$49.500	= $45.000

Order Processing Cost Report

Actual		Applied
Salaries	$ 9.000	
Depreciation	4.000	
Other fixed costs	1.800	
Other variable costs	4.900	Applied: $15.000 + ($1.20 x 4.500)
Total costs	$19.700	= $20.400

General and Administrative Cost Report

Actual		Budgeted
Salaries	$ 5.000	
Depreciation	6.000	
Other fixed costs	1.200	
Other variable costs	500	
Total costs	$12.700	Budgeted: $13.000

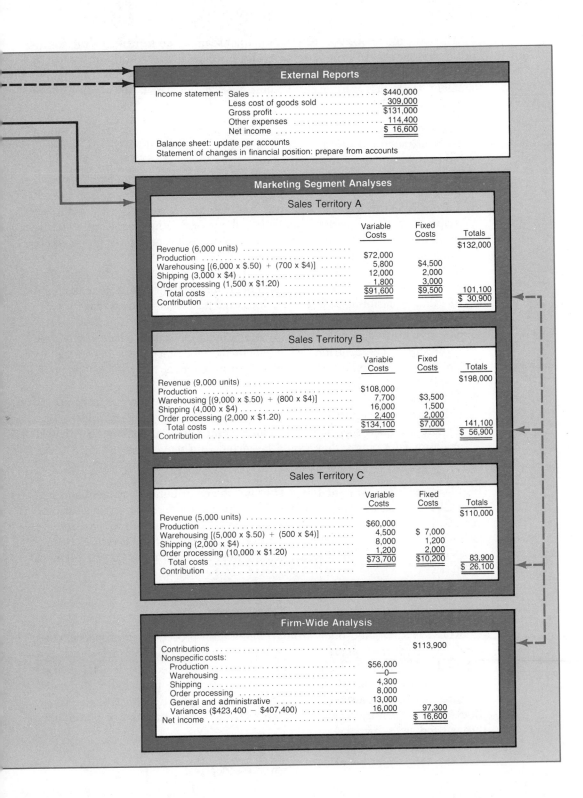

External Reports

Income statement: Sales $440,000
Less cost of goods sold 309,000
Gross profit $131,000
Other expenses 114,400
Net income .... $ 16,600

Balance sheet: update per accounts
Statement of changes in financial position: prepare from accounts

Marketing Segment Analyses

Sales Territory A

	Variable Costs	Fixed Costs	Totals
Revenue (6,000 units)			$132,000
Production	$72,000		
Warehousing [(6,000 x $.50) + (700 x $4)]	5,800	$4,500	
Shipping (3,000 x $4)	12,000	2,000	
Order processing (1,500 x $1.20)	1,800	3,000	
Total costs	$91,600	$9,500	101,100
Contribution			$ 30,900

Sales Territory B

	Variable Costs	Fixed Costs	Totals
Revenue (9,000 units)			$198,000
Production	$108,000		
Warehousing [(9,000 x $.50) + (800 x $4)]	7,700	$3,500	
Shipping (4,000 x $4)	16,000	1,500	
Order processing (2,000 x $1.20)	2,400	2,000	
Total costs	$134,100	$7,000	141,100
Contribution			$ 56,900

Sales Territory C

	Variable Costs	Fixed Costs	Totals
Revenue (5,000 units)			$110,000
Production	$60,000		
Warehousing [(5,000 x $.50) + (500 x $4)]	4,500	$ 7,000	
Shipping (2,000 x $4)	8,000	1,200	
Order processing (10,000 x $1.20)	1,200	2,000	
Total costs	$73,700	$10,200	83,900
Contribution			$ 26,100

Firm-Wide Analysis

Contributions		$113,900
Nonspecific costs:		
Production	$56,000	
Warehousing	—0—	
Shipping	4,300	
Order processing	8,000	
General and administrative	13,000	
Variances ($423,400 − $407,400)	16,000	97,300
Net income		$ 16,600

495

The basic model for the analysis of market segment performance is the contribution model developed in Chapter 4. In Illustration 14-2, contribution analysis is applied to a marketing territory. Part A of the illustration is the contribution statement, while Part B is the cost-volume-profit graph. The following features of the illustration should be noted:

1. All variable costs, including physical distribution costs and variable selling costs, are subtracted from revenue in order to compute the segment contribution to fixed costs.
2. Specific fixed costs of the segment are separated into short-run fixed costs and long-run fixed costs.
3. Economic depreciation charges are used. **Economic depreciation** is the anticipated change in market value during the period. While many firms will use historical, cost-based depreciation, it is more relevant for decision-making purposes to use a measure of economic depreciation.
4. Three contribution zones are identified on the cost-volume-profit graph. The short-run justification point separates the negative contribution zone from the marginal contribution zone. The long-run justification point separates the positive contribution zone from the marginal contribution zone.
5. The sales dollar approach is used, since segments typically produce a broad mix of products. The contribution statement therefore includes a Percentage of Total Revenue column to aid in the construction of the cost-volume-profit graph.
6. The example does not include tax consequences, since income taxes are an obligation of the entire firm and attach only at the firm-wide level. However, if there are taxes specific to the segment, such as local income taxes levied against a sales outlet, they would be included in the analysis.

The Segment's Investment Base. Thus far, the contribution statement and segment CVP analysis have not considered the investment base required to earn the contribution. A common means of considering the efficiency with which assets are used is to compare contribution to assets used. This comparison is termed **return on investment (ROI)**. In the past, many firms calculated the ROI of a segment as follows:

$$ROI = \frac{Segment\ net\ income}{Segment\ assets}$$

ROI was a full, and often arbitrary, allocation procedure. Nonspecific costs were allocated to the segment to arrive at net income, and the costs of assets shared and used in common by segments were also fully allocated. While ROI defined in terms of segment net income is a measure of relative profitability, a parallel measure that is more useful to management is **contribution on specific assets (COSA)**, or **return on assets managed (ROAM)**. This measure of profitability is calculated as follows:

$$COSA = \frac{Segment\ contribution}{Segment\ specific\ assets}$$

Illustration 14-2   Market Segment Analysis
Part A   Contribution Statement, Midwest Sales Territory

			Percent of Total Revenue
Revenue		$8,000,000	100%
Less variable costs:			
Variable standard cost of goods sold (assumes a given product mix)	$4,160,000		52%
Variable standard physical distribution costs (assumes a given product and customer mix)	640,000		8
Variable sales commissions	400,000		5
Total variable costs		5,200,000	65%
Contribution to segment short-run fixed costs		$2,800,000	35%
Less segment short-run fixed costs:			
Fixed manufacturing costs	$ 700,000		
Fixed physical distribution costs	300,000		
Selling and advertising	200,000	1,200,000	
Contribution to segment long-run fixed costs		$1,600,000	
Less segment long-run fixed costs:			
Depreciation on plant and equipment (based on change in market value) ...	$ 550,000		
Lease expense (truck fleet)	150,000	700,000	
Segment contribution (to nonspecific costs)		$ 900,000	

Illustration 14-2
Market Segment Analysis

Part B
CVP Analysis

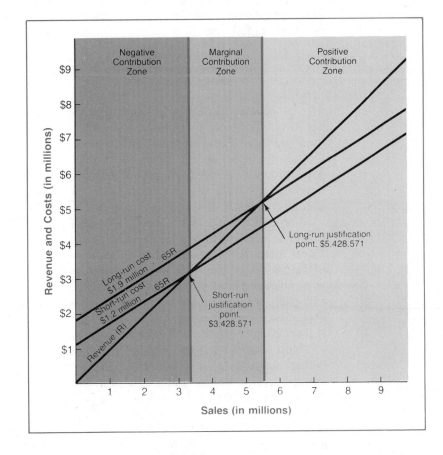

Specific assets are those assets which directly support the operations of the segment and which would not be needed if the segment were discontinued. These assets include assets managed by the segment, as well as those assets managed at higher corporate levels which directly and specifically benefit the segment. While many firms measure these assets at their depreciated historical costs, a more relevant approach is to consider the assets' opportunity costs as indicated by their market values. To illustrate, assume that the Midwest Sales Territory analyzed in Illustration 14-2 has the following specific assets:

Inventory	$ 500,000
Receivables (net of specific payables)	600,000
Average market value of plant and equipment during period ...	2,000,000
Total specific assets	$3,100,000

The Midwest Sales Territory's performance could then be measured as follows:

$$\text{COSA} = \frac{\$900{,}000 \text{ segment contribution}}{\$3{,}100{,}000 \text{ total specific assets}} = 29.03\%$$

An alternative, and possibly superior, method of comparing contribution to segment assets is the **residual income approach.** This approach, which subtracts from net income a cost of capital charge for the value of the assets used, is illustrated as follows:

Net income	$50,000
Cost of capital charge (.12 × $300,000)	36,000
Residual income	$14,000

The residual income of $14,000 indicates that the firm is successful, since it has $14,000 of income beyond that needed to meet its cost of capital. In effect, this $14,000 is "super income." The return on investment approach for the same firm also indicates success, since the ROI of 16.7% ($50,000 net income ÷ $300,000 assets) exceeds the cost of capital. Note that a firm with a positive net income may have a negative residual income when its net income is not large enough to meet its cost of capital.

Just as ROI is modified to become COSA for application to segments, residual income is modified to become **residual contribution** when applied to segments. A cost of capital charge is included only for assets specific to the segment. This cost of capital charge may have both variable and fixed components. For example, receivables and inventory will often vary in proportion to sales, and thus the cost of capital charge for these assets is a variable cost. The investment in plant and equipment is fixed, however, with respect to volume. Therefore, the cost of capital charge on these assets is a fixed cost.

Illustration 14-3 is an extension of Illustration 14-2, in that a 12% cost of capital charge has been added. In Part A, the variable costs now include the cost of capital on inventory and receivables. The long-run fixed cost section now includes the cost of capital charge on plant and equipment. In Part B, segment CVP analysis is expanded to include the cost of capital charge. Since the variable cost percentage increases and fixed costs increase, the justification points now occur at higher volumes.

Illustration 14-3 Market Segment Residual Analysis
Part A Residual Contribution Statement for the Midwest Sales Territory

			Percent of Total Revenue
Revenue		$8,000,000	100.00%
Less variable costs:			
Variable standard cost of goods sold	$4,160,000		52.00%
Variable standard physical distribution costs	640,000		8.00
Variable sales commissions	400,000		5.00
Variable cost of capital charge:			
Inventory (.12 × $500,000)	60,000		.75
Net receivables (.12 × $600,000)	72,000		.90
Total variable costs		5,332,000	66.65%
Residual contribution to segment short-run fixed costs		$2,668,000	33.35%
Less segment short-run fixed costs:			
Fixed manufacturing costs	$ 700,000		
Fixed physical distribution costs	300,000		
Selling and advertising	200,000	1,200,000	
Residual contribution to segment long-run fixed costs		$1,468,000	
Less segment long-run fixed costs:			
Depreciation on plant and equipment (based on change in market value)	$ 550,000		
Cost of capital charge on plant and equipment (.12 × $2,000,000)	300,000		
Lease expense, truck fleet	150,000	1,000,000	
Segment residual contribution (to nonspecific costs)		$ 468,000	

Illustration 14-3
Market Segment
Residual Analysis

Part B
CVP Analysis

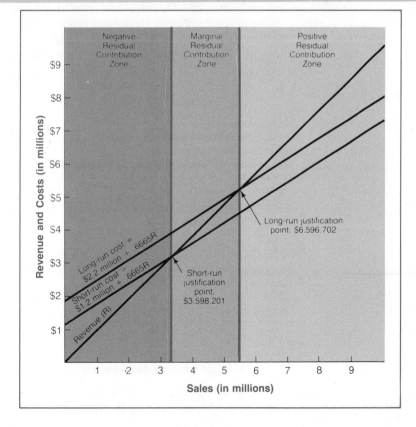

The residual income approach to segment contribution analysis offers the following advantages over the COSA approach:

1. Justification of a segment requires that it produce a contribution at least equal to the cost of capital for assets used by the segment.
2. Analysis is performed in one dimension—cost—rather than cost and then investment in assets. Thus, the cost of the asset investment can be directly included in a CVP graph.
3. The investment in assets, like any other cost, can be analyzed as to its fixed and variable components.
4. The residual contribution approach has more meaning to managers and should result in better planning and control of asset investment. Rather than having their contributions compared to their asset bases at year end, managers are encouraged to control their inventories more closely, since they are charged 1% per month for them. The cost of capital charge puts inventory cost on the same basis as any other cost, rather than as a secondary consideration. The concept of a cost of capital charge is consistent with other management accounting procedures, such as capital budgeting, discussed in Chapter 7, and inventory management models, discussed in Chapter 15.
5. The residual contribution approach offers a means of comparing the profitability of owning assets and leasing assets. Although lease payments cover depreciation and an interest factor, the profitability of segments using leased assets is inflated when the COSA approach is used, since leased assets are not included in the investment base. Under the residual contribution approach, however, depreciation and a cost of capital charge are included. This advantage is illustrated in the following example for Segment A, which leases $500,000 of fixed assets, and Segment B, which owns $500,000 of fixed assets:

	Segment A	Segment B
Return on investment:		
Segment contribution to long-run fixed costs	$200,000	$200,000
Less segment fixed costs:		
Lease expense (includes depreciation and interest factor)	125,000	
Depreciation		50,000
Segment contribution	$ 75,000	$150,000
Segment specific assets	$300,000	$800,000[a]
COSA (contribution ÷ assets)	.25	.1875
Segment residual contribution approach:		
Segment contribution to long-run fixed costs	$160,000[b]	$160,000[b]
Less segment fixed costs:		
Lease expense	125,000	
Depreciation		50,000
Cost of capital charge on fixed assets (.12 × $500,000)		60,000
Segment residual contribution	$ 35,000	$ 50,000

[a] Includes $500,000 fixed asset.
[b] Includes $40,000 cost of capital charge on variable and short-run fixed asset investment.

6. The residual income approach avoids the "averaging-down bias" that may occur with ROI approaches. If a segment has a cost of capital of 10% and an

ROI of 14%, a new opportunity to earn a 12% return would lower the overall ROI and could discourage a manager from accepting the proposal. Under the residual contribution approach, there would be added contribution, since the project earns 12% and is charged 10% for funds. Assuming that the opportunity is the best available, the residual contribution approach would encourage acceptance of the proposal.

PLANNING PROMOTIONAL EFFORTS

Promotional costs, including advertising and selling costs, are not managed by minimizing them but by directing them at the most potentially profitable market segments. In a sense, promotional efforts are ammunition which needs to be aimed at high contribution targets. The budgetary control of promotional costs is important, but, in most cases, it is secondary to their careful deployment to market segments.

Analysis of a Sales Plan

A modular data base should supply the necessary revenue, variable cost, specific fixed cost, and asset investment information with which to test alternative sales plans. In addition to the level of promotional expenditures, the alternative sales plans must specify the following information:

1. Sales projections in units and sales prices. Using the modular data base, the contribution to fixed costs of the units sold can be determined by deducting product-related variable costs from the projected sales prices.
2. Estimated use of nonproduct-related factors of cost variability, which allows customer-related costs to be estimated. For instance, physical distribution costs can be estimated on the basis of projected customer mix.
3. Segments in conformity with the fixed cost attachment levels used by the modular data base.

Illustration 14-4[2] is an example of analyzing a sales plan for the Southwest Sales Territory, which sells three products. Part A contains the revenue and cost information in the modular data base. Part B applies the data to the projected sales and accompanying activity within the Southwest Sales Territory.

Illustration 14-4
Planning Segment Contribution, 19X2

Part A
Revenue and Cost Information for Products X_1, X_2, and X_3

	X_1	X_2	X_3
Revenue per unit	$40.00	$50.00	$25.00
Standard variable production cost per unit	$20.00	$28.00	$13.00
Inventory holding cost (18% interest ÷ 12 = 1.5% of variable cost per month)	.30	.42	.20
Inventory handling	2.30	1.58	.80
	$22.60	$30.00	$14.00
Contribution per unit	$17.40	$20.00	$11.00

Other variable costs:
  Transportation: $.80 per ton-mile
  Receivable interest cost: 1-month average payment period at a cost of capital of 18% annual rate (or 1.5% of revenue).
  Order-processing cost: $1.20 per invoice equivalent.

[2] Adapted from Frank J. Mossman, W. J. E. Crissy, and Paul M. Fischer, *op. cit.*, pp. 125-127. Reprinted by permission of John Wiley & Sons, Inc.

Specific fixed costs:		
Controllable short-run fixed cost of district office	$18,000	
Noncontrollable long-run fixed cost of district office	12,000	
Total	$30,000	
Promotional costs:		
Advertising	$40,000	
Promotion	15,000	
Sales salaries and travel	60.000	
Sales commissions	4% of sales	

Revenue:		
10,000 X_1 × $40	$400,000	
6,000 X_2 × $50	300,000	
4,000 X_3 × $25	100,000	$800,000
Less variable product-related costs:		
10,000 X_1 × $22.60	$226,000	
6,000 X_2 × $30.00	180,000	
4,000 X_3 × $14.00	56,000	
Transportation (80,000 ton-miles × $.80)	64,000	
Invoice costs (1,800 invoice equivalents × $1.20)	2,160	
Receivable carrying cost (.015 × $800,000 revenue)	12,000	
Sales commissions (.04 × $800,000 revenue)	32,000	572,160
District residual contribution to segment short-run fixed costs		$227,840
Less short-run fixed costs:		
District office	$18,000	
Advertising	40,000	
Promotion	15,000	
Sales salaries and travel	60,000	133,000
Segment residual contribution to long-run fixed costs		$94,840
Less long-run fixed costs		12,000
Segment contribution		$82,840

Care must be taken in the apportioning of promotional efforts among segments. It is often tempting to direct efforts to those segments currently contributing the most. However, this strategy may not be optimal, since directing more effort to such a segment may be less beneficial than directing efforts to less contributing segments with significant potential for improving their contribution. To illustrate, the following analysis is performed for the three sales districts in the Southwest Sales Territory. It is assumed that advertising and promotion are specific to districts.

	District A		District B		District C	
	19X1	19X2	19X1	19X2	19X1	19X2
Segment contribution	$50,000	$80,000	$30,000.00	$46,840.00	$85,000.00	$101,000.00
Advertising and promotional expenses	10,000	20,000	9,000.00	11,000.00	15,000.00	22,000.00
Contribution per dollar of promotion	5	4	3.30	3.60	5.70	4.60
Change in contribution		$30,000		$16,840.00		$16,000.00
Change in promotion		10,000		2,000.00		7,000.00
Incremental contribution per incremental dollar of promotion		3		8.40		2.30

While District B has the lowest average contribution per dollar of promotion in 19X2, it is the most responsive to an increment in promotion expenditures. Therefore, it is the best candidate for added effort.

Variance Analysis

The information needed on a projected basis is also needed on an actual basis, so that variances may be analyzed. In variance analysis, the actual performance of a segment is compared to the original budget plan in order to identify any need for corrective action and to improve future planning. Cost variances for production or physical distribution functions are ignored, since such variances are analyzed within cost centers and are not charged to sales segments. Although sales performance is analyzed using only the standard costs charged to sales segments, the variances isolated may not be the responsibility of the segment's manager. For example, the volume sold may not be entirely controllable by the manager.

In Illustration 14-5, the actual sales performance of the Southwest Sales Territory, which was budgeted in Illustration 14-4, is analyzed. The actual volume, price, and revenue amounts are as follows:

Unit	Volume	× Price	= Revenue
X_1	11,000	$38	$418,000
X_2	4,500	50	225,000
X_3	5,500	23	126,500
Total			$769,500

Illustration 14-5   Variance Analysis for a Sales Segment

Sales price variance:

Product	Actual Revenue	Actual Units	Budgeted Price	Actual Units at Budgeted Price	Variance	
X_1	$418,000	11,000	$40 per unit	$440,000	$22,000 U	
X_2	225,000	4,500	50	225,000	——	
X_3	126,500	5,500	25	137,500	11,000 U	$33,000 U
Total	$769,500	21,000		$802,500		

Sales mix variance:

Product	Actual Volume	Actual Volume in Budgeted Mix	Unit Variance	Budgeted Contribution	Variance	
X_1	11,000	10,500 (.5 × 21,000)	500 F	$17.40 per unit	$8,700 F	
X_2	4,500	6,300 (.3 × 21,000)	1,800 U	20.00	36,000 U	
X_3	5,500	4,200 (.2 × 21,000)	1,300 F	11.00	14,300 F	13,000 U
Total	21,000	21,000				

Sales volume variance (21,000 units actual versus 20,000 budgeted equals 1,000 units favorable in the budgeted mix):

Product	Units in Budgeted Mix	Budgeted Contribution	Variance	
X_1	500 F (.5 × 1,000 F)	$17.40 per unit	$ 8,700 F	
X_2	300 F (.3 × 1,000 F)	20.00	6,000 F	
X_3	200 F (.2 × 1,000 F)	11.00	2,200 F	16,900 F
Total	1000 F			

Total variances .... $29,100 U

The variances are isolated in Illustration 14-5 in the price-mix-volume order used for multiple raw materials inputs in Chapter 10. The straining process used in Chapter 10 may also be applied. First, the difference in price is isolated, reducing the actual quantity and mix of units to the budgeted price. Then, the difference between budgeted and actual mix is isolated. In units, this variance is always zero, since it is caused by the differential contribution among units. Since the price variances have already been isolated, the mix differences are analyzed, using the budgeted contribution. Finally, the difference in volume is isolated, using the budgeted mix and the budgeted contribution per unit, since the price and mix variances have already been isolated.

DECENTRALIZATION AND TRANSFER PRICING

In previous sections, measurement of the performance of market segments, defined in terms of product lines, categories of customers, or geographical location, was discussed. These market segments may influence the organizational structure of a firm. For example, most automobile companies have established a separate division for each of their major auto and truck lines. Other firms have established their organizational structures to reflect geographical distinctions, such as foreign operations and domestic operations.

Centralized versus Decentralized Organizational Structures

The organizational structure of a firm is the result of management's philosophy regarding where decisions should be made. If a centralized approach is taken, the important decisions will be made by managers at corporate headquarters, and operations will be more tightly controlled. If there is a shortage of experienced managerial talent in an organization, the centralized approach allows the existing talents to be used most effectively. A centralized structure allows a firm to achieve consistent policies in such important areas as pricing the firm's main products and in dealing with crisis situations. In addition, a centralized structure may help a firm achieve significant economies of scale in the acquisition and utilization of resources. For example, borrowing sizable amounts of cash at the corporate level may result in lower interest rates than segment managers could secure independently, and the centralized receipt and disbursement of cash may minimize idle cash balances.

The alternative philosophy of decision making is evident in a decentralized organizational structure in which more of the major decisions are made by managers at lower levels in the organization. The authority to make some decisions is usually delegated when it becomes more and more difficult for a few individuals to give adequate attention to all of the activities in a growing organization. Better decisions may also result from decentralization because managers at the division level can quickly react to changes in the environment of each individual segment, and thus take advantage of new opportunities and minimize the adverse effects of sudden unfavorable developments.

Another advantage which may result from decentralization is that lower-level managers may be motivated to improve their performance, since the job itself becomes more challenging, and the financial rewards and other perquisites are likely to be greater. These managers can also improve their managerial skills as a result of their decision-making experiences. Successful segment managers thus form a pool of management talent that can be tapped as openings arise in top-level management positions.

Few organizations are completely centralized or completely decentralized. In practice, most firms have characteristics of both organizational structures. For example, it is not unusual for a firm to be centralized with respect to some decisions and, at the same time, to allow other decisions to be made at the divisional or plant level.

The degree of decentralization determines the basis on which top-level management evaluates the performance of segment managers. If a segment manager has been given the authority to acquire materials and labor resources and to manufacture products, but has no authority to sell the segment's products in the marketplace, the manager of such a cost center should be evaluated on how well production schedules are met and costs controlled. If the segment manager also has the responsibility for marketing the product, that manager would be held responsible for revenues as well as costs, and the segment would be a contribution center. Extending decentralization further would involve giving the segment manager significant responsibility for acquiring and disposing of assets, resulting in an investment center. Managers of investment centers would be evaluated on the basis of their ROI, COSA, or segment residual contribution, after a charge for the cost of their controllable capital investment is deducted.

Implications of Decentralization for Transfer Pricing

In many organizations, products and services will be transferred from one segment to another. The unit price associated with such a transferred product or service is referred to as its transfer price. If the firm is decentralized and the segments are regarded as contribution centers, the dollar amount of goods transferred from one segment to another will be treated as revenue to the seller and as a cost to the purchaser.

When financial statements for the entire firm are prepared, revenues from the intersegment transfers on the books of the selling segment are completely offset by the purchase cost entry on the books of the purchasing segment. Similarly, any receivable for intersegment transfers is eliminated against the corresponding payable when a statement for the entire firm is prepared. These eliminations are easily made, since the debit for the purchase (or the receivable) on the books of one segment will be completely offset by the credit for the sale (or the liability) on the books of the other segment, regardless of the unit transfer price.

When segment financial statements are aggregated for the purpose of preparing a financial statement for the entire firm, any inventories on hand which were transferred at a price lower than full cost must be brought up to full cost, and any inventories transferred at a price greater than full cost must be reduced to cost by eliminating the segment profit on these internal sales. Full cost includes both variable cost and an allocation of fixed costs.

Decentralized firms use a variety of transfer prices. Some firms use transfer prices based on costs, and most firms that choose this approach use full cost. Only a few firms use variable cost as the transfer price. It is often desirable, however, to establish a transfer price at a level which may be different from cost. The most popular transfer pricing methods are based on a market price, such as the product's selling price or cost plus a profit margin to approximate the selling price. In keeping with the basic philosophy of decentralization, other firms do not specify transfer prices but let the segment managers involved in the transfer determine a mutually acceptable price. A few firms use more complicated transfer pricing procedures, such as dual pricing, in which the selling segment records the transfer at one price and the purchasing segment uses a different price, and shadow pricing, in which linear programming formulations are used to incorporate opportunity costs.

Segment managers use transfer prices to evaluate their alternatives in purchasing, producing, and selling. Top management's evaluation of the segment manager's performance is influenced by transfer prices, since the transfer prices used affect the segment contributions. Ideally, top management would like to achieve goal congruence by selecting a transfer price which will motivate segment managers to make decisions that benefit the firm as a whole, even though these managers view their objective as being the maximization of the profits of their own segments.

In many situations, it is difficult to select for each segment a single transfer price that will accomplish the objectives of each segment as well as the firm as a whole. Top management may be forced to decide which objective is to receive top priority and then select a transfer price consistent with that objective, even though it may not be optimal for all purposes. In the following paragraphs, the merits of alternative transfer prices will be evaluated, and guidelines for selecting the best transfer price for achieving management's objectives will be discussed.

Variable Cost. Throughout this text, the importance of variable costs and contribution margins in making good decisions has been emphasized. If a segment has sufficient unused capacity which can be used to produce the output demanded by another segment, then the variable cost of the producing segment represents the sacrifice made by the firm in making the goods available to other segments. The consistent use of variable cost as the transfer price throughout the firm means that each segment adds its own variable costs to the transfer price, and the resulting total represents the variable cost for the entire firm. If other transfer prices are used, the total variable cost for the firm will not be reflected in the transfer price of a product or component which has passed through several other segments upstream in the organization.

Variable costs may be useful for decision-making purposes, but they have some definite drawbacks. The calculation of the variable cost itself may pose problems. Since the variable cost may be constant only over some relevant range, there may be some difficulty in deciding which variable cost figure should be used. Moreover, if the segment supplying the product has other alternatives, i.e., if the product can be sold on the outside market or if the production facilities can be used to manufacture other products, then the variable cost represents only part of the sacrifice made in transferring the product to another segment in the firm. In this case, the use of the variable cost as the transfer price could lead to a transfer of components within the firm when it would be more profitable to sell them to outsiders.

When variable cost is used as the transfer price, segments engaged primarily in producing components and products for other segments must be organized as cost centers, which reduces some of the possible benefits from decentralization. For example, the use of variable cost as a transfer price makes it difficult to evaluate the performance of producing segment managers, except as managers of cost centers. Segments supplying products to other segments within a firm will show large losses, since their "revenues" will only cover their variable costs, with no margin to cover their fixed costs. Some decentralized firms provide corporate "subsidies" to producing segments. These subsidies are equal to a segment's fixed costs, which enables the segment to break even. Other firms require the purchasing segment to pay an amount equal to the variable cost of the products transferred plus a lump sum payment to cover segment fixed costs. If the entire output of the supplier is transferred, the lump sum would cover all the fixed costs. If only a portion of the output is transferred, the lump sum payment would usually be set at that same portion of total fixed costs.

The performance of managers whose segments buy much of their material from other segments and sell most of their output outside the firm will also be difficult to evaluate when the variable cost is used as the transfer price. Such segments will appear to be very profitable, since they pay only the variable cost for any internally purchased items. While top-level management can partially adjust for these large profit levels by increasing the target profit level against which the segment manager will be measured, it will be difficult to compare managers of upstream or downstream segments in vertically integrated firms. It will also be difficult to compare the results of segment operations with results achieved by outside firms dealing in the same products.

Full Cost. Although full cost is readily available on the books of firms using absorption costing, full cost has little to recommend it as a transfer price. It does provide inventory valuations that are required for most external reporting purposes. Also, it may be accepted by segment managers as an objectively determined transfer price, since it is the same number which appears on external reports.

The primary disadvantage of using full cost as the transfer price is that the full cost is not useful for most decisions. Unless top-level managers can provide appropriate directions to segment managers, the managers are likely to make decisions which are not optimal from the standpoint of the firm's profits. For example, the manager of a supplying segment will normally want to sell the segment's output outside the firm in order to receive the outside selling price, rather than transfer the output to another segment and receive only the full cost. Since the segment supplying the product must be treated as a cost center, the use of full cost as the transfer price creates problems in evaluating the performance of the manager.

Market Price. If the market is perfectly competitive, the external sales price of a segment's product is popular as a transfer price, since it achieves goal congruence in decision making and facilitates performance evaluation in a decentralized firm. The external selling price in these circumstances provides the proper measure of the transfer's real gain or loss to the company as a whole. Using the selling price as the transfer price also results in segment profit figures which closely approximate the results which would be achieved if the segments were separate, independent entities.

In some cases, an external selling price may not exist for the product being transferred because the company does not sell the product separately to the outside market. For example, the major U. S. automakers did not sell their first automatic transmissions to other manufacturers, and the segments producing these transmissions accordingly had no selling price available to use as a transfer price. In these situations, the selling price of a similar product can sometimes be used as an approximation of a market price, with appropriate adjustments made for any quality differences or differences in features which might exist between the product produced internally and the similar product being sold in the external market. Another approach would be to compute a hypothetical selling price by using the firm's standard pricing formula, which often is stated as full cost plus a profit percentage.

Products produced by one segment and transferred to another are often slightly different from products produced for sale to outside firms. Certain costs may also not be incurred on internal transfers. For example, credit and collecting expenses that are recovered through the external selling price are not relevant on transfers of goods to other segments of the firm. To deal with this situation, the cost of such services may be deducted from the external selling price in order to establish an internal transfer price.

Another problem when using selling price as the transfer price arises when the outside market in which the product is sold is not a perfectly competitive market. According to economic theory, profits are maximized when firms equate marginal costs with marginal revenues. In a perfectly competitive market, marginal revenue is equal to the selling price, and correct output decisions will be made if output is expanded until marginal costs equal the selling price. If a segment faces a downward-sloping demand curve, however, marginal revenue rather than selling price must be used in decision making. When the selling price must be reduced in order to sell additional units in the outside market, the use of the selling price as the transfer price will result in misleading comparisons of the gains achieved by selling units outside versus transferring units to another segment.

Interactions between markets may also reduce the usefulness of a product's selling price as the basis for establishing a segment's transfer price. If the products of one segment are competitive with or serve as complements to another segment's products, then the selling price does not measure the entire revenue impact on the firm. A reduced selling price of a competitive product may increase the revenues of one segment and, at the same time, reduce the demand for another segment's products. A complementary product can have the opposite effect on sales by other segments.

Negotiated Transfer Price. The approach to setting transfer prices that is most consistent with the underlying philosophy of decentralized decision making is to allow the segment managers involved in the transfer of a product to negotiate with each other to determine the price at which the product is to be transferred. A mutually negotiated transfer price presumably is satisfactory to both segment managers and should benefit both divisions. Negotiating the transfer price also provides segment managers with experience in bargaining. This experience can be an important aspect of the firm's management development program, while at the same time can assure the firm that the consequences of ineffective bargaining will not be as severe as if a segment manager struck a poor bargain with an outside firm.

A negotiated transfer price has some potential disadvantages. Negotiations are costly in terms of managerial time and talent. A process must also be worked out to arbitrate unresolved differences, usually involving corporate headquarters personnel. Instead of generating cooperation between segments, the bargaining process may generate hard feelings.

A negotiated transfer price may not be the optimal transfer price from the overall firm standpoint. The price may reflect only the relative bargaining abilities of the two segment managers or the relative size and clout of the two segments. Moreover, a negotiated transfer price, though satisfactory to the two negotiating segments, may have negative implications for other segments.

Dual Prices. Faced with the dilemma that no single transfer price is without some drawbacks, some firms use two different prices to record a transfer between segments. When this procedure is used, the external selling price is recorded on the books of the segment supplying the product, and the variable cost is recorded on the books of the segment acquiring the product. Using the selling price for the supplying division provides segment profit figures that are more comparable to those of other segments selling to the outside. Charging the acquiring segment with the variable cost may facilitate better decision making within that segment. Although the advantages of both the market price and the variable cost methods may be realized, the disadvantages of both methods may make the dual pricing procedure undesirable.

Guideline Price. The preceding discussion should make it clear that there is no single transfer price which is appropriate for every conceivable set of circumstances. Nevertheless, it is possible to establish a general transfer pricing guideline. This guideline price may be stated as follows:

Guideline price = Variable cost + Contribution given up by making the transfer

The flexibility in this pricing formula is provided by the contribution element. If there are no alternative uses for the resources devoted to making the product being transferred, no contribution margin is sacrificed, and the appropriate transfer price is the variable cost. On the other hand, if there is a strong external market for the product, the segment transferring the product is sacrificing the entire contribution margin which could be earned on an outside sale. In that case, the appropriate transfer price is the variable cost plus the entire contribution margin, and it is equal to the selling price.

To illustrate how the guideline price can be applied in a variety of circumstances, the operations of United Electronics will be examined. United Electronics is an integrated electronics firm which has several decentralized segments. The costs and selling prices of the main products of three of these segments or divisions are shown in Illustration 14-6. The Circuits Division produces driver circuits and a variety of other integrated circuits; the Monitor Division produces monitor displays used in a variety of small computers; and the Computer Division manufactures a small microcomputer word processor.

Illustration 14-6
Product Cost and Margin
Sheets of United
Electronics

Circuits Division	
	Driver Circuit
Selling price	$50 per unit
Less product variable costs (materials, direct labor, and other costs)	20 per unit
Product contribution margin	$30 per unit
Less depreciation and other fixed costs	15
Product profit margin before taxes	$15 per unit
Current production and sales volume	3,000 circuits
Production capacity	5,000 circuits

Monitor Division	
	Monitor
Selling price	$550 per unit
Less product variable costs:	
2 Driver Circuits at $50 each	$100 per unit
Other variable costs	200
Total variable costs	$300 per unit
Product contribution margin	$250 per unit
Less fixed costs	150
Product profit margin before taxes	$100 per unit
Current production and sales volume	1,800 monitors
Production capacity	3,000 monitors

Computer Division	
	Word Processor
Selling price	$1,000 per unit
Less product variable costs:	
Monitor	$ 500 per unit
Other variable costs	200
Total variable costs	$ 700 per unit
Product contribution margin	$ 300 per unit
Less fixed costs	150
Product profit margin before taxes	$ 150 per unit
Current production and sales volume	1,000 units
Production capacity	1,000 units

All the divisions now buy their component requirements from other firms. The Computer Division manager purchases special monitors with amber-colored screens from Baker Co., at $500 each, to install in the microcomputer. United's own Monitor Division produces a monitor with a green screen, but the Monitor Division manager determines that an amber-colored monitor can be provided to the Computer Division at the same cost as the standard monitor.

Since the Monitor Division has 1,200 units of excess capacity, it can easily provide the 1,000 monitors required by the Computer Division. The additional costs incurred would be equal to the Monitor Division's variable costs of $300. If Monitor's $550 selling price is used as the transfer price, the manager of the Computer Division would have no incentive to acquire the monitors internally, since the monitors can be purchased for $500 outside the company. Any price lower than $500 would encourage the Computer Division to buy from the Monitor Division. Although the transfer price need not be as low as Monitor's variable costs, a transfer price of $300 is the lowest possible price. The $300 price does not provide any additional contribution margin to the Monitor Division. The manager of that division, however, would probably be willing to supply the extra monitors, since it does not cost anything to do so, and the Monitor Division manager probably would prefer to keep the work force busy and the plant operating at high levels of activity.

A segment manager faced with excess capacity often can find other opportunites to use that capacity. The Monitor Division manager might consider reducing the selling price of the standard monitor to increase the demand. If the demand curve shown in Illustration 14-7 represents the demand curve for monitors, the Monitor Division manager should reduce the selling price from $550 to $480. As shown in Illustration 14-7, selling 2,800 monitors at $480 each would generate $54,000 more contribution margin than would be earned by selling 1,800 monitors at $500.

Illustration 14-7
Demand for Monitors

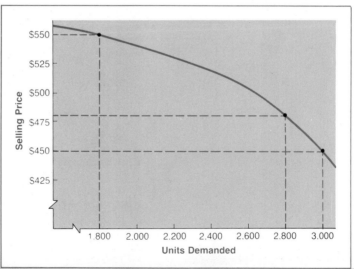

	$550	$480	$450
Selling price	$550	$480	$450
Demand	1,800 units	2,800 units	3,000 units
Total revenue:			
1,800 units at $550	$990,000		
2,800 units at $480		$1,344,000	
3,000 units at $450			$1,350,000
Less total variable costs ($300 per unit)	540,000	840,000	900,000
Total contribution margin	$450,000	$504,000	$450,000

To apply the transfer pricing guideline in this case, the $54,000 potential additional contribution margin that the Monitor Division would sacrifice by manufacturing 1,000 monitors for the Computer Division should be added to the variable cost of the monitors to arrive at the proper transfer price. If the $54,000 margin is to be recouped on the transfer of 1,000 units, $54 must be added to the $300 variable costs to arrive at a transfer price of $354 per unit. The Computer Division manager would be motivated to buy the monitors from the Monitor Division, since the $354 transfer price is still well below the price at which the monitors can be obtained on the outside.

When a third division sells components to outside firms, it is more difficult to achieve goal congruence in determining a guideline transfer price. The diagram in Illustration 14-8 illustrates this situation, using the divisions of United Electronics. In this illustration, the only monitors satisfactory for the Computer Division's product are those available from two other firms: Able Company, which purchases the two driver circuits in each monitor from the Circuits Division and charges $515 for its monitor; and Baker Co., which offers an equivalent monitor for $500 but does not buy any circuits from United. The manager of the Computer Division, if acting independently, will buy the monitors from Baker Co., which offers the lowest price. The Computer Division manager may not be aware that Able's monitors use United's driver circuits and Baker's do not. As shown in Illustration 14-8, however, the net cash inflow to the firm would be $45 less if monitors are purchased from Able Company, since $60 of contribution margin is earned by the Circuits Division on each monitor that Able Company manufactures.

Illustration 14-8
Effect of Sales to External
Suppliers by Another
Division

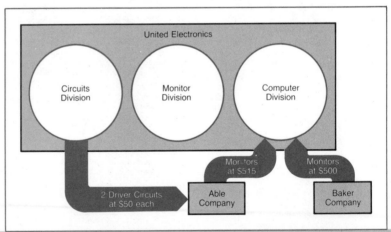

Out-of-Pocket Variable Costs to United Electronics		
	Purchase by Computer Division	
	From Able Company	From Baker Company
Cash payment for the monitor	$515	$500
Less net cash received on the sale of 2 driver circuits to Able Company:		
Revenue ($50 × 2)	$100	
Less variable cost ($20 × 2)	40	
Contribution margin	60	—
Net out-of-pocket costs to United	$455	$500

To achieve goal congruence in this situation, corporate management could offer the Computer Division a $60 "subsidy" for each monitor purchased from Able Company. This subsidy would bring the net cost to the Computer Division down to $455, and the Computer Division manager would make a decision which not only maximizes the Division's profits but the company's profits as well.

The net figure of $455 also provides the proper signals to the Computer Division manager with respect to searching out other sources for monitors. As long as the price of other monitors is above $455, United would be better off if the Computer Division buys from Able Company, and the Computer Division manager will be motivated to buy Able monitors. If monitors can be purchased for less than $455, the Computer Division manager should buy those monitors in order to maximize United's profits.

If the $60 subsidy is charged against the Circuits Division, the effect is the same as if the transfer price were based on the variable cost. If the $60 subsidy is not charged to the Circuits Division, the corporate policy is equivalent to a dual pricing policy.

As more divisions interact with each other and with outside firms, it becomes more and more difficult to trace through the interaction and arrive at optimal decisions. One way of dealing with these complicated situations is to formulate the company's planning problem as a linear programming problem. Appendix 14-1 shows how United Electronics could use linear programming to schedule production, plan sales, and establish transfer prices.

APPENDIX 14: LINEAR PROGRAMMING APPROACH TO PLANNING IN A DECENTRALIZED COMPANY

To illustrate the use of linear programming in transfer pricing situations, the data provided for United Electronics will be used. It will also be assumed that each of the divisions in United can sell its product to outside firms. In this example, both the Circuits Division and the Monitor Division can produce products which are equivalent to products which the other divisions can purchase outside the firm. United's customers for the finished products are therefore indifferent as to whether the products contain United's components or purchased components.

To formulate this problem, the following notation will be used:

C_1 = circuits sold to outside firms
M_1 = monitors with purchased circuits sold to outside firms
M_2 = monitors with United circuits sold to outside firms
W_1 = sales of word processors with monitors containing purchased circuits and transferred from the Monitor Division
W_2 = sales of word processors with monitors containing United circuits and transferred from the Monitor Division
W_3 = sales of word processors with monitors purchased from Able Company
W_4 = sales of word processors with monitors purchased from Baker Co.

Illustration A14-1 shows the calculation of the corporate contribution margin for each of United's products. United's total corporate contribution margin is the objective function to be maximized, which is stated as follows:

$$\text{Maximize } Z = 30C_1 + 250M_1 + 310M_2 + 500W_1 + 560W_2 + 345W_3 + 300W_4$$

Illustration A14-1
Contribution Margins with
Internal Transfers

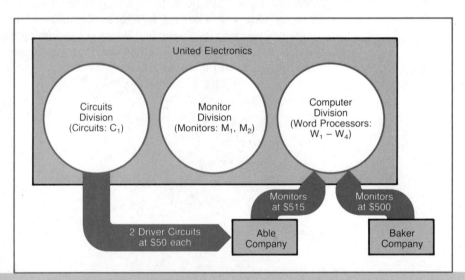

Unit Contribution Margin of United Electronics Products							
	C_1	M_1	M_2	W_1	W_2	W_3	W_4
Selling price	$50	$550	$550	$1,000	$1,000	$1,000	$1,000
Less variable costs:							
Misc. var. costs	$20	$200	$200	$ 200	$ 200	$ 200	$ 200
Purchased circuits at $50		100					
Transferred circuits at $20			40				
United monitors with purchased circuits					300		
United monitors with United circuits						240	
Able monitors							455	
Baker monitors								500
Total var. costs	$20	$300	$240	$ 500	$ 440	$ 655	$ 700
Contrib. margin	$30	$250	$310	$ 500	$ 560	$ 345	$ 300

For each division, there is a production constraint resulting from limited production capacity and a demand constraint based on the maximum outside demand for each product, given the current selling price. The capacity limitation for the Circuits and Monitor Divisions is noted in Illustration 14-6. Since the current sales volume of circuits and monitors reflects all output being sold to outside firms, the sales volume for each product also represents the product's maximum external demand. However, United's word processor is so popular that the estimated demand and production capacity for this product have been increased to 4,000 units.

Based on the division capacities and product demands given in Illustration 14-6, the production and demand constraints are as follows:

- Production capacity for circuits: $C_1 + 2M_2 + 2W_2 + 2W_3 \leq 5,000$ units
- Demand for circuits: $C_1 \leq 3,000$ units
- Production capacity for monitors: $M_1 + M_2 + W_1 + W_2 \leq 3,000$ units
- Demand for monitors: $M_1 + M_2 \leq 1,800$ units
- Production capacity and demand for word processors:
  $$W_1 + W_2 + W_3 + W_4 \leq 4,000 \text{ units}$$
  $$C_1, M_1, M_2, W_1, W_2, W_3, W_4 \geq 0$$

Although it is not difficult to formulate the objective function and the constraints, it would be very difficult to arrive at an optimal solution manually. A computer program, however, can easily solve this linear programming problem. The solution shown in Illustration A14-2 indicates that, to maximize United's profits, none of the circuits manufactured by the Circuits Division should be sold outside ($C_1 = O$). Instead, the Division's entire output of 5,000 circuits [$2 \times (M_2 + W_2)$] should be transferred to the Monitor Division.

Illustration A14-2
United Electronics'
Planning Problem—
Linear Programming
Solution

Planning Problem:

Maximize $Z = 30C_1 + 250M_1 + 310M_2 + 500W_1 + 560W_2 + 345W_3 + 300W_4$

Subject to:

			Constraint No.
$C_1 + 2M_2 + 2W_2 + 2W_3$	$\leq$	5,000	1
C_1	$\leq$	3,000	2
$M_1 + M_2 + W_1 + W_2$	$\leq$	3,000	3
$M_1 + M_2$	$\leq$	1,800	4
$W_1 + W_2 + W_3 + W_4$	$\leq$	4,000	5
$C_1, M_1, M_2, W_1, W_2, W_3, W_4$	$\geq$	0	

Solution:	Constraint No.	Slack	Shadow Price
$C_1 = 0$	1	0	$ 30
$M_1 = 500$	2	3,000	0
$M_2 = 1,300$	3	0	200
$W_1 = 0$	4	0	50
$W_2 = 1,200$	5	0	300
$W_3 = 0$			
$W_4 = 2,800$			

Value of Objective Function = $2,040,000

The Monitor Division will satisfy the external demand for its monitors by selling 1,800 units of its production to outside customers ($M_1 + M_2$). The remaining 1,200 units produced will be transferred to the Computer Division (W_2). To satisfy its requirements for 6,000 driver circuits (2 circuits for each of the 3,000 monitors produced), 5,000 United circuits will be transferred to the Monitor Division, and the remaining 1,000 circuits ($2 \times M_1$) will be purchased.

The Computer Division will produce 4,000 word processors to meet current market demand for this product. As noted above, 1,200 units (W_2) will contain United monitors, and 2,800 (W_4) will have monitors purchased from Baker Co.

This optimal production and marketing plan, which would be developed at corporate headquarters, represents a centralized approach to planning and decision making. The division managers' input to this planning process would be limited to providing information on selling prices and costs, production capacities, and market demands. Once the planning problem has been solved, corporate headquarters would tell the divisions how many units should be manufactured, sold, and/or transferred, and where components should be acquired.

A step toward decentralization could be taken by developing guideline prices. This procedure would encourage the division managers to evaluate their alternatives from their own divisional perspective, and to take actions which would not only benefit their own division but the company as a whole.

To formulate an optimal guideline transfer price, the contribution margin forgone by making the transfer must be added to the variable cost of the product transferred. This forgone contribution margin for each division's product is given by the shadow price for that division's production capacity constraint. For each unit of Circuit Division capacity devoted to producing a product for transfer to another division, $30 is sacrificed and must be added to the $20 variable cost. The resulting transfer price is $50, which is also the outside selling price of circuits. Accordingly, circuits should be transferred to the Monitor Division at their selling price. The Monitor Division manager should purchase circuits externally if equivalent circuits can be acquired for less than $50. The Circuit Division manager will then use the available capacity·to manufacture circuits which will be sold to outside customers at $50.

The shadow price for the Monitor Division's capacity is $200 per unit. When this amount is added to the $300 variable cost of monitors, a transfer price of $500 is obtained. This guideline price is somewhat less than the Monitor Division's external selling price of $550, since the external market demand for its monitors (1,800 units) is already saturated.

As is the case for circuits, the $500 transfer price provides proper signals to managers in both the Monitor and the Computer Divisions. If the Monitor Division manager can find a customer who will pay more than $500 for monitors, the monitors should be sold to that customer rather than transferring them to the Computer Division. Similarly, if the Computer Division manager can find a source of monitors at a price less than $500, the monitors should be purchased externally at that lower price.

If United sets these transfer prices and provides the suggested production and marketing plans to its division managers, not only will actions that optimize the corporation's profits be taken, but each division manager will discover that there is no other plan for the division that will generate higher divisional profits. The transfer prices will also provide proper signals for exploiting profitable new opportunities. A set of segment income statements incorporating these transfer prices, together with the corporate income statement, is shown in Illustration A14-3.

	Circuit Division	Monitor Division	Computer Division	Eliminations	Corporate Statement
Revenues	$250,000[a]	$1,590,000[d]	$4,000,000[g]	$850,000[j]	$4,990,000
Less variable costs	100,000[b]	900,000[e]	2,800,000[h]	850,000[k]	2,950,000
Contribution margin	$150,000	$ 690,000	$1,200,000	-0-	$2,040,000
Less fixed costs	75,000[c]	450,000[f]	550,000[i]	——	1,075,000
Income from operations	$ 75,000	$ 240,000	$ 650,000	——	$ 965,000

[a] 5,000 units @ $50 = $250,000
[b] 5,000 units @ $20 = $100,000
[c] 5,000 units (capacity) @ $15 = $75,000 (see Illustration 14-6)
[d] Outside sales (1,800 units @ $550) . . . . $ 990,000
  Divisional transfers (1,200 units @ $500)   600,000
                                                     $1,590,000

[e] Miscellaneous variable costs (3,000 units @ $200) $600,000
  Purchased circuits (1,000 units @ $50)   50,000
  United circuits (5,000 units @ $50)   250,000
                                                            $900,000

[f] 3,000 units (capacity) @ $150 = $450,000 (see Illustration 14-6)
[g] 4,000 units @ $1,000 = $4,000,000
[h] Miscellaneous variable costs (4,000 units @ $200) . . . . $ 800,000
  Purchased monitors (2,800 units @ $500)   1,400,000
  United monitors (1,200 units @ $500)   600,000
                                                            $2,800,000

[i] Fixed costs at previous capacity (1,000 units @ $150) . . . . $150,000 (see Illustration 14-6)
  Costs to increase capacity to 4,000 units   400,000
  Total fixed costs for 4,000 units (present capacity) $550,000

[j] Divisional transfers from Circuit Division $250,000
  Divisional transfers from Monitor Division   600,000
                                                             $850,000

[k] United circuits (5,000 units @ $50) $250,000
  United monitors (1,200 units @ $500)   600,000
                                                             $850,000

Exercise Consolidated Gold Fields Ltd. operates gold mines in South Africa. For purposes of control, the firm is organized into 3 operating segments: Mining, Smelting, and Minting. The Mining Division embraces all the firm's mines. Smelting is performed in a centralized smelter which serves several mines. The Smelting Division purchases ore from the Mining Division and other mines and sells 99.999% pure gold ingots to the Minting Division and other customers. On the average, 4 tons of ore are required to yield one ounce of fine gold. The Minting Division mints special commemorative and collectors coins from the ingots purchased and markets them worldwide. Since the demand for collectible gold coins is limited, the Smelting Division primarily sells 20-oz. gold bars to jewelers and investors. A schematic of the firm's operations is as follows:

External Purchases	Mining Division	External Sales
	Variable cost (external sales) .... $30 per ton Variable cost (internal transfers) .... 27 Fixed cost 25	Gold Ore $65 per ton

Gold Ore

	Smelting Division	
Gold Ore $64 per ton	Variable cost (not including cost of gold ore)... $30 per ton Fixed cost 15	Gold Bars $430 per oz.

Gold Bars

	Minting Division	
Gold Bars $410 per oz.	Variable cost (not including cost of gold bars).. $40 per oz. Fixed cost 37	Gold Coins $550 per oz.

Unit fixed costs listed above have been determined on the basis of capacity. The capacity of each division and the market demand limits are as follows:

	Production Capacity	Maximum Market Demand
Mining Division	330,000 tons	45,000 tons
Smelting Division	320,000 tons	78,000 ounces
Minting Division	35,000 ounces	18,000 ounces

(1) Construct the objective function and all constraints necessary to plan Consolidated's operations, using the following notation:

G = tons of gold ore sold externally
I_1 = ounces of gold ingots sold externally; processed from ore transferred from the Mining Division
I_2 = ounces of gold ingots sold externally; processed from ore purchased externally
C_1 = ounces of coins sold; gold transferred in from Smelting Division from ore mined internally
C_2 = ounces of coins sold; gold transferred in from Smelting Division from ore purchased externally
C_3 = ounces of coins sold; gold purchased externally

(2) Assume that the linear programming solution to Consolidated's planning problem provided the following values:

Solution Values			Shadow (Dual) Prices	
Variable	Value	Division	Production Capacity	Market Demand Limitations
G	10,000 tons	Mining	$35 per ton	0 per ton
I_1	78,000 oz.	Smelting	10.50 per ton	$20 per oz.
I_2	0	Minting	0 per oz.	100 per oz.
C_1	2,000 oz.			
C_2	0			
C_3	16,000 oz.			

Calculate the gross margin which Consolidated would earn if the operations for the next period were carried out in accordance with the linear programming solution given. (Any unabsorbed fixed overhead is written off by Consolidated against operations.)

(3) Assume that Consolidated implements the operating plan implied by the linear programming solution given in (2). Determine the optimal transfer price for gold ore transferred to the Smelting Division from the Mining Division. Use the transfer pricing guideline, together with the opportunity costs provided by the linear programming solution given in (2).

1. In constructing a flexible budget for physical distribution activities, the factor of variability chosen to explain cost behavior should be chosen with what objectives in mind?

2. Explain how the modular data base for physical distribution costs handles actual and standard costs so as to comply with responsibility accounting.

3. Explain the two basic models by which the contribution of a segment may be compared to its specific investment base.

4. If a segment has a negative residual contribution, is it making no contribution to the remaining fixed costs of the firm?

5. There are several advantages of the residual income approach over the COSA approach. Among the more technical advantages are that it provides a means of comparing the profitability of owning and leasing assets and it avoids the averaging-down bias. Explain these two features.

6. Assuming that residual contribution analysis is being applied to sales segments, what should be the financial objective in deciding which segments receive added promotional efforts?

7. What are the variances that are computed for a sales segment, and what is the best order in which to compute them?

8. Why does a firm that transfers units between segments need transfer prices?

9. In a segmental contribution analysis, what problems might arise when the variable cost per unit is used as a transfer price?

10. The engine division of a lawn mower manufacturer currently sells 40% of its output to other firms for $120 per unit in an imperfectly competitive market. Of the engines manufactured, 60% go to the Mower Division at the $120 price. The remaining variable costs of a mower are $80. It appears that in the coming months, a mower will sell for only $197. Is it necessarily wise to maintain the transfer price?

11. Define and illustrate a dual transfer price.

EXERCISES

Exercise 1. U.A.T. Electronics produces and distributes cordless electronic telephones at its California plant. All sales are mail order. The firm would like to develop cost functions for its warehousing and order-processing functions in order to better forecast and control cost. Data for two representative months are as follows:

	April	August
Warehousing:		
Salaries and wages	$20,240	$22,000
Depreciation	8,600	8,600
Rent expense	9,700	18,500
Heat, light, and power	4,660	11,325

	April	August
Order-processing:		
Salaries and wages	$31,610	$33,400
Supplies	7,200	12,900
Other	4,940	6,200

U.A.T.'s managers feel that warehousing costs vary with the average number of units carried in inventory, and that order-processing costs vary with the number of orders shipped. The average inventory was 8,000 units in April and 14,500 units in August. The number of orders processed in April and August were 17,000 and 22,000, respectively.

Production costs for the coming year have already been analyzed, and the result of that study is the following standard cost sheet:

Materials	$65
Direct labor (4 hrs. @ $7 per DLH)	28
Variable overhead (4 hrs. @ $5 per DLH)	20
Fixed overhead (4 hrs. @ $10 per DLH*)	40

*Based on normal production of 60,000 DLHs per year.

(1) Use the high-low method to develop cost budgets for both the warehousing and order-processing functions.
(2) Assume that a local golf course has offered to buy 400 of the units for a price of $115 per unit. The units would be held in inventory roughly two months before delivery. Should U.A.T. accept the order?

Exercise 2. VGS Inc. is a holding company involved in the recording, production, distribution, and promotion of recording artists. The company concentrates primarily on new wave, jazz-fusion, and rockabilly artists. The company's physical distribution subsidiary, Windborne Company, has been plagued by losses, caused primarily by an inefficient and haphazard order-processing system. Costs incurred by the order-processing department are summarized as follows:

Salaries	$127,000
Supplies	17,400
Telephone	12,000
Rent	21,000
Heat, light, and power	7,000

VGS Inc. has hired an outside consultant to examine the order-processing department and make recommendations. The consultant feels that the operation is disorganized and can be greatly improved with simple procedural changes. The operation budget is as follows:

Order-processing cost = $99,700 + ($1.40 × orders processed) + [$125 × (average order size − 400 units)]

During the past year, 25,000 orders were processed. The average order size was 700 units. Calculate the total variance for the order-processing department.

Exercise 3. Wickstrom Company manufactures and sells natural and synthetic fiber carpeting throughout the United States. The firm has recently launched an intensive marketing effort in the southeastern United States, its newest sales area. Revenue and cost data for the Southeastern Sales Region include the following:

Revenues	$6,300,000
Variable cost of goods sold	60% of revenues
Fixed costs:	
Manufacturing	$1,275,000
Physical distribution	430,000
Selling and administrative	510,000
Sales commissions	2% of revenues

The firm's investment in assets related to the Southeastern Sales Region is comprised of the following:

Inventory	$ 750,000
Receivables net of payables	1,580,000
Market value of plant and equipment	205,000

Determine the Southeastern Sales Region's contribution to nonspecific costs and the segment's contribution on specific assets (COSA).

Exercise 4. Wickstrom Company, referred to in Exercise 3, would like to change its method of evaluating segmental performance from the COSA method to the residual contribution approach.

Use the data supplied in Exercise 3 to prepare a residual contribution statement for the Southeastern Sales Region. Wickstrom requires an 8% return on all investments. It may be assumed that the level of net receivables and inventory varies directly with sales.

Exercise 5. Wheeling Nurseries Inc. operates two identical lawn and garden shops on the northern and southern borders of a large metropolitan area. For purposes of control, the two stores are treated as separate segments within a common corporation. For the year just ended, each segment had the following operating results:

	North Segment	South Segment
Revenue	$215,000	$215,000
Less variable costs:		
Variable cost of goods sold	$123,000	$123,000
Variable administrative costs	24,000	24,000
Variable distribution costs	15,000	15,000
Total variable costs	$168,000	$168,000
Contribution to segment fixed costs	$ 47,000	$ 47,000
Less segment fixed costs	28,000	28,000
Segment contribution	$ 19,000	$ 19,000
Segment identifiable assets	$126,667	$126,667
Contribution on specific assets	15.0%	15.0%

Wheeling would like to expand its operations at both locations and has negotiated the acquisition of a 15-acre plot of land adjacent to each store. Wheeling expects to use the land to grow ornamental bushes, shrubs, and trees for resale. The plot adjacent to the northern store would be purchased for $75,000. The plot adjacent to the southern store would be leased on a 30-year lease for $9,000 per year. Wheeling expects to generate an incremental annual contribution of $15,000 from each plot.

(1) Calculate the contribution of each segment and each segment's contribution on specific assets (COSA) after acquisition of the land.

(2) Using a cost of capital of 10%, calculate the residual contribution of each segment after acquisition of the land.

Exercise 6. Universal Foods manufactures two kinds of snacks—*Jeepers!* and *Gee Whiz!* Budgeted sales were 166,000 and 249,000 units for *Jeepers!* and *Gee Whiz!*, respectively, for the first month of the current year. Planned selling prices and contribution margin ratios were as follows:

	Jeepers!	Gee Whiz!
Planned selling price	$1.50	$.90
Contribution margin ratio	70%	60%

Actual sales data for the first month included the following:

	Jeepers!	Gee Whiz!
Sales	160,000 units	250,000 units
Revenues	$248,000	$230,000

(1) Use the data to determine Universal's sales price variance for the first month of the year.

(2) Calculate Universal's sales mix variance for the first month of the year.

(3) Determine Universal's sales volume variance for the first month of the year.

Exercise 7. The Optics Division of Fujo Camera Company produces 50mm lenses for use with 35mm cameras. These lenses are sold to outside customers and are also transferred to the Camera Division of Fujo, which produces camera bodies and assembles the lenses and bodies into complete cameras. Internal statements reported the following results for 19X3:

	Optics Division	Camera Division	Total
Sales	$23,000,000	$39,000,000	$62,000,000
Less cost of goods sold:			
Beginning finished goods inventory	-0-	-0-	-0-
Cost of goods manufactured	$20,000,000	$39,000,000	$59,000,000
Less ending finished goods inventory	-0-	(6,500,000)	(6,500,000)
Cost of goods sold	$20,000,000	$32,500,000	$52,500,000
Gross margin	$ 3,000,000	$ 6,500,000	$ 9,500,000
General, selling, and administrative expenses traceable to segment	1,140,000	1,690,000	2,830,000
Segment margin	$ 1,860,000	$ 4,810,000	$ 6,670,000
General, selling and administrative expenses—common			2,920,000
Income before taxes			$ 3,750,000

During 19X3, the Optics Division produced 500,000 lenses and transferred 300,000 of these to the Camera Division. The remaining 200,000 were sold to outside customers. Lenses are transferred internally at their full cost of $40 per unit plus a normal profit margin of 15% of cost. The Camera Division produced

300,000 units and sold 250,000 at a price of $156 each. There were no beginning work in process or finished goods inventories in either department.

    (1) Calculate the value of the ending finished goods inventory as it would appear on the firm's corporate balance sheet, which is prepared on a basis consistent with GAAP (generally accepted accounting principles).

    (2) Prepare an income statement for 19X3 for Fujo Camera Company on a basis consistent with GAAP.

Exercise 8. Marion Corporation is composed of two divisions—A and B. Division A supplies all of its output to Division B. The product supplied by Division A, Part No. 250, is transferred at its full cost of $13 plus a 20% markup on cost to cover nonmanufacturing costs, which are all fixed. Product cost data and sales information for the two divisions are as follows:

Division A		Division B	
Materials	$ 3	Materials	$15.60
Direct labor	2	Other	4.00
Variable overhead	2	Direct labor	3.00
Fixed overhead*	6	Variable overhead	3.00
Standard cost per unit	$13	Fixed overhead*	2.00
		Standard cost per unit	$27.60

---

* Based on normal capacity of 10,000 units produced and sold per month.

The manager of Division B has received an offer from another manufacturer who would supply a substitute for Part No. 250 for $14 per unit. Marion Corporation expects to produce and sell 144,000 units of Division B output during the coming year.

    (1) Assume that the productive capacity of Division A would remain idle if the offer were accepted. Would the purchase of the part from an outside manufacturer improve the operating performance of Division B? Would it be optimal for the entire firm?

    (2) Assume that the part can be purchased externally for $10 per unit. From the point of view of the firm, should the manager of Division B accept the offer?

    (3) Assume that a second firm has offered to supply the part to Division B for $9 per unit. If this offer were accepted, Marion would lease Division A's production capacity for $300,000 per year. Division A's fixed costs would be unchanged if the production capacity were leased. Should the firm accept the offer?

Exercise 9. Drummond Corporation is composed of three autonomous divisions: the Farm Equipment Division, the Industrial Equipment Division, and the Clark Diesel Division. Each of Drummond's divisions is a profit center. Purchasers of farm and industrial equipment are given the option to purchase the diesel engine of one of several different manufacturers. A substantial discount is given if the customer selects a Clark diesel. In the industry, Clark diesels have a good reputation for reliability and ease of maintenance.

Drummond Corporation has recently acquired Electrogenerator Company, a firm which manufactures electrical generators powered by gas and diesel engines. Electrogenerator will become a fourth division and profit center. Drummond would like the Clark Diesel Division to supply some 4-cylinder LD4 diesel engines to Electrogenerator, since Clark is currently operating at only 70% of its annual capacity of 200,000 direct labor hours.

The current standard cost sheet for the LD4 diesel engine is as follows:

Materials	$118 per engine
Direct labor (17.5 hrs. @ $6 per hr.)	105
Variable overhead (17.5 hrs. @ $2 per hr.)	35
Fixed overhead (17.5 hrs. @ $8 per hr.)	140
Total standard cost	$398 per engine

In addition to the above cost of this engine, Clark Division would incur the following additional costs if the LD4 engine were provided to Electrogenerator:

Cost of modifying engine cooling system for sustained operation	$45 per engine
Freight and insurance	18
Total	$63 per engine

The division manager of Electrogenerator Division has approached the sales manager of the Clark Diesel Division to negotiate an acceptable transfer price for 2,700 LD4 engines for the coming year. Electrogenerator currently offers the following diesel engines on its generators:

Type	Delivered Cost
Grummings Diesel	$497
Carter Diesel	508
Mosstown Diesel	503

Electrogenerator's past experience has shown that price is usually an important factor in a customer's engine selection. Electrogenerator quotes to its customers a diesel price equal to its delivered cost plus 10%.

Calculate the range of transfer prices within which the negotiated transfer price will probably fall. Identify the competing objectives of the division managers.

Problem 14-1. Tredia Motor Sales distributes light trucks on the west coast of the United States. The company's operations are divided into two segments for control purposes—Southern California and the Pacific Northwest, which includes Northern California, Oregon, and Washington. The firm is forecasting income for 19X7, its third full year of operations. Budgeted deliveries (sales) to dealers for the upcoming year are as follows:

	Deliveries	Average Price
Southern California	1,280 units	$7,900
Pacific Northwest	770	8,200

The cost of goods sold for the budgeted sales mix is 65% of revenues for both segments.

The firm has collected data on shipping and order-processing costs incurred in two prior years, adjusted for predicted changes in cost. These data are as follows:

Shipping Costs

	19X5	19X6
Salaries	$510,000	$514,000
Insurance	85,000	108,000
Freight charges	204,000	259,000
Other administrative costs	51,000	65,000
	$850,000	$946,000

Order-Processing Costs

	19X5	19X6
Salaries	$187,530	$186,900
Rent	48,200	48,000
Supplies	27,700	30,350
Utilities	4,470	4,450
	$267,900	$269,700

	19X5	19X6
Units shipped	1,400	1,640
Orders processed	155	165

Shipping costs vary with the number of units shipped, and order-processing costs vary with the number of orders handled. A multiple regression analysis of warehousing costs resulted in the following cost function:

Warehousing costs = $430,000 + ($215 × average inventory) + ($370 × orders processed)

During 19X7, Tredia expects to maintain average inventories of 215 trucks and 190 trucks in the Southern California and Pacific Northwest segments, respectively. Orders are expected to total 140 for the Southern California segment and 110 for the Pacific Northwest segment.

Units shipped will equal expected deliveries. All fixed costs are specific only to the entire firm. Administrative costs not allocable to either segment are budgeted at $1,315,000 for 19X7.

Required
(1) Use the high-low method to determine the cost functions for both shipping costs and order-processing costs.
(2) Prepare forecast statements of segment contribution for both sales areas for 19X7, as illustrated in the text. Also prepare a firmwide statement of net income.

Problem 14-2. Livingstone Co. manufactures a product known as *Stanley* at its plant in Africa. Standard production costs per unit of *Stanley* are summarized as follows:

Materials	$ 7
Direct labor	4
Variable overhead	8
Fixed overhead*	3
Total standard production cost	$22

* Based on a normal yearly output of 95,000 units.

Flexible budgets for the firm's physical distribution activities were prepared by the firm's accountants at the same time as the standard cost sheet. The results of these studies are as follows:

Activity	Budget
Shipping	$96,000 + $.12 per ton-mile
Warehousing	$56,000 + $3.75 per unit in average inventory
Order processing	$71,000 + $16.90 per invoice equivalent

Livingstone sells *Stanley* to two different kinds of customers: multinational companies and workers' cooperatives. During 19X2, Livingstone produced and sold 60,900 units of *Stanley* to multinational firms and 26,100 units to workers' cooperatives at an average price of $28 per unit.

Variable production and physical distribution costs are charged to each segment on the basis of relevant usage. Fixed production costs and one half of the fixed physical distribution costs are allocable only to the entire firm. The remaining fixed physical distribution costs are charged to each segment in proportion to their unit sales.

Actual costs incurred by Livingstone Co. during 19X2 are summarized in the following table:

	Production	Ware-housing	Shipping	Order Processing	General and Administrative	Total
Materials	$ 548,100	—	—	—	—	$ 548,100
Direct labor	375,840	—	—	—	—	375,840
Indirect materials	102,600	$ 5,220	$ 18,300	—	—	126,120
Indirect labor	72,400	37,400	11,040	—	—	120,840
Heat, light, and power	184,310	14,000	8,720	$ 7,100	$ 24,480	238,610
Salaries	142,420	28,000	31,710	50,500	97,300	349,930
Depreciation	84,000	—	—	—	—	84,000
Freight	—	—	22,400	—	—	22,400
Insurance	18,070	—	8,390	—	—	26,460
Supplies	20,300	—	—	18,390	11,100	49,790
Other variable	364,530	—	—	7,820	13,300	385,650
Other fixed	—	—	2,450	2,920	4,700	10,070
	$1,912,570	$84,620	$103,010	$86,730	$150,880	$2,337,810

Activity and other relevant measures include the following:

	Total	Multinationals	Cooperatives
Average inventory	9,800 units	5,800 units	4,000 units
Invoice equivalents	900 invoices	380 invoices	520 invoices
Ton-miles shipped	181,000 ton-miles	90,000 ton-miles	91,000 ton-miles

Required (1) Calculate the total variance from budget for Livingstone's production department and also for each physical distribution activity. Formal cost reports need not be prepared.

(2) Prepare a cost and revenue analysis for both sales segments and for the entire firm, as shown in Illustration 14-1. All cost variances attach only to the entire firm.

Problem 14-3. Brentwood Co. manufactures stainless steel cable in three diameters —1/4", 3/8", and 1/2". The cable is sold to a wide variety of manufacturers, retailers, and services. For control purposes, the firm's operations are divided into two segments—the Eastern United States and the Western United States.

To plan its activities during the coming year, Brentwood has asked you to analyze projected data for the Eastern segment. Brentwood expects to sell the following quantities of cable to its Eastern customers:

	1/4"	3/8"	1/2"	Totals
Manufacturers	185,000 ft.	375,000 ft.	300,000 ft.	860,000 ft.
Retailers and services	740,000	562,500	75,000	1,377,500
	925,000 ft.	937,500 ft.	375,000 ft.	2,237,500 ft.

Standard costs and revenues for the various sizes of cable are projected as follows:

Cable Size	Revenue	Materials	Direct Labor	Variable Overhead	Fixed Overhead
1/4"	$.45	.07 per foot	.03 per foot	.05 per foot	.12 per foot
3/8"	.65	.16	.04	.09	.15
1/2"	.98	.28	.05	.15	.20

Fixed production costs for the entire firm are projected as follows:

		% Allowable to Eastern Division	
	Amount	Short Run	Long Run
Supervision	$120,000	40%	45%
Depreciation*—equipment	78,000	30	40
Heat, light, and power	54,000	25	25
Rent—factory building	60,000	0	-
Property taxes	18,000	0	-

* Estimated change in market values.

Physical distribution costs are controlled by preparing flexible budgets at the beginning of each year. The coming year's flexible budgets, along with projected activity data for the Eastern segment, are as follows:

	Manufacturers	Retailers and Services
Warehousing cost	$42,000 + 14% of the full cost of avg. inventory	$42,000 + 14% of the full cost of avg. inventory
Order-processing cost	$32,000 + $24 per order	$30 per order
Shipping cost	$29,000 + $.80 per ton-mile	$1.50 per ton-mile
Orders	215 orders	2,750 orders
Ton-miles	103,000 ton-miles	36,000 ton-miles

Orders from retailers and services tend to be smaller, more complicated, have longer payment lags, have more errors which account for the higher order-processing costs, and are not large enough to capture economies of scale in shipping. Hence, the shipping cost is higher.

Average inventories equal 20% of annual production, and production equals expected sales. If the Eastern segment were eliminated, only 25% of the physical distribution fixed costs would be saved in the short run. An additional 5% would be eliminated in subsequent years.

General, administrative, and selling expenses applicable to the Eastern segment total $82,000 (all long-run costs). The projected balance sheet for the firm at December 31, 19X8, together with segmental data, is as follows:

	Amount	% Allocable to Eastern Segment		Amount	% Allocable to Eastern Segment
Cash	$ 150,000[a]	40%	Accounts payable	$ 217,500[a]	40%
Accounts receivable	458,000[a]	50	Bonds payable	1,000,000	0
Inventory	370,000[a]	50			
Land	320,000	0	Common stock	1,200,000	0
Equipment (net)	1,688,000[b]	40	Retained earnings	568,500	
	$2,986,000			$2,986,000	

[a] These assets and liabilities vary proportionately to sales.
[b] The market value of land and equipment is estimated at 125% of book value.

Required   (1) Prepare a projected contribution statement for the Eastern segment, using the data supplied. Prepare supporting schedules for the variable cost of goods sold, variable warehousing costs, short and long-run fixed production costs, and short and long-run fixed physical distribution costs.
(2) Prepare a cost-volume-profit graph for the Eastern segment for the coming year.
(3) Calculate the Eastern segment's projected contribution on specific assets (COSA) for the coming year.

Problem 14-4. Brentwood Company in Problem 14-3 has asked you to analyze its operations for the coming year. The firm requires a 15% return on all assets.

Required   (1) Prepare a pro forma residual contribution statement for the Eastern segment for the coming year. Include the short- and long-run contribution.
(2) Prepare a cost-volume-profit graph for the coming year.

Problem 14-5. Communications Systems International designs and manufactures data transmission networks for office equipment. One half of the firm's sales are made abroad, and for control purposes, the firm is segmented into a Domestic Sales Division and a Foreign Sales Division. The firm's most current balance sheet (December 31, 19X7) is as follows:

Cash	$ 201,250	Accounts payable	$ 232,710
Accounts receivable	526,100	Accrued expenses	19,700
Prepayments	53,500	Bonds payable	400,000
Land	910,000	Common stock ($2 par)	812,000
Buildings	837,000	Paid-in capital in excess of par	755,000
Less accumulated depreciation	(62,000)	Retained earnings	818,940
Manufacturing equipment	515,500		
Less accumulated depreciation	(125,000)		
Office equipment	220,000		
Less accumulated depreciation	(38,000)		
Total assets	$3,038,350	Total liabilities and equity	$3,038,350

The following additional data are provided by the firm's accounting staff:

- Current assets and liabilities could be reduced by 30% and 25% if the Ch. 14 529 Domestic Sales Division and the Foreign Sales Division, respectively, were eliminated. There would be no further reductions in the long run.

The level of current assets and liabilities specific to a segment vary directly with the sales level.

- There would be no reduction in land in the short run, even if one division were eliminated. In the long run, land could be reduced by only 15% if either division were closed.
- All production occurs in one building. If one division were eliminated, unused space could be leased immediately as warehouse space for $25,000 per year.
- Production equipment could be reduced by the following amounts if one division were closed:

	Short Run	Long Run
Domestic sales	25%	35%
Foreign sales	15	20

- All office equipment pertains to either the manufacturing operation or domestic sales and would be reduced by 40% if the Domestic Sales Division were eliminated. All export sales are made from the firm's New York sales office, which has a short-term lease for all space and equipment at an annual cost of $107,000.
- A shutdown of either segment would not affect either long-term liability or equity balances.

Sales last year totaled $795,000 for the Domestic Sales Division and $910,000 for Foreign Sales Division. The variable cost of goods sold averages 55% for both divisions. The only other variable cost is a 4% sales commission paid on foreign sales only.

Depreciation expense is incurred by each division in proportion to its percent of assets and approximate changes in market values. A summary of expenses include the following:

Item	Domestic Sales	Foreign Sales	Total
Depreciation expense:			
Manufacturing equipment	?	?	$ 25,000
Office equipment	?	?	15,000
Interest expense			48,000
Salaries	40%	25%	275,000
Other	20%	20%	108,000

Communications Systems International requires a 10% return on all assets.

Required   (1) Determine the contribution on specific assets (both short-run and long-run) for both the Domestic Sales Division and the Foreign Sales Division.

(2) Calculate the residual contribution for both divisions.

Problem 14-6. Packaging Concepts Corporation has brought together its marketing and accounting managers to plan the firm's promotional efforts for its Container Division for the coming year. The firm has three principle products: a 2-liter plastic bottle; a two-piece, 12-oz. aluminum can; and a 1-liter glass bottle. Forecast revenue and variable cost data for the three products are summarized as follows:

	2-liter Plastic Bottle	12-oz. Aluminum Cans	1-liter Glass Bottle
Quantity per case	12	24	12
Revenue per case	$1.38	$1.26	$2.40
Variable production cost per case	$ .65	$0.40	$1.70
Shipping weight per case	1 lb.	.50 lbs.	8 lbs.

On the average, receivables are outstanding for two months, and all sales are on credit. Inventory quantities average 10% of annual sales. Warehousing costs (not including interest or depreciation) are estimated at 15% of the full-cost inventory value. On the basis of past statistical analysis, the firm has calculated its variable order cost to be $14 per order. Average order sizes vary for the various products:

2-liter plastic bottles	$1,278
12-oz. aluminum cans	2,100
1-liter glass bottles	1,500

The firm has prepared the following analysis of shipments, based on data for the past eight months:

Shipping Distance	Frequency	Shipping Distance	Frequency
200 miles per order	.35	800	.15
400	.40	1,600	.10

Shipping costs in the next year are expected to average $.08 per ton-mile.

Fixed costs specific to the Container Division, excluding depreciation, are as follows:

Manufacturing costs	$695,000
Physical distribution costs:	
Warehousing	65,000
Order processing	87,000
Shipping	47,000
General and administrative	135,000

For the next year, the firm has estimated the following selling expenditures for its Container Division: advertising, $41,000; promotion, $15,000; travel expenses, $20,000.

The firm expects to maintain a cash balance equal to 3% of annual revenues. Cash, receivables, and inventory are the only current assets. Payables average $450,000. The market value of plant, property, and equipment specific to the Container Division, net of depreciation, totals $2,800,000. These long-lived assets are expected to decline 15% in market value over the next year.

On the basis of the above promotional expenses, the firm's marketing managers anticipate the following sales:

2-liter plastic bottle	700,000 cases
12-oz. aluminum cans	1,300,000
1-liter glass bottle	1,000,000

Required

(1) Use the information provided to calculate the firm's total expected shipping charges at the anticipated level of sales.

(2) Prepare a pro forma residual contribution statement for the coming year. Use a 12% cost of capital.

Problem 14-7. The Container Division of Packaging Concepts Corporation has just completed the year which was forecast in Problem 14-6. A strong economy led to increased demand for the segment's products and results have been good. A summarized version of the firm's original budget, under the residual contribution approach, is as follows:

	Budget - 1/1/19X7	Actual
Revenues	$5,004,000	$6,700,000
Variable costs:		
Variable production costs	$2,675,000	$3,685,000
Warehousing costs (1.5% of cost of goods sold)	50,550	62,300
Order costs ($14 per order)	43,904	60,060
Shipping costs ($.08 per ton-mile)	190,740	293,480
Variable cost of capital:		
Net receivables (12% per year)	46,080	111,000
Inventory (1.2% of cost of goods sold)	40,440	51,792
Cash (.36% of revenues)	18,014	27,400
Total variable costs	$3,064,728	$4,291,032
Segment contribution to fixed costs	$1,939,272	$2,408,968
Fixed costs:		
Production	$ 695,000	$ 631,000
Physical distribution	199,000	209,000
Selling, general, and administrative	211,000	183,000
Depreciation expense	420,000	422,000
Cost of capital (long-lived assets)	336,000	336,000
Total fixed costs	$1,861,000	$1,781,000
Segment residual contribution	$ 78,272	$ 627,968

Although sales were well above the original estimate, the sales mix conformed to the firm's expectations. Sales equaled production, and there were no changes in inventories during the year. Additional data for the year are summarized as follows (standard usage for actual sales volume):

> Orders: 4,200 orders processed
> Shipments: 3,190,000 ton-miles
> Average receivables: $975,000

Required

Prepare a flexible budget for the firm, based on the actual level of activity. Compare your budget with the firm's actual results, and prepare a summary of variances.

Problem 14-8. Conquest Bicycle Co. is composed of two semi-autonomous divisions: the Frame Division and the Assembly Division. Each of the divisions is operated as a profit center. The company was founded originally to produce only racing bicycle frames. These frames are highly regarded for their strength, precision, and light weight. After several years of successful production, the firm decided to expand its physical plant to produce finished 10-speed bicycles. The 10-speed bikes are assembled by adding components purchased from several outside manufacturers to Conquest frames. All production and marketing activities associated with producing finished bicycles are grouped within the Assembly Division.

The Frame Division is currently operating at full capacity of 3,000 frames per year. About 50% of the Frame Division's annual output is sold externally. Internal transfers to the Assembly Division are made at the current market price of $225 per frame.

The Assembly Division, since it operates as a profit center, has negotiated with a Japanese company to provide frames at $180 each. The frames are substantially equivalent to those produced by the Frame Division. The Frame Division, however, is unwilling to supply frames at less than its current market price of $225 per frame.

The standard cost of frames is as follows:

Materials	$ 40
Direct labor (5 hrs. @ $7 per hr.)	35
Variable overhead (5 hrs. @ $4 per hr.)	20
Fixed overhead (5 hrs. @ $3 per hr.)	15
Standard cost per frame	$110

The Frame Division, faced with the necessity of supplying the remaining 50% of its production to the external market, has engaged a consultant to determine the demand for its product. The market for bicycle frames is a narrow one, composed primarily of racers and serious enthusiasts. The consultant has developed the following demand curve for the firm's frames:

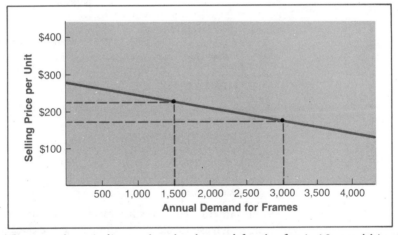

The consultant indicates that the demand for the firm's 10-speed bicycles, in contrast, is horizontal up to the limits of its production capacity of 1,500 bicycles.

Required (1) Using the general guideline for establishing transfer prices, calculate the optimal transfer price for bicycle frames.

(2) Assume that because the Frame Division refuses to sell frames to the Assembly Division at any price less than the $225 it currently receives from outside customers, the Assembly Division buys its frames from the Japanese supplier, and the Frame Division sells its entire output to outside customers. How much profit will Conquest Bicycle Co. sacrifice (or gain) as compared to the profits it would earn if frames for its 10-speed bicycles were manufactured by the Frame Division?

(3) Making the same assumptions as in (2), how much profit will each of the divisions sacrifice (or gain)?

Problem 14-9. Gibralter Company manufactures heat exchangers for industrial use. The company consists of three autonomous divisions: Tube Industries, which manufactures copper and stainless steel tubing; Fabralloy, which fabricates the radiators which are a major part of a heat exchanger; and Environmental Controls, which produces the completed heat exchanger. Tube Industries sells tubing to outside customers as well as to Fabralloy. Fabralloy also sells completed radiators to outside customers and to Environmental Controls.

All three divisions operate as profit centers, and transfers between divisions are priced at market price. All divisions except for Tube Industries are operating at full capacity and can sell all they produce at the existing market price. Tube Industries has substantial excess capacity.

Cost and market price data for each division are as follows:

Tube Industries

Unit cost of tubing:

Variable cost	$.18 per foot	
Fixed cost	.04	
	$.22 per foot	
Market price	$.35 per foot	

Fabralloy

Unit cost of a radiator:

Variable cost (including 150 ft. of tubing @ $.35 per ft.)	$250
Fixed cost	40
	$290
Market price	$340

Environmental Controls

Unit cost of heat exchanger:

Variable cost (including 4 radiators @ $340 per radiator)	$2,000
Fixed cost	350
	$2,350
Market price	$2,800

Environmental Controls has received an offer from Ibiza Company to supply radiators which are substantially identical to the ones supplied by Fabralloy Company for $350 per unit. Tube Industries currently supplies Ibiza Company with all of its tubing needs, 150 feet per radiator at its current market price. Environmental Controls' managers feel that it would be foolish to purchase radiators externally for $350, when they are available internally for $340.

Required

(1) From the standpoint of maximizing Gibralter Company's overall profits, is it desirable for Environmental Controls to acquire its radiators from Ibiza Company, or from Fabralloy?

(2) Assume that Fabralloy and Tube Industries were operating with substantial slack capacity due to a downturn in industry demand. Would this change your answer to (1)?

Problem 14-10. Heidegger Corporation has recently acquired a new operating division, the Carnap Division. The Carnap Division manufactures refrigeration units for appliances. Heidegger's other division, the Wittgenstein Division, produces the *Thermo-King* line of appliances. Wittgenstein Division recently began a large marketing campaign to increase its market share of refrigerators and freezers. It anticipates a 20% increase (from 10,000 to 12,000 units) in the number of refrigeration units it requires. Carnap currently has sufficient capacity to supply these 2,000 additional units. Wittgenstein Division now purchases the refrigeration units from its regular supplier for $145 each. The standard cost sheet for each division's product and relevant sales data are as follows:

	Carnap Division	Wittgenstein Division
Materials	$ 60	$430[b]
Direct labor	25	70
Variable overhead	40	40
Fixed overhead	30[a]	70[c]
Standard cost per unit of output	$155	$610

[a] Based on expected capacity of 15,000 units per year.
[b] Includes $145 cost of refrigeration unit.
[c] Based on expected capacity of 12,000 units per year.

Projected annual sales for 19X3:		
External	13,000 units	12,000 units
Internal	2,000	
Projected selling price for 19X3	$165 per unit	$625 per unit

Both the Carnap and Wittgenstein Divisions have profit responsibility. In an effort to increase incentives for each divisional manager, Heidegger has adopted a system of dual pricing for intersegmental transfers. The Carnap Division will be credited with a transfer price of $165, and Wittgenstein will be charged Carnap's variable cost for 2,000 refrigeration units transferred.

Required (1) Compute the gross margins for 19X3 for the Carnap and Wittgenstein Divisions, reflecting the dual transfer prices and the gross margin for the Heidegger Corporation.
(2) Assume that Carnap could sell the 2,000 additional refrigeration units to a foreign refrigerator manufacturer for $150 each. This sale would not affect its domestic market of 13,000 units. Calculate the optimal transfer price, using the transfer price guideline. Discuss possible disfunctional consequences of the dual pricing system in this situation.

Fifteen

Operations Research Techniques and Managerial Accounting

Operations research (OR) techniques are quantitative methods and quantitative models that are used in the planning and control of a firm's activities. Since the primary objective of operations research techniques is to reduce costs and increase profits, a major source of the data inputs to OR models is the accounting information system. Once the models have been implemented, the results are monitored and accounting performance reports are prepared. In these reports, the actual results can be compared with achievements of prior periods and with planned performance.

In two previous chapters, two operations research tools—linear programming and financial simulation models—were used to develop better profit plans. These techniques have also been applied to a wide variety of other planning problems, including production scheduling, facility location, transportation scheduling, media selection, and capital budgeting. In this chapter, three additional quantitative techniques for planning and control—inventory control models, PERT/CPM project planning and control models, and labor learning curve models—are presented.

INVENTORY CONTROL MODELS

The most widely discussed inventory control models concentrate on minimizing inventory-related costs by developing rules for deciding how much to order

(order quantity) and when to order (order point). Some order systems are based on placing orders at fixed time intervals, such as the end of every month, and then ordering enough to replenish the inventory to a given maximum level. A more common system is to establish a fixed, optimal **order quantity** often called the **economic order quantity (EOQ)**. The order point is then established in terms of a specified inventory level. When this level is reached, an order for the predetermined EOQ is placed.

The Basic EOQ Model

In determining the optimal order quantity, the EOQ model balances the costs of carrying large inventories against the costs of frequent ordering. If many small orders are placed, the average level of inventory over the year will be small, thus reducing the costs of carrying that inventory. However, frequent orders will generate large order costs for the year. Conversely, if only a few large orders are placed over the course of the year, order costs will be reduced, but the average inventory will be large, and the inventory carrying costs will be excessive.

The EOQ is the order size that will minimize the sum of the total inventory carrying costs and the total order costs. To show how the EOQ is derived, the following notations will be used:

Q = quantity actually ordered (in units per order)
H = unit variable holding (or carrying) costs (per year)
O = variable order cost (per order)
D = total demand (in units per year)
A = average level of inventory (in units)
N = total number of orders placed during the year
T = total variable inventory-related costs (per year)

Using these notations, the total variable inventory-related cost, T, for a given item is:

$$T = HA + ON \qquad (15.1)$$

The basic EOQ model is based on the assumption that the demand for an item is fairly uniform over the year, and orders can be placed to be delivered just as the firm runs out of inventory. Part A of Illustration 15-1 shows the variation in inventory levels for an electronic circuit board, Part 505, which is carried in the inventory of Jones Co. The demand in the illustration is not absolutely uniform, but the fluctuations are so minor that they can be ignored.

In the basic EOQ model, the minimum inventory level is zero (just after the last unit in inventory is used), and the maximum inventory is equal to Q (just after the zero inventory is replenished by the receipt of the quantity ordered). Since the demand is assumed to be uniform, the average level of inventory, A, is determined as follows:

$$A = \frac{0 + Q}{2}$$

$$A = \frac{Q}{2} \qquad (15.2)$$

The basic EOQ model is also based on an assumption that all the units demanded from inventory will be supplied. Therefore, the total demand, D, must be ordered. Since the number of units ordered each time an order is placed is constant, the number of orders placed, N, will be:

$$N = \frac{D}{Q} \qquad (15.3)$$

When the expression for A, given in Formula 15.2, and the expression for N, given in Formula 15.3, are substituted into Formula 15.1, the following definitional equation results:

$$T = (H \times \frac{Q}{2}) + (O \times \frac{D}{Q}) \qquad (15.4)$$

Formula 15.4 gives the actual variable costs for the year for any order quantity. The graph in Part B of Illustration 15-1 shows how the annual variable holding costs (HA), the annual variable order costs (ON), and the total variable inventory-related costs (T) vary as a function of different order quantities (Q). The graph also shows that the lowest value for T is where Q equals 20 units. This value for Q is the EOQ.

Illustration 15-1

The Basic EOQ Model

Part A

Variation of Inventory Levels over Time

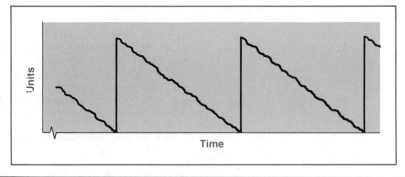

Illustration 15-1

The Basic EOQ Model

Part B

Total Variable Inventory-Related Costs for Different Order Quantities

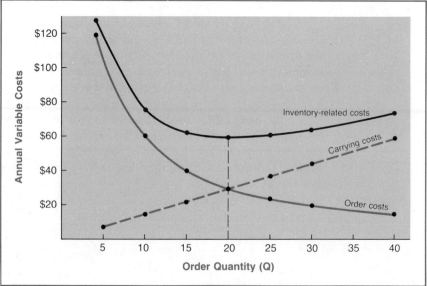

	Holding Costs			Order Costs			
(1)	(2)	(3)	(4)	(5)	(6)	(7)	(8)
			Total			Total	Total
	Average	Variable	Variable	Number of	Variable	Variable	Variable
Order	Inventory	Holding	Holding	Orders Placed	Order	Order	Inventory-Related
Quantity	Level	Costs	Costs	per Year	Costs	Costs	Costs
(Q)	(Q ÷ 2)	(H)	[(2) × (3)]	(100 ÷ Q)	(O)	[(5) × (6)]	[(4) + (7)]
5 units	2.5 units	$3 per unit	$ 7.50	20.00	$6 per order	$120.00	$127.50
10	5.0	3	15.00	10.00	6	60.00	75.00
15	7.5	3	22.50	6.67	6	40.02	62.52
20	10.0	3	30.00	5.00	6	30.00	60.00
25	12.5	3	37.50	4.00	6	24.00	61.50
30	15.0	3	45.00	3.33	6	19.98	64.98
40	20.0	3	60.00	2.50	6	15.00	75.00

As shown in Illustration 15-2, differential calculus may be used to determine the EOQ. The first derivative of T with respect to Q is determined, set equal to zero, and solved for Q. The resulting value of Q is the EOQ, which provides the minimum total inventory-related costs. Therefore, the EOQ inventory model is stated as follows:

$$EOQ = \sqrt{\frac{2DO}{H}}$$ (15.5)

Illustration 15-2
Derivation of the
Economic Order Quantity
(EOQ)

1. Rearrange the terms in Formula 15.4 to emphasize that T is a simple function of Q.

$$T = (H \times \frac{Q}{2}) + (O \times \frac{D}{Q})$$

$$T = (\frac{H}{2} Q) + ODQ^{-1}$$

2. Take the first derivative of T with respect to Q.

$$\frac{dT}{dQ} = \frac{H}{2} - ODQ^{-2}$$

3. Find the value of Q which gives the minimum T by setting the first derivative equal to zero and solving for Q.

$$\frac{H}{2} - ODQ^{-2} = 0$$

$$\frac{OD}{Q^2} = \frac{H}{2}$$

$$Q^2H = 2DO$$

$$Q^2 = \frac{2DO}{H}$$

$$Q = \sqrt{\frac{2DO}{H}} \text{ (the economic order quantity, EOQ)}$$

(Evaluating the second derivative confirms that the value for Q is a minimum.)

If the EOQ is ordered, the minimum total cost incurred is determined by substituting the optimal Q into Formula 15.4 and factoring out the EOQ term, as follows:

$$T = (\frac{H}{2} \times \sqrt{\frac{2DO}{H}}) + \frac{OD}{\sqrt{\frac{2DO}{H}}}$$

$$T = \sqrt{\frac{2DO}{H}} \times \left[\frac{H}{2} + \frac{OD}{\left(\sqrt{\frac{2DO}{H}}\right)^2}\right]$$

$$T = \sqrt{\frac{2DO}{H}} \times H$$

$$T = \sqrt{2DOH} \qquad\qquad\qquad (15.6)$$

Substituting the values of 100 for D, $6 for O, and $3 for H gives the following EOQ:

$$EOQ = \sqrt{\frac{2 \times 100 \times \$6}{\$3}} = \sqrt{400} = 20 \text{ units}$$

The resulting minimum total cost is:

$$T = \sqrt{2 \times 100 \times \$6 \times \$3} = \$60 \text{ per year}$$

Determining the Proper Cost Input Data. Throughout the text, variable cost data have been emphasized as the relevant data for most managerial applications. Variable costs are also the relevant data for determining EOQs, since fixed costs cannot influence the choice of the proper order quantity. This variable cost information might come from flexible budgets, which segregate fixed costs from variable costs. In other cases, special industrial engineering studies might be undertaken to provide estimates of the appropriate variable holding costs and variable order costs. A third possible way of securing these cost estimates is to perform statistical regression analyses on total cost data or to use one of the other cost estimation procedures, described in Chapter 3, for isolating the variable components of cost.

The unit variable holding cost parameter must be defined in terms of the extra cost incurred when one additional unit is carried in inventory for a year. The key to determining the proper value for H is to include any cost which increases in total as more units are held for a longer period of time. Examples of such variable costs include the cost of rented warehouse space (when the rent is based on actual space utilized), personal property taxes (when the property tax is based on the average size of inventories), insurance, the cost of taking physical inventories, and the cost of deterioration, damage, loss, and obsolescence of inventory stock.

Another component of H is the cost of capital tied up in inventory. This cost, usually expressed as a percentage of the unit cost, should be the same cost of capital which is used in capital budgeting decisions. From a capital budgeting point of view, putting more money into carrying larger inventories is simply another investment that the firm makes. Such an investment should bring the same return, in terms of reduced costs or increased profits, as any other investment of comparable risk.

To arrive at the appropriate addition to the unit variable holding cost, the incremental cost of increasing inventory by one unit should be multiplied by the cost of capital. The incremental cost would include the purchase price of the item and all other incremental outlays involved in the acquisition of the additional unit, such as freight and handling. For example, if the delivered cost of an item being stocked in inventory is $10, the cost of inspecting each item at the time of receipt is $.50 per unit, and the cost of capital is 20%, the cost of capital tied up in inventory would be $2.10 per unit per year (20% of $10.50).

The variable order costs, O, similarly reflect only unit incremental costs. Only those costs which would increase if one additional order were placed are included in O. Any fixed costs, such as supervisory salaries, are ignored. While many of the relevant variable costs are identified with the purchasing function, such as the costs of typing the purchase order and the cost of forms, costs in other functional areas are also involved in processing, receiving, and paying orders. For example, a purchase requisition originating in an inventory control department may trigger the issuance of a purchase order; the receipt of the shipment will ordinarily involve additional paperwork in the receiving department; and the accounting department must insure that the invoice requesting payment reflects an authorized transaction, that the goods have been received, and that the invoice is for the proper amount. These costs are incurred once for every order processed and thus represent variable costs which should be included in O.

The demand for an item, D, may be derived from a detailed master budget or profit plan. While perpetual inventory records can provide data on the past demand for each item, the past sales or usage of an item must be modified to reflect any anticipated future changes. Some firms forecast future demand judgmentally. Other firms utilize forecasting models, such as statistical regression models or moving average time-series models, to estimate future demand.

Determining the Order Point. For the basic inventory model, the inventory is assumed to be replenished just as the last unit is requisitioned or sold. For this scenario to occur, an order must be placed far enough in advance of the inventory depletion that the processing of the order can be completed and the item delivered at the proper time. The length of time required to accomplish order processing and delivery is referred to as the **lead time.** If the usage of the inventoried part or product during this lead time is determined, then placing an order when the inventory reaches this point will allow for replenishment by the time the inventory reaches the zero level.

For the basic EOQ model, the order point is set at an amount equal to the average usage during the lead time. For example, if a firm operates 50 weeks during the year, annual demand is 1,000 units at a uniform rate of 20 units per week, and the lead time is 2 weeks, then 40 units will be demanded during the 2-week lead time. Accordingly, the order point for this item is 40 units. If an order is placed when the inventory level is equal to 40 units, the order replenishing the inventory should arrive just as the inventory drops to zero.

Application of EOQ to Manufacturing. The basic inventory model has also been applied in determining the optimal production run size in manufacturing operations. In this context, O (the variable order costs in a purchasing application) would be interpreted as the unit cost of setting up the machinery for the production run, along with any other cost incurred once for each production run. The interpretation of the H and D parameters are much the same as in a purchasing situation—H is now the variable cost of carrying one manufactured unit in inventory for one year, and D is the total number of units to be manufactured (total demand) for the year. Operations research texts provide a complex formula for determining the optimal manufacturing lot size, but if the rate of production is much faster than the rate at which units are demanded and removed from inventory, the basic EOQ formula will give good results.

Quantity Discounts. Frequently, suppliers offer lower prices for large orders. Such quantity discounts are difficult to incorporate directly into the EOQ model, since they introduce a break in the total relevant cost curve at the point where the quantity discount takes effect. If the discount is large enough, the reduced costs will more than offset the higher costs of holding the larger inventories.

The easiest way of dealing with quantity discounts is to calculate first the EOQ and the total costs associated with that order size. These costs are then compared to the total costs associated with ordering the lowest quantity in the range eligible for a given quantity discount. This comparison of total costs is repeated for each different quantity discount offered.

To illustrate the analysis involving a quantity discount, assume that the supplier of the circuit board used by Jones Co. in the previous illustration provides the following price list:

> 0 - 24 units .... $10.00 per unit
> 25 or more units .... 9.95 per unit

If a quantity discount is offered and the values of D, O, and H do not change,[1] then ordering quantities greater than the EOQ will increase the combined holding and order costs associated with the larger order quantity. However, the quantity discount will offset some or all of these increased costs. Using the values for D, O, and H given earlier, the EOQ for the circuit board was calculated as 20 units, and the total holding and order costs were $60 per year. If Jones orders in quantities of 25, the total holding and order costs, using Formula 15.4, would be $61.50 per year [$3 × (25 ÷ 2) + $6 × (100 ÷ 25)]. However, a discount of $5 ($.05 per unit × 100 units) would be earned, making the net cost $56.50 per year ($61.50 − $5). Because of the savings from the quantity discount, Jones would increase its order size from 20 to 25 units.

The Safety Stock Model

The basic EOQ model, in which all units demanded are assumed to be filled from inventory, can be modified to reflect the occurrence of stockouts. Two possible variations of the basic model may be formulated, which differ as to how stockouts are to be handled.

---

[1] If H is calculated by applying a holding cost percentage to the net cost of the product, H will drop slightly because the quantity discount reduces the product net cost.

The **backorder model** assumes that demand which occurs when the inventory is temporarily out of stock will always be filled when the next order is received. If out-of-stock situations can be handled at modest cost, the backorder model is appropriate. Appendix 15A describes the backorder model in more detail.

If not being able to fill demand as it occurs involves large cost penalties, the **safety stock model** is appropriate. The use of this model offers protection against stockouts by providing for additional inventory, called **safety stocks,** for meeting unforeseen increases in demand during lead times or unexpected increases in the length of the lead time. Demand during the lead time is critical in avoiding stockouts, since inventories are at their lowest level at that time. Variability in demand at other times is absorbed by the higher inventory levels existing earlier in the inventory cycle.

Illustration 15-3 shows inventory levels of a video circuit board, Part 630, for which there is significant variability in the demand during lead times over several cycles. An order point of 5 units, with demand of 4, 3, and 6 units, results in inventory levels of 1 unit, 2 units, and zero units, respectively. During the last cycle, there is a one-unit stockout.

Illustration 15-3
The Safety Stock Model—Variation of Inventory and Stockout Levels over Time

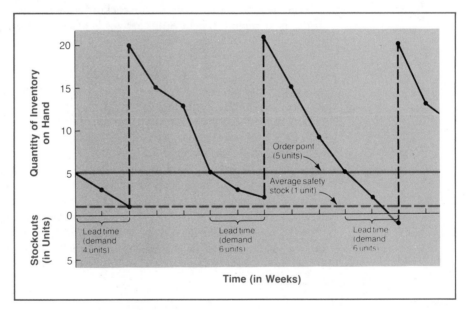

To determine how large a safety stock to carry, the degree of uncertainty connected with the demand during the lead time is quantified in terms of a probability distribution. Such a probability distribution for Jones Co.'s video circuit board is shown in Part A of Illustration 15-4. The expected value of the demand during the lead time is 3.4 units, but as many as 6 units and as few as zero units may be demanded. If stockouts are to be avoided completely, an order must be placed when the inventory level reaches 6 units. For an order point of six units, the average safety stock is 2.6 units (6-unit order point − 3.4-unit average demand).

Setting the order point equal to the maximum demand during the lead time is a very conservative policy. While it avoids stockouts completely, it requires that an extra 2.6 units (the safety stock) be carried over the entire year in order to protect against occasional stockouts of one or two units. To determine whether this policy is justified requires a balancing of the costs of carrying the safety stock against the cost of stockouts and the benefits of avoiding stockouts.

For each possible order point, the number of expected stockouts is determined. Since the maximum demand during the lead time is 6 units, and stockouts can only occur if the demand exceeds the quantity that is on hand when the order is placed, no stockouts will occur if an order point of 6 units is established. If an order point of 4 units is selected, Jones Co. will be out of stock by 2 units whenever the demand is 6 units. Similarly, the firm will be one unit short whenever 5 units are demanded during the lead time and the order point is 4 units.

Each stockout possibility is weighted by its probability of occurrence in order to determine the expected number of units which will be out of stock in one inventory cycle. This number is then multiplied by the unit stockout cost per cycle ($4) and the number of cycles per year (D ÷ Q = 5). The result is the annual stockout cost which would be expected for that order point.

The cost of stockouts depends on the manner in which stockouts are handled and on the type of inventory. In the backorder model, an order to be filled as soon as the next replenishment order arrives is placed in a special backorder file. For this model, the stockout cost will consist of the additional clerical costs that must be incurred. For finished goods in the safety stock model, the major component of stockout costs usually consists of the profits lost when disappointed customers cancel existing (and possibly future) orders. For raw materials or purchased parts, the most significant component of stockout costs is the extra operating costs incurred in the factory when production schedules must be rearranged because the necessary raw materials or parts cannot be supplied from inventory.

The cost of stockouts and the cost of carrying safety stocks for each possible order point for Jones Co. are shown in Part B of Illustration 15-4. For each order point, there is a different level of safety stock. Specifying either the order point or the safety stock determines the other. The average safety stock which results from a given order point is the difference between the quantity on hand when the order is placed (the order point) and the average or expected value of demand during the lead time. To determine the annual cost of carrying a level of safety stock, the average safety stock is multiplied by the cost of holding one unit in inventory for a year.

Illustration 15-4
The Safety Stock Model—Determination of Optimal Safety Stock

Part A
Probability Distribution of Demand During 2-Week Lead Time

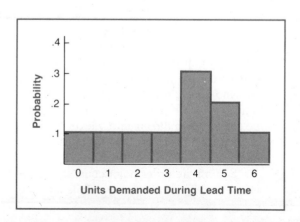

Order Point	Units Demanded	Stockout Costs (1) Expected Number of Units Out of Stock (per Cycle)	Stockout Costs (2) Total Annual Stockout Costs [(1) × \$4[a] × 5[b]]	Costs of Carrying Safety Stock (3) Safety Stock for Given Order Point (Order Point − 3.4)	Costs of Carrying Safety Stock (4) Total Annual Holding Costs [(3) × \$3[c]]	(5) Combined Annual Stockout and Holding Costs [(2) + (4)]
6	6 or less	0.0 (0 × 1)	0	2.6 units	\$7.80	\$7.80
5	6 5 or less	0.1 (1 × .1) 0.0 (0 × .9) 0.1	\$2.00	1.6 units	\$4.80	\$6.80
4	6 5 4 or less	0.2 (2 × .1) 0.2 (1 × .2) 0.0 (0 × .7) 0.4	\$8.00	.6 units	\$1.80	\$9.80

[a] Stockout unit cost per cycle
[b] Inventory cycles per year
[c] Annual cost of holding one unit in inventory (H)

The optimal order point is the one which minimizes the sum of the related annual stockout costs and the annual cost of carrying the resulting safety stock. The inventory-related costs for Jones Co. are minimized by ordering when the inventory of video circuit boards reaches 5 units. With this order point, the average safety stock is 1.6 units, and stockouts of one unit can be expected to occur during the lead time in 10% of the inventory cycles.

One measure of the adequacy of a given safety stock policy is the **service level,** which is the probability of meeting all demand during the lead time. For Jones Co., the service level is 90% (100% − 10% stockouts). Another measure of adequacy is the **service ratio,** which is the ratio of the expected number of units supplied during the lead time to the expected number of units demanded during the lead time. Since carrying a safety stock of 1.6 units results in expected stockouts of .1 units per inventory cycle, the remainder of the average demand is 3.3 units (3.4 units demanded − .1 units out-of-stock), and the service ratio is 95% (3.3 ÷ 3.4).

Notice that the service level and the service ratio do not reflect the costs of running out of stock. Since these indicators of service can be calculated directly from the lead time demand probabilities, inventory managers may decide on the safety stock to be carried by simply specifying a given service level or service ratio as their objective. Although this procedure bypasses the problem of estimating unit stockout and carrying costs, it does not necessarily provide the optimal (minimum cost) safety stock level.

The safety stock model illustrated is based on the assumption that the order quantity (Q) is obtained from the basic EOQ model. In reality, however, the order quantity may be slightly larger than optimal as a result of the influence of two factors. If stockouts lead to losses in demand, the annual demand will be slightly overstated, and the order quantity will be too large. In addition, the larger the order quantity, the fewer the number of inventory cycles in a year, and hence the lower the annual stockout costs. Nevertheless, both direct mathematical analysis and simulation studies indicate that the amount of this overstatement is not likely to be large for most situations.

In the discussion of the safety stock model, the uncertainty present in demand during the lead time was measured by specifying directly the probability distribution of demand.[2] This distribution reflects both the variability in daily demand and the variability in the length of the lead time, due to such factors as variations in the time required by suppliers to fill orders and delays during shipping. This joint probability distribution may be constructed directly from historical data on the demand or from separate probability distributions for daily demand and the length of the lead time.

Other Approaches to Managing Inventories

The inventory models described up to this point have concentrated on minimizing inventory-related costs through developing optimal order-quantity and order-point policies. However, management should consider not only inventory order policies, but also other approaches to keeping its inventory costs down. Several of these inventory approaches are briefly described in the following sections.

The ABC System. The ABC approach is based on the division of items being carried in inventory into three basic categories—A, B, and C. Inventory management techniques appropriate for each class are then selected. These techniques range from simple control techniques for low-value items to more elaborate approaches for items in which there is a significant dollar investment. Illustration 15-5 shows a typical breakdown of inventory into the three classes, based on the inventory carried by Jones Co.

Illustration 15-5
ABC Inventory System

	Unit Cost	Annual Demand	Class' Proportion of Total Items	Class' Proportion of Total Demand
Class A				
Type I circuit board	$150	$100,000 per year		
Microprocessor chip	80	80,000	10%	75%
Class B				
Type II circuit board	10	25,000	15	15
Class C				
Resistors	.50	5,000		
Capacitors	1.00	1,000	75	10

Class A inventory items are defined as those items which account for the major portion of the dollar value of the inventory. These items typically have either a high unit price or a moderate unit price and a high unit volume. Since usually about

---

[2] More elaborate safety stock models specify that the distribution of demand during the lead time will conform to some standard statistical distribution, such as the normal distribution. In these cases, stockout probabilities may then be determined from tables for the given distribution.

10% of the items carried in the inventory are Class A items, a firm can afford to apply elaborate inventory management techniques to these items. Formal inventory order-quantity and order-point models are developed, parameter values needed for the models are carefully estimated, perpetual inventory records are maintained, and good physical security is provided in order to prevent theft and misuse of these items.

Class C items are the low-cost, low-volume items. About 75% of the items a firm carries in inventory generally fall into Class C. Because of the large number of individual low-volume items which constitute Class C, elaborate record keeping and the development of formal models cannot be justified. Instead, simple schemes, often based on physical observation, are used to trigger orders.

The two-bin system is a typical technique used for Class C items. In this system, a given reserve quantity of inventory is placed in a physically distinct rear bin, and the remainder of the inventory is placed in the front bin. Orders are then filled from the stock in the front bin. When the front bin is empty, an order is placed and the bin of reserve stock is moved to the front.

Class B items are the items which fall between the two extreme classes. Simple inventory models which are inexpensive to develop and convenient to use may be applied to Class B items, and moderate inventory control measures are implemented.

Close Coupling to Suppliers. The basis for a close coupling to suppliers is that if suppliers can be relied upon to provide needed items just before they are demanded, inventories can be reduced to negligible amounts. A major portion of the Japanese automobile manufacturers' production cost advantage in the 1970s and 1980s was attributable to an ability to secure needed parts, components, and subassemblies from suppliers whose parts and warehouses were located adjacent to the automobile assembly plants. By providing these suppliers with advance notice of parts needed, the parts could be moved quickly from the suppliers' production facilities to the user's assembly plant, with little buildup of inventories. In this way, Japanese managers reduced both the uncertainty and the length of the lead time, and thereby achieved significant reductions in inventories.

Materials Requirements Planning (MRP) Systems. In the past, it was quite common in manufacturing operations to estimate separately the annual demand for each major part, component, and subassembly. The prior year's usage of each item was determined and then adjusted simply for overall changes in production of the firm's major products. To allow for the uncertainty in the number of individual parts which would be needed and to provide for flexibility in production scheduling, large component inventories and large work in process inventories of subassemblies were maintained. With the increased use of computers in production management, the demand for parts, components, and subassemblies can be derived by processing the scheduled production of final products against bills of material which show the composition requirements for each product. By stabilizing product design and adhering to production schedules, the need to maintain large inventories to buffer uncertainty in demand is minimized.

PLANNING AND CONTROLLING PROJECTS WITH PERT AND CPM

Managers involved in planning a complicated project with many interrelated activities may use PERT or CPM as a planning tool. In the late 1950s, the Navy and a team of consultants developed **PERT (Program Evaluation and Review Technique)** for planning and controlling the building of the Polaris submarine. About the same time, engineers in private industry developed **CPM (Critical Path Method)** for planning, scheduling, and coordinating the construction of new chemical plants.

Initially, project planning with CPM networks will be illustrated. PERT will be used later to show how additional information can be developed. The major distinction between the two techniques is that PERT incorporates a probabilistic estimate of the time required to complete each activity, while CPM uses only a single best estimate. Both CPM and PERT depict the activities involved in a project in a flow diagram, or **network.** The results of analyzing the network can then be used to schedule personnel assignments and materials purchases, to isolate critical activities for further study, and to monitor ongoing activities in order to exercise control over the timely completion of a project. Although PERT and CPM originally were limited to planning the time required to complete a project, the techniques can be extended to incorporate the costs of a project.

To construct a PERT or CPM network, a project must be broken down into the individual activities which make up the total project. Each of these activities is represented in the network by an arrow and identified by two numbers—one at the tail and a higher number at the head of the arrow. These numbers, which are usually enclosed in circles in the network diagram, are referred to as the **nodes** in the network. The nodes represent **events**—the completion of one activity and the start of another. The specific numbers have no numerical significance, but are used for identification purposes only.

If one activity must be completed before some other activity can be started, the same number is used as the head of the first activity's arrow and the tail of the second activity's arrow. To illustrate, the following network shows that activity A, or activity 1,2, must be completed before activity B, or activity 2,3, can be started:

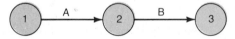

For some projects, two different activities may be preceded by the same prior activity and followed by the same successor activity. For example, if independent activities C and D can be started when activity B is completed, and both C and D must be completed before activity E can be started, the network would appear as follows:

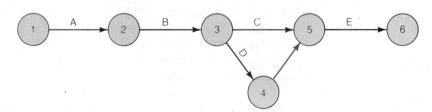

In this network, activity 3,5 could refer to either C or D. The potential ambiguity from having parallel paths in a network can be eliminated by adding a node for a **dummy activity,** which requires zero time, in one of the parallel paths. In the following example, a dummy activity, activity 4,5, is added and is represented by the brown arrow:

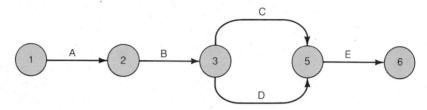

CPM Networks

The activities in a simplified CPM network for an actual project involving the rebuilding of a tool grinder are shown in Part A of Illustration 15-6.[3] The network itself is shown in Part B. Notice that since assembling the head (activity 5,9) and assembling the cross slides (activity 7,9) can be done at the same time, a dummy activity (activity 5,7) is inserted in the network.

Illustration 15-6
CPM Network for
Rebuilding a Tool Grinder

Part A
Required Activities and
Time Estimates

Illustration 15-6
CPM Network for
Rebuilding a Tool Grinder

Part B
CPM Network

	Activity	Duration of Activity
1, 2	Unload and test unit	1.2 days
2, 3	Disassemble electrical parts and motor	0.2
3, 4	Clean and disassemble machine	1.2
3, 8	Inspect electrical parts and paint motor	1.2
8, 9	Assemble and install electrical parts and motor	0.9
4, 5	Secure head parts from manufacturers	8.5
4, 6	Machine and scrape slides and table	5.5
6, 7	Machine and scrape gibbs	1.8
5, 7	Dummy	0.0
5, 9	Assemble head	1.0
7, 9	Assemble cross slides	0.9
9, 10	Test and load for shipping	0.8

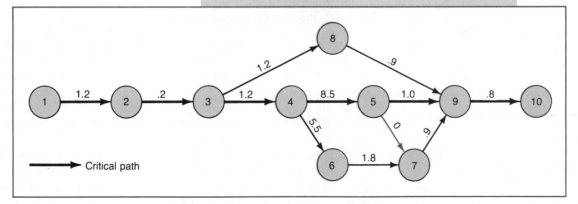

Critical path

[3] Adapted from Figure 2 in Russell D. Archibald, *PERT/CPM Management System for the Small Subcontractor,* Small Business Administration Technical Aids for Small Manufacturers, No. 86 (Washington, D.C.: March-April, 1964), p. 2.

Once the individual activities in the project have been identified and the time required to complete them has been estimated, the time required to complete the entire project can be determined. This total time is the sum of the individual activity times for those consecutive activities which form the longest path, called the **critical path,** through the network. Any delay in the completion of an activity on this path will delay the completion of the project, and if management wishes to rush the project's completion, one or more of the activities on the critical path must be expedited.

For a small network, all of the various paths through a network can be easily identified by inspection, and the longest path can be quickly determined. In the grinder rebuilding network shown in Illustration 15-6, there are four paths through the network. These paths and the time required to complete the activities on these paths are as follows:

Paths	Completion Times
1,2,3,4,5,9,10	12.9 days
1,2,3,4,5,7,9,10	12.8
1,2,3,8,9,10	4.3
1,2,3,4,6,7,9,10	11.6

The longest (critical) path is the first of the four paths listed. If all the activities actually require the length of time originally estimated, the rebuilding will be completed in 12.9 days, which is the length of the critical path through the network.

For the more complex networks encountered in practice, **algorithms** have been developed which identify the critical path without resorting to trial and error or a complete enumeration approach. These algorithms, which are described in operations research texts, have been incorporated in programs that are available for most computers. The practicing accountant typically will not be involved in using these algorithms, but will be involved in analyzing the activities of accounting-related projects, providing the input data for the computer program, and interpreting the computer printouts.

The data from the computer printout showing the events on the critical path for the grinder rebuilding project are reproduced in Illustration 15-7. The algorithms on which this illustration is based work as follows:

1. The **early finish (EF) time** for each event is calculated. Starting at the beginning of the project with an EF time of zero (or the calendar date when the project is to be started), the duration of each activity is added to the EF time for the preceding event to arrive at the EF time for the event at the completion of the activity. If there are several preceding events, the latest EF time is used, since the activity in question cannot be started until all the prior activities have been completed.

2. The **late finish (LF) time** for each event is calculated, working backward through the network. The LF time for the last event is assumed to be equal to the EF time for that event. The LF time for each of the other events is calculated by subtracting the activity's duration from the LF time of the following event. If there are several following events, i.e., several activities that begin a given node, the earliest LF time within that set of events is used.

(Delaying the event further could cause some other path to become critical and delay the completion of the project.)

3. The slack for each event is calculated. Slack is the difference between the EF and the LF times. Since events which have no slack are on the critical path, the critical path can be identified by following the sequence of events with zero slack through the network.

In Illustration 15-7, the events on the critical path are identified as events 1,2,3,4,5,9,10, as noted previously. In addition, the illustration includes the earliest time that each event can be expected to occur. This earliest event time is the sum of the activity times for the longest path through the network from the start of the project to that event. The earliest time for the event which represents the completion of the last activity in the network is also the earliest the project can be completed. Accordingly, the earliest expected completion time for this project is 12.9 days.

For each activity not on the critical path, some delay or slack can be tolerated without causing a delay in finishing the project. As management reviews a CPM report, possibilities for directing resources away from activities with large amounts

Illustration 15-7
CPM Report for the Tool Grinder Project

Event Analysis

Event No.	Earliest Expected Time	Slack
1	0.00	0.00 (on critical path)
2	1.20	0.00 (on critical path)
3	1.40	0.00 (on critical path)
8	2.60	8.60
4	2.60	0.00 (on critical path)
6	8.10	1.30
7	11.10	0.10
5	11.10	0.00 (on critical path)
9	12.10	0.00 (on critical path)
10	12.90	0.00 (on critical path)

Activity Report

Activity From	To	Earliest Start	End	Latest Start	End
1	2	0.00	1.20	0.00	1.20 (critical activity)
2	3	1.20	1.40	1.20	1.40 (critical activity)
3	8	1.40	2.60	10.00	11.20
3	4	1.40	2.60	1.40	2.60 (critical activity)
4	6	2.60	8.10	3.90	9.40
6	7	8.10	9.90	9.40	11.20
5	7	11.10	11.10	11.20	11.20
4	5	2.60	11.10	2.60	11.10 (critical activity)
7	9	11.10	12.00	11.20	12.10
5	9	11.10	12.10	11.10	12.10 (critical activity)
8	9	2.60	3.50	11.20	12.10
9	10	12.10	12.90	12.10	12.90 (critical activity)

of slack and toward the activities on the critical path may become evident. Since any reduction in time on a critical path activity will shorten the project's completion time, such reallocations of resources will be advantageous if there are benefits to completing the project early or there are penalties associated with delays in completing the project.

Illustration 15-7 also shows the earliest time an activity can be started and the earliest time an activity can be completed. The earliest time an activity can be started is when the last predecessor activity has been completed. If there is some slack associated with a given activity, the start of the activity can be delayed without jeopardizing the timely completion of the project. The earliest time a given activity can be completed is equal to the time required for completion, i.e., the activity's duration, plus the activity's earliest start time.

PERT Networks

Since the time required to complete an activity is only a manager's best estimate, the uncertainty involved in that estimate is quantified in PERT by requiring the manager to provide a best estimate, an optimistic estimate, and a pessimistic estimate of the time required to perform each activity. These three estimates are presumed to describe a distribution of possible activity durations. The best estimate is the most likely time, or mode, of the distribution, and the optimistic and pessimistic times set the lower and upper limits of the distribution. Because these distributions are often not symmetrical, the normal distribution is not a good description of activity durations. Instead, the beta distribution is used. The parameters of the beta distribution can be set so that it will be symmetrical and looks very much like the normal distribution, or it can be skewed to either the left or the right. Illustration 15-8 shows several different shapes for a beta distribution, depending on the optimistic, most likely, and pessimistic estimates.

The statistical formulas for the mean and the standard deviation of the beta distribution are quite complicated, but two simple formulas which very closely approximate the mean and the variance (square of the standard deviation) of a beta distribution have been developed. These formulas are as follows:

$$\text{Mean}(t) = \frac{a + 4m + b}{6} \tag{15.7}$$

$$\text{Standard deviation}(\sigma) = \frac{b - a}{6} \tag{15.8}$$

where a is the optimistic (minimum) time, m is the most likely time (mode), and b is the pessimistic (maximum) time. If the optimistic, most likely, and pessimistic estimates for the grinder rebuilding activity 1,2 are .9, 1.2, and 1.8 days, respectively, then:

$$t = \frac{.9 + 1.2 + 1.8}{6} = 1.25$$

$$\sigma = \frac{1.8 - .9}{6} = .15$$

$$\sigma^2 = .0225$$

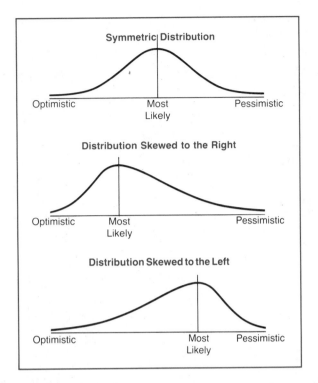

Illustration 15-8
Alternative Shapes for a
Beta Distribution

Symmetric Distribution

Optimistic   Most   Pessimistic
                   Likely

Distribution Skewed to the Right

Optimistic   Most   Pessimistic
                   Likely

Distribution Skewed to the Left

Optimistic   Most   Pessimistic
                                   Likely

If managers are asked to provide only a single estimate of an activity time, they might respond with the most likely value (the mode) or with the mean of their subjective probability distribution. If the distribution is skewed to the right or the left, the mean and the mode will be different values. For the CPM network calculations in Illustrations 15-6 and 15-7, the single estimates are assumed to correspond to the most likely values shown in Part A of Illustration 15-9. Part A also shows the optimistic and pessimistic times for completing each activity in the project, as well as the mean and the standard deviation of each activity. For the activities with skewed distributions, the expected times in Illustration 15-9 will differ from the values shown earlier, and the expected project completion time will also be slightly different.

Assuming that there are likely to be a large number of activities in the network and that the activities are independent, the total expected time and the total variance for any sequence of activities in the network can be computed by simply summing the expected (or mean) time and the variance for each of the individual activities. These calculations have the most significance for the sequence of activities on the critical path.

Part B of Illustration 15-9, the activity report for the PERT network, shows the degree of flexibility available in scheduling the individual activities based on the PERT time estimates. The earliest expected time, the slack, the variance, and the standard deviation for each event in the network for rebuilding the grinder is shown in Part C of Illustration 15-9. Since the last event (event 10) represents the completion of the project, the expected time for completing the project is 13.33 days. The standard deviation associated with this estimate is .8606.

Illustration 15-9   PERT Activity Time Estimates and Reports
Part A   Probabilistic Activity Time Estimates

Activity		Optimistic	Most Likely	Pessimistic	Mean	Standard Deviation
1,2	Unload and test unit	0.9 days	1.2 days	1.8 days	1.2500	.1500
2,3	Disassemble electrical parts and motor	0.1	0.2	0.4	0.2167	.0500
3,4	Clean and disassemble machine	0.9	1.2	1.5	1.2000	.1000
3,8	Inspect electrical parts and paint motor	0.8	1.2	1.5	1.8333	.1167
8,9	Assemble and install electrical parts and motor	0.6	0.9	1.2	0.9000	.1000
4,5	Secure head parts from manufacturers	7.0	8.5	12.0	8.8333	.8333
4,6	Machine and scrape slides and table	4.5	5.5	7.5	5.6667	.5000
6,7	Machine and scrape gibbs	1.5	1.8	2.0	1.7833	.0833
5,7	Dummy	0.0	0.0	0.0	0.0000	.0000
5,9	Assemble head	0.8	1.0	1.4	1.0333	.1000
7,9	Assemble cross slides	0.8	0.9	1.3	0.9500	.0833
9,10	Test and load for shipping	0.7	0.8	0.9	0.8000	.0333

Illustration 15-9
PERT Activity Time
Estimates and Reports

Part B
Activity Report

Activity		Earliest		Latest	
From	To	Start	End	Start	End
1	2	0.00	1.25	0.00	1.25 (critical activity)
2	3	1.25	1.47	1.25	1.47 (critical activity)
3	8	1.47	2.65	10.45	11.63
3	4	1.47	2.67	1.47	2.67 (critical activity)
4	6	2.67	8.33	4.18	9.85
6	7	8.33	10.12	9.85	11.63
5	7	11.50	11.50	11.63	11.63
4	5	2.67	11.50	2.67	11.50 (critical activity)
7	9	11.50	12.40	11.63	12.53
5	9	11.50	12.53	11.50	12.53 (critical activity)
8	9	2.65	3.55	11.63	12.53
9	10	12.53	13.33	12.53	13.33 (critical activity)

Illustration 15-9
PERT Activity Time
Estimates and Reports

Part C
Event Analysis

Event No.	Earliest Expected Time	Slack	Total Variance	Total Standard Deviation
1	0.00	0.00	.00	
2	1.25	0.00	.02	.1500 (on critical path)
3	1.47	0.00	.03	.1581 (on critical path)
8	2.65	8.98	.04	.1965
4	2.67	0.00	.04	.1871 (on critical path)
6	8.33	1.52	.29	.5339
7	11.50	0.13	.73	.8541
5	11.50	0.00	.73	.8541 (on critical path)
9	12.53	0.00	.74	.8599 (on critical path)
10	13.33	0.00	.74	.8606 (on critical path)

The standard deviation of the expected time for project completion can be used to set a confidence interval which, for a given level of confidence, provides the range within which the completion time is expected to fall. For the grinder project, a 95% confidence interval would be from 11.64 to 15.02 days [13.33 days $\pm$ (1.96 standard deviations $\times$ .8606 days), or 13.33 days $\pm$ 1.69 days].

The standard deviation for the distribution of completion times, .8606, can also be used to calculate the probability of finishing within a given period of time or earlier (or later). For example, the probability of finishing the grinder rebuilding in 12 days or less is represented by the area in the left tail of a normal distribution up to 1.55 standard deviations ($1.33 \div .8606$) below the mean, since 12 days is 1.33 days ($13.33 - 12$) less than the expected time. A table of cumulative probabilities for the normal distribution, Table 3 in the appendix at the end of the text, indicates that this probability is approximately .06 or 6%. Although the individual activity distributions are not normal, the sum of many activities, i.e., the total time for the critical path, will be approximately normal.

Incorporating Costs into PERT and CPM Networks

The planning and control of the time required for completing a project is important, but unless the costs of performing the activities are included, the planning and control cycle will be incomplete. The basic CPM and PERT models can be modified to incorporate estimates of the cost as well as the time required to complete each activity. The actual times and costs can then be compared to the scheduled times and the budgeted costs at regular intervals.

Work on many activities can be expedited to hasten completion, but a cost penalty for such items as overtime premiums and assigning additional workers will be incurred. In planning projects, managers may be asked to provide not only the estimates for the time and cost required to complete each activity at a normal pace, but also a set of expedited, or crash, times and costs. Crash times and costs for the grinder rebuilding project are shown in Part A of Illustration 15-10, and the CPM activity report based on crash times is shown in Part B.

If activities on the critical path are shortened, another path through the network may become critical. For example, if activity 5,9 for the grinder project were to be shortened by more than .1 days, the parallel path involving the dummy activity 5,7 and the real activity 7,9 which takes .9 days would become critical. Alternatively, if activity 4,5 is shortened by more than 1.3 days, the critical path including activities 4,5 and 5,9 will no longer be critical, but the path including activities 4,6, 6,7, and 7,9 will become critical.

The total cost of completing a project is the sum of the costs of all the activities in the project. The normal cost of the grinder rebuilding project is $3,780, and the cost of completing the project if all activities are crashed is $4,369. As indicated in Illustration 15-7, the normal time required to complete the project is 12.9 days, the sum of times required to complete those activities on the critical path— 1,2,3,4,5,9,10. When the activities are crashed, a new critical path emerges— 1,2,3,4,6,7,9,10—and the time required to complete the project is reduced to 10.4 days.

It should be noted that crashing some activities does not contribute to reducing the time required to complete the grinder rebuilding project. For example, activity 3,8 is not on the critical path of normal or crash times, and decreasing the time of completing this activity does not enter into expediting the project's completion. Crashing this activity only increases the amount of slack and increases the project's cost.

Activity	Normal Duration	Normal Cost	Crash Duration	Crash Cost
1,2 Unload and test unit	1.2 days	$250	0.9 days	$289
2,3 Disassemble electrical parts and motor	0.2	40	0.1	50
3,4 Clean and disassemble machine	1.2	350	1.2	350
3,8 Inspect electrical parts and paint motor	1.2	360	1.0	400
8,9 Assemble and install electrical parts and motor	0.9	200	0.9	200
4,5 Secure head parts from manufacturers	8.5	200	6.5	350
4,6 Machine and scrape slides and table	5.5	1,200	5.5	1,200
6,7 Machine and scrape gibbs	1.0	500	1.4	650
5,7 Dummy	0.0	0	0.0	0
5,9 Assemble head	1.0	250	1.0	250
7,9 Assemble cross slides	0.9	250	0.9	250
9,10 Test and load for shipping	0.8	180	0.4	280
		$3,780		$4,269

Illustration 15-10
Analysis of Normal and
Crash Costs for
Rebuilding a Tool Grinder

Part B
Activity Report for
Rebuilding a Tool Grinder
(Activities Crashed)

Activity From	To	Earliest Start	Earliest End	Latest Start	Latest End
1	2	0.00	0.90	0.00	0.90 (critical activity)
2	3	0.90	1.00	0.90	1.00 (critical activity)
3	8	1.00	2.20	8.00	9.20
3	4	1.00	2.20	1.00	2.20 (critical activity)
4	6	2.20	7.70	2.20	7.70 (critical activity)
4	5	2.20	8.70	2.50	9.00
6	7	7.70	9.10	7.70	9.10 (critical activity)
5	7	8.70	8.70	9.10	9.10
5	9	8.70	9.70	9.00	10.00
8	9	2.20	3.00	9.20	10.00
7	9	9.10	10.00	9.10	10.00 (critical activity)
9	10	10.00	10.40	10.00	10.40 (critical activity)

Event No.	Earliest Expected Time	Slack
1	0.00	0.00 (on critical path)
2	0.90	0.00 (on critical path)
3	1.00	0.00 (on critical path)
8	2.20	7.00
4	2.20	0.00 (on critical path)
6	7.70	0.00 (on critical path)
5	8.70	0.30
7	9.10	0.00 (on critical path)
9	10.00	0.00 (on critical path)
10	10.40	0.00 (on critical path)

A cost-effective way of shortening the time required to complete a project is to concentrate on the activities which are on the critical path. Those activities on the critical path which have the lowest cost per day of reduction in time are selected for crashing. The cost ratios for all of the activities which can be crashed in the grinder rebuilding project are as follows:

Activity	Increase in Cost	Reduction in Time	Cost-Benefit Ratio
1,2	$ 39	.3 days	$130 per day
2,3	10	.1	100
3,8	40	.2	200
4,5	150	2.0	75
6,7	150	.4	375
9,10	100	.4	250

For this project, management has determined that all of the activities listed above can be shortened by any amount from the normal time to the crash time, in increments of .1 days, at a proportionate increase in cost. For example, activity 1,2 can be shortened by .1 days for $13, by .2 days for $26, or by .3 days for $39. To shorten the completion time of this project in the most cost-effective way, activity 4,5 should be selected first for crashing, since it has the lowest cost-benefit ratio, $75 per day. If a second activity needs to be crashed, activity 2,3 should be chosen, since its cost-benefit ratio is $100 per day.

To further illustrate crashing, assume that management requires that the completion time for the grinder rebuilding project be shortened by 1.5 days, at the lowest cost. Activity 4,5 should first be shortened by 1.3 days at a cost of $97.50 (1.3 days × $75 per day). At this point, parallel subpaths 4,5,9 and 4,6,7,9 are both critical. Further reductions in activity 4,5 would also require that activity 6,7 be shortened simultaneously at a combined cost of $450 per day. An approach that is less costly is to shorten activity 2,3 by .1 days at a cost of $10 (.1 x $100 per day), and then shorten activity 1,2 by .1 days at a cost of $13 (.1 × $130 per day). These changes will shorten the critical path by the required 1.5 days and add $120.50 to the project's cost. Thus, the scheduled completion time becomes 11.4 days and the cost becomes $3,900.50. The CPM report for this set of crashed times and costs is shown in Illustration 15-11.

THE LEARNING CURVE

The **learning curve model** is a mathematical model that can be used to predict the reductions in direct labor times and costs which result from the increased efficiencies achieved by individuals as they become more adept at performing a new task. The learning curve model first received attention in the shipbuilding and aircraft industries during World War II. During production runs of fighter planes and bombers, for example, it was noticed that as the total number of planes produced doubled, the average time for producing the total output dropped to about 80% of the former cumulative average time. If the average time for producing the first 25 fusilage sections was 1,000 hours per section, by the time 50 sections had been completed, the average time for all 50 sections would have dropped to 800 hours (80% of 1,000) per section. Accordingly, the total time required to produce 50 sections would be 40,000 hours (50 × 800 hours per section).

If management wishes to estimate how much time would be required to produce another 50 sections, after the first 50 sections had been produced, the 80% learning curve model could be used. Since the production of 50 more

Activity		Duration of Activity	Cost
1,2	Unload and test unit	1.1 days	$ 263.00
2,3	Disassemble electrical parts and motor	0.1	50.00
3,4	Clean and disassemble machine	1.2	350.00
3,8	Inspect electrical parts and paint motor	1.2	360.00
8,9	Assemble and install electrical parts and motor	0.9	200.00
4,5	Secure head parts from manufacturers	7.2	297.50
4,6	Machine and scrape slides and table	5.5	1,200.00
6,7	Machine and scrape gibbs	1.8	500.00
5,7	Dummy	0.0	0.00
5,9	Assemble head	1.0	250.00
7,9	Assemble cross slides	0.9	250.00
9,10	Test and load for shipping	0.8	180.00
			$3,900.50

CPM Report

Activity		Earliest		Latest	
From	To	Start	End	Start	End
1	2	0.00	1.10	0.00	1.10 (critical activity)
2	3	1.10	1.20	1.10	1.20 (critical activity)
3	8	1.20	2.40	8.50	9.70
3	4	1.20	2.40	1.20	2.40 (critical activity)
4	6	2.40	7.90	2.40	7.90 (critical activity)
4	5	2.40	9.60	2.40	9.60 (critical activity)
6	7	7.90	9.70	7.90	9.70 (critical activity)
5	7	9.60	9.60	9.70	9.70
7	9	9.70	10.60	9.70	10.60 (critical activity)
5	9	9.60	10.60	9.60	10.60 (critical activity)
8	9	2.40	3.30	9.70	10.60
9	10	10.60	11.40	10.60	11.40 (critical activity)

Event No.	Earliest Expected Time	Slack
1	0.00	0.00 (on critical path)
2	1.10	0.00 (on critical path)
3	1.20	0.00 (on critical path)
8	2.40	7.30
4	2.40	0.00 (on critical path)
6	7.90	0.00 (on critical path)
5	9.60	0.00 (on critical path)
7	9.70	0.00 (on critical path)
9	10.60	0.00 (on critical path)
10	11.40	0.00 (on critical path)

sections would double the cumulative quantity produced to date, management could expect that the cumulative average time per section for the first 100 sections would again drop to 80% of its former value, or 640 hours per section (80% of 800 hours). If the average time for the first 100 sections was 640 hours per section, the total time for all 100 sections would be 64,000 hours. The time required for the second 50 sections would be equal to the total time for producing the first 100 sections less the total time for producing the first 50 sections, or 24,000 hours (64,000 hours − 40,000 hours). These computations and a plot of the cumulative average times for this 80% learning curve are shown in Illustration 15-12.

(A) Starting Date for Lot	(B) Quantity in Lot	(C) Cumulative Quantity	(D) Average Time for Cumulative Quantity (.8 × Previous Value for "D")	(E) Total Time for Cumulative Quantity [(C × D)]	(F) Total Time for Lot (E − Previous Value for "E")
July 1	25	25	1,000 hrs.[a]	25,000 hrs.	25,000 hrs.[a]
Sept. 1	25	50	800	40,000	15,000
Oct. 15	50	100	640	64,000	24,000

[a] Time for first lot

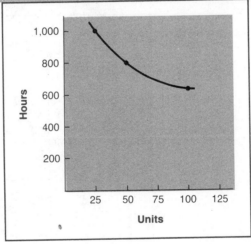

Since the quantities for which production times are needed will not usually coincide with quantities which double the cumulative production quantities, as they do in Illustration 15-12, a more flexible approach to determining production times is needed. Such an approach is the use of log-log paper, on which the plots of cumulative average times and cumulative total times appear as straight lines. In Illustration 15-13, the data for the example in the previous paragraph are plotted. The cumulative average times are plotted on both arithmetic and logarithmic scales in Part A, and the cumulative total times are plotted on both scales in Part B.

The appropriate total time for any cumulative quantity can be read from these graphs, and the time required to produce any subsequent number of units can be calculated. For example, if the time for 30 more sections had been needed after 50 sections had been produced, the cumulative total time for 80 sections could be read from the graph in Part B (approximately 55,000 hours), and the time required for the next 30 units (80 − 50) could be calculated as 15,000 hours (55,000 hours − 40,000 hours).

Illustration 15-13   Graphs of Learning Curves
Part A   Graphs of Cumulative Average Time

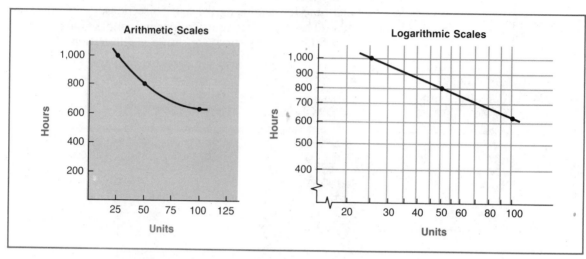

Illustration 15-13   Graphs of Learning Curves
Part B   Graphs of Cumulative Total Time

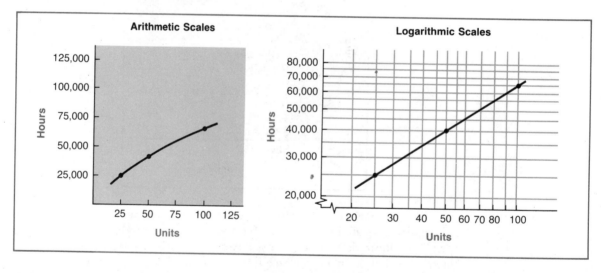

Learning Curve Formulas

Mathematical formulas can be used to determine more accurate cumulative times than can be obtained by using graphs. The basic formula for the cumulative average time required to produce a given number of units is as follows:

$$A = kq^b \qquad\qquad \textbf{(15.9)}$$

where k represents the theoretical time required to produce the first unit, q is the number of units, and b represents the amount of learning which characterizes a given production process. If q equals 1, then q^b equals 1 and A equals k, regardless of the value of b. The parameter b is determined by the following formula:

$$b = \frac{\text{logarithm of the learning curve percent}}{\text{logarithm of 2}} \qquad \text{(15.10)}$$

Although q is defined in terms of individual units, production is sometimes carried out by working on batches of units. In such cases, it may be more convenient to let q refer to the total number of batches produced. A will then be the average time for q batches, and k will be the time required to produce the first batch.

The value of 2 in the denominator of the formula for b corresponds to the fact that the learning curve percentage is defined in terms of doubled cumulative quantities. Since the value for b is the ratio of two logarithms, either common logarithms (to the base 10) or natural logarithms (to the base e, or ln) can be used in these computations. Since many calculators have natural, but not common, logarithmic functions, natural logarithms will be used in illustrations.

The value for b for an 80% learning curve is:

$$b = \frac{\ln .8}{\ln 2} = \frac{-.22314}{.69315} = -.3219$$

This value for b is the same for any 80% learning curve, regardless of the specific product involved. THe value for k, however, depends on the time required to produce the first unit of the product. For products requiring a great deal of labor to produce, k will be a large value; for smaller products, k will be a smaller value. For a given product, the value for k can be calculated by substituting values for A, q, and b into the cumulative average time formula, if the average time and the learning curve percent for producing any one quantity were known. Rearranging Formula 15.9 and substituting the value of A for a q of 25 gives the value for k as follows:

$$k = \frac{A}{q^b} = \frac{1,000}{25^{-.3219}} = \frac{1,000}{.3548} = 2,818$$

The values for k and b can now be used to calculate the values for A for any desired cumulative quantity. For example, the cumulative average time for the first 80 units can be calculated as follows:

$$A = 2,818 \times 80^{-.3219} = 687.6 \text{ hours per unit}$$

The total time required for 80 units would then be 55,008 hours (687.6 $\times$ 80 units). The total cumulative time to produce q units can be determined by multiplying Formula 15.9 by q, as follows:

$$T = Aq$$
$$T = kq^b \times q$$
$$T = kq^{b+1} \qquad \text{(15.11)}$$

In some applications, it is useful to know the time required to produce a given unit, i.e., the incremental time. The time required for the qth unit can be calculated as the total time required to produce q units, less the total time required to produce q minus 1 units. For example, the time required for the 80th fusilage section is equal to the total time for producing 80 sections, less the total time required for producing 79 sections. These times are calculated by using Formula 15.11, as follows:

$$T = 2{,}818 \times 80^{-.3219 + 1} = 55{,}008 \text{ hours}$$
$$T = 2{,}818 \times 79^{-.3219 + 1} = 54{,}541 \text{ hours}$$

The time required to produce the 80th unit is thus 467 hours (55,008 hours − 54,541 hours), which is much less than the time required for the first unit, 2,818 hours. For large qs, the incremental time required to produce a given unit can be estimated by computing the marginal time for the qth unit. The formula for the marginal time, M, can be derived by taking the first derivative of the total time with respect to q, as follows:

$$M = \frac{dT}{dq} = (b + 1) \times k \times q^b \qquad \qquad \textbf{(15.12)}$$

Using this formula, the time required to produce the 80th unit is computed as follows:

$$M = .6781 \times 80^{-.3219} \times 2{,}818 = 466 \text{ hours}$$

The marginal time in the instantaneous rate of change, or slope, of the time curve at a single point. Since the slope does not change very much for an increase of one unit when q equals 80, the approximation is very good at this point on the curve.

The formula for the marginal time is almost the same as the formula for the average time ($A = kq^b$). The only difference is that the coefficient for the marginal time is $(b + 1)(k)$, rather than b. Because both formulas involve raising q to the b power, the 80% ratio of cumulative average times for any two doubled quantities for an 80% learning curve will also be observed as the ratio of the marginal times for any two doubled cumulative quantities.

As long as the hourly rate paid to direct labor does not change, the formulas for A, T, and M can be used for determining cumulative average cost, cumulative total cost, and marginal cost, as well as times. The value for b will remain the same in either application, but the value for k must be expressed in dollars if costs are desired. The parameter k becomes the theoretical labor cost of producing the first unit. For example, if the labor cost to produce planes is $10 per hour, the value for k would be $28,180. Using this value for k in Formula 15.11, the total labor cost of producing the first 79 planes would be $545,410.

Estimating Parameter Values in the Learning Curve Formulas

One way that management might estimate the parameter values for b and k is to base the estimates on the values actually experienced for a similar product in previous production runs. To illustrate, assume that management is just beginning to build fusilage sections which are quite similar to the ones previously described, except that the new sections are smaller than the other sections. The appropriate value of k for the new sections would be proportionately smaller, say approximately 2,395.3 hours (85% of 2,818 hours). Similarly, although an 80% learning curve characterized previous production, if management believed that learning would be less on production of a new, different product, such that an 82% learning curve would be achieved, the appropriate value for b for the new product would be −.2863 (ln .82 ÷ ln 2). The accuracy of these estimates would depend on the ability of managers to make these judgmental forecasts.

Another approach to estimating parameter values is to wait until some production has taken place, and then use the data collected during the early portion of the actual production run to make the estimate. Appendix 15B shows how statistical regression analysis can be used to provide parameter estimates from production data.

Applications of Learning Curves

Although learning curves were first applied in the shipbuilding and aircraft industries, the improvement in labor productivity due to learning has also been documented in numerous other industries, such as the manufacturing of large musical instruments, steel, glass, paper, and electrical products. Although the specific parameter values for each application will vary, operations that have a high degree of labor content will generally show a greater amount of learning, i.e., a lower learning curve percent, than operations which are predominantly machine-paced.

Although the log-linear model described is the most commonly used learning curve model, variations of the particular shape of the learning curve may occur in different applications. One variation which is sometimes seen in practice is shown in Illustration 15-14. This modification of the learning curve model is based on the assumption that reductions in the marginal time will no longer occur after a certain point, or **steady-state phase,** has been reached. Beyond this point, the time required to produce an additional unit is assumed to be constant. When manage-

**Illustration 15-14
The Learning Curve
Model with a Steady-
State Phase**

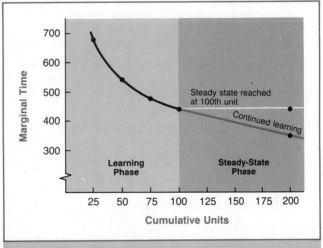

Cumulative Units	Marginal Time	
	With Steady State Reached at the 100th Unit	With Continued Learning
25	678	678
50	542	542
75	476	476
100	434	434
200	434	347

ment believes, or the operating data show, that a steady state has been reached, the accountant must be careful not to extend the learning curve model into the steady-state region when labor times and costs are being predicted.

Most users of the learning curve model apply it only to direct labor costs and to manufacturing overhead based on direct labor. Unless otherwise indicated, the learning curve should not be assumed to apply to materials. In some instances, however, reductions in materials costs may occur as production output increases. Such reductions occur as a result of lower spoilage, improved yields, or, in the case of purchased parts, because of quantity discounts available as parts are purchased in larger lot sizes. Even though reductions in unit materials costs may occur, it is unlikely that the same rate of decrease observed for labor times and costs would also apply to materials. Either a separate improvement rate should be computed for materials, or a composite, weighted-average rate of improvement covering both materials and labor should be determined and applied to the calculation of total prime costs.

Accounting Implications

If production times will be significantly influenced by learning curves, the expected reductions in labor-related costs should be incorporated in planning, control, decision making, and financial reporting. For most planning activities, such as capital budgeting, cost-volume-profit analysis, and budgeting, the unit variable cost of manufacturing a product is assumed, with stable prices, to remain constant over time. This assumption will not be valid, however, when learning reduces the labor-related cost of each successive unit produced. For example, in evaluating capital investments, management must take into account the longer periods of time over which cash flows occur as the initial units are produced and sold. This longer time period will reduce the net present value for those units.

Since the total cost function is no longer linear in a learning curve situation, simple algebra is no longer adequate for calculating break-even points. Instead, the total cost formula, Formula 15.11, can be used as the basis for a simple computer program to calculate total profits. The quantity of product to be manufactured and sold, q, may then be varied in a programmed loop or by an iterative trial-and-error approach until the break-even point is reached.

Learning may also have a significant effect on the monthly profits and cash flows incorporated in a firm's master budget and profit plan. The time required for completing each successive batch of units must be carefully projected, using learning curve formulas to determine the timing for the scheduling of labor, the purchase of materials, and the delivery of finished units to customers.

Learning curves can also be used to improve labor cost control during the early production period prior to the achievement of the steady-state phase. Learning curve formulas can be used to establish cost targets which are better estimates of the costs that should be incurred for the production of each batch of products. If cost standards are based on the first units produced, the standards will be too loose for subsequent units. Steady-state standards, on the other hand, will be unrealistically tight during the early, start-up phase of production.

When improvements in production times due to learning are significant, firms which are successful in developing new products with relatively short product lives may dominate the market because of product design and production cost advantages. Such firms may have progressed so far along their learning curve that competitors who enter the market later are never able to catch up. These product innovators often adopt an aggressive price strategy, reducing the product price as their production costs drop. Such a strategy may discourage other firms from entering the market, since meeting a continuously declining market price with higher production costs would result in incurring losses over the product's entire life cycle.

Other firms may adopt a stable pricing strategy which establishes a price based on the cumulative average production cost for the total number of units expected to be produced and sold. If such a strategy is followed, the cost of producing the first units is likely to be in excess of the selling price. Income statements prepared during this period would report substantial losses. Inventories of finished goods would have to be written down to market, even though the sales of the product over the entire life cycle are expected to generate substantial profits. To avoid this problem with the financial statements, the excess of the actual cost of production of a given unit over the product's selling price may be recorded in a deferred asset account, Deferred Production Costs, and written off in later periods when the initial phase of high production costs has passed. This accounting practice would recognize no profits (or losses) during the initial periods.

A less conservative approach is to defer the excess of the actual costs over the cumulative average costs for all units expected to be produced and sold. If this accounting practice is followed, the long-run average profit will be reported for each unit manufactured and sold. The deferred production costs account will increase until the incremental unit production cost equals the overall cumulative average cost. Beyond this point, the actual production costs for a unit will be less than the cumulative average cost for all units to be produced, and the difference should be credited to the deferred cost account. If the estimates of the learning rate and the total number of units to be manufactured and sold are correct, the deferred cost account will have a zero balance when the last unit has been produced and sold. If the learning rate or the market for the product has been overestimated, then interim write-downs of this asset account will be required. This method of accounting will not be acceptable, however, unless it can be demonstrated that the estimated learning rates are actually being achieved and that the forecasted sales volume is likely to be sold.

APPENDIX 15A: THE BACKORDER MODEL

In the basic EOQ model, no stockouts are assumed to occur. One variation of this basic model is the backorder model, which permits stockouts. In this model, the inventory is deliberately allowed to decrease to zero and is left at that level for a period of time. During this time, the quantity demanded is backordered. The backordered demand is then filled as soon as the next replenishment order is received. Although extra costs are incurred in processing these backordered units, there is a savings in holding costs achieved, since there are no inventory holding costs associated with the backordered units. The backorder model balances the extra backorder processing costs against the savings in holding costs for backordered units.

Part A of Illustration 15A-1 shows how inventory levels of Jones Co.'s circuit boards would vary over time with a backorder model. An order quantity of 25 units, including backorders of 9 units in each inventory cycle, results in a maximum inventory level of 16 units.

In the backorder model, the total variable inventory-related costs, T, are equal to the sum of (1) the annual variable holding costs, (2) the annual variable order costs, and (3) the annual variable backorder costs. If B denotes the total number of units backordered in each inventory cycle and Q is the order quantity, the maximum inventory in the backorder model is Q minus B, and the average inventory is Q minus B divided by 2. In this model, the average backordered quantity, $Q \div 2$, is backordered for the portion of the inventory cycle equal to $B \div Q$. If P is the unit variable backorder cost per year ($5.33 per unit), D is the value for total demand (100 units), O is the value for variable order cost ($6 per order), and H is the value for unit variable holding cost ($3 per unit), the total variable inventory-related costs incurred, with backorders allowed, can be stated as follows:

$$T = \left[\left(\frac{Q-B}{2}\right)\left(\frac{Q-B}{Q}\right)H\right] = \left[\left(\frac{D}{Q}\right)O\right] + \left[\left(\frac{B}{2}\right)\left(\frac{B}{Q}\right)P\right]$$

$$T = \frac{(Q-B)^2 H}{2Q} + \frac{DO}{Q} + \frac{B^2 P}{2Q} \tag{15A.1}$$

Part B of Illustration 15A-1 shows how the total variable inventory-related costs vary for several different values of Q and B if the variable backorder cost is assumed to be $5.33 per unit. When no backorders are permitted (line 1), the total backorder cost will be zero, and the minimum total cost is $60 for an order quantity of 20 units, with the total annual order costs equal to the total annual inventory holding costs. This solution was optimal for the basic EOQ model illustrated in the chapter.

When backorders are permitted, the optimal order quantity increases from 20 to 25 units, and 9 units are backordered in each cycle. For this backorder model, the minimum combined annual total costs are reduced from $60 for the basic EOQ model to $48. In the backorder model, the minimum annual combined total costs will be achieved when the total annual order costs equal the sum of the total annual inventory holding costs and the total annual backorder costs.

Differential calculus can be used to find the optimal values for Q and B which minimize the total cost as determined by Formula 15A.1. The first derivatives of T with respect to Q and B are taken, the first derivatives are set equal to zero, and the resulting equations are solved for Q and B. To simplify the computation of these values, it is convenient to calculate first the fraction, F, as follows:

$$F = \frac{P}{P+H} \tag{15A.2}$$

Illustration 15A-1
The Backorder Model

Part A
Variation of Inventory
and Backorder Levels
over Time

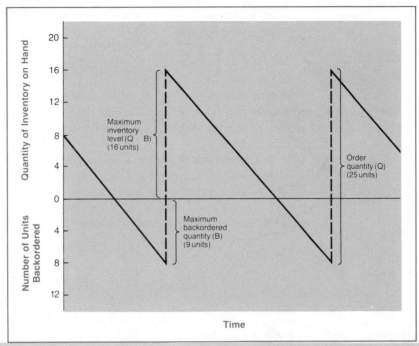

Illustration 15A-1
The Backorder Model

Part B
Total Variable Inventory-
Related Costs for the
Backorder Model with
Various Order Quantities

	Quantity Ordered = 15 units	Quantity Ordered = 20 units	Quantity Ordered = 25 units	Quantity Ordered = 30 units
Backordered quantity = 0:				
Total holding (carrying) costs	$22.50	$30.00	$37.50	$45.00
Total order costs	40.00	30.00	24.00	20.00
Total backorder costs	0	0	0	0
Total inventory-related costs	$62.50	$60.00	$61.50	$65.00
Backordered quantity = 9:				
Total holding (carrying) costs	$ 3.60	$ 9.08	$15.36	$22.05
Total order costs	40.00	30.00	24.00	20.00
Total backorder costs	14.40	10.80	8.64	7.20
Total inventory-related costs	$58.00	$49.88	$48.00	$49.25
Backordered quantity = 18:				
Total holding (carrying) costs	$ .90	$ .30	$ 2.94	$ 7.20
Total order costs	40.00	30.00	24.00	20.00
Total backorder costs	57.60	43.20	34.56	28.80
Total inventory-related costs	$98.50	$73.50	$61.50	$56.00

The economic (optimal) order quantity, EOQ, and the economic (optimal) backorder quantity, EBQ, can be computed by using the following formulas:

$$EOQ = \sqrt{\frac{2DO}{H}}\sqrt{\frac{1}{F}}$$

$$EOQ = \sqrt{\frac{2DO}{HF}} \qquad \text{(15A.3)}$$

$$EBQ = \sqrt{\frac{2DO}{H}}\left[\sqrt{\frac{1}{F}} - \sqrt{F}\right] \qquad \text{(15A.4)}$$

If these optimal inventory policies are adopted, the total variable inventory-related costs for the year will be:

$$T = \sqrt{2DOH}\ \sqrt{F}$$
$$T = \sqrt{2DOHF}$$

(15A.5)

Notice that as the unit variable backorder cost, P, becomes very large, F approaches the value 1.0, and the EOQ for the backorder model as given in Formula 15A.3 approaches the same value as that given for the basic EOQ model in Formula 15.5.

If the additional variable costs for processing backordered units are $5.33 per backordered unit per year, then: $F = .64$ [$5.33 \div ($5.33 + $3)$]; $\sqrt{F} = .8$; and $\sqrt{1 \div F} = 1.25$. Substituting these values in Formulas 15A.3, 15A.4, and 15A.5 gives an optimal order quantity of 25 units, an optimal backorder quantity of 9 units, and total variable inventory-related costs of $48 per year, as follows:

$$EOQ = \sqrt{\frac{2 \times 100 \times \$6}{\$3}} \times 1.25 = 20 \times 1.25 = 25 \text{ units}$$

$$EBQ = \sqrt{\frac{1,200}{3}} \times (1.25 - .8) = 20 \times .45 = 9 \text{ units}$$

$$T = \sqrt{2 \times 100 \times \$6 \times \$3} \times .8 = \$60 \times .8 = \$48 \text{ per year}$$

If the backorder model is used because it is a satisfactory description of the inventory-related costs, the order point calculation appropriate for the basic EOQ model must be modified slightly. In the basic EOQ model, the order is placed when the inventory level reaches a point equal to the value of the demand (usage) during the lead time. In the backorder model, the order should be placed at the point which will allow the demand during the lead time to deplete the inventories completely and to build up backorders to the optimal backorder quantity. To determine this point, the optimal backorder quantity is subtracted from the demand during the lead time. This difference, if positive, is the order point in terms of units in inventory. A negative difference is the order point in terms of cumulative backordered units. If an order is placed at this point, the predetermined optimal backorder quantity will be reached just as the next replenishment order is received.

APPENDIX 15B: ESTIMATING LEARNING CURVE PARAMETERS USING REGRESSION ANALYSIS

Part A of Illustration 15B-1 lists the cumulative average times for the production of an aircraft tail section. The ten data points include observations covering the first 3 units through the first 30 units. Part B of this illustration shows computer-generated plots of both the raw data and the natural logarithms of the data. To find the best fit to these data, a least squares regression can be performed. The values for Y are the natural logarithms of the cumulative average times, and the values for X are the natural logarithms of the cumulative production quantities. The results of the regression are summarized in Part C of Illustration 15B-1.

Illustration 15B-1
Regression Estimates
of Learning Curve
Parameters

Part A
Data for Production
of Tail Sections

Cumulative Production	Cumulative Average Time	Cumulative Production (ln of units)	Cumulative Average Time (ln of hours)
3 units	146.075 hours	1.0986	4.98412
5	126.763	1.6094	4.84232
10	105.114	2.3026	4.65505
14	96.376	2.6391	4.56826
16	93.967	2.7726	4.54294
17	90.858	2.8332	4.50930
19	87.482	2.9944	4.47143
22	84.304	3.0910	4.43443
26	81.334	3.2581	4.39856
30	79.115	3.4012	4.37090

Illustration 15B-1   Regression Estimates of Learning Curve Parameters
Part B   Graphs of Production Data

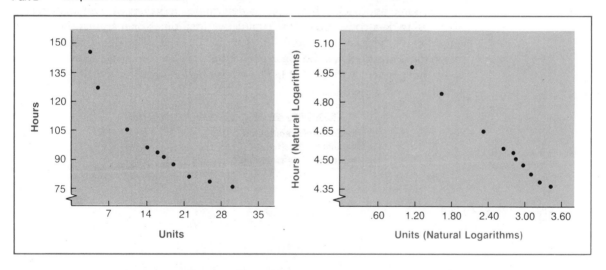

Illustration 15B-1   Regression Estimates of Learning Curve Parameters
Part C   Regression Output (log-transformed data)

The regression equation is: $Y = 5.28 - .270X_1$

Constant	Column	Coefficient	Standard Deviation of Coefficient	T Ratio = Coef./Stan. Dev.
	—	5.27853	.01016	519.24
X_1	C6	−0.270056	.003783	−71.37

The standard deviation of Y about the regression line is: $S = .08218$, with $(10 - 2) = 8$ degrees of freedom (D. F.)

$R^2 = 99.8\%$
$R^2 = 99.8\%$, adjusted for D. F.

Durbin-Watson statistic = 1.30

To interpret the regression results, take the logarithms of both sides of Formula 15.9, as follows:

$$A = kq^b$$
$$\ln A = \ln k + b\left(\ln q\right)$$

If Y is substituted for $\ln A$ and X is substituted for $\ln q$, the above equation is a linear equation of the form, $Y = c + bX$. As given in Part C of Illustration 15B-1, the intercept is an estimate of $\ln k$ in Formula 15.9. Since $\ln k$ is equal to 5.28, k is the antilog of 5.28. Using natural logarithm tables, or the antilog key (the e^x key) on a calculator, the antilog of 5.28 is determined to be 196.34.

The slope coefficient shown in Part C, $-.2701$, is an estimate of b. Since the logarithm of the learning curve percent is equal to b multiplied by the logarithm of 2, the natural logarithm of the learning curve percent is equal to $-.1872$ ($-.2701 \times .6931$). The antilog of $-.1872$ is .829, which indicates that the production of these tail sections involves an 82.9% learning curve.

The same approach can be used to determine the values of the parameters b and k, using data consisting of the cumulative total times or marginal times. The logarithms of the total or marginal times should be used as the dependent variable (Y) in the regression, and the logarithm of the cumulative quantity should be used as the independent variable (X). The interpretation of the regression results is shown in the following table:

Dependent Variable	Intercept	Slope
logarithm of average time	log k	b
logarithm of total time	log k	b + 1
logarithm of marginal time	log (b + 1) (k)	b

1. Describe the types of costs which determine inventory size. What are the objectives of inventory control models with regard to cost?

2. What two questions related to inventory are answered by inventory control models?

3. Why is the cost of the units purchased for inventory not included as part of the inventory ordering cost?

4. Give examples of the types of costs included in the unit variable holding costs (H).

5. What types of costs are included in the variable order cost (O)?

6. How would the basic EOQ model be applied to determine the optimal size of a manufacturing run?

7. You have been asked to determine the level of safety stock for copier paper at a local office supply store. What information do you need to make your decision?

8. If a goal of EOQ inventory control models is to minimize total inventory costs, why do Materials Requirements Planning systems sometimes generate lower total costs than EOQ-based systems?

9. In what ways are the PERT and CPM methods alike? How do they differ?

10. What is the critical path of a PERT or CPM network?

11. What is meant by a production process in which an 80% learning curve applies?

12. How does the learning curve phenomenon complicate the determination of cost standards and the break-even point?

Exercise 1. Seafarer Outboard Motor Company manufactures a line of small outboard motors for recreational use. The outboard motors are four-cycle engines, and each engine is filled with motor oil just prior to completion. The firm's expected production for the coming year is summarized as follows:

Engine Size	Quantity	Oil Capacity
7.5 HP	7,000 units	2.0 qts.
15.0	18,000	2.5
25.0	4,000	3.0

The firm orders motor oil in 50-gallon drums from a variety of suppliers. Lead times are short (3 days), delivery is reliable, and no safety stock is maintained. The engines are produced on parallel assembly lines, so that average daily oil usage is constant throughout the 365-day year. Inventory-related costs for the next year are as follows:

Variable holding costs . . . . $20 per barrel per year
Variable order costs . . . . . $ 8 per order

(1) Determine the firm's economic order quantity for motor oil.
(2) Calculate the order point for motor oil.
(3) Calculate the total variable cost associated with ordering and holding motor oil inventories.

Exercise 2. W P Co. distributes Strotz beer in western Pennsylvania. Deliveries of Strotz's "Old Munich" brand lager account for 60% of the firm's activity. The distributing company would like you to analyze the cost effectiveness of its inventory policy for this brand. Currently, W P Co. places orders twice a month and orders the quantity it expects to deliver in the subsequent period. A safety stock of 5% of annual demand is maintained. Inventory-related data for the coming 365-day year are as follows:

Annual demand	20,000 cases
Variable order cost	$40 per order
Variable holding cost	$.90 per case per year
Lead time	4 calendar days

(1) Determine the economic order quantity and the order point, assuming that no safety stock will be maintained.
(2) W P Co. has decided that because daily deliveries of Strotz beer are relatively constant in amount, it is unnecessary to hold safety stocks of this product. If the company implements the order policies determined in (1), what will its annual cost savings be, compared to its present policies?

Exercise 3. (*Note: This exercise is based, in part, on Appendix 15A*). Grey Star Company distributes a silicon boat wax through mail-order. The company has asked you to determine how many units it should carry in its inventory in order to minimize its inventory costs. The firm's accountant has provided you with the following data related to a 250-day work year:

Annual demand	75,000 units
Variable cost per order	$40 per order
Variable holding cost	$.72 per unit per year
Lead time	4 days

(1) Determine the economic order quantity and the order point for boat wax, using the basic EOQ model.
(2) The management of Grey Star wishes to evaluate an inventory policy which would allow backorders. The cost analyst estimates that the variable cost of a backordered unit is $1.15 per unit per year. Determine the optimal order quantity, order point, and the backorder quantity Grey Star can expect, using the backorder model.
(3) Compare the annual variable costs related to the two inventory and order policies.

Exercise 4. Soho Lumber Company is planning its inventory policy for its principal products for the coming year. Exterior-grade, 1/2" plywood is the company's primary product in dollar value and accounts for 25% of sales. Lead time for plywood orders is ten days. On the basis of past sales records, the company has developed the following probability distribution for demand during the lead time:

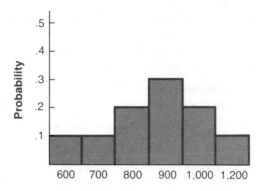

Demand During Lead Time
(in Sheets of Plywood)

The cost of a stockout is $1 per sheet. The firm will face 13 inventory cycles during the next year, based on the EOQ-determined order size. Holding costs of plywood are $.50 per sheet per year.

(1) Determine the combined annual stockout and holding costs for order points of: 1,200, 1,100, 1,000, and 900 sheets of plywood.
(2) What is the firm's optimal safety stock?

Exercise 5. Polly Company wishes to determine the optimal amount of safety stock it should carry for Product D. The following information is available:

Stockout cost	$15 per unit
Carrying cost of safety stock	$4 per unit per year
Number of orders	5 per year

On the basis of past experience, the firm has estimated the following probabilities for demand during the lead time:

Units Demanded	Probability
100	.05
90	.20
80	.25
70	.30
60	.10
50	.10

(1) Calculate Polly Company's expected demand during the lead time.
(2) (a) Determine the optimal order point for the firm.
    (b) Calculate the firm's service level and service ratio at this order point.

Exercise 6. Brady Sporting Goods Inc. buys baseballs at $20 per dozen from its wholesaler. Brady expects to sell 36,000 dozen baseballs evenly throughout the year. Brady desires a 10% return on its inventory investment. In addition, rent, insurance, and property taxes for each dozen baseballs in inventory are $.40 per year. The administrative cost involved in handling each purchase order is $10.

Brady's distributor has started a program in which purchasers are offered a discount of 1% off wholesale price on orders of 600 dozen baseballs or more.

(1) Calculate the EOQ, ignoring the quantity discount.

(2) Assuming that Brady can secure additional warehouse space at the price paid currently, determine whether or not the quantity discount should be taken.

Exercise 7. The following summary provides data on activities which are required to replace the radar dish of a jet aircraft:

Activity	Time Required	Activity	Time Required
A (1,2)	2 hours	E (4,5)	2
B (2,3)	5	F (4,6)	9
C (2,4)	7	G (5,6)	3
D (3,5)	7		

(1) Draw the CPM network describing the radar dish replacement activities.

(2) Determine the total time required to perform the activities on each path through the network.

(3) Which path is the critical path? How long will it take to replace the radar dish?

Exercise 8. Scientists at FaroTech have developed the following set of activities for the laboratory testing and evaluation of a new synthetic vitamin:

Activity	Time Required	Activity	Time Required
A (1,2)	1 week	H (5,7)	10
B (1,3)	2	I (4,9)	12
C (2,4)	4	J (7,8)	1
D (2,5)	8	K (7,9)	5
E (2,6)	4	L (8,10)	12
F (3,6)	7	M (9,10)	6
G (6,8)	8		

(1) Draw the CPM network which describes the testing and evaluation process.

(2) The following listing was obtained when the above data were input into a CPM computer program. Using the data from this listing, identify the critical path. How long will it take FaroTech to complete the testing?

Activity		Earliest		Latest	
From	To	Start	End	Start	End
1	2	0	1	0	1
1	3	0	2	3	5
2	4	1	5	10	14
2	5	1	9	1	9
2	6	1	5	8	12
3	6	2	9	5	12
6	8	9	17	12	20
5	7	9	19	9	19
7	8	19	20	19	20
4	9	5	17	14	26
7	9	19	24	21	26
8	10	20	32	20	32
9	10	24	30	26	32

Exercise 9. Capt. Joshua Slocum is the commander of a passenger ship, the *Atlantic Conveyor*. The ship has struck an iceberg on its maiden voyage, and is taking on water at an alarming rate, in spite of efforts to pump out the water. Capt. Slocum, whose career is at stake, is optimistic and believes that it will take 3 hours for seawater to flood the ship's engine room, short-circuiting the electrical system and causing the pumps to shut down. Thereafter, Slocum believes, it will take only 2 hours for seawater to reach the C-deck, the highest level at which watertight doors exist, and an additional 1.5 hours for the ship to roll over and sink.

I. M. Bright, the ship's insurer, is pessimistic and believes it will take only 1 hour for water to reach the engine room, another hour to reach the C-deck, and one more hour for the ship to roll over.

Chief Engineer Wright is the ship's designer and is regarded as the expert in this matter. Wright feels that the most likely times are 2.5 hours for water to reach the engine room, 1.5 hours to reach the C-deck, and 1.25 hours for the ship to sink.

(1) Assuming that the three events described are analogous to three consecutive events in a PERT network, and that the 3 time estimates for each event describe the shortest, longest, and most likely times, what is the expected time that it will take the ship to sink?

(2) If 4.5 hours are required to remove all passengers from the ship, what is the probability that all the ship's passengers will be saved?

Exercise 10. Wein Company is preparing a quarterly cash budget as part of its yearly continuous budgeting system. The activities involved in preparing a cash budget are described as follows, along with the controller's estimates, in working days, of the time required to perform each activity.

Activity	Description of Activity	Immediate Preceding Activities*	Time Estimates Optimistic	Most Likely	Pessimistic
A	Assign staff to budget groups	—	0.1	0.2	0.5
B	Determine selling and administrative expenses for the next quarter	A	5.0	7.0	11.0
C	Review production standard costs in light of expected efficiency and inflation factors	A	1.5	2.0	3.0
D	Develop the next quarter's sales forecast	A	1.5	3.0	4.0
E	Prepare a production budget for the next quarter	D	0.3	0.5	0.7
F	Determine cash collections on account	D	0.2	0.4	0.5
G	Develop a materials purchases budget, in units, and unit labor and overhead requirements	E	0.5	0.8	0.9
H	Restate purchases of materials, labor, and overhead required in dollars	C,G	0.1	0.2	0.3
I	Determine cash payments for production costs and selling and administrative expenses	B,H	0.1	0.2	0.5
J	Summarize projected cash flows in a cash budget	F,I	0.7	0.8	1.2

* Preceding activity or activities which must be completed before the designated activity can be started.

(1) Draw the PERT network for the cash budgeting system.
(2) Identify the critical path through the network.
(3) Determine the expected time required to prepare the next quarter's cash budget.
(4) The controller needs the cash budget for presentation at the next executive meeting in nine working days. What is the probability that the cash budget will be completed in time to meet this deadline?

Exercise 11. The following normal and crash times and costs are required for completing each activity along the critical path of a CPM network:

	Normal		Crash	
Activity	Time	Cost	Time	Cost
A	1.2 days	$ 215	0.8 days	$ 335
B	2.2	140	2.1	154
C	0.8	180	0.5	216
D	1.9	400	1.2	519
E	2.4	275	2.0	299
Total	8.5 days	$1,210	6.6 days	$1,523

(1) Determine which activities should be expedited, if the manager needs to complete the project in 7.5 days and wishes to shorten the project time at the least cost. (Assume that each activity can be shortened by any amount of time up to its crash time at a proportionate increase in cost. Also assume that shortening these activities will not cause any other path through the network to become critical.)
(2) What is the total cost of performing activities A through E, if they are expedited in accordance with your solution to (1)?

Exercise 12. Portable Computer Co. (PCC) has developed a new, battery-powered, flat screen personal computer, the FS-1. The time required to assemble the first computer was 20 hours, and the assembly process is characterized by an 80% learning curve.

(1) Using graph paper with arithmetic (linear) scales, plot the cumulative average time and the marginal time for assembling FS-1 computers. Show the times for units 1 through 128.
(2) If PCC has already assembled its first four FS-1 computers, how long will it take to assemble the next 60 computers?

Exercise 13. Patrick O'Reilly has just been employed in the Accounting Department of Interstate Manufacturing Co. to reconcile interplant transfers. It took Patrick from 9:00 a.m. until noon to complete his first reconciliation. Patrick performs one of these interplant reconciliations each morning. After observing his performance during the first two weeks, the Accounting Department supervisor determined that Patrick's performance is closely approximated by a 95% learning curve.

Assuming that 10 working days have elapsed since Patrick started performing this task, how many more days will it take until Patrick reduces the reconciliation time to 2 hours?

Problem 15-1. Nightingale Company is the exclusive American distributor of *Yukon Pete,* a premium Canadian whiskey. Nightingale Company expects to ship 1,500,000 cases in 19X9, an increase of 25% over the current year's shipments (19X8). Nightingale has asked you to review its current inventory policies and costs, and suggest possible changes.

Yukon Pete shipments are received by road freight (70%) and by rail (30%). Freight charges are levied according to weight and volume and average $3 per case by road and $2 per case by rail. As each case is received, it is inspected by Nightingale employees for breakage. If complete, the case is run through machinery which fixes federal liquor tax labels to the bottles. The cost of the inspection/labeling operation is budgeted at $13,700 per month plus $.40 per case inspected. Inspectors from the Bureau of Alcohol, Tobacco, and Firearms make 6 surprise visits each year to audit the labeling operation. The cost of each audit, $600, is charged to Nightingale. Cases which are damaged on arrival are returned to the distiller, who reimburses Nightingale for the freight in and freight out paid. Through mishandling, breakage also occurs after inspection, and this annual breakage cost is 2% of the purchase price (excluding freight) of the average inventory.

Additional data for selected months are reproduced in the following table:

	February	June	September
Number of purchase orders	5	5	8
Average inventory (cases)	7,000	12,000	12,000
Order size (cases)	20,000	20,000	12,500
Property tax on warehouse	$11,000	$11,000	$11,000
Property tax on inventory	2,042	3,500	3,500
Depreciation on warehouse	3,500	3,500	3,500
Charges for leased warehouse equipment	4,000	4,200	5,100
Insurance on warehouse	850	850	850
Insurance on inventory	4,083	7,000	7,000
Clerical costs	8,000	8,000	8,600
Employee payroll	9,700	9,700	9,700
Warehouse utilities	4,700	5,200	5,200
Advertising costs	27,000	22,000	13,000

A case of *Yukon Pete* costs $70. Nightingale requires an 8% aftertax return on its inventory investment.

(1) Calculate the variable order cost (O) and the unit variable holding cost (H) for Nightingale in 19X8.
(2) Use the simple EOQ model to calculate the optimal order size for 19X9. Assume that there will be no significant change in inventory-related costs from 19X8 to 19X9.
(3) The firm's current inventory policy is to order inventory in round lots of 12,500 cases per order. Calculate the possible savings in annual inventory costs if the firm switches to an EOQ-based ordering system. No safety stocks would be carried under either system.

Problem 15-2 (*Note: This problem is based in part on Appendix 15A*). Garman Company distributes *Adler* radial tires in the eastern United States. The tires are designed for high-performance sedans, are costly, and sell in relatively low volumes. The firm uses a backorder model to determine order sizes and order points. Shipments from Germany are sent via air freight, which allows Garman to fill customer orders relatively quickly, in spite of backorders.

Air freight is very costly, and Garman is considering revising its current inventory policy. Under the new system, purchase orders would be received by ship. Since lead times would jump from 3 days to 20 working days, a safety stock of 10% of demand during the lead time would be carried, and no backorders would be allowed. Relevant cost and demand information is summarized as follows:

Expected 19X3 sales	125,000 tires over the 250-working-day year
Order costs for shipping by air or sea	$50 per order
Unit variable holding costs	12% of the delivered cost of a tire (per year)
Backorder costs	$5 per unit per year
Shipping costs:	
Shipment by sea	$1.50 per unit, including insurance
Air freight	$10 per unit, including insurance

The expected cost of the tires during the coming year is $90 per tire, excluding shipping charges.

Required

(1) Determine the optimal order size, backorder amount, and the total variable order, holding, and backorder costs under the current system.

(2) Determine whether Garman's order and inventory-related costs would be lower under the current air shipment/backorder policy or a sea shipment/ basic EOQ model with safety stocks.

(3) If Garman orders large quantities of tires, the manufacturer would give the following quantity discounts:

1/2% discount on orders of 50,000 to 74,999 units
5% discount on orders of 75,000 units or more

Should Garman take advantage of this discount by increasing the order quantity from the optimal order size in your answer to (2)?

Problem 15-3. Soho Bottlers Inc. produces, distributes, and markets *Orange Soft,* a popular orange-flavored soft drink. The firm's production manager is determining the materials requirements for the coming year. The manager is especially concerned with the sugar requirements and inventories, since processed sugar is an important raw material in the formulation of soft drinks.

The firm cannot predict demand with certainty, but it has developed the following sales forecasting model based on historical data and economic trends:

$$Y = 300 + 2X_1 + 100X_2$$

where Y is annual demand, in thousands of cases, X_1 is disposable income of consumers in Soho's market, in millions, and X_2 is a dummy variable reflecting summer weather (0 for a normal summer and 1 for a hot summer).

Soho's economic consultant believes that consumer disposable income in the coming year will be $150 million. The long-range weather forecast for next year is for a hot summer.

The firm estimates that it costs $20 to place an order for sugar, and that the holding costs for sugar are $.35 per pound per year. Each case of Orange Soft produced requires 1.75 pounds of processed sugar.

Required (1) Calculate the expected demand for Orange Soft next year, and the sugar required to produce this quantity of soft drink.
(2) Based on the expected demand, calculate the economic order quantity for processed sugar.
(3) Determine the total variable inventory-related cost associated with this order quantity.

Problem 15-4. Yorkshire Candy Company manages its inventories of raw materials, using the simple EOQ model. The firm uses large amounts of processed chocolate in its operations, and is planning materials purchases for the coming year. The firm knows that 2,000,000 pounds of chocolate will be required next year. A pound of chocolate costs Yorkshire $.85.

Although it is difficult to estimate the cost of placing an order, the following is the firm's best estimate regarding this item:

Order preparation	$18
Payment of order	6
	$24

Inventory holding costs were last estimated three years ago. At that time, they were calculated as follows:

Insurance	$.02 per lb. per year
Storage	$.15 per lb. per year
Spoilage and deterioration	4% of annual average inventory
Cost of funds invested in inventory	12%

Required (1) Calculate the optimal quantity that the firm should order each time it places an order. Also calculate the total annual inventory cost incurred by the firm.
(2) Assume that Yorkshire has grossly understated its true inventory holding costs, and that actual costs are double those originally estimated. Determine the EOQ and the total inventory cost, using this revised information.
(3) What annual inventory cost would the firm have incurred if it had failed to discover the understatement of inventory cost? What is the maximum amount the firm should pay to discover this error?

Problem 15-5. Conservative Company manufactures asphalt roofing shingles at its plant in Tacoma. The shingles come in many colors, but in a single grade. Conservative's *Series 200* shingle is a high-quality shingle with a long life. Before every production run, production equipment must be cleaned and adjusted. Data relevant to determining setup costs are as follows:

Cleaning time	8 hours @ $60 per hour
Adjustment of machinery	5 hours @ $36 per hour

Standard costs for the units produced during the year were as follows:

	Standard Costs[a] for Series 200
Selling price	$11.00 per bale
Direct materials	6.10 per bale
Direct labor	.20 hours @ $10 per DLH[b]
Variable overhead	.20 hours @ $ 7 per DLH
Fixed overhead	.20 hours @ $ 4 per DLH

[a] Does not include setup costs
[b] DLH = Direct Labor Hours

During the coming year, Conservative expects to produce and sell 500,000 bales of *Series 200* shingles. Variable holding costs per bale are estimated as follows:

Storage	$.41 per unit per year
Insurance	.10 per unit per year

In addition, Conservative demands a 12% return on funds invested in inventory.

Required

(1) Determine the optimal production run for *Series 200* shingles. Use the basic EOQ model.

(2) Calculate the total relevant inventory-related costs which Conservative would expect to incur, based on the size of the production run determined in (1) and implied by the use of the basic EOQ model.

(3) (a) Calculate the daily rate of demand for shingles over the 250-working-day year and the length of a single inventory cycle.

(b) Calculate the unit and percentage error in Conservative's production run size, as it was estimated in (1).

(4) Because inventories at Conservative are not instantaneously replenished, average inventories of shingles over each inventory cycle will be somewhat less than is assumed by the basic EOQ model. The actual average inventory is equal to one half of the scheduled production run size multiplied by F, where F is $1 - (D \div P)$, D is the daily demand rate for the product, and P is the daily production rate.

(a) Calculate the actual total inventory-related costs which Conservative will incur.

(b) Calculate the dollar and percentage error in Conservative's annual cost estimate, as it was estimated in (2).

(5) The correct optimal production run size, OPQ, is determined as follows:

$$OPQ = \sqrt{\frac{2DO}{FH}}$$

where F is the fraction defined in (4).

(a) Calculate the correct optimal production lot size, using the above formula, and round the run size to the nearest 100 bales.

(b) Calculate the unit and percentage error in Conservative's production run size, as it was estimated in (1).

cont.

(6) (a) Calculate the (minimum) total inventory-related costs which Conservative would have incurred if it had implemented the production run size calculated in (5a).

(b) What is the maximum amount Conservative should pay to a consultant to give it the correct production-run model; i.e., what would it have been worth to Conservative to know the information given in (4) and (5)?

Problem 15-6 (CMA adapted, 12/74). Starr Company manufactures a portable drill powered by a special purchased battery. To determine the optimum number of batteries to order, Starr uses the basic EOQ model, ignoring safety stock considerations. It then determines how much safety stock to carry.

Starr Company uses 30,000 electric batteries annually (300 working days.) The lead time for an order is five days. The annual cost of carrying one battery in inventory is $10. Management has also estimated that the cost of being out of stock is $20 for each battery they are short. Because the batteries are frequently faulty, Starr sets up a special line to test each battery when an order of batteries is received from its supplier. It costs $1,450 to set up this test line and an additional $2 to run each battery through the required tests. Other costs related to processing a purchase order amount to $50 per order.

Starr Company has analyzed the usage during past periods by examining the inventory records, which indicate the following patterns:

Usage During Lead Time	Number of Times Quantity Was Used
440 units	6
460	12
480	16
500	130
520	20
540	10
560	6
	200

Required
(1) Ignoring safety stock considerations, calculate the order quantity, using the basic EOQ model.
(2) Calculate the optimal safety stock level of batteries. Use the number of order cycles for the year which is implied by the order quantity calculated in (1).
(3) Calculate the order point for batteries.
(4) What factors should Starr Company incorporate in its estimate of out-of-stock costs?

Problem 15-7. The engineering staff at Analog Industries has provided the information shown at the top of page 582 for the completion of the firm's most popular product, an inexpensive watch.

Required
(1) Draw the CPM network describing the assembly of Analog's watch.
(2) Determine the critical path through the network.
(3) Assuming that the assembly procedures described are followed and that the time requirements are met, what is the total elapsed time if 500 watches are assembled and inspected sequentially?

Activity	Description	Immediate Preceding Activities	Time Required
A	Secure materials from stores	—	.15 hours
B	Extrude case, band, and crystal from raw plastic	A	.13
C	Test movement for accuracy	A	.03
D	Cut and trim watchband links	B	.05
E	Polish crystal to remove scratches	B	.02
F	Insert movement in case	B,C	.01
G	Join crystal to case	E,F	.01
H	Assemble watchband links	D	.07
I	Join watchband to case	G,H	.03
J	Final inspection	I	.02

Problem 15-8. Precision Products operates a research laboratory engaged in designing energy-related products. The following PERT network shows the activities involved in one of these development projects, a laser communications device:

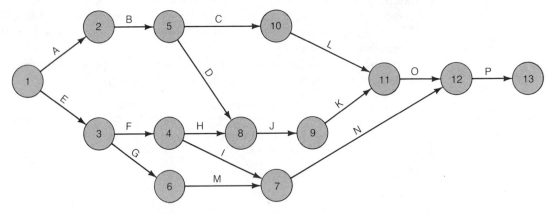

The following times necessary to complete each activity have been estimated by the researchers involved in the project:

Activity		Optimistic	Most Likely	Pessimistic
A	(1,2)	5 weeks	7 weeks	14 weeks
B	(2,5)	1	2	4
C	(5,10)	10	12	24
D	(5,8) (Dummy)	0	0	0
E	(1,3)	5	8	10
F	(3,4)	10	16	20
G	(3,6)	1	1	1
H	(4,8)	3	4	7
I	(4,7) (Dummy)	0	0	0
J	(8,9)	2	6	7
K	(9,11)	5	6	10
L	(10,11)	3	4	5
M	(6,7)	10	12	16
N	(7,12)	1	2	5
O	(11,12)	8	10	11
P	(12,13)	3	4	5

(1) Calculate the expected (mean) time, the standard deviation, and the variance for each activity.

(2) Using the information calculated in (1), determine the project's critical path.

(3) Determine a 90% confidence interval for the project completion time.

Problem 15-9. Grandolf Engines Inc. is in the midst of completing two large marine diesel engines for a Korean shipyard. Heavy demand in world shipping has lead the buyer of the ship in which these engines will be installed to offer a substantial bonus for early completion of the ship. The shipyard, in turn, has offered Grandolf a $50,000 bonus if the engines can be completed and delivered within 16 weeks. The tasks remaining to complete the engines are summarized in the following CPM network:

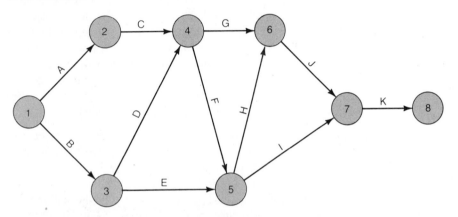

The firm's accountants have gathered the following additional data on estimated crash costs and times in an effort to reschedule these remaining activities to secure the bonus:

Activity	Normal Time	Normal Cost	Crash Time	Crash Cost
A	3 weeks	$ 36,000	2 weeks	$ 48,000
B	4	54,000	3	69,000
C	3	27,000	2.5	37,000
D	7	60,000	5	88,000
E	8	118,000	7	133,000
F	3	17,000	1.5	29,000
G	5	42,000	4	51,000
H	0	0	0	0
I	6	74,000	4	86,000
J	1	10,000	1	10,000
K	2	37,000	1	50,000

Required (1) Determine the critical path through the network and the normal time required to complete the engines.

(2) Prepare a table summarizing the incremental cost of shortening each relevant activity by one week.

(3) If Grandolf wishes to complete the project in 16 weeks, which activities should be crashed and by what amount? Assume that activities can be reduced up to *Ch. 15* 583

the crash time at an additional cost proportional to the increase in time required to crash the activity.

(4) How much would Grandolf gain or lose if it reduced the activity times as specified in (3) and secured the bonus?

Problem 15-10. Adler Co. produces carved marble columns, pilasters, cornices, and statues for churches, museums, and public buildings. The firm recently received an invitation to bid on 40 marble columns to be used in constructing a neoclassical courthouse in Kansas. Each column consists of six substantially identical sections. The order will be carved in 10 batches of 24 sections each. The firm believes, on the basis of past experience, that an 85% learning curve will apply to this production order.

Adler Co. has just completed an order for marble columns which are similar to (but smaller than) those ordered for the Kansas courthouse. The cumulative average time per batch for the smaller columns had dropped to 150 labor hours per batch by the time the seventh, and final, batch had been completed.

Adler believes that although the learning rate will be about the same for both columns, the larger size of the Kansas courthouse columns will cause the k parameter (the theoretical time required for the first batch) to be twice as large as the value of k for the smaller columns just completed.

<u>Required</u>

(1) Using the learning curve formula for the cumulative average time, estimate the theoretical time required to carve the first batch of the small columns.

(2) Calculate the total time which it will take Adler to produce the 10 batches of Kansas courthouse columns.

(3) Adler's standard pricing formula sets the selling price for a job equal to 125% of its estimated production cost. Materials costs for the Kansas courthouse columns total $70,000. Labor and overhead are charged to production at a rate of $11.50 per direct labor hour. What selling price should Adler quote for the Kansas courthouse job, if it uses its standard pricing formula?

Problem 15-11. Beckwith Co. plans to set up a new production line to manufacture a new product in batches of 300 units each. The firm's production engineers believe that labor-related costs are subject to an 80% learning curve. The firm's marketing manager, however, is reluctant to plan on any improvements due to learning because of the tight labor market which is expected to result in abnormally high turnover of Beckwith's labor force. During its first year of production and sales of this new product, 2,400 units are expected to be produced and sold.

After the first batch of 300 units was produced, the following standard costs were established, reflecting the actual cost of producing these units:

Materials	$35 per unit
Direct labor (3 hours @ $6 per direct labor hour)	18
Variable overhead (3 hours @ $2 per direct labor hour)	6
Fixed overhead* (3 hours @ $7 per direct labor hour)	21
Standard cost	$80 per unit

* Based on normal production line activity of 7,200 direct labor hours per year.

To break into the market, Beckwith's marketing manager has priced the new product at the low price of $105 per unit. Expected selling and administrative costs related to the new product total $46,000 for the coming year; these costs are essentially fixed costs. The book value of assets related to this product is $200,000.

Required (1) Assuming that the labor turnover will prevent any increased efficiency due to learning and that the cost incurred for the first batch will be typical of all production during the coming year:
    (a) Calculate the forecasted dollar income before taxes from the production and sale of 2,400 units.
    (b) Calculate the pretax return on investment for the product.
    (c) Calculate the break-even point in units. If units are produced in batches of 300, for which batch will the cumulative production and sales first show a profit?

(2) Assuming that Beckwith is able to achieve labor efficiencies corresponding to an 80% learning curve:
    (a) Calculate the forecasted dollar income before taxes from the production and sale of 2,400 units. Assume that any excess production capacity can not be used for any other product.
    (b) Calculate the pretax return on investment for the product.
    (c) Prepare a table showing the total cumulative revenues and costs for each of the first eight batches. For which batch will the cumulative production and sales first show a profit?

Problem 15-12.[4] In the spring of 1968, Lockheed Aircraft Corp. began work on the development of a new wide-bodied commercial jet aircraft, the L-1011 Tri Star. Lockheed initially estimated its break-even point at about 200 aircraft, and had originally anticipated production of 220 units over the period from late 1971 to late 1977. By 1971, firm orders had been received for 103 planes, with an additional 75 optional orders. By this time, Lockheed was experiencing a severe liquidity crisis occasioned, in part, by cost overruns on military contracts. Lockheed appealed to Congress for a loan guarantee to secure funds to carry on the Tri Star program. Congressional hearings were held, and eventually the loan was granted.

It appears that the best estimate of total nonrecurring, pre-production outlays on the Tri Star program amounted to about $900 million, and it was initially expected that this would be expended over a period of about 42 months. Knowledgeable industry sources estimated in 1971 that the cumulative average production cost after production of the 150th Tri Star would be about $15.5 million, but that, because of the effect of learning, by the time 300 planes would have been produced, this cost would have dropped to $12.0 million. Although the original price of the Tri Star in 1968 is said to have been $14.7 million, the price had increased to about $15.5 million in 1971 because of escalator clauses.

Required (1) Estimate the improvement factor (learning curve percent) for the Tri Star program.
(2) Calculate the value of the b parameter in the learning curve formulas corresponding to the learning curve percent determined in (1).
(3) Calculate the value of the parameter k, (the theoretical cost of the first unit) for Lockheed Tri Stars.

cont.

4 U. E. Reinhardt, "Break-Even Analysis for Lockheed's Tri Star: An Application of Financial Theory," *The Journal of Finance* (September, 1973), pp. 821-838.

(4) Lockheed projected a total free-world market of 775 wide-bodied aircraft. It hoped to capture 40% of this market. Assuming that Lockheed was subject to a 50% tax rate, calculate the total aftertax profitability of the Tri Star program.

(5) The estimate of 775 aircraft may have been somewhat too optimistic, since it was based on an assumed annual growth of 10% in air travel. Considering that air travel actually declined in 1970-71, a more realistic estimate of the growth in air travel might have been 5% a year over the next decade, in which case the total market would be only 323 aircraft. Using this more conservative estimate of total demand and a market share of 40%, what is the aftertax profitability of the Tri Star program?

Problem 15-13 (*Note: This problem is based in part on Appendix 15B*). Fray Co. produces special color cameras for the graphic arts industry. In early January, Fray began design work on a new camera, QuickColor 80. Nine months later, production began. By the following June, 650 cameras had been produced, and Fray believed it had reached a steady-state productivity level. Data on cumulative output and cumulative average times for selected observations are summarized as follows:

Observation	Cumulative Average Time	Cumulative Output
1	151.2 hours per unit	2 units
2	61.6	10
3	22.7	50
4	16.8	80
5	11.0	140
6	9.0	400
7	5.4	500
8	3.5	1500

Required

(1) After transforming the data for the first seven observations to logarithms, estimate the k and b parameters in the average time formula, $A = kq^b$, using least squares regression analysis.

(2) Based on the regression estimates in (1), calculate the learning curve percent which seems to characterize production of this camera.

(3) Based on the regression estimates in (1), estimate the total time required to produce 650 cameras.

(4) Assuming that Fray had reached the steady-state productivity level with the production of 650 cameras, calculate the average time required to produce a camera once the steady state had been reached. Base this estimate on the average time required to produce the 651st through the 1,500th cameras. Use the 8th observation to calculate the total time for producing 1,500 cameras and the total time calculated in (3) for producing 650 cameras.

(5) If 2,000 QuickColor 80 cameras will be built before the camera is significantly redesigned or replaced with a new model, calculate the total time required by Fray to produce the 2,000 cameras.

Appendix: Tables

n/r	9%	10%	11%	12%	13%	14%	15%	16%
1	.9174	.9091	.9009	.8929	.8850	.8772	.8696	.8621
2	.8417	.8264	.8116	.7972	.7831	.7695	.7561	.7432
3	.7722	.7513	.7312	.7118	.6931	.6750	.6575	.6407
4	.7084	.6830	.6587	.6355	.6133	.5921	.5718	.5523
5	.6499	.6209	.5935	.5674	.5428	.5194	.4972	.4761
6	.5963	.5645	.5346	.5066	.4803	.4556	.4323	.4104
7	.5470	.5132	.4817	.4523	.4251	.3996	.3759	.3538
8	.5019	.4665	.4339	.4039	.3762	.3506	.3269	.3050
9	.4604	.4241	.3909	.3606	.3329	.3075	.2843	.2630
10	.4224	.3855	.3522	.3220	.2946	.2697	.2472	.2267
11	.3875	.3505	.3173	.2875	.2607	.2366	.2149	.1954
12	.3555	.3186	.2858	.2567	.2307	.2076	.1869	.1685
13	.3262	.2897	.2575	.2292	.2042	.1821	.1625	.1452
14	.2992	.2633	.2320	.2046	.1807	.1597	.1413	.1252
15	.2745	.2394	.2090	.1827	.1599	.1401	.1229	.1079
16	.2519	.2176	.1883	.1631	.1415	.1229	.1069	.0930
17	.2311	.1978	.1696	.1456	.1252	.1078	.0929	.0802
18	.2120	.1799	.1528	.1300	.1108	.0946	.0808	.0691
19	.1945	.1635	.1377	.1161	.0981	.0829	.0703	.0596
20	.1784	.1486	.1240	.1037	.0868	.0728	.0611	.0514
21	.1637	.1351	.1117	.0926	.0768	.0638	.0531	.0443
22	.1502	.1228	.1007	.0826	.0680	.0560	.0462	.0382
23	.1378	.1117	.0907	.0738	.0601	.0491	.0402	.0329
24	.1264	.1015	.0817	.0659	.0532	.0431	.0349	.0284
25	.1160	.0923	.0736	.0588	.0471	.0378	.0304	.0245
26	.1064	.0839	.0663	.0525	.0417	.0331	.0264	.0211
27	.0976	.0763	.0597	.0469	.0369	.0291	.0230	.0182
28	.0895	.0693	.0538	.0419	.0326	.0255	.0200	.0157
29	.0822	.0630	.0485	.0374	.0289	.0224	.0174	.0135
30	.0754	.0573	.0437	.0334	.0256	.0196	.0151	.0116
35	.0490	.0356	.0259	.0189	.0139	.0102	.0075	.0055
40	.0318	.0221	.0154	.0107	.0075	.0053	.0037	.0026
45	.0207	.0137	.0091	.0061	.0041	.0027	.0019	.0013
50	.0134	.0085	.0054	.0035	.0022	.0014	.0009	.0006

n/r	17%	18%	19%	20%	21%	22%	23%	24%
1	.8547	.8475	.8403	.8333	.8264	.8197	.8130	.8065
2	.7305	.7182	.7062	.6944	.6830	.6719	.6610	.6504
3	.6244	.6086	.5934	.5787	.5645	.5507	.5374	.5245
4	.5337	.5158	.4987	.4823	.4665	.4514	.4369	.4230
5	.4561	.4371	.4190	.4019	.3855	.3700	.3552	.3411
6	.3898	.3704	.3521	.3349	.3186	.3033	.2888	.2751
7	.3332	.3139	.2959	.2791	.2633	.2486	.2348	.2218
8	.2848	.2660	.2487	.2326	.2176	.2038	.1909	.1789
9	.2434	.2255	.2090	.1938	.1799	.1670	.1552	.1443
10	.2080	.1911	.1756	.1615	.1486	.1369	.1262	.1164
11	.1778	.1619	.1476	.1346	.1228	.1122	.1026	.0938
12	.1520	.1372	.1240	.1122	.1015	.0920	.0834	.0757
13	.1299	.1163	.1042	.0935	.0839	.0754	.0678	.0610
14	.1110	.0985	.0876	.0779	.0693	.0618	.0551	.0492
15	.0949	.0835	.0736	.0649	.0573	.0507	.0448	.0397
16	.0811	.0708	.0618	.0541	.0474	.0415	.0364	.0320
17	.0693	.0600	.0520	.0451	.0391	.0340	.0296	.0258
18	.0592	.0508	.0437	.0376	.0323	.0279	.0241	.0208
19	.0506	.0431	.0367	.0313	.0267	.0229	.0196	.0168
20	.0433	.0365	.0308	.0261	.0221	.0187	.0159	.0135
21	.0370	.0309	.0259	.0217	.0183	.0154	.0129	.0109
22	.0316	.0262	.0218	.0181	.0151	.0126	.0105	.0088
23	.0270	.0222	.0183	.0151	.0125	.0103	.0086	.0071
24	.0231	.0188	.0154	.0126	.0103	.0085	.0070	.0057
25	.0197	.0160	.0129	.0105	.0085	.0069	.0057	.0046
26	.0169	.0135	.0109	.0087	.0070	.0057	.0046	.0037
27	.0144	.0115	.0091	.0073	.0058	.0047	.0037	.0030
28	.0123	.0097	.0077	.0061	.0048	.0038	.0030	.0024
29	.0105	.0082	.0064	.0051	.0040	.0031	.0025	.0020
30	.0090	.0070	.0054	.0042	.0033	.0026	.0020	.0016
35	.0041	.0030	.0023	.0017	.0013	.0009	.0007	.0005
40	.0019	.0013	.0010	.0007	.0005	.0004	.0002	.0002
45	.0009	.0006	.0004	.0003	.0002	.0001	.0001	.0001
50	.0004	.0003	.0002	.0001	.0001	.0000	.0000	.0000

Table 2

Present Value of an Annuity of $1.00 Received per Period

n/r	1%	2%	3%	4%	5%	6%
1	.9901	.9804	.9709	.9615	.9524	0.9434
2	1.9704	1.9416	1.9135	1.8861	1.8594	1.8334
3	2.9410	2.8839	2.8286	2.7751	2.7233	2.6730
4	3.9020	3.8077	3.7171	3.6299	3.5460	3.4651
5	4.8534	4.7135	4.5797	4.4518	4.3295	4.2124
6	5.7955	5.6014	5.4172	4.2421	5.0757	4.9173
7	6.7282	6.4720	6.2303	6.0021	5.7864	5.5824
8	7.6517	7.3255	7.0197	6.7327	6.4632	6.2098
9	8.5660	8.1622	7.7861	7.4353	7.1078	6.8017
10	9.4713	8.9826	8.5302	8.1109	7.7217	7.3601
11	10.3676	9.7869	9.2526	8.7605	8.3064	7.8869
12	11.2551	10.5753	9.9540	9.3851	8.8633	8.3838
13	12.1337	11.3484	10.6350	9.9857	9.3936	8.8527
14	13.0037	12.1063	11.2961	10.5631	9.8986	9.2950
15	13.8651	12.8493	11.9379	11.1184	10.3797	9.7122
16	14.7179	13.5777	12.5611	11.6523	10.8378	10.1059
17	15.5623	14.2919	13.1661	12.1657	11.2741	10.4773
18	16.3983	14.9920	13.7535	12.6593	11.6896	10.8276
19	17.2260	15.6785	14.3238	13.1339	12.0853	11.1581
20	18.0456	16.3514	14.8775	13.5903	12.4622	11.4699
21	18.8570	17.0112	15.4151	14.0292	12.8212	11.7641
22	19.6604	17.6581	15.9369	14.4511	13.1630	12.0416
23	20.4558	18.2922	16.4436	14.8568	13.4886	12.3034
24	21.2434	18.9139	16.9355	15.2470	13.7986	12.5504
25	22.0232	19.5235	17.4132	15.6221	14.0939	12.7834
26	22.7952	20.1210	17.8768	15.9828	14.3752	13.0032
27	23.5596	20.7069	18.3270	16.3296	14.6430	13.2105
28	24.3164	21.2813	18.7641	16.6631	14.8981	13.4062
29	25.0658	21.8444	19.1885	16.9837	15.1411	13.5907
30	25.8077	22.3965	19.6004	17.2920	15.3725	13.7648
31	26.5423	22.9377	20.0004	17.5885	15.5928	13.9291
32	27.2696	23.4683	20.3888	17.8736	15.8027	14.0840
33	27.9897	23.9886	20.7658	18.1477	16.0026	14.2302
34	28.7027	24.4986	21.1318	18.4112	16.1929	14.3681
35	29.4086	24.9986	21.4872	18.6646	16.3742	14.4982
40	32.8347	27.3555	23.1148	19.7928	17.1591	15.0463
45	36.0945	29.4902	24.5187	20.7200	17.7741	15.4558
50	39.1961	31.4236	25.7298	21.4822	18.2559	15.7619

n/r	7%	8%	9%	10%	11%	12%
1	0.9346	0.9259	0.9174	0.9091	0.9009	0.8929
2	1.8080	1.7833	1.7591	1.7355	1.7125	1.6901
3	2.6243	2.5771	2.5313	2.4869	2.4437	2.4018
4	3.3872	3.3121	3.2397	3.1699	3.1024	3.0373
5	4.1002	3.9927	3.8897	3.7908	3.6959	3.6048
6	4.7665	4.6229	4.4859	4.3553	4.2305	4.1114
7	5.3893	5.2064	5.0330	4.8684	4.7122	4.5638
8	5.9713	5.7466	5.5348	5.3349	5.1461	4.9676
9	6.5152	6.2469	5.9952	5.7590	5.5370	5.3282
10	7.0236	6.7101	6.4177	6.1446	5.8892	5.6502
11	7.4987	7.1390	6.8051	6.4951	6.2065	5.9377
12	7.9427	7.5361	7.1607	6.8137	6.4924	6.1944
13	8.3577	7.9038	7.4869	7.1034	6.7499	6.4235
14	8.7455	8.2442	7.7862	7.3667	6.9819	6.6282
15	9.1079	8.5595	8.0607	7.6061	7.1909	6.8109
16	9.4466	8.8514	8.3126	7.8237	7.3792	6.9740
17	9.7632	9.1216	8.5436	8.0216	7.5488	7.1196
18	10.0591	9.3719	8.7556	8.2014	7.7016	7.2497
19	10.3356	9.6036	8.9501	8.3649	7.8393	7.3658
20	10.5940	9.8181	9.1285	8.5136	7.9633	7.4694
21	10.8355	10.0168	9.2922	8.6487	8.0751	7.5620
22	11.0612	10.2007	9.4424	8.7715	8.1757	7.6446
23	11.2722	10.3711	9.5802	8.8832	8.2664	7.7184
24	11.4693	10.5288	9.7066	8.9847	8.3481	7.7843
25	11.6536	10.6748	9.8226	9.0770	8.4217	7.8431
26	11.8258	10.8100	9.9290	9.1609	8.4881	7.8957
27	11.9867	10.9352	10.0266	9.2372	8.5478	7.9426
28	12.1371	11.0511	10.1161	9.3066	8.6016	7.9844
29	12.2777	11.1584	10.1983	9.3696	8.6501	8.0218
30	12.4090	11.2578	10.2737	9.4269	8.6938	8.0552
31	12.5318	11.3498	10.3428	9.4790	8.7331	8.0850
32	12.6466	11.4350	10.4062	9.5264	8.7686	8.1116
33	12.7538	11.5139	10.4644	9.5694	8.8005	8.1354
34	12.8540	11.5869	10.5178	9.6086	8.8293	8.1566
35	12.9477	11.6546	10.5668	9.6442	8.8552	8.1755
40	13.3317	11.9246	10.7574	9.7791	8.9511	8.2438
45	13.6055	12.1084	10.8812	9.8628	9.0079	8.2825
50	13.8007	12.2335	10.9617	9.9148	9.0417	8.3045

n/r	13%	14%	15%	16%	17%	18%
1	0.8850	0.8772	0.8696	0.8621	0.8547	0.8475
2	1.6681	1.6467	1.6257	1.6052	1.5852	1.5656
3	2.3612	2.3216	2.2832	2.2459	2.2096	2.1743
4	2.9745	2.9137	2.8550	2.7982	2.7432	2.6901
5	3.5172	3.4331	3.3522	3.2743	3.1993	3.1272
6	3.9975	3.8887	3.7845	3.6847	3.5892	3.4976
7	4.4226	4.2883	4.1604	4.0386	3.9224	3.8115
8	4.7988	4.6389	4.4873	4.3436	4.2072	4.0776
9	5.1317	4.9464	4.7716	4.6065	4.4506	4.3030
10	5.4262	5.2161	5.0188	4.8332	4.6586	4.4941
11	5.6869	5.4527	5.2337	5.0286	4.8364	4.6560
12	5.9176	5.6603	5.4206	5.1971	4.9884	4.7932
13	6.1218	5.8424	5.5831	5.3423	5.1183	4.9095
14	6.3025	6.0021	5.7245	5.4675	5.2293	5.0081
15	6.4624	6 1422	5.8474	5.5755	5.3242	5.0916
16	6.6039	6.2651	5.9542	5.6685	5.4053	5.1624
17	6.7291	6.3729	6.0472	5.7487	5.4746	5.2223
18	6.8399	6.4674	6.1280	5.8178	5.5339	5.2732
19	6.9380	6.5504	6.1982	5.8775	5.5845	5.3162
20	7.0248	6.6231	6.2593	5.9288	5.6278	5.3527
21	7.1015	6.6870	6.3125	5.9731	5.6648	5.3837
22	7.1695	6.7429	6.3587	6.0113	5.6964	5.4099
23	7.2297	6.7921	6.3988	6.0442	5.7234	5.4321
24	7.2829	6.8351	6.4338	6.0726	5.7465	5.4509
25	7.3300	6.8729	6.4641	6.0971	5.7662	5.4669
26	7.3717	6.9061	6.4906	6.1182	5.7831	5.4804
27	7.4086	6.9352	6.5135	6.1364	5.7975	5.4919
28	7.4412	6.9607	6.5335	6.1520	5.8099	5.5016
29	7.4701	6.9830	6.5509	6.1656	5.8204	5.5098
30	7.4957	7.0027	6.5660	6.1772	5.8294	5.5168
31	7.5183	7.0199	6.5791	6.1872	5.8371	5.5227
32	7.5383	7.0350	6.5905	6.1959	5.8437	5.5277
33	7.5560	7.0482	6.6005	6.2034	5.8493	5.5320
34	7.5717	7.0599	6.6091	6.2098	5.8541	5.5356
35	7.5856	7.0700	6.6166	6.2153	5.8582	5.5386
40	7.6344	7.1050	6.6418	6.2335	5.8713	5.5482
45	7.6609	7.1232	6.6543	6.2421	5.8773	5.5523
50	7.6752	7.1327	6.6605	6.2463	5.8801	5.5541

n/r	19%	20%	21%	22%	23%	24%
1	0.8403	0.8333	0.8264	0.8197	0.8130	0.8065
2	1.5465	1.5278	1.5095	1.4915	1.4740	1.4568
3	2.1399	2.1065	2.0739	2.0422	2.0114	1.9813
4	2.6386	2.5887	2.5404	2.4936	2.4483	2.4043
5	3.0576	2.9906	2.9260	2.8636	2.8035	2.7454
6	3.4098	3.3255	3.2446	3.1669	3.0923	3.0205
7	3.7057	3.6046	3.5079	3.4155	3.3270	3.2423
8	3.9544	3.8372	3.7256	3.6193	3.5179	3.4212
9	4.1633	4.0310	3.9054	3.7863	3.6731	3.5655
10	4.3389	4.1925	4.0541	3.9232	3.7993	3.6819
11	4.4865	4.3271	4.1769	4.0354	3.9018	3.7757
12	4.6105	4.4392	4.2784	4.1274	3.9852	3.8514
13	4.7147	4.5327	4.3624	4.2028	4.0530	3.9124
14	4.8023	4.6106	4.4317	4.2646	4.1082	3.9616
15	4.8759	4.6755	4.4890	4.3152	4.1530	4.0013
16	4.9377	4.7296	4.5364	4.3567	4.1894	4.0333
17	4.9879	4.7746	4.5755	4.3908	4.2190	4.0591
18	5.0333	4.8122	4.6079	4.4187	4.2431	4.0799
19	5.0700	4.8435	4.6346	4.4415	4.2627	4.0967
20	5.1009	4.8696	4.6567	4.4603	4.2786	4.1103
21	5.1268	4.8913	4.6750	4.4756	4.2916	4.1212
22	5.1486	4.9094	4.6900	4.4882	4.3021	4.1300
23	5.1668	4.9245	4.7025	4.4985	4.3106	4.1371
24	5.1822	4.9371	4.7128	4.5070	4.3176	4.1428
25	5.1951	4.9476	4.7213	4.5139	4.3232	4.1474
26	5.2060	4.9563	4.7284	4.5196	4.3278	4.1511
27	5.2151	4.9636	4.7342	4.5243	4.3316	4.1542
28	5.2228	4.9697	4.7390	4.5281	4.3346	4.1566
29	5.2292	4.9747	4.7430	4.5312	4.3371	4.1585
30	5.2347	4.9789	4.7463	4.5338	4.3391	4.1601
31	5.2393	4.9824	4.7490	4.5359	4.3407	4.1614
32	5.2430	4.9854	4.7512	4.5376	4.3421	4.1624
33	5.2462	4.9878	4.7531	4.5390	4.3431	4.1632
34	5.2489	4.9898	4.7546	4.5402	4.3440	4.1639
35	5.2512	4.9915	4.7559	4.5411	4.3447	4.1644
40	5.2582	4.9966	4.7596	4.5439	4.3467	4.1659
45	5.2611	4.9986	4.7610	4.5449	4.3474	4.1664
50	5.2623	4.9995	4.7616	4.5452	4.3477	4.1666

Table 3
Areas in One Tail of the Normal Curve

This table shows the black area:

z	.00	.01	.02	.03	.04	.05	.06	.07	.08	.09
0.0	.5000	.4960	.4920	.4880	.4840	.4801	.4761	.4721	.4681	.4641
0.1	.4602	.4562	.4522	.4483	.4443	.4404	.4364	.4325	.4286	.4247
0.2	.4207	.4168	.4129	.4090	.4052	.4013	.3974	.3936	.3897	.3859
0.3	.3821	.3783	.3745	.3707	.3669	.3632	.3594	.3557	.3520	.3483
0.4	.3446	.3409	.3372	.3336	.3300	.3264	.3228	.3192	.3156	.3121
0.5	.3085	.3050	.3015	.2981	.2946	.2912	.2877	.2843	.2810	.2776
0.6	.2743	.2709	.2676	.2643	.2611	.2578	.2546	.2514	.2483	.2451
0.7	.2420	.2389	.2358	.2327	.2296	.2266	.2236	.2206	.2177	.2148
0.8	.2119	.2090	.2061	.2033	.2005	.1977	.1949	.1922	.1894	.1867
0.9	.1841	.1814	.1788	.1762	.1736	.1711	.1685	.1660	.1635	.1611
1.0	.1587	.1562	.1539	.1515	.1492	.1469	.1446	.1423	.1401	.1379
1.1	.1357	.1335	.1314	.1292	.1271	.1251	.1230	.1210	.1190	.1170
1.2	.1151	.1131	.1112	.1093	.1075	.1056	.1038	.1020	.1003	.0985
1.3	.0968	.0951	.0934	.0918	.0901	.0885	.0869	.0853	.0838	.0823
1.4	.0808	.0793	.0778	.0764	.0749	.0735	.0721	.0708	.0694	.0681
1.5	.0668	.0655	.0643	.0630	.0618	.0606	.0594	.0582	.0571	.0559
1.6	.0548	.0537	.0526	.0516	.0505	.0495	.0485	.0475	.0465	.0455
1.7	.0446	.0436	.0427	.0418	.0409	.0401	.0392	.0384	.0375	.0367
1.8	.0359	.0351	.0344	.0336	.0329	.0322	.0314	.0307	.0301	.0294
1.9	.0287	.0281	.0274	.0268	.0262	.0256	.0250	.0244	.0239	.0233
2.0	.0228	.0222	.0217	.0212	.0207	.0202	.0197	.0192	.0188	.0183
2.1	.0179	.0174	.0170	.0166	.0162	.0158	.0154	.0150	.0146	.0143
2.2	.0139	.0136	.0132	.0129	.0125	.0122	.0119	.0116	.0113	.0110
2.3	.0107	.0104	.0102	.00990	.00964	.00939	.00914	.00889	.00866	.00842
2.4	.00820	.00798	.00776	.00755	.00734	.00714	.00695	.00676	.00657	.00639
2.5	.00621	.00604	.00587	.00570	.00554	.00539	.00523	.00508	.00494	.00480
2.6	.00466	.00453	.00440	.00427	.00415	.00402	.00391	.00379	.00368	.00357
2.7	.00347	.00336	.00326	.00317	.00307	.00298	.00289	.00280	.00272	.00264
2.8	.00256	.00248	.00240	.00233	.00226	.00219	.00212	.00205	.00199	.00193
2.9	.00187	.00181	.00175	.00160	.00164	.00159	.00154	.00149	.00144	.00139

From *Tables of Areas in Two Tails and in One Tail of the Normal Curve*, by Frederick I. Croxton. Copyright, 1949, by Prentice-Hall, Inc.

Table 4
Percentiles of the t Distribution T table (One-tail)

Degrees of Freedom (d.f.)	.10	.05	.025	.01	.005	.0005
1	3.078	6.314	12.706	31.821	63.657	636.619
2	1.886	2.920	4.303	6.965	9.925	31.598
3	1.638	2.353	3.182	4.541	5.841	12.924
4	1.533	2.132	2.776	3.747	4.604	8.610
5	1.476	2.015	2.571	3.365	4.032	6.869
6	1.440	1.943	2.447	3.143	3.707	5.959
7	1.415	1.895	2.365	2.998	3.499	5.408
8	1.397	1.860	2.306	2.896	3.355	5.041
9	1.383	1.833	2.262	2.821	3.250	4.781
10	1.372	1.812	2.228	2.764	3.169	4.587
11	1.363	1.796	2.201	2.718	3.106	4.437
12	1.356	1.782	2.179	2.681	3.055	4.318
13	1.350	1.771	2.160	2.650	3.012	4.221
14	1.345	1.761	2.145	2.624	2.977	4.140
15	1.341	1.753	2.131	2.602	2.947	4.073
16	1.337	1.746	2.120	2.583	2.921	4.015
17	1.333	1.740	2.110	2.567	2.898	3.965
18	1.330	1.734	2.101	2.552	2.878	3.922
19	1.328	1.729	2.093	2.539	2.861	3.883
20	1.325	1.725	2.086	2.528	2.845	3.850
21	1.323	1.721	2.080	2.518	2.831	3.819
22	1.321	1.717	2.074	2.508	2.819	3.792
23	1.319	1.714	2.069	2.500	2.807	3.767
24	1.318	1.711	2.064	2.492	2.797	3.745
25	1.316	1.708	2.060	2.485	2.787	3.725
26	1.315	1.706	2.056	2.479	2.779	3.707
27	1.314	1.703	2.052	2.473	2.771	3.690
28	1.313	1.701	2.048	2.467	2.763	3.674
29	1.311	1.699	2.045	2.462	2.756	3.659
30	1.310	1.697	2.042	2.457	2.750	3.646
40	1.303	1.684	2.021	2.423	2.704	3.551
60	1.296	1.671	2.000	2.390	2.660	3.460
120	1.289	1.658	1.980	2.358	2.617	3.373
∞	1.282	1.645	1.960	2.326	2.576	3.291

Table is taken from Tables of Fisher & Yates: *Statistical Tables for Biological, Agricultural and Medical Research*. Published by Longman Group Ltd. London. (previously published by Oliver & Boyd Ltd. Edinburgh) and by permission of the authors and publishers.

INDEX

Guidelines for decision making, 9

H

Heteroscedasticity, 87
High-low analysis, *illus.,* 66
High-low method, 66-67
Homoscedasticity, 87

I

Income,
  before tax, 192-193
Income statement,
  budgeted, *illus.,* 454
  format of, 191-192
  pro forma, *illus.,* 517
Incremental,
  costs, 11
  revenues, 11
Incremental analysis, 265, *illus.,* 266
Inflation,
  adjusting cash flows, 274-276
  adjusting the cutoff rate, 273
  ignoring, 272
  impact on capital project
    evaluations, 272-276
Internal rate of return, *def.,* 220, *illus.,*
  221, 261
  calculating, 247
Inventory control model, 536
  ABC system, 546-547
  backorder, 565-568
  close coupling to suppliers, 547
  cost input data for EOQ, 540
  EOQ, 536
  materials requirements planning
    (MRP) systems, 547
  safety stock, 542-546
Investigation of variances, 344-348
Investment base,
  segment's, 496-501
Investment tax credit, 228
ITC options, *illus.,* 230

J

Job cost card, *illus.,* 43
Job order cost applications, 318-319
Job order costing, 40-44, *def.,* 39,
  illus., 41
Joint cost allocations,
  for product costing, 406-409
  relative net realizable value, *illus.,*
    410
  relative sales value, *illus.,* 408
  weighted physical units, *illus.,* 407
Joint costs,
  allocated by physical units, 406-407

allocated by relative net realizable
  value method, 408-409
allocated by relative sales value,
  407-408
allocated by weighted physical
  units, 406
linear programming application,
  424-426
Joint production costs,
  allocation of, 402-411
Joint products, *def.,* 402
  break-even analysis, *illus.,* 405
  combined break-even point, *illus.,*
    405
  contribution margin, *illus.,* 405
  cost control and performance
    evaluation, 403-404
  cost-volume-profit analysis, 404
  linear programming applications,
    424-426
  management decisions involving,
    403-406
  processing beyond split-off,
    405-406
  separable costs, 404
Journal entries for actual process
  costing, *illus.,* 373
Justification point,
  division, 117
  product, 114

L

Labor
  direct, 26
Labor and overhead variances, 335
Labor variance,
  control graph for investigation of,
    illus., 348
Late finish time, *def.,* 550
Learning curve, 557-565
  accounting implications, 564-565
  applications of, 563-564
  estimating parameters using
    regression analysis, 568-570
  graphs, *illus.,* 560
  model, *def.,* 557
  regression estimates of
    parameters, *illus.,* 569
  steady-state phase, *illus.,* 563
Learning curve formulas, 560-562
  estimating parameter values in,
    562-563
Lease,
  operating, 285-289
  sale/loan, 283-284
Leasing, 282-289
Least squares regression, *illus.,* 69
Linear programming, 140, *illus.,* 141,
  145, 146
  applications to joint products and
    joint costs, 424-426

approach to planning in
  decentralized company,
  513-519
Linear regression,
  multiple, 79
  simple, 67-74
Long-run product justification point,
  114

M

Main products, *def.,* 402
Manufacturing costs, *def.,* 26, *illus.,*
  36
  schedule, 37
  total, 35
Manufacturing operations, *illus.,* 403
Marginal contribution zone, *def.,* 115
Margin of safety, 110
Market segment, *def.,* 490
  residual analysis, *illus.,* 499
Market segment analysis, *illus.,* 497
Master budget, *def.,* 451
  preparation of, 451-457
Materials, *def.,* 26
  process cost applications, 317
  standards for, 303
Materials requirements planning
  system (MRP),
  inventory control, 547
Materials spending variance, 303
Materials variance, 303-305, 332
  sequence of determining, *illus.,* 334
Matrix algebra,
  overhead allocations using,
  427-431
Measuring output with EPUs, 359-361
Mixed costs, 27
Mixed overhead, 30
Models,
  basic EOQ, 536
  financial simulation, 461-465
  inventory control, 536
Modified volume variance, 318
Modular data base, 492-496, *illus.,*
  494
  uses of, *illus.,* 492
Money,
  time value of, 219
Monthly flows, 237-248
Multicollinearity, *def.,* 81
Multiple linear regression, 79
Multiple regression analysis, *illus.,* 80
Mutually exclusive projects, 265

N

Negative contribution zone, 114
Net present value, *def.,* 219, *illus.,*
  221
Nondiscretionary fixed costs, *def.,* 30

Table 1
Present Value of $1.00

n/r	1%	2%	3%	4%	5%	6%	7%	8%
1	.9901	.9804	.9709	.9615	.9524	.9434	.9259	.9346
2	.9803	.9612	.9426	.9246	.9070	.8900	.8573	.8734
3	.9706	.9423	.9151	.8890	.8638	.8396	.7938	.8163
4	.9610	.9238	.8885	.8548	.8227	.7921	.7350	.7629
5	.9515	.9057	.8626	.8219	.7835	.7473	.6806	.7130
6	.9420	.8880	.8375	.7903	.7462	.7050	.6302	.6663
7	.9327	.8706	.8131	.7599	.7107	.6651	.5835	.6227
8	.9235	.8535	.7894	.7307	.6768	.6274	.5403	.5820
9	.9143	.8368	.7664	.7026	.6446	.5919	.5002	.5439
10	.9053	.8203	.7441	.6756	.6139	.5584	.4632	.5083
11	.8963	.8042	.7224	.6496	.5847	.5268	.4289	.4751
12	.8874	.7885	.7014	.6246	.5568	.4970	.3971	.4440
13	.8787	.7730	.6810	.6006	.5303	.4688	.3677	.4150
14	.8610	.7579	.6611	.5775	.5051	.4423	.3405	.3878
15	.8613	.7430	.6419	.5553	.4810	.4173	.3152	.3624
16	.8528	.7284	.6232	.5339	.4581	.3936	.2919	.3387
17	.8444	.7142	.6050	.5134	.4363	.3714	.2703	.3166
18	.8360	.7002	.5874	.4936	.4155	.3503	.2502	.2959
19	.8277	.6864	.5703	.4746	.3957	.3305	.2317	.2765
20	.8195	.6730	.5537	.4564	.3769	.3118	.2145	.2584
21	.8114	.6598	.5375	.4388	.3589	.2942	.1987	.2415
22	.8034	.6468	.5219	.4220	.3419	.2775	.1839	.2257
23	.7954	.6342	.5067	.4057	.3256	.2618	.1703	.2109
24	.7876	.6217	.4919	.3901	.3101	.2470	.1577	.1971
25	.7798	.6095	.4776	.3751	.2953	.2330	.1460	.1842
26	.7720	.5976	.4637	.3607	.2812	.2198	.1352	.1722
27	.7644	.5859	.4502	.3468	.2678	.2074	.1252	.1609
28	.7568	.5744	.4371	.3335	.2551	.1956	.1159	.1504
29	.7493	.5631	.4243	.3207	.2429	.1846	.1073	.1406
30	.7419	.5521	.4120	.3083	.2314	.1741	.0994	.1314
35	.7059	.5000	.3554	.2534	.1813	.1301	.0676	.0937
40	.6717	.4529	.3066	.2083	.1420	.0972	.0460	.0668
45	.6391	.4102	.2644	.1712	.1113	.0727	.0313	.0476
50	.6080	.3715	.2281	.1407	.0872	.0543	.0213	.0339